Improving
The Long-Term Effects
of Psychotherapy

MODELS OF DURABLE OUTCOME

Improving The Long-Term Effects of Psychotherapy

MODELS OF DURABLE OUTCOME

Edited by
PAUL KAROLY
and JOHN J. STEFFEN
University of Cincinnati

GARDNER PRESS, INC., New York
Distributed by HALSTED PRESS
A Division of John Wiley & Sons, Inc.
New York • Toronto • London • Sydney

GARDNER PRESS, INC.

19 Union Square West

New York, New York 10003

Distributed solely by the Halsted Press Division of

John Wiley & Sons, Inc., New York.

Library of Congress Cataloging in Publication Data
Main entry under title:

Improving the long-term effects of psychotherapy.

   1. Psychotherapy. I. Karoly, Paul.
II. Steffen, John.
RC480.5.I49   616.8'914   79-18430
ISBN 0-470-26854-9

Book Design
By Publishers Creative Services Inc.

This book is dedicated to our parents,
Dora and Harry Karoly;
Cesa Ré and the late Eugene Charles Steffen

CONTENTS

CONTRIBUTORS

Sharon S. Brehm, Department of Psychology, University of Kansas, Lawrence, Kansas

Raymond B. Cattell, Emeritus, Department of Psychology, University of Illinois, Champaign, Illinois

J. Thomas DeVoge, Department of Psychology, Veteran's Administration Medical Center, Cincinnati, Ohio; and Department of Psychology, University of Cincinnati, Cincinnati, Ohio

Steven T. Fishman, Institute for Behavior Therapy, New York, New York

Sharon M. Hall, Department of Psychiatry, School of Medicine, University of California, San Francisco, California

Paul Karoly, Department of Psychology, University of Cincinnati, Cincinnati, Ohio

Mark Kempner, Health Planning Council of Greater Boston, Boston, Massachusetts

Edward B. Klein, Department of Psychology, University of Cincinnati, Cincinnati, Ohio

Barry S. Lubetkin, Institute for Behavior Therapy, New York, New York

Eric J. Mash, Department of Psychology, The University of Calgary, Calgary, Alberta, Canada

David A. McAllister, Department of Psychology, University of Kansas, Lawrence, Kansas

William R. Meyers, Department of Psychology, University of Cincinnati, Cincinnati, Ohio

Michael S. Neale, Department of Psychology, Yale University, New Haven, Connecticut

John J. Steffen, Department of Psychology, University of Cincinnati, Cincinnati, Ohio

Leif G. Terdal, University of Oregon Health Sciences Center, Portland, Oregon

Paul L. Wachtel, Department of Psychology, City College of the City University of New York, New York, New York

Robert W. Wildman, Geriatric Division, Central State Hospital, Milledgeville, Georgia

Robert W. Wildman II, Department of Psychology, Radford College, Radford, Virginia

Richard A. Winett, Department of Psychology, Virginia Polytechnic Institute and State University, Blacksburg, Virginia

PREFACE

The study of the long-range effects of psychotherapy inevitably begins as a conceptual stepchild, heir to the frailties of its ancestors. Psychotherapy researchers admit that knowledge of the immediate effects of varied psychological interventions is incomplete and unreliable, as is their very ability to delineate the boundaries of the domain they seek to study. Further limitations derive from the fact that the meaningfulness of long-range change is dependent on such parameters as the chronic versus phasic nature of the original problem, the method of detecting and labeling the client's complaint, the person- and systems-centered incentives for change, and the complex interaction of client, therapist, and mode of intervention. Despite frequent arguments to the contrary, the level of experimental questions in psychotherapy research is still quite primitive (does treatment x assist class of patients y as indexed by instruments a, b, and c?), while our fund of information remains "disappointingly meager" (Frank, 1979).

Therefore, shouldn't logic dictate that we tackle "first things first"? Isn't maintenance of therapeutic gain a little like eating your cake before you've had it?

The editors and contributors have taken the position, implicitly and expressly, that the behavioral, attitudinal, and cognitive components of therapy-based change have a life of their own and deserve a theory (or theories) of their own. Just as the highest level of automotive technology can never render a car safe from the assaults of bad drivers, ubiquitous potholes, and fuel shortages, a time-limited psychological process such as psychotherapy must be seen as merely a beginning—which can either be auspicious or misguided. There is no disease to be removed, but rather a set of skills, attitudes or reaction tendencies to be *added and left to develop* outside their place of origin (Phillips, 1978).

To a large extent, the success of psychotherapy over the short run depends on the vagaries of technique interacting with problem characteristics, while the long-range adjustment of the individual appears dependent on qualitatively different although related processes—including the clients' emergent style of storing and processing information about the self and the posttherapy environment and the reaction of that molar and molecular environment to the client's newly acquired patterns of thought and behavior. While several of the contributors to this volume aptly demonstrate how a clearer grasp of the parameters of treatment and the nature of clinical disorders can contribute to the establishment of long-range success, others proffer the equally important (but less familiar) message: that a parallel consideration of the systematic determinants of long-range change (e.g., personal, dyadic, social, ecological, developmental, and political) can inform our theories of time-bound psychotherapy as well as our clinical intervention strategies.

In a sense, this volume is a call to arms, directed at those who believe that immediate technological solutions to the maintenance problem are the only practical solutions; at those who believe in simple and sovereign explanations; at those who believe that a concern with long-range outcomes is a luxury practicing clinicians can ill afford; and at those who believe in the essential imponderability of the cycle of human growth and stability. The purpose of this volume is to lay the groundwork for a challenge to these well-entrenched viewpoints.

This volume grew out of the editors' combined teaching and clinical experiences. In a graduate seminar on the psychology of long-term behavior change, one of us (P.K.) learned that speaking the language of the laboratory and of the consulting room allowed him both to erect conceptual bridges and to detect the structural weaknesses in bridges already in use. The facilitators of this learning were (and are) his thoughtful and uncompromising graduate students—to whom a very great debt is owed. In teaching an introductory course in behavior modification, one of us (J.J.S.) was continuously goaded into clarifying and justifying the application of learning principles until their inherent limitations and often unrecognized strengths took on greater meaning to him. One fact was obvious to both of us: that the promissory notes written since the turn of the century by thinkers from Freud and Wolpe would never be negotiable until the question of the durability of our psychological interventions was more fully and honestly addressed.

We trust that this volume will help foster the emergence of a psychology of therapeutic maintenance. The variety of views represented by the contributors to this text was expressly sought and encouraged, for we are still in the discovery phase of our work. We would like to take this opportunity to acknowledge the various chapter authors for their outstanding creative efforts. Finally, to Diane Kopriwa, who typed much of the original manuscript, we extend our sincerest appreciation.

Paul Karoly
John J. Steffen
Cincinnati, Ohio

REFERENCES

Frank, J. D. The present status of outcome studies. *Journal of Consulting and Clinical Psychology,* 1979, *47,* 310–316.

Phillips, E. L. *The social skills basis of psychopathology.* New York: Grune & Stratton, 1978.

Improving
The Long-Term Effects
of Psychotherapy

MODELS OF DURABLE OUTCOME

PART I

Overview

C H A P T E R

1

TOWARD A PSYCHOLOGY OF THERAPEUTIC PERSISTENCE

JOHN J. STEFFEN AND PAUL KAROLY

At a time when psychotherapy is undergoing a critical appraisal both from within (Garfield & Bergin, 1978) and from without (Gross, 1978), all facets of this developing enterprise must be closely examined and evaluated. Proper examination, of course, requires that we know what activities constitute psychotherapy, since numerous nonpsychotherapeutic activities (e.g., chemotherapy, lobotomy, nude encounter marathons) are often presented to the public, and sometimes the profession, as legitimate forms of psychological intervention. A serious appraisal of our activities as therapists cannot take place within a context of confusion regarding the parameters of our practice. Defining psychotherapy, however, proves to be a difficult task, one which provokes chaos in a field already beset with confusion and controversy. This definitional problem arises from the fact that there are numerous competing theoretical systems and disciplines within the field, each claiming sole proprietorship.

THE SCOPE OF PSYCHOTHERAPY

It is not impossible, however, to begin to formulate a general description of therapy that would be acceptable to most. In so doing our goal should be to delineate both the activities and expectations of all participants in the psychotherapeutic encounter. While it appears relatively simple to develop an operational description of therapeutic endeavors, the clarification of therapeutic expectations may be more problematic.

We can begin with Strupp's (1978) informal definition of psychotherapy. He states:

Psychotherapy is an interpersonal process designed to bring about modifications of feelings, cognitions, attitudes, and behavior which have proven troublesome to the person seeking help . . . . as ordinarily understood, the psychotherapist is a trained professional person who has acquired special skills. (p. 3)

This description is helpful since it allows us to distinguish between psychotherapy and medical interventions, such as chemotherapy, through the stipulation that therapy is an "interpersonal process." Some might argue, however, that chemotherapy may achieve some or all of its effect through an interpersonal influence process (Shapiro & Morris, 1978). While this may be true, its *intended* effect is presumably achieved mainly through pharmacological, not interpersonal, channels. The distinction between traditional psychotherapy practices and those that can be best characterized as "fringe" is somewhat more problematic. History has proven that "fringe" practices sometimes later emerge as acceptable, and may even become well entrenched within the mainstream (e.g., hypnosis, psychoanalysis, behavior modification). The argument has been made, however, that such "fringe" practices as sensitivity training and nude encounter marathons are directed primarily toward the normal individual who is seeking personal growth and not at the person in emotional turmoil. This argument then, further limits our definition of psychotherapy to the modification of the problematic facets of an individual's life.

PSYCHOTHERAPEUTIC EXPECTATIONS

At this point, while we may generally agree as to what constitutes the practice of psychotherapy, we are left with the problem of identifying the expectations of both therapist and patient regarding the essential characteristics of therapy practice.

While consideration of expectations within the psychotherapeutic context may seem alien to many behaviorally oriented practitioners, the importance of such variables to outcome and maintenance cannot be denied. Bandura (1977) has recently implicated the alteration of self-efficacy expectations as crucial for instigating therapeutic change and its maintenance. It has also become de rigueur to measure an assortment of therapist and patient expectations throughout the course of therapy (so-called process measures) for assessment of their contribution in most recent outcome evaluation investigations. We do not deny the importance of these factors to the process of therapy; for our current interests, however, we will limit our discussion to the expectations held by therapists and patients regarding outcome and maintenance. Strupp and Hadley (1977) have pointed out that there are at least three different perspectives involved in mental health and psychotherapeutic outcome: those of the patient, those of the therapist, and those of the society within which they live. Strupp and Hadley (1977) note that the problems presented by the patient and their consequent outcomes may have different meanings depending on the perspective from which the problems are viewed. Conflict among perspectives is possible. For example, while society and the therapist may agree that a certain outcome is desirable, the patient may not. In addition to this form of outcome expectation, both patient and therapist may have a more basic expectation as to whether or not therapy will be effective. Thus while patient, therapist, and society may all agree regarding the desirability of a particular outcome, such agreement does not ensure the belief, by any of the interested parties, that the outcome is possible. While the relation between expectations and therapeutic change is quite clouded, it is certainly reasonable to anticipate that positive expectations would be more facilitative of change than would negative expectations.

Outcome expectations are not the only ones held by participants in psychotherapy. Most patients today are sufficiently informed about the various modes of therapy to have specific expectations about the way therapists should act. Therapists too have their own expectations (and "rules") about proper patient behaviors. Some therapists even expect that the patient will occasionally act in a fashion counterproductive to adaptive change, and consider resolution of this "resistance behavior" to be of paramount importance for successful therapy. There are also structural expectations that are held by patients and therapists, such as those regarding length of sessions, duration of treatment, and therapist and patient attire.

The importance of these structural expectations to the therapeutic process has been recognized for quite some time. Indeed, almost 20 years has passed since Goldstein's (1962) investigations on therapeutic expectations were first introduced. Given the recent reemergence of expectations as a much-touted variable possibly moderating therapeutic change and maintenance, we wonder if Goldstein's work would qualify for the "Rip van Winkle Award" for important contributions to the field that have been undeservedly neglected. In very brief summary, Goldstein's (1962) vintage research indicated that modification of therapist and patient expectancies regarding therapy was both possible and potentially powerful in influencing therapeutic outcome. We will leave speculations concerning the reason for our neglect of this early work to historians, since that is not the focal point of this volume.

A final characteristic that we need to address concerns the therapist's and the patient's expectations regarding the duration of the changes brought about in therapy. Concern, or more precisely the lack of concern, among mental health professionals regarding this expectation is a major impetus for the compilation of the chapters of this book. A thoughtful person might suspect that both therapists and patients would anticipate that any emotional or behavioral changes effected during treatment would endure well beyond the termination of therapeutic contact. Judging from the published works of clinicians and clinical researchers, the expectation of long-term improvement in personal adjustment remains a tacit and generally untested assumption. Perhaps one cause of this neglect is the fact that the empirical evaluation of therapeutic effectiveness is a relatively new enterprise. Clinical practitioners and researchers who have studied short-term therapeutic outcome rarely agree among themselves on the design and evaluation of outcome investigations. Considerable effort has been spent sifting through the complex of factors that must be manipulated or controlled in such research. The addition of therapeutic maintenance compounds this complexity since the potential interplay of variables and factors is drawn out over time. We do not wish to devalue the essential work that has been directed toward the evaluation and perfection of psychotherapeutic systems by raising this concern. Rather we feel that the prevailing conditions permeating outcome research are such that clinicians and investigators alike are tempted to ignore the more long-term effects of the changes they help foster in their patients. While we all expect that the magnitude of effort expended in the name of psychotherapy will produce a harvest of change that will never diminish, we seldom evaluate the durability of that change nor do we anticipate any of the impediments to lasting change that may emerge as a natural result of the passage of time. Attempts to measure change within the boundaries of therapeutic contact are certainly difficult enough to design and enact without expanding the temporal parameter. Yet, do we not expect the products and services we purchase to carry some guarantees of lasting usefulness offered by their producers and providers? Should it not be considered appropriate for therapists to make similar offers? We would like to suggest at this point that what has been implicit within the therapeutic contract be made explicit. In other words, under normal and anticipated circumstances, how long should therapeutically induced change last? While it would certainly be desirable, we cannot expect that therapists could presently offer any guarantees to the patient on the durability of their efforts. However, we would consider any steps in this direction as essential if we claim and intend to provide a professional service to our patients. Before we discuss in any further detail our concerns with the maintenance of change, we would like briefly to survey the current state of outcome research.

THE STATE OF OUTCOME RESEARCH

Eysenck's (1952) scathing review of the effects of psychotherapy stands as the historical inspiration behind most recent attempts to evaluate the outcome of therapeutic practices. While many of Eysenck's analyses and conclusions have themselves been sharply questioned (Bergin, 1971; Kiesler, 1966), no one can deny his major contribution to the instigation of a profusion of outcome studies. Eysenck's early paper generated a continuing series of charges and countercharges concerning the adequacy of psychotherapy. While his analyses have been questioned, he did manage to unearth a variety of conceptual and methodological concerns that had not been previously addressed. From the time of his review to the present, hundreds of psychotherapy outcome studies have been published. Most of these, however, have been inadequately designed, limiting the comparative and evaluative conclusions that can be drawn from their findings (Kazdin & Wilson, 1978). If any one accomplishment can be attributed to this flood of research, it is that the once taken-for-granted curative powers of the therapist have been placed under the empirical scrutiny of the researcher. While most of the widely practiced modes of therapy have been examined in at least case study form, few firm conclusions can be stated regarding the absolute or comparative efficacy of one mode versus another. Kazdin and Wilson (1978) have recently made several valuable suggestions concerning the development of adequate and informative outcome evaluation designs. Apparently, until some uniform evaluative practices are adopted there will still remain the possibility that a team of investigators can examine 17 studies comparing "behavior therapy" and "psychotherapy," and upon finding that behavior therapy was superior in 6 and did not differ from psychotherapy in the remaining 11, conclude that the two modes are equally effective (Luborsky, Singer, & Luborsky, 1975).

Aside from the fact that there are no uniformly accepted standards tor evaluating outcome studies, a more general interpretive problem prevails: investigators from different perspectives seldom agree on what constitutes a meaningful outcome. Measurement anarchy stems from the differences among therapy adherents concerning the "true" goals of psychotherapy. Thus while some value intrapsychic change, others tout behavior change, and seldom do the twain agree. Several authors have recently suggested that in place of a rather provincial attitude toward outcome, investigators should employ a variety of measures and methods of tracking change (Waskow & Parloff, 1973).

However, many investigators do not employ appropriate multivariable statistical analyses. Movement from unidimensional to multidimensional outcome constructs poses an additional dilemma: that is, at what level of interpretation do the multiple dimensions converge, if they do at all? Let us consider the statistical and interpretive problems in turn.

The literature is replete with calls for multidimensional measurement and almost equally so with calls for the use of "sophisticated multivariate statistical analyses." One might even conclude that the use of multivariate analyses will surely deliver us from the evils of parochialism in outcome research. Multivariate messiahs abound, collecting disciples prepared to sacrifice their Fs and ts for *eigenvalues*.

Yet, these multivariate disciples frequently run their multivariate analyses, disregard the multivariate Fs and correlation matrices, and conclude by reporting a string of univariate statistics (which they find easier to interpret).

Cattell (1978) has recently presented some guidelines concerning the design of factor-analytic studies, and Gabriel and Glavin (1978) have presented a thorough discussion of the uses of multivariate procedures in behavioral research including a worked-through example of methods to identify relations among the dependent measures (a practice often neglected). Attention to articles such as these, as well as thoughtful consultation of one or more of the many texts on multivariate analyses (e.g., Bennett & Bowers, 1977; Maxwell, 1977; Namboodiri, Carter, & Blalock, 1975; Overall & Klett, 1972) will help outcome investigators avoid the technical pitfalls of blind obedience to multivariate messiahs.

A related but considerably more insidious problem with multidimensional measurement concerns the construct validity and relatedness of outcome measures. It is now a well-known and oft-reported fact that associations among the diverse measures used to assess outcomes are often quite limited. Patients may show improvement on one set of measures but not on others. The investigator is then forced to decide which measures of change (or nonchange) are the more meaningful. Generally, this decision is swayed toward selection of those measures which are consistent with the investigator's theoretical orientation. In a spirit of ecumenism, behavior therapists will, for example, resort to a host of outcome measures from behavioral observations to subjective self-report. However, this ecumenical spirit soon dissipates in the light of conflicting findings. Rather than question the validity of the construct system that has led to selection of the chosen measures, more often than not the diligent researcher will denigrate the results of those measures which do not support the theoretical underpinnings of the research. What an investigator may fail to realize in this situation is that it may well be an improper and incomplete understanding of the construct under investigation, and not any specifiable portion of it, that is contributing to the equivocal results. Recent work reported by Mintz, Luborsky, and Christoph (1979) on the associations among diverse measures of psychotherapy outcome provides some clarity to this concern about discordant outcome. Mintz et al. (1979) took a variety of self-report outcome measures from 73 patients, their therapists, and independent evaluators in an effort to evaluate the products of psychotherapy. They found considerable agreement among the patients, therapists, and evaluators regarding outcome. While their study of outcome agreement is buttressed by rather thoughtful statistical analyses, their findings must be limited only to the putative concordance among self-report measures of outcome. On the side of providing a clearer picture regarding the constructs involved in assessing outcome, Mintz et al. (1979) report compelling evidence that there are two major dimensions in this regard: posttreatment adjustment and rated benefits. Adjustment refers to the patient's overall health at the termination of treatment; the rated benefits dimension refers to estimates of the patient's change instigated through therapy. Their findings suggest that adequate assessment should include more than just an overall estimate of change (rated benefits); it should also provide some index of the patient's post treatment adjustment. Of course, this type of analysis should be extended to other domains of outcome such as more specific measures derived from behavior observations and self-monitoring.

GENERALIZATION, TRANSFER, AND MAINTENANCE

If agreement among investigators is minimal with regard to the modes and methods of a single outcome evaluation, one could not expect anything close to consensus for the evaluation of temporally extended outcomes. However, the efforts of such investigators as Mintz et al (1979) will certainly facilitate agreement among researchers concerning the important evaluative dimensions of change. We would now like to explore the concept of therapeutic maintenance in sufficient detail to provide an interpretative frame for the following chapters in this book. Questions have been raised thus far on the nature of psychotherapeutic change and the somewhat limited agreement among investigators about the proper form such change should take. At this point, a tentative characterization of the maintenance of change is in order. As the reader will later note, the contributors to this book do not apply a uniform definition of maintenance. There is, however, considerable overlap with regard to their focus on this issue: maintenance, quite simply, refers to the continuation of changes instigated in therapy beyond the formal termination of treatment. As we will see, there are several features to this usage, the more important ones being time and change. However, any discussion on the interrelated dimensions of time and change should be preceded by a discussion on what is *not* considered maintenance, since a common confusion occurs when the terms "maintenance" and "generalization" are used interchangably.

Generalization of change has a specific referent within psychological research: either stimulus or response generalization. Kimble (1961) has defined stimulus generalization as the "ability of different stimuli to evoke a conditioned response" (p. 328). Stimulus generalization is demonstrated in the learning laboratory when a subject displays the same response (e.g., GSR increase) to different stimuli (e.g., tones of different frequencies). This phenomenon is frequently demonstrated in the natural environment as well. For example, a child who has just learned to say "da da" in the presence of his father will call all adult males in this fashion. In the therapeutic context, this would refer to the ability of stimulus conditions, other than those under which the patient was trained, to occasion whatever adaptive responses the patient has acquired. The patient may have learned an effective assertive response toward her spouse. Stimulus generalization would then be said to have occurred if she later exhibits the same response toward some other person.

Response generalization, on the other hand, occurs "when a certain response is conditioned to a particular stimulus and related responses are also automatically conditioned to the same stimulus" (Kimble, 1961, p. 360). In the learning experiment, when a response (e.g., digital extension) is initially trained to a stimulus (e.g., mild shock) and experimental conditions are then altered to allow responses of different forms, the elicitation of a new but related response (e.g., digital flexion) to the original stimulus demonstrates response generalization.

If we can accept the extrapolation from simple stimuli to complex social settings and from simple responses to social behavior, this form of generalization occurs quite frequently in the natural environment, assuming that multiple responses are available to people in most social settings. Upon seeing her mother's face, a 7-month-old infant may display any one of a related class of smiles ranging from a slight upturn of her closed mouth to a wide-open mouth.

In the therapeutic context, response generalization could be demonstrated in a variety of ways, especially when the treatment is focused on response acquisition (e.g., social skills and assertion training, participant modeling, self-instructional therapy). Clients who are engaged in social skills training programs are often taught different approaches to conversational initiation through behavioral rehearsal and evaluative feedback. Often, specific strategies which include verbal and nonverbal elements are practiced within the therapeutic context for implementation in the natural setting. Response generalization might occur under those circumstances where the client uses the practiced strategy as an outline or plan for initiations. While the general situation remains the same (meeting someone), the client's initiation attempts may vary with regard to verbal content and non verbal display.

Demonstrations of generalization, however, have not been sought over any considerable length of time. Whether in the learning laboratory or the natural setting, a sufficient (and, actually, preferred) generalization test should occur shortly after the initial training. Short intervals between initial training and subsequent testing are preferred by demonstrators since the beneficial effects of training may erode (be forgotten) over time. When evaluating or testing for clinical maintenance, the status of the temporal parameter is elevated to a position of importance: the changes instigated through therapeutic interventions are expected to persist over time as well as generalize over settings (stimuli) and activities (responses).

Investigations on the transfer of training, an extension from the learning laboratory research on generalization, do appear to have some relevance to therapeutic maintenance (Hall, 1966, pp. 472–546). Transfer of training refers to the influences or effects of learning a particular task that carry over to subsequently learned tasks. Transfer effects are seen as positive, negative, or neutral. Positive effects involve facilitation of second task learning by the previous learning experience. Negative effects refer to the hindering of subsequent learning by prior learning. Neutral, or zero, effects occur when past learning has no effect on subsequent learning. Perusal of the literature suggests several possible applications of transfer of training research to the practice of psychotherapy. Indeed, Goldstein, Heller, and Sechrest (1966), in their outstanding effort to bridge the research-to-practice gap in psychotherapy, have provided several useful suggestions for applying the findings from transfer reserach to therapy. Two examples of hypotheses they have derived are:

HYPOTHESIS 5.1: Transfer of learning from psychotherapy to extratherapy situations will be greater when the therapy stimuli are representative of extratherapy stimuli. (p. 226)

HYPOTHESIS 5.4: A cognitive structure which enables an individual correctly to anticipate and organize his experience will facilitate learning and retention of new or more elaborate behavior sequences. (p. 240)

Hypothesis 5.1 directly follows an earlier suggestion by Osgood (1949) that the more similar first-task stimuli and responses are to the second-task stimuli and responses, the greater the magnitude of positive transfer.

While neither Goldstein et al. (1966) nor Osgood (1949) suggests any temporal limits to transfer effects, such a consideration would be necessary if one were to apply these suggestions for the enhancement of therapeutic maintenance. An important question would be if there were any temporal limits to positive transfer effects: Does the facilitative effect of training on task 1 erode as greater periods of time elapse between task 1 and a later task 2? Ellis (1965, 1969) has provided an interesting, albeit incomplete, perspective on this question. In reviewing his earlier work and that of Bunch (1939), Ellis (1965, 1969) concluded that, over time:

transfer of training remains approximately constant as long as performance on the transfer task does not depend on memory for specific items in the original task. Where transfer does depend on memory for specific items, or under conditions of cue reversal, transfer will vary as a function of time elapsing between tasks. (Ellis, 1965, p. 41)

Thus, transfer of specific, remembered facets of the original task showed an erosion over time in the studies reviewed by Ellis. On the other hand, the general facilitative effect of earlier training did continue to have a temporally extended, beneficial effect on subsequent (and similar) learning tasks. Extrapolation of these findings from the learning laboratory to psychotherapy suggests that maintenance of change will not necessarily take the form of specifically retained information over time, but rather that the subsequent acquisition of new (and hopefully adaptive) modes of response will be facilitated by some general learning set that prepares the individual for future learning. Of course, any extension of research based on the acquisition of paired associates to the acquisition of complex modes of acting and thinking under complex environmental conditions must be tempered with caution. We know too little about what is learned in therapy; nor can we approach with equal sophistication the measurement specificity of the paired-associate learning experiment when we cast our view upon the therapeutic encounter.

Goldstein et al.'s (1966) Hypothesis 5.4, in light of the previous discussions, appears to extend our speculation concerning the relevance of transfer of training research to the maintenance of therapeutically induced change. This hypothesis is derived from the work of Ausubel (1963) on what he calls "advance organizers." Advance organizers take the form of prior information which allows the person to assimilate new information. Since Karoly (see Chapter 7) discusses the relevance of this line of thought with regard to the contribution of individual differences to the facilitation of maintenance, our discussion here will be brief. It should be sufficient to note that provisions in therapy should be made regarding the anticipation of the effects of future life experiences on the patient's emotional wellbeing. Within this current analysis, transfer of training effects may be more enduring and positive if patients are given some means of anticipating future circumstances which may threaten their relatively symptom-free status.

One concern has remained unclear, however, throughout this discussion: If the long-term duration of change is important, how long must this change last before it is considered durable?

While many recent outcome studies have included a reassessment of the patient's status on the initial complaint at points in time beyond treatment termination, selection of specific follow-up periods are more the product of the whim of the outcome investigator than they are of any clear-cut conceptual considerations. Determination of appropriate follow-up time intervals depends on several factors relevant to the treatment program. The nature of the treated problem, for example, should contribute to the follow-up decision. If this problem has shown a cyclical history, such as certain forms of depression or alcohol abuse, the temporal locations of follow-ups should not be so short as to overlook possible relapse. Also, as Hunt and Matarazzo (1973) have shown with regard to the treatment of a variety of addictive disorders, there appears to be a gradual erosion of treatment success over time that resembles the forgetting curve in learning research. This erosion might suggest that frequent follow-ups are necessary to charting potential outcome declines for those particular disorders (see also Mash and Terdal's discussion in Chapter 4). Since the authors of the current chapters all approach this problem from somewhat different perspectives, we shall not pursue the matter at any greater length here.

Our concern with the passage of time and the fact that all change may well be a natural temporal process will be our next focus (see also Chapter 9).

TIME AND CHANGE

If we accept the position that the *temporal* parameter is important for consideration of maintenance, we are forced into a dilemma when we include the concept of *change* as a crucial element. We have previously noted some of the problems in measuring change throughout the course of psychotherapy, particularly the less-than-unanimous agreement as to what constitutes acceptable change. When we extend our attention to outcome beyond the course of treatment, we must face straight-on the problem of sorting the differential changes that occur within our patients over time. Elaboration of this problem has plagued philosophers as well as scientists (Watzlawick, Weakland, & Fisch, 1974). When the thoughtful therapist contemplates the myriad of forces that impel the person to act in certain ways, as well as the effects the individual may have on the environment, a clear conceptualization of change becomes essential. If we adhere to a somewhat antiquated understanding of change in psychotherapy, we can easily view the patient as similar to any inanimate physical object, and assume a psychotherapeutic *"law of behavioral inertia"*: patients do not move (change) unless impelled to do so by an external force (the efforts of the therapist). Similarly, once moved, the patient will never cease such motion unless he meets another external force (the precipitant for a further problem). The fallacy in this assumption is that the patient lies helpless to change in the face of compelling external events. A more apt physical analogy would consider the fact that change within our patient can easily occur independent of our therapeutic ministrations and of capricious environmental events. This view of the person as an independent and active participant in his world has become increasingly popular within developmental psychology (Riegel, 1976) and social learning theory (Bandura, 1977), encouraging investigators in their respective fields to reconsider the conceptually limited "law of inertia" mentioned above. Indeed, change within the therapeutic context must be approached from several simultaneous directions. Throughout the therapeutic contact the therapist and patient hope to bring about some degree of change within the patient. Whether practicing behavior therapy or psychoanalysis, the therapist attempts to alter the way the patient experiences his world and to foster an actual change in his living circumstances, seeking change for the patient's external reality. A dilemma arises when we consider that we and our world are in a constant state of flux: nothing can ever remain the same, although change may seem momentarily imperceptible. Constant change defines our existence, so that even our experience of hard-core physical reality (such as the desk before us) is actually defined more through change than stasis. It is not unreasonable to assume that change permeates our patients' lives regardless of the potency of our interventions. Therefore, what is the distinction between change that is therapeutic and change that is not? Further, at what point does change, in any form, become perceptible? By whom should the change be noticed? While facile answers to questions like these are not readily available, their explication is important if we are to understand the meaning of change in our patients' lives.

Our assumptions about maintenance dictate that we seek change in the form of adaptive interpersonal and intrapersonal functioning. However, judgments of adaptiveness cannot be made independent of the physical and social context within which the individual dwells. The complexity and importance of our social and physical contexts, independent of therapeutic ones, weigh most heavily in promoting and maintaining change. The influence of the world outside the consulting room has long been recognized by adherents of community mental health and behavior therapy. Yet the impact of this world on the patient is seldom evaluated, let alone used as part of the therapeutic process. When attempting to foster change within the patient or between the patient and his environment, the therapist should at the very least be aware of the potential impact of the environment both as a contributor and impediment to therapeutic change. The force of the patient's life outside of therapy can easily overwhelm the best designed program. This may occur not just during treatment, but after treatment as well. The longer time passes after treatment is terminated, the more fragile therapeutically induced change becomes in the face of powerful and, potentially, countertherapeutic environmental influences on the patient. Treatment programs that have limited initial impact on the patient are less likely to endure over time; those that have had a greater impact, both on the patient and on his environment, are more likely to endure, provided that they have also anticipated the cycle of person–situation interactions most likely to occur in the patient's future.

To summarize our analysis thus far, we have briefly touched on the relation between the passage of time and change. We have made the assumption that cycles of change and stability are the natural condition of developing persons.

Therapeutically induced change must compete with the processes of change that occur both within the patient and between the patient and environment. As time passes from the point of treatment termination, powerful intraindividual and environmental processes come to the fore. Unless treatment can alter the patient's construal style, living style, and/or physical and social world sufficiently, therapeutically fostered change will probably not endure.

LIFESTYLE AND MAINTENANCE

We have let a term slip into the previous discussion that bears a focal relevance to the remainder of this chapter. At this stage, it behooves us to discuss the concept of lifestyle and its meaning with regard to therapeutic, intraindividual, and environmental change. We maintain that sufficient therapeutic change should be assessed from at least three perspectives: the intrusion of the problem into the patient's cognitive life; the function of the problem within the patient's environment; and the degree to which the patient's current lifestyle supports the problem. While these perspectives are interrelated, we feel that they represent areas of concern distinct enough to warrant separate identification and discussion.

By intrusion we refer to the degree to which the problem interferes with the patient's ability to exhibit adaptive cognitive and instrumental functioning. It is well known, for example, that excessive anxiety can impair an individual's performance on complex cognitive tasks. Also, certain problems can have a major debilitative impact on the quality of the patient's mental life: obsessional and depressive disorders undoubtedly occupy the affected patient with thoughts that impede normal everyday living. On the other hand, some problems take up a considerably smaller amount of the patient's thought time. If we were to apply some arbitrary scale of therapeutic change, we would suggest that the more thought intrusive the problem, the more change units would be required for sufficient change. To this end, we would make the following prediction regarding the relation between maintenance of change, cognitive intrusion, and therapeutic change: the more pervasively the patient's problem is interwoven into his internal world, the more therapeutic change is required in order to be lasting.

The second perspective is a familiar one to most adherents of behavior therapy, especially those who subscribe to conditioning-based learning theories. This dimension is particularly relevant when we consider the supportive role an individual's environment can play in maintaining his maladaptive behavior. In this regard, when we refer to environment we mean the patient's social, as opposed to physical environment. Many behavior therapy treatment programs, particularly those for children and severely disturbed adults, focus on altering the style with which the patient interacts with significant others. Apparently the patient and those around him often fall into patterns of interaction which support the continuation of the patient's unproductive lifestyle. In those cases where such environmental support represents a major source of control, endurance of therapeutic change will be minimal unless the social environment is directly altered or the patient is instructed in how to change it. For this dimension, we would expect that problems which serve some function in the social environment or which are maintained through environmental support would require greater therapeutic effort (i.e., more change units) than would less involved problems.

The final parameter we will discuss here represents a link among lifestyles, maintenance, and change. In the previous discussion we highlighted the roles of intraindividual and environmental influences as elements to examine in determining the potential sufficiency of therapeutic change. The third parameter, the degree to which the patient's lifestyle supports the presenting problem, contains facets of each of the two previously discussed. While an explicit and clear definition of lifestyle is difficult, we will use this term to refer to the idiosyncratic and characteristic approach that the person takes toward living in his physical and social world. Thus an individual's lifestyle would be optimally described by meticulously recording his everyday activities. Included in such an observation would be a description of both the settings within which the individual negotiates his activities, as well as a characterization of the encounters he has with others. In fact, the efforts by Roger Barker and his colleagues (Barker, 1963) in describing the everyday activities of ordinary people comes closest to the ideal of recording lifestyles as we interpret this term. Barker's work, which has been almost completely neglected in the mental health field, provided invaluable insights into the interrelations among people, their social environments, and their routine activities. However, the picture of lifestyle produced by observations of activities neglects an important element of the individual's style of living: the ways in which he plans, organizes, and anticipates his actions. An individual's lifestyle, reflected in what he does and how he does it, represents only a small portion of a hierarchically structured phenomenon. At any moment in time, an individual can have a plan for what he will do in the next hour, the next month, the next year, and so on through the course of his life. His plans can also include one or many facets of his life; he may have different plans for work, family life, and leisure time. These plans that individuals have about what they will be doing, in which areas of their lives, and at what moments of their life are an integral part of the individual's lifestyle.

Given this characterization of lifestyle, as daily and routine actions, it is not too difficult to imagine how lifestyle may come to support a patient's problems. The way we structure our daily lives, the people we see, and the settings we enter can all become tightly interwoven with our problems in living. An implicit goal of most therapies is to bring about changes in the ways patients conduct their lives. Ostensibly, these changes should directly impact on the problems that patients present. However, when we do affect our patients' problems, we are probably accomplishing more than the simple elimination of symptoms.

We would like to suggest here that there is a direct link between sufficient change for long-lasting therapeutic effects and the degree to which the patient's lifestyle supports his presenting problem: the more closely intertwined the patient's lifestyle is with his problem, the more degrees or units of therapeutic change are necessary. To this end, it is well understood that individuals adopt certain lifestyles or living patterns dependent on their presenting problems.

While it would certainly be unwise to posit a lifestyle uniformity assumption here, certain individuals sharing common problems apparently follow similar lifestyles. Thus we can rather clearly demonstrate that there is a particular lifestyle that supports some problems, such as alcohol or drug abuse. Addicted individuals frequently count among their friends those who engage in similar abuses and pursuits.

One major source of difficulty in determining the precise relation between lifestyle and presenting problem stems from a lack of clarity with regard to the causative structure. Are lifestyles structured about problems, or do lifestyles create problems? While this is a question amenable to empirical investigation (and one that must be more clearly spelled out), the relation between the two may well be birdirectional. That is, the individual's lifestyle and presenting problem may interact in a mutual system of support such that neither can be viewed as causative of the other. What is certainly clear, however, is that they are linked in some fasion: determination of the nature of the linkage remains to be revealed by future research.

Maintenance obviously becomes a matter of central concern since change will indeed be short-lived unless the nexus between lifestyle and the clinical problem is broken. In this regard, a sufficient amount of therapeutically induced change will be necessary to alter this relation. What would be necessary is elimination of the problem which would consequently disrupt the lifestyle supporting it. Alternatively, alteration of the lifestyle may eliminate the presenting problem.

We are suggesting here that any form of intervention whose effects the therapist intends to endure must directly or indirectly disrupt the client's living pattern. Change, if it is to last, must be nurtured within the client's social world. The wisdom of behavior change agents such as Tharp and Wetzel (1969) and Fairweather, Sanders, Cressler, and Maynard (1969), who developed change programs that radically altered their clients' living patterns, is quite obvious given this consideration. When a radical form of intervention which disrupts the client's daily living patterns is not feasible or necessary, alternative means of intervention must be selected which have some impact on the client's everyday world.

Self-control procedures represent an approach toward lifestyle alteration that has become increasingly accepted in this regard. Where direct environmental intervention by the therapist is difficult, the client is enlisted as the major agent of change. In either case, whether the therapist or client attempts environmental change, such intervention is important for maintenance.

The degree of lifestyle disruption adequate for instigation of long-lasting change depends in part on the severity of the presenting complaint. Successfully maintained change for the chronic alcoholic or drug abuser would require a more broad-based change than that for the spider phobic or situationally unassertive client. In many cases of alcohol and drug abuse the client adopts a patterns of living to support the abuse. A further complication arises in that drug or alcohol abuse seldom is the only problem the client exhibits: both disorders have wide-ranging social, familial, and vocational effects. On the other hand, the spider phobic generally does not experience considerably more difficulty than that associated with the phobia. We would assume, given this analysis, that considerably more effort (units of change) would be required on the therapist's and patient's part to alter the alcoholic lifestyle than would be required to alter a monosymptomatic phobia lifestyle.

While we have only briefly presented each of the three parameters we feel are relevant to the maintenance of change, in-depth consideration of each is important. Further, identification of parameters that may influence the maintenance of change should not end with the three we have highlighted here.

Before we proceed with a presentation of the plan and structure of this book, we would like to note several obvious points regarding maintenance. First, therapists and investigators need to devote more direct energy toward ensuring that therapeutically induced change endures. While the therapeutic contract seldom contains a warranty against relapse, the rise of consumerism in our society may lead us to devise methods of offering clients more information relevant to their choosing a therpaist and evaluating the quality of the services received. Second, the therapist cannot uncritically expect that adaptive change will endure, especially if we view change as a natural by-product of life. In planning for maintenance, the therapist should follow the leads suggested by Goldstein et al. (1966) and the contributors to this present work.

The therapist interested in promoting long-lasting change should be aware of all the concerns we have addressed above. We should repeat, however, that the points we have made regarding therapeutic change and maintenance are primarily speculative at this point. As investigators direct their interest toward maintenance problems, greater clarity on these matters should be obtained.

PLAN OF THE BOOK

A number of themes have been introduced thus far: the active organism conception, interactionism, multiple success indicants, the cyclicity of change and stability, lifestyles, and the contextual embeddedness of psychological disorders. Although they may appear loosely related, a moment's thought will reveal the unifying thread in the concept of a *system*. While systems notions are not new to psychology (cf. Kantor, 1959) or to "mental health" (Hayes-Roth, Longabaugh, & Ryback, 1977; Kilburg, 1977), the movement toward a systems-oriented, "unified" model of clinical intervention and outcome has been quite limited. One contributor to the conceptual myopia is the widespread tendency to elevate the separate "elements" of the system to positions of preeminence, based on theoretical or disciplinary loyalties. A second and more basic deterrent to unification is the absence of a consensually formulated model for identifying, quantifying, and manipulating the "complex of interacting elements" in human networks, personal and interpersonal.

Talk, they say, is cheap. And "systems talk" may be the most convenient of all—for it seems glibly to encompass *everything*. Any discussion of systems that does not clearly specify constituents and which fails to generate hypotheses amenable to empirical test is not worth the reader's time. In the present volume, the chapters have been organized to acquaint readers with the basic ingredients of clinical growth and development, both inside and outside the client. Similarly, a critical and hypothesis-generating attitude pervades the chapters.

In the first section, following the "Overview" (Part I) are several chapters which introduce the learning theory "foundations" of contemporary, action-oriented treatment. Wildman and Wildman review in Chapter 2 the findings from applied behavior-analytic programs of treatment. Their presentation is thorough and incisive, yielding a set of 16 suggestions for "programming" generalization of behaviorally based interventions. In Chapter 3, Fishman and Lubetkin describe the intricacies of individual behavior therapy practice in such a way as to make clear that it is anything but a mechanical, or purely technique-oriented enterprise. Asserting that maintenance and transfer of gains from behavioral interventions are a "reflection of the sound practice of clinical behavior therapy," Fishman and Lubetkin illustrate both the potential of the learning theory model and the need to supplement it with knowledge of the client's unique perspectives and with a sensitivity to oft-neglected "relationship" factors. In the final chapter of Part II, Mash and Terdal present an insightful critique of contemporary models of follow-up assessment, touching on several of the questions raised in the present chapter. These authors offer guidelines on the design of psychotherapy outcome research that should help to reduce the often arbitrary, noncontextual, and oversimplified nature of the maintenance data upon which behavioral investigators have too readily rested their claims of relative superiority.

Part III of the book includes in-depth presentations covering the role of the person (amid the temporal and situational context) in long-range therapeutic change. In Chapter 5, Paul Wachtel (one of the most respected commentators on matters behavioral and psychodynamic) looks at the "philosophies" of behavioral intervention and suggests that a more *person-centered* focus might well be in order, particularly as it may shed light on the question of the generalizability of therapeutic learning. The patient's perceptions, expectancies, interests, and values are seen as central in defining both pathology and needed change. Wachtel draws important parallels between clinically sophisticated accounts of behavior therapy, psychodynamic intervention, and family therapy which may help to highlight the emergent "systems" philosophy in contemporary clinical theory. A most thorough attempt to relate intrapsychic concepts to treatment design and evaluation is provided by Raymond B. Cattell in Chapter 6. Cattell's *structured learning theory* represents a singular conceptual effort to quantify psychodynamic concepts, to relate intrapsychic adjustment (or balance) to environmental enabling conditions, and to provide a means of assessing the structural nature of "personality change" subsequent to therapeutic intervention. Cattellian concepts of "integration learning," the "dynamic lattice," and the *P* technique of intensive clinical investigation, along with his explicit interactional view of learning and development, would seem to offer much to the theory-starved field of psychotherapeutic maintenance— even to those who would reject the Freudian-inspired rendering of so-called dynamic source traits. In Chapter 7, Karoly attempts to provide an empirically based outline of the client's active contribution to long-range therapeutic learning, by drawing upon the implications of what Mischel (1973) has termed "person variables"—the internalized products of an individual's social learning history which influence how the environment impacts on him/her and which regulate his/her active mastery of the inconstant conditions of living. How and what a client thinks, does, feels, expects, wants, remembers, and forgets jointly influence the short- and long-range results of treatment. Without postulating an unconscious or instinctual source of energy or inherent stability, Karoly offers a person-centered analysis of therapeutic learning organized around several "tasks" of therapy. The organizational scheme may provide a less arbitrary framework for the inclusion of "personality variables" in future psychotherapy research. Following this chapter is Sharon M. Hall's conceptual and empirical analysis of the self-management literature (Chapter 8). The most discussed and perhaps the most elusive person variable, self-management deals with the processes through which individuals either sustain or alter their goal-directed activities for adaptive purposes, often in conflict with environmental contingencies. Self-management training is strongly endorsed as a primary means of providing clients with generalizable skills "which could be used during and especially after therapy to produce long-lasting, self-determined change." Hall reviews the clinical research on self-management (focusing on addictive disorders) and offers a working model of adherence to self-management programs that should prove to possess great heuristic value in the years ahead. An in the final chapter of Part III, Edward B. Klein provides an adult developmental perspective on therapy, incorporating the all-important temporal dimension in his account of therapeutic growth and change. Specifically, Klein argues that "change is normal" (in many cases) and that pathology-oriented conceptions of human crises fail to provide true historical continuity for the clinical appraisal of a client's "life structure." In his presentation, Klein offers a tentative adult development model of evolving life tasks—based on recent research into the lives of a small group of American men (Levinson, Darrow, Klein, Levinson, & McKee, 1978). Particularly helpful is the glimpse into the conduct of both adult development research and clinical practice based on special sensitivity to developmental crises, the exploration of values and choices, and treatment termination.

Part IV of this volume takes the reader into systems domains rarely addressed by the clinical practitioner or the psychotherapy outcome researcher. By definition, systems interact with other systems and

generally move toward stable interrelationships (Berrien, 1968). The personal components in the context of individual therapy must be considered only a part of the "larger context"—of extended extratherapy dyadic, social, familial, subcultural, and political realities. The contributors to Part IV of this book offer exciting perspectives on the broader systems in which maladaptive behavior patterns are not only created and nurtured, but (hopefully) changed through the ministrations of knowledgeable professionals and paraprofessionals.

J. T. DeVoge (Chapter 10) argues that the interpersonal relationship between doctor and patient has not been fully appreciated (particularly by behavioral practitioners), nor has its transfer-enhancing potential been completely understood or exploited. After offering a critique of the "behavioral view of the social world," DeVoge reviews the conceptual and tactical implications for the process of long-range behavior change of Leary's (1957) structural model of reciprocal interpersonal exchange. DeVoge presents his own model of reciprocal role training as a therapeutic procedure designed to "enable a client to adjust to the social consequences of a newly acquired behavioral repertoire." In Chapter 11, Brehm and McAllister review the contributions of contemporary social psychology to the process of change and maintenance. Several theoretical orientations (e.g., dissonance, reactance, overjustification, self-perception, intrinsic motivation) are integrated into their presentation, with the goal of demonstrating how a composite of social psychological perspectives can contribute to an improved clinical product vis-a-vis outcome and long-range durability of learning. Winett and Neale (Chapter 12) offer an intriguing analysis of flexible work schedules in their ecologically oriented presentation, which illustrates how the structure of the workplace directly influences the quality of family life. Earlier in this chapter, we raised the issue of lifestyle change as a central component of posttherapy adjustment. Winett and Neale illustrate the potential of a "systems-centered," community-based intervention designed to restructure a "target environment" in such a way as to enhance the adaptive capabilities of dual-worker families with young children. And in the final chapter of this volume, Meyers and Kempner review the oft-neglected literature in health planning as a necessary fund of knowledge for the psychologist who would function as clinician–administrator in the "aftercare system." Psychologists have expended great efforts in denying the validity of the "medical model." Unfortunately, whether or not it is epistemologically correct to incorporate "mental health" concepts within a general health rubric, federal legislation nonetheless ties mental health dollars to facilities (hospitals and community clinics) that provide health services under the management of physicians, accountants, and citizen boards. Meyers and Kempner will introduce the reader to the Health Systems Agency (HSA), Public Law

93–641, the "certificate of need review," and a host of health planning concepts that will better equip the psychologist to function adequately in the mental health system—functioning which is vital to the long-range tenure of the posttherapy client in the community.

Taken together, the 13 chapters of the present volume represent a fundamental curriculum in the psychology of therapeutic persistence.

REFERENCES

Ausubel, D. P. *The psychology of meaningful verbal learning.* New York: Grune & Stratton, 1963.

Bandura, A. *Social learning theory.* Englewood Cliffs, N.J.: Prentice-Hall, 1977.

Barker, R. G. (Ed.). *The stream of behavior: Explorations of its structure and content.* New York: Appleton-Century-Crofts, 1963.

Bennett, S., & Bowers, D. *An introduction to multivariate techniques for social and behavioral sciences.* New York: Halsted, 1977.

Bergin, A. E. The evaluation of therapeutic outcomes. In A. E. Bergin & S. L. Garfield (Eds.), *Handbook of psychotherapy and behavior change: An empirical analysis.* New York: Wiley, 1971.

Berrien, F. K. *General and social systems.* New Brunswick, N. J.: Rutgers University Press, 1968.

Bunch, M. E. Transfer of training in the mastery of an antagonistic habit after varying intervals of time. *Journal of Comparative Psychology,* 1939, *28,* 189–200.

Cattell, R. B. *The scientific use of factor analysis in behavioral and life sciences.* New York: Plenum, 1978.

Ellis, H. C. *The transfer of learning.* New York: Macmillan, 1965.

Ellis, H. C. Transfer and retention. In M. H. Marx (Ed.), *Learning: Processes.* London: Macmillan, 1969.

Eysenck, H. J. The effects of psychotherapy: An evaluation. *Journal of Consulting Psychology,* 1952, *16,* 319–324.

Fairweather, G. W., Sanders, D. H., Cressler, D. L., & Maynard, H. *Community life for the mentally ill: An alternative to institutional care.* Chicago: Aldine, 1969.

Gabriel, R. M., & Glavin, G. B. Multivariate data analysis in empirical research: A look on the bright side. *Pavlovian Journal of Biological Science,* 1978, *13,* 93–112.

Garfield, S. L., & Bergin, A. E. (Eds.). *Handbook of psychotherapy and behavior change: An empirical analysis* (2nd ed.). New York: Wiley, 1978.

Goldstein, A. P. *Therapist–patient expectancies in psychotherapy.* New York: Pergamon, 1962.

Goldstein, A. P., Heller, K., & Sechrest, L. B. *Psychotherapy and the psychology of behavior change.* New York: Wiley, 1966.

Gross, M. L. *The psychological society: A critical analysis of psychiatry, psychotherapy, psychoanalysis and the psychological revolution.* New York: Random House, 1978.

Hall, J. F. *The psychology of learning.* Philadelphia: Lippincott, 1966.

Hayes-Roth, F., Longabaugh, R., & Ryback, R. Mental health: Systems and nonsystems. *International Journal of Mental Health,* 1977, *5,* 5–31.

Hunt, W. A., & Matarazzo, J. D. Three years later: Recent developments in the experimental modification of smoking behavior. *Journal of Abnormal Psychology,* 1973, *81,* 107–114.

Kantor, J. R. *Interbehavioral psychology.* Bloomington, Ind.: Principia Press, 1959.

Kazdin, A. E., & Wilson, G. T. *Evaluation of behavior therapy: Issues, evidence, and research strategies.* Cambridge, Mass.: Ballinger, 1978.

Kiesler, D. J. Some myths of psychotherapy research and the search for a paradigm. *Psychological Bulletin,* 1966, *65,* 110–136.

Kilburg, R. General systems theory and community mental health: A view from the boiler room. *International Journal of Mental Health,* 1977, *5,* 73–102.

Kimbel, G. A. *Hilgard and Marquis' conditioning and learning.* New York: Appleton-Century-Crofts, 1961.

Leary, T. *Interpersonal diagnosis of personality.* New York: Ronald Press, 1957.

Levinson, D. J., Darrow, C. H., Klein, E. B. Levinson, M. H., & McKee, B. *The seasons of a man's life.* New York: Knopf, 1978.

Luborsky, L., Singer, B., & Luborsky, L. Comparative studies of psychotherapy: Is it true that everyone has won and all must have prizes? *Archives of General Psychiatry,* 1975, *32,* 995–1008.

Maxwell, A. E. *Multivariate analysis in behavioural research.* London: Halsted, 1977.

Mintz, J., Luborsky, L., & Christoph, P. Measuring the outcomes of psychotherapy: Findings of the Penn Psychotherapy Project. *Journal of Consulting and Clinical Psychology,* 1979, *47,* 319–334.

Mischel, W. Toward a cognitive social learning reconceptualization of personality. *Psychological Review,* 1973, *80,* 252–283.

Namboodiri, N. K., Carter, L. F., & Blalock, H. M., Jr. *Applied multivariate analysis and experimental designs.* New York: McGraw-Hill, 1975.

Osgood, C. E. The similarity paradox in human learning: A resolution. *Psychological Review,* 1949, *56,* 132–143.

Overall, J. E., & Klett, C. J. *Applied multivariate analysis.* New York: McGraw-Hill, 1972.

Riegel, K. F. The dialectics of human development. *American Psychologist,* 1976, *31,* 689–700.

Shapiro, A. K., & Morris, L. A. Placebo effects in medical and psychological therapies. In S. L. Garfield & A. E. Bergin (Eds.), *Handbook of psychotherapy and behavior change: An empirical analysis* (2nd ed.). New York: Wiley, 1978.

Strupp, H. H. Psychotherapy research and practice: An overview. In S. L. Garfield & A. E. Bergin (Eds.), *Handbook of psychotherapy and behavior change: An empirical analysis* (2nd ed.). New York: Wiley, 1978.

Strupp, H. H., & Hadley, S. W. A tripartite model of mental health and therapeutic outcomes. *American Psychologist,* 1977, *32,* 187–196.

Tharp, R. G., & Wetzel, R. J. *Behavior modification in the natural environment.* New York: Academic Press, 1969.

Waskow, I.E., & Parloff, M. B. (Eds.). *Psychotherapy change measures* (DHEW Publication No. ADM 74–120). Washington, D.C.: U.S. Government Printing Office, 1975.

Watzlawick, P., Weakland, J. H., & Fisch, R. *Change: Principles of problem formation and problem resolution.* New York: W. W. Norton, 1974.

PART **II**

Learning Theory
Foundations

C H A P T E R

2

MAINTENANCE AND GENERALIZATION OF INSTITUTIONAL BEHAVIOR MODIFICATION PROGRAMS

ROBERT W. WILDMAN II AND ROBERT W. WILDMAN

An applied behavior analysis, as defined by Baer, Wolf, and Risley (1968) in the first issue of the *Journal of Applied Behavior Analysis*, "will make obvious the importance of the behavior changed, its quantitative characteristics, the experimental manipulations which analyze with clarity what was responsible for the change, the technologically exact description of all procedures contributing to that change, the effectiveness of those procedures in making sufficient change for value, and the generality of that change" (p. 97). This approach, often popularly termed "behavior modification" (Goodall, 1972), has demonstrated its effectiveness in altering a wide range of behavior patterns manifested by a extremely heterogeneous assortment of clients. These demonstrations include, as examples, the control of overeating (Stuart, 1967), the elimination of towel hoarding in a psychotic patient (Ayllon, 1963), the reduction of disruptive and aggressive behaviors (Bostow & Bailey, 1969), and the improvement of marital happiness (Azrin, Naster, & Jones, 1973).

One part of the Baer et al. (1968) definition of an applied behavior analysis quoted above is the determination of the generality of the resulting change in behavior. Kazdin and Bootzin (1972) have expressed the opinion that the generalization of the treatment effects of one form of behavior modification procedure, the token economy, to situations in which the token economy is not in operation would be expected to be the very raison d'etre for such procedures. However, they list numerous studies which fail to demonstrate such generality. In fact, many workers regard a return to pretreatment behavior patterns upon the reversal of experimental conditions (the A-B-A or A-B-A-B design) as part of the demonstration of a functional relationship (e.g., Bijou, Peterson, Harris, Allen, & Johnston, 1969). And in the multiple-baseline design, improvement in one behavior at the time an intervention is applied to another behavior is regarded as a failure to demonstrate experimental control over the responses (e.g., R. V. Hall, Cristler, Cranston, & Tucker, 1970).[1]

Lindsley (1964) has distinguished between therapeutic and prosthetic interventions. Briefly, a therapeutic intervention is one whose effects transcend the treatment situation. Such is not the case with prosthetic interventions. Reviews of the behavior modification literature by Kazdin and Bootzin (1972) and O'Leary and Drabman (1971) strongly suggest that the question of whether behavior modification procedures are prostehtic or therapeutic interventions is an unresolved one. The contention that the effects of behavior modification procedures show "little, if any, generalization" was one of the key points in Russell's (1974) strongly worded critique of behavior modification methods. Unless behavior modifiers are able to demonstrate that they have the technology to make the behavioral changes which they engender also give evidence of transfer to extratherapy times and settings, it seems likely that Russell's (1974) viewpoint will prevail.

The question of whether or not the effects of behavior modification procedures are generalizable would appear to be a particularly important one for personnel working in institutional settings. In a time of limited budgets, the extensive use of such elaborate procedures as behavior modification typically entails would seem to be of dubious economy and practicality, unless the results of such efforts are at least somewhat far-reaching and durable. It is incumbent upon behavior modifiers to search for ways to make the effects of their work "carry over" to times and places outside the treatment setting.

The present report is a review of the literature relevant to the generality of the effects of behavior modification in institutional settings. While work from many types of institutions will be covered in this review, studies conducted in classroom settings will predominate. This emphasis results from the fact that generally there are better opportunities for follow-up to behavior modification programs in educational settings than in other types of institutions. For example, following a token economy classroom program the students usually can be observed later in a regular classroom. The fate of patients discharged from a token economy ward in a state hospital is not typically so easily determined.

WHAT IS GENERALIZATION?

The concept of generalization or transfer of training is a multifaceted one. O'Leary and Drabman (1971) have identified four types of generalization:

1. *Generalization across behaviors:* Will behavior modification procedures applied to one behavior within a subject influence other behavior patterns within the same subject?

2. *Generalization across situations:* If one is successful in establishing or modifying behavior in one situation, will that behavior pattern similarly be established or modified in an independent situation?

3. *Generalization across time:* Will behavior taught or changed at one point in time also manifest itself at a subsequent point in time?

4. *A combination* of the above forms of generalization.

From the standpoint of learning theory, items 2 and 3 above are instances of stimulus generalization, whereas item 1 involves a response generalization process (R. V. Hall, 1966).

The preceding list of types of generalization would appear to be a basic as opposed to an exhaustive one. Other investigators have described other, although possibly less significant, forms of generalization. For example, Surratt, Ulrich, and Hawkins (1969), Broden, Bruce, Mitchell, Carter, and Hall (1970), and Kazdin (1973a) discussed generalization across subjects. This form of generalization is perhaps a manifestation of the modeling paradigm explicated by Bandura (1969).

GENERALIZATION OF NONTOKEN CLASSROOM BEHAVIOR MODIFICATION PROGRAMS

R. V. Hall, Lund, and Jackson (1968) manipulated the amount of study behavior manifested by several economically deprived students, three, of whom were in the same elementary school classroom. This was accomplished by changing the occasions on which teacher attention was delivered.

It was determined during a baseline phase that teacher attention was primarily delivered following the occurrence of nonstudy, disruptive behaviors. During baseline the percentage of observation intervals during which study behaviors were observed was at a very low level. But making teacher attention contingent on studying greatly increased the percentage of study behaviors observed. A functional relationship between the occasions on which attention was delivered and the students' behavior was demonstrated by reversing the contingencies in the classroom; that is to say, teacher attention was delivered following episodes of nonstudying by the experimental subjects. This reversal resulted in study behaviors' decreasing to near the percentage that had been observed under the baseline condition. Study behavior was then again reinforced, and the percentage of intervals in which studying was observed increased. Postchecks on the behavior of two of the students were conducted following the formal termination of the R. V. Hall et al. (1968) programs. During these postchecks, it was found that studying continued to occur at the same higher percentages which had been attained at the conclusion of the second reinforcement phase. However, it is not certain that this finding should be interpreted as evidence of generalization of the effects of the experimental procedure across time. The subjects remained for the year with the same teachers who had been involved in the project. It was during the remainder of that school year that the postchecks were conducted. It seems likely that these teachers, having learned more effective means for controlling the behavior of their previously disruptive pupils, would have continued to reinforce studying with attention and to ignore nonstudying behavior. This seems particularly likely in view of the fact that the teachers were reported to have found the reversal phase to be aversive and that one teacher spontaneously (and apparently successfully) applied these same procedures to pupils who were not formally designated as experimental subjects. The generalization of treatment effects from the R. V. Hall et al. (1968) study may thus have actually represented an instance of "reprogramming the environment," a technique for achieving generalization which is discussed later in this review.

Madsen, Becker, and Thomas (1968) demonstrated that they could reduce the percentage of observation intervals in which disruptive behaviors were noted for several pupils by making teacher attention contingent on appropriate behaviors. But as in the R. V. Hall et al. (1968) study, an increased percentage of disruptive behaviors resulted when the teacher again dealt with the class as she had done during the initial baseline period. One might conclude from this that the behavior modification procedure had not made the students "well-behaved children" in the sense of imparting to them an enduring personality trait.

In a class of educable mental retardates, the students' use of an obscene gesture ("naughty finger") was a problem. Sulzbacher and Houser (1970) instituted a special 10-minute recess in the afternoon. The class was told that they would lose 1 minute of that recess each time the teacher saw or heard of the use of a "naughty finger." During the time the recess contingency was in effect, the frequency of the teacher's observing the gesture declined markedly below baseline rates. But that rate began climbing again when the recess contingency was removed. Thus the Sulzbacher and Houser (1970) procedure did not demonstrate generalization across time.

It seems clear that the application of learning principles to problems in the classroom may be extremely effective in controlling the behavior of students where and while such a program is in operation. But this success does not guarantee that these behavioral changes will generalize to other times and settings. In this discussion, the classroom is being used simply as a standard environment in which to measure the strength of generalization. A similar lack of generalization has also been noted in other settings and with different patient populations (Ullmann & Krasner, 1965). However, it might be speculated that the procedures used in the studies just mentioned were in some way too weak to produce generalization consistently. The token economy is a technique held in awe by many. Perhaps the effects of this more powerful procedure will routinely generalize.

GENERALIZATION OF TOKEN ECONOMY PROGRAMS

O'Leary and Drabman (1971), in their review of classroom token economies, note that generalization of treatment effects has been found in some programs but not in others. It would seem to be useful to examine several programs from each group in an attempt to determine what critical differences, if any, might exist between those token economies whose effects generalize and those whose effects do not.

Token Economies Which Have Not Demonstrated Generalization

Kuypers, Becker, and O'Leary (1968) established a token economy in a special adjustment class for third- and fourth-graders. Following the baseline phase, a list of rules was written on the blackboard. The teacher explained that each child in the room would be rated on a scale from 1 to 10 in accordance with the extent to which he or she followed the rules written on the board. The ratings the children received could be exchanged later for prizes. This procedure was followed only during the afternoon session.

The children were also rated by their teachers during other parts of the day, but the teacher was told to "emphasize" to them that the ratings they received in other classes would not influence the number of points they received during the afternoon token economy session. During the token economy phase, the mean percentage of intervals in which "deviant" behaviors were observed fell from 54% to 27.8%. However, during a 2-week return-to-baseline condition, the percentage of intervals in which disruptive behaviors were observed increased to 41.5%. "Little, if any, generalization of improved behavior from the afternoon period when the token system was in effect to the morning period when the token system was not in effect" (Kuypers et al., 1968, p. 105) was noted. Thus, the Kuypers et al. (1968) token program did not demonstrate generalization across either time or situation.

A classroom token economy for institutionalized adolescent female offenders has been reported by Meichenbaum, Bowers, and Ross (1968). The girls were told that they could earn money by behaving appropriately in an afternoon class. On a periodic schedule, each girl received a slip of paper showing the percentage of her behavior which was judged to have been appropriate during the preceding period. They were paid different amounts of money on the basis of this percentage. These determinations, as well as the other observations collected during the study, were done on a time-sampling basis. The girls were explicitly informed that while their behavior would be observed during the morning session, the appropriateness or inappropriateness of their behavior during the morning would have no bearing on the amount of money they received during the afternoon sessions. This procedure was effective in increasing the percentage of appropriate behavior manifested by the girls during the afternoon session. But these effects did not generalize across time and situations to the morning session. There were excellent indications that the students discriminated between the token and nontoken conditions very well. In fact, Meichenbaum et al. (1968) reported that one girl threatened in regard to the morning session, "If you don't pay us, we won't shape up." A variant of the token procedure was thus introduced into the morning sessions. This step immediately increased the percentage of intervals in which appropriate classroom behavior was observed to a level comparable to that obtained during the afternoon class.

O'Leary, Becker, Evans, and Saudargas (1969) gave children points in accordance with the extent to which they followed classroom rules. As in the Meichenbaum et al. (1968) program, these points were exchangeable for backup reinforcers, prizes. The children were told at the beginning of the token period that they would be rated in this fashion four times each afternoon. In contrast to the Kuypers et al. (1968) and Meichenbaum et al. (1968) reports, there was no mention in this program whether the children were told that their behavior during other portions of the day would have no bearing on the number of tokens they received during the afternoon. The token procedure had the effect of dramatically reducing the percentage of disruptive behaviors during the afternoon session. No sustained generalization of treatment effects to the morning session was observed. However, there appeared to be a temporary effect on the morning session in that the percentage of disruptive behaviors was lowered for the first few days the token system was in operation. It may be that not explicitly informing the subjects of the lack of any contingency between their behavior during the morning session and the number of tokens they would receive made it more difficult for them to discriminate between the token and nontoken conditions. However, the data clearly indicate that that discrimination was ultimately achieved. Generalization across behaviors was suggested but not demonstrated by this program. The subjects made greater than expected gains on the California Achievement Test during the time the token economy was in operation, and average daily attendance was greater during the token than during the nontoken periods.

Wolf, Giles, and Hall (1968) operated an afterschool remedial classroom for underachieving fifth- and sixth-graders from deprived backgrounds. Points were given to the students for the completion of academic work within the token economy classroom and for earning good grades in their regular school. These points could later be exchanged for such reinforcers as candy, novelties, and trips to places of interest. One experiment carried out within the context of this program involved manipulating the number of tokens dispensed for the completion of various academic assignments. This procedure had a dramatic effect on the number of exercises within each area completed. For example, when two subjects were paid a large number of tokens for reading a certain book, the number of stories read from that book was relatively high. But when the same activity was reinforced at a lower rate, the number of stories read fell to near zero. The dramatic effectiveness of this procedure was perhaps enhanced by the fact that subjects in the study were carefully briefed as to the number of tokens available for the completion of different work. A later experiment in the program addressed itself to the question of the effect of the high token rewards for one class of behavior on the frequency of occurrence of other classes. Generally, the number of less rewarded tasks completed declined during the course of the study. However, the authors noted an exception to this pattern. The frequency of reading did not decline to baseline rates after the completion of a period in which it had been richly rewarded for a number of subjects. Thus Wolf et al. (1968) had designed a token economy in which, for most subjects, generalization across behaviors did not occur. Of course, much of this effect may have resulted from the fact that the behaviors under study were incompatible with each other;

obviously, when one is reading, that person cannot also be completing arithmetic problems. So as the rate of one behavior was increased, a drop in other behaviors was the nearly inevitable result. During the period in which the remedial classroom was in operation, the students made significantly greater gains in report card grades than did the members of a carefully matched control group. It is, however, unclear as to whether or not this finding indicates generalization across situations since the students were actually paid tokens for good report card grades. An important finding of the Wolf et al. (1968) report was that the experimental subjects demonstrated significantly greater improvement on the Stanford Achievement Test than did the control group. It should be pointed out that academic work in the project under discussion was reinforced only when it was done correctly. Other programs in which purely topographical behaviors (e.g., remaining in seat, looking at a book) were reinforced were by and large not successful in demonstrating genuine academic improvements (e.g., Barrish, Saunders, & Wolf, 1969; R. V. Hall, Panyan, & Rabon, 1968; Homme, deBaca, Devine, Steinhorst, & Rickert, 1963). On the other hand, reinforcing academic behaviors may have the indirect effect of reducing the percentage of disruptive intervals (Ayllon & Roberts, 1974; Winett & Roach, 1973). A most significant illustration of this latter principle is contained in a study by Ayllon, Layman, and Kandel (1975). Three hyperactive children were taken off their medication, resulting in dramatic increases in the disruptive behaviors symptomatic of hyperactivity. The children were then reinforced for correct academic work in the areas of math and reading. Percentages of correct academic work rose dramatically, and behaviors suggestive of hyperactivity fell to the level of the period when the children had been on medication. These findings assume particular importance when it is considered that the children had not made academic progress while on medication. Hay, Hay, and Nelson (1977) replicated the effect noted by Ayllon and Roberts (1974) and Winett and Roach (1973). Their data also suggest that the reinforcement of academic behaviors may produce effects on both academic and on-task behaviors which generalize to times when only on-task behaviors are reinforced and to times when no contingencies whatever are in effect.

Other classroom token economies in which generalization was not demonstrated include those of Bushell, Wrobel, and Michaelis (1968), and Herman and Tramontana (1971).

Token Economies Which Have Demonstrated Generalization

Hewett, Taylor, and Artuso (1969) involved emotionally disturbed children in a project which evaluated the effectiveness of an "engineered classroom." The backbone of the procedure in the engineered classroom was a system of awarding checkmarks, exchangeable for tangible rewards, for starting and working on academic tasks. Four separate classes were involved in the Hewett et al. (1969) study. A control class (C) did not use the token system during any part of the year. An experimental class (E) was run on the token system during the entire year. Two other classes had the token system in operation only during half of the year: class CE began without the token system but switched to it at midyear, while class EC began with the system in operation but the use of tokens was discontinued at the beginning of the spring semester. The dependent measures employed in the study were the percentage of time during observation periods the students "attended" to academic tasks and pre- and post-test comparisons on the California Achievement Test. The percentage of attending behaviors in the control class remained at a relatively low level throughout the course of the academic year. In contrast, the experimental class's attending behavior climbed to a high percentage and stabilized at that level. Class CE began the year with a relatively low level of attending behaviors. This percentage increased dramatically with the introduction of the token economy. The results for class EC were quite unusual. This class obtained its highest percentages of attending behaviors *following the removal* of the token economy. Similarly, the arithmetic scores for this group continued to increase during the nontoken period. The mere passage of time or the increasing maturity of the students would not appear to be an acceptable explanation for these findings in that neither of these phenomena were observed in the control class. The authors advanced several hypotheses to account for these unexpected results, such as the increased competency of the teachers and the possibility that the token period had in some way "readied" the students to cope with the more traditional educational approach. But these suggestions do not explain why such continued improvement was not observed following the removal of token contingencies in other programs. It would seem to be potentially fruitful to examine the procedures used in the Hewett et al. (1969) token economy in more detail in an effort to determine what specific aspects of the program may have contributed to the generalization of effects across time (to the nontoken period) and across behaviors (improvements in academic achievement when only attending was systematically rewarded).

A previous report of the engineered classroom (Hewett, 1967) was, regretably as far as the purposes of the present chapter are concerned, written in an anecdotal fashion as opposed to specifying precisely which procedures were used. However, one possible difference between this and other token economy classrooms may lie in the fact that Hewett (1967) explicitly lists "appreciation for social approval and avoidance of disapproval" (p. 459) as one of the "standards required for learning" which may be promoted through the use of behavior modification in the classroom. The author states that while the token system is the backbone of the reward procedures in the engineered classroom, every effort is made to bring the children under the control of rewards "at the higher levels of the hierarchy," such as teacher approval. Of course, teacher approval is not a stimulus event which is completely absent from other token economy classrooms. But the fact that Hewett (1967) specifically mentions bringing the children under the control of this reinforcer would seem to suggest that teacher approval may have been paired with the delivery of tokens on a more systematic basis in this classroom than was the case in others. Some support for this suggestion, again anecdotal, comes from the author:

> The engineered class design is not viewed as an end in itself. Observations suggest that the value of checkmarks and tangible exchange items soon gives way to the satisfaction of succeeding in school and receiving recognition as a student from peers, teachers, and parents. Transition programs have been worked out where children started in the engineered classroom have gradually been reintroduced into regular classes. While this stage is not fully developed, it appears to be a natural evolutionary development in the program. (Hewett, 1967, p. 466)

It would seem that this procedure could well have the effect of establishing teacher approval as a powerful secondary reinforcer. Perhaps continued improvement in the EC class was maintained by this newly acquired reinforcer. A much more rigorous test of this hypothesis comes from a study by Chadwick and Day (1971). They treated 25 minority group students in a token economy classroom. Points were awarded for engaging in academic activities, correct academic work, and for "appropriate personal and social classroom behavior related to academic performance." Teacher approval and attention were paired with both the delivery of points and their exchange for tangible backup reinforcers. In contrast to the baseline period, the token phase was marked by: (1) an increase in the percentage of class time the students spent working; (2) an increase in the amount of work completed per unit time; and (3) an improvement in accuracy of academic work. The token system was then withdrawn, but the "systematic use of social reinforcement" applied during the token phase was continued unchanged. During the posttoken phase, the amount of academic work completed per unit time and its accuracy continued at the same high level as was observed when the token economy was in operation. However, the percentage of time the subjects devoted to studying declined to near baseline rates. No data on the impact of this program on disruptive behaviors were presented. Significant increases on the California Achievement Test over the course of the entire project were noted.

Galloway and Mickelson (1971) also paired social reinforcement from the teacher with the delivery of material rewards. They reported their observation that "It was the authors' experience . . . that when material reinforcement was combined with social reinforcement and with success in the task at hand, the children did not demand material reinforcement for all responses" (pp. 153–154). The pairing of teacher approval with the delivery of reinforcement would appear to be a particularly important factor in generalization from behavior modification procedures, in that it has been demonstrated that the very act of dispensing tokens increases a teacher's rate of social contacts with her students (Mandelker, Brigham, & Bushell, 1970).

O'Leary and Becker (1967) operated a token economy classroom in which ratings were given for appropriate behavior. During the year the token system was in effect, the number of times per day the ratings were given was gradually reduced. Also, a progressively greater delay of reinforcement was introduced by requiring the students to save their tokens for progressively longer periods of time before they could be exchanged for backup reinforcers. The token system had the effect of greatly decreasing the percentage of deviant behavior observed in the classroom for all students. This effect was not disrupted by the less frequent awarding of ratings nor by the increased delay of reinforcement. Further, anecdotal reports strongly suggested that the effects of the O'Leary and Becker (1967) token economy generalized across time and situations to nontoken portions of the day. Some of the students were quoted as saying "that next year they would be old enough to behave and work well without the prizes." Consistent with their statements, the teachers of 11 of 16 of the subjects reported the following year that they had not been bothered by disruptive behavior on the part of students who had participated in the experimental classroom. Systematic observations indicated that the subjects' percentage of deviant behavior in the regular classroom was 36%. This compares quite favorably with the 79% which had been observed during the baseline period preceding the introduction of the token economy (O'Leary & Drabman, 1971). Nay and Legum (1976) also experienced success in fading out the reinforcement program they used in reducing out-of-seat behavior and inappropriate verbalizations in a class for educable mental retardates. Partial reinforcement was also used in an attempt to achieve generalization of the effects of training a chronic psychiatric patient to speak in a nondelusional manner (R. L. Patterson & Teigen, 1973). R. L. Patterson and Teigen (1973) reported mixed results from this effort. The utility of partial reinforcement in promoting generalization appears to relate to the well-known fact that responses acquired on partial schedules of reinforcement are more resistant to extinction than are those obtained on continuous schedules (Kimble, 1961). However, behaviors learned on partial schedules do ultimately extinguish. It might be speculated that partial reinforcement makes the desirable behaviors sufficiently resistant to extinction to be manifested a number of times in the environment to which the students are returned, thus making it possible for them to come under the control of "natural" reinforcers. But the conclusion that leaning the schedule of reinforcement is conducive to the occurrence of generalization must be tempered by the results of a study by Reiss (1973). He found that increasing the rate of token reinforcement for a counting task dispensed by one experimenter had the effect of increasing the subjects' work rate in the presence of a second experimenter who continued to reinforce counting at the original rate. No generalization of effect was found for a second group in which the first experimenter increased the amount of work required for reinforcement. It was further found that disruptive behaviors increased in the presence of both experimenters for the group that was reinforced at the less favorable rate. However, the rate of reinforcement for the group of whom more work was required was extremely unfavorable. The rate of reinforcement was in fact so low that it was virtually impossible to earn tokens from Experimenter A. Therefore, this condition may actually have been experienced by the subjects as extinction instead of the leaning of the schedule of reinforcement. The increase in disruptiveness may thus be attributed to "emotional behavior."

Walker, Mattson, and Buckley (1971) employed in their token economy classroom several of the features which had been found to promote generalization in previous reports. As was the case in the Hewett et al. (1969) program, teacher attention and praise were systematically paired with the points the previously disruptive students received. And as in the O'Leary and Becker (1967) report, the intervals between reinforcements for appropriate behavior and the successful completion of academic tasks were gradually lengthened throughout the time a student was in the classroom. And the actual amount of reinforcement was also lowered. Thus it required more academic work and more good behavior at the end of the project to earn a given amount of tangible rewards than was the case when a student first entered the special class. Further, when it was known that a student was soon to return to a regular classroom on a full-time basis, the conditions in the special class were shifted more and more to approximate those to which the child would be returning. And the child's regular teacher was provided with a special program to follow in dealing with that particular student. At three months following the complete severing of ties with the special classroom, it was found that the subjects had retained a mean of 72% of the gains they had made during the project.

In a follow-up to the Walker et al. (1971) report, Walker and Buckley (1972) conducted an investigation of various measures which attempt to maintain the effects of a token economy classroom into the child's regular class. Forty-four subjects whose behavior in regular classrooms had been disruptive were treated in a token economy classroom (Walker et al., 1971). This had the effect of doubling the percentage of appropriate behavior. Four strategies were employed with groups of 11 students following reintroduction into regular classrooms:

1. *Peer reprogramming:* Appropriate behavior by the subject allowed the entire class to earn reinforcement. Token economy personnel visited the classroom for sessions in which reinforcement was earned.

2. *Equating stimulus conditions:* Token economy personnel gave the regular teachers step-by-step instructions on the handling of the subjects. They consulted with her regularly.

3. *Teacher training:* The classroom teachers read material on behavior modification. There were no consultations.

4. *Control:* Standard classroom conditions.

Walker and Buckley (1972) concluded that peer reprogramming and equating stimulus conditions produced a significantly higher percentage of maintenance of treatment effects than did the control procedure following 2 months in the regular classroom. Teacher training did not produce significantly higher rates, and 67% of the treatment effects were maintained in the control condition. However, the authors' interpretation of their data has been questioned by Cone (1973) on the basis of their failure to consider baseline levels of appropriate behavior. Ayllon and Michael (1959), Ayllon and Azrin (1968), Surratt et al. (1969), Staats, Minke, Goodwin, and Landeen (1967), and Wildman and Wildman (1972) have also shown that behavior modification procedures can be applied successfully by relatively untrained individuals who work under the supervision of personnel who are well versed in these techniques. In the Staats et al. (1967) program, adult volunteers and high school seniors used extrinsic rewards to teach retarded children reading skills. The students learned an average of 593.5 new words, of which 70.9% were retained on a posttest. But Walker and Buckley's (1972) data make the use of untrained therapists without close supervision seem to be a much more uncertain undertaking.

Walker and Buckley's (1972) strategy of reprogramming the environment to which a subject will be returned received support from the later research of Rincover and Koegel (1975). This study focused on four autistic children whose acquisition of a motor response failed to generalize to an extratreatment setting. Generalization was accomplished by successively introducing stimuli from the original training setting until a stimulus was hit upon which proved capable of controlling the learned response. Obviously, the more reprogramming of the transfer environment which is accomplished, the more likely it is that the controlling stimulus or stimuli will be included.

A well-controlled study of the effectiveness of reprogramming the environment to which a student will be returned was presented by Walker, Hops, and Johnson (1975). One group of disruptive children was placed in a token economy classroom for the first 4 months of a school year. The children were returned to a regular classroom for the last 5 months of the school year, but the regular classroom teacher was given training in behavior modification and feedback on the teacher's and child's performance. In other words, the regular classroom was "reprogrammed." A second group of subjects received only the token classroom intervention during the final 5 months of the school year. The students who had been exposed to both the token economy classroom and the regular classroom maintenance strategy showed a significantly higher level of appropriate behavior during the first 4 months of the next school year in a regular, nonreprogrammed classroom than did the students who were exposed only to the token classroom. These findings lend support to the position that reprogramming the natural environment helps promote long-term generalization. However, Walker et al. (1975) themselves point out that one could suggest that their study is confounded by the argument that the reprogrammed regular classroom was actually a continuation of the behavior modification program. If one accepts this hypothesis, it might be concluded that the group whose behavior was most appropriate the year following the program had actually received 9 months of behavior modification, whereas the other group had gotten only 5. This argument suggests the possibility that length of time in a behavior modification program may play a role in the generalization of its effects.

Koegel and Rincover (1977) performed a study which speaks to the issue of reprogramming the environment to which the subject will be returned. They used candy as a reward in teaching autistic children to make various motor movements in response to the appropriate command. The durability of responding in an extratherapy setting was assessed. Predictably, intermittent reinforcement in the therapy setting contributed to the durability of responding in the generalization situation. Also, the use of *noncontingent* reinforcement in the extratherapy setting resulted in increased maintenance of responding. Thus, in reprogramming the environment, the dispensing of rewards which were utilized during training (even if experimental control in the extratherapy setting is so limited that they must be applied noncontingently) should be considered.

Another form of reprogramming the environment was demonstrated by Lewittes and Israel (1975). In the initial portion of their study, a rapid smoking procedure was successful in reducing the number of cigarettes smoked by two college roommates. Then, each roommate agreed to smoke three cigarettes for each one smoked by the other. Each individual's subsequent responsibility for the health and well-being of the other was carefully explained. Following the pairing of their cigarette consumption rates, neither roommate smoked another cigarette during the 6-month follow-up period.

A procedure which shows some promise for promoting generalization from token economy classrooms has been reported by McKenzie, Clark, Wolf, Kothera, and Benson (1968). In a special education class composed of 10 underachieving elementary school students, they had the students' parents agree to make the amount of the students' allowance contingent on the grades they brought home from the special class. This was done on a weekly basis in the special class, but the time periods between gradings were extended following the subjects' reintroduction into regular classrooms. Making the students' allowances contingent on their grades had the effect of significantly increasing their percentages of attending behaviors during both reading and arithmetic lessons. This improvement is particularly impressive when it is considered that this is in comparison to a condition in which such "natural" classroom reinforcers as free-time activities and special privileges were awarded for study behaviors. When 6 of the 10 subjects were transferred to regular classrooms, their performances were satisfactory in the new setting, as judged by the fact that all 6 were promoted to the next grade by the regular teacher at the conclusion of the following year. Presumably the parents continued to make the amount of the children's allowances contingent on their grades in the regular classes. Thus control of an effective system for increasing students' study behavior was successfully shifted from token economy personnel to the parents. A similar procedure was successfully employed at "Achievement Place" (Bailey, Wolf, & Phillips, 1970). Coleman (1973) also had desirable behaviors at school rewarded by money at home. This procedure maintained a high rate of working in both math and reading classes, even during a phase of the study in which some of the formal aspects of the procedure were faded out. Forehand and Atkeson (1977) have reviewed the literature relating to generalization when parents are used to implement behavior modification procedures. Their review suggests ways in which parents can be used optimally in the attainment of generalization (cf. also Koegel, Glahn, & Nieminen, 1978).

Another factor promoting generalization has been proposed by Thomas, Nielsen, Kuypers, and Becker (1968). They devised a token system for one disruptive, underachieving 6-year-old student. This token system involved a pupil (Rich) who was paid tokens for correctly reading words during tutoring sessions and for completing classroom workbook assignments. Concurrently with the token and tutorial procedures, the regular teacher began making social reinforcement contingent on appropriate behavior for the entire class. Rich made both behavioral and academic gains during the course of this project. And there were strong indications that these gains generalized to a nonexperimental summer school. In fact, Rich asked that the length of time he spent in summer school be increased. This was in dramatic contrast to his previous responses to academic situations. The authors speculated that the fact that the experimental procedure had succeeded in teaching Rich a skill, in this case reading, had opened up to him an opportunity for earning positive reinforcement which had previously been denied to him. While this conclusion is rather loosely stated, it is consistent with the warning of Ayllon and Azrin (1968) that it is not fruitful to shape an individual to perform behaviors which will not be reinforced and thus maintained by the environment to which that person will be returned. Reading was a behavior which was reinforced by Rich's natural environment, and thus it was maintained. Vaal (1972) decreased the percentage of verbalizations of too low volume to be audible which were manifested by two 11-year-old girls in a special classroom. This was accomplished by responding only to appropriate verbalizations; unintelligible statements resulted in the experimenter's staring at the subject until she repeated the statement in an understandable manner. The teacher of another classroom reported that "when the Ss first came to his room for English [which was approximately the same time that the study was undertaken], he experienced some difficulty in hearing the Ss when they responded. He stated that the unintelligible responses gradually diminished until both Ss were responding appropriately 100% of the time" (p. 449). Apparently Vaal (1972) had succeeded in teaching his subjects a behavior, speaking loud enough to be heard, which was functional in a variety of settings and thus generalized. Another example of this effect is contained in the report by Hauserman, Walen, and Behling (1973). They reinforced children for sitting with a " "new friend" each day in the school cafeteria. They found evidence of the generalization of the effects of this procedure to a free-play period in which the choice of companion was not consequated. It would seem that their experimental manipulation had the effect of teaching subjects to interact with children who later became natural reinforcers. A similar explanation could be advanced for Altman's (1971) finding that "cooperative responses" acquired in an experiment also had the effect of increasing "associate play responses" during a free-play period. Similarly, Bennett and Maley (1973) reinforced social interactions in chronic mental patients and observed an increase in social behaviors in nontreatment settings. This factor, the importance of teaching useful skills, appears to account for the generalization which has been demonstrated in the training of "social skills" (cf. Bellack, Hersen, & Turner, 1976, who worked with chronic schizophrenics).

Another example of the generalization of the effects of training behaviors which will be reinforced in the natural environment is contained in the report of Frederiksen, Jenkins, Foy, and Eisler (1976). Two adult psychiatric patients were taught to decrease the frequency of inappropriate verbal behavior, e.g., threatening, and increase the frequency of appropriate verbal behavior, e.g., nonthreatening requests. This result was accomplished through the use of social skills training which utilized instructions, modeling, behavioral rehearsal, and the giving of feedback. The effects of this procedure generalized to training and novel scenes role-played with a different partner and to the subjects' reactions to events on the ward.

O'Leary, Drabman, and Kass (1973) conducted a project which had been inspired by their hypothesis that small reinforcers which are freely available to all classroom teachers would be more effective in producing generalizable behavioral changes than would large, extrinsic reinforcers. They had noted that in previous reports in which such freely available reinforcers as free time (Osborne, 1969) and access to a play area (Salzberg, Wheeler, Devar, & Hopkins, 1971) were employed, little or no regression to baseline rates of behavior was found following the withdrawal of the experimental procedure. Why generalization was not found in the previously cited Sulzbacher and Houser (1970) study is not readily apparent. The O'Leary et al. (1973) procedure involved the removal of disruptive children from their regular classes for 1 hour per day. That hour was spent in a special "resource room class" in which the students earned points for good behavior and the correct completion of academic assignments. The students used these points to pay for time in a play area during the latter portion of the resource room period. Disruptive behavior decreased in the resource rooms. However, this effect did not generalize to the students' regular classes. Even so, 8 weeks following the termination of the token system it was found that the number of disruptive behaviors in one of the special classes was 56% lower than had been the case during a baseline period. Remarkably similar findings were reported by Ascare and Axelrod (1973). They rewarded on-task behavior with points which were exchangeable for free-play time at the end of the day. This was done in four "open" classrooms. In all four classrooms, the points phase was associated with an increase in attending to classwork. When the points and contingencies were withdrawn during a 9-day return-to-baseline condition, percentages of on-task behavior fell sharply in three of the classes. However, it fell from a mean of 75% to only 67% in the fourth class. A very tentative conclusion from the O'Leary et al. (1973) and the Ascare and Axelrod (1973) studies and the previous reports they cite might be that the use of small, freely available reinforcers may promote generalization across time, but appears to provide no increment in generalization of treatment effects across situations. However, Grandy, Madsen, and de Mersseman (1973) obtained some generalization across settings in a study which employed free time as a reinforcer for not talking-out and for the students' remaining in their seats during class. Generalization across time was also noted, particularly after several reversals and reinstatements of the contingencies had occurred.

Drabman, Spitalnik, and O'Leary (1973) had teachers award tokens to third-grade students for the completion of academic assignments and for appropriate classroom behavior. The students were then instructed to rate independently the number of tokens they should receive. They were given a bonus point for matching the teacher's rating. A discrepancy between student and teacher ratings of more than 1 point resulted in no tokens being awarded. Teacher ratings were then gradually faded out by having the teacher check fewer and fewer of the students' self-ratings. Finally, during the "self-evaluation" phase of the study, the students completely determined the number of tokens they should receive. "The teachers continued to praise general matching and honesty. That is, they praised the child if he seemed to evaluate himself veridically, but there was no specific check of how the child's rating correlated with the teacher rating. Marked over-evaluations would receive very occasional reprimands" (p. 13). Introduction of token reinforcement was associated with a reduction in disruptive behaviors, from a mean of .86 per 20-second observational interval during baseline to .28, and an increase in academic behavior, from an average of 83 Sullivan reading items correct per hour to 130 during token reinforcement. For some unknown reason, the effects of this procedure on disruptive behavior generalized from the token period to a 15-minute no-token control period, even though the teacher "announced at the beginning of each of the four periods whether the period was a token period or not" (p. 12). Disruptive behaviors decreased from .86 per 20-second observational interval to a mean of .26 during the control period. Perhaps the shortness of the control periods (15 minutes) and the fact that they were held in the same classroom as the token periods contributed to the finding of generalization in this case. The gains that were achieved during the token phase of the study were maintained as the teacher ratings were faded out. During the phase of the Drabman et al. (1973) study in which all token were awarded on the basis of ratings done by the students themselves, disruptive behaviors averaged only .19 per observational interval, and a mean of 158 academic items was completed. In the control period, the figure was .09 disruptive behaviors, a reduction from .86 during baseline. An increase in academic behaviors during the control periods was also noted. A tentative conclusion from the Drabman et al. (1973) report is that the students learned "self-control" and were able to use reinforcement to motivate their own desirable behaviors. This result would certainly qualify as an instance of generalization. But the fact that the students were given occasional feedback about the accuracy of their self-ratings is, in the authors' judgment, a methodological shortcoming of the study which makes the self-evaluation results Drabman et al. obtained more difficult to explain. But the interpretation that having students observe and rate their own behavior promotes the generalization of desirable behavior changes is consistent with the results of a previous study (Kaufman & O'Leary, 1972) in which self-observation and self-evaluation were employed, and in which no mention was made of the subjects' receiving feedback on the accuracy of their self-ratings. Turkewitz, O'Leary and Ironsmith (1975) performed a general replication of the Drabman et al. (1973) report in which backup reinforcers were withdrawn during the course of the study. Turkewitz et al. (1975) demonstrated generalization of the program's effects to the no-token control period and also maintenance of the improved academic and social behavior following the complete removal of all backup reinforcers. However, generalization of appropriate social behavior to the regular classroom did not occur. The importance of self-observation in weight control has been demonstrated by S. M. Hall, Hall, Borden, and Hanson (1975). Following a formal behavioral weight reduction program, subjects were assigned to follow-up conditions. Those subjects placed in a follow-up condition which involved continued self-observation lost weight during the posttreatment period, whereas subjects placed in a control condition following treatment gained weight.

A cautionary note would appear to be in order at this point. Unspecified individual differences may enter into whether the effects of a behavior modification procedure generalize or not. Birnbrauer, Wolf, Kidder, and Tague (1965) supervised a highly successful token economy classroom for retarded students at the Rainier School in Washington State. The pupils were reinforced with checkmarks for the correct completion of academic work and for "cooperative behavior." This token system was withdrawn for all subjects for at least 21 days. Birnbrauer et al. (1965) summarize the effects of this temporary termination of the token system as follows:

To recapitulate: (1) Five of the 15 Ss included in this analysis gave no measurable indication in 21 days that token reinforcement was necessary to maintain their cooperation and level of accuracy . . . . (2) One S (S3) steadily increased in percentage of errors during NT [nontoken period] . . . to a level four times that obtained in B and B2 [first and second token periods] . . . ; another S (S4) also increased markedly in percentage of errors during NT but may have been responding to the change in routine *per se*. The decreases in accuracy would have been alarming by most standards . . . . (3) Four Ss declined in accuracy in NT at least to the point where the effect was educationally significant was measured by their advancing in one program, sight vocabulary . . . . (4) Three Ss (Ss 6, 8, and 9), were clearly more cooperative and more accurate with token reinforcement than without it. In fact, their disruptive behavior in NT was such that dropping them from school would have been in order under ordinary circumstances . . . . (5) The token reinforcement system and programs were not sufficient to bring another S's behavior under sufficient control for him to benefit from education . . . . (6) The tokens were sufficiently powerful to contain disruptive peer interactions, substantially reducing the need for time-out procedures. (7) The effects of loss of tokens for errors ranged from no apparent effect to a considerable increase in accuracy. (pp. 233–234).

Individualized student responses to a token system have also been described by Broden, Hall, Dunlap, and Clark (1970), Koch and Breyer (1974), and McLaughlin and Malaby (1974).

The preceding review of classroom token economies makes Baer, Wolf, and Risley's (1968) statement that "Generalization should be programmed rather than expected or lamented" (p. 97) seem particularly apt. Even so, there are a few instances in the literature in which generalization was found in the absence of the reported use of any specific devices to obtain it (e.g., Blanchard & Johnson, 1973; Hunt & Zimmerman, 1969). But in general it would appear that some programming for generalization is necessary. This review may make it possible to advance a number of tentative "rules" for the promotion of generalization from classroom token economy programs. These "rules" would appear to be:

1. Do not instruct the subjects that rewards will only be available at certain times or under certain conditions (Kuypers et al., 1968; Meichenbaum et al., 1968; O'Leary et al., 1969).

2. Do not attempt to achieve generalization among incompatible behaviors by reinforcing or richly reinforcing only one of the behaviors (Wolf et al., 1968).

3. Pair attention and social reinforcement with the delivery of tokens and their exchange for backup reinforcers (Chadwick & Day, 1971; Galloway & Mickelson, 1971; Hewett, 1967; Hewett et al., 1969; Walker et al., 1971).

4. Over the course of a token economy program, decrease the number of times per day ratings are given (O'Leary & Becker, 1967; R. L. Patterson & Teigen, 1973; Walker et al., 1971).

5. Over the course of a token economy program, progressively increase the delay between the earning of tokens and their exchange for tangible reinforcers (O'Leary & Becker, 1967).

6. Decrease the actual amount of reinforcement awarded for each unit of academic work or appropriate behavior (Walker et al., 1971).

7. Give those individuals who exercise control over the environment to which the subject will be returned specific, step-by-step instructions on how to maintain treatment gains (Walker & Buckley, 1972; Walker et al., 1971).

8. Treat the subject in an environment which as much as possible approximates the environment to which the child will be returned (Walker et al., 1971).

9. Attempt to involve the students' parents in the treatment program and in the maintenance of treatment gains (McKenzie et al., 1968).

10. Insofar as is possible, focus the token system on the instruction of skills which will be reinforced and maintained by the environment to which the child will be returned (Bennett & Maley, 1973; Hauserman et al., 1973; Thomas et al., 1968; Vaal, 1972).

11. Employ small, readily available reinforcers (Ascare & Axelrod, 1973; Grandy et al., 1973; O'Leary, Drabman, & Kass, 1973; Osborne, 1969; Salzberg et al., 1971).

12. Involve the subjects in the observation and rating of their own behavior, and then fade out the external ratings (Drabman et al., 1973; Kaufman & O'Leary, 1972).

The literature relating to the generalization of token economies with mental patients bears a striking resemblance to that of its use in the classroom. Kazdin and Bootzin (1972) present its status as follows: "In summary, although token economies have been dramatically effective at changing behavior within the psychiatric hospital, there is little evidence that improvement is maintained outside the institution" (p. 360).

Several investigators have employed some of the same procedures with mental patients that have been proven to be effective in promoting generalization from classroom token economy programs. For example, Atthowe and Krasner (1968) report pairing verbal praise with the delivery of tokens, and Schaefer and Martin (1969) discuss the gradual fading out of a token system for psychotics. However, it is extremely difficult to assess the effectiveness of these procedures because the usual measures of generalization, discharge and readmission rates, are often greatly confounded by unrelated changes in administrative policy (Kazdin, 1977b).

It might of course be argued that some of the preceding studies in which generalization was not specifically programmed did not demonstrate generalization because they were conducted within a group format. That is, it may be that behavior modification conducted on an individual basis is inherently more likely to generalize. Possibly, individualized behavior modification, because it is "tailor-made" for the subject, is more effective than are group methods at actually changing the person, regardless of where he might be or the time. To investigate this possibility, it would appear to be useful to examine several behavior modification projects which have been conducted on an individual basis.

INDIVIDUAL BEHAVIOR
MODIFICATION PROJECTS

Wahler (1969) dealt individually with two children who presented behavior problems both in school and at home. One child was referred because he was "stubborn and disruptive." The other boy was treated for "low motivation for schoolwork." The boys' parents were given training in the use of differential attention. The first child's parents were told to attend to cooperative behaviors and to employ time-out procedures for disruptive behaviors. The parents of the second boy were instructed to make their attention contingent on studying. This regime resulted in a great increase in the amount of target behaviors observed in the home for both boys. But no changes in the relative amounts of appropriate and inappropriate behaviors were noted in the school situations. Thus these two individually conducted behavior modification programs failed to produce generalization across situations. Only when the boys' teachers began to employ differential attention to their behaviors did the amount of appropriate behaviors increase and the amount of inappropriate behaviors decrease in the school setting.

MacDonald, Gallimore, and MacDonald (1970) were able to increase the attendance at school of six "chronic nonattenders" by making individual "deals" with them whereby certain natural reinforcers in their environments, such as their allowance and access to a pool hall, were made contingent on attendance at school. This was accomplished through the cooperation of "mediators" who exercised some controlling function over each of the children. During a 2-week absence of the attendance counselor who had supervised the "deals," the attendance record of three of the boys continued at the high rate established during the first intervention phase. But attendance figures for the other three boys fell dramatically back to baseline rates. Thus this procedure did not have the invariant effect of making subjects "chronic attenders." It could be speculated that generalization across time was demonstrated for three of the students because the mediators continued to enforce the experimental contingencies, even in the absence of supervision from the attendance counselor. The reader will recall that such an occurrence was cited as the likely explanation for the maintenance of treatment effects in the McKenzie et al. (1968) report.

One part of a report relating to the use of multiple-baseline research tactics (R. V. Hall et al., 1970) involved a project with a 10-year-old girl whose life circumstances had caused her to have heavy commitments in the areas of practicing the clarinet, completing projects for Campfire Girls, and reading books for school. The girl admitted that if she were adequately to meet these commitments it would be necessary for her to devote approximately 30 minutes per evening to each of these activities. However, baseline measurements revealed that the girl devoted only a mean of 13.5 minutes per day to practicing the clarinet, a mean of 3.5 minutes per day to completing Campfire work, and 11 minutes to reading. The girl was placed by the mother under a contingency such that she would have to go to bed 1 minute early each evening for each minute less than 30 she spent practicing the clarinet that day. The first day under this condition Lisa spent 26 minutes practicing the clarinet. Following this, time devoted to clarinet practice was at or near 30 minutes per day for the remaineder of the study. However, this procedure did not have any apparent effect on her Campfire work or on her reading. Both of these behaviors remained at the low baseline rates. The same contingency as had been used with clarinet practice was then simultaneously applied to Campfire projects. Her mean time of working on these projects jumped to approximately 29 minutes per day. There was no effect of this on either her high rate of clarinet practice or low rate of reading. Reading was only increased when the same contingency was also applied to this behavior. This report illustrates a failure of behavior modification procedures to generalize across behaviors. They appeared to have failed to make the girl "responsible" enough to work to meet her commitments spontaneously.

It would appear that the step of employing behavior modification on an individual basis is not enough to ensure its generalizability. It is possible that, as was the case with token economy programs, special steps to program generalization will have to be taken in this area too in order to accomplish this objective. It would seem reasonable that some indication of what these steps might be could be obtained by reviewing those individualized behavior modification studies in which generalization has been achieved.

Individual Behavior Modification Projects Which Have Demonstrated Generalization

Buell, Stoddard, Harris, and Baer (1968) employed priming and social reinforcement by teachers to increase a 3-year-old girl's use of playground equipment. Reinforcement for using the equipment was made intermittent toward the end of the study. These tactics not only increased the subject's use of playground equipment, but simultaneous increases in desirable social behaviors were also observed. Other than the intermittent use of reinforcement, possible reasons for this generalization across behaviors are that the subject's extended time on the equipment in close proximity to other children placed her in a situation in which social behavior was likely to be reinforced, and the experimental procedures may have had the unplanned but desirable effect of altering the teachers' responses to her social behaviors.

G. R. Patterson and Brodsky (1966) utilized a variety of conditioning procedures in treating the disruptive and inappropriate behaviors of a kindergarten boy (Karl). The behavioral improvements attained were maintained following the termination of all of the conditioning programs. This generalization may, at least in part, have been achieved through the authors' "reprogramming" of the boy's social environment. More specifically, Karl's peers were reinforced with candy for initiating social contacts with him. And Karl was reinforced for responding appropriately to these social overtures and for initiating social contacts on his own. This procedure may have had the effect of teaching the boy more appropriate means for obtaining social reinforcement, such as attention. Since that reinforcement remained available following the completion of the study, and the pro-social behaviors which were thus reinforced were incompatible with his previous disruptive behaviors, this technique may have contributed to the demonstration of generalization across time. A partial reprogramming of the environment to which the subject was returned was also conducted by R. L. Patterson and Teigen (1973). Cooper (1973) was successful in eliminating the crying and complaining of a 6-year-old girl. This was done by reprogramming both the school and home environments. Lisa's teacher and mother were instructed to attend to positive statements about school but to ignore her crying and complaints about school and imaginary illnesses. Two postchecks conducted over 3 months following the termination of the school psychologist's involvement in the treatment program revealed that the maladaptive behaviors had not returned. Lovaas, Koegel, Simmons, and Long (1973) also found that the results of their work with autistic children generalized only when the child was returned to an environment which was favorable for such generalization.

A fourth-grade boy with a low rate of attending behavior was treated by Walker and Buckley (1968) in a special classroom setting. They gave him points, exchangeable for models at a later time, for intervals of attending behaviors. Attending behavior was defined for the purposes of the Walker and Buckley (1968) study as the subject's looking at the assigned page. The intervals of attending behavior required to obtain reinforcement were gradually lengthened throughout the course of the study, beginning at 30 seconds and ending at 600. The longer intervals which maintained the desirable behaviors made it possible for the reinforcement contingencies to be handled by a regular classroom teacher. The subject's attending behavior was thus maintained by transferring control of the program to the teacher in his regular class. In this way, generalization across time and settings was obtained by bringing the subject's behavior under the control of a schedule of reinforcement which his natural environment could be programmed to continue. Hopkins (1968) has also experienced success with progressively "leaning" the schedule of contrived reinforcement in order to promote generalization. Another example of reporgramming the subject's natural environment in order to achieve generalization across situations has been reported by Stolz and Wolf (1969). They used operant reinforcement procedures to demonstrate that a 16-year-old functionally blind male could make visual discriminations. Generalization of this "seeing" behavior to the extraexperimental setting was promoted by withdrawing assistance to him in selecting food in the cafeteria and by imposing a 10-second time-out period when he failed to make appropriate visually guided responses while eating lunch. The subject learned to function appropriately under both of these sets of contingencies. However, it is not clear whether these findings demonstrate generalization or whether these techniques constituted separate conditioning sessions. This question becomes particularly relevant when it is considered that both of these behavioral effects were reversed when conditions in the natural environment were returned to the way they had been prior to the institution of the procedures designed to promote generalization.

Kale, Kaye, Whelen, and Hopkins (1968) conducted a study with three "withdrawn" mental patients. They prompted and reinforced with cigarettes social responses (verbal greetings) to an experimenter (E_1). The prompts were then faded out and the reinforcement schedule was leaned. This dramatically increased the number of social responses all three subjects made to E_1, even during a phase of the experiment in which reinforcement was not given for these responses. But the effects of this treatment did not generalize to a second experimenter (E_2). Then, five other experimenters (E_3–E_7) reinforced the subjects for greetings. When E_2 was subsequently reintroduced, all three subjects then manifested a relatively high frequency of social behaviors in response to him. It could be speculated that the subjects' receiving reinforcements from a variety of experimenters, presumably characterized by a variety of stimulus patterns, made it more difficult for them to discriminate between those individuals (S^Ds) who had marked the occasion for the availability of reinforcement and those who had not, thus promoting stimulus generalization. A similar effect was noted by Garcia (1974) in teaching conversational speech to retarded children. Stokes, Baer, and Jackson (1974) argued that the methodology of Kale et al. (1968) confounded the issue of the number of trainers with the length of time in training. Stokes et al. (1974), using handwaving instead of verbal greetings, and working with retarded children, attempted to investigate the effects of multiple trainers while controlling for length of training. Their results, in the authors' judgment, did not provide a conclusive answer to the question of whether or not the two issues are completely independent of each other.

Lovaas and Simmons (1969) reduced self-destructive behavior in several retarded children by punishing such responses with electric shock. One boy in their program had been punished by only one of the experimenters. He ceased self-destructive responses in the presence of that experimenter, but this procedure did not influence his rate of self-injurious behavior in the presence of other personnel. The suppression of self-destructive responses in the presence of all other experimenters was immediately achieved following one application of contingent shock by a second staff member. The use of more than one therapist in order to promote generalization has also been reported in the behavior therapy area (Elliott, Smith, & Wildman, 1972). Another procedure employed by Lovaas and Simmons (1969) was pairing the word "no" with shock. Following this, "no", which had previously been demonstrated to be a neutral stimulus, served to suppress behavior in extraexperimental settings.

The tactic of involving a variety of individuals in the training procedures has also been successfully utilized by Whitman, Mercurio, and Caponigri (1970). They treated two withdrawn retarded children by reinforcing them with candy for cooperative play with each other. This was done during special training sessions. The effects of treatment generalized across settings to the children's regular classroom, but the two subjects played only with each other. At this point two other students from the classroom were introduced into the training sessions. Following this, the two experimental subjects began playing with a number of their classmates, including some who had in no way been involved in the treatment procedure. That is, the subjects began interacting socially with children they had never been reinforced for playing with. Generalization across behaviors was also observed in that the two children began engaging in social activities which had not been part of the training procedure. Unfortunately, after the training sessions were discontinued, the time the two subjects spent in social interactions during 15-minute observation periods in the classroom declined.

The tactic of utilizing a variety of individuals to implement contingencies was carried a step further by Emshoff, Redd, and Davidson (1976), who worked with four delinquent adolescents. The adolescents were praised and awarded redeemable points for making positive statements about other adolescents. For two subjects, the same trainer always conducted the sessions and training always took place during the same time and activity and in the same location. For the other two subjects, trainers, time, places, and activities were varied across training sessions. All four subjects greatly increased the number of their peer-directed positive comments during the experimental sessions. Those subjects who had been exposed to a variable stimulus pattern during training showed generalization of the program's effects across situations to the residential home, and across time to the 3 weeks following the program's termination. No generalization was observed in the two subjects who always worked with the same trainer during the same activity.

Schwartz and Hawkins (1970) treated a girl in an elementary classroom for excessively touching her face, slouching in her chair, and speaking at an inaudible volume. This was accomplished by making videotapes of parts of class periods and showing the tapes to the girl after school. The girl timed the duration of appropriate behaviors she manifested on the tape, and she was rewarded for these periods. Each of the three major problems was successfully attacked in turn. The effects of training did not generalize across behaviors. Training the girl not to touch her face did not, for example, reduce the percentage of time she spent slouching in her chair. However, when all three classes of desirable behaviors had been increased, the effects of treatment generalized across time to an amazing degree. The girl stopped touching her face, slouching, and talking in a low voice during portions of the day in which tapes had never been made. And these reductions in undesirable behaviors were still in evidence at a postcheck conducted 4 weeks following the end of training. As a possible explanation of this finding of generalization, Schwartz and Hawkins (1970) cite laboratory studies showing that delay of reinforcement leads to greater resistance to extinction.

Verbal behaviors and responses to instructions are classes of responses in which generalization from training is frequently observed, often even in cases in which such generalization was not specifically programmed. For example, Lovaas, Berberich, Perloff, and Schaeffer (1966), in their classic report on teaching speech to autistic children, reported that their subjects learned to imitate Norwegian words, even though only the imitation of English words had been rewarded. Lovaas et al. (1966) concluded from this finding that "children may be able to acquire new behaviors on their own" (p. 707). Wheeler and Sulzer (1970) reinforced a speech-deficient child for using a certain sentence form in response to picture cards. The subject subsequently employed that sentence form a high percentage of the time in response to both the cards used in training and "generalization cards," responses to which had never been reinforced. Whitman, Zakaras, and Chardos (1971) found extensive generalization of the effects of training two severely retarded children to follow sets of instructions. The children began responding appropriately to a second list of instructions at a frequency which was almost as high as the list for which correct responses were reinforced.

Bernal, Jacobson, and Lopez (1975) worked with a young retardate who was thought to have had no possibility for the development of speech or conceptual behavior. He was taught to attend to stimuli and point on cue. He developed learning sets and became able to verbalize appropriately 45 words. The effects of this training were found to have endured at the time of a 9-month follow-up, and it was demonstrated that the subject could even be taught to expand these skills further. Other examples of the unprogrammed generalization of the effects of the instruction of verbal behaviors are contained in the reports of Martin (1975), and Fichter, Wallace, Liberman, and Davis (1976). Johnston and Johnston (1972) report a series of experiments which was performed in a classroom setting with children who manifested "low operant rates of correctly articulating two or more consonant speech sounds." The subjects were reinforced with stickers, exchangeable for a subsequent choice of activity or snack, for correctly articulating consonant sounds during structured activities. This had the effect of increasing the number of correct pronunciations of sounds with which the subjects had previously had difficulty, and decreasing the number of incorrect pronunciations. However, these effects did not generalize to an independent-play period. Only when the children were reinforced for correct articulations during the play period did the number of correct responses increase during that period. The same results were found when a subject himself counted his correct responses. Not only did the effects of reinforcement during one period fail to generalize, but the subjects tended not even to count during the other period. In both of these cases the same teachers and peers were present in both settings.

Generalization to another setting was, however, found when subjects were reinforced for properly monitoring and praising or correcting each others' speech in one of the settings. That this was the result of the speech's coming under the stimulus control of the specific monitor was documented by the fact that the percentage of correct articulations declined when another child was substituted for the monitor in the generalization situation. Thus the monitor had been a discriminative stimulus for correct articulations. These findings would seem to suggest that, whenever possible, an individual who will be in the situation to which generalization is desired should be involved in a controlling function in the training process. Apparently the mere presence of the individual may not suffice in all cases.

This review of individualized behavior modification projects has revealed a number of procedures which may be effective in promoting generalization. Some of these are similar to tactics which have been found effective in the previously reviewed token economy programs, such as reprogramming the environment to which the subject(s) will be returned (Cooper, 1973; G. R. Patterson & Brodsky, 1966; R. L. Patterson & Teigen, 1973; Stolz & Wolf, 1969), gradually increasing behavioral demands and delay of reinforcement as the project progresses (Hopkins, 1968; Schwartz & Hawkins, 1970; Walker & Buckley, 1968), and involving the subject's parents in the treatment procedures (Cooper, 1973).

Other procedures, however, have been newly revealed by the review of individual programs:

13. Strengthen behaviors which will bring the subject into an environ-

ment in which other appropriate behaviors will be reinforced (Buell et al., 1968).

14. Utilize a number of individuals to implement the experimental contingencies (Elliott et al., 1972; Kale et al., 1968; Lovaas & Simmons, 1969; Whitman et al., 1970).

15. Vary stimulus conditions during training (Emshoff et al., 1976).

16. Enlist the active involvement in the training sessions of someone who will be present in the generalization situation (Johnston & Johnston, 1972).

Several of the principles emerging from this review were recognized earlier by Goldstein, Heller, and Sechrest (1966), who wrote in an individual psychotherapy context. The reader who is interested in the theoretical aspects of generalization should review the Goldstein et al. (1966) chapter. Gruber (1971), working within the context of conditioning therapy, has suggested another: generalization appears to be promoted by the client's lack of awareness of the contingencies involved in treatment. This tactic may in some ways parallel Rule No. 1 of this review ("Do not instruct the subjects that rewards will only be available at certain times or under certain conditions"). Liberman, McCann, and Wallace (1976) give a case study from their work with adult psychotics. From their experience with this patient class, they advance 10 "rules" for the promotion of generalization, 9 of which are identical to or rather closely parallel those put forward by the present authors. The 10th, a cognitive factor, is:

Involve the patient in setting goals of treatment and in choosing from among alternative treatment methods. This helps to shift the perceived focus of control from external to internal, and makes more likely that the patient will attribute clinical progress to his or her own efforts. (Liberman et al., 1976, p. 495)

A comprehensive review of the generalization literature has been contributed recently by Stokes and Baer (1977). Their suggestions for the promotion of generalization generally parallel those advanced in the present report, but the different approach taken, and the high level of scholarship displayed in the Stokes and Baer (1977) review, recommend it to the serious student of generalization.

T. Ayllon and his students have recently conducted a series of case studies in which several of the rules for promoting generalization discussed in the present review were utilized in treating clinical problems. Ayllon, Smith, and Rogers (1970) dealt with a case of school phobia. Rule No. 8, "Treat the subject in an environment which as much as possible approximates the environment to which the child will be returned," was carried to its ultimate by actually conducting the treatment in the home and by gradually introducing the subject into the very classroom to which she would be returned. A key element in Ayllon et al.'s (1970) procedure involved the mother, at great inconvenience to herself, returning home and personally walking to school with Valerie when she did not go voluntarily. Thus, the parents were involved in treatment (Rule No. 9). The effects of this treatment generalized across time to the extent that Val's attendance at school rose from approximately 10% before treatment to perfect attendance during the year following treatment. Generalization across behaviors was noted in reports from the school personnel:

> While previously she was an average C student, she now has A's and B's. Her teacher remarked that Val is well-behaved in class and helpful to the teacher. While she is pleased to volunteer for small errands and clean-up duties to assist the teacher, she has also shown sufficient social skills to be chosen as the school guide for a new girl admitted into her classroom. (p 136)

This final treatment effect would appear to result from the fact that Ayllon et al. (1970) shaped behaviors which brought the child into an environment in which appropriate behaviors were reinforced (Rule No. 13).

Ayllon and Skuban (1973) treated an autistic child who was negativistic and manifested a high rate of temper tantrums. The procedure they successfully utilized involved giving the subject, Mike, coins for obeying instructions from adults. Tantrums were punished by a period of time-out from the opportunity to earn positive reinforcement. Aspects of Ayllon and Skuban's (1973) treatment designed to enhance generalization included (1) treating Mike in the natural environment (stores and parks, Rule No. 8); (2) pairing praise with the delivery of material reinforcers (Rule No. 3); and (3) increasing the requirements for reinforcement (Rule No. 6). Also, a variable ratio was established between the number of times Mike was praised and the number of material reinforcements he received. Over the course of the study, the timers and other mechanical devices were gradually faded out (Rule No. 8).

The most extensive use of techniques to promote generalization is contained in a study reported by Ayllon and Kelly (1974). Mona, an 11-year-old retardate, was found to speak normally outside of her classroom with her peers, but she did not respond verbally to prompts by her teacher in class. Using primary reinforcement, she was shaped to respond appropriately to mands (Skinner, 1957) in an extraclassroom setting. Social attention from the investigator was paired with the delivery of primary reinforcement (Rule No. 3). Also, elements of the stimulus pattern of the classroom, other students, desks, a blackboard, etc., were gradually added during the course of training to the treatment setting, a counselor's office (Rule No. 8). A group contingency was placed on the appropriate verbal responding of all of the students in the training setting; they were given M&Ms when each child answered appropriately. Primary reinforcement was then shifted from a continuous to an intermittent schedule (Rule No. 6). Social reinforcement continued to be dispensed for each correct response to a mand. The training in the counselor's office resulted in Mona's responding appropriately to questions in that setting almost 100% of the time. She was then reintroduced into the classroom, with the individual who had served as trainer substituting for the teacher. Correct responding occurred to all mands on this trial. Mona was rewarded on an intermittent schedule for this performance. However, when the teacher resumed control of the classroom and the reinforcement procedure was discontinued, verbalizations fell to baseline rates. Appropriate responding was then rapidly reshaped in the classroom, and the teacher was gradually faded back in as the reinforcing and controlling agent. Ayllon and Kelly (1974) report that at the conclusion of their study Mona was responding appropriately to the teacher nearly 100% of the time. The teacher utilized social reinforcement to maintain this performance. Thus, although the procedures designed to promote generalization—intermittent reinforcement and equating stimulus conditions—did not result in complete and immediate transfer of training to the classroom, they may well have made it easier to bring Mona's verbalizations under the teacher's control after she was returned to the natural environment. Long-term generalization over time and across settings was demonstrated in the Ayllon and Kelly (1974) report. The subject was found to respond appropriately to mands over 90% of the time in three different classrooms the following year. "Indeed, the Music Teacher had a problem with Mona's tendency to talk too much during class!" (p. 11). Some of these same procedures were also utilized successfully with a selectively mute child by Rosenbaum and Kellman (1973) and Conrad, Delk, and Williams (1974). And Koegel and Rincover (1974) taught autistic children to respond appropriately in one-to-one tutoring sessions. While this was successfully accomplished, there was little or no generalization of the results of this treatment to a classroom environment. Such generalization was, however, achieved by thinning the schedule of reinforcement delivered during the tutorial sessions (Rule No. 6) and by gradually fading in other students (Rule No. 8). Jackson and Wallace (1974) worked with a 15-year-old retarded girl who spoke at a volume which was too low to be understood. They were successful in shaping her to speak louder in a laboratory situation. However, this training produced no generalization to the classroom setting. Then elements of the classroom setting, e.g., students and the teacher, were brought into the laboratory situation (Rule No. 8) and the teacher began reinforcing voice loudness in the classroom (Rule No. 7). Also, more verbal behavior was required prior to each reinforcement (Rule No. 6). Following the implementation of these "rules," the subject's level of voice intensity in the classroom increased to within the range of the other students.

Ayllon, Simon, and Wildman (1975) obtained a very rapid, unanticipated cessation of chronic soiling behavior in a 7-year-old boy. Their strategy for maintaining this desirable behavioral change involved his being rewarded with an outing for weeks during which he did not soil himself. The authors faded themselves out and the mother was faded in as the reinforcing agent (Rules No. 8 and 9).

THE SPECIAL CASE OF CORRESPONDENCE TRAINING

A special form of generalization is concerned with the extent to which verbal and nonverbal behaviors correspond. This form of generalization is of particular importance because so many of society's attempts to modify and control the behavior of its members, e.g., teaching and psychotherapy, seek to change nonverbal behavior through the manipulation of verbal behavior.

Risley and Hart (1968) reinforced with food preschool children's reports of playing with certain classroom materials. Reports of the use of these play materials went up dramatically, but actual use of the material remained little changed. However, when the report of the use of the material was reinforced only when the child had actually played with the object, correspondence between saying and doing was achieved quickly. This change was accomplished either by the children's increasing the use of the material or decreasing their verbal reports of such use. Interestingly, after a number of sequences of reinforcing first reports and then only true reports, reinforcement of the report of playing with a material alone was sufficient to bring the motor behavior into line with the verbal report. The parameters of correspondence training with children have been investigated further by Rogers-Warren and Baer (1976) and Karoly and Dirks (1977).

Tracey, Briddell, and Wilson (1974) worked with chronic adult female psychiatric patients. During group meetings, the patients were rewarded with social reinforcement and tokens for making positive statements about a ward activity. Following the beginning of the delivery of reinforcement for such statements, their rate during group meetings increased. Significantly, the rate of actual participation in such activities also increased, even though neither the activities themselves nor verbalization–activity correspondence had been reinforced. Tracey et al. (1974) suggest that they were successful in modifying motor behavior with adults without correspondence training because adults have experienced the requirement that verbalizations match motor behavior repeatedly in the natural environment. The children in the Risley and Hart (1968) study had to be given such training before their motor behavior was brought under this form of verbal control.

Given the importance of "telling the truth" in our society, the findings presented here on verbal–nonverbal correspondence appear most encouraging. In some subjects, perhaps adults and more advanced children, such correspondence is observed even in the absence of the use of special procedures to obtain it. And in less advanced children such correspondence may be trained (Risley & Hart, 1968). In this connection, Israel and O'Leary (1973) produced data suggesting that the verbal–nonverbal pattern is more effective method to teach correspondence than is a nonverbal–verbal sequence (cf. also Israel, 1978, for a review of conceptual and methodological issues in correspondence training).

THE POSSIBILITY OF
NEGATIVE GENERALIZATION

Levine and Fasnacht (1974) warned that the use of token reinforcement could undermine intrinsic motivation to perform desirable behaviors, thus causing decreases from preintervention rates when the behavior modification program is withdrawn. Feingold and Mahoney (1975) performed a study designed to examine this possible pheonomenon. Children's play with follow-the-dots pictures was recorded. The children were then awarded points for increased performance on the pictures. Following removal of the reinforcement program, number of dots connected was again recorded. No decrease in dots connected from before the token program to the final baseline following the program's removal was observed, thus casting doubt on the position that a point contingency may cause a long-term decline in the rate of desirable behaviors that are no longer reinforced. Further arguments against the overjustification hypothesis come from studies reviewed earlier in this chapter in which *positive* generalization was demonstrated. However, it has not been definitely proven that such negative effects cannot occur, and Feingold and Mahoney (1975) warn workers to be on the lookout for such possible undesirable effects of token economy programs (cf. also Chapter 11).

CONCLUSION

This review has made the authors' initial question of whether all behavior modification procedures are prosthetic or therapeutic interventions seem quite naive. Apparently, behavior modification produces a lasting effect only when certain programming steps are incorporated into the treatment design. This chapter has suggested at least 16 ways in which this programming for generalization may be accomplished. Hopefully, future research and/or a more careful reading of existing reports will reveal additional methods for making the treatment effects of behavioristic techniques more long-lasting. Obviously, not all of these procedures for achieving generalization can be used in any one study. Each investigator can, however, use those which are applicable to his own setting and experimental design.

It seems that an important study which needs to be conducted at this point in behavior modification's growth would involve setting up two token economy classrooms. One classroom would focus solely on achieving immediate behavioral changes; the other would utilize as many of the "rules" for achieving generalization as is possible in that setting. A comparison of the members of the two classes on a variety of measures of generalization would say much about the fruitfulness of the "rules" for achieving generalization which have been abstracted by the current authors. Part of this objective was achieved by Jones and Kazdin (1975). They employed a token reinforcement program to reduce the inappropriate motor behaviors of students in a special education classroom. Several strategies were utilized to program response maintenance: praise was paired with the delivery of tokens used to reinforce attentive behavior (Rule No. 3); delivery of backup reinforcers was made intermittent (Rule No. 6); and a group contingency was implemented. The inappropriate motor behaviors were observed to remain at a low rate 12 weeks after the termination of all contingencies. Unfortunately, no control class was included, but a review of the literature suggests strongly that the obtained generalization would not have occurred in the absence of procedures designed to promote it.

Also, the individual "rules" proposed in this paper could be investigated separately, as has already been done by Kazdin and Polster (1973) in regard to the effects of intermittent reinforcement (Rule No. 6) on generalization. One adult male retardate was rewarded with tokens on a continuous schedule of reinforcement for social interactions; another subject was rewarded on an intermittent schedule. When the token reinforcement was withdrawn, the subject who had received continuous reinforcement ceased interacting socially with peers, but the retardate on the intermittent schedule continued to do so. The Kazdin and Polster (1973) study appears to provide strong support for the utility of Rule No. 6 in promoting generalization of the effects of behavior modification. Tests of the other "rules" should also be devised and executed in order that the list may be revised and improved.

Generalization may also relate to individual differences in "self-control," specifically in a student's or patient's ability to continue to implement with respect to his own behavior reinforcement contingencies utilized during training. Rozensky and Bellack (1974) have discussed the dimensions of such an ability/inability to administer "self-reinforcement" sucessfully, and Pawlicki and Morey (1976) have described a "low-cost instrument for 'thinning' self-directed schedules of reinforcement." This device, called the "CARROT," allows a patient to determine when reinforcement is called for by various schedules. Thinning the schedule of reinforcement is an important technique in the promotion of generalization of the effects of behavior modification procedures (Rules 4, 5, and 6), and having patients themselves administer the thinning phase should make the process of achieving generalization more efficient.

Another phenomenon which is being observed when a broad perspective is taken in the evaluation of a token economy program is the vicarious effects of the reinforcement of target subjects on the behavior of their nontarget peers (Kazdin, 1977a). Interestingly, the effect of vicarious reinforcement is not always in the same direction as that of the direct reinforcement. For example, Kazdin (1977a) found that verbal reinforcement for *both* inattentive and attentive behaviors increased the percentage of attentive behaviors in the nontarget student!

It is the authors' belief that clinicians should be alert to the possibility that behavior modification procedures may have effects which not only generalize from but actually transcend the behavioral objectives of the program. Parker (1974) presents data which suggest this exciting potentiality. He found improvements on a measure of self-concept for students who had participated in a contingency management program. And Gray, Graubard, and Rosenberg (1974) speak of involvement in a truly unique behavior modification project as improving the subjects' "self-confidence" and "self-respect." As Kazdin (1973b) recommends, it may be very important for the future development of behavior modification for workers also to collect data on behaviors which are not the target of the specific program being implemented. That the collection of such data may demonstrate the existence of exciting, added benefits of contingency management programs is illustrated by the report of Firestone (1976) relating to his work with an aggressive 4½-year-old male nursery school student. Time-out was successfully utilized to decrease the percentage of time the subject spent engaged in physically aggressive behavior. Because Firestone (1976) also collected data on nontarget behaviors, it was discovered that the time-out contingency applied only to physically aggressive behaviors had the additional effect of decreasing verbally aggressive behaviors and of increasing the percentage of time the subject spent in cooperative interactions with other children. An even more exciting demonstration of the unexpected additional benefits of behavior modification programs is illustrated by the manner in which McLaughlin and Malaby (1974) conclude their report of the successful use of behavior modification to increase the percentage of academic assignments completed by a 10-year-old pupil:

> In several sessions with the building principal it was learned that it was his opinion that the attitude of the pupil studied had improved greatly. He based his opinion on his in-class contacts with the pupil in math and social studies, as well as his out-of-class contacts with the pupil. Since no objective data were gathered in this category, the results must be viewed with some reservation. (p. 194)

Finally, it occurs to the present authors that cognitive factors may play a role in generalization. For example, explaining to a child that the same good behaviors which resulted in rewards in a special classroom will also "pay off" in the regular classroom may help the effects transfer to the natural environment. The use of analogies might also be found to promote generalization across many settings. Research into the effects of "cognitive restructuring" on the transfer of gains from behavior modification programs would seem to be in order (see Chapters 7 and 8).

NOTE

1. Kazdin and Kopel (1975) have challenged the assumptions underlying the multiple-baseline design. They point out that it assumes that treatment effects will have only specific influence on the target behavior, while extraneous variables will have generalized effects across many behaviors. There is, of course, no logical basis for predicting that the two classes of events, "treatment" and "extraneous," would operate so differently in terms of generality of effect.

ACKNOWLEDGMENTS

Much of the present chapter appeared previously in the authors' "The Generalization of Behavior Modification Procedures: An Evaluative Review—With Special Emphasis on Classroom Applications," which was published in *Psychology in the Schools* (1975, *12*, 432–448). Gratitude is extended to the Clinical Psychology Publishing Company for granting permission to reproduce this material here. Appreciation is also expressed to Kathleen Kelly, Luciano L'Abate, J. Brien O'Callaghan, Kim Pisor, and Steven Simon for their insightful and helpful comments on an earlier draft of the manuscript, and to Dianne Purvis for extensive clerical assistance in the preparation of this report.

REFERENCES

Altman, K. Effects of cooperative response acquisition on social behavior during free-play. *Journal of Experimental Child Psychology,* 1971, *12,* 387-395.

Ascare, D., & Axelrod, S. Use of behavior modification procedures in four "open" classrooms. *Psychology in the Schools,* 1973, *10,* 243-248.

Atthowe, J. M., & Krasner, L. Preliminary report on the application of contingent reinforcement procedures (token economy) on a "chronic" psychiatric ward. *Journal of Abnormal Psychology,* 1968, *73,* 37-43.

Ayllon, T. Intensive treatment of psychotic behavior by stimulus satiation and food reinforcement. *Behaviour Research and Therapy,* 1963, *1,* 53-61.

Ayllon, T., & Azrin, N. H. *The token economy: A motivational system for therapy and rehabilitation.* New York: Appleton-Century Crofts, 1968.

Ayllon, T., & Kelly, K. Reinstatement of verbal behavior in a functionally mute retardate. *Professional Psychology,* 1974, *5,* 385-393.

Ayllon, T., Layman, D., & Kandel, H. J. Behavioral-education alternative to drug control in hyperactive children. *Journal of Applied Behavior Analysis,* 1975, *8,* 137-146.

Ayllon, T., & Michael, J. The psychiatric nurse as a behavioral engineer. *Journal of the Experimental Analysis of Behavior,* 1959, *2,* 323-334.

Ayllon, T., & Roberts, M. D. Eliminating discipline problems by strengthening academic performance. *Journal of Applied Behavior Analysis,* 1974, *7,* 71-76.

Ayllon, T., Simon, S., & Wildman, R. W., II. Instructions and reinforcement in the treatment of encopresis: A case study. *Journal of Behavior Therapy and Experimental Psychiatry,* 1975, *6,* 235-238.

Ayllon, T., & Skuban, W. Accountability in psychotherapy: A test case. *Journal of Behavior Therapy and Experimental Psychiatry,* 1973, *4,* 19-30.

Ayllon, T., Smith, D., & Rogers, M. Behavioral management of school phobia. *Journal of Behavior Therapy and Experimental Psychiatry,* 1970, *1,* 125-138.

Azrin, N. H., Naster, B. J., & Jones, R. Reciprocity counseling: A rapid learning-based procedure for marital counseling. *Behaviour Research and Therapy,* 1973, *11,* 365-382.

Baer, D. M., Wolf, M. M., & Risley, T. R. Some current dimensions of applied behavior analysis. *Journal of Applied Behavior Analysis,* 1968, *1,* 91-97.

Bailey, J., Wolf, M., & Phillips, E. Home-based reinforcement and the modification of pre-delinquents' classroom behavior. *Journal of Applied Behavior Analysis,* 1970, *3,* 223-233.

Bandura, A. *Principles of behavior modification.* New York: Holt, Rinehart & Winston, 1969.

Barrish, H. H., Saunders, M., & Wolf, M. M. Good behavior game: Effects of individual contingencies for group consequences on disruptive behavior in a classroom. *Journal of Applied Behavior Analysis,* 1969, *2,* 119–124.

Bellack, A. S., Hersen, M., & Turner, S. M. Generalization effects of social skills training in chronic schizophrenics: An experimental analysis. *Behaviour Research and Therapy,* 1976, *14,* 391–398.

Bennett, P. S., & Maley, R. F. Modification of interactive behaviors in chronic mental patients. *Journal of Applied Behavior Analysis,* 1973, *6,* 609–620.

Bernal, G., Jacobson, L. I., & Lopez, G. N. Do the effects of behaviour modification programs endure? *Behaviour Research and Therapy,* 1975, *13,* 61–64.

Bijou, S. W., Peterson, R. F., Harris, F. R., Allen, K. E., & Johnston, M. S. Methodology for experimental studies of young children in natural settings. *Psychological Record,* 1969, *19,* 177–210.

Birnbrauer, J. S., Wolf, M. M., Kidder, J. D., & Tague, C. E. Classroom behavior of retarded pupils with token reinforcement. *Journal of Experimental Child Psychology,* 1965, *2,* 219–235.

Blanchard, E. B., & Johnson, R. A. Generalization of operant classroom control procedures. *Behavior Therapy,* 1973, *4,* 219–229.

Bostow, D. E., & Bailey, J. B. Modification of severe disruptive and aggressive behavior using brief timeout and reinforcement procedures. *Journal of Applied Behavior Analysis,* 1969, *2,* 31–37.

Broden, M., Bruce, C., Mitchell, M., Carter, V., & Hall, R. V. Effects of teacher attention on attending behavior of two boys at adjacent desks. *Journal of Applied Behavior Analysis,* 1970, *3,* 199–203.

Broden, M., Hall, R. V., Dunlap, A., & Clark, R. Effects of teacher attention and a token reinforcement system in a junior high school special education class. *Exceptional Children,* 1970, *36,* 341–349.

Buell, J., Stoddard, P., Harris, F. R., & Baer, D. M. Collateral social development accompanying reinforcement of outdoor play in a preschool child. *Journal of Applied Behavior Analysis,* 1968, *1,* 167–173.

Bushell, D., Jr., Wrobel, P. A., & Michaelis, M. L. Applying "group" contingencies to the classroom study behavior of preschool children. *Journal of Applied Behavior Analysis,* 1968, *1,* 55–61.

Chadwick, B. A., & Day, R. C. Systematic reinforcement: Academic performance of under-achieving students. *Journal of Applied Behavior Analysis,* 1971, *4,* 311–319.

Coleman, R. G. A procedure for fading from experimenter–school-based to parent–home-based control of classroom behavior. *Journal of School Psychology,* 1973, *11,* 71–79.

Cone, J. D. Assessing the effectiveness of programmed generalization. *Journal of Applied Behavior Analysis,* 1973, *6,* 713–718.

Conrad, R. D., Delk, J. L., & Williams, C. L. Use of stimulus fading procedures in the treatment of situation specific mutism: A case study. *Journal of Behavior Therapy and Experimental Psychiatry,* 1974, *5,* 99–100.

Cooper, J. A. Application of the consultant role to parent–teacher management of school avoidance behavior. *Psychology in the Schools,* 1973, *10,* 259–262.

Drabman, R. S., Spitalnik, R., & O'Leary, K. D. Teaching self-control to disruptive children. *Journal of Abnormal Psychology,* 1973, *82,* 10–16.

Elliott, T. N., Smith, R. D., & Wildman, R. W., II. Suicide and systematic desensitization: A case study. *Journal of Clinical Psychology,* 1972, *28,* 420–423.

Emshoff, J. G., Redd, W. H., & Davidson, W. S. Generalization training and the transfer of prosocial behavior in delinquent adolescents. *Journal of Behavior Therapy and Experimental Psychiatry*, 1976, *7*, 141–144.

Feingold, B. D. & Mahoney, M. J. Reinforcement effects on intrinsic interest: Undermining the overjustification hypothesis. *Behavior Therapy*, 1975, *6*, 367–377.

Fichter, M. M., Wallace, C. J., Liberman, R. P., & Davis, J. R. Improving social interaction in a chronic psychotic using discriminated avoidance ("nagging"): Experimental analysis and generalization. *Journal of Applied Behavior Analysis*, 1976, *9*, 377–386.

Firestone, P. The effects and side effects of timeout on an aggressive nursery school child. *Journal of Behavior Therapy and Experimental Psychiatry*, 1976, *6*, 79–81.

Forehand, R., & Atkeson, B. M. Generality of treatment effects with parents as therapists: A review of assessment and implementation procedures *Behavior Therapy*, 1977, *8*, 575–593.

Frederiksen, L. W., Jenkins, J. D., Foy, D. W., & Eisler, R. M. Social-skills training to modify abusive verbal outbursts in adults. *Journal of Applied Behavior Analysis*, 1976, *9*, 117–125.

Galloway, C. G., & Mickelson, N. I. Modifications of behavior patterns of Indian children. *Elementary School Journal*, 1971, *72*, 150–155.

Garcia, E. The training and generalization of a conversational speech form in nonverbal retardates. *Journal of Applied Behavior Analysis*, 1974, *7*, 137–149.

Goldstein, A. P., Heller, K., & Sechrest, L. B. *Psychotherapy and the psychology of behavior change*. New York: Wiley, 1966.

Goodall, K. Shapers at work. *Psychology Today*, 1972, *6*(6), 53–63, 132–134, 136–138.

Grandy, G. S., Madsen, C. H., Jr., & de Mersseman, L. M. The effects of individual and interdependent contingencies on inappropriate classroom behavior. *Psychology in the Schools*, 1973, *10*, 488–493.

Gray, F., Graubard, P. S., & Rosenberg, H. Little brother is changing you. *Psychology Today*, 1974, *7*(10), 42–46.

Gruber, R. P. Behavior therapy: Problems in generalization. *Behavior Therapy*, 1971, *2*, 361–368.

Hall, J. F. *The psychology of learning*. Philadelphia: Lippincott, 1966.

Hall, R. V., Cristler, C., Cranston, S. S., & Tucker, B. Teachers and parents as researchers using multiple baseline designs. *Journal of Applied Behavior Analysis*, 1970, *3*, 247–255.

Hall, R. V., Lund, D., & Jackson, D. Effects of teacher attention on study behavior. *Journal of Applied Behavior Analysis*, 1968, *1*, 1–12.

Hall, R. V., Panyan, M., & Rabon, D. Instructing beginning teachers in reinforcement procedures which improve classroom control. *Journal of Applied Behavior Analysis*, 1968, *1*, 315–322.

Hall, S. M., Hall, R. G., Borden, B. L., & Hanson, R. W. Follow-up strategies in the behavioral treatment of overweight. *Behaviour Research and Therapy*, 1975, *13*, 167–172.

Hauserman, N., Walen, S. R., & Behling, M. Reinforced racial integration in the first grade: A study in generalization. *Journal of Applied Behavior Analysis*, 1973, *6*, 193–200.

Hay, W. M., Hay, L. R., & Nelson, R. O. Direct and collateral changes in on-task and academic behavior resulting from on-task versus academic contingencies. *Behavior Therapy*, 1977, *8*, 431–441.

Herman, S. H., & Tramontana, J. Instructions and group versus individual reinforcement in modifying disruptive group behavior. *Journal of Applied Behavior Analysis,* 1971, *4,* 113–119.

Hewett, F. M. Educational engineering with emotionally disturbed children. *Exceptional Children,* 1967, *33,* 459–467.

Hewett, F. M., Taylor, F. D., & Artuso, A. A. The Santa Monica Project: Evaluation of an engineered classroom design with emotionally disturbed children. *Exceptional Children,* 1969, *35,* 523–529.

Homme, L. E., deBaca, P. C., Devine J. V., Steinhorst, R., & Rickert, F. J. Use of the Premack Principal in controlling the behavior of nursery school children. *Journal of the Experimental Analysis of Behavior,* 1963, *6,* 544.

Hopkins, B. L. Effects of candy and social reinforcement, instructions, and reinforcement schedule leaning on the modification and maintenance of smiling. *Journal of Applied Behavior Analysis,* 1968, *1,* 121–129.

Hunt, J. G., & Zimmerman, J. Stimulating productivity in a sheltered workshop setting. *American Journal of Mental Deficiency,* 1969, *74,* 43–49.

Israel, A. C. Some thoughts on correspondence between saying and doing. *Journal of Applied Behavior Analysis,* 1978, *11,* 271–276.

Israel, A. C., & O'Leary, K. D. Developing correspondence between one's words and deeds. *Child Development,* 1973, *44,* 575–581.

Jackson, D. A., & Wallace, R. F. The modification and generalization of voice loudness in a fifteen-year-old retarded girl. *Journal of Applied Behavior Analysis,* 1974, *7,* 461–471.

Johnston, J. M., & Johnston, G. T. Modification of consonant speech-sound articulation in young children. *Journal of Applied Behavior Analysis,* 1972, *5,* 233–246.

Jones, R. T., & Kazdin, A. E. Programming response maintenance after withdrawing token reinforcement. *Behavior Therapy,* 1975, *6,* 153–164.

Kale, R. J., Kaye, J. H., Whelen, P. A., & Hopkins, B. L. The effects of reinforcement on the modification, maintenance, and generalization of social responses of mental patients. *Journal of Applied Behavior Analysis,* 1968, *1,* 307–314.

Karoly, P., & Dirks, M. J. Developing self-control in preschool children through correspondence training. *Behavior Therapy,* 1977, *8,* 398–405.

Kaufman, K. F., & O'Leary, K. D. Reward, cost, and self-evaluation procedures for disruptive adolescents in a psychiatric hospital school. *Journal of Applied Behavior Analysis,* 1972, *5,* 293–309.

Kazdin, A. E. The effect of vicarious reinforcement on attentive behavior in the classroom. *Journal of Applied Behavior Analysis,* 1973, *6,* 71–78. (a)

Kazdin, A. E. Methodological and assessment considerations in evaluating reinforcement programs in applied settings. *Journal of Applied Behavior Analysis,* 1973, *6,* 517–531. (b)

Kazdin, A. E. Vicarious reinforcement and direction of behavior change in the classroom. *Behavior Therapy,* 1977, *8,* 57–63. (a)

Kazdin, A. E. *The token economy.* New York: Plenum, 1977. (b)

Kazdin, A. E., & Bootzin, R. R. The token economy: An evaluative review. *Journal of Applied Behavior Analysis,* 1972, *5,* 343–372.

Kazdin, A. E., & Kopel, S. On resolving ambiguities of the multiple-baseline design: Problems and recommendations. *Behavior Therapy,* 1975, *6,* 601–608.

Kazdin, A. E., & Polster, R. Intermittent token reinforcement and response maintenance in extinction. *Behavior Therapy,* 1973, *4,* 386–391.

Kimble, G. A. *Hilgard and Marquis' conditioning and learning.* New York: Appleton-Century-Crofts, 1961.

Koch, L., & Breyer, N. L. A token economy for the teacher. *Psychology in the Schools*, 1974, *11*, 195–200.

Koegel, R. L., Glahn, T. J. & Nieminen, G. S. Generalization of parent-training results. *Journal of Applied Behavior Analysis*, 1978, *11*, 95–109.

Koegel, R. L., & Rincover, A. Treatment of psychotic children in a classroom environment: I. Learning in a large group. *Journal of Applied Behavior Analysis*, 1974, *7*, 45–49.

Koegel, R. L., & Rincover, A. Research on the difference between generalization and maintenance in extra-therapy responding. *Journal of Applied Behavior Analysis*, 1977, *10*, 1–12.

Kuypers, D. S., Becker, W. C., & O'Leary, K. D. How to make a token system fail. *Exceptional Children*, 1968, *35*, 101–109.

Levine, F. M., & Fasnacht, G. Token rewards may lead to token learning. *American Psychologist*, 1974, *29*, 816–820.

Lewittes, D. J., & Israel, A. C. Responsibility contracting for the maintenance of reduced smoking: A technique innovation. *Behavior Therapy*, 1975, *6*, 696–697.

Liberman, R. P., McCann, M. J., & Wallace, C. J. Generalization of behaviour therapy with psychotics. *British Journal of Psychiatry*, 1976, *129*, 490–496.

Lindsley, O. R. Direct measurement and prosthesis of retarded behavior. *Journal of Education*, 1964, *147*, 62–81.

Lovaas, O. I., Berberich, J. P., Perloff, B. F., & Schaeffer, B. Acquisition of imitative speech by schizophrenic children. *Science*, 1966, *151*, 705–707.

Lovaas, O. I., Koegel, R., Simmons, J. Q., & Long, J. S. Some generalization and follow-up measurs on autistic children in behavior therapy. *Journal of Applied Behavior Analysis*, 1973, *6*, 131–166.

Lovaas, O. I., & Simmons, J. Q. Manipulation of self-destruction in three retarded children. *Journal of Applied Behavior Analysis*, 1969, *2*, 143–157.

MacDonald, W. S., Gallimore, R., & MacDonald, G. Contingency counseling by school personnel: An economical model of intervention. *Journal of Applied Behavior Analysis*, 1970, *3*, 175–182.

Madsen, C. H., Becker, W. C., & Thomas, D. R. Rules, praise, and ignoring: Elements of elementary classroom control. *Journal of Applied Behavior Analysis*, 1968, *1*, 139–150.

Mandelker, A. V., Brigham, T. A., & Bushell, D. The effects of token procedures on a teacher's social contacts with her students. *Journal of Applied Behavior Analysis*, 1970, *3*, 169–174.

Martin, J. A. Generalizing the use of descriptive adjectives through modeling. *Journal of Applied Behavior Analysis*, 1975, *8*, 201–209.

McKenzie, H. S., Clark, M., Wolf, M. M., Kothera, R., & Benson, C. Behavior modification of children with learning disabilities using grades as tokens and allowances as back-up reinforcers. *Exceptional Children*, 1968, *34*, 745–752.

McLaughlin, T. F., & Malaby, J. E. The utilization of an individual contingency program to control assignment completion in a token classroom: A case study. *Psychology in the Schools*, 1974, *11*, 191–194.

Meichenbaum, D. H., Bowers, K. S., & Ross, R. R. Modification of classroom behaviour of institutionalized female adolescent offenders. *Behaviour Research and Therapy*, 1968, *6*, 343–353.

Nay, W. R., & Legum, L. Increasing generalization in a token program for adolescent retardates. *Behavior Therapy*, 1976, *7*, 413–414.

O'Leary, K. D., & Becker, W. C. Behavior modification of an adjustment class. *Exceptional Children*, 1967, *33*, 637–642.

O'Leary, K. D., Becker, W. C. Evans, M. D., & Saudargas, R. A. A token reinforcement program in a public school: A replication and systematic analysis. *Journal of Applied Behavior Analysis,* 1969, *2,* 3–13.

O'Leary, K. D., & Drabman, R. Token reinforcement programs in the classroom: A review. *Psychological Bulletin,* 1971, *75,* 379–398.

O'Leary, K. D., Drabman, R. S., & Kass, R. E. Maintenance of appropriate behavior in a token program. *Journal of Abnormal Child Psychology,* 1973, *1,* 127–138.

Osborne, J. G. Free time as a reinforcer in the management of classroom behavior. *Journal of Applied Behavior Analysis,* 1969, *2,* 113–118.

Parker, H. C. Contingency management and noncomitant changes in elementary-school students' self-concepts. *Psychology in the Schools,* 1974, *11,* 70–79.

Patterson, G. R., & Brodsky, G. A behaviour modification programme for a child with multiple problem behaviors. *Journal of Child Psychology and Psychiatry,* 1966, *7,* 277–295.

Patterson, R. L., & Teigen, J. R. Conditioning and post-hospital generalization of nondelusional responses in a chronic psychotic patient. *Journal of Applied Behavior Analysis,* 1973, *6,* 65–70.

Pawlicki, R. E., & Morey, T. M. A low cost instrument for "thinning" self-directed schedules of reinforcement. *Behavior Therapy,* 1976, *7,* 120–122.

Reiss, S. Transfer effects of success and failure training from one reinforcing agent to another. *Journal of Abnormal Psychology,* 1973, *82,* 435–445.

Rincover, A., & Koegel, R. L. Setting generality and stimulus control in autistic children. *Journal of Applied Behavior Analysis,* 1975, *8,* 235–246.

Risley, T. R., & Hart, B. Developing correspondence between the nonverbal and verbal behavior of preschool children. *Journal of Applied Behavior Analysis,* 1968, *1,* 267–282.

Rogers-Warren, A., & Baer, D. M. Correspondence between saying and doing: Teaching children to share and praise. *Journal of Applied Behavior Analysis,* 1976, *9,* 335–354.

Rosenbaum, E., & Kellman, M. Treatment of a selectively mute third-grade child. *Journal of School Psychology,* 1973, *11,* 26–29.

Rozensky, R. H., & Bellack, A. S. Behavior change and individual differences in self-control. *Behaviour Research and Therapy,* 1974, *12,* 267–268.

Russell, E. W. The power of behavior control: A critique of behavior modification methods. *Journal of Clinical Psychology,* 1974, *30,* 111–136.

Salzberg, B. H., Wheeler, A. J., Devar, L. T., & Hopkins, B. L. The effect of intermittent feedback and intermittent contingent access to play on printing of kindergarten children. *Journal of Applied Behavior Analysis,* 1971, *4,* 163–171.

Schaefer, H. H., & Martin, P. L. *Behavioral therapy.* New York: McGraw-Hill, 1969.

Schwartz, M. L., & Hawkins, R. P. Application of delayed reinforcement procedures to the behavior of an elementary school child. *Journal of Applied Behavior Analysis,* 1970, *3,* 85–96.

Skinner, B. F. *Verbal behavior.* New York: Appleton-Century-Crofts, 1957.

Staats, A. W., Minke, K. A., Goodwin, W., & Landeen, J. Cognitive behavior modification: 'Motivated learning' reading treatment with subprofessional therapy technicians. *Behaviour Research and Therapy,* 1967, *5,* 283–299.

Stokes, T. F., & Baer, D. M. An implicit technology of generalization. *Journal of Applied Behavior Analysis,* 1977, *10,* 349–367.

Stokes, T. F., Baer, D. M., Jackson, R. L. Programming the generalization of a greeting response in four retarded children. *Journal of Applied Behavior Analysis,* 1974, *7,* 599–610.

Stolz, S. B., & Wolf, M. M. Visually discriminated behavior in a "blind" adolescent retardate. *Journal of Applied Behavior Analysis,* 1969, *2,* 65–77.

Stuart, R. B. Behavioral control of over-eating *Behaviour Research and Therapy,* 1967, *5,* 357–365.

Sulzbacher, S. I., & Houser, J. E. A tactic to eliminate disruptive behaviors in the classroom: Group contingent consequences. In R. Ulrich, T. Stachnik, & J. Mabry (Eds.), *Control of human behavior* Glenville, Ill.: Scott, Foresman, 1970.

Surratt, P. R., Ulrich, R. E., & Hawkins, R. P. An elementary student as behavioral engineer. *Journal of Applied Behavior Analysis,* 1969, *2,* 85–92.

Thomas, D. A., Nielsen, L. J., Kuypers, D. S., & Becker, W. C. Social reinforcement and remedial instruction in the elimination of a classroom behavior problem. *Journal of Special Education,* 1968, *2,* 291–305.

Tracey, D. A., Briddell, D. W., & Wilson, G. T. Generalization of verbal conditioning to verbal and nonverbal behavior: Group therapy with chronic psychiatric patients. *Journal of Applied Behavior Analysis,* 1974, *7,* 391–401.

Turkewitz, H., O'Leary, K. D., & Ironsmith, M. Generalization and maintenance of appropriate behavior through self-control. *Journal of Consulting and Clinical Psychology,* 1975, *43,* 577–583.

Ullmann, L. P., & Krasner, L. *Case studies in behavior modification.* New York: Holt, Rinehart & Winston, 1965.

Vaal, J. J. The decrease of unintelligible verbal responses through the use of operant conditioning techniques. *Psychology in the Schools,* 1972, *9,* 446–450.

Wahler, R. G. Setting generality: Some specific and general effects of child behavior therapy. *Journal of Applied Behavior Analysis,* 1969, *2,* 239–246.

Walker, H. M., & Buckley, N. K. The use of positive reinforcement in conditioning attending behavior. *Journal of Applied Behavior Analysis,* 1968, *1,* 245–250.

Walker, H. M., & Buckley, N. K. Programming generalization and maintenance of treatment effects across time and across settings. *Journal of Applied Behavior Analysis,* 1972, *5,* 209–224.

Walker, H. M., Hops, H., & Johnson, S. M. Generalization and maintenance of classroom treatment effects. *Behavior Therapy,* 1975, *6,* 188–200.

Walker, H. M., Mattson, R. H., & Buckley, N. K. The functional analysis of behavior within an experimental class setting. In W. C. Becker (Ed.), *An empirical basis for change in education.* Chicago: Science Research Associates, 1971.

Wheeler, A. J., & Sulzer, B. Operant training and generalization of a verbal response form in a speech-deficient child. *Journal of Applied Behavior Analysis,* 1970, *3,* 139–147.

Whitman, T. L., Mercurio, J. R., & Caponigri, V. Development of social responses in two severely retarded children. *Journal of Applied Behavior Analysis,* 1970, *3,* 133–138.

Whitman, T. L., Zakaras, M., & Chardos, S. Effects of reinforcement and guidance procedures on instruction-following behavior of severely retarded children. *Journal of Applied Behavior Analysis,* 1971, *4,* 283–290.

Wildman, R. W., & Wildman, R. W., II. The subdoctoral psychologist. *The Clinical Psychologist,* 1972, *26*(1), 11–12.

Winett, R. A., & Roach, A. M. The effects of reinforcing academic performance on social behavior: A brief report. *Psychological Record,* 1973, *23,* 391–396.

Wolf, M. M., Giles, D. K., & Hall, R. V. Experiments with token reinforcement in a remedial classroom. *Behaviour Research and Therapy,* 1968, *6,* 51–64.

CHAPTER

3

MAINTENANCE AND GENERALIZATION OF INDIVIDUAL BEHAVIOR THERAPY PROGRAMS: CLINICAL OBSERVATIONS

STEVEN T. FISHMAN AND BARRY S. LUBETKIN

The ultimate proof of the efficacy of any system of psychotherapy lies not only in its ability to effect change in a client's functioning, but also in its ability to ensure that such change will stand the test of time. It is surprising that although behavior therapy boasts a scientific foundation and is a system committed to refinement of its methods by empirical study, there has been a paucity of follow-up investigations in its literature. The small amount of follow-up work that does exist has been done in conjunction with laboratory analogue studies employing research subjects rather than in clinically based studies using clinical populations. The relationship between such laboratory "equivalencies" and actual clinical practice is assumed, but has never been unequivocally established. In spite of this apparent limitation, behavior therapy has enjoyed considerable attention since its inception in the mid-1950s, and has emerged as a viable psychotherapeutic system: one viewed as an alternative to the more traditional or evocative psychotherapy approaches.

Since its beginnings, behavior therapy has undergone a number of modifications. Predominant among these has been a metamorphosis from a neobehavioristic, S–R mediational model (Eysenck, 1960, 1964; Wolpe, 1958) based on orthodox learning theory to a more multiform or multimodal model (Lazarus, 1971, 1977b) which for the most part has found a theoretical home in social learning theory (Bandura, 1969). It is this latter, more broad-based system which includes inductions on the cognitive, affectual, and behavioral levels which best characterizes present-day clinical behavior therapy. Mahoney (1974, 1977) and Meichenbaum (1974, 1977) have heralded the beginning of cognitive behavior therapy which evolved from the wedding of traditional behavior therapy with the cognitive therapies (e.g., Beck, 1976; Ellis, 1962); even though others (e.g., Bandura, 1969; Mischel, 1968) can be considered harbingers of the movement toward a more comprehensive system. As Mahoney (1977) observed, each system had problems standing independently because its respective outcomes were wanting. Since these systems have a natural affinity for one another, it was only reasonable that they would join forces to ensure the front-line practitioner a more durable and efficient system of psychotherapy.

Additional significant changes in the development of behavior therapy include: movement from a system that was aimed mainly at the alleviation of rather limited, circumscribed problems to one that treats nearly the entire spectrum of emotional and behavioral problems; evolution from a rather brief, short-term approach to one requiring many more sessions and considerably more between-session activity; growth from a system that was technique oriented to one that is especially concerned with the effects of the "nonspecifics" or "extratreatment" variables on treatment outcomes; and development from a system that was very "problem centered" to a system that attempts to impart more general (i.e., self-control) coping strategies for everyday living.

These changes generally ensure greater efficiency in the system at large, but the real work of transfer and maintenance, the central theme of this chapter, lies with the individual practitioner. In using these terms, the following conditions should be met if transfer and maintenance can be considered effected: any alteration in the client's functioning that occurs as a direct consequence of treatment interventions must stand independent of any further therapeutic anchors, must be spontaneously incorporated into the client's everyday functioning, and should endure long after regular therapeutic contacts have been phased out or terminated.

From a clinical perspective, we content that transfer and maintenance of therapy gains are *merely a reflection of the sound practice of clinical behavior therapy.* Concern for these phenomena must be programmed into each phase of the psychotherapeutic sequence. Consequently, this chapter will address each phase of the therapist–client contact, specifically, assessment, treatment proper, the "consolidation period," termination, and follow-up will be discussed with this perspective in mind.

BEHAVIORAL ASSESSMENT AND PROBLEM CONCEPTUALIZATION

The efficacy of behavior therapy is only as good as the behavioral assessment that precedes it. The principal concern of the behavior therapist during the assessment phase is to cull out the determinants (both overt and covert) that elicit and act to perpetuate the client's problematic behavior (Goldfried & Pomeranz, 1968; Kanfer & Saslow, 1965). The real art of behavior therapy surfaces when the therapist uses this information in conceptualizing the overall problem and formulates a treatment program based on his conceptualization. Unfortunately, problem conceptualization and subsequent treatment formulation are not as straightforward as some therapists would like to believe. There are several factors which have to be taken into consideration during the assessment period which ultimately affect treatment planning and bear directly on the issues of generalization and maintenance.

Setting Priorities for Treatment

In our experience, most clients present multifaceted problems; consequently, several factors have to be taken into consideration in determining treatment focus. An initial decision must be made concerning the *urgency* of the various aspects of the client's symptom picture. For instance, one of the authors had a client, a young man recently enrolled in one of the local universities, presenting a long and continuing history of sexual exhibitionism. This client's other problems included drug usage (that had a disinhibiting effect on his exhibitionism), profound stuttering, severe interpersonal-social anxiety, and academic difficulties. Ideally one might assume that if the client could better control his stuttering and if he could feel considerably more comfortable with his own peers in social contacts, that the exhibitionism would abate. But the reality of the situation was that this client was exposing himself with such frequency that he was being arrested every other week. Because of the urgency and severity of the exhibitionism, it became apparent that the only sensible way to treat this individual was by treating the exhibitionism directly—with the thought of returning to the other problems when time permitted.

Second, consideration has to be given to the *expectations* the client brings to treatment. After conducting a thorough assessment of the client's functioning, it may be obvious to the therapist that the most significant and fundamental problems are different from the ones that the client has anticipated focusing on. The therapist will run the risk of alienating the client and increasing resistance by insisting that focus be on one area. A more reasonable approach would be to focus on the less desirable area or the one that will lead to a greater cooperative effort on the part of the client until such time that a relationship and trust is established.

Third, therapeutic attention has to be given to the most *crucial* or the "core" area which when ameliorated can lend to a generalization effect (Mischel, 1968), or what Fensterheim (1972) calls a "ripple effect" across the client's other problematic areas. For instance, one client seen by one of the authors reported experiencing generalized and pervasive anxiety, gastrointestinal difficulties, marital and sexual problems, and was unemployed because the company which had previously employed him for 15 years was forced into bankruptcy. The financial pressures were mounting and the marital difficulties were being exacerbated. The core problem was the client's lack of employment. The therapist addressed this area directly and intensively, via relaxation training and behavioral rehearsal for improving the client's interview skills, as well as by contingency contracting to ensure he would search the "want ads" and the employment agencies with regularity. Once this client was able to acquire a position that was almost comparable to his previous one, all the other problem areas he had presented upon initial contact either improved dramatically or dropped out. Of course, this is a rather obvious example and other cases may call for finer assessment discrimination. But the point remains: it is rather inefficient if a therapist finds himself merely "potshotting" areas of treatment focus rather than devoting the necessary time to formulating a viable treatment plan based on a global conceptualization of the client's problems.

Misassessment

There are other, subtler factors that have to be parcelled out during the assessment period lest the behavior therapist find himself down the proverbial "garden path," and having to battle resistance on the part of the client. Many practicing behavior therapists are too wedded to the prima facie problems that the client brings to therapy. As these authors have found from their clinical experience, many times "under material" may be directly responsible for maintaining the manifest behavior, such as would be the case when a client is deriving a secondary gain from his overt problems. By definition, secondary gains are manifest problems that are being maintained by the principle of negative reinforcement, and in a sense serve as a "cover" for a more severe problem. More specifically, learning theory would suggest that it is reinforcing to be removed from an event or situation that is fear provoking, so by avoiding confronting such problems or situations directly a client is perpetuating his problems.

A case example should suffice to illustrate this phenomenon. A 54-year-old woman who had been in therapy for a number of years with a "traditional" therapist was referred to one of the authors because she had a "stairs" phobia. She literally could not walk up or down two or three steps unattended without displaying a serious panic reaction. It appeared to be a straightforward problem and theoretically one that behavior therapy can adequately address. A regimen of systematic desensitization, both imaginal and in vivo, was initiated. The client began making genuine progress with the phobia, and each week the therapist and client could be seen parading up and down stairs in one of the local department stores practicing the in vivo exposure. Subsequently, the client began exhibiting some of the classical signs of countercontrol (e.g., too tired to practice, not following her home prescriptions, missing appointments). The in vivo program was then suspended, and it was back to the drawing board to reassess this client's problem. After further in depth exploration, the client finally revealed that as an adolescent she and her girlfriends would go to dances that apparently were held in places that necessitated her walking up staircases. She recalled that invariably her girlfriends were all asked to dance and she, being somewhat unattractive, remained on the sidelines feeling hurt and rejected. It was while leaving one of these social events that she developed a full-blown anxiety reaction on the steps, and from that time on she continued avoiding staircases. In fact, she used the phobia as a justification for getting out of other social occasions that might eventuate in embarrassment or discomfort.

The examples of the secondary gain phenomenon are boundless. Sometimes a family member inadvertently reinforces the maladaptive functioning of a client and thereby unwittingly perpetuates the pattern. One example should suffice. A 52-year-old, unmarried woman was referred for serious agoraphobic symptoms. Specifically, she could not walk outside her home or place of business without aid, which was in the form of holding onto a companion's arm. While she had always experienced a certain degree of "free-floating" anxiety, the debilitating panic feelings had recent onset. She had lived with her unmarried sister for most of her adult life, but recently their relationship had become increasingly strained. The client was threatened by the sister's growing need for independence and her fear that she would have to move out of the house and "be on her own." During the course of behavioral treatment, several hierarchically arranged in vivo practice assignments were suggested to the client. These included increasing the physical distance between her and a companion by the use of various strategies (e.g., coping self-talk, anxiety distraction procedures, use of varying lengths of strings to assist her in moving further away from companions while maintaining some sense of contact). Despite such efforts and firm, yet sensitive, encouragement from the therapist, the client steadfastly resisted implementing most of the assignments. Indeed, it appeared that her investment in remaining dependent (and ensuring her sister's guilt and loyalty) was prepotent over her desire to overcome her phobia. Only when a prolonged program of assertion and independence training was initiated, as well as intensive cognitive restructuring (to help her dispute her notion that she was a relatively worthless human being without the approval of her sister), was she able to practice and benefit from the homework prescriptions.

Once the behavior therapist becomes aware of the functional relationship between the maladaptive pattern and the family member's role in perpetuating it (like the one above), the family member is then cast into the role of "the benevolent saboteur." She is given explicit instructions by the therapist as to how she may subtly begin shifting the locus of control back to the client, so that the client can begin functioning in a more independent way. For instance, if the client has to go somewhere, the benevolent saboteur can back out at the very last minute, and more often than not the client, albeit reluctantly, will do the task independently. Of course, the family member is taught to appreciate the "canon of gradualness" and begins fading herself from the client by incremental steps.

Other examples of secondary gain include successful business people and professionals who present circumscribed phobias and who, with further probing, reveal that they feel like "imposters" in their chosen occupations. They feel that they have achieved the heights they have by "slipping through" with their incompetence unnoticed. Obviously underlying these circumscribed phobias are rather profound feelings of insecurity for which clients have compensated by achieving well in their chosen fields. However, they have failed to integrate their occupational successes sufficiently to alter their basic self-concept. Lazarus (1971) offered an example of an individual who developed a bridge phobia to avoid having to go to work only after being promoted to a position he felt ill-equipped to deal with. Additionally, many assertion difficulties are masked by some circumscribed problems. As an illustration of this point, one of the authors saw an actress in treatment who presented a flying phobia that was interfering with both her personal and professional functioning. After the client began realizing excellent progress with her problem she began to resist further movement, and the therapist found that flying represented an act of assertion of freedom for this young woman. Her underlying fear was that if she were to exercise too many of her individual prerogatives, it might ultimately lead to the dissolution of her marriage to her rather controlling husband. Most clients like this find it more acceptable to develop and present a phobia or some other similar problem than to risk failure, ridicule, rejection, or social embarrassment.

There are several signs that a secondary gain phenomenon may be operating on a client's life problems. As we have indicated, the client in the course of treatment begins "resisting" in some way (e.g., late for appointments, not doing homework, missing appointments) when treatment is directed at the manifest problem. As the practitioner suspends treatment and returns to further probing and exploration of the client's spheres of functioning, he typically finds or uncovers some problems that are being hidden by the overt problems. Another indicator is that the client often describes his manifest problems in a de facto way and does not appear to be overtly distressed by their reality. Such problems are conveniently masking problems that are more severe; so as a result, clients are relatively comfortable with the more obvious (and more acceptable) ones. Frequently, when clients are asked how their life will be different when they successfully overcome their problems, they might instantly respond with optimistic predictions such as: "Things will be great," "I'll be free," "I'll be able to make new friends," etc. Skilled probing by the therapist will often uncover terror at the prospect of change, fears of others' expectations, or other well-ingrained fears once their problems disappear. Contrary to what would be predicted from a psychodynamic perspective, once therapy interventions focus on the real underlying problems, the symptomatic or presenting problems do not spontaneously drop out. The overt problems have been perpetuated by prolonged avoidance and have in fact built sufficient habit strength. They therefore remain as autonomous problems. Rather, the client will then have to "allow" the therapist to focus on the overt problem without further significant interruption or resistance.

Another area that is typically overlooked in assessment is the degree and extent to which the client is invested in his own problems. If the presenting problem is one of long duration, the client has probably centered his lifestyle, and in fact most of his everyday functioning, around the particular problem. This type of client, like the client deriving a secondary gain from his problem, resists treatment. But countercontrol tactics begin near the final stages of the treatment process when it appears that termination is imminent: that is, the time when the client is facing change, unfamiliar feelings, independent functioning, and a possible change in lifestyle.

One client seen in treatment by one of the authors presented a rather severe small animal phobia. The woman had had the phobia for approximately 25 years, and she centered her whole existence around her phobia. She moved from a neighborhood that had many dogs running loose in the streets to a location that was relatively dog free. As she began progressing, she began resisting treatment. She reported "being afraid" to be without her phobia because it had provided structure for her functioning (e.g., who she could visit or where she could go). In a sense, the client was afraid to be without it. She would be functioning on "unfamiliar" ground which caused her more anxiety than the phobia, which she has successfully managed by well-planned avoidance behavior. It became necessary to counsel the client on how to function on an everyday level without the phobia. The author used a number of imagery techniques (Lazarus, 1977a) to help the client project into the future without the phobia.

The same phenomenon exists with clients who are grossly overweight. Once they lose significant amounts of weight, there is a greater onus on them to function in the interpersonal-social sphere where heretofore they had a "built-in" excuse not to. Loss of a significant amount of weight does not ensure that the client will function with greater facility or comfort in social situations. Considerable attention has to be given to this area if a therapist is to do a complete and thorough job with a client, but more importantly, to ensure the transfer and maintenance of the client's gains. Without such additional attention there is a rather high probability that the client will lapse into his old and familiar patterns of behavior.

One strategy that these practitioners have employed to counter this "twilight resistance" and to prepare the client for an altered lifestyle is to install an additional step in the therapeutic sequence called "the consolidation phase of treatment." This phase of the treatment sequence, an important one because it speaks to the essence of this volume, maintenance and transfer, will be discussed later in this chapter.

Contextual Analysis

A necessary part of the assessment process, and one that is not particularly new to behavior modification, is to assess the problem relative to the environment in which it occurs. The physical environment may be a significant contributing factor in eliciting and maintaining the problematic behavior. This type of assessment procedure has been used mainly with a child population (Tharp & Wetzel, 1969) but is seen as an important dimension in an adult population as well.

Physical environment is an important variable in helping to understand the nuances of a client's behavior. For instance, aggressive behavior might be perfectly appropriate for someone who resides in a community where aggression is necessary for survival. The goal of treatment might not be to eliminate the aggressive behavior, but rather to help sharpen the client's discriminatory skills to differentiate appropriate settings to exhibit aggressive behavior from inappropriate ones. If a college student has no other effective means of relating to a group of peers (that is, he is lacking the necessary social skills) and relates to them by participating in drug parties, then treatment would be approached in a very different manner than merely targeting the drug problem as the focus of therapy. The same holds true for the occurrence of homosexual behavior in prisons where it is considered acceptable, but not necessarily so outside of prisons where such practice is not fully sanctioned by our society. Problems are defined, and their normative boundaries set, by the context in which they occur. Of course, understanding the behavior helps to direct the treatment focus along dimensions that are relevant to the individual client.

Many times therapy entails the restructuring of the environment that triggers or gives rise to particular behavioral responses. Once a desirable change is effected in the client's behavior, then he may in fact be urged to change his previous environment and the attendant stimulus constellation that tempts him. For instance, these authors (Lubetkin & Fishman, 1974) treated a 22-year-old PhD graduate student in physics for a drug dependency (i.e., heroin problem). The problem was not of long duration, but seemed to be elicited and perpetuated by the young man's environment. Many of his closest friends were involved with drug usage, and when they socialized together they would invariably use heroin. These authors were successful in treating the drug problem, but additionally urged that the young graduate student leave the campus where the temptation to use drugs was almost inescapable by virtue of his social network. He and his wife relocated abroad where the client completed his doctoral studies. A 1-year follow-up revealed him to be drug free. Indeed, it appears that many times transfer of treatment gains is not possible in a client's existing environment. To ensure lasting change in a circumscribed aspect of functioning, a change in the environment is sometimes necessitated.

It is always a good practice to include significant others in the treatment planning, execution, and follow-up, to facilitate transfer and maintenance of gains into the client's familial context. It is a well-documented fact that there is a high risk, or even a significant probability, once a client leaves treatment and the guidance of the therapist that progress either stalls or breaks down. This is particularly true of agoraphobes where dependency is a core issue. If the therapist focuses solely on the avoidant behavior and fails to concentrate on the underlying insecurities, then the risk of relapse is high. Mathews (1978) developed a home-based treatment for agoraphobes where the locus of control was shifted from the therapist very early in the treatment process to a significant other who merely followed the directions of the therapist in helping the client (e.g., with home practice). A similar program exists at Butler Hospital in Rhode Island under the direction of David Barlow, where patients are treated for obsessive-compulsive disorders using a "response prevention" paradigm. In the later stages of therapy, after the client has shown considerable progress, therapists go into the home to facilitate generalization of progress into that environment. As in the Mathews program, they enlist the aid of a significant other to act as a facilitator or trainer for the patient. It must be underscored that such procedures contribute to greater transfer and maintenance of gains, but they are not the ultimate solution to the problem. It is imperative that the ultimate locus of control lie with the individual client, and not a therapist, a significant other, or a group, because if there are any future threats to the client's support systems the risk of relapse becomes high (cf. Chapter 8).

TREATMENT

Setting the Stage

It is crucial that the client be properly prepared and expectations established before commencing with treatment. He is alerted to the fact that behavior therapy is hard work and presupposes his motivation and cooperation, but more important, that he is to be an *active* participant in the change process. Essentially, he is instructed that he will virtually be in therapy all the time between formal sessions (i.e., practicing tapes, recording data, carrying out behavioral prescriptions).

It is during this preparatory phase that the client is introduced to the notion of the "canon of gradualness," which in principle underlies the workings of behavior therapy, and more globally sets the tempo for the process of change. Specifically, individuals change or progress by incremental steps, and each small step is self-reinforced and serves as an impetus for subsequent steps. The client learns to build on his successes until such time that progress becomes generalized over other spheres of his functioning. Often the client is further made aware of the various dimensions of the change progress by graphically portraying it. It is depicted as a positively accelerated time line that is replete with peaks, valleys, and numerous plateaus. The message is clear: *the client ought not expect uninterrupted positive progress toward his desired goals.* Rather, in all likelihood he will experience some slippage and backsliding through the course of his therapy. If the client is inoculated against the panic and disappointment which might ensue from these inevitable occurrences, he is better able to manage such setbacks more philosophically without undue catastrophizing.

Sometimes it is useful to present the change pattern of another client whose problems are similar to his and with whom he can identify. Reasonable causal explanations accompany descriptions of the slippage points, and again the point is underscored that these are normal and to be expected. Marlatt and Gordon (1979) have provided a good model for inoculation against posttherapy problems.

In working with relapse in alcoholics, Marlatt looks at the "abstinence violation effect": an individual's reaction to a slip. He observes that alcoholics who resume drinking after a period of abstinence often interpret the slip as either another affirmation of their hopelessness or as an excuse to "go off the wagon" and resume abusive drinking. Marlatt incorporates into his program a training component to help clients effectively cope with setbacks without undoing realized treatment gains. The superstitious notion has existed for too long among many psychotherapists that if failure is discussed with clients, then that will increase the probability of failure's actually occurring. We submit that for many clients just the opposite is true!

It is often useful to "anticipate the anticipator," and to have a discussion about problems that the client anticipates occurring during the therapy. One phobic client recently seen anticipated balking at in vivo exercises and predicted stalling therapeutically if asked to become more independent of his spouse. By emphasizing the step-by-step nature of the change process and by showing the client how he was ultimately responsible for the pace of his change, he was reassured. He was further assured that he would never be coerced into doing anything for which he felt ill-prepared. Another client suffering from intermittent impotence was skeptical about the long-term effects of therapy. While involved in other forms of psychotherapy he reported a history of several periods in which he functioned sexually without problems followed by periods of total dysfunction. He needed assurance that behavior therapy could provide a more consistent, durable change. By recreating an approximate change curve of his previous experiences, we were able to explicate the meaning of, and probable causation of, many of his setbacks (including unreasonable sexual standards and unexpressed anger feelings toward partners). In this manner we were able to outline the various strategies that he would have to acquire in order to prevent such future relapses. By anticipating the anticipator and by preidentifying the various pitfalls that may occur as therapy evolves, resistance to change is diminished and the client becomes a more cooperative partner in the change process.

It is also useful to instruct clients to keep track of the pressures they bring to bear on themselves during therapy with self-defeating questions and comments like "How long is this going to take?" "Why aren't I feeling better faster?" "At this rate I'll be in therapy when I'm 75!" Clients can be taught to identify such destructive cognitions and to counter them by noting what roadblocks they are setting up to their own progress. The "permission-giving" process should also hold for any doubts or uncomfortable feelings that they may be experiencing in regard to the procedures employed or the nature of the therapeutic relationship.

Homework Assignments

A cornerstone of behavior therapy treatment is the assignment of relevant and manageable homework. The purpose of such homework is twofold: to ensure the client's active involvement in the change process; and more important, to help pave the way for the transfer of new coping strategies into the client's functioning. Our task here is not to list and discuss the myriad of possible homework assignments that a behavior therapist is likely to suggest to his clients. (The reader is referred to Shelton & Ackerman, 1974, for a comprehensive review of the topic.) Rather, it is our purpose to define the problems that both client and therapist encounter when developing homework assignments, and further, to discuss the role that such outside work has on the transfer and maintenance of problem improvement.

Lazarus (1971) has suggested that there are at least eight reasons why a client chooses not to carry out homework assignments, or to carry them out incompletely. He offers the following explanations: the assignment is seen as irrelevant, too threatening, or too time-consuming; there is a lack of clarity as to who is responsible for the change; there is resistance to the therapy; sabotaging from another source (family member, friend); and the old standby, secondary gains. Let us look at several of these separately, keeping in mind that there is frequently a good deal of overlap in each category.

Irrelevant or incorrect homework assignments usually follow from a misassessment of the client's disturbance or a misreading of what is most essential to the client at the particular point in therapy. It may not be useful, for example, to encourage a client with a high degree of social evaluative anxiety to practice smiling at strangers if he first needs to learn appropriate social conversational skills. Smiling may lead to an increase in the probability of occasional spontaneous conversations which will surely lead to feelings of humiliation and failure in the ill-prepared client. Another example is when a therapist is doing assertion training with clients who experience high levels of anxiety when risking disapproval from others, and he elects to use a number of "shame and risk" exercises. These exercises are designed to help clients alter cognitions in a rational, constructive way by "behaving themselves into feeling differently." One client with interpersonal-social anxiety as his presenting problem was encouraged to enter several restaurants each day, order only a glass of water, drink it, thank the waitress, and leave. After many such efforts, the client began to recognize philosophically that he could risk the possibility of being negatively evaluated by others without diminishing value in himself. The generalizability, however, of such altered cognitions to more relevant life circumstances is open to question. It does not necessarily follow that because a client is less personally and socially self-conscious with strangers that this new-found freedom will generalize to significant others in his life. Many cognitively oriented therapists, however, make such an inferential leap. It is becoming increasingly evident in clinical practice that beliefs, attitudes, and values are *less universal* than was heretofore believed. In order to maximize transfer of new cognitions into a client's life situations, the behavior therapist must cognitively restructure along dimensions that have relevance and meaning for a particular client.

Homework tasks can be intimidating for a client if the therapist overestimates the response capability of the client. Even when clients are assigned what appear to be rather "benign" tasks like practicing with relaxation tapes, they can find such assignments overwhelming if they have a fear of losing emotional control in a state of deep relaxation. For this reason, it is good practice for therapists to administer such exercises with a client in his office before sending him home for independent practice, in case trouble shooting for that technique is indicated.

Occasionally a client will complain that a particular homework assignment is too time-consuming, and therefore will either not carry it out or will do it incompletely. One college student client having difficulty with studying and motivation was assigned a rather complicated operant-based study program which included about an hour a day of studying. While the program would have benefited him greatly, the time commitment required to carry it out was too great. Indeed, the client began to panic that he was spending "so much time practicing how to study that there would be little time left to actually study."

Sometimes clients involved in behavior therapy are unwilling to accept responsibility for their role in the change process. This is especially true in an active-directive approach like behavior therapy where the therapist is continually giving suggestions, outlining alternatives, prompting and directing change. Such a style often leads to a client's becoming dependent on the therapist for his next directive. The "do me" mentality is especially evident among clients with various hypochondriacal complaints who have an expectation for cure that is equivalent to that expected with physical conditions. As noted throughout this chapter, therapists can counteract this tendency on the part of some clients by encouraging independence in thought and behavior. Clients are often encouraged, for example, to create their own homework assignments, to provide a rationale for each task, and to determine criteria to assess whether the task is carried out partially or completely. Attribution theory (cf. Davison & Valins, 1969) would support the notion that if responsibility for change is "owned" by the client and not attributed to some external resource, then change will be more enduring.

BEHAVIOR THERAPY STRATEGIES

As noted earlier in this chapter, the multiform behavior therapist approaches client problems in a comprehensive fashion, emphasizing *holistic treatment* programs rather than concentrating only on manifest problem behaviors. Further, the thrust of this perspective is on helping the client develop self-control/self-management coping skills to increase the durability of change rather than solely focusing on problem elimination. It seems apparent that in clinical practice, the more dimensions or functionally related aspects of a problem that are assessed and ameliorated, the greater the likelihood of maintenance of that improvement. Lazarus (1977b), in developing multimodal therapy, has been a major spokesman for this approach. It is his contention, and these authors are in accord, that therapy is educational, and that the more people learn, the more coping responses they possess and the less likely they are to relapse.

It is beyond the scope of this chapter to survey the gamut of individual strategies that comprise the behavior therapist's armamentarium, particularly in the light of the recent inclusion of a multitude of new cognitive and affectual techniques into the system. A number of excellent resources already serve that purpose (e.g., Goldfried & Davison, 1976; Meichenbaum, 1977). Rather, we will sample and discuss some of the techniques, particularly as they relate to the issues at hand, transfer and maintenance. Additionally, we will illustrate the multiform approach, addressing the treatment of a highly prevalent problem in most clinical settings, interpersonal-social anxiety.

Generally, the behavior therapy approaches have evolved from therapist-administered or -directed techniques to more client-administered or self-control strategies (Goldfried & Merbaum, 1973). To illustrate the change in focus, let us select the one technique that has been most widely used and researched in behavior therapy, systematic desensitization (SD). As Wolpe (1958) originally conceptualized the method, in keeping with his theoretical rationale as well, systematic desensitization is administered under the explicit control of the therapist. Once the client has successfully "mastered" the anxiety associated with a particular object or situation, he is sent out to face these situations with little, if any, discomfort. Goldfried (1971) modified the systematic desensitization technique in line with a self-control perspective. Specifically, the original SD structure was maintained (i.e., relaxation training and hierarchy construction) but the procedure was modified in such a way as to provide the client a vehicle in which he can learn to cope with increasing levels of anxiety. The Goldfried technique, "prolonged exposure" as he terms it, acts to facilitate transfer of a newly learned coping skill (i.e., relaxation) into the client's everyday functioning. Other examples of changes in the basic techniques reflecting a similar shift in emphasis in the direction of self-control and transfer include: change from differential muscular relaxation (Jacobson, 1929) to cue-mediated relaxation procedures (Bernstein & Borkovec, 1973); systematic desensitization with a rational-emotive component (Meichenbaum & Cameron, Note 1); rational restructuring (Goldfried & Goldfried, 1975); and a host of multicomponent packages for stress, anger, and pain inoculation (Novaco, 1975; Suinn & Richardson, 1971; Meichenbaum & Cameron, Note 1).

Social avoidance distress (Watson & Friend, 1969) or interpersonal-social anxiety is characterized by an avoidance and in most cases an excessive degree of anxiety that crosscuts a wide range of social situations, such as new group situations, the opposite sex, and authority figures, or for that matter any situation where a client's performance is evaluated or scrutinized. Most clients with interpersonal-social anxiety are severely debilitated in their functioning because of the pervasive nature of their anxiety and the added discomfort generated by self-deprecatory activity. Until only recently, most of the analogue research in the area concentrated on social skills deficits (McFall & Marston, 1970) to the exclusion of cognitive and affectual modalities. Studies by Borkovec, Fleischman, and Caputo (1973) and Glasgow and Arkowitz (1975) demonstrated, in simulated dating situations, that low-frequency daters were rated on a number of measures by a panel of independent judges to have social skills equivalent to the high-frequency daters. Low-frequency daters, however, rated themselves on self-report measures as having patently deficient social skills. Clearly, even though these researchers did not make it explicit, the cognitive modality plays an important role in affecting the avoidant behavior in low-frequency daters. At all costs they must "avoid looking foolish" or risk being rejected, both of which are unacceptable to the socially anxious individual.

Since studies seem to suggest the multiform nature of social anxiety, and our clinical work would bear this out, the most efficacious way to approach this insidious problem would be in a multiform fashion. Table 3-1 represents the wide array of possible techniques in the three modalities that can be used in the treatment of this problem. It must be underscored that to

Table 3-1
Multiform treatment of Interpersonal-Social Anxiety

Anxiety component	Behavioral skill deficits	Irrational perspectives on self and the world

1. Relaxation training
   a. differential muscular relaxation
   b. sensory awareness
   c. hypnosis
	1. Education about importance of assertiveness and rationale
	2. Role-playing and behavioral rehearsal of various situations
	3. Script building
		1. Correct sexual and relationship myths and misconceptions
		2. Rational-emotive procedures
		3. Development of risk-taking philosophy

2. Systematic desensitization Prolonged exposure with rational restructuring and coping strategies 3. Implosion and high-arousal flooding 4. Chemotherapy	4. In vivo modeling 5. Identifying personal rights 6. Exhortation 7. Intimacy training 8. Teaching nonverbal communication skills 9. Reversal of real or anticipated sexual dysfunction 10. Assertion exerise: "saying no," "making requests," "giving compliments," etc.	4. Antiawfulizing homework 5. Shame and risk exercises 6. Thought stopping for self-depreciation 7. Time projection and other active imagery techniques 8. Coverant control procedures 9. Problem solving

maximize the chances for transfer of treatment gains into the client's functioning, treatment programming must be individualized; that is, it must be relevant to the client with whom the behavior therapist is working.

We will not review the various techniques delineated under each category, but rather we will discuss general treatment issues that are relevant to each of the three categories.

Anxiety Component

Anxiety plays a central role in causing the socially self-conscious individual to avoid, or to exhibit stiff or awkward behavior in, social contexts. Clinically, it appears that control of anxiety can best be maintained if clients are taught both *task*-relevant and *problem*-relevant relaxation procedures. Clients should be taught procedures which they can employ unobtrusively in real-life situations. Breathing exercises, imagery techniques, and cue-mediated procedures seem best suited for men and women who want to remain alert and communicative in social settings. For these clients who have pan-anxiety mediated by a fear of losing control, along with interpersonal anxiety, techniques such as differential progressive relaxation (see Jacobson, 1929) would be contraindicated. Such methods suggest that clients focus attention on the body and musculature, when deemphasizing such self-focus is crucial. Various distraction and externalization methods would be more appropriate. It is important to make the distinction between perceived somatic and cognitive anxiety dimensions. Frequently, dimension-relevant relaxation procedures will be more effective in lowering anxiety and maintaining improvement than will dimension-irrelevant procedures.

As illustrated earlier, the prolonged exposure systematic desensitization procedure (Goldfried, 1971) is especially useful for the socially anxious client because of the pervasive nature of the problem. The technique affords the training ground for learning to apply the relaxation skill to his everyday interpersonal and social functioning. Meichenbaum, Gilmore, and Fedoravicius (1971) further modified the technique to include a rational-emotive component or self-instructional statements as an aid in the reduction of anxiety in social settings. To illustrate, take a young male college student attempting to approach a young woman at a university "mixer." Almost without exception, such a scene will generate excessive anxiety in the socially anxious client. As he imagines himself in the situation and begins experiencing anxiety in the therapy setting, he is equipped with cue words like "calm control" that mediate relaxation, and with self-instructional statements like "stay relaxed," "I can handle this," and the like. The combination of the two components facilitates his approach to the young lady and helps to minimize his discomfort. It is important for ensuring maintenance that the client have many opportunities to rehearse coping self-statements in vitro. Desensitization scenes are often taped (Nawas, Fishman, & Pucel, 1970), and clients are encouraged to practice them at home on a regular basis.

In addition, it is felt that both desensitization and flooding scenes ought to make use of dominant client representational systems (see Bandler & Grinder, 1975) in order to increase generalizability from in vitro to in vivo activities. In other words, the visual-sensory modality, which has been most often used in imagery-based techniques, may not necessarily be the dominant modality in mediating the clients' fear reaction. Other systems, such as auditory, olfactory, gustatory, and especially kinesthetic, may be important mediators of anxiety for particular clients. Bandler and Grinder (1975) encourage beginning with the client's major representational system (usually determined from an interview and practice-imagery scenes) and then encompassing all appropriate systems.

Behavioral Skill Deficits

It is felt that it is incomplete therapy, destined to fail, if unassertive, interpersonally anxious individuals are not provided with a solid rationale for developing new interpersonal skills. Lange and Jakubowski (1976) make a similar point. Simply doing assertion training, of any variety, with a client without ensuring that the client *understands why* the new skills are important will usually lead to cosmetic changes at best. This is particularly true with clients who have strong moral and parental restrictions against assertion in relationships. Aggressive clients must be shown how they are having problems with assertion, and they are often terrified at open, honest expressions of feeling. They often deny any problems with assertion. Clients must be taught to distinguish between politeness and unassertiveness, between selfishness and self-interest. Once clients recognize that self-respect and an increased sense of mastery over their environment follow from more appropriately assertive behavior, they will be willing to accept and practice new skills. Therapists ought not to make the assumption that clients are "automatically" educated about the usefulness of assertive behavior and attitudes. Often, judicious self-disclosure is useful in conveying the importance of assertive behavior. Many clients resent the basic idea in assertion training of behaving oneself into feeling differently and opt for the notion of feeling more confident before proceeding to risk new interpersonal behaviors. Clients who have not had the idea of behavior rehearsal leading to cognitive and affectual change adequately explained to them will resist the procedures, or simply "go through the motions" of assertion exercises with little real investment in change. It should be explained that the client has often been waiting for years for new feelings to develop and has wasted many precious opportunities: behaving himself into feeling differently will let him take advantage of current opportunities.

It is imperative for maintenance of interpersonal gains that clients have the opportunity to anticipate and practice problematic situations which may arise in their lives after therapy is terminated. During role-playing, behavioral rehearsal, and problem-solving training (see Goldfried & D'Zurilla, 1969), clients are encouraged constructively to anticipate (as contrasted with destructive, fearful anticipation) potential problems which may arise as a consequence of implementing skills learned in therapy. One male client, fearful of the potential negative consequences of persistently asking his boss for raise, reviewed with the therapist, and role-played, all possible reactions from his boss and, finally, how he might react to each of them. He was also coached on how to handle appropriately the boss's possible negative reactions to his persistence. The goal here is to provide clients with knowledge of, and experiential practice with, all their options in order that they may proceed confidently, reassured that they are prepared for a variety of possibilities. After each role-play or problem-solving phase, the client is encouraged to identify general principles of behaving that he can apply to other problematic situations. Often he is encouraged to find other examples of how he might apply these principles in his daily living. Every effort is also made to involve at least one family member or relative who would be willing to continue practicing new skills with the client between sessions and after termination. Sometimes this is fellow therapy group member.

Irrational Thinking

Many clients with interpersonal-social anxiety problems may learn to control anxiety and may learn to overcome behavioral skill deficiencies, but still relapse after therapy is terminated. These clients often require cognitive restructuring procedures (Ellis, 1962; Meichenbaum, 1977) to help correct erroneous and illogical ideas and attitudes that may be inhibiting social effectiveness. It is felt that no matter which cognitive restructuring procedure is used in the consulting room (e.g., Socratic argument, rational-emotive procedures, rational restructuring, or bibliotherapy), maintenance of gains is invariably enhanced by in vivo procedures. For example, clients are often encouraged to keep daily thought diaries in order to maintain the connection between uncomfortable feelings and cognitions. A portion of each session is then devoted to closely examining erroneous ideas and misappraisals, how they affect feelings and behavior, and learning to substitute more useful self-enhancing beliefs for such ideas. A number of procedures can be used for this purpose. For example, with Goldfried and Goldfried's rational restructuring procedure, clients are asked to imagine themselves in anxiety-producing situations; then, once they begin experiencing in vitro anxiety, they are asked what they are telling themselves about the situation at that moment. In the case of social anxiety, clients typically reply either "I'm going to make a fool out of myself" or "She's going to reject me." Of course, such self-utterances can only translate themselves into anxious feelings which interfere with effective social functioning. The client, while continuing to imagine the same situation, is then asked to change his self-statement in such a way as to reduce his self-created anxiety. This of course is accomplished by the client's altering his self-defeating internal statements to more positive or self-enhancing statements.

This rational restructuring method has the advantage of the prolonged exposure technique (Goldfried, 1971) described earlier. It affords the client a vehicle for rehearsing coping skills that can be extrapolated into his everyday experiences.

Many clients debilitated by social fears generate a good portion of their anxiety by their own negative imagery. Usually in anticipation of any social event, the client vividly imagines himself making a fool out of himself and being subjected to merciless ridicule from others. Obviously, with such self-defeating imagery the client brings his own self-generated brand of anxiety into the social event and then realizes his worst fears— he behaves in an awkward, self-conscious manner. A host of "imagery reconstruction" methods can be used for this purpose, such as covert modeling (Cautela, Flannery, & Hanley, 1974; Kazdin, 1975) or a number of others found in a recent text by Lazarus (1977b).

CONSOLIDATION PERIOD

In the latter stages of treatment, when the client reports and exhibits observable signs of progress over a reasonable period of time, the client is then shifted into what we term the "consolidation phase" of the psychotherapeutic sequence. This particular phase is more crucial if transfer and ultimate maintenance of gains are to be incorporated into the client's everyday functioning. Typically the client will begin coming into each session announcing successes that he had enjoyed that particular week. It becomes evident that he is employing, to his betterment, the specific techniques, cognitive and behavioral, rather consistently and spontaneously. Up until this point in therapy the therapeutic process was under the active direction of the behavior therapist. During this phase the client is allowed to plateau with only minimal treatment demands being imposed upon him. In essence, he is allowed a period of time to consolidate his treatment gains. It is also a time during which the behavior therapist takes a decidedly more passive role in treatment planning and problem resolution. The ultimate control for future treatment programming is shifted to the client. The latter is highlighted by such statements from the therapist as "What would you like or think that you would like to accomplish for next week?" "Why don't you just continue doing what you're doing?" "How do you think you should handle that problem?" For instance, when doing assertion training for a socially anxious individual, a list of life's assignments are developed with the help of the client. These are essentially a hierarchy of in vivo assignments ordered in terms of increasing difficulty (e.g, asking a question in class, starting a conversation with someone in line at a supermarket, or asking a boss to diminish a workload) that are specific to that client. Once the list is successfully negotiated and the client begins benefiting from other aspects of treatment, explicit assignments for the week are no longer given. Rather, the client begins applying his accumulated therapeutic experiences, as well as the principles gleaned from his therapy, to his everyday functioning. Problems of the week are no longer discussed or role-played in detail, but are discussed in a more general way like "What happened?" "How did you handle it?" "What did you learn from the experience?" "Have you ever encountered something like that before?" In addition to giving the client greater responsibility for treatment strategizing and planning, the consolidation period is also a time during which formal treatment sessions can begin to be spaced and the therapist "faded" until the time of termination of that client.

There are several other reasons that underscore the importance of this intermediate phase between treatment and termination in the therapeutic sequence. First, it allows for the continued practice of the newly acquired coping skills with sights set on building habit strength with each until their usage is truly automatic and spontaneous. Second, it allows the client to internalize and "own" his successes, for the positive feelings of accomplishment can never catch up to the client's behavioral accomplishments if the demands to do more are ever-present. Third, it affords the client the opportunity to incorporate his new cognitive and behavioral and affectual responses into his lifestyle. This of course serves to minimize a client's fears of a radically altered lifestyle.

TERMINATION

Assuming that the consolidation period has eventuated in continued but independent progress, and the gains enjoyed up to that point have been maintained, then termination is considered and discussed with the client. Needless to say, this time is always difficult for the client and the therapist alike. Several points have to be stressed to the client regarding termination. First, even though the word "termination" implies finality, it is important that the client need not be made to feel that termination is permanent or that such an agreement ends any future professional contacts with the therapist. The client should be led to believe that the channels of communication are always open and available to him—that the therapist is always within telephone reach. Second, it is important that the client be made to realize that there is never going to be a time when he is totally free of life's problems or all emotional discomforts. Hopefully, at the time of termination his current problems are well within manageable limits and he has cultivated a number of varied strategies to cope more effectively with the problems focused on in the course of therapy. Third, if problems raised at the time of discussion about termination are new material for the therapist (and were only touched on lightly during the course of the assessment and treatment phases) and determined not to be of central importance, then one can only assume that the client is feeling the pains of separation and required reassurrance or some other mechanism like those discussed below.

MECHANISMS FOR FOLLOW-UP TREATMENT

As indicated above, it is not good practice to close the doors behind the client upon termination. At the same time, it is imperative that the therapist impart the impression to the client that at this point he has the response capabilities for functioning effectively and non-self-defeatingly outside of the regularly scheduled treatment sessions and that all future progress would be merely refinements of his gains to date. Most important, however, it is imperative for greater insurance that his gains will stand the test of time that the client make the attribution for his progress to himself rather than to the therapist.

At the time of termination, any one of a number of mechanisms can be implemented to help ensure the transfer and maintenance of progress. First, it is always a good practice at the time of termination to ask the client's spouse, parents, or mate to come in so that they can be apprised of the changes the client has realized and the effects these changes may have on the family constellation or the relationship. In addition, it should be clearly specified how these significant others can change to accommodate the client's changes. Finally, it is important to specify clearly the conditions of termination so they will not be misinterpreted. If these significant others have been active in the treatment program thus far, then they can be equally as active in the termination phase. Briefly, for instance, a spouse can recognize the early warning signs of a client's depression, such as loss of appetite, less concern for physical appearance or clothes coordination. With this information she can help the therapist to resolve the sources of her husband's depression; or if not, she can urge the client to telephone the therapist before the depression becomes too incapacitating. Second, the client can be instructed to telephone the therapist on a specified date after termination to apprise the therapist of his level of functioning. Often, brief troubleshooting or a bit of encouragement can forestall a major slippage. This frequently takes the form of reminding the client of self-control or self-management prescriptions that he has been neglecting to follow. Third, throughout the development of behavior therapy, practitioners have had clients return intermittently for a brief reinstatement of treatment techniques used in the course of formal therapy. It was thought that such booster sessions would inoculate clients against relapse and ensure the durability of treatment gains. Recently, the efficacy of booster sessions has been called into question by Kazdin and Wilson (1978) on the ground that they are conceptually inaccurate. Specifically, in the past booster sessions were arbitrarily scheduled by the therapist, usually inconsistent with the needs and functioning level of the client. For this reason, their purpose is not best served. The control for scheduling of booster sessions should lie with the client, and should be done so when he begins experiencing some sign of slippage or a slackening of control over his previously maladaptive patterns. Therapists must make every effort to assist clients in identifying, processing, and reacting to early warning signs of slippage. In this way, clients can be taught to use therapy follow-up or booster sessions judiciously and most beneficially. An example of such training should be informative. A 30-year-old female obsessive-compulsive client with a long history of checking and rechecking her activities in order to reduce the likelihood of mistakes was successfully treated with a combination of in vitro and in vivo flooding and cognitive restructuring. The client was helped to create a list of useful hints to help break the obsessive thought-neutralizing (or undoing) stimulus cycle. Items on the list included such exercises as asking herself "How crucial is it that I do this activity perfectly?" and writing out a several-sentence answer including evidence that it was not crucial; practice in generating distracting imagery was also included. After successfully practicing these "stopgap" exercises during the final therapy session, the client was encouraged to review these exercises whenever she felt "trapped" in the obsessive thought cycle. She was to do this regularly whenever appropriate, and was encouraged to contact the therapist only if none of the exercises worked in reducing her anxiety. The client had booster sessions scheduled on four separate occasions up to 16 months after terminating treatment. Each session was scheduled as a consequence of the client's not reaching a predetermined criterion for using her exercises successfully. Booster sessions mainly involved troubleshooting the reasons for excessive failure, prescribing modifications, etc. Follow-up indicated continued improvement without the need for further booster visits.

Another practice with which several therapists have had good success, particularly in helping to sustain therapy gains, is yearly "checkups" for good therapeutic maintenance. Just as the phrase implies, the client, once terminated, continues to return on at least a once-per-year basis, merely to discuss with his therapist his current functioning and objectives, and particularly the means by which he is coping with his problems. The various problem areas dealt with in his former therapy are reviewed as well as the specific strategies he had acquired at the time. The therapist's notes from the assessment phase are sometimes shared with the client to underscore gains made. Practice sessions for the techniques assessed at the time as either being devalued, not actively used, or seeming to be losing their potency, are encouraged. A final method for sustaining progress was suggested by Keefe, Kopel, and Gordon (1978) and by Kazdin and Wilson (1978), and is termed by the present authors as "fail-safe" planning. Specifically, during the session prior to the final session, the behavior therapist and the client anticipate what could interfere with the client's current functioning over the next several years and he is asked to imagine such occurrences. He is then asked to write down in columnar fashion each anticipated problem and in the columns beside it to remediate that particular problem on the cognitive, affectual, and behavioral levels. For instance, the client may suggest that he will have to give a speech which he would speculate would generate considerable anxiety, even though he had made excellent progress in the interpersonal-social sphere in the course of his behavior therapy. He would write in the problem column "give a speech." In the cognitive column he may indicate the following remedial steps: "not anticipate in advance or engage in 'what if' statements," or "practice imagining myself giving a speech which meets with good success." In the affect column he can remind himself once again to reinstate the use of his relaxation tapes; in the behavioral column he can prepare and practice "task-relevant" exercises, including role-playing with his wife, memorizing certain trouble spots in the speech, and practicing the use of props. After writing up his complete "fail-safe" plan, he puts it away for safekeeping, just in case.

SUMMARY AND CONCLUSIONS

Behavior therapy has reached a level of theoretical and procedural sophistication where behavior therapists can now more comfortably divert their attention from the refinement of their techniques to the more "non technical" aspects of treatment. Ultimately, these aspects of treatment bear on the efficacy of individual treatment programs and on behavior therapy in general. Two such clinical issues, that of transfer and maintenance of individual treatment programs, were the subject of the present chapter.

It was our intent to provide a more comprehensive perspective on the issues of transfer and maintenance than heretofore has been advanced in the behavior therapy literature. Our perspective is predicated on the notion that concern for these phenomena presupposes the efficacy of the assessment and treatment that precedes it.

Strategies directed toward the ends of transfer and maintenance are introduced during the assessment and conceptualization phase, during which client expectations are determined and priorities for treatment are established. These phases are further marked by the exploration of potential causes for misassessment, such as secondary gains and contextual reinforcers, each of which act to perpetuate manifest problems.

The potential for maintenance and generalization of treatment outcomes is further enhanced by realistically "setting the stage" for therapy. This process includes the explication of the "canon of gradualness," inoculating clients against slippage, and "anticipating the anticipator," all of which serve to minimize the myriad of possible problems that surface with homework assignments, behavioral prescriptions, and any other similar out-of-office activities.

The evolution of behavior therapy to present-day multiform approaches (e.g., educative methods and coping skills training) is illustrated and further exemplified by the treatment of one problem area, interpersonal-social anxiety, wherein skill deficits, affectional disturbances, and self-defeating cognitions are assessed and remediated. The "consolidation phase" of therapy, during which the client takes progressively more responsibility for treatment programming until the time of his termination, is described. Finally, follow-up planning and a variety of relapse control programs are suggested.

A final word is in order. Throughout the progression of this chapter we continue to rediscover an old psychotherapeutic truth: despite its scientifically based methods and procedures, behavior therapy is only as *effective* as the skills the individual practitioner possesses in administering them; and more important, it is only as *lasting* as the skills the individual practitioner possesses in dealing with the "nontechnical" aspects of treatment.

REFERENCE NOTE

1. Meichenbaum, D., & Cameron, R. *Stress inoculation: A skills training approach to anxiety management.* Unpublished manuscript, University of Waterloo, 1973.

REFERENCES

Bandler, R., & Grinder, J. *The structure of magic I: A book about language and therapy.* Palo Alto, Calif.: Science and Behavior, 1975.

Bandura, A. *Principles of behavior modification.* New York: Holt, Rinehart & Winston, 1969.

Beck, A. T. *Cognitive therapy and the emotional disorders.* New York: International Universities Press, 1976.

Bernstein, D. A., & Borkovec, T. D. *Progressive relaxation training.* Champaign, Ill.: Research Press, 1973.

Borkovec, T. D., Fleischman, D. J., & Caputo, J. A. The measurement of anxiety in an analogue social situation. *Journal of Consulting and Clinical Psychology,* 1973, *41,* 157–161.

Cautela, J. R., Flannery, R. B., & Hanley, E. Covert modeling: An experimental test. *Behavior Therapy,* 1974, *5,* 494–502.

Davison, G. C., & Valins, S. Maintenance of self-attributed and drug-attributed behavior change. *Journal of Personality and Social Psychology,* 1969, *11,* 25–33.

Ellis, A. *Reason and emotion in psychotherapy.* New York: Lyle Stuart, 1962.

Eysenck, H. J. (Ed.). *Behaviour therapy and the neuroses.* New York: Pergamon, 1960.

Eysenck, H. J. The nature of behaviour therapy. In H. J. Eysenck (Ed.), *Experiments in behaviour therapy.* London: Pergamon, 1964.

Fensterheim, H. The initial interview. In A. A. Lazarus (Ed.), *Clinical behavior therapy.* New York: Brunner/Mazel, 1972.

Glasgow, R. E., & Arkowitz, H. the behavioral assessment of male and female social competence in dyadic heterosexual interactions. *Behavior Therapy,* 1975, *6,* 488–498.

Goldfried, M. R. Systematic desensitization as training in self-control. *Journal of Consulting and Clinical Psychology,* 1971, *37,* 228–234.

Goldfried, M. R., & Davison, G. C. *Clinical behavior therapy.* New York: Holt, Rinehart & Winston, 1976.

Goldfried, M. R., & D'Zurilla, T. J. A behavioral-analytic model for assessing competence. In C. D. Spielberger (Ed.) *Current topics in clinical and community psychology.* (vol. 1). New York: Academic Press, 1969.

Goldfried, M. R., & Goldfried, A. P. Cognitive change methods. In F. H. Kanfer & A. P. Goldstein (Eds.), *Helping people change.* New York: Pergamon, 1975.

Goldfried, M. R., & Merbaum, M. (Eds.). *Behavior change through self-control.* New York: Holt, Rinehart & Winston, 1973.

Goldfried, M. R., & Pomeranz, D. M. Role of assessment in behavior modification. *Psychological Reports,* 1968, *23,* 75–87.

Jacobson, E. *Progressive relaxation.* Chicago: University of Chicago Press, 1929.

Kanfer, F. H., & Saslow, G. Behavioral analysis: An alternative to diagnostic classification. *Archives of General Psychiatry,* 1965, *12,* 529–538.

Kazdin, A. E. Covert modeling, imagery assessment, and assertive behavior. *Journal of Consulting and Clinical Psychology,* 1975, *43,* 716–724.

Kazdin, A. E., & Wilson, G. T. *Evaluation of behavior therapy.* Cambridge, Mass.: Ballinger, 1978.

Keefe, F., Kopel, S., & Gordon, S. B. *Behavioral assessment.* New York: Springer, 1978.

Lange, A., & Jakubowski, P. *Responsible assertive behavior.* Champaign, Ill.: Research Press, 1976.

Lazarus, A. A. *Behavior therapy and beyond.* New York: McGraw-Hill, 1971.

Lazarus, A. A. *In the mind's eye: The power of imagery therapy to give you control over your life.* New York: Rawson, 1977. (a)

Lazarus, A. A. *Multimodal behavior therapy.* New York: Springer, 1977. (b)

Lubetkin, B. S., & Fishman, S. T. Electrical aversion with a chronic heroin user. *Journal of Behavior Therapy and Experimental Psychiatry,* 1974, *5,* 193–197.

Mahoney, M. J. *Cognition and behavior modification.* Cambridge, Mass.: Ballinger, 1974.

Mahoney, M. J. Reflections on the cognitive-learning trend in psychotherapy. *American Psychologist,* 1977, *32,* 5–13.

Marlatt, G. A., & Gordon, J. R. Determinants of relapse: Implications for the maintenance of behavior change. In P. Davidson (Ed.), *Behavioral medicine: Changing health lifestyles.* New York: Brunner/Mazel, 1979.

Mathews, A. M. Recent developments in the treatment of agoraphobia. *Behavioral Analysis and Modification,* 1978, *2,* 64–75.

McFall, R. M., & Marston, A. R. An experimental investigation of behavioral rehearsal in assertive training. *Journal of Abnormal Psychology,* 1970, *76,* 295–303.

Meichenbaum, D. *Cognitive behavior modification.* Morristown, N.J.: General Learning Press, 1974.

Meichenbaum, D. *Cognitive behavior modification.* New York: Plenum, 1977.

Meichenbaum, D., Gilmore, J., & Fedoravicius, A. Group insight vs. group desensitization in treating speech anxiety. *Journal of Consulting and Clinical Psychology,* 1971, *36,* 410–421.

Mischel, W. *Personality and assessment.* New York: Wiley, 1968.

Nawas, M. M., Fishman, S. T., & Pucel, J. C. A standardized desensitization program applicable to group and individual treatment. *Behaviour Research and Therapy,* 1970, *6,* 63–68.

Novaco, R. *Anger control: The development and evaluation of an experimental treatment.* Lexington, Mass.: Lexington Books, 1975.

Shelton, J. L., & Ackerman, J. M. *Homework in counseling and psychotherapy.* Springfield, Ill.: Charles C. Thomas, 1974.

Suinn, R. M., & Richardson, F. Anxiety management training: A nonspecific behavior therapy program for anxiety control. *Behavior Therapy,* 1971, *2,* 498–510.

Tharp, R. G., & Wetzel, R. J. *Behavior modification in the natural environment.* New York: Academic Press, 1969.

Watson, D., & Friend, R. Measurement of social evaluative anxiety. *Journal of Consulting and Clinical Psychology,* 1969, *34,* 448–457.

Wolpe, J. *Psychotherapy by reciprocal inhibition.* Stanford, Calif.: Stanford University Press, 1958.

CHAPTER

4

FOLLOW-UP ASSESSMENTS IN BEHAVIOR THERAPY

ERIC J. MASH AND LEIF G. TERDAL

Stealing food, hoarding towels, and wearing an excessive amount of clothing were three behaviors exhibited by a 47-year-old chronic schizophrenic woman treated around 1960 using behavior modification procedures. This program, carried out on an experimental ward of the Saskatchewan Hospital, Weyburn, Saskatchewan, under the direction of Dr. Teodoro Ayllon, subsequently was reported in the first issue of the first behavior therapy journal (Ayllon, 1963), and also appeared in one of the first behavior modification textbooks (Ullmann & Krasner, 1965). Familiar to most students of behavior therapy, this report rapidly became a "classic" in the behavior modification literature.

As the behavior therapy movement grew and developed beyond the case study phase (Mash, 1976), several writers challenged such early demonstrations with respect to their conceptual adequacy, durability, and relevance (see Mahoney, Kazdin, & Lesswing, 1974). Consequently, it was with great interest and curiosity that a 10-year follow-up of the patient described above was noted. Sherwood and Gray (1974) presented recent descriptive data for the 1960 case report with reference to both general functioning and status of the specific behaviors treated. Data were obtained from clinic files, interviews with staff, correspondence with the staff of other institutions, and direct observations. The passages below present the findings of Sherwood and Gray:

Since 1962 the patient's diagnosis has varied from chronic to hebephrenic to paranoid schizophrenia, depending on the bias of the different psychiatrists making the diagnosis. Psychiatric descriptions deal almost exclusively with her verbal behaviour with an emphasis on its delusive content. The patient has repeatedly claimed that there are fires (occasionally also Jesus or God) in her body. Her several bouts of water intoxication have been interpreted as attempts to quench these fires.

The nurses' progress reports prove to be more helpful in the assessment of the patient's actual behaviour. Except for a leave of a month and a half in 1961 (following the termination of Ayllon's project), the patient has continued to reside in the same institution. Many of these reports are concerned with the various weight-reducing diets that have been part of her program since the experiments ended. Her reactions to these diets are generally described as verbally resistive and aggressive. Apart from such outbursts, however, she has not been described as disruptive. Indeed, she has been seclusive over the years, in general interacting only with a select few of the older staff members. Her main activities until recently have been watching television or movies, praying, and lying or sitting on her bed or in some other out of the way place. It is reported that she often gives somatic complaints as excuses for not taking part in other activities. Over the years she has been treated with various chemotherapies (primarily the major tranquilizers), occupational therapy, and ECT.

Currently (and for the three years before this investigation) she works five hours a day in a hospital workshop making artificial flowers that are used to decorate wedding cars. The workshop supervisor describes her work as extremely slow but perfectionistic. Her average level of production is 10 flowers per day. For this she is paid the sum of $1.50 per week which can be spent in the canteen. Her physical condition is good except for her very obvious weight problem. Her medication at the time of this study consisted of Largactil 50 mg. t.i.d. and Stelazine 4 mg. b.i.d.

Food Stealing. In the first experiment (Ayllon, 1963) the behaviour of stealing food from the trays of other patients was eliminated in two weeks when positive reinforcement (a meal) was withdrawn as a consequence of stealing. Ayllon reported that in the 14 months after this program was instituted the patient's weight went down from 250 pounds to 180 pounds.

The patient's weight chart shows that she actually stabilized at approximately 150 pounds in July of 1961. At this time she was granted a 30-day leave with relatives. When she came back a month and a half later she weighted 196 pounds. This trend continued on the regular ward until one year later she weighted 310 pounds. Apart from temporary fluctuations, the patient's weight has been maintained at high levels ever since.

In August 1972, despite maintenance on a reducing diet, she weighed 270 pounds. The reasons for this seem apparent in view of her current situation. She is on an open ward with free access to almost the whole hospital, including the canteen. Canteen staff report that she is usually there once a day, but is only allowed to buy diet candy and low calorie soft drinks. More important, however, the numerous references to food stealing in the nursing notes suggest that this behaviour re-established itself shortly after the termination of the experimental program, and has continued unabated ever since. Although nursing staff will ask her to return food if they catch her stealing, supervision at meal times is not rigorous, and there are no consistent consequences applied after instances of this kind of behaviour. Since it seems reasonable to suppose that her obesity is not a result of the $1.50 per week spent on diet products, we may assume that it is a function of additional food acquired by theft, just as it was in 1959.

Towel Hoarding. In Ayllon's (1963) second experiment a program of satiation was begun to eliminate the towel hoarding behaviour which the patient had exhibited for the previous nine years. From a baseline range of 19 to 29 towels, satiation was continued until the patient had more than 600 towels in her room; at which point she began to remove them. This continued until the average number of towels in her room over a 12-month period was 1.5 towels per week. It is clear from nursing reports that this behaviour has not recurred since the patient was a subject in the research project. This fact was further substantiated by direct observations made by the senior author. According to ward nurses, however, she still engages in hoarding behaviour of a minor kind (locks of hair, toilet paper, etc.) from time to time.

Excessive Dressing. In the third experiment food reinforcement was contingent upon the removal of unnecessary clothing. As a consequence, in the space of ten weeks, the weight of her clothing went from 25 pounds to 3 pounds.

Clinic files indicate this behaviour has not markedly recurred. There is one reference in the nursing notes, dated November 1962, to an incident of excessive dressing. It was noted that she removed excess clothing when the staff "firmly insisted." Direct observation and staff interviews confirm that she does not currently wear an excessive amount of clothing. As a rule her standard outfit consists of undergarments, one pair of stockings, one pair of shoes, one dress, one sweater, one artificial flower worn in her hair and a slightly excessive amount of lipstick and rouge (pp. 421–422)[1]

In summary, 10 years later Ayllon's patient was still institutionalized and obese, although two of the three behaviors treated did not recur over the 10-year follow-up. Of equal interest to this report was the brief accompanying comment made by Dr. Ayllon (Ayllon, 1974), who while not overly impressed with the conclusions to be drawn from this follow-up, noted that the reemergence of treated behavior was to be expected as long as there were accompanying changes in the posttreatment environment.[2] It would therefore be necessary to maximize generalization by ensuring that "the treatment and post-treatment environments share some of the same stimulus or contingency conditions" (p. 428). Implicit in Ayllon's remarks is that all good behavior therapists would today do this, and he states that although it was not done with the early 1960 case study, "behavioral research (see the *Journal of Applied Behavioral Analysis*) has become much more sophisticated since its humble beginnings" (p. 428).

This follow-up report, and the response to it, highlight several of the important issues and questions associated with long-term assessment in behavior therapy that will be dealt with in this chapter. These issues are of a conceptual, methodological, practical, and ethical nature and all contribute to the frequently encountered difficulties involved in conducting *meaningful* follow-up investigations. To date, discussions and empirical accounts of follow-up in behavior therapy have almost without exception been governed by an overriding principle that we have termed the "follow-up fallacy," which is: "the longer it is—the better it is." The 10-year follow-up study described above, although extremely interesting, suggests that length may not be the sine qua non for follow-up assessment. Without an adequate consideration of purposes and method, the conclusions to be drawn from follow-up investigations of any length will necessarily be limited. In this chapter, we hope to demonstrate that behavioral researchers and practitioners must go beyond naive recommendations and verbal exhortations to conduct longer follow-up investigations, and begin to develop a conceptual framework and methodological guidelines for the conduct of follow-up assessments that are appropriate to the purposes at hand.

It is with some trepidation that we attempt, as others have, to deal with the issues involved in follow-up assessment—*lasciate ogni speranza voi ch'entrate* (inscription over Dante's hell—"Abandon hope all ye who enter"). Strupp (1973), in discussing various outcome problems including that of lasting change, observes that the literature has not been particularly helpful in clarifying them. He also notes that the scant attention given by researchers to the outcome problem recently is not because the problem has lost its importance. Rather, it is the realization that a new approach to the issue must be found before the question of therapy effectiveness can be meaningfully addressed.

Discussions of follow-up assessment in the behavioral literature (e.g., Atthowe, 1973; Cochrane & Sobol, 1976; Hersen & Bellack, 1977; Kazdin & Wilson, 1978; Zielinski, 1978) have shown remarkable consensus on two issues: first, the importance of conducting follow-up evaluations; and second, the lack of adequate follow-up information across a wide range of treatments and problems.

This discrepancy between the perceived importance of follow-up and the nonavailability of meaningful information highlights the issues and disagreements surrounding the conduct of follow-up investigations in psychotherapy generally and behavior therapy in particular.

IMPORTANCE OF FOLLOW-UP

The extent to which behavioral intervention programs produce *lasting* measurable effects continues to be a prevalent concern for researchers and practitioners alike. Investigations into the generalizability of treatment effects over "significant" time periods have been viewed as a necessary sign of maturity in a rapidly developing field (Bachrach & Quigley, 1966; Cautela, 1968; Conway & Bucher, 1976; Franks & Wilson, 1976), and the measurement of such temporal generalization (e.g., maintenance), or follow-up assessment, is of particular importance to behavioral assessors. For example, Hersen and Bellack (1977) state that "the measurement area that requires the most attention at this time is the one concerned with assessing generalization of treatment effects" (p. 539). Presumably, treatments whose effects are short-lived are insufficient in meeting the needs of both the client and the society at large, although it is conceivable that in some situations even "short-term relief" may be a worthwhile outcome.

The importance of examining long-term effects is highlighted by the discrepancy often found between status at termination and status at follow-up. Although some behavior therapists have reported correspondence between short- and long-term outcomes (e.g., Lazarus, 1963; Wolpe, 1958), these claims for success are often derived from uncontrolled clinical practice. It should be noted, however, that others using similar uncontrolled observations have reported a lack of maintenance. For example, Poser (1977) reports that seven of eight cases were viewed by the therapist at the time of termination as distinctly improved, but by the time of follow-up 5–10 years later only two of eight gave clear evidence of having completely overcome the target symptom. There is also a good deal of empirical evidence suggesting that short-term outcomes may not predict later functioning.

The literature is consistent in pointing out that as time following therapy increases, the magnitude of the treatment effect decreases. For example, Smith and Glass (1977) reported a small but statistically significant inverse relationship between number of months posttherapy for follow-up and size of effect. The relative effects of differing treatments also seem to diminish with time (Hall & Hall, 1977; C. B. Taylor, Farquhar, Nelson, & Agras, 1977) and as Kazdin and Wilson (1978) state, "in light of contemporary literature, durability rather than short-term outcome appears to be the great equalizer of treatments" (p. 121). Thus diminishing effects both within and across treatments with time suggest the importance of examining changes over longer time intervals.

LACK OF INFORMATION

The availability of relevant information about temporal generalizability should be an inherent result of the ongoing evaluative assessments that characterize behavioral treatments (Mash & Terdal, 1976). For example, several features of behavioral interventions such as an emphasis on objective measurement and evaluation of treatment outcomes (Baer, Wolf, & Risley, 1968; Johnson & Bolstad, 1973; Kazdin, 1973), utilization of single-subject designs (Hersen & Barlow, 1976), and a concern for the social significance or therapeutic importance of change (Baer et al., 1968; Kazdin, 1977; Risley, 1970; Wolf, 1978) suggest special promise for the accumulation of meaningful follow-up data. To date this is a promise unfulfilled. Although it is possible that more outcome and follow-up data have been collected by behavior therapists than therapists of other persuasions, it is not the relative quantity of data that is of the moment but their probative strength. As noted by Kazdin and Wilson (1978), "the relative paucity of follow-up data in clinical research makes the long-term effects of many techniques a matter of speculation" (p. 121).

The stringent standards applied to the evaluation of short-term effects have often been abandoned in the face of the exigencies and practical constraints characteristically associated with evaluation of continuing and long-term treatment outcomes. A number of recent reviews of behavioral treatments both in general (Cochrane & Sobol, 1976; Conway & Bucher, 1976; Kazdin & Wilson, 1978; Keeley, Shemberg, & Carbonell, 1976; Flynn Wood, Michelson, & Keen, Note 1; Peterson & Hartmann, Note 2) and in specific areas such as drug abuse (Callner, 1975; Gotestam, Melin, & Ost, 1976), asthma (Knapp & Wells, 1978), obesity (D. B. Jeffrey, 1976), alcoholism (Nathan, 1976), and marriage and family therapy (Gurman & Kniskern, Note 3), to name but a few, have concluded with few exceptions that behavioral researchers have not addressed follow-up questions seriously, and that the methodological shortcomings of most investigations make it virtually impossible to draw any definitive conclusions regarding the durability of treatment effects over time.[3]

The approach to follow-up study taken by most behavioral investigators has paralleled that of investigators in related areas and has been haphazard, unsystematic, uncontrolled, and typically based on custom, dogma, personal predilection, availability of therapist, patient, research personnel, and economics (Robins, 1972). It is not uncommon for there to be no direct attention given to the assessment of long-term effects, with the therapist adopting a "train and hope" attitude toward maintenance (Stokes & Baer, 1977). Alternatively, brief and uncontrolled telephone contacts some time after treatment have also been used (e.g., Alban & Nay, 1976; Blanchard, 1975).

One might argue that this state of affairs for follow-up assessment reflects the fact that behavior therapy is a relatively new approach to treatment (although aging rapidly), and that increasing attention to follow-up will occur as the field develops further. If such a trend exists, it is certainly not evident from the literature. In reviewing both experimental and case studies that appeared in the journal *Behavior Therapy* from 1970 to 1977, Flynn et al. (Note 1) found that of 289 experimental studies 67% had no follow-up at all, 24% had one follow-up, 7% had two or three, and the remainder had up to nine follow-ups. Of the 33% of the studies with follow-up, for 24% the length was 1–50 days, for 27% it was between 51–150 days, and for 43% at least 151 days.[4] In looking at follow-up for case studies over the same time period, it was found that a greater number of the case studies had follow-up (60%) and that follow-up intervals tended to be longer. A most disconcerting finding of this study was a marked decline in the use of follow-up, with fewer and shorter follow-ups over the years that were surveyed. Although such data must be interpreted carefully since alternative publication outlets, changing editorial policies and reviewers, and so forth, may produce spurious findings, the study seems to suggest rather strongly the absence of a trend toward more attention to follow-up!

WHY THE DISCREPANCY?

Our discussion thus far indicates that the practice of follow-up assessment in behavior therapy seems inconsistent with its recognized importance. One might argue that this discrepancy is a function of the familiar and recurrent methodological and practical problems associated with the measurement of long-term outcomes in psychotherapy generally (Bergin & Garfield, 1971; Kazdin & Wilson, 1978; Luborsky, Singer, & Luborsky, 1975; Meltzoff & Kornreich, 1970; Rachman, 1971; Sargent, 1960; Schwartz, Myers, & Astrachan, 1973), and is not unique to behavior therapy. From a methodological standpoint Meltzoff and Kornreich (1970) have noted such problems in outcome research as design flaws, inappropriate controls and/or inadequate sampling, experimenter bias, lack of objective, reliable, and valid criterion measures, and suitable analysis and interpretation of data. Follow-up assessments may also be confounded due to the influence of intercurrent therapeutic experience,[5] the occurrence of life crisis (or their absence) at the time of evaluation, client biases in reporting, and motivational changes. Similarly, Turkat and Forehand (Note 4) suggest that the lack of unity regarding the efficacy of behavior therapy reflects the use of differing designs, different outcome measures, and variations in the populations used. One could argue that overcoming some of these methodological difficulties might lead to some consensus regarding psychotherapy outcomes. However, methodological rigor does not seem sufficient. In their review of psychotherapy research Meltzoff and Kornreich (1970) conclude, "in general, the better the quality of research, the more positive the results obtained" (p. 177), whereas Forehand and Atkeson (1977), in reviewing behavioral family interventions, state, "unfortunately, the more rigorous the method of assessment, the less positive the results have been" (p. 575).

If the methodological and design problems of follow-up assessment were not sufficient to make the task a difficult one, practical and ethical problems also abound: many behavior therapy studies conclude with a frank admission that follow-up, although important, was impractical (e.g., Bucher, Reykdal, & Albin, 1976). Such things as patient mobility, changing therapists and/or assessors, and personnel costs are common occurrences, and ethical concerns relating to intrusion must also be considered.

Considering the enormous amount of attention that has been given to problems of outcome research (e.g., Bergin, 1971) the purpose of this chapter will not be to discuss them again. Rather, it is our contention that although many of the above issues certainly apply to follow-up in behavior therapy, the theoretical and methodological underpinnings of behavior therapy require that follow-up assessments be conceptualized and conducted in a manner different from that of other therapy approaches. It is our belief that behavioral practitioners and researchers have failed to do this, and as a result have not provided meaningful guidelines for carrying out long-term follow-up from a behavioral perspective.

It has been noted that strategies for treatment in behavior therapy seemed to develop much more rapidly than strategies for assessment (Mash & Terdal, 1976). Also, behavior therapists tend to be more catholic in their use of assessment techniques than in their use of treatment techniques (Wade, Baker, & Hartmann, Note 5). In considering follow-up assessment, a similar state of affairs seems to exist. Behavioral investigators are rapidly developing technologies that will supposedly serve to promote therapeutic maintenance (e.g., Stokes & Baer, 1977) while remaining traditional in their approach to problems of long-term assessment with these strategies. It is our belief that unless adequate attention is given to conceptualizing and providing guidelines for the conduct of *behavioral follow-up assessment,* much of the current work on therapeutic maintenance in behavior therapy will be inconclusive at best.

It is the purpose of this chapter to consider follow-up assessment from a behavioral perspective. In this regard we will consider various definitions of follow-up, examine varying purposes for which follow-up assessments are conducted, present a model for follow-up assessment that we believe to be consistent with behavioral treatments, and describe classes of setting variables within behavior therapies that influence follow-up. We will then consider a number of issues and specific strategies involved in follow-up assessment and will attempt to show how one's approach to follow-up will depend on the interacting influences of purposes, conceptualization, and setting events.[6]

DEFINING FOLLOW-UP ASSESSMENT

The follow-up question within behavior therapy typically asks "Are the effects of treatment durable?" or "Do treatments have a lasting effect?" Implicit in these questions, and indeed characteristic of definitions of follow-up assessments in general, is the importance of examining some *temporal* relationship between "treatment" and "outcome." Apart from the problems involved in defining what constitutes "treatment" and "outcome" (the criterion question), there are the additional problems associated with defining time intervals and their effects. Presumably, for follow-up the temporal dimension of interest differs from that usually considered in examining treatment–outcome relationships in that the duration of time between the two events is "longer." Consequently, evaluative follow-up assessments are no different from any outcome study, with the exception that the time base is longer and measurement over longer time intervals seems to produce special problems and constraints. To name just a few, the longer the time span, the less likely there is to be a treatment effect, and the less likely there are to be differences between experimental and control groups (Hall & Hall, 1977). The likelihood of subject attrition increases (Costello, Bechtel, & Griffen, 1973) as does that of "spontaneous recovery" (Eysenck, 1965). The longer the time, the greater the likelihood that there will be shifts in the normative standards used in evaluating and reporting outcomes (e.g., Boyd, Paul, Scholle, & Mitchell, Note 6). These problems suggest the special importance of time for the assessment of outcomes.

Robins (1972) has noted that the term "follow-up" has been used in many ways, "but that one concept common to all uses is that some measure has been taken at two or more points in time" (p. 415). In considering follow-up in its broadest meaning, Robins states that the interval may be short or long, measures may be taken only at the beginning and end or recurrently throughout the time interval, and the kinds of things measured at the beginning and end may be the same or different. However, Robins places two additional restrictions on the use of the term "follow-up": "First, the time interval must be of sufficient length so that there has been an opportunity for an important amount of change to occur," and "second, the measurements at either end of a time interval must be independent of each other" (p. 415). These restrictions point up the need, in the case of the former, to specify and develop guidelines for determining such factors as "sufficient length" and "important amount," and in the latter, to examine possible interdependencies of measures that could lead to spurious relationships and erroneous conclusions.

The question of permanence of treatment effect also implies that follow-up is only relevant where some *initial effect* of treatment has been noted to occur. For example, Kazdin and Wilson (1978) state, "obviously, it is premature to raise questions of follow-up in areas where the ability of treatments to make initial changes in target behaviors has not been demonstrated. Demonstrations that changes can be achieved make salient the issue of durability" (pp. 42–43). This view implies a contiguity between treatment and effect that often is the case, but does not acknowledge the possibility that long-term effects may occur even though immediate change is not evident. The latter situation, to be discussed later in this chapter, suggests that follow-up assessment may also be relevant, even in the absence of immediate effects.

Also implicit in the question "Are treatment effects durable?" is a *standard of comparison*. That is, the question of whether individuals have improved more permanently also asks, "than would have been expected if not treated," or "relative to the improvement observed in groups receiving an alternative treatment." Although on the same continuum, the former statement reflects the more typically asked follow-up question, and comparative follow-up assessments (e.g., Sloane, Staples, Cristol, Yorkston, & Whipple, 1975) are relatively rare.

Follow-up questions are typically raised (Conway & Bucher, 1976; Forehand & Atkeson, 1977; Zielinski, 1978) within the broader context of "generalization," that is, does treatment influence the treated behavior in nontreated situations, other nontreated behaviors, individuals that are not treated, and the treated behavior during periods of time when "treatment" is no longer in effect (temporal generalization or follow-up)? Although most discussions have tended to consider situation, response, person, and temporal generalization independently, Conway and Bucher (1976) have quite appropriately outlined and conceptualized the interdependencies among the differing types of generalization. In the present context it is important to point out that in spite of attempts to do so, it is not likely that we can talk about follow-up assessment independently of these other areas of generalization, although many writers have done so. For example, Zielinski (1978) states that "maintenance is a particular form of generalization. It is behaving similarly in situations that vary only over time" (p. 353). This view implies a situational isomorphism across time that is uncharacteristic of most human situations. Situations will vary with time, and unless this is taken into account it is likely that follow-up assessments will be confounded with the effects of a changing context.

From the above discussion we can state that follow-up has typically been concerned with the monitoring of initial change following treatment, over some specified "time interval," relative to some "standard of comparison." Further, it is often the case that such monitoring has occurred with minimal consideration for dimensions other than the passage of time. Although this statement delineates some of the dimensions important to follow-up assessment, it does not define it since in actuality there are many types of follow-up assessment. How we define follow-up, and ultimately the strategies we use in implementing follow-up assessment, will depend on the purpose for which follow-up is intended.

PURPOSES OF FOLLOW-UP

Our discussion of the concept of follow-up assessment thus far, and its most common usage, has been as one criterion for estimating the effectiveness of treatment. Presumably, treatments that are more durable are "better," although it will of course be necessary to consider other factors such as costs, side effects, and consumer acceptability (Kazdin, 1977; Wolf, 1978). Follow-up assessments that ask whether changes have occurred in relation to some intervention, and whether they continue to occur, may be referred to as *evaluative follow-up* (E-FU). E-FUs also ask whether changes can be attributed to the intervention when they are conducted within the framework of a systematic between- or within-subject experimental design, and how the changes that occurred with this intervention compare with another treatment (comparative outcome research). E-FUs may also vary in terms of whether they are examining effects in individual clients, in groups of clients treated individually, and in groups of clients treated collectively as part of an institutional or community program. In the first instance we may be interested in such things as the long-term effectiveness of a program of automated systematic desensitization in the treatment of a fear of high places; in the second, with the effectiveness of this program in treating many individuals with similar fears; in the third, with the effectiveness of an institutional token economy, a classroom contingency management system, programs in work settings, community interventions, ecological interventions to alter energy consumption, etc. In all of these cases, however, the major goal of E-FU typically involves making judgments regarding the intervention itself, rather than maximizing immediate therapeutic benefits for the client(s). The two goals, of course, are in no way mutually exclusive; however there are times when, in order to draw direct conclusions, E-FU requires that the conditions of assessment be maintained in spite of the fact that individual clients might profit from altered and alternative procedures.

Follow-up assessments whose primary purpose is with maximizing gains made by individuals or groups of individuals following treatment may be referred to as *diagnostic follow-up* (D-FU). D-FUs are primarily directed at obtaining information that will permit program changes to be made, should behavior change diminish or should situational context change. D-FU might also focus on the detection of early warning signals that may predict deterioration of effect, and therefore suggest some alteration of the program in spite of the fact that behavior change has been maintained to that point. D-FUs also attempt to obtain information that might be useful in the reformulation of treatment or the design of a new treatment.

In some cases follow-up assessments may be intentionally treatment oriented in their purpose, and may be termed *therapeutic follow-up* (T-FU). With T-FUs, the assessment itself is presumed to have some value in enhancing the persistence of treatment effects. Some behavioral programs of family intervention (e.g., Patterson, 1976) have provided long-term assessment with the implication that such contact may serve to promote maintenance. Martin and Twentymen (1974) note that telephone calls to individuals following treatment may be effective in such a maintenance role, and that such calls may become increasingly more effective as the time interval following treatment increases. In such contacts assessments are often accompanied by "booster" or "refresher" sessions that attempt to reestablish some of the initial therapeutic conditions. It should be noted that T-FU may not always be intentional or planned. Periodic assessments may communicate individual concern over time and reinforcement for continued progress, although this may not have been the specific intent of the follow-up.[7] Since T-FUs have not been systematically studied within behavior therapy, and may be viewed as a source of confound within some experimental investigations, the mechanisms whereby T-FU may serve to promote maintenance are not well understood, nor is it clear whether such changes are long-term or occur only during the time that the discriminative cues associated with the assessment condition are reestablished. In any event, there are many reports in the behavioral literature of follow-up assessments that have therapeutic intent as their purpose, and T-FU should receive further study.

There are also a range of situations in which the purpose of follow-up is to answer a predominantly research question that is only indirectly related to the purposes described above. Such *investigative follow-up* (I-FU) may take a number of forms, but often resemble longitudinal studies in other areas of research (e.g., Stone & Onqué, 1959). For example, normative information regarding certain kinds of behavior disorders may be obtained in order to determine outcomes for given behavior problems under particular environmental circumstances. A study in which children whose parents showed particular interaction styles were followed over x number of years in order to assess the possible behavioral effects of noncontingent positive reinforcement as a prepotent response, for example, would be an instance of I-FU. Such I-FUs often have implication for the theory related to treatment in contrast to E-FUs where the major point of interest is outcome. So if a theory predicted the mechanism of treatment to operate through a practice effect, then follow-up may be done to see if there is an enhancement of effect with time which may then have some bearing on the theory. Indirectly, this would of course have implications for the effectiveness of the treatment as well, but this would not be the primary intent of the study.

In outlining E-FU, D-FU, T-FU, and I-FU, it is not our intent to describe categories that exhaust all possible purposes. Nor is it our intent to communicate that these categories are mutually exclusive or noncomplementary. There are many situations where more than one purpose is evident, and in fact this may be the rule rather than the exception. We believe, however, that these categories represent some of the more common purposes for which follow-up is conducted, and that it is of paramount importance that purposes be made explicit in the development of specific follow-up strategies. As we shall see, such considerations as the choice of dependent measures, frequency and length of follow-up intervals, and experimental design must depend in part on the purposes of follow-up. There are many reports in which the methods used for follow-up are incompatible with the purposes at hand, for example, the failure to obtain measures of situational context where D-FU is the major purpose.

The purposes outlined above represent, to varying degrees, either formative evaluations in which follow-up assessment is part of an informational loop, or summative evaluations which represent terminal judgments on the merit of an intervention program. In theory all follow-up assessment in behavior therapy should be formative, and it is usually inappropriate to use follow-up information as the basis for a dichotomous all-or-nothing judgment about the success or failure of a treatment. In practice there are many instances in which summative evaluation is the rule and the information derived from follow-up assessment is not used to modify or alter the intervention. This may be due to the frequent lack of continuity for successive follow-up investigations, or more typically may reflect the kinds of information obtained during follow-up. When outcomes are represented strictly in terms of broad categories of "improved" or "not improved," or only in terms of behavior reduction (e.g., decrease in tantrums), the direct yield for program modification or improvement is minimal.

E-FUs, as they are typically conducted, tend to be summative evaluations, whereas D-FU, T-FU, and I-FU tend to represent more of an ongoing and self-regulating information system. In this regard, E-FU assessment, as currently practiced in behavior therapy, tends to be inconsistent with some of the explicit goals of behavior therapy assessment (Mash & Terdal, 1976). The direct relevance of E-FU for the formulation or reformulation of treatment is not always apparent, and this would apply to E-FU with individuals, groups of clients treated individually, or groups of individuals treated within an overall program. It is believed that some reformulation of what should constitute follow-up assessment in behavior therapy may be necessary if E-FUs, especially and to some extent D-FUs, T-FUs, and I-FUs, are to be made more functional and directly relevant to treatment. Behavioral assessors have often approached follow-up assessment using a conceptualization that is incompatible with many of their own assumptions and practices. In the next section we will describe an implicit, but often unelaborated, framework for behavior therapy follow-up assessment.

A BEHAVIORAL FRAMEWORK FOR FOLLOW-UP ASSESSMENT

Adherence to a particular treatment model should influence both the types of evaluation questions asked as well as the methods employed to answer them. Kazdin and Wilson (1978) note that "evaluation of behavior therapy is closely tied to both the conceptual model and the scientific foundation on which it is based" (p. 8). The same should apply to follow-up assessments in that evaluation of effects for intervals following treatment should be consistent with behavioral models that describe the maintenance of change over time.

Writing from a behavioral viewpoint, Kazdin and Wilson (1978) indicate that "conventional approaches to outcome evaluation have been rooted in the quasi-disease model of abnormal behavior with its emphasis on such qualitative concepts as cure, spontaneous remission and relapse" (p. 129). Nonbehaviorally oriented psychotherapy researchers have also warned against the dangers of medical analogizing, and have noted that behavioral researchers have continued this approach. For example, Strupp (1973) has observed that learning theory based therapists have continued to develop and use efficacy measures along "mental health" lines. It is our view that behavior therapists have approached follow-up assessment in a "conventional" manner, in that treatment and treatment effects are frequently viewed in a global and qualitative all-or-none fashion, often reflecting such notions as cure, relapse, spontaneous remission, and improvement.[8] In order to highlight what we see as the major differences between conventional and behavioral views of follow-up assessment we shall present two models; the first we refer to as treatment termination and the second as programming generalization.

Treatment Termination

In research on psychotherapy, follow-up assessment is most typically viewed as the measurement of the persistence of effects over time, following the termination of treatment. This view, believed to reflect traditional psychotherapy approaches, and some early behavioral applications, is depicted in Figure 4–1a. In this figure the broken horizontal line (C) refers to unmeasured contextual events, and the solid line and circles (R) refer to measured target responses. There are several generalizations characterizing this "treatment termination" model:

1. Treatment occurs at a fixed point in time that precedes and is distinct from follow-up. This distinction is typically based on the presence or absence of regular contact with a professional therapist.

2. Treatment is directed at some target response, and does not attempt to influence directly the surrounding contextual events. These targets are often conceptualized as intrapsychic personality conflicts which are not necessarily affected by environmental events and consequently may be altered directly, independent of environmental change.

3. Measures of outcome are typically restricted only to target responses, and since these are viewed as internal events, the use of indirect and discrete measures involving verbal response to personality inventories and/or projective tests is common.

4. Changes are expected to occur primarily during the time that treatment is in effect, although some later consolidation of effects within the individual is possible.

5. With effective treatment, changes will persist after termination and should continue in spite of the influence of everyday circumstances which are given a relatively unimportant role (Sargent, 1960)[9]

6. If maintenance is not found, the inference is that the *previously* occurring treatment was not powerful enough in producing resolution of personality conflict.

7. Follow-up assessments are primarily evaluative in purpose (E-FU), and in the absence of maintenance provide little information relevant to treatment reformulation.

FOLLOW-UP ASSESSMENT

a. Treatment Termination
   Discrete Measures: Response

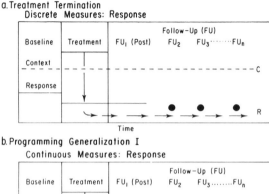

b. Programming Generalization I
   Continuous Measures: Response

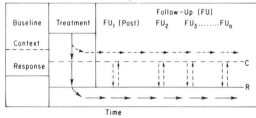

c. Programming Generalization II
   Continuous Measures: Response and Context

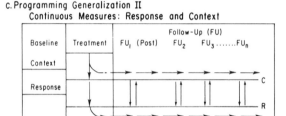

Figure 4-1. Three models for follow-up assessment: treatment termination (a), programming generalization I (b), and programming generalization II (c). Broken horizontal lines represent unmeasured events; solid horizontal lines are measured events. (C = contextual events for response; R = response).

The treatment termination model of follow-up assessment is consistent with the traditional therapeutic approaches that have as their goal the production of change in the personality structure of the individual. Within this model "treatment" is viewed as a discrete, time-limited, and distinct event. Also implicit in this view is that the variables affecting behavior during treatment are qualitatively different from those operative following treatment (e.g., psychotherapeutic relationship). Although such qualitative distinctions tend to be uncharacteristic of behavioral approaches generally (Bandura, 1969), such a view seems to be perpetuated in behavioral approaches to follow-up. Although Kazdin and Wilson (1978) provide a consistent behavioral conceptualization for treatment evaluation in general, they also state:

From a social learning perspective, outcome evaluation must distinguish among the initial induction of therapeutic change, its transfer to the natural environment, and its maintenance over time. It is important to distinguish among these different phases of treatment since they *appear to be governed by different variables* and require different intervention strategies at different times. (p. 132; italics added)

While basically agreeing with the above statement, we would comment that the lack of transfer and maintenance of behavior that is found in many studies does not necessarily suggest that qualitatively different variables are operative, although this is possible. Such a view would not be consistent with most behavioral accounts of environment–response relationships. In addition, sharp distinctions between varying phases of treatment provides implicit support for a treatment termination model of follow-up. For example, in discussing the immediate effectiveness of a treatment that does not maintain itself, Kazdin and Wilson (1978) state that it showed "no superiority at a subsequent follow-up owing to the dissipation of the initial therapeutic effect over time" (p. 132).

A treatment termination view of follow-up seems incompatible with several behavioral assessment principles as well (Ciminero, Calhoun, & Adams, 1977; Cone & Hawkins, 1977; Hersen & Bellack, 1976; Mash & Terdal, 1976). The direct relevance of follow-up assessment for treatment is not evident, since such assessments are almost exclusively evaluative and do not provide information for treatment reformulation. More specifically, follow-up assessment provides little direct information about setting events, since such events are viewed merely as a background for treatment effects that they have already occurred, rather than as contemporaneous controlling events for behavior. Finally, the lack of continuity between treatment and follow-up often leads to varying measurement conditions over time, making the two phases highly discriminable and consequently especially susceptible to reactive measurement and differential demand characteristics.

The treatment termination model described above seems incompatible with several of the current assumptions and practices of behavior therapy and assessment, especially with the behavioral notion that generalization over time must be "programmed."

Programming Generalization

Numerous behavioral writers have pointed out that the impact of a time-limited treatment may be puny compared to the steady diet of environmental conditions to which the individual is likely to be exposed (Baer, et al., 1968; Bijou & Peterson, 1971). This notion, which characterizes Ayllon's (1974) comments in response to the case study reported at the beginning of this chapter, has led to the view that generalization must be programmed (Atthowe, 1973; Conway & Bucher, 1976; Stokes & Baer, 1977). This view is expressed in its most extreme form by Stokes and Baer (1977) who state:

In other words, behavioral research and practice should act as if there were no such animal as "free" generalization—as if generalization never occurs "naturally, but always requires programming." (p. 365)

With the social learning assumption that changes cannot be expected to persist over time in the face of opposing and more current circumstances, generalization must be programmed. How this is to be done is a matter of some importance, and although numerous suggestions have been offered as to "how to do it" (Atthowe, 1973; Stokes & Baer, 1977), the concept of "programming generalization" itself has not been well defined. In the present context we raise the question of whether programming generalization is really any different from what we ordinarily describe as treatment. Stokes and Baer (1977) state:

Generalization will be considered to be the occurrence of relevant behavior under different, non-training conditions (i.e., across subjects, settings, people, behaviors, and/or time) *without the scheduling of the same events in those conditions as has been scheduled in the training conditions.* (p. 350; italics added)

If we accept such a definition, programming of generalization over time could occur in one of two ways. The first, which seems implicit in the above definition, is through the implementation of procedures during the training condition that are removed during the nontraining condition without the substitution of other procedures (e.g., treatment termination), and second, through the provision of events during the nontraining conditions that are different from those present during training. However, if we adopt this latter approach, then how is nontraining different from training other than with respect to the point in time at which each occurs? The only difference seems to be in relation to relevant events that are present at a given point in time that serve to influence the behaviors in question. Are we not again defining treatment in terms of the presence or absence of professional therapist contact, and if so, is this not consistent with some of the more traditional approaches to follow-up?

It is our view that programming generalization, or more simply, treatment, involves the provision of ongoing, contemporaneous, and presumably measurable contextual events that serve to influence behavior. Both initial effects *and* later effects (sometimes referred to as maintenance) should be directly related to the continued representation of this programming. For the present, these contextual events are conceptualized in their broadest meaning as being overt or covert, constant or changing, planned or unplanned. From an assessment standpoint, in any *particular* instance it will be necessary to define the relevant context in terms of events that have some demonstrated or hypothesized functional relationship to the behavior under consideration.

Efforts to program generalization obscure the arbitrary boundary between treatment and follow-up such that it is difficult to determine when therapy stops and follow-up begins. For example, when treatment consists of the use of agents in the environment as therapists (Aragona, Cassady, & Drabman, 1975; Tharp & Wetzel, 1969), direct environmental restructuring (Tuso & Geller, 1976), the continued use of self-recording (Hall, Hall, Borden, & Hanson, 1975), self-directed mastery (Bandura, Jeffery, & Gajdos, 1975), or cognitive strategies for change (Stunkard & Mahoney, 1976), all of which persist and exert influences following the involvement of a primary therapist, at what point can we say that treatment terminates?

The view of follow-up assessment believed to be most characteristic of current behavioral practice is depicted in Figure 4–1b. Here the effects of programming are presumed to exist but a major omission is that they are *not* measured directly and continuously over time. Note that in this figure broken horizontal lines refer to unmeasured events or context, and solid horizontal lines to measured events or responses. Here treatment is directed at both context and behavior. Treatment does not terminate but is assumed to have continued representation over time, that serves to maintain behavior change. Lack of maintenance, when it occurs, may be directly attributed to a breakdown in programming.

The major limitation of this framework, typical of most behavioral follow-up assessments, is the failure to obtain ongoing and repeated measures of programming. This omission renders this approach functionally equivalent to the treatment termination model, in spite of the incompatibility of assumptions. Without information about context, treatment effects are presumed to persist as a function of previously occurring treatment. In the absence of behavioral maintenance we can only say that what was done at an earlier point in time was not sufficient to produce persisting effects. Without ongoing information about contextual events and programming, the emphasis in follow-up assessment remains predominantly evaluative.

A more appropriate representation for follow-up assessments in behavior therapy is shown in Figure 4–1c. Identical to the framework just discussed in its assumptions, this framework differs in its operations of measurement. Here, measures of both behavior and context are obtained. *Follow-up assessment is viewed simply as ongoing measurement of behavior and relevant context over extended periods of time, rather than the measurement of effects following the termination of treatment.* During this extended measurement period, primary therapist involvement may terminate, but this event is viewed as no more or less important than other relevant contextual changes that occur at some later point in time, for example, the discontinuation of the use of self-instructions by a client or of a time-out procedure by a parent. Such an approach permits the examination of covariations in behavior and continuing representations of treatment, and gives information as to possible reasons for changes in target responses. In addition, since continuing functional analysis provides a basis for ongoing treatment reformulation, follow-up assessments have more direct relevance for treatment. The view being advocated here is not dissimilar to those positions eschewing the arbitrary dichotomization between process and outcome research in psychotherapy (Kiesler, 1966; Paul, 1969) and described by Hersen and Barlow (1976), who state that "measures of change within treatment could be continued throughout treatment until an 'outcome' point is reached" (p. 20).

With a programming generalization conceptualization of follow-up, it is clear that several classes of events will determine what constitutes an appropriate assessment strategy. Given the ongoing interplay between context and behavior, it will be necessary to consider such factors as the nature of the intervention target, setting characteristics, population characteristics, and characteristics of the intervention strategy, if we are to assess meaningfully the durability of treatment effects. Thus far we have described purposes and concepts in follow-up. We shall now turn to a general consideration of several classes of events that will influence most aspects of follow-up. We have designated these as setting variables in follow-up assessment since they are almost without exception factors that, along with conceptualization and purposes, have direct implications for such things as the choice of appropriate follow-up intervals, the selection of dependent measures, the instructions to subjects at follow-up, etc. After briefly outlining these variables, we will then focus our discussion on specific issues and methods in the conduct of follow-up assessment, and will attempt to show how follow-up strategies will ultimately depend on how follow-up is conceptualized, the specific purpose for which it is intended, and a range of setting variables associated with the conduct of the investigation.

SETTING VARIABLES
IN FOLLOW-UP ASSESSMENT

Population and Intervention Target

Issues and strageties of follow-up assessment will depend on the nature of the *population* of interest and the *target problems* typically represented in these populations. For example, the demands of follow-up are quite different in considering child versus adult populations. Many children's problems seem to be age related, and problems present at one age will not necessarily be found at another. In this regard, while the problems manifested by children at varying ages may be different, there may be some correlation between numbers of problems at different ages. However, this correlation may not appear until children are of school age (MacFarlane, Allen, & Honzik, 1954). Rates of behavioral change are faster with young children and there will be differences in the availability of children versus adults at follow-up. By no means exhaustive, these points serve to illustrate the kinds of factors that will likely influence follow-up assessment. In this instance the dependent measures we employ for long-term study will be quite different with children because the likelihood of instrument decay is higher.

It is obvious that assessment with persons with differing diagnoses, such as severely disturbed or institutionalized individuals, will also create differential demands at follow-up, as will differing population characteristics related to a range of demographic variables, particularly age, socioeconomic status, and level of education. In addition, other population characteristics such as attitudes and expectancies will also be important. Population characteristics are obviously a consideration in any study. However, in the present context of follow-up it will be necessary to consider unique population characteristics from the standpoint of *specific issues* associated with the assessment of outcomes over extended time periods. This will be true of the other setting variables to be described.

Related directly to population characteristics are factors related to the intervention target itself. Problem behaviors that tend to be self-limited and show some time course will require a different follow-up strategy from those that seem to be more long-standing problems. For target behaviors in which periodicity is the norm, longer assessments may be needed in order to gain adequate perspective. Other characteristics of the behavior will also influence the choice of dependent measures. For example, Lazarus (1961) has reported using behavioral tests as outcome measures in the treatment of specific phobias, while using verbal self-report in assessing outcome for the treatment of impotence.

For some populations, initial severity of the problem behavior will also influence follow-up. For example, Fo and O'Donnell (1975) note that follow-up results may depend on the severity of delinquent behavior prior to treatment. The nature of the target for intervention will likely influence the meaningfulness of follow-up generally in that initial goals of treatment and assessment may be quite different from long-term goals. Consequently, although a treatment program emphasizing self-care skills in a retarded population might require short-term measures of shirt buttoning and shoe lacing, it is unlikely that long-term follow-up of these specific behaviors would be relevant. Rather, other types of independent living skills would be important. This situation is not unlike the 10-year follow-up on towel hoarding in a schizophrenic woman. Given the costs associated with follow-up, careful consideration must be given to the selection of target behaviors to be considered. Intervention target characteristics, as a factor in follow-up, are inextricably related to base rate problems and the need to identify the projected course of a given behavior over time under particular contextual circumstances.

Nature of Intervention

Characteristics of the intervention will also affect follow-up. This would include such things as whether an individual or group procedure is used, characteristics of the therapist, and whether the intervention is intended to produce a terminal level of behavior (e.g., elimination of a problem, loss of x number of pounds) versus continued improvement (e.g., social skills training). In the latter case, more frequent measures of behavior and context might be required over longer intervals. Some interventions may not require any E-FU *per se,* for example, where it has been established that the effect of the treatment seems limited to the time it is in effect. The use of certain psychostimulants, such as Ritalin for hyperactivity, would fall into this category, although in such instances D-FU and/or I-FU would be quite meaningful.

In some instances the intervention may be intended to produce changes in behavior that enable other changes to occur. Teaching survival skills in a classroom setting would likely require long-term follow-up for academic performance rather than classroom behavior *per se.* Still other interventions, shaping programs for example, may be directed at part of a behavioral chain. In this case, follow-up might be directed at the final response in the behavioral chain rather than intermediate efforts.

The relationship between the intervention strategy and the primary maintaining variables for a given behavior may also have direct implications for follow-up. For example, Davidson (1978) presents data to suggest that particular therapeutic regimes are maximally effective in attenuating different types of anxiety (i.e., cognitive versus somatic). With respect to follow-up, it is possible that therapies producing change indirectly, but not directly, affecting primary maintaining variables may be of a more temporary nature. For example, treatment of cognitive anxiety via progressive relaxation may have immediate but short-term effects. The same might be true in relation to treatments for certain types of hyperactivity that focus on behavior problems in contrast to attional deficit (Mash &

Dalby, 1979). The question of treatment–disorder matching in relation to I-FU is of potential importance and worthy of further study.

Nature of Maintenance Strategy

As noted previously, we view the distinction between treatment and maintenance to be an arbitrary one. From the standpoint of intervention, however, maintenance strategies may be viewed simply as treatments in which there is some explicit statement of concern for "long-term" effects. Since this is invariably a goal for any treatment, we see no need to import special status to maintenance strategies or ways of programming generalization as they are labeled in the literature. However, a number of treatments that are purported to enhance the likelihood of long-term effects have been described in the literature. These approaches have direct relevance for follow-up assessment and will therefore be discussed briefly at this point under a separate heading.

An extensive description of generalization and maintenance strategies (both explicit and implicit) in behavior therapy has been presented by Stokes and Baer (1977). These methods include "train and hope," sequential modification, introduction to natural maintaining contingencies, training of sufficient exemplars, training loosely, using indiscriminable contingencies, programming common stimuli, mediating generalization, and training "to generalize." Stokes and Baer (1977) also point out the importance of "systematic measurement and analysis of variables that may have been functional in any apparently unprogrammed generalization" (p. 365). We have indicated the importance of such ongoing systematic measurement of relevant context for "programmed" generalization as well. The view that contributions to a technology of generalization will emerge from a better understanding of critical variables that function to produce maintenance (Stokes & Baer, 1977) is consistent with the ongoing measurement approach to follow-up assessment being presented in this chapter.

Atthowe (1973) has also described a variety of maintenance strategies including the use of booster treatments (Lemere & Voegtlin, 1950; Lovibond, 1964), mass exposure, treatment packages, self-regulation strategies, intermittent reinforcement, overlearning, creation of conditioned reinforcers and stimuli, increasing the amount of work or lengthening the chain of behaviors required for reinforcement, gradually reducing the magnitude of the reinforcer, "thinning" the schedule of reinforcement, and fading old stimuli while substituting more natural ones. Additional maintenance strategies have involved teaching coping and problem-solving skills (Intagliata, 1978), suggestions for enlisting family support (Stunkard & Mahoney, 1976), and treatments based on environmental restriction (Suedfeld, 1977).

In some ways the number of alternative suggestions put forth for maintenance is surprising in light of the general inconclusiveness or lack of follow-up information described earlier. If this flurry of proposals for enhancing long-term effectiveness is any indication, it would suggest that behavior therapists' own appraisals of long-term outcomes with existing methods is even more pessimistic than currently existing data would indicate. It would seem that more attention might be directed at the development of a technology for follow-up assessment if treatments are to follow from empirically supported outcomes rather than conjecture. However, until such empirical information becomes available, strategies based on theory, such as those mentioned above, will probably be necessary.

The maintenance strategies listed above represent both time-limited (e.g., mass exposure) as well as ongoing environmental arrangements (e.g., family support systems). In either case it is believed that the measurement of the effects of programming for both relevant context and behavior will be important. There are many reports in which a lack of maintenance is attributed to insufficient time-limited treatment rather than changing context, and it is only via the measurement of contemporaneous representations of programming that the reasons for behavior change can be understood. There have been few studies in which "program adherence" has been assessed directly. The few studies that have assessed program adherence have done so during the course of time-limited treatment, but not at follow-up, even with assessments as long as 1 year after treatment (e.g., Stalonas, Johnson, & Christ, 1978).

Situational Factors

The range of settings in which behavior therapy follow-up assessments have been conducted includes psychiatric hospitals, institutions for retarded individuals, delinquent and adult criminal offenders, university settings, medical hospitals, outpatient clinics, nursing homes, and educational settings. It is evident that follow-up assessments will invariably be influenced in their design and implementation by special characteristics associated with particular settings including such things as type of personnel, staff turnover, admitting and discharge procedures, and institutional resources, to name just a few. Follow-up assessments should be planned to take into account characteristics inherent to particular settings. For example, the structure of schools involves grade levels and classroom changes. Therefore, outcome measures that are appropriately used with different informants (e.g., teachers) and/or classroom arrangements should be planned in advance. There are many reports describing incomplete or "impossible to do" follow-up assessments resulting from predictable setting constraints that may have been avoided had follow-up been planned with setting variables in mind.

Practical Constraints

Points similar to those raised with regard to situational factors apply to practical constraints. Personnel turnover, time, money, individual clinicians' resources, and physical resources are ever-present concerns with long-term evaluation. Numerous and often uncontrollable subject characteristics such as mobility and available time commitment should also be considered. It is not our intent here to outline all of the familiar practical difficulties involved in long-term outcome assessments. We view practical constraints to be setting variables that need to be considered in planned follow-up. Behavioral assessment follow-up strategies must be developed so they can be readily implemented. There is evidence that many clinicians have failed to use behavioral assessment strategies extensively because of their impracticality, and there is this danger in behavioral follow-up assessment as well. Unless practical constraints are routinely considered, we are in danger of designing a technology that will not be used.

Ethical Considerations

Follow-up assessments may be viewed as an intrusion or invasion of privacy, and for this reason should be carefully planned. For some individuals, follow-up as it is currently carried out might be a reminder of bad times when they wish to avoid the stigma of having sought treatment for a problem. Ethical concern about withholding treatment from a control group is always a problem which is further magnified when longer time intervals are the variables of interest. For example, some studies have reported negative reactions from control groups and resentment over being placed in the untreated condition.

We have thus far attempted to identify and present a behavioral framework for follow-up, discussed the varying purposes of follow-up assessment in behavior therapy, and briefly outlined several classes of setting variables that seem to be operative with all follow-up assessments. It is believed that concepts, purposes, and setting variables will influence and interact with the procedures involved in the design and implementation of planned follow-up assessment. We will now address ourselves to a discussion of some of the more specific issues and strategies involved in the conduct of behavioral follow-up assessment. Where possible, we will attempt to make recommendations for follow-up assessment under particular circumstances.

ISSUES AND STRATEGIES
IN FOLLOW-UP ASSESSMENT

Length of Follow-Up

As mentioned previously, behavioral investigators have taken the arbitrary position that the longer the follow-up, the better it is. This thinking reflects the treatment termination model with its emphasis on the long-term persistence of effects for the evaluation of previously occurring treatment. Within a programming generalization framework, the focus shifts from how long to when and how often follow-up should be conducted. There are many reports in the literature that designate a particular follow-up interval as acceptable with little rationale as to why. Bergin and Suinn (1975), in their review of behavior therapy in the *Annual Review of Psychology,* state, "finally, it is time to extend research for longer follow-up periods instead of limiting reports to a single post-testing" (p. 543), but do not provide guidelines for *how much longer.* Gulanick, Woodburn, and Rimm (1975) state, "a 12 week follow-up, while acceptable, is also quite short," without specifying criteria for such terms as "acceptable" and "short." Keeley et al. (1976), in their review of operant follow-up studies, report that only 6.2% of the studies reviewed report "long-term follow-up," defined as "at least 6 months post-treatment." However, they present no rationale as to why 6 months was long-term and any thing shorter was inadequate.

The choice of an appropriate follow-up interval is a crucial concern, especially so in light of the costs and frustrations involved in conducting follow-up, and the direct relationship between length of follow-up interval and likelihood of experimental contamination and confound (Costello et al., 1973). In determining the follow-up interval, such considerations as the purpose of follow-up assessment, features of the behavior under consideration (e.g., frequency, intensity, duration), predicted and known treatment outcomes, consequences of remission, practical considerations and costs, and ultimately the terminal objective for a behavior in relation to sociocultural norms, all seem important.

When the purpose of follow-up assessment is to evaluate the general effectiveness of a treatment (i.e., E-FU) rather than to determine whether additional treatment reformulation is necessary for an individual client (such as D-FU), the follow-up interval is likely to be longer and probably fixed at varying time intervals. Follow-up intervals that are set at 6 months, 12 months, etc., make sense only in relation to evaluative outcome criteria. For D-FU the intervals will likely be determined by performance demands arising at various measurement intervals.

Probably the major area in which the selection of an appropriate follow-up assessment interval seems important is with respect to features of the behavior under consideration such as the base rate of occurrence, intensity, and likelihood of spontaneous remission. Specific guidelines are needed in order to establish optimal follow-up intervals and to avoid situations where intervals are either too short or too long (Hartmann, Roper, & Gelfand, 1977; Mash, 1976). Initially, such guidelines may be developed through face validity considerations: 1 week for dating skills or stealing is probably too short, and 10 years for enuresis is probably too long. However, as more follow-up studies are conducted, such guidelines will hopefully be developed on the basis of actuarial data, a great deal of which are already available. If, for example, half of the relapses in treating enuresis occur in the first 6 months following discharge (P.D. Taylor & Turner, 1975) and there are almost none after 1 year, frequent initial follow-up assessments followed by more sporadic assessments would seem appropriate. However, such a pattern of follow-up assessment must be viewed as behavior specific rather than as a general guideline (Callner, 1975). For some behaviors, perhaps those of a skill acquisition nature that require time to take effect, frequent early follow-up may not be fruitful. It is likely, as suggested by Nathan (1976) in a review of behavioral approaches to alcoholism, that initially behavior therapists will need to conduct frequent follow-up assessments in order to develop cost-effectiveness statements of intensive versus intermittent follow-up for specific behavior disorders.

Until such cost-effectiveness statements are generated, decisions regarding follow-up intervals may have to be based on such factors as predictions regarding outcomes for particular treatments (e.g., aversive stimulation for self-injurious behavior should be immediately effective, whereas social skills training may take longer), the consequences of remission (e.g., treatment for high-rate interpersonal aggression may require more immediate follow-up than a program for teaching dating skills), and practical considerations and costs.

Frequency of Follow-up

There is a general consensus among behavioral researchers that single end point observations of behavior are limited (once is not enough), and that repeated observations are necessary in order to establish trends. For example, Chassen (1962) states:

It becomes apparent that mere end-point observations for the purpose of estimating change in the patient-state after say, the introduction of some form of treatment places generally severe limitations on the precision of the estimation of change. For random fluctuation in the patient state can then be easily mistaken for systematic change. To overcome this difficulty frequent repeated observations must be made of each patient in the study. (p. 615)

Where there is periodicity in the course of behavior, and where cyclical manifestations of severity arising from exogenous or endogenous factors occur, the need for repeated measurement over an adequate time base is especially necessary (Subotnik, 1972).

Behavioral investigators, particularly those conducting group designs in which posttreatment assessment is followed by a single follow-up measure, have by such infrequent assessment limited themselves to an examination of linear trends only. From the point after treatment, behavior is usually expected to get better or to maintain itself, and it is seldom the case that deterioration; (Gurman & Kniskern, Note 3; Strupp, Hadley, Gomes, & Armstrong, Note 7) or nonlinear trends are even considered (Bergin & Suinn, 1975). There is no reason to assume a nonlinear trend following treatment, and it is important that repeated measures are taken to look for other trends which might provide information as to some of the possible controlling variables for behavior. For example, Kingsley and Wilson (1977) report that individual behavior therapy for obesity produced significantly greater weight loss posttreatment than a group social pressure treatment, but at a 1-year follow-up the advantage was for the social pressure treatment.[10] Silverman, Martin, Ungaro, and Mendelsohn (1978) report the use of a behavioral program for the treatment of obesity combined with "symbiotic gratification fantasy" treatment. Although there was no difference between groups immediately following treatment, there was a difference at follow-up. R. W. Jeffery, Wing, and Stunkard (1978) report no relationship between weight at post-treatment and weight at a 1-year follow-up. Harris and Hallbauer (1973) report no difference between controlled eating and exercise groups at termination, but the exercise group showed more weight loss at a 7-month follow-up than the comparison group. In contrast to these studies on obesity that suggest changes from termination to follow-up that may be of a delayed or nonlinear nature, Marks, Rachman, and Hodgson (1975) report that the initial response of obsessive-compulsive patients appears to be an accurate predictor of long-term success. Again, these types of data point up the need for repeated measurement over time, the frequency of which will vary with behavior being considered and the purpose of the follow-up.

In this regard, single-subject or intensive designs (Chassen, 1962; Hersen & Barlow, 1976) hold special promise. However, such designs have held promise for many years now, and the majority of follow-up reports in the behavioral literature continue to employ group designs. If a repeated-measures notion of follow-up assessment is to be accepted, it will be important for behavioral researchers to put aside the idea that single-subject designs are demonstrative rather than evaluative (Gurman & Kniskern, 1978) and accept the notion that long-term evaluation may be achieved through systematic replication. The recent work by Hersen and Barlow (1976) will hopefully contribute to this acceptance although it may be some time before this issue is resolved (Jones, 1978). In any case, it is generally accepted that repeated observations are necessary for follow-up. How frequent for particular behaviors is yet to be determined.

One additional comment on the frequency of assessment seems important. Although repeated observations have characterized much behavioral intervention on a short-term basis, the apparent costs associated with continued frequent measurement have often resulted in abandonment of this approach at follow-up assessment. There are many instances in the literature where frequent and repeated measurement during treatment is followed by a single data point or postcheck measure, such as daily measurement for 3 months, then 1-day assessments at 3 months, 6 months, 9 months, etc. It is recommended that some attempt should be made to match the frequency and density of follow-up assessment with the earlier assessment intervals used. Such matching will permit an examination of changes in level, slope, and trends in the behavior under investigation. Without such matching, the reactivity of follow-up assessment could greatly increase the likelihood that spurious findings may result.

A key issue in the discussion of both length and frequency of follow-up intervals, and especially so with the continuous-measures approach to assessment being put forth in this chapter, is the determination of the point at which measurement is discontinued. First, cost-effectiveness analysis following frequent and long-term data collection should lead to optimal intervals for particular behaviors and treatments. At some point it should be possible to conclude that follow-up intervals of a particular length are acceptable. This decision may be based on several considerations. First, a particular interval may be shown to be predictive of outcome level at some later point in time. Second, observations beyond a particular interval for certain problems may introduce factors such as maturation, instrument decay, situational changes, and changing norms for a behavior that would make further follow-up inconclusive. Finally, termination of follow-up assessments will be dictated by the level of the behavior in relation to mutually agreed upon sociocultural normative data and subjective evaluation (Kazdin, 1977). In considering the effectiveness of behavioral treatments assessed through follow-up we are dealing with a predominantly definitional problem involving value judgments about the kinds of outcomes a given investigator or public consumers deem worthwhile.[11]

Standardized Follow-Up Assessment

There are two ways in which standardization seems important to follow-up assessment: (1) standardization of measures and conditions of measurement *across time* for an individual or group of individuals within the same study; and (2) standardization of measures and conditions of measurement *across studies* involving similar treatments and/or treatment targets (McNamara & MacDonough, 1972).

Standardization Across Time. Use of similar measurement conditions across time within the same study, or stated another way, the degree to which there is temporal congruence of measurement, is a basic design requirement for any study of change. Clearly, if either the measuring instrument or conditions change, we are unable to determine whether changes were real or a function of measurement error. In spite of this essential and basic requirement the literature on behavior therapy is fraught with instances in which later follow-up assessments differ from the assessments conducted earlier. These measurement differences take a number of common forms, with an almost total lack of elaboration on the reasons for a shifting measurement approach.

The follow-up measures are *different* in kind from those given initially. Many studies use initial assessments involving observation, self-monitoring, and questionnaires, that are later followed by an assessment involving only unstructured self-report, such as a telephone interview in which the client reports that things are "okay."

Only a small and selected proportion of the measures used initially is repeated at the time of follow-up. This is probably the most common instance of changing measurement conditions characteristic of follow-up studies in behavior therapy. There are numerous examples in which pre- and posttreatment measures may include direct observation, a behavioral test, physiological measures, and multiple self-report questionnaires, to be followed by the use of only one or two of these measures at follow-up (Kazdin, 1975, 1976; Twentyman & McFall, 1975). The measures selected from the initial battery are almost exclusively self-report, and the reason for such selection, when given, is usually associated with practical considerations such as time, expense, and probability of subject participation. Such selectivity of follow-up measures seems especially characteristic of studies in which subjects are likely to show high mobility (e.g., end of term for college students, being discharged from an institutional setting, the end of an elementary school year), and the only way of reaching individuals may be via telephone contact or mail. A common characteristic of studies using partial measures at follow-up is to overgeneralize in drawing conclusions. For example, "the treatment was shown to be effective [five measures], and these gains were maintained at a 6-month [two measures] and a 12-month [one measure] follow-up" is a typical statement of this variety which tends to obscure some of the measurement limitations.

There is a change in the time base for measurement. The first point above referred to a change in the kind of measuring instruments, the second to a change in the number of measures. Another common change involves a change in the time unit of measurement, often accompanied by a change in the measure as well. In one report of a program for smoking (Best, 1975) a 1-week follow-up period requiring daily recording of smoking rate was used, which was followed by 1-, 2-, 3-, and 6-month follow-ups in which subjects were asked to estimate their smoking rates during the preceding week. Sutherland, Amit, Golden, and Roseberger (1975), also in a program for smoking, used daily self-recording initially, followed by 9-week and 25-week contacts by telephone. In both of these studies there is a change in both the time base of measurement as well as the measuring instrument.

The lack of standardization described above seems almost exclusively related to practical considerations such as the availability of experimenter, client, or subject time. Since such limitations are likely to persist in follow-up assessments, it seems appropriate to make several recommendations given such limitations.

Where it is likely that a "nonpreferred measure" such as report via telephone or weekly retrospective estimates of behavior are to be used in follow-up, such measures should be used throughout the course of intervention in addition to the other measures that may be used on a short-term basis. Such use will ensure that a consistent measure (albeit not the best) will at least be available throughout. In addition, through the use of such measures at a time when "better" measures are also being used, it may be possible to obtain better estimates of their reliability and validity. So, for example, when using direct observations of a given behavior it might also be advantageous to ask the individual to make weekly estimates of the behavior as well and to also obtain such estimates from significant others in the person's environment. This should provide a greater degree of confidence in these measures if they are to be used exclusively at some later point in time, although the absence of collateral monitoring systems during follow-up would limit direct comparability.

Since more expeditious measures are likely to be used for follow-up, greater effort should be invested in developing more reliable and valid self-report procedures (Cautela & Upper, 1976; Nelson, Note 8) and also in forming a pool of such measures for follow-up that are appropriate to particular treatments and disorders. The development of standardized follow-up questionnaires, interviews, and telephone contacts (Patterson, 1974; Poser, 1977; Rinn, Vernon, & Wise, 1975), along with studies examining the psychometric properties of such instruments, would be a step in this direction.

There is a need for the development of cost-effectiveness statements for varying follow-up assessment procedures with different *populations* and *problems.* The use of existing data, for example, to compare percentages of varying subject populations participating in follow-up with different assessment demands would be a step in the right direction. Basic information such as the proportion of subjects participating in follow-up assessment following different treatments and assessments is not available in a single source at the present time. Such a data-based approach for formulating general guidelines is recommended in lieu of a priori assumptions that potentially uncooperative subjects require that a less demanding follow-up assessment be conducted to ensure complete data return (Best, 1975). Such assumptions may be accurate for some populations and problems, but clearly not for others.

Special attention should be given to creating a comparable time base for measurement at follow-up assessment. Rather than single measures at 6 months, for example, if daily measures were used during baseline, their use should be daily at the 6-month interval.

Attempts should be made to compare the effect of giving a measure as part of an assessment battery, in contrast to giving the measure in isolation. If a person's self-report of anxiety is to be used as a follow-up measure by itself, a comparison of this measure given by itself with results obtained when the measure is given concomitant with a behavioral assessment of speech performance should be made. Clearly, knowledge of the performance measure may affect initial questionnaire response, which may be later affected by knowledge that no performance measure will be given.

Standardization Across Studies. The lack of standardization of measurement instruments and conditions within studies as described above compounds the problems involved in attempting to make comparisons of findings across studies. Evans and Nelson (1977) note that the "clinical significance of much of the outcome data in child behavior therapy cannot be determined because of the still unstandardized, unquantified, and unrepeatable form in which it is reported" (p. 660). Kanfer (1972) has discussed the lack of standardization that generally characterizes behavioral assessment procedures. Bergin and Suinn (1975), in reviewing research on outcome in behavior therapy, point up the difficulties in interpreting outcome studies for a particular treatment technique when differing measures are used. They emphasize that there is a great need for more research relying on standardized measures. Peter Nathan (1976), in his review of behavioral treatments for alcoholism, states:

At present researchers use such a wide variety of follow-up procedures employed over such a range of follow-up periods that direct comparisons of treatment efficacy of different methods over time is impossible. The development of standard behavioral procedures for follow-up . . . would enable this direct comparison. (p. 39)

In a review of behavioral approaches to drug abuse (Callner, 1975), and in reviews of related areas of research such as parent–child interaction (Bell & Hertz, 1976), similar recommendations have been made.

Standardization of measures has both advantages and disadvantages but would appear desirable if we wish to compare long-term outcomes across various studies. It is believed that the development and availability of a psychometrically sound pool of follow-up measures for specific populations and problems would facilitate much cross-study comparison. However, as long as loosely developed follow-up measures, such as those using informal telephone contact, for example, are the norm rather than the exception, there is likely to be heterogeneity across studies. There is no reason for one investigator to believe that his telephone call is any less reliable or valid than the other person's.

It should be noted that the use of standardized follow-up measures could have a major benefit. It would potentially eliminate the necessity of standardizing follow-up intervals in studies examining similar treatments and would render these studies more directly comparable. It would permit the use of several different studies to create a continuous series of measures for follow-up and would generate the type of cost-effectiveness analyses of intermittent versus continuous follow-up recommended by Nathan (1976) and others. It would create opportunities for systematic replication, with some studies using 1-month intervals, others 2-month, others longer.

At the same time that standardization is recommended, it is likely that since practical exigencies seem prepotent in the planning of follow-up assessments, and the range of practical exigencies is so diverse from study to study and situation to situation, nonstandardized measures and measurement conditions are likely to continue. Under such circumstances it seems that suggestions to render different measures comparable through the use of multivariate statistical procedures, as recently suggested by Weinrott (Note 9), should be pursued.

Reactivity of Follow-Up Assessment

Follow-up assessments share the same reactivity problems inherent in short-term assessments[12] and also possess some unique problems that are generated by the longer time base typically involved.

First, the measures of performance obtained on a particular follow-up occasion may be unrepresentative of behavior at that point in time. Such unrepresentativeness may be attributed to the influence of observers or examiners, the assessment context, the nature of the previous therapeutic contact, and demand characteristics associated with a particular phase of treatment. Second, the factors operative in producing this unrepresentativeness may differ across successive measurement occasions. In this latter instance, follow-up assessment is probably unique only in the sense that the expanded time base involved in follow-up enhances the likelihood that such influences are likely to be different with time. It is unlikely that the same observer will be involved. Similarly, the client–therapist relationship is different and the expectations for success of treatment will no doubt have changed. Further, even though raters may be blind as to treatment condition, knowledge that performance is occurring at 1 year following primary intervention may influence their ratings (e.g., Blackwood, Strupp, & Bradley, 1975).

Although problems concerned with the reactivity of measurement have received extensive discussion in the behavioral literature (Johnson & Bolstad, 1973) and will not be covered in detail here, it should be noted that such discussions have focused primarily on observational measures (Mash & Hedley, 1975) and short-term effects. There is little information regarding the reactivity associated with other types of measures including the interview (Morganstern, 1976), telephone contacts, and questionnaires. One study has suggested that there may be differential effects of the examiner depending on the particular measure used, e.g., verbal report, observation, and so on (Tittler, Anchor, & Weitz, 1976).

Since nonobservational measures are becoming more common in behavioral assessment, and are typically the norm in follow-up assessments— Callner (1975) reported that 87% of the studies reviewed employed self-report measures for follow-up—behavioral assessors should address their attention to reactivity for these other types of measures. Some writers (Hersen & Barlow, 1976) note that demand characteristics may be greater with self-report than observation measures. Although this assumption has not been tested directly, the study of demand characteristics associated with verbal report measures seems especially important. In addition, more attention should be directed toward the development and use of procedures that would likely minimize reactive effects at the time of follow-up assessment. For example, making follow-up assessment less discriminative through the use of frequent assessments throughout, the use of unobtrusive measures when possible (Twentyman & McFall, 1975), the random selection of days for follow-up assessment, and the use of collateral data sources and agents would be steps in this direction.

Related to the reactivity question for follow-up are the special questions of demand characteristics, sets, and expectancies (Rosen, 1976). Since follow-up data collection often has an explicit discriminative function (Surratt, Ulrich, & Hawkins, 1969), the likelihood of particular demand characteristics and expectancies seems high. There is little work elaborating on the nature of such demand characteristics and expectancies in relation to follow-up. For example, Johnson and Eyberg (1975) assume that demand characteristics to "look good" are not going to be present at follow-up, in that there seems to be no readily apparent reason for this type of distortion. However, it might be argued that since follow-up may have some aversive properties, as evidenced by the often surprisingly high rates of refusal to participate, "looking good" may be the quickest way to avoid an unpleasant situation. In any event, it is clear that expectancies are likely to change over the course of treatment (Rosen, 1976), and such changing expectancies may lead to spurious findings. For example, Kazdin and Wilcoxon (1976), in discussing systematic desensitization, suggest that assessments of expectancy for change that occur after treatment may themselves be influenced by therapeutic impact. In summary, there is a need to investigate systematically what special demand characteristics and expectancies are created by follow-up assessment and to measure changing attitudes and expectancies directly over the course of intervention (Kazdin & Wilcoxon, 1976).

Selecting Follow-Up Measures

Kazdin and Wilson (1978) have noted that "the lack of adequate measures of treatment outcome has possibly been the most serious deficiency of the treatment literature to date" (p. 112). In considering outcome research in general, an examination of the kinds of measures used to assess outcome, the units of measurement used with respect to their degree of specificity, and the number of measures employed are all important considerations. These considerations are not specific to follow-up assessment, but since they are consistent with the general theme of this chapter regarding the expanded time base for measurement as being the major defining property of follow-up, it would seem appropriate to discuss selectively some of the issues involved in the choice of outcome measures when longer time periods are a factor.

In contrast to studies involving the measurement of short-term outcomes, which have relied extensively on "direct" behavioral measures such as observation by trained observers, studies including follow-up assessments have been characterized by the use of verbal report measures including both self-report and report by significant others (Lesser, 1976).

Although some investigators have argued for the use of self-report measures as a necessary (Eyberg & Johnson, 1974; Johnson & Christensen, 1975; Johnson & Eyberg, 1975; Wolf, 1978) but *perhaps* not sufficient index of outcome (Patterson, Weiss, & Hops, 1976), this reliance on verbal report information has been a constant source of criticism by reviewers of follow-up research on behavior therapy (Callner, 1975; Gordon, 1975; Keeley, et al., 1976; Nathan, 1976).

The extensive use of verbal report measures has *not* been indicative of their preferred status as an outcome measure. Rather, their use in almost all instances relates to the difficulties involved in implementing direct observation over longer time periods and with low base-rate behaviors, in contrast to the belief that verbal report measures provide a better estimate of outcome. The difficulties in the employment of direct observation for follow-up assessment, as described in the literature, center around but are not restricted to the actual or anticipated time and effort involved for the client *and* therapist. Given the prevalent use of verbal report measures, one must seriously question whether the frequently proposed, outright rejection of studies using only verbal report as too "soft," and the attempt to include observational measures in all long-term assessments of outcome, represent realistic alternatives. A more fruitful direction would be an attempt to develop verbal report measures that are more reliable and less subject to distortion (Nelson, Note 8), and alternatively to develop observational measures that are more practical, such as not requiring that a fleet of expensively trained and maintained observers be available, or that the client and/or therapist give up their weekends and summer vacations to provide a sufficient amount of data to meet sampling considerations.

With respect to the development of better verbal report measures, general behavioral assessment principles involving such qualities as the specificity of report required with respect to situational or setting events and molecularity of behavioral descriptions would be important. The quality of self-report information is enhanced by assessments which are less global (Patterson, et al., 1976). For example, Walter and Gilmore (1973) report that although parents accurately described no change in their children's behavior, they still answered yes to the question "Has your child improved?"

In spite of the fact that more specific verbal report seems desirable, there are situations defined by readily apparent long-term outcomes where verbal report is not only likely to be reliable, but probably less reactive and therefore preferred over direct observation. It is unlikely that daily, long-term, in vivo observations by two trained observers recording in the home the number of encopretic incidences of a young child is going to yield better information about the long-term effects of treatment than a telephone call in which the parent is asked whether the child had any "accidents" over the past 6 months (Plachetta, 1976). In any event, more systematic attempts to evaluate the reliability, validity, and reactivity of a variety of verbal report measures for differing problems and situations are needed. Attempts to increase the use of more specific, structured, and standardized verbal reports, and the use of collateral data sources (Eyberg & Johnson, 1974) and informants (Lovibond & Caddy, 1970; Wickramasekera, 1976) to substantiate verbal report, appear to be fruitful directions.

It is possible that in their zeal for including direct observation of behavior as a necessary outcome measure, behavioral assessors may have become unrealistic in the development of observational measures that have utility for long-term assessment, both from the standpoint of practicalities of implementation and usefulness of obtained information. There is likely an inverse relationship between the degree of sophistication of an observational measure with respect to number of behaviors sampled, amount of training of observers required, and resources for data analysis and its usefulness for long-term follow-up assessment. First of all, it is less likely to be used since the continued maintenance of resources cannot be expected, except perhaps with large research centers. Second, although the specificity of multiple-category code systems provides greater reliability on a short-term basis, such specificity increases susceptibility to measurement decay over long time periods. This is especially so when we are dealing with rapidly changing behavior, as is the case with young children. It is believed that observational measures which include broader response classes, which may be defined in several ways (Mash, 1976; Wahler, House, & Stambaugh, 1976) and may include topographically dissimilar responses at different points in time, may be more appropriate for long-term follow-up assessments. The fact that some response classes have been shown to possess structural stability (Wahler, 1975) offers tentative support for this approach.

The degree of confidence gained in finding convergence on a number of outcome measures over time suggests the use of multiple measures, both verbal report and direct observation. Unfortunately, most behavioral studies have resulted in a lack of convergence of measures over time, and to some extent this lack of convergence increases in likelihood as the time base for measurement increases (Patterson et al., 1976). Such findings are difficult to interpret in the absence of long-term information on reliability for the measures typically employed in behavioral studies. Test–retest reliabilities are necessary (Hartmann, Note 10; Nelson & Hay, Note 11) in that, to the extent that measures differ in such temporal reliability, the expectancy for convergence is less and the source of such unreliability will need identification (e.g., changing demand characteristics, instrument decay).

There is also a need for the development of contextual measures appropriate to follow-up. Given many of the programming generalization strategies currently employed in attempting to produce maintenance, measures tapping natural support systems would seem appropriate. Gottlieb (1978), for example, has presented a measure for examining informal social support systems for single mothers. These types of measures would seem useful for follow-ups involving extended assessment.

Subject Attrition

There is little question that loss of subjects at the time of follow-up assessment is a prevalent concern and one which increases as the length of the follow-up interval increases (Costello et al., 1973). Subject attrition may occur for a number of reasons but appears to cluster in two categories, the first in which subjects cannot be located and the second in which subjects refuse to participate in follow-up assessment. For evaluative follow-up assessments both conditions create methodological difficulties that have been frequently discussed, such as changing sample size or a lack of comparability of findings; and therefore these difficulties should be minimized. The refusal to participate in follow-up assessment creates additional concerns and poses some interesting questions.

Investigators have interpreted subjects' refusal to participate in follow-up assessment in different ways, often diametrically opposed. For example, Gottman and Leiblum (1974) state, "a good indication of successful termination occurs when an ex-client finds that he has far more important things to do than come to therapy, and when therapy checkup sessions are just a big pain in the neck to the client" (p. 157). Conceivably, refusal under such circumstances would suggest that things are going well and the client does not want to be bothered. The finding by Reid and Patterson (1976) that treatment dropouts showed greater treatment effects than those not dropping out provides indirect support for this notion. However, such individuals may also show a higher initial level of deviance (Johnson & Christensen, 1975). Alternatively, refusal may clearly reflect a dissatisfaction with the results of treatment and an unwillingness to be involved further. In some instances an unwillingness to participate in follow-up assessment may be *directly* related to treatment failure. If the follow-up assessment involves a behavioral performance measure with confrontation of an unpleasant situation (a behavioral avoidance test, or speech performance analogue), refusal may more directly reflect treatment failure than refusal to complete a questionnaire (especially in situations where the time demands are somewhat equivalent). The same subject who returns a questionnaire may be unwilling to participate in an avoidance test.

The above statements suggest that behavioral investigations should give more attention to identifying the reasons for subjects' failure to participate in follow-up assessment. Most studies do not report such information, and such unelaborated statements as "15% of subjects were 'lost to follow-up,'" or "8 of 22 families refused to participate fully for one reason or another," are common. Some studies look for differences between those participating and those not participating in follow-up. So, for example, Johnson and Christensen (1975) found that families participating in follow-up were more cooperative *throughout* treatment with no other differences. Such information may lead to early identification of possible treatment or follow-up dropouts; however, it will still be necessary to identify conditions that will promote continuation for follow-up assessment. Information about reasons for refusal may permit the development of a taxonomy of situations, demands, etc., which provide the setting events for participation with various clients, problems, and procedures. Such information may then be used to set up conditions which will minimize attrition. Several recommendations may prove fruitful in enhancing the likelihood of participating in follow-up.

1. The "repeated measures over time" view of follow-up assessment should serve to make the treatment–follow-up phases less discriminable and distinct, thus reducing the likelihood that follow-up assessment is viewed as less important than earlier assessments. Follow-up assessments should be perceived as "measurement as usual."

2. The importance of long-term measurement should be explained early in the program so that it does not appear something that is tacked on at the end of treatment.

3. The rationale for long-term assessment should be made explicit. Although some writers (e.g., Suedfeld, 1977) have had success with instructions emphasizing the need for accurate feedback, it is not likely that "for the good of science"-type explanations, or explanations that emphasize altruistic motives such as "it will help us to help other people," will be very effective in promoting participation. For example, subjects have been found to be more likely to terminate prematurely when an experimental purpose is given for a study than a therapeutic purpose (Fiester & Rudestam, 1975). Since evaluative assessment frequently carries experimental connotations, an attempt should be made to emphasize the diagnostic and therapeutic role of continuous measurement for long periods of time.

4. Researchers must themselves give priority to follow-up assessment. Such recognition is apparent in studies (Hagan, Foreyt, & Durham, 1976) that use deposit contracts contingent on completion of the program but notably absent in many studies requiring treatment deposits which are returned after treatment but *before* follow-up assessment (Gulanick, Woodburn, & Rimm, 1975).

5. Attempts should be made to match the practical demands of follow-

up assessment to the characteristics and circumstances of the population under study. The choice of assessment measures should be determined in part by the likelihood of later compliance with procedures. Too many studies employ batteries of assessment that are unrealistic for long follow-up, in spite of the fact that long-term follow-up is planned. High attrition rates under such circumstances are not uncommon.

CONCLUSIONS

Behavior therapists are currently faced with many of the methodological and practical problems that have plagued other investigators interested in conducting long-term outcome research. In this chapter we have attempted to describe a framework for follow-up assessment in behavior therapy that is consistent with current behavioral assumptions and practices, especially those related to the need for programming generalization (e.g., Marholin, Siegel, & Phillips, 1976). We have also identified several common purposes and setting variables in follow-up assessment and have attempted to show how these dimensions combine to influence the specific follow-up assessment strategies employed. It is hoped that more attention will be given to the development of realistic guidelines for the conduct of follow-up assessments in behavior therapy, and that such guidelines will replace the frequent exhortations to conduct longer treatment follow-ups, made without adequate rationale or practical suggestions as to how this might be accomplished. The need for follow-up assessments that are systematic and planned in advance (e.g., Jones, Timbers, & Davis, Note 12) seems especially important. It is believed that unless an adequate technology for follow-up assessment is developed, many of the current efforts to enhance therapeutic maintenance will likely be inconclusive. Therefore, concomitant efforts in both areas seem necessary.

NOTES

1. Reprinted with permission of the authors and the *Canadian Journal of Behavioural Science*. Also, see Sherwood and Gray (1974) for follow-up on other patients treated on Ayllon's experimental ward.

2. Ayllon's comment does not account for why two of the three behaviors did not recur, unless of course one assumes that for these behaviors the posttreatment environment did not change. This seems unlikely, and such explanations if invoked would be something of a tautology.

3. The proclivity of area-specific review articles in behavior therapy to end with the statement "Finally, there is a need to collect follow-up information over longer periods of time" has made the phrase something of a cliche. One needs only to turn to the last page to find it, usually under "Recommendations."

4. Smith and Glass (1977), in their review of psychotherapy outcome studies, report that the average length of follow-up for behavioral programs was shorter (approximately 2 months) than for nonbehavioral studies (approximately 5 months).

5. For example, Cox, Freundlich, and Meyer (1975) report that placebo follow-up data were contaminated by the fact that two of the women had quit their stress-related jobs, another had sought relaxation training at the clinic, one had gotten a divorce, another was in the hospital, and another man was undergoing chiropractic massage for his headaches. All this had taken place during a 4-month period for control subjects, whereas there were no such occurrences in the experimental group.

6. It is not our purpose to deal with the question of whether or not the data would support the long-term efficacy of behavioral treatments. Readers interested in this question should consult the excellent review by Kazdin and Wilson (1978).

7. It should be noted that under such circumstances follow-up assessment may be mistaken for therapy and this could be a potential confound from the standpoint of a "no-treatment" control group.

8. It has been said that "analogies prove nothing that is quite true, but they can make one feel more at home" (Freud, 1933).

9. Points (4) and (5) reflect the medical concepts of cure and improvement. However, Robins (1972) notes that medical treatments do not necessarily have cure as a goal. There are incurable illnesses with spontaneously occurring remission and exacerbation (e.g., arthritis) where the question of follow-up is not cure or improvement but whether treatment has increased the proportion of the follow-up intervals during which the patient can function effectively. There are self-limited illnesses from which almost all recover (e.g., influenza) where the follow-up question is not improvement but whether the course of the disease was milder as a result of treatment. In fact, Robins (1972) notes that "at the present level of medical knowledge, the medical syndromes for which the relevant measure of treatment is whether the patient is cured at follow-up or even much improved is a small minority of the total" (p. 429).

10. Many group comparisons speak to the relative advantage of one treatment versus another at termination and at follow-up. It should noted that relative advantages do not indicate the time course of behavior, even though many studies imply improvement or deterioration. In actuality, a relative advantage of one group at follow-up may reflect any one of a number of changes for each group that may only be assessed through repeated measurement.

11. On a similar note, such subjectivity is reflected in the following statement: "And the question is how a patient ends being a patient. . . . as long as I am busy being a doctor, I need patients, and every time a person stops acting like a patient, I have to get rid of him, because he is not fulfilling whatever it is I need" (Ram Dass, 1974, p. 21).

12. Smith and Glass (1977) report a significant relationship between the reactivity of the measure used to assess outcome and the magnitude of effect. The more reactive the measure, the larger the effect. They also report that behavioral researchers tended to use more reactive outcome measures than those reported in nonbehavioral studies.

ACKNOWLEDGMENTS

The authors would like to thank Sherry Pitcher, Ann Garner, Russell Barkley, and Charles Costello for their helpful comments on an earlier draft of this chapter. During the preparation of this chapter, the first author was supported by Canada Council Leave Fellowship No. W760087 and was a visiting associate professor of medical psychology at the Child Development and Rehabilitation Center of the University of Oregon Health Sciences Center. An abbreviated version of this chapter previously appeared in *Psychological Reports* (1977, *41*, 1287–1308).

REFERENCE NOTES

1. Flynn, J. M., Wood, R., Michelson, L., & Keen, J. *Publication trends in behavior therapy, 1970–1977.* Paper presented at the meeting of the Association for the Advancement of Behavior Therapy, Atlanta, December 1977.
2. Peterson, L., & Hartmann, D. P. *Some treatment-methodological problems in current child behavior therapy research.* Paper presented at the meeting of the Association for the Advancement of Behavior Therapy, San Francisco, November 1975.
3. Gurman, A. S., & Kniskern, D. P. *Deterioration in marital and family therapy: Empirical and conceptual issues.* Paper presented at the meeting of the Society for Psychotherapy Research, San Diego, 1976.
4. Turkat, I. D., and Forehand, R. Unpublished manuscript, University of Georgia at Athens, 1978.
5. Wade, T. C., Baker, T. B., & Hartmann, D. P. *The views and practices of behavior therapists.* Unpublished manuscript, University of Utah, 1978.
6. Boyd, J., Paul, E., Scholle, K., & Mitchell, J. *Comparison of maternal attitudes toward the behavior of pre-school children, 1953–1975.* Unpublished manuscript, Pace University, 1978.
7. Strupp, H. H., Hadley, S. W., Gomes, B., & Armstrong, S. *Negative effects in psychotherapy: A review of clinical and theoretical issues together with recommendations for a program of research.* Unpublished manuscript, Vanderbilt University, 1976.
8. Nelson, R. O. *Self-report measures in behavior therapy.* Paper presented at the meeting of the Association for the Advancement of Behavior Therapy, New York, December 1976.
9. Weinrott, M. Personal communication. November 1976.
10. Hartmann, D. P. *Must the baby follow the bathwater: Psychometric principles—behavioral data.* Paper presented at the meeting of the American Psychological Association, Washington, D.C., September 1976.
11. Nelson, R. O., & Hay, L. R. *Temporal stability coefficients: Relevant for behavioral assessment.* Paper presented at the meeting of the American Psychological Association, Washington, D.C., September 1976.
12. Jones, R. J., Timbers, G. D., & Davis, J. L. *A model follow-up procedure for tracking the post-treatment adjustments of juvenile offenders.* Paper presented at the meeting of the Association for the Advancement of Behavior Therapy, Atlanta, December 1977.

REFERENCES

Alban, L. S., & Nay, W. R. Reduction of ritual checking by a relaxation-delay treatment. *Journal of Behavior Therapy and Experimental Psychiatry*, 1976, *7*, 151–154.

Aragona, J., Cassady, J., & Drabman, R. S. Training overweight children through parental training and contingency contracting. *Journal of Applied Behavior Analysis*, 1975, *8*, 269–278.

Atthowe, J. M., Jr. Behavior innovation and persistence. *American Psychologist*, 1973, *28*, 34–41.

Ayllon, T. Intensive treatment of psychotic behaviour by stimulus satiation and food reinforcement. *Behaviour Research and Therapy*, 1963, *1*, 53–61.

Ayllon, T. Comments on "Two classic behaviour modification patients" a decade later. *Canadian Journal of Behavioural Science*, 1974, *6*, 428.

Bachrach, A. J., & Quigley, W. Direct methods of treatment. In I. A. Berg & L. A. Pennington (Eds.), *Introduction to clinical psychology*. New York: Ronald Press, 1966.

Baer, D. M., Wolf, M. M., & Risley, T. R. Some current dimensions of applied behavior analysis. *Journal of Applied Behavior Analysis*, 1968, *1*, 91–97.

Bandura, A. *Principles of behavior modification*. New York: Holt, Rinehart & Winston, 1969.

Bandura, A., Jeffery, R. W., & Gajdos, E. Generalizing change through participant modeling with self-directed mastery. *Behaviour Research and Therapy*, 1975, *13*, 141–152.

Bell, R. Q., & Hertz, T. W. Toward more compatability and generalizability of developmental research. *Child Development*, 1976, *47*, 6–13.

Bergin, A. E. The evaluation of therapeutic outcomes. In A. E. Bergin & S. L. Garfield (Eds.), *Handbook of psychotherapy and behavior change: An empirical analysis*. New York: Wiley, 1971.

Bergin, A. E., & Garfield, S L. (Eds.), *Handbook of psychotherapy and behavior change: An empirical analysis*. New York: Wiley, 1971.

Bergin, A. E., & Suinn, R. M. Individual psychotherapy and behavior therapy. *Annual Review of Psychology*, 1975, *26*, 509–556.

Best, J. A. Tailoring smoking withdrawal procedures to personality and motivational differences. *Journal of Consulting and Clinical Psychology*, 1975, *43*, 1–8.

Bijou, S. W., & Peterson, R. F. The psychological assessment of children: A functional analysis. In P. McReynolds (Ed.), *Advances in psychological assessment* (vol. 2). Palo Alto, Calif.: Science and Behavior Books, 1971.

Blackwood, G. L., & Strupp, H. H., & Bradley, L. A. Effects of prognostic information on global ratings of psychotherapy outcome. *Journal of Consulting and Clinical Psychology*, 1975, *43*, 810–815.

Blanchard, E. B. Brief flooding treatment for a debilitating revulsion. *Behaviour Research and Therapy*, 1975, *13*, 193–195.

Bucher, B., Reykdal, B., & Albin, J. Brief physical restraint to control pica in retarded children. *Journal of Behavior Therapy and Experimental Psychiatry*, 1976, *7*, 137–140.

Callner, D. A. Behavioral treatment approaches to drug abuse. *Psychological Bulletin*, 1975, *82*, 143–164.

Cautela, J. R. Behavior therapy and the need for behavioral assessment. *Psychotherapy: Theory, Research and Practice*, 1968, *5*, 175–179.

Cautela, J. R., & Upper, D. The behavioral inventory battery: The use of self-report measures in behavioral anaylsis and therapy. In M. Hersen & A. S. Bellack (Eds.), *Behavioral assessment: A practical handbook*. New York: Pergamon, 1976.

Chassen, J. B. Probability processes in psychoanalytic psychiatry. In J. Scher (Ed.), *Theories of the mind*. New York: The Free Press of Glencoe, 1962.

Ciminero, A. R., Calhoun, K. S., & Adams, H. E. (Eds.). *Handbook of behavioral assessment*. New York: Wiley, 1977.

Cochrane, R., & Sobol, M. P. Myth and methodology in behaviour therapy research. In M. P. Feldman & A. Broadhurst (Eds.), *Theoretical and empirical bases of the behaviour therapies*. London: Wiley, 1976.

Cone, J. D., & Hawkins, R. P. (Eds.), *Behavioral assessment: New directions in clinical psychology*. New York: Brunner/Mazel, 1977.

Conway, J. B., & Bucher, B. D. Transfer and maintenance of behavior change in children: A review and suggestions. In E. J. Mash, L. A. Hamerlynck, & L. C. Handy (Eds.), *Behavior modification and families*. New York: Brunner/Mazel, 1976.

Costello, R. M., Bechtel, J. E., & Griffen, M. B. A community's efforts to attack the problem of alcoholism: II. Base rate data for future program evaluation. *International Journal of the Addictions,* 1973, *8,* 875–888.

Cox, D. J., Freundlich, A., & Meyer, R. G. Differential effectiveness of electromyograph feedback, verbal relaxation instructions, and medication placebo with tension headaches. *Journal of Consulting and Clinical Psychology,* 1975, *43,* 892–898.

Davidson, R. J. Specificity and patterning in biobehavioral systems: Implications for behavior change. *American Psychologist,* 1978, *33,* 430–436.

Evans, I. M., & Nelson, R. O. Assessment of child behavior problems. In A. R. Ciminero, K. S. Calhoun, & H. E. Adams (Eds.), *Handbook of behavioral assessment*. New York: Wiley, 1977.

Eyberg, S. M., & Johnson, S. M. Multiple assessment of behavior modification with families: Effects of contingency contracting and order of treated problem. *Journal of Consulting and Clinical Psychology,* 1974, *42,* 594–606.

Eysenck, H. J. The effects of psychotherapy. *International Journal of Psychiatry,* 1965, *1,* 99–142.

Fiester, A. R., & Rudestam, K. E. A multivariate analysis of the early dropout process. *Journal of Consulting and Clinical Psychology,* 1975, *43,* 528–535.

Fo, W. S. O., & O'Donnell, C. R. The buddy system: Effect of community intervention on delinquent offenses. *Behavior Therapy,* 1975, *6,* 522–524.

Forehand, R., & Atkeson, B. M. Generality of treatment effects with parents as therapists: A review of assessment and implementation procedures. *Behavior Therapy,* 1977, *8,* 575–593.

Franks, C. M., & Wilson, G. T. (Eds.). *Annual review of behavior therapy: Theory & practice*. New York: Brunner/Mazel, 1976.

Freud, S. *New introductory lectures in psychoanalysis* (1932). New York: Norton, 1933.

Gordon, S. B. Multiple assessment of behavior modification with families. *Journal of Consulting and Clinical Psychology,* 1975, *43,* 917.

Götestam, K. G., Melin, L., & Ost, L. Behavioral techniques in the treatment of drug abuse: an evaluation review. *Addictive Behaviors,* 1976, *1,* 205–226.

Gottlieb, B. H. The development and application of a classification scheme of informal helping behaviors. *Canadian Journal of Behavioural Science,* 1978, *10,* 105–115.

Gottman, J. M., & Leiblum, S. R. *How to do psychotherapy and how to evaluate it: A manual for beginners.* New York: Holt, Rinehart & Winston, 1974.

Gulanick, N., Woodburn, L. T., & Rimm, D. C. Weight gain through self-control procedures. *Journal of Consulting and Clinical Psychology,* 1975, *43,* 536-539.

Gurman, A. S., & Kniskern, D. P. Research on marital and family therapy: Progress, perspective and prospect. In S. L. Garfield & A. E. Bergin (Eds.), *Handbook of psychotherapy and behavior change: An empirical analysis* (2nd ed.). New York: Wiley, 1978.

Hagen, R. L., Foreyt, J. P., & Durham, T. W. The dropout problem: Reducing attrition in obesity research. *Behavior Therapy,* 1976, *7,* 463-471.

Hall, S. M., & Hall, R. G. Outcome and methodological considerations in behavioral treatment of obesity. In J. P. Foreyt (Ed.), *Behavioral treatments of ob-obesity.* New York: Pergamon, 1977.

Hall, S. M., Hall, R. G., Borden, B. L., & Hanson, R. W. Follow-up strategies in the behavioral treatment of overweight. *Behaviour Research and Therapy,* 1975, *13,* 167-172.

Harris, M. B., & Hallbauer, E. S. Self-directed weight control through eating and exercise. *Behaviour Research and Therapy,* 1973, *11,* 523-529.

Hartmann, D. P., Roper, B. L., & Gelfand, D. M. An evaluation of alternative modes of child psychotherapy. In B. B. Lahey & A. E. Kazdin (Eds.), *Advances in clinical child psychology.* New York: Plenum, 1977, Vol. 1.

Hersen, M., & Barlow, D. H. *Single case experimental designs: Strategies for studying behavior change.* New York: Pergamon, 1976.

Hersen, M., & Bellack, A. S. (Eds.), *Behavioral assessment: A practical handbook.* New York: Pergamon, 1976.

Hersen, M., & Bellack, A. S. Assessment of social skills. In A. R. Ciminero, K. S. Calhoun, & H. E. Adams (Eds.), *Handbook of behavioral assessment.* New York: Wiley, 1977.

Intagliata, J. C. Increasing the interpersonal problem-solving skills of an alcoholic population. *Journal of Consulting and Clinical Psychology,* 1978, *46,* 489-498.

Jeffery, R. W., Wing, R. R., & Stunkard, A. J. Behavioral treatment of obesity: S. Martin, & J. P. Foreyt (Eds.), *Obesity: Behavioral approaches to dietary management.* New York: Brunner/Mazel, 1976.

Jeffery, R. W., Wing, R. R., & Stunkard, A. J. Behavioral treatment of obesity: The state of the art. *Behavior Therapy,* 1978, *9,* 189-199.

Johnson, S. M., & Bolstad, O. D. Methodological issues in naturalistic observation: Some problems and solutions for field research. In L. A. Hamerlynck, L. C. Handy, & E. J. Mash (Eds.), *Behavior change: Methodology, concepts and practice.* Champaign, Ill.: Research Press, 1973.

Johnson, S. M., & Christensen, A. Multiple criteria follow-up of behavior modification with families. *Journal of Abnormal Psychology,* 1975, *84,* 135-154.

Johnson, S. M., & Eyberg, S. Evaluating outcome data: A reply to Gordon. *Journal of Consulting and Clinical Psychology,* 1975, *43,* 917-919.

Jones, R. R. A review of: "Single-case experimental designs: Strategies for studying behavior change" by Michel Hersen and David H. Barlow. *Journal of Applied Behavior Analysis,* 1978, *11,* 309-313.

Kanfer, F. H. Assessment for behavior modification. *Journal of Personality Assessment,* 1972, *36,* 418-423.

Kazdin, A. E. Methodological and assessment considerations in evaluating reinforcement programs in applied settings. *Journal of Applied Behavior Analysis,* 1973, *6,* 517–531.

Kazdin, A. E. Covert modeling, imagery assessment, and assertive behavior. *Journal of Consulting and Clinical Psychology,* 1975, *43,* 716–724.

Kazdin, A. E. Effects of covert modeling, multiple models, and model reinforcement on assertive behavior. *Behavior Therapy,* 1976, *7,* 211–222.

Kazdin, A. E. Assessing the clinical or applied importance of behavior change through social validation. *Behavior Modification,* 1977, *1,* 427–452.

Kazdin, A. E., & Wilcoxon, L. A. Systematic desensitization and nonspecific treatment effects: A methodological evaluation. *Psychological Bulletin,* 1976, *83,* 729–758.

Kazdin, A. E., & Wilson, G. T. *Evaluation of behavior therapy: Issues, evidence, and research strategies.* Cambridge, Mass.: Ballinger, 1978.

Keeley, S. M., Shemberg, K. M., & Carbonell, J. Operant clinical intervention: Behavior management or beyond? Where are the data? *Behavior Therapy,* 1976, *7,* 292–305.

Kiesler, D. J. Some myths of psychotherapy research and the search for a paradigm. *Psychological Bulletin,* 1966, *65,* 110–136.

Kingsley, R. G., & Wilson, G. T. Behavior therapy for obesity: A comparative investigation of long-term efficacy. *Journal of Consulting and Clinical Psychology,* 1977, *45,* 288–298.

Knapp, T. J., & Wells, L. A. Behavior therapy for asthma: A review. *Behaviour Research and Therapy,* 1978, *16.* 103–115.

Lazarus, A. A. Group therapy of phobic disorders by systematic desensitization. *Journal of Abnormal Social Psychology,* 1961, *63,* 504–510.

Lazarus, A. A. The results of behaviour therapy in 126 cases of severe neurosis. *Behaviour Research and Therapy,* 1963, *1,* 69–79.

Lemere, F., & Voegtlin, W. An evaluation of the aversion treatment of alcoholism. *Quarterly Journal of Studies on Alcohol,* 1950, *11,* 199–204.

Lesser, E. Behavior therapy with a narcotics user: A case report: Ten-year follow-up. *Behaviour Research and Therapy,* 1976, *14,* 381.

Lovibond, S. H. *Conditioning and enuresis.* Oxford: Pergamon, 1964.

Lovibond, S. H., & Caddy, G. R. Discriminated aversive control in the moderation of alcoholics' drinking behavior. *Behavior Therapy,* 1970, *1,* 437–444.

Luborsky, L., Singer, B., & Luborsky, L. Comparative studies of psychotherapies: Is it true that everyone has won and all must have prizes? *Archives of General Psychiatry,* 1975, *32,* 995–1008.

MacFarlane, J. W., Allen, L., & Honzik, M. P. *A developmental study of the behavior problems of normal children between twenty-one months and fourteen years.* Berkeley and Los Angeles: University of California Press, 1954.

Mahoney, M. J., Kazdin, A. E., & Lesswing, N. J. Behavior modification: Delusion or deliverance? In C. M. Franks & G. T. Wilson (Eds.), *Annual Review of Behavior Therapy* (vol. 2), New York: Brunner/Mazel, 1974.

Marholin, D., II, Siegel, L. J., & Phillips, D. Treatment and transfer: A search for empirical procedures. In M. Hersen, R. M. Eisler, & P. M. Miller (Eds.), *Progress in behavior modification* (vol. 3), New York: Academic Press, 1976.

Marks, I. M., Rachman, S., & Hodgson, R. Treatment of chronic obsessive-compulsive neurosis by in-vivo exposure. *British Journal of Psychiatry,* 1975, *127,* 349–364.

Martin, B., & Twentyman, C. Teaching conflict resolution skills to parents and children. In E. M. Mash, L. C. Handy, & L. A. Hammerlynck (Eds.), *Behavior modification approaches to parenting.* New York: Brunner/Mazel, 1976.

Mash, E. J. Behavior modification and methodology: A developmental perspective. *Journal of Educational Thought,* 1976, *10,* 5–21.

Mash, E. J., & Dalby, J. T. Behavioral interventions for hyperactivity. In R. Trites (Ed.), *Hyperactivity: Etiology, measurement, and treatment.* Baltimore, Md.: University Park Press, 1979.

Mash, E. J., & Hedley, J. Observer effect as a function of prior history of social interaction. *Perceptual and Motor Skills,* 1975, *40,* 659–669.

Mash, E. J., & Terdal, L. G. (Eds.), *Behavior therapy assessment: Diagnosis, design and evaluation.* New York: Springer, 1976.

McNamara, J. R., & MacDonough, T. S. Some methodological considerations in the design and implementation of behavior therapy research. *Behavior Therapy,* 1972, *3,* 361–378.

Meltzoff, J., & Kornreich, M. *Research in psychotherapy.* New York: Atherton Press, 1970.

Morganstern, K. P. Behavioral interviewing: Initial stages of assessment. In M. Hersen & A. S. Bellack (Eds.), *Behavioral assessment: A practical handbook.* New York: Pergamon, 1976.

Nathan, P. E. Alcoholism. In H. Leitenberg (Ed.), *Handbook of behavior modification and behavior therapy.* Englewood Cliffs, N.J.: Prentice-Hall, 1976.

Patterson, G. R. Interventions for boys with conduct problems: Multiple settings, treatments, and criteria. *Journal of Consulting and Clinical Psychology,* 1974, *42,* 471–481.

Patterson, G. R. The aggressive child: Victim and architect of a coercive system. In E. J. Mash, L. A. Hamerlynck, & L. C. Handy (Eds.), *Behavior modification and families.* New York: Brunner/Mazel, 1976.

Patterson, G. R., Weiss, R. L., & Hops, H. Training of marital skills: Some problems and concepts. In H. Leitenberg (Ed.), *Handbook of behavior modification and behavior therapy.* Englewood Cliffs, N.J.: Prentice-Hall, 1976.

Paul, G. L. Behavior modification research: Design and tactics. In C. M. Franks (Ed.), *Behavior therapy: Appraisal and status.* New York: McGraw-Hill, 1969.

Plachetta, K. E. Encopresis: A case study utilizing contracting, scheduling and self-charting. *Journal of Behavior Therapy and Experimental Psychiatry,* 1976, *7,* 195–196.

Poser, E. G. *Behavior therapy in clinical practice: Decision making, procedure and outcome.* Springfield, Ill.: Charles C Thomas, 1977.

Rachman, S. *The effects of psychotherapy.* New York: Pergamon, 1971.

Ram Dass. *The only dance there is.* New York: Anchor Books, 1974.

Reid, J. B., & Patterson, G. R. Follow-up analyses of a behavioral treatment program for boys with conduct problems: A reply to Kent. *Journal of Consulting and Clinical Psychology,* 1976, *44,* 229–302.

Rinn, R. C., Vernon, J. C., & Wise, M. J. Training parents of behaviorally-disordered children in groups: A three years' program evaluation. *Behavior Therapy,* 1975, *6,* 378–387.

Risley, T. R. Behavior modification: An experimental-therapeutic endeavor. In L. A. Hamerlynck, P. O. Davidson, & L. E. Acker (Eds.), *Behavior modification and ideal mental health services.* Calgary, Alberta: University of Calgary, 1970.

Robins, L. N. Follow-up studies of behavior disorders in children. In H. C.

Quay & J. S. Werry (Eds.), *Psychopathological disorders of childhood.* New York: Wiley, 1972.

Rosen, G. M. Subjects' initial therapeutic expectancies and subjects' awareness of therapeutic goals in systematic desensitization: A review. *Behavior Therapy,* 1976, *7,* 14–27.

Sargent, H. D. Methodological problems of follow-up studies in psychotherapy research. *American Journal of Orthopsychiatry,* 1960, *30,* 495–506.

Schwartz, C., Myers, K., & Astrachan, M. The outcome study in psychiatric evaluative research: Issues and methods. *Archives of General Psychiatry,* 1973, *29,* 98–102.

Sherwood, G. G., & Gray, J. E. Two "classic" behaviour modification patients: A decade later. *Canadian Journal of Behavioural Science,* 1974, *6,* 420–427.

Silverman, L. H., Martin, A., Ungaro, R., & Mendelsohn, E. Effect of subliminal stimulation of symbiotic fantasies on behavior modification treatment of obesity. *Journal of Consulting and Clinical Psychology,* 1978, *46,* 432–441.

Sloane, R. B., Staples, F. R., Cristol, A. H., Yorkston, N. J., & Whipple, K. *Psychotherapy versus behavior therapy.* Cambridge, Mass.: Harvard University Press, 1975.

Smith, M. L., & Glass, G. V. Meta-analysis of psychotherapy outcome studies. *American Psychologist,* 1977, *32,* 752–760.

Stalonas, P. M., Johnson, W. G., & Christ, M. Behavior modification for obesity: The evaluation of exercise, contingency management and program adherence. *Journal of Consulting and Clinical Psychology,* 1978, *46,* 463–469.

Stokes, T. F., & Baer, D. M. An implicit technology of generalization. *Journal of Applied Behavior Analysis,* 1977, *10,* 349–367.

Stone, A. A., & Onqué, G. *Longitudinal studies of child personality.* Cambridge, Mass.: Harvard University Press, 1959.

Strupp, H. *Psychotherapy: Clinical, research and theoretical issues.* New York: Jason Aronson, 1973.

Stunkard, A. J., & Mahoney, M. J. Behavioral treatment of eating disorders. In H. Leitenberg (Ed.), *Handbook of behavior modification and behavior therapy.* Englewood Cliffs, N.J.: Prentice-Hall, 1976.

Subotnik, L. Spontaneous remission: Fact or artifact? *Psychological Bulletin,* 1972, *77,* 32–48.

Suedfeld, P. Using environmental restriction to initiate long-term behavior change. In R. B. Stuart (Ed.), *Behavioral self-management: Strategies, techniques and outcome.* New York: Brunner/Mazel, 1977.

Surratt, P. R., Ulrich, R. E., & Hawkins, R. P. An elementary student as a behavioral engineer. *Journal of Applied Behavior Analysis,* 1969, *2,* 85–92.

Sutherland, A., Amit, Z., Golden, M., & Roseberger, Z. Comparison of three behavioral techniques in modification of smoking behavior. *Journal of Consulting and Clinical Psychology,* 1975, *43,* 443–447.

Taylor, C. B., Farquhar, J. W., Nelson, E., & Agras, S. The effects of relaxation therapy upon high blood pressure. *Archives of General Psychiatry,* 1977, *34,* 339–345.

Taylor, P. D., & Turner, R. K. A clinical trial of continuous, intermittent, and overlearning "bell and pad" treatments for nocturnal enuresis. *Behaviour Research and Therapy,* 1975, *13,* 281–293.

Tharp, R. G., & Wetzel, R. J. *Behavior modification in the natural environment.* New York: Academic Press, 1969.

Tittler, B. I., Anchor, K. N., & Weitz, L. J. Measuring change in openness:

Behavioral assessment techniques and the problem of the examiner. *Journal of Counseling Psychology,* 1976, *5,* 473–478.

Tuso, M. A., & Geller, E. S. Behavior analysis applied to environmental/ecological problems: A review. *Journal of Applied Behavior Analysis,* 1976, *9,* 526.

Twentyman, C. T., & McFall, R. M. Behavioral training of social skills in shy males. *Journal of Consulting and Clinical Psychology,* 1975, *43,* 384–395.

Ullman, L. P., & Krasner, L. *Case studies in behavior modification.* New York: Holt, Rinehart & Winston, Inc., 1965.

Wahler, R. G. Some structural aspects of deviant child behavior. *Journal of Applied Behavior Analysis,* 1975, *8,* 27–42.

Wahler, R. G., House, A. E., & Stambaugh, E. E. *Ecological assessment of child problem behavior.* New York: Pergamon, 1976.

Walter, H. I., & Gilmore, S. K. Placebo versus social learning effects in parent training procedures designed to alter the behavior of aggressive boys. *Behavior Therapy,* 1973, *4,* 361–377.

Wickramasekera, I. Aversive behavior rehearsal for sexual exhibitionism. *Behavior Therapy,* 1976, *7,* 167–176.

Wolf, M. M. Social validity: The case for subjective measurement or how applied behavior analysis is finding its heart. *Journal of Applied Behavior Analysis,* 1978, *11,* 203–214.

Wolpe, J. *Psychotherapy by reciprocal inhibition.* Stanford, Calif.: Stanford University Press, 1958.

Zielinski, J. J. Maintenance of therapeutic gains: Issues, problems and implementation. *Professional Psychology,* 1978, *9,* 353–360.

PART III

The Interface of Person, Environment, and Time

C H A P T E R

5

ON THE MAINTENANCE AND GENERALIZATION OF CHANGE IN BEHAVIOR THERAPY AND BEHAVIOR MODIFICATION PROGRAMS:
A Commentary

PAUL L. WACHTEL

The terms "behavior therapy" and "behavior modification" are often used interchangeably. The chapters by Fishman and Lubetkin and by Wildman and Wildman illustrate well why one must be cautious in doing so. Ostensibly, the difference between the two chapters centers on whether the treatment is administered on an individual basis or in an institutional setting. But the more significant difference between them involves different philosophies of treatment and different conceptions of the nature of disordered behavior and the nature of behavior change. It turns out that the "behavior modification" approach reflected in Wildman and Wildman's chapter does tend frequently to be associated with institutional settings, and the "behavior therapy" approach discussed by Fishman and Lubetkin often is implemented on an individual basis. Such an association is not entirely accidental, as will perhaps become clearer as we proceed, but it is not an intrinsic difference. The spirit of the approach described by Wildman and Wildman can readily be seen in certain kinds of individual treatment programs, and the treatment philosophy exemplified by Fishman and Lubetkin can certainly be found in some programs within institutions.

The approaches discussed in the two chapters are not, of course, *entirely* different. The overlap is substantial enough, for example, that proponents of both coexist (sometimes uneasily) in the same professional associations and read and publish in the same journals. They are part of a broadly "behavioral" approach and are seen by the professional community and by the public at large as sharing a common domain in a larger mapping of the field of mental health or psychotherapeutics. I shall in fact have occasion to consider some of their similarities later in this chapter. I would like to begin this commentary chapter, however, by addressing some of the differences and considering the implications of those differences for our understanding of how therapeutic change is maintained (and indeed for understanding more clearly what we mean by maintenance or by change).

One is struck immediately by the difference in tone and style between the two chapters. Wildman and Wildman begin immediately with a definition and proceed to present in highly technical prose a summary of a large body of empirical research. Fishman and Lubetkin begin with an historical account of the evolution of a field and move to a description of the therapeutic process and the clinical and conceptual problems it presents. At the center of Fishman and Lubetkin's presentation are the *people* who have come for help. At the center of Wildman and Wildman's are the *behaviors* that were observed and influenced. One finishes Fishman and Lubetkin's chapter with the feeling one has come to *know* a number of people who have consulted them and the human predicaments they have experienced. No such sense of familiarity is gained with any of the individuals who passed through the programs described by Wildman and Wildman. These authors choose instead to present an abstract and impersonal account. They are scientists, not storytellers. They are concerned with delineating casual efficacy, not with depicting personal experience.

Along with this difference in style appears a second difference, which I think is not entirely unrelated: the individuals described by Fishman and Lubetkin *have come to them* for help. And the process of assessment described by those authors is one in which the patients or clients are helped to describe and articulate what *they* (the clients) want to see changed. The therapist may suggest working on particular target behaviors as a bit of technical advice (e.g., regarding where change is more likely to be achieveable to begin with, or which changes logically follow from which), but the basic aims or goals of the work are the client's. Moreover, every effort is made to enlist the client as an active and cooperating coparticipant, whose stake in the outcome is, after all, ultimately greater than the therapist's.

In contrast, for many of the programs described by Wildman and Wildman the subjects were not volunteers. They did not ask for the assistance of the therapeutic agents. Moreover, in many instances they also had no say as to what the target behaviors would be, what in their repertoire would be changed.

The presumption of those running these programs, one assumes, was that the program was in the best interests of those who were put through it. But in many instances the concern about the behavior was felt, or at least initially expressed, by *others*. One must at least wonder whether the convenience of those responsible for initiating the program was not as salient a factor as the needs of its subjects in determining both whether to implement it and what sort of target behaviors to address. Or in those instances where such a way of putting it seems too harsh, one can ask whether the therapist's view as to what is good, what one should strive for, act like, and value, is not being substituted for the person's own sense of what he wants and needs.

This of course raises enormously complex and important ethical and epistemological questions. I am tempted to address these because I am at once sympathetic to the issues raised by critics of these programs and concerned that they have not sufficiently addressed the benefits such programs can potentially provide or the realistic alternatives presently faced by those who might be "saved" from them. Very real abuses of power have occurred in such programs, but the insensitivity to these issues on the part of many behavior modifiers seems to have provoked excessive and reactive judgments on the part of some critics, such that a proper dialectical evaluation of the opposing goods and harms has been hampered. In particular, both proponents and critics of these programs have tended to accept uncritically the notion that reinforcements "control" behavior, and this has confused discussion of the ethical issues (see Wachtel, 1977a, chap. 10 and 12). A full discussion of these issues, however, is beyond the scope of the present commentary, and the reader is encouraged to consult the growing literature on this topic (e.g., Gaylin, 1974; Holland, 1976; London, 1977; Wexler, 1973).

I do wish, however, to address one aspect of this matter which does seem germane to our present focus. That is that the degree to which the patient, client, or subject sees the changes in his behavior as in his own interest and the degree to which he perceives himself as having desired and chosen those changes are likely to be critical determinants of how lasting the change will be. Fishman and Lubetkin seem quite sensitive to this issue, and concern with enlisting the client's active participation and with gearing their therapeutic program to the client's own aims. Wildman and Wildman, writing from a different tradition, seem much less attentive to it. In their summary list of 16 rules for promoting generalization, only number 12 even vaguely resembles what we are discussing here. They do cite Liberman, McCann, and Wallace's (1976) suggestion that patients be involved in setting goals and choosing among alternative treatment methods, but they seem to distinguish it from the nine other suggestions by those authors which parallel their own.

In some respects the entire issue of generalizability is different depending on whether the person has come to you about something he himself finds troubling or is having contingencies applied to him because someone else wants to see certain behaviors changed. In the latter instance, it is hardly surprising that if you are trying to influence, by extrinsic rewards, behavior the person has not himself expressed concern about, you must apply those rewards wherever you want the particular behavior, or at least you must leave the person uncertain as to whether the contingency is in effect or not. When children in a classroom are expected to behave appropriately according to *someone else's* standards, and are told there will be consequences for doing so or not doing so only at certain times, why would *anyone* expect them to behave "appropriately" at the times they have been told do not "count." Of course, if you want to maintain the behavior in this way, you must maintain either the contingencies or the *appearance* of the contingencies (for, as seems to be often overlooked, it is never contingencies per se that influence behavior, but contingencies as perceived).

More interesting, it seems to me, from the point of view of maintenance of therapeutic change is the question of how to assure that behavior which is valued by the person behaving can occur in those contexts in which the person would like them to occur. Where one is addressing behavior which the person does not at first acknowledge as in his interest or as what he wants to do, then one of your tasks is to create circumstances which enable that change in self-attribution to occur. (Here again, issues of paternalism, of "brainwashing," and so forth need to be addressed as well, but will not be in this presentation.) The implicit claim of many behavior modification programs does seem to be that the target individuals' own interests are being served, that even where initially external social values are being imposed, it will eventually be more rewarding to the person to endorse those values and act in ways that the program is trying to promote. Where this is not at all the case (where, say, the concern is simply with getting the person to be more cooperative with those in power, to stop doing what is disruptive not because you will ultimately find a path to a better life that way, but because such behavior is simply not allowed), then it is unlikely that any behavior modification program can yield results which endure beyond the point where the contingencies continue to be—or to appear to be—applied.

Such instances are, or should be, the trivial limiting case. Yet because issues of what people really *want,* or of in whose *interest* certain changes are understood to be implemented, are not sufficiently addressed by most writers on behavior modification, these trivial cases can be confused with the more interesting and important case in which maintenance and generalization of change means more than just keeping the same set of contingencies in classroom A and classroom B. Surely we are concerned with issues of fading out reinforcements, for example, for reasons other than just making coercion less expensive. We hope to fade them out because we hope that they will become *unnecessary,* that the person will, after a while, *want* to study or *want* to behave in a friendly, rather than an aggressive or withdrawn way. Regardless of where one stands metaphysically—and this *is* a metaphysical question, regardless of which side you are on—on the issue of whether behavior can ever, in an ultimate way, be described as the result of reinforcement contingencies, one must also address (in whatever terms one likes) the seemingly simple-minded or naive distinctions of the previous sentence.

Resolution of the apparent paradox of the A-B-A design is related to these considerations. The A-B-A design is intended to show that whatever change occurred did so for the reasons the behavior modifier thought. If the changed contingencies where responsible for the new behavior, then reinstating the old contingencies should reverse the change, and reinstituting the new ones should again result in the new pattern of behavior. The difficulty with this approach, of course, is that it seems to have built into it the assumption of nondurability of change. That is, if reversing the contingencies is expected to reverse the behavior change, then the change is dependent on the maintenance of the contingency. The person has not changed; he has just accommodated temporarily to new circumstances, or as Wildman and Wildman put it in discussing a study attempting to reduce disruptive behaviors, "One might conclude . . . that the behavior modification procedure had not made the students well behaved children in the sense of imparting to them an enduring personality trait."

If one takes a longer time perspective, however, and considers as well that specific changes in behavior can bring about changes in opportunities and in how others react to one, and can lead to a reassessment of what one wants or enjoys, then one might predict that *after a while* the change would become independent of the original contingencies. And such a prediction could be perfectly consistent with an understanding that at least initially the change in contingencies was a critical factor in bringing the change about.

A good example is a report by Allen, Hart, Buell, Harris, and Wolf

(1964) of a change in the play behavior of a nursery school girl. The girl had intended to spend most of her time in the company of the teachers and had largely avoided play with peers when the teacher was not participating. It was found that the contingencies in operation in the classroom operated so as to provide her with more teacher contact ("comforting"?) when she was withdrawn from the other children. On those occasions when she did play, she apparently did not seem as "needy" and so teacher contact was not provided. She was thus, in a sense, rewarded (assuming teacher contact to be an important reward for her at that point) for being apart from children and had the reward withdrawn when she did interact. When the contingencies were reversed, the behavior changed dramatically. And in accord with the A-B-A design, when the old contingencies were reinstituted, her behavior reverted to the old pattern.

What is most interesting in the present context is that after the therapeutic contingencies had again been employed for a while (teacher would join the group of children she was playing with, although not selectively responding just to her, since that would just lure her away from the group), the teacher attention in response to her peer play was gradually faded out, *and she continued to show high levels of peer play.* It seems likely that this procedure, by encouraging her to spend more time playing with other children, enabled her to feel more comfortable with them, and that after a while she began to experience these interactions as more rewarding. The relative value to her then of the rewards associated with teacher contact and those associated with peer contact very likely shifted, so that pursuing whatever would bring teacher contact no longer was her primary aim.[1]

In instances such as this, one can still understand behavior as responsive to[2] reinforcement contingencies, but a change in the nature of the contingencies that are relevant can be seen as itself one of the therapeutically meaningful variables. Bandura's (1969) discussion of the use of concrete reinforcers with schizophrenics, and the shift to social reinforcers later in the treatment, is also relevant in this context. One of the *problems* with schizophrenics, in the view of many, is the degree to which their behavior is guided by concrete rather than social reinforcers. If the use of the former is designed as a way of ultimately enhancing the relevance of the latter, then *that* change—rather than a change in the probability of occurrence of any particular behavior—may be the most therapeutically relevant change of all.

Discussion of many of these issues may be obscured by too sharp a distinction between internal and external determinants of behavior (Wachtel, 1978) or between attributes of the person and features of the environment. Independent variable/dependent variable designs tend to shape our perceptions of casuality in ways that obscure the degree to which the environment can itself be viewed as a function of our personalities, as well as the reverse (cf. Bandura, 1978; Wachtel, 1973, 1977b).

On the one hand, this means that concern about whether the "person" has really changed, rather than his behavior in a particular environment, may put the matter too starkly. Not just behavior modifiers, but also family therapists and even some interpersonally oriented psychodynamic theorists have recognized the degree to which our behavior must be described contextually. The idea of fixed traits, manifesting themselves regardless of context, is not really a very common one these days, even among the trait theorists (see Chapter 6).

Nonetheless, it remains a legitimate concern of the therapeutic agent to try to assure that the changes brought about will be manifested in an appropriately broad range of contexts. I say "appropriately" broad because for different purposes a greater or lesser degree of generalization is required. One might hope that the reduction in disruptive behavior manifested by an aggressive and hard-to-control child in the classroom would generalize not just to other classrooms but to his behavior, say, in supermarkets (where he would no longer leave a trail of tumbled cans in the aisles) or in the playground (where the same might hold for playmates instead of cans). If, however, the aim was to increase time spent quietly reading or doing arithmetic problems, one might be less concerned about the supermarket or playground as relevant contexts. (Indeed, one would worry if the behavior "generalized" to them.)

From the framework of the kind of programs discussed by Wildman and Wildman, the first kind of "generalization" would seem unlikely, perhaps even far-fetched. The "contingencies" in the supermarket would seem, by and large, to be too different from those of the classroom even to expect such a generalization. Some exclusively operant behavior modification programs may in fact achieve such broadly generalizable results (the Allen et al., 1964, study noted earlier may well be an example, although for reasons that probably require an extension of the simplest kind of operant framework). In general, operant programs have more narrowly focused goals, not just in target behavior but in context, and they tend to be most effective when their aims are limited. Indeed, it is precisely with regard to narrow and modest (although often important) changes that such programs can show a superiority over other kinds of behavior change efforts.

The approach described by Fishman and Lubetkin, in contrast, seems far better suited for achieving the broader sort of change. Changing contingencies in a classroom is unlikely to affect supermarket behavior, but a full behavioral analysis might well reveal some underlying variables (say, involving a clear sense of how to be assertive without being aggressive, or related to some aspect of the child's interactions with his mother) that are relevant to the child's behavior in both settings. Like the family therapist or the psychodynamic therapist, the behavior therapist operating in the way Fishman and Lubetkin describe might well find it reasonable to attempt some intervention, not immediately and obviously related to the specific contingencies in either setting, which would be expected to have an impact on behavior in both contexts. They would, however, probably also be more willing to consider the possibility that such a "general" intervention would *not* be appropriate. If their behavioral analysis pointed to a focus on the specific contingencies in one or both settings, that too would be consistent with their frame of reference.

Several interesting parallels between the methods described by Fishman and Lubetkin and those of therapists from other orientations are worth noting. For example, it would be interesting to compare their emphasis on informing the client that he should expect some slippage and backsliding in the therapy with the method used by some family therapists of actually *prescribing* relapses (see Haley, 1977).[3] An interesting parallel with Haley's work is also evident in Fishman and Lubetkin's description of their "consolidation" period. Haley often makes a point of feigning puzzlement and lack of understanding of why anything has changed, with the aim of creating circumstances in which the clients see the change as initiated by themselves, rather than by the therapist. An explicit effort to assure that the patient takes the change as his own accomplishment is seen as necessary by both.[4] Fishman and Lubetkin's point that "feeling of accomplishment can never catch up to the client's behavioral accomplishments if the demands to do more are ever-present" has a counterpart in the concern fo some psychodynamic therapists regarding the wording of interpretations in a way that avoids seeming demanding and accusatory and that facilitates the patient's sense that he can cope with what is being presented (Wachtel, in press).

From the very beginning the approach described by Fishman and Lubetkin attempts to have change occur not just within the session but in the client's life circumstances. Generalization is, in this sense, not something that one tries to bring about after having first achieved change in the context of the sessions. Change *in the person's natural setting* is part of the strategy from the beginning; if change occurs at all, it occurs there.[5] This would seem to be in sharp contrast to the classical psychoanalytic approach in which there is no assigning of "homework" to do between sessions and often little direct examination of just how the person is applying the work of the sessions in his daily life. It is, however, quite consistent with those versions of psychodynamic psychotherapy which are based on a conception of cyclical processes in which conflicts, motives, and fantasies are not strictly "internal" events, inhabiting a separate and largely autonomous "inner world," but are viewed as influenced by, as well as influencing, the manifest events of the person's life (Wachtel, 1977a). From this latter perspective, one might suggest that the most useful way to understand how therapeutic change is maintained and generalized would be to consider how the person learns both to choose environments congenial to the new behavior and to program whatever environment he enters to react to him in a way that maintains and enhances the desired changes. The environment, in this view, is not simply an independent variable. It is largely our own creation, and skill in creating facilitative environments may be the most important thing we learn in therapy, although it is not often addressed as such (see Chapters 7 and 8).

Wildman and Wildman tend to treat environmental variables rather exclusively from an independent variable perspective, as do most of those who conduct the therapeutic experiments they describe. Unfortunately, this way of viewing things is not always inaccurate for the situations described (although I think it is almost always inadequate for understanding how to be maximally facilitative to the people one hopes to serve). It is not inaccurate because many of these experiments create power relationships in which the ability of the person to choose and influence his environment is in fact severely limited. Such truncating environments are unfortunately not uncommon in this world, and although Wildman and Wildman are describing a relatively benign variety of them, they nonetheless do place limits on human possibilities and on our understanding of the possibilities for expanding and enhancing change processes (Wachtel, 1972, 1973).

Fishman and Lubetkin seem much more aware of the interactional or transactional processes which are at the heart of the most extensive therapeutic change (although one wonders about their—to my mind—odd use of the term "physical" environment on several occasions). Their concern to involve the client's family in the change process, and to alert the family members as to how their own actions might help or impede the client's maintaining the desired changes, seems very useful. I think that greater consideration of the *ambivalence* of family members regarding the apparently desired changes, and of the family members' *stake* in the old way of interacting (however much it is also a source of distress), might enhance their effectiveness, but such considerations do not seem to be alien to the spirit of their approach. (I do have qualms, however, about their suggestion that family members be instructed to trick the agoraphobic patient into going out on her own. Such "benevolent sabotage," as they put it, may be justified if there is no other way of achieving the desired therapeutic gain; but if alternatives are available, its use raises serious ethical questions, and may also ultimately work against the spirit of trust that is so important for maximal therapeutic effectiveness.)

A full examination of the relation between the kind of behavioral approach presented by Fishman and Lubetkin and the approaches of interpersonally oriented psychodynamic theorists would be interesting to pursue. Fishman and Lubetkin's brand of behavior therapy seems particularly close to the border between behavioral and traditional approaches, and indeed illustrates how ambiguous that border is. Concepts of resistance and ambivalence seem to have gained ready entry to a conceptual DMZ, and even notions of people wanting things they are not aware of wanting seem to have gotten by the border guards in a way that would have been unthinkable some years back. I still think there are major and important benefits that would derive from a more explicit and extended effort to incorporate psychodynamic perspectives into their work (as I find that there are valuable aspects of what they suggest that would enhance my own efforts to incorporate behavioral methods). But I must forgo at this point a more complete discussion of the relation between approaches and of what the psychodynamic perspective of the relation between approaches and of what the psychodynamic perspective can add (and/or has *already* added) to the approach they describe (the interested reader is referred to the detailed discussion of these issues in Wachtel, 1977a). Instead I will simply end by thanking the editors for inviting me to read and comment on these two interesting chapters.

NOTES

1. Obviously, other explanations of this change are possible as well. Even if one views the A-B-A design as having shown the contingency change to have been an active behavior-change agent, one need not view the results from the standard operant conditioning perspective. (One could, for example, speculate that the series of contingency changes led her to view the teachers as manipulative, fickle, or unreliable, and that she therefore turned away from them in disgust or disappointment and turned to the children instead. Or conversely, that seeing how much effort they were exerting to help her, her self-esteem was raised and she could more confidently venture to play with other children.) Procedures can be effective for reasons other than those supposed by those who employ them. I have heard some critics claim that such procedures simply suppress the child's natural inclinations and force her to comply outwardly while learning a schizoid-like style that hides her true feelings. Such criticisms may be warranted on some occasions but seem to me excessive in the present instance. The disappearance of the child's hypochondriacal complaints and the apparent increase in zest and enthusiasm seem to me to argue against such an understanding here.

2. It is not by accident that I use this term rather than "controlled by." See Wachtel, 1977a, chaps. 10 and 12.

3. My own therapist, a rather idiosyncratic psychoanalyst, told me at one point that he thought I would make progress in certain areas only *after* the therapy was

completed, and over a period of years. Perhaps not surprisingly, this is how it happened.

4. Wildman and Wildman seem to me, in this regard, to dismiss far too readily the questions about clients' attribution of change raised by Levine and Fasnacht (1974), Davison, Tsujimoto, and Glaros (1973), and others. The Feingold and Mahoney (1975) study they cite has many limitations and hardly puts the issue to rest.

5. Strictly speaking, only *some* of the procedures employed by behavior therapists fit this description. Systematic desensitization, for example, is primarily an office procedure, and accordingly there has been a good deal of concern with the question of how readily the gains in imaginal desensitization generalize to the actual feared situations—as well as an increasing tendency to stress in vivo desensitization from the very beginning of treatment.

REFERENCES

Allen, K. E., Hart, B., Buell, J., Harris, F., & Wolf, M. Effects of social reinforcement on isolate behavior of a nursery school child. *Child Development,* 1964, *35,* 511–518.

Bandura, A. *Principles of behavior modification.* New York: Holt, Rinehart & Winston, 1969.

Bandura, A. The self system in reciprocal determinism. *American Psychologist,* 1978, *33,* 344–358.

Davison, G. C., Tsujimoto, R., & Glaros, A. Attribution and the maintenance of behavior change in falling asleep. *Journal of Abnormal Psychology,* 1973, *82,* 124–133.

Feingold, B., & Mahoney, M. Reinforcement effects on intrinsic interest: Undermining the over justification hypothesis. *Behavior Therapy,* 1975, *6,* 367–377.

Gaylin, W. On the borders of persuasion: A psychoanalyst looks at coercion. *Psychiatry,* 1974, *37,* 1–9.

Haley, J. *Problem solving therapy.* San Francisco: Jossey-Bass, 1977.

Holland, J. Ethical considerations in behavior modification. *Journal of Humanistic Psychology,* 1976, *16,* 71–78.

Levine, F. M., & Fasnacht, G. Token rewards may lead to token learning. *American Psychologist,* 1974, *29,* 816–820.

Liberman, R., McCann, J., & Wallace, C. Generalization of behavior therapy with psychotics. *British Journal of Psychiatry,* 1976, *129,* 490–496.

London, P. *Behavior control* (rev. ed.). New York: New American Library, 1977.

Wachtel, P. L. Cognitive style and style of adaptation. *Perceptual and Motor Skills,* 1972, *35,* 779–785.

Wachtel, P. L. Psychodynamics, behavior therapy, and the implacable experimenter: An inquiry into the consistency of personality. *Journal of Abnormal Psychology,* 1973, *82,* 324–334.

Wachtel, P. L. *Psychoanalysis and behavior therapy.* New York: Basic Books, 1977.(a)

Wachtel, P. L. Interaction cycles, unconscious processes, and the person–situation issue. In D. Magnusson & N. Endler (Eds.), *Personality at the crossroads: Toward an interaction psychology.* Washington, D.C.: Hemisphere Publications, 1977.(b)

Wachtel, P. L. Internal and external determinants of behavior in psychodynamic theories. In L. Pervin & M. Lewis (Eds.). *Perspectives in interactional psychology.* New York: Plenum, 1978.

Wachtel, P. L. What should we say to our patients? On the wording of therapists' comments. *Psychotherapy: Theory, Research and Practice,* in press.

Wexler, D. B. Token and taboo: Behavior modification, token economics and the law. *California Law Review,* 1973, *61,* 81–109.

C H A P T E R

THE STRUCTURED LEARNING ANALYSIS
OF THERAPEUTIC CHANGE
AND MAINTENANCE*

RAYMOND B. CATTELL

The theme put forward in the present chapter is one which rests on two major developments over the last generation which are called *structured measurement* and *structured learning theory*.

Psychological testing developed in two very different ways, as unmixable to any clear thinker as oil and water. In the first, or "intuitive" approach, a psychologist would conceive a concept, perhaps suggested by a word in the dictionary or some discussion, and directly make up a test or questionnaire to assess his or her conception of it. In the second, or "structural" approach, he or she would find by correlational and sophisticated factor-analytic methods (perhaps lasting some years) the structure in personality itself, and then set out to build batteries validated against the dis-

*Editor's Note: For those unfamiliar with the terminology employed by Cattell and his associates, a glossary is provided at the end of this chapter. Words or phrases followed by an asterisk (*) can be found in the glossary.

covered factors. These two approaches can be illustrated in the intelligence field by the Binet, WISC, WAIS, etc., for the first, and Spearman's test of "g" and modern Culture Fair Intelligence Tests (IPAT, 1959, 1973) for the second. In personality they are illustrated in the first case by numerous questionnaires which are perhaps best left nameless, and in the structured, factored domain by those of Guilford, Scheier, Krug, Nesselroade, the 16 PF, and the recent Cattell and Schuerger O–A (Objective–Analytic) Battery.

Through such scales and batteries as the latter, one can measure such traits* as ego strength, anxiety, verbal ability, superego strength, tension on a particular drive (erg),* level of depression, and so on. The advantage of factor-structured measures is that the concepts are operationally "clean" and correspond to *source traits,** about the life course, inheritance, learning origins, and general criterion associations of which psychological knowledge is centered and constantly increasing. By contrast, the various ad hoc scales and intelligence tests, however popular, are "mixed" measures about which a truly reliable understanding or calculation is not possible.

The skilled use of *structured* measures in clinical work is discussed in *Personality Theory in Action* (Cattell & Schuerger, 1978) and in the handbooks of Cattell, Eber, and Tatsuoka (1970), Karson and O'Dell (1976), and others; and in the questionnaire domain, by the present writer's *Personality and Mood by Questionnaire* (Cattell, 1973a). The use of structured methods requires in the clinician only an elementary statistical background in order to understand: reliability and validity concepts (particularly the difference of concept and concrete validities); standardization with age correction; and the combining of weights on the source traits in predictions, as explained in the next section. At the same time it *does* demand a real understanding of the psychological meaning of source traits.

STRUCTURED LEARNING THEORY

Base in the Behavioral Equation

To imagine that the application of reflexology to therapy in what is too broadly called "behavior therapy" will solve most therapeutic problems is like claiming the 19th-century use of carbolic acid to be the big advance in modern surgery. In both there are elements of true utility, but the genuine advances depend on much more complex concepts. In expounding the complexities of structured learning theory here (alas, in all-too-condensed a space) there is no intention to denigrate the fine research in the Watson–

Skinner branch of psychology, but rather to be clear that it still is not enough, and that the learning theory building needs the second story—that of structured learning theory (cf., also Karoly's critique of insufficiencies in S–R concepts, in Chapter 7).

Before we even look at the differences of theory it is obvious that in practice alone there is a considerable difference between, on the one hand, extinguishing an aversion to cats or creating by emetic drugs an aversion to whiskey or reducing an exhibitionist compulsion, and on the other, *changing personality* as a structure, for example, in bringing about some basic recovery in a schizophrenic or a dangerous criminal. Many of the former instances included in the statistics of success of behavior therapy are little more than modification of whims, admittedly leaving the personality (structure) in which they developed unchanged. We are blandly told that there is no evidence of the person's developing "substitute" or "dynamically equivalent" symptoms, as in the case of a child conditioned out of enuresis who may develop the habit of nail biting. These statements have no more logical worth than a man's assurance that because he cannot find his wife in the next room, she must have vanished from the face of the earth. In short, no experimenter has monitored the infinity of an individual's behavior; and the psychologist working on the principles of the dynamic calculus is right in questioning whether the removal of a narrow symptom by reflexological learning principles is the last one will hear of it.

Four major principles, all of importance for practice, distinguish structured learning theory from reflexological conceptions: (1) that the *existing source traits* of the individual enter substantially into any learning or relearning, over and above coexcitation (classical conditioning) or instrumental learning components; (2) that an adequate learning theory must account not only for specific reflex learnings, but for the growth of the massive *unitary source traits* which the personality researcher measures every day, and finds theoretically and practically sound in predicting behavior; (3) that among the existing traits which affect learning are, particularly, the dynamic traits* (*ergs and sentiments);* therefore, discussing "reinforcement" *in the abstract,* without regard to the structural position of the ergic tension reductions involved, ignores important information (as does, say, a black-and-white photo of a colored scene); and (4) that a person's learning cannot be adequately measured by change in a specific piece of behavior, but only by changes in the *trait terms* and in the *behavioral indices* (weights) of the "behavioral specification equation."*

All four of these points can be most neatly expressed for the psychologist by use of the behavioral specification equation, which for simplicity we will reduce, as follows, to the case of just three source traits, T_1, T_2, and T_3:

$$a_{ijk} = b_{jk1}T_{1i} + b_{jk2}T_{2i} + b_{jk3}T_{3i} \qquad (1)$$

If the reader will take the subscripts in stride he will see a simple statement that any bit of behavior normally derives from more than one trait and dynamic purpose. The bs (behavioral indices) are weights (found from correlations with the behavior a_{jk}), saying how much each of the traits enters into (i.e., is important in defining) the given behavior. The bs have subscripts 1, 2, and 3 to show that they are of different sizes, peculiar to T_1, T_2, and T_3. They also have in common the subscript jk to show that the involvement of the trait is peculiar also the particular behavior j and situation k. Thus, a_{ijk} is individual i's score, a, in the performance, response, or symptom j, to situation k. Both a and the T scores are in standard scores for any individual, i, and the bs will range from $+1.0$ to -1.0.

For the various personality traits in the 16 PF and the O–A Battery these behavioral index sizes have been found for school achievement, for certain job performances, and (implicitly in the mean profiles of various clinical groups; Tatsuoka & Cattell, 1970) for the appearance of some clinical syndromes. These predictive regression weights (as the statistician will call them) have long been worked out for intelligence on a great variety of school and other performances. But psychology still awaits more clinical research to extend the predictions from dynamic and temperament trait behavioral indices to more varied criterion prognoses. In particular we need predictive indices for ego strength,* thereby facilitating prognosis for various disorders and various kinds of therapy. Evidence is available from the 16 PF on changes in ego strength after therapy (Cattell & Rickels, 1968) and on prognosis for delinquency based on ego strength (Cartwright, Tomson, & Schwartz, 1975; Pierson, Barton, & Hey, 1964), while more extensive data is about to be published. Thus the clinician with an ordinary basic training in psychometrics will find the central behavioral equation increasingly useful in transcending rough guesses through the use of research-based (more accurate) estimates. As one becomes more sophisticated regarding the nature and properties of the primary source traits, he or she will also find the model of weighted outcomes (aided by knowledge of the usual life courses of the factors) particularly helpful in clarifying clinical formulations on individual cases.

Expression in Two Profiles ("Vectors") of Change

The equation explaining a behavioral act will also explain the amount of learning in an act or performance. However, in this case the effects of two structured learning principles, coexcitation and means–end learning (CE and ME for short), need to be included. Skinner's operant conditioning may be taken as identical with ME; but as the theory now stands, classical conditioning is hypothesized to be a mixture of CE and ME action. Adherence to the term "means–end" (ME) rather than "operant conditioning" is more than breath saving: it holds the important principle in mind that learning new behavior occurs as a means to the end of achieving a particular ergic goal. The factoring of the dynamic traits—a particular class of Ts above—shows clearly that humans possess distinct ergic (rhymes with allergic) tensions corresponding to the mammalian ergs of sex, fear, gregariousness, hunger, parental-protector behavior, and so on. These we represent by Es. For the research evidence on ergs, see Cattell and Child (1975).

If the change in a_{ijk} wrought by one learning experience (e.g., one run in a rat maze) is represented by $d.a_{ijk}$ then (if for simplicity we leave coexcitation effects aside and also keep to only three ergs as we did the three personality ability traits) the amount of learning may be described as:

$$d.a_{ijk} = b_{jk1}T_{1i} + b_{jk2}T_{2i} + b_{jk3}T_{3i} + b_{jke1}E_{1i} + b_{jke2}E_{2i} + b_{jke3}\bar{E}_{3i}$$
$$(2)$$

where $\bar{E}$ is the *reduction* in ergic tension of E, which is the reward (reinforcement of a_{jk}) occurring to the given erg at the time. That reinforcement acts in this way is witnessed by innumerable experiments. That T_1, T_2, etc., join in the prediction of learning is shown by the work of Cattell and Butcher (1969), Cattell and Sealy (Note 1), Barton, Dielman, and Cattell (1972), and many others. As regards a year's gain in school performance, the contribution from the Ts is roughly three times greater than that from the reinforcement (the E terms).

Now, as mentioned in contrasting classical reflexological learning theory and structured learning theory, the former is content to speak and calculate in terms of improvement of *a reflex response* or some highly specific learning, whereas the newer theory recognizes that the teacher and the far-sighted clinician should be interested in changes in the total personality (i.e., in the measured, functionally unitary ability, personality, and dynamic traits). We need not digress here into the three principles (Cattell & Dreger, 1977) accounting for the common learning rates which connect several diverse $d.a_{jk}$s (as in equation 2 above) into growth in a single factorial trait, but we shall direct our attention henceforth to the unitary source traits themselves, such as C or ego strength, Q_3 or self-sentiment, and F or surgency.

It is obvious that the man in the street, the dramatist, and the clinician interested in long-term therapy see personality change in terms of change in such traits. ("John is more sociable and talkative [surgent] than before he traveled abroad." "King Lear is losing his self-control." "Therapy has reduced both anxiety and depression in Alice.") It is therefore amazing that among the hundreds of thousands of research articles available today it is hard to find half a dozen that give evidence of life (or therapeutic) influences *producing statistically significant changes in factorially identified major source traits.*

In 1965 the present writer measured 1000 18-year-olds leaving school in New Zealand on the 16 factors of the 16 PF. He returned 4 years later to retest them on the same. What happened to them in between as regards job success, marriage, bereavements, illnesses, etc., was recorded; and a number of significant general personality factor changes were found. For example, those who married shifted towards desurgency ($F-$) compared to those who did not. Ego strength (C) built up in those who joined some moral guidance (e.g., church) group. And dominance, E, increased in those who received job promotion. Parenthetically, the considerable labor in rerecruiting most of 1000 subjects, and the fact that PhD candidates all over the country prefer a research cut to 6 months, may explain why psychology lacks other researches of this kind. As we shall see, however, a few clinical studies have used recognizable factor source traits for retests over time.

To this point in the argument, therefore, we are saying that structured learning theory differs from reflexological theory in basing its observations no longer on conditioned reflexes but on changes in the *total personality profile,* based on the meaningful measures of unitary traits provided by 50 years of research on personality structure. But next it adds a more radical development. If a group of individuals are trained in, say, public speaking, and a factoring of their performance (along with, say, 20 other performances, and some personality measures) is compared with that of an untrained control group, we are likely to find that they have altered not only on some profile *factors* (e.g., $H-$, shyness), but also on the *behavioral index weights* for the traits on that performance. The postlearning behavioral equation will compare with the prelearning behavioral equation in (1) above as shown by:

$$a'_{ijk} = b'_{jk1}T'_{1i} + b'_{jk2}T'_{2i} + b'_{jk3}T'_{3i} \tag{3}$$

where the primes indicate new values. In snort, the learning needs to be recognized as expressing itself not only in a change in the total T profile, but also in a change in the way the individual combines his ability and personality resources in effecting the performance (a change of "style"). In terms of the model, we say that the reflexologist loses a good deal of information when he records learning merely as change in a_{jk}, and that human growth can be fully contained only in the vector description of learning, as a change in the vector (profile of scores), T_{1i}, T_{2i}, etc., and the vector b_{hj1}, b_{hj2}, etc., which defines the *environmental interaction.*

In ordinary terms we are saying that *learning is a multidimensional change in the individual in response to a multidimensional learning situation, the changing relations to which are expressed in a multidimensional statement of relationships.* That such a greater complexity of conception is necessary for human learning becomes evident from the behavioral equation. But in principle it is also true that even the lowly rat pushed into a Skinner box is learning more than the experimenter intended. The laws predicting the learning which the experimenter measures are unlikely to reach a comprehensive and accurate nature until the complete context of learning changes is taken into account in the analysis.

To recapitulate before proceeding, structured learning theory requires going beyond current learning theory in the following respects:

1. It recognizes that the kind of learning important to the clinician is likely to invoke the total personality and can only be encompassed by (a) measures on primary *source traits spanning the whole personality* and (b) recognition of the *changing behavioral indices* which show how a person alters his involvements of traits in various specific kinds of behavior.

2. It recognizes that not only classical and instrumental (or CE and ME) influences, but also the person's total existing personality–ability profile, just mentioned, must enter into any equation to estimate and explain learning.

3. It points out that in the second part of the equation, "reinforcement" is not a sufficient principle. Means–ends (ME) learning needs to be located and recorded in terms of the rewards (tension reductions) for particular ergs (and other dynamic structures, notably the sentiments and the ego) both because these determine present learning and because subsequent events (e.g., retrieval) are likely to depend on the character of the ergic (emotional) satisfactions in the learning.

MEASURING THERAPEUTIC CHANGE BY RATINGS OR BY MEASURED SOURCE TRAIT PROFILES?

The logical, but little-practiced design to discover sources of therapeutic change first requires reliably measuring such change as a dependent variable, and second, comparing the change on such measures of a control group and of a group under some defined form of therapy. And it would be best to begin with long-term therapy, both because short-term changes lack guarantee of permanence and because measuring instruments are currently so insensitive that indubitable change from short therapy is rarely statistically established.

Before the evidence of change on particular traits is examined it is necessary to ask a fundamental question which psychotherapists and psychiatrists have grievously neglected, namely, "In what direction do we measure recovery toward mental health?" The question is complex to the point of being philosophical, and is certainly not to be handled by the casual, brash subjectivity accepted as evidence in most studies evaluating therapeutic gain. In two articles invited on this topic (Cattell, 1970, 1973b) I have attempted some conceptual but operational criteria as follows:

1. "Getting better" is not a single dimension of change but requires research to see what typically happens—especially in natural recovery rather than therapy—on *all* personality dimensions.

2. It is not possible to fix the desired direction of change as "return to the population average" of mental health. In some traits we do not even know which is the "good" pole; and in all traits it is uncertain whether increase is good indefinitely, or only to an optimum point. Intelligence is a trait on which most people agree that more is better, but on which, if we could influence the score of a mental defective, we would raise intelligence not only to the average but beyond. Probably most therapists would vote the same for traits like emotional stability (ego strength, C), capacity to mobilize (U.I.23), reduction of ergic tension (Q_4) and some others. But in others, like anxiety, (QII), surgency (F), and guilt proneness (O), an optimum would be considered most healthy (in the last case, somewhere between the guilt-ridden depressive and the happy but dangerous psychopath).

3. Even when one shifts from vague traits to psychometrically precise ones, it is evident that subjectivity is still not in some respects avoided. The solution I have proposed to this in an article entitled "The Measurement of the Healthy Personality and the Healthy Society" (Cattell, 1973b) is that we recognize that what is functionally "mental health" (not merely what people regard as the norm) is different for different societies and cultures. Furthermore, although this goes further into social psychology than we can afford to go here, a formula is offered for this definition of health in the individual in relation to health in the society.

4. To pursue the last in operational research is theoretically possible, but it is certainly not likely to be pursued to its final technical completeness in our time. We must be satisfied with "estimates" of that goal for the present. With that "estimate" for (3) we can nevertheless take our stand on (1) and (2)—that improvement is to be evaluated *as a composite of several personality measures.* Granted this, our fourth point is that ratings by the clinician or social worker of the patient's recovery by criteria of "Can he hold this job?" "Has he returned to his wife?" and "Does he get along better with people?" are not as sound a basis as many suppose, compared to measurements on well-defined personality traits.

This may seem a paradoxical assertion for one who has always asked for operational realism. After all, are these not the *criteria* that mere tests are designed to predict? Can the test be better than the criterion? First, I would point to the overwhelming accumulation of evidence, as cited elsewhere in this article, that both the questionnaire factor scores and the objective (T-data)* source trait scores, correlate very widely with life criteria measures of all kinds. Second, I would point out that when these correlations have fallen low it has proved to be due to *unreliability of the criterion* rather than of the test. In short, except under very rarely obtained conditions (Cattell, 1957), the reliability of life observation data is less than that of tests. (The same is true of medicine, where a patient's report of, say, dizziness, tinnitus, and fatigue are less reliable indications of high blood pressure than a test.)

Although holding a job, being adjusted in the family, and so on are the criteria of importance in estimating therapeutic progress, I am challenging the majority who lean on them by my claim that personality tests predict these criteria (when exhaustively observed) better than the kind of *casual observation* of the things themselves by a single social worker. The basis for saying this is the finding of poor interobserver reliability (be it social worker or psychiatrist), and the higher level of test-criterion correlation reached when very good life observation (Cattell, Pierson, & Finkbeiner, 1976) can be made systematically. Since no research on clinical gain that the writer knows has employed the equivalent of two or three private detectives per patient, the assessment of personality improvement by personality tests is our best bet at present.

THE POTENCY OF SOURCE TRAIT SCORES IN DIAGNOSTIC DIFFERENTIATION AND THE MONITORING OF THERAPEUTIC CHANGE

Our next concern is to decide what test score changes constitute an improvement. After what has been said at the beginning, it is obvious that we are not going to concern ourselves with unstructured measures like the Rorschach, the Bender-Gestalt, the Bernreuter, or the like. By a fantastic expenditure of man-hours that would have been far better employed on a clearer theoretical basis, a few significant relations have been built up on such tests to aid diagnosis and prognosis; but as such psychometrists as Thurstone, Cronbach, and the present writer have pointed out, the signs are as statistically weak as they are obscure to any *general personality theory.* The greater part of the efficacy of these and similar evaluations is in the mind of the crystal ball user, and vanishes whenever statistically challenged. On the other hand the correlations of clinical diagnoses and outcomes with the factored measures has been substantial—indeed, no less substantial than that of factored intelligence tests with school achievement, brain injury measures, drug action, and other objective criteria. As long as 17 years ago a clear separation of diagnosed neurotics and controls was achieved with a discriminant from a dozen factors on the O-A Kit batteries, as shown in Figure 6-1.

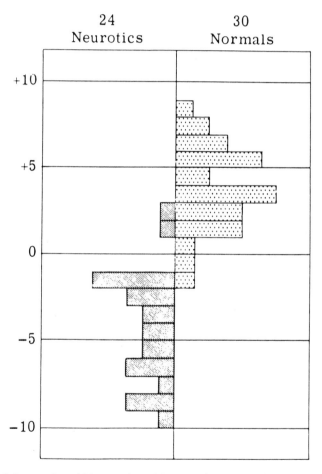

Figure 6-1. Separation of 24 neurotic and 30 normal cases, as shown by histogram, using discriminant function on scores from the Objective-Analytic (O-A) Battery (vertical axis = score on the O-A composite). Reproduced with permission from Cattell & Scheier (1961), *The Meaning and Measurement of Neuroticism and Anxiety;* New York: Ronald Press, 1961.

Neurotics can be understood in terms of deviations on normal traits, but the *Clinical Analysis Questionnaire* (adding 12 abnormal "disease" process scales to the 16 PF) has been necessary for diagnosing psychoses.

Many of the same personality factors can be measured either by questionnaires or by objective tests (see Table 6-1), and although at first sight the only advantage of the O-A (T-data) source trait measures might seem to be the freedom from the faking or motivational distortion that affects questionnaires, there is accumulating evidence that clinical separations are superior on O-A. Thus schizophrenics have been found (Cattell & Killian, 1967; Cattell, Schmidt, & Bjersted, 1972; Cattell & Schuerger, 1978; Tatro, 1968) to differ from normals at the $p < .01$ level or beyond on a number of universally indexed factors* such as U.I.16 − , U.I.19 − , U.I.21 − , U.I.23 − , U.I.25 − , U.I.32 − , and U.I.33 − , together producing a very high degree of diagnostic separation. A discriminant function separating neurotics from schizophrenics was also calculated by Schmidt in which the former are less deviant on U.I.25, more on U.I.21, higher on U.I.24, and so on.

Character disorders are different again in total pattern, showing lower realism (U.I.25 −), some introversion (U.I.32 −), and higher apathy (U.I.27). As between paranoid and nonparanoid schizophrenics, although both are strongly characterized by low U.I.16 (low ego) and low U.I.19 (independence), the simple, hebephrenic, and catonic alike differ from paranoid by showing more regression (U.I.23 −) and more introversion (U.I.32 −). Similar differences, but less powerful in producing separation, have been found in the factored questionnaires such as the 16 PF and the High School Personality Questionnaire (HSPQ).

All these data so far have shown the power of factored source trait measurement in diagnosis, rather than therapy, and leave us only with the logical inference—rather than actual evidence—that therapy would reduce the deviations on U.I.16, 19, 23, 24, and so on. However, a pioneer study by Rickels and a group of psychoanalytic therapists (Rickels, Cattell, Weise, Gray, Yee, Malin, & Aaronson, 1966) using both therapy and mild chemotherapy (meprobamate) has shown that reduction on such factors as were hypothesized and measured indeed occurs, as shown in Table 6-1.

The psychometrically interesting point here is that it does not matter whether the source traits are measured by factored questionnaires or by factored objective tests, although only the objective test, the U.I.23 Regression battery, climbs to a significance of $p < .001$. Similar findings of change under therapy have been established for increase of ego strength (*C* factor in the 16 PF) and rise in *E* and *F* factors (Hunt, Ewing, LaForge, & Gilbert, 1959), while Pierson (1965) and Pierson et al. (1964) have shown changes in young delinquents in institutions.

Table 6-1
Measurable Changes in U.I.23 (Mobilization vs. Regression)
and U.I. 24 (Anxiety Produced by Therapy): Comparison of
Anxiety and Regression Change under Therapy
on Questionnaire and Objective Test Measures[a]

Measure	Initial score(1)	Final score (2)	Change (2) − (1)
I. PAT Verbal Anxiety			
Patients	46.09	43.02	− 3.07*
Controls	26.13	26.77	0.64
O–A Anxiety Battery			
Patients[b]	0.361	0.198	− 0.163*
Controls	− 0.361	− 0.472	− 0.111
O–A Regression Battery			
Patients	0.440	0.114	− 0.326**
Controls	− 0.458	− 0.611	− 0.153*

SOURCE: Cattell et al., 1966. © Copyright 1978 by R. B. Cattell and J. M. Schuerger, *Personality theory in action: Handbook for the O–A personality kit.* Champaign, Ill.: Institute for Personality and Ability Testing. Adapted with permission.

[a]N = 46 patients; N = 53 normal controls.

[b]*Numerical agreement of these two initial values for patients and controls is accidental. All scores are raw scores and have no comparability immediately from objective to questionnaire values, being unstandardized.*

*$p < 0.05$.

**$p < 0.001$.

The structured approach to states and traits has shown that although anxiety is a single factor, depression has seven primaries and (in T data) four secondaries. A recent study by Patrick, Price, and Cattell (Note 2) shows (see table 6–2) that all four of the latter distinguish clinical depressives form normals with substantial significances. The next step is now being taken—of finding the meaning of these source traits to aid our understanding the different forms and prognoses of depression.

The above illustrations must suffice here to reveal to the reader unfamiliar with these developments the sheer pragmatic potency of structured measurement. However, a much fuller basis for understanding will be found in Barton and Cattell (1972), Barton, Cattell, and Vaughan (1973), Cattell (1966, 1969, 1970, 1977), Cattell and Killian (1967), Cattell and Scheier (1961), Cattell and Schuerger (1978), Karson and O'Dell (1976), Krug (1977), Rickels et al. (1966), and various articles now in press.

Table 6-2
Significance of Differences of Depressives and Controls
on Four Source Traits Measured on the O–A Battery[a]

Source trait (factor)	Sample and size	Mean score on trait	Sigma on trait	Degrees of freedom	t value	Significances of depressive − Normal differences 1-tailed significance
U.I.19 (independence)	Depressives (31)	−2.396	4.305	59	4.69	$p = .0001$
	Normal (30)	2.476	3.782			
U.I.20 (evasiveness)	Depressives (31)	2.556	6.805	59	3.42	$p = .001$
	Normal (30)	−2.641	4.866			
U.I.25 (reality control)	Depressives (31)	−0.652	2.881	59	1.96	$p = .053$
	Normal (30)	0.674	2.370			
U.I.30 (somindence)	Depressives (31)	0.564	2.610	59	1.93	$p = .054$
	Normal (30)	−0.598	2.105			

Source: Patrick, Price, & Cattell (Note 2)

[a] Depressive significantly higher on U.I.20 and U.I.30; depressives significantly lower on U.I.19 and U.I.25. Note that although the subjects are in standard scores.

THE RELATIONS OF DYNAMIC AND GENERAL PERSONALITY MEASURES IN DIAGNOSIS AND THERAPY

A time lag of 10–20 years has separated the discovery of unitary source traits, along with the validation of structured measurements by psychometric research, and the introduction of the source trait measures into courses in clinical psychology. Although such lags, costly to the general public, are familiar in medicine and other areas, it is incumbent alike on the psychometrists and the therapists to seek the causes and arrange better communication.

One reason for the lag is that clinicians have been brought up to see clinical problems purely in dynamic terms (with the exception of intelligence, largely restricted to child clinic diagnosis—and there is no record of use of an intelligence test by Freud). Clinical discussions of cases, indeed, have not been essentially different from the refined personality analysis by novelists over the last few centuries, except for embellishment by some polysyllabic terms known only to the establishment. If therapists have become aware at all of the demonstrated roles of deviations on *general personality* traits like intelligence, introversion, ego strength, superego strength, surgency, anxiety, and regression, they have been at a loss to digest them into their theoretical schemas.

It is this failure of these strange new trait concepts—a couple dozen of them—to fit into the vocabulary of conflict, repression, projection, transference, and the like within the dynamic approach that accounts primarily for their being left out of clinical practice. In a moment we shall show that they integrate perfectly well; but while we are considering socioprofessional lag as such, the second main obstacle must be admitted. It is that only a few more alert clinical courses have given training in structural psychometrics, training that is very necessary because the T-data batteries and the *Motivational Analysis Test (MAT)* measures we are about to discuss are not as simple to give as an interview. They require training to administer much as in experimental psychology, and instruction in scoring and predictive calculation that only a good psychometrics course can give.

Let us leave this problem to progressive faculties and consider the more basic question of the relation of dynamics to general personality traits. Briefly, it is that the general traits are causal, on the one hand, in posing limits of endowment, for example in intelligence, in U.I.1, in extraversion of temperament (U.I.32) and retrieval capacity in U.I.21, with which the individual must work out his dynamic problems. These we may call *given capacity traits*. On the other hand, these deviating traits represent (in such dimensions as ego strength, regression, and anxiety level) the end products of the adjustment process, such that Scheier and Cattell (1961) named them neurotic *process traits*. They might equally be called *product traits,* as standing products of the neurotic process. It is these latter that should be directly monitored as deviations whose change shows how well the therapy is working in untangling dynamic problems.

However, this is not all that structured measurement can do, for in the last decade it has progressed in the MAT and *School Motivation Analysis Test* (SMAT) to objective motivational measurement of specific drive tensions (ergs) and acquired sentiment* levels, e.g., to wife, job, home, hobby, etc. Quite recently it has progressed to measuring control structures, such as the superego and self-sentiment (also by the objective devices such as memory, projection, word association, and GSR). The MAT and SMAT devices, with their division of scores into integrated and unintegrated motivation components, have been very skillfully used by a number of clinicians. But a gap still remains between the psychometrist and the couch which is an entirely logical one, namely that, although dynamic, the MAT measures are still of *common* traits, not *unique* traits. That is to say, they measure the level of ergic tension in John Smith's sex erg, or the strength of his interest in the job; but the therapist of the dynamic school still feels the story is incomplete unless he or she knows *to whom* a sex drive of that intensity is being directed and what the particular boss on the job is like.

If the individual's adjustment to particulars of the external world is to be manipulated with the help of the therapist in the interest of dynamic readjustment, it is of course important that he know these particular cathexes. The mistake in the past, made equally by the psychoanalyst and the behavior therapist, has been in assuming that this is *all* that he needs to know. Research on the deviation of clinical cases shows that in understanding the problem comprehensively the clinician needs to know (1) where the individual stands on general personality factors both of *capacity* and *neurotic process-product* (measured, for example, on the 16 PF, the Clinical Analysis Questionnaire [CAQ] or the objective–analytic [O–A] scales); and (2) what the dimensions of the dynamic conflict are with respect to magnitude and the area within the dynamic system (as shown by the sentiment, erg, and ego levels on the integrated and unintegrated components on, say, the MAT).

Given this quantitative information on general personality from objective, standardized measures, the therapist still rightly considers that the penetration into unique traits (with their particular object cathexes) is also needed, and that he must consequently return to supplement his dynamic scores by couch methods. But nearly 20 published researchers (see Birkett & Cattell, 1978; Cattell & Child, 1975; Kline & Grindley, 1974; Lebo & Nesselroade, 1978) show that a new method—the P technique*—is available that will *quantitatively* and in a positive, correlational fashion open up all the particular, unique, and individual motivations and cathexes in the life of the individual. The therapist, if he wishes to go the whole way into purely unique attachments, with quantitative and objective dynamic analysis, can today do so. The theoretical and psychometric bases of the P technique have been demonstrated to be sound. Although the reader must be referred elsewhere (Cattell & Child, 1975) for the technical sources, it should be added here, in perspective, that the method, demanding 30–100 occasions (visits) by the patient, is still a "deluxe" one—perhaps comparable to aviation as a form of public travel in 1925—and will require the concentrated efforts of clinicians to shorten it and bring it to wider practicality.

THERAPEUTIC METHODS CONCEIVED IN THE FRAMEWORK OF STRUCTURED LEARNING THEORY

The last few sections above have been a necessary detour, based on our opening position that if sources of therapeutic advance are ever to be evaluated and further discovered, greater accuracy has to be brought to the before and after measures. Our final position is that, manipulatively, handling the individual dynamic problem may be the means to advance, but that advance needs to be *evaluated on a complete profile of personality and dynamic factors.* Further, we have taken the position that although a sound theoretical conclusion can ideally be drawn as to what directions of factor change represent progress, we must rely for the present on the questionnaire findings as to the directions in which pathological clinical cases differ significantly from healthy controls. Those directions can be specified in questionnaire factors as a move toward higher C (ego strengh), F (surgency), and Q_3 (sentiment strength), and reduction of Q_4 (ergic tension) and of the tendency to use defense mechanisms such as projection. In O–A battery factors the direction of recovery is very clearly one of rises on U.I.16 (ego standards), U.I.19, U.I.21, U.I.23 (capacity to mobilize), and U.I.25 (reality contact), and reduction in U.I.24 (anxiety). On the MAT, the changes are similar.

With this concreteness of checks available, let us now return to the inferences for handling therapy from structured learning theory. The basic position is that *therapy is a branch of structured learning.* However, relative to what, say, educators think of as learning theory, it has much more to do with relearning and extinction of acquired systems. If the acquisition of sentiments (such as the MAT finds in the factors for home, career, sweetheart, etc.) is appropriate to the stimuli and satisfactions in the environment, there is (in the sense which we call "environment balance") a first degree of adjustment. But a sweetheart changes her mind or a job is closed, and a relearning becomes necessary. The possibility of maladjustment begins thus (as far as sentiments are concerned), with a change of environment. However, the same principles will apply where the satisfaction gap has existed from the beginning. This is chronically the case as far as the second type of dynamic structure is concerned, namely, ergs (factorially defined innate drives). For these, with their primitive goals, are perpetually "maladjusted" in some degree as far as a complex civilization is concerned. They are gradually incorporated into acquired sentiment systems from which they get much of their discharge. From studies on these, by the dynamic calculus (Cattell & Child, 1975) we can determine what has been defined as the *ergic investment* of a given sentiment system (as a vector retraining numerically the particular ergic quality of the satisfaction). The psychoanalytic notion of the cathexis of an object approaches the concept of the ergic investment of a sentiment object, but of course lacks instrumental quantification and the discovery and demonstration of the unitary ergs actually involved in the vector.

The first step in therapy is recognizing the nature and magnitude of the discrepancy between the demands of the client's existing dynamic structures and the environmental outlets. This gap can arise from ergs or sentiments, and may have been long in existence as in, say, the sex needs of a late adolescent, or may have been created by a sudden change of environment as in a woman who is widowed. The therapy may call either for building up inadequate sentiments, as with delinquents and some addicts, or for reducing and perhaps extinguishing those present.

If we pause to look at the latter, one of the many important differences of Skinnerian reflexological and structured learning theory is immediately apparent. Reflexological therapy proceeds to apply the law for extinction of a conditioned reflex, whereas the latter examines (see Cattell & Birkett, 1979; Cattell & Child, 1975) the dynamic lattice* structure in the given individual. Structured learning theory concentrates on rewarding the ergs that were present in the particular investments of the unfortunate sentiment. It does so by attaching to other, alternative, old or new, systems the dynamics which are discerned from examining the dynamic lattice. To a therapist unskilled in structured learning analysis, the latter steps may seem obscure; but the illumination of the dynamic lattice by P technique (or other testing devices) will have revealed the necessary steps to the structural therapist.

Although maladjustments begin with a discrepancy between dynamic needs and the environment, we expect if we follow the *adjustment process analysis* chart in Figure 6-2 (Cattell & Child, 1975; Cattell & Scheier, 1961), that in many cases they will end in the deadlock of an internal conflict. Unless relieved, this is followed by anxiety, depression, and the multiplication

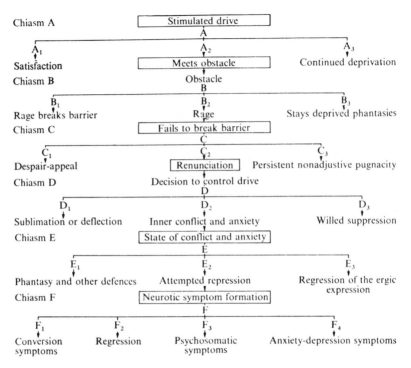

Figure 6-2. The adjustment process analysis chart.

of defenses, such as defined by Anna Freud (1936), and neurotic symptoms. How does structured learning theory deal with this?

To tackle this basic issue in the next section we need to consolidate for a couple of pages what knowledge we possess about the nature of the ego structure, since it is centrally involved in integration learning* (Cattell, 1977) and what might be called demolition learning. Let us consider the evidence on the nature and incidence of the *C* or ego strength factor. That a deficiency in this structure lies close to the heart of the adjustment problem is called to our attention by the *universality* of significantly low scores on *C* in all forms of psychopathology thus far measured (see the 40 very diverse clinical groups given profiles in Cattell, Eber, & Tatsuoka, 1970; p. 260). As with certain other particular factors found deficient, and discussed in terms of *capacity* and *process* (eventually product) traits (Cattell & Scheier, 1961), the deviation here is one produced in part by a process. But it is then brought to bear in part in the role of a capacity. Conflicts of emotional education and incompatibilities in sentiment and ergic structures are the *processes* that have weakened the ego. Eventually the ego becomes so poor as a *capacity* that the maladjustment expressed in the ensuing unwise handling of the dynamic traits becomes worse, as shown at the E and F crossroads in Figure 6-2.

As we shall clarify in the more practical injunctions of the next section, the therapist's first task is to help the client see reality and the tactical steps needed to discover actual satisfactions and outlets. But once the process in the adjustment process analysis chart has "nose-dived" into the D, E, and F levels, the provision of outlets (although a desirable prophylactic) is not enough; for now structural changes are necessary in demolishing rigid defenses and in strengthening the ego. Accordingly, at this point we need to study the ego. The quantitative and correlational evidence on the ego structure has now amplified Freud's preliminary clinical insights (see Birkett, 1979; Cattell & Birkett, 1979; Gorsuch & Cattell, 1977; Horn, 1966). The evidence points to the ego structures exerting its control through developing the following four process skills: (1) bringing about an *impulse inhibition* long enough for consideration of alternatives; (2) sensing the strength of the dynamic traits demanding satisfaction; (3) examining the possibilities in the external situation in terms of long-term satisfactions, and doing so in relation to retrieval of memories of past action outcomes in that region; and (4) reaching a decision and putting it into effect by marshalling "allies" to the ego, such as by *cue evocation of trait strengths* (CET) that will join positively with the ego term in the behavioral equation.

One would expect that gains in ego strength could be initiated by training the client in what can very broadly be called cognitive process habits. We say "broadly" because it includes in (2) and (4) the sensing, recognition, and appraisal of emotional needs by improved recognition of feelings and by finding names for them. But it also covers better recognition of social and other relations in the external world, and a better awareness (by retrieval) of the past consequences of various behaviors. Psychoanalysis, it seems from the present perspective, concentrates a little too much (as far as the *average* modern client is concerned) on the fact that some of these cognitive connections have become repressed and can no longer be made. Although structured learning theory recognizes and incorporates repression and dissociation of cognitive elements, e.g., those attached to certain ergs, it nevertheless argues that in the majority of present-day average nonpsychotic clients the deficient cognitive connections are still open and are capable of being made. Saying that the ego achieves its control by CET, and by cognitive manipulations in general, nevertheless recognizes additionally that cognitive connections (engrams) will run the gamut from easy accessibility through a moderate difficulty of retrieval and so on to repressed "unconsciousness." In ways not yet understood, ego conflict and conflict in other areas create relative cognitive inaccessibilities. The factoring of manifestations of conflict by Cattell and Sweney (1964) and of perceptual defense mechanisms by Cattell and Wenig (1952) clearly locates this form of defensive capacity among other defense mechanisms. One must therefore explicitly recognize in structured learning theory a continuum of cognitive accessibilities among past engrams, and the correctness of the psychoanalytic perception of a need for techniques for making them accessible. Granted that in extreme cases the techniques of bringing connections out of complete cognitive inaccessibility become necessary, we nevertheless suggest that in perhaps 80% of clients it is possible to work by ordinary cognitive connection procedures, even in the penumbra of borderline accessibilities.

In connection with understanding the ego role it is necessary to give the perspective of structured learning theory (Cattell, 1966, 1977) that three main forms of the learning process exist: (1) coexcitation (a major element in the classical paradigm); (2) means–end learning (in the instrumental paradigm, but with a structuring in a new model of ergic goals; and (3) integration learning. The last is largely overlooked in classical reflexological learning theory because it scarcely exists in animal learning. It requires the existence of an ego structure, consciously weighing the various compromises in terms of long-term satisfaction. It effectuates itself through manipulation by the ego of largely internal stimuli in such a way as to maximize long-term ergic (and therefore sentiment) satisfaction. It is in the learning that takes place under this third principle that the adjustment learning of the neurotic has broken down, and needs to be restored to greater efficiency.

Incidentally, while concentrating on the role of the ego in learning (and that of learning in reinforcing the ego) let us not overlook the commonly overlooked genetic component in ego motivation. The behavior genetic research evidence (Cattell, Blewett, & Beloff, 1955) shows an unmistakable genetic contribution to ego strength, which we theorize operates mainly in the first process—halting impulses for consideration. Mammalian species—man, dog, chimpanzee—obviously differ in this genetic endowment; but the importance for dealing with individual humans is that different children will reach the same inner maturational level of such control at different ages. As psychoanalysis recognized, the attempt to demand ego control with unusually powerful conflicting forces, or at too early an age, produces a "trauma" in which undesirable and rigid habits of ego defense become installed. Considerable research is needed in structured learning theory to understand the interaction of these individual differences on genetic endowment with the learning acquisition of the ego structure. However, what is broadly evident is that the ego, like any other sentiment structure, grows by reinforcement through the means-ends principle. The better it succeeds in finding satisfactions for ergs and sentiments of a long-term nature, the stronger it becomes as a unitary dynamic entity.

STRUCTURED LEARNING SOURCES OF
LONG-TERM THERAPEUTIC CHANGE

It will be evident that the position of the structured learning theorist is that much behavior therapy, reconditioning, and extinguishing of restricted symptoms and specific behaviors, is in general unlikely to lead to long-term therapeutic change.

Some of the procedures in a broader based therapy may also fail to do so. We have stated that the first task of the therapist is to seek to reduce the discrepancy between needs and circumstances by helping the client, as an intelligent observer, to find satisfactory outlets. An appreciable part of this process, however, will not succeed in carrying over to the next life situation that the client gets into, and so is not of long-term significance. We cannot count on "transfer of training". But that part of the teaching of the four main tasks of the ego (listed above) that does succeed in the present situation is likely to do so.

The task of long-term therapy is likely to embrace the whole personality, and therefore to be most appropriately stated and evaluated in terms of restoring to normal levels the large deviation on certain common personality factors which measurement has shown to exist. These deviations, however, are in part different for neurotics on the one hand, and psychotics on the other; so we shall give some separate consideration to these two problems, with more being given to neurotics, since psychotherapeutic treatment of psychotics has as yet little to show.

If psychosis may be discussed here briefly, it would be with the view that hereditary and physiological influences play a much larger part therein than in the neuroses. The hereditary influences presumably operate in the form of rather extreme values for the *capacity* factors above, as met by most people, leading to relatively normal degrees of dynamic conflict and exhaustion becoming insupportable, and causing a solution by breakdown of reality contact. However, some of the deviations could occur also as products of process factors. On objective tests the deviations of psychotics (Cattell & Schuerger, 1978) are such that psychotics are significantly lower on U.I.19 (independence), U.I.21 (exuberance), U.I.23 (capacity to mobilize), U.I.24 (anxiety), U.I.25 (reality contact), U.I.30 (somindence), and higher on U.I.28 (asthenia). However, it must be remembered that neurotics also deviate from normal ($p < .001$) in the same direction on U.I.19, 21, and 23. These three are therefore probably best considered the debilitating results of extensive mental conflict.

What seems more peculiar to psychosis, therefore, is lack of reality contact U.I.25 – (which conclusion is supported by Eysenck's results), along with U.I.30, somindence, a significant but smaller deviation on anxiety, U.I.24, and distinctly higher on asthenia, U.I.28. Incidentally, the indications are that a few thorough researches with these source traits would provide effective discriminant functions among schizophrenics, manics, depressives, and psychopaths. For instance, in a recent study, Patrick, Price and Cattell (Note 2) found U.I.30, somindence (restricted emotionality) particularly deviant in depressives. We do not know enough about U.I.30 and U.I.28 at present to see what they mean for therapeutic steps with psychotics (assuming U.I.25, 28, and 30 are not just debilitation indicators), but in the U.I.25 we see inner tensions of a special kind (not just anxieties) gradually withdrawing the individual's attention away from reality contact.

In the questionnaire domain the psychotic deviations on normal personality traits are (Cattell, Eber, & Tatsuoka, 1970, p. 274) C – (ego weakness), $E-$ (submissiveness), $F-$ (desurgency), $O-$ (guilt proneness), and strangely, Q_3 (higher self-sentiment) on most, plus the specific deviations on the disease process scales—schizophrenia, depressive, etc.—on the Clinical Analysis Questionnaire. At first the strange deviation on Q_3, self-sentiment, may be understood as a narcissistic withdrawal and bolstering of the self-image; the $E-$, $F-$, and perhaps O as debilitative consequences of conflict; but the $C-$ deviation is a dynamic one, specifically indicating a strong need for a therapeutic buildup of the ego, as discussed above.

It is with the neurotic (including the addict) that, as every therapist knows, a promise of relearning exists that is generally absent in the psychotic, whose reality perceptions and contacts have broken down. Consequently, it is in this setting that we shall discuss the essential therapeutic steps indicated by structured learning theory. Before doing so, we may briefly note the personality structure characteristics as we did with the psychotic. In objective tests, neurotics share with psychotics, but to a lesser degree, the debilitative product traits U.I.19($-$), 21($-$), and 23($-$); but in addition, in a discriminative degree, lower ego standards (U.I.16$-$), lower cortertia (U.I.22$-$), higher overreactivity (U.I.29), and especially higher anxiety (U.I.24) relative to the general population. In Q data, additional to low E and F and high O, as with psychotics they show low superego $G-$, high premsia (emotional sensitivity), $I+$, very high ergic tension, Q_4, and, of course, higher second-order anxiety scores (Cattell et al., 1970, p. 266). This pattern, incidentally, indicates that there is more to the neurotic problem than either the psychoanalyst (Freud: "anxiety is the central problem of the neurosis") or the behavior therapist, attacking some by-product symptom of the dynamic maladjustment, conceives. The much replicated finding of high premsia (*I*) requires explanation, and can contingently be interpreted as an undisciplined habit of counting both on eating one's cake and having it, i.e., a habitual pleasure principle adoption of incompatible goals.

For a perspective on the therapeutic process we shall turn to the adjustment process analysis chart in Figure 6-2, mentioned above in introducing the nature and functions of the ego factor.

We began with the situation, present alike to normals and neurotics, of an environment–personality *imbalance*, which can arise either from environmental deprivation or from dynamic traits growing stronger by either internal, viscerogenic appetite, or environmental stimulation. The most natural first outcome here, as shown at *chiasm* (crossroad or choice point) A in the chart, is that the ego either finds a mode of satisfaction or, thwarted, resorts to pugnacity ("aggression") which may channel to outlet C_3, persistent nonadjustive impulse expression and pugnacity. This describes the clinical status of the delinquent, and if we include action from complexes down at chiasm F, also of the character disorder and acting-out case.

What structured learning theory indicates for therapy at this point is: (1) learning greater incorporation of ergs within sentiment structures, which themselves are more or less socially acceptable, whereas simple ergic expressions are not; (2) building up ego strength; and (3) helping the client assemble those sentiments to bring to the aid of the ego that which a survey of the dynamic structure reveals to be its most effective allies.

The learning in (1) is normally the task of teacher and parent, and child guidance clinics encounter many cases where the problem is simply that stable, acceptable sentiments and the superego sentiment have not been taught and/or acquired. This should quickly be revealed by HSPQ and SMAT measures. If, on the other hand, (2) and (3) are the problem, we are dealing with a situation more skillfully handled by a psychologist, measuring the relative sentiment strengths—although in life, a friend, a pastor, or a school counselor often does the job.

It is when the D chiasm is passed and E is reached (on one major or a collection of lesser dynamic problems) that we enter the domain of neurosis. This domain is, in terms of the dynamic calculus and its concepts, one of *conflict-produced impairment of the cognitive connections to ergic resources*. As stated above, this is not a matter only of the *absolute* repression effects discovered by Freud, but of *degrees of inaccessibility* of cognitive connections, produced not by one defense device but by any of several. Unfortunately, the combination of sophisticated correlational factor-analytic designs and clinical clarity in the operational representation of defenses, both of which are needed for objective research in this domain, seems to have been missing. At any rate, the exploratory location of types of defense mechanism by Cattell and Wenig (1952), which supported and added to Anna Freud's analyses, and the identification of forms of expression of conflict (Cattell & Sweney, 1964) has not been followed up to to augment reliable evidence about the unitary habit systems involved. Consequently, there are no objective measures to allow current practice to assess what forms of defense and cognitive distortion are operating at chiasm F in a given patient.

Let us, for brevity, refer to this stage of the adjustment process analysis, and the domain of dynamic characteristics produced there, as "dissociated dynamic structure," more fully described above as those showing conflict-produced impairment of cognitive connections with ergic sources (and with other sentiments). Structured learning has to incorporate in its practice certain auxiliary principles which, incidentally, are not heeded in reflexological behavior therapy. The knowledge which personality structure measurement methods give of the strengths of the ergic tension and sentiment strength, and the strength of the controlling ego, are here not sufficient to enable structured learning advocates to bring stimulation and reward in the right places because certain systems are inaccessible. Structured learning advocates must avail themselves of those methods of making the inaccessible accessible which practicing clinicians have learned over three generations such as persistent free association, hypnotism, dream and humor interpretation, and perhaps uses of psychoactive drugs yet to be discovered.

The theory does, however, have resources for *finding* domains of conflict that were formerly lacking. As Sweney (1967, 1969), Horn (1966) Birkett, (1979) and others have shown, an excess of the U over the I (of the unintegrated—"I wish"—over the integrated motive) component in any MAT measurement of an interest domain is a sign of conflict, at least of unfulfilled needs, that generally correlates with other diverse evidences of conflict. The opposite sign (I greater than U) has some ambiguity, sometimes indicating excellent, ego-directed realization of needs and sometimes a recession of basic ergic interest from an acquired expression structure.

Some very recent work on motivation components (Cattell & Birkett, 1979) supports another second-order factor, beyond U and I, which has been indexed as B for "blocking interest." It loads heavily on the large GSR response, along with poor memory for the stimulus cues, interference in reminiscence, and low fluency on the topic. Until this is checked by a third research, it is admittedly going out on a technical limb to attempt an interpretation. But the present writer would suggest that we *may* have here the indicator we are looking for of the existence of degree of dissociation in a given dynamic area.

The structured learning therapy in nondissociative areas follows the ordinary three learning mechanisms of (1) coexcitation (CE), (2) means–end learning (ME), and (3) integration learning, through action of the ego structure. Coexcitation, by deliberate and repeated copresentation (of external stimuli or evoked ideas) to establish cognitive connections needs no illustration. Means–end learning raises the question of whence the reward is to come for a desired positive behavior or the willed (ego) suspension of undesirable behavior. What structured learning offers here is a view of possibilities beyond direct ergic reward, or money, or the counters offered to subjects in much reflexology learning. It proposes that the map—the dynamic lattice—of the individual's existing sentiment strengths and the current levels of his ergic tensions should be examined to see where resources of reward lie *within* the individual, as well as outside.

A frequent complaint of the therapist, particularly with delinquents who have not yet been sent to jail or addicts who have not begun to reap the consequences of their addition, is that there seems insufficient motivation in the client for change. Here again structured personality measurement, in its dynamic aspects, may be the answer. It is surely likely in most cases to reveal some unexpressed ergic tension (as a high U score) that can with a little situational manipulation be brought to bear. Therapists so far have not had the audacity to raise with public opinion the possibility of improving their recovery rates by exposing their clients voluntarily or involuntarily (depending on whether he is a neurotic or a criminal) to the kinds of manipulable deprivations used effectively in brain washing in Vietnam and elsewhere, where the easy manipulability of the ergs of fear, hunger, and sleep-seeking was exemplified. These are beyond ethical practice, but at least they illustrate that the leverage of sufficient motivation within the individual is a primary requisite, and one may add that it can created within acceptable limits by study of the individual's dynamics. The role of strength of motivation in the undoing of dissociative tangles must also not be overlooked, whatever the adjunct devices used.

A principle in the task of what we may call "demolition" is that older learnings will, by the imprinting effect, be naturally stronger than engramming acquired under the same motivation strength at a later period. Freud recognized this particularly in perverted fixations of the sex erg in infancy, but the nature and magnitude of the association of such engramming properties with age has been astonishingly neglected by classical experimental learning theory. Again, this has been largely because of its inability, by bivariate designs, to reveal the nature of ergic patterns. Much has yet to be discovered, therefore, as structured learning advances, on demolition and relearning of early imprintings.

As psychoanalysis has well recognized, the overcoming of resistances and undoing of rigid defenses is only a beginning to be followed by the process of finding reality-acceptable and effective expressions. However, therapeutic resistance is apt to peter out before this is accomplished. Such a failure is not entirely due to the bankruptcy of the patient, but to lack of clear guidelines in theory, as well as to the reluctance of pure rationalists to accept religious value systems as an ultimate adjustment. As to guidelines in theory, structured learning theory is reasonably clear on the principles operating in new sentiment formation.

However, the principal sequel to the demolition work on defenses and release of ergic resources is not so much the establishment of new sentiment structures as the strengthening of the ego. Since the impoverishment of the ego (which our factored tests of C show to be the most universal trait deviation across clinical disorders) began through failure and unreward in its attempted controlling functions, the release of original functions and possibilities at the time of demolition of rigid defenses should be the means, even though not immediately, of strengthening it. The evidence that this occurs is shown by the results of therapy on a substantial sample of students (Hunt et al., 1959) as well as in a middle-class group of clients undergoing psychoanalytic treatment and chemotherapy (Cattell, Rickels, Weise, Gray, & Yee, 1966; Rickels & Cattell, 1969). That training in the four main processes of ego action (Birkett, 1979) will also improve ego strength scores has not yet been shown, although Birkett makes a strong case for it. In any event, it is surely evident that one of the explicit aims of therapy must be the increase of the ego strength factor. Demolition and reeducation of the dynamic defense fixation is only one contributory step to this. Theoretically one can expect that demolition without C-factor elevation might lead only to a fresh dynamic tangle in the next situation, and the same should happen even more readily in the reflexological therapy of extinguishing symptoms.

Growth on C is, however, only one—although perhaps the most important—dimension in what we defined as learning, when we called it "a multidimensional change in relation to a multidimensional learning situation." When we divided the known significant deviations of neurotics from normals (Cattell & Scheier, 1961) into *contributory* and process-product traits, we did so on still fragmentary evidence that the former were capacity limits, predisposing some among all those with similar dynamic conflicts, to become neurotic. We should not expect these capacity values to change very much. But the result of therapy should become apparent not only in the process-product factor *C*, but also in others. The Rickels studies show this trait change positively occurring in reduction of U.I.24 (anxiety) and U.I.23 (regression). With the release of the convenient objective measures in the O–A Kit (Cattell & Schuerger, 1978) it will be easier first to explore results of therapy on other dimensions, similar in kind to U.I.23 and 24, and also to score those process-product trait deviations on which reduction to normality may be considered an evaluation of success of long-term therapy.

In looking over this chapter the reader may recognize that structured learning is not merely the equivalent in scientific culture of that phase of "demolition" of existing practices that we have recognized in individual therapy. It is a new learning, calling for (1) the introduction of structured learning theory on a broader basis than behavior therapy and (2) precisioning some psychoanalytic and Jungian insights in a framework of factor-analytic models and verification of concepts.

If a conservative fails to see what this adds, we would assert that structured personality measurement, and the structured learning that uses it as a foundation, add what surgery gained when it moved on from its pre-Vesalian ignorance of anatomy. And the quantification of change in structured learning theory brings to the psychotherapist some of the gains which medical therapy experienced when blood tests, X-rays, and sphygmomanometers made possible reasonably precise evaluation of, and intervention in, functional processes.

GLOSSARY

dynamic lattice—The dynamic lattice is Cattell's term for the complex interrelationship of traits within the personality. Ergs are the most basic elements in the lattice. Sentiments are subsidiary to (serve) the ergs of an individual.

dynamic, ability, and temperament traits—Dynamic traits are those reaction tendencies that reflect motivations and interests, and therefore goal-directedness. Ability traits have to do with how effectively a person confronts environmental challenges on the way toward achieving a goal. Temperament traits reflect constitutional dimensions of behavior such as tempo, style, force, emotional level, duration, etc.

ego strength—A source trait, ego strength (referred to as *C*) reflects good emotional stability and the capacity to cope with emotional difficulties.

erg—An innate source of reactivity (drive) that orients the person to certain classes of objects, causes the person to experience a specific emotion in regard to the objects, and directs the person toward a specific goal activity. Among the ergs

Cattell discusses are sex, fear, self-assertion, hunger, gregariousness, curiosity, parental protectiveness, pugnacity, acquisitiveness, and self-indulgence. An erg is a constitutional, dynamic, source trait (q.v.). *Ergic* (rhymes with allergic) *tension* refers to the aroused, unexpressed tension from specific ergic structure sources.

integration learning—Similar to the Freudian notion of secondary process, integration learning refers to the individual's use of cognitive skills to rearrange conflicting needs so that, by inhibition and compromise, a new response is found that yields the largest discoverable total satisfaction. Also called integrated end (IE) learning or integrative learning.

P technique—The P technique is a factor-analytic procedure which involves multiple measures of a single person over a number of different occasions. The P technique is useful for detecting purely idiosyncratic individual structures and structural changes in the person over time (including emotional or organismic states).

sentiments—A sentiment is a dynamic source trait built up through experiential or cultural inputs. Sentiments are organized around particular social institutions, like school, career, home, religion, or sports. The *self-sentiment* is the structure centered upon the person's view of himself or herself.

source traits—Traits that are determined by factor-analytic methods to be the single, unitary influence on a set of overt behaviors. Cattell believes source traits potentially to be the basic building blocks of human personality. Source traits are distinguished from *surface traits,* a set of characteristics which are correlated but do not form a factor. Surface traits are believed produced by the interaction of source traits and environmental determinants.

specification equation (also behavioral equation)—The specification equation is a linear equation or formula which specifies how an individual's behavior (or test score) may be predicted in a given situation by adding together the relevant traits (T), each weighted by its behavioral index (b). The behavioral index is equivalent to a factor loading (varying between -1.0 and $+1.0$) which shows how much the trait enters into the behavior in question. If the sign is $-$, the trait tends to inhibit the response.

T data, L data, and Q data—According to Cattell, there are three sources of data about personality: objective tests, or specially created situations in which a person's behavior can be objectively observed and measured (T data); observer ratings of behavior in everyday, real-life settings (L data); and questionnaires (Q data).

trait—An underlying unity in the person accounting for enduring individual differences in his or her reaction tendencies. Traits may be shared by groups of individuals or may be unique to the person. Traits are built up through the workings of biology (physiological and genetic factors) and/or the environment (learning and conditioning).

Universal Index (U.I.) System—A system devised by Cattell to allow investigators to refer to identified source trait patterns without applying traditional verbal labels. Factors are simply given Universal Index (or U.I.) numbers. Objective test scores can also be referenced and given a *Master Index* (or M.I.) number for the scores, and a *T number* for the actual test materials. The following is a list of factors mentioned in the text by U.I. numbers, each with a rough verbal equivalent: U.I.1—general intelligence; Spearman's "g" factor; U.I.16—unbound, assertive ego versus disciplined ego (carefulness, frustration-tolerance); U.I. 19—independence versus subduedness; U.I.21—exuberance versus quietness (suppressibility); U.I.22—cortical alertness (what Cattell calls "cortertia") versus slowness of reactivity (what Cattell calls "pathemia"); U.I.23—capacity to mobilize versus regression; U.I.24—high unbound anxiety versus low general anxiety (good adjustment); U.I.25—realism (reality contact) versus psychoticism; U.I.27—grudgingness (low aspiration level) versus trustingness; U.I.28—low psychophysical momentum ("asthenia") versus casualness; U.I.29—cooperativeness versus uncooperativeness; U.I.30—stolid temperament versus tenseness; U.I. 32—extraversion ("exvia") versus introversion ("invia"); U.I.33—pessimism versus optimism.

REFERENCE NOTES

1. Cattell, R. B., & Sealy, P. *The general relation and changes in personality and interest to changes in school performance.* Washington, D.C.: Project No. 1411, U.S. Department of Health, Education and Welfare, 1965.
2. Patrick, S. V., Price, P. L. & Cattell, R. B. A discriminant function for diagnostically separating depressive disorders, based on the OA Kit measures. Unpublished manuscript. University of Hawaii at Manoa, 1979.

REFERENCES

Barton, K., & Cattell, R. B. Personality before and after a chronic illness. *Journal of Clinical Psychology,* 1972, *28,* 464–467.

Barton, K., Cattell, R. B., & Vaughn, G. M. Changes in personality as a function of college attendance or work experience. *Journal of Counseling Psychology,* 1973, *20,* 162–165.

Barton, K., Dielman, F. E., & Cattell, R. B. Personality, motivation, and I.Q. measures as predictors of school achievement and grades. *Psychology in the Schools,* 1972, *9,* 47–51.

Birkett, H. *The structure of the ego, factor-analytically determined on a basis of past and present clinical concepts.* Unpublished doctoral dissertation. University of Hawaii, 1979.

Birkett, H., & Cattell, R. B. Diagnosis of the dynamic roots of a clinical symptom by P-technique: A case of episodic alcoholism. *Multivariate Experimental Clinical Research,* 1978, *3,* 173–194.

Cartwright, D. T., Tomson, B., & Schwartz, H. *Gang delinquency.* Monterey, Calif.: Brooks/Cole, 1975.

Cattell, R. B. *Personality and motivation structure and measurement.* New York: Harcourt, 1957.

Cattell, R. B. Evaluating therapy as a total personality change: Theory and available instruments. *American Journal of Psychotherapy,* 1966, *20,* 69–88.

Cattell, R. B. *The diagnosis of schizophrenia by questionnaires and objectives* personality tests. In D. V. Sarka (Ed.), *Schizophrenia: Current concepts and research.* New York: PJD Publications, 1969.

Cattell, R. B. A factor analytic system for clinicians: The integration of functional and psychometric requirements in a quantitative and computerized diagnostic system. In A. R. Mahrer (Ed.), *New approaches to personality classification.* New York: Columbia University Press, 1970.

Cattell, R. B. *Personality and mood by questionnaire.* San Francisco: Jossey-Bass, 1973.(a)

Cattell, R. B. The measurement of the healthy personality and the healthy society. *The Counselling Psychologist,* 1973, *4,* 13–18. (b)

Cattell, R. B. Structured learning theory applied to personality change. In R. B. Cattell & R. M. Dreger (Eds.), *Handbook of modern personality theory.* Washington, D.C.: Hemisphere (Wiley), 1977.

Cattell, R. B. *Personality and learning theory.* New York: Springer, 1978.

Cattell, R. B., & Birkett, H. *Controlled psychotherapy by objective diagnosis and applied structured learning theory* New York: Springer, 1979.

Cattell, R. B., Blewett, D. B., & Beloff, J. R. The inheritance of personality: A multiple variance analysis determination of approximate nature-nuture ratios for primary personality factors in Q-data *American Journal of Human Genetics,* 1955, *7,* 122–146.

Cattell, R. B., & Butcher, H. J. *The prediction of achievement and creativity.* Indianapolis: Bobbs Merrill, 1968.

Cattell, R. B., & Child, D. *Motivation and dynamic structure.* New York: Halsted Press, 1975.

Cattell, R. B., & Dreger, R. M. *Handbook of modern personality theory.* Washington, D.C.: Hemisphere (Wiley), 1977.

Cattell, R. B., Eber, H. J., & Tatsuoka, M. *Handbook for the sixteen personality factor questionnaire.* Champaign, Ill.: Institute for Personality and Ability Testing, 1970.

Cattell, R. B., & Killian, L. R. The pattern of objective test personality factor differences in schizophrenia and the character disorders. *Journal of Clinical Psychology,* 1967, *23,* 343–348.

Cattell, R. B., Pierson, G. R., & Finkbeiner, C. Alignment of personality source traits from questionnaires and observer ratings. *Multivariate Experimental Clinical Research,* 1976, *2,* 63–88.

Cattell, R. B., & Rickels, K. The relationship of clinical symptoms and IPAT factored tests of anxiety, regression, and asthenia. *Journal of Nervous and Mental Disease,* 1968, *146,* 147–160.

Cattell, R. B., Rickels, K., Weise, C., Gray, B., & Yee, R. The effects of psychotherapy upon measured anxiety and regression. *American Journal of Psychotherapy,* 1966, *20,* 261–269.

Cattell, R. B., & Scheier, I. H. *The meaning and measurement of neuroticism and anxiety.* New York: Ronald Press, 1961.

Cattell, R. B., Schmidt, L. R., & Bjersted, A. Clinical diagnosis by the objective-analytic (O-A) personality batteries. *Journal of Clinical Psychology,* Monograph Suppls., 1972 (no. 34), *28,* 239–312.

Cattell, R. B., & Schuerger, J. M. *Personality theory in action: Handbook for the O-A personality kit.* Champaign, Ill.: Institute for Personality and Ability Testing, 1978.

Cattell, R. B., & Sweney, A. B. Measurable components on the structure of conflict manifestations. *Journal of Abnormal and Social Psychology,* 1964, *68,* 479–490.

Cattell, R. B., & Wenig, P. Dynamic and cognitive factors controlling misperception. *Journal of Abnormal and Social Psychology,* 1952, *47,* 797–809.

Freud, A. *The ego and the mechanisms of defense.* London: Hogarth, 1936.

Gorsuch, R. L., & Cattell, R. B. Personality and socio-ethical values: The structure of self and superego. In R. B. Cattell & R. M. Dreger (Eds.), *Handbook of modern personality theory.* New York: Wiley/Halsted, 1977.

Horn, J. L. Motivation and dynamic calculus concepts from multivariate experiment. In R. B. Cattell (Ed.), *Handbook of multivariate experimental psychology.* Chicago: Rand McNally, 1966.

Hunt, J. McV., Ewing, T. N., Laforge, R., & Gilbert, W. N. An integrated approach to research on therapeutic counseling with samples of results. *Journal of Counseling Psychology,* 1959, *6,* 46–54.

Institute for Personality and Ability Testing. *The culture fair intelligence tests: Scales 1, 2, and 3.* Champaign, Ill.: Author, 1959, 1973.

Karson, S., & O'Dell, J. W. *The clinical use of the 16 PF.* Champaign, Ill.: Institute for Personality and Ability Testing, 1976.

Kline, P., & Grindley, J. A 28-day case study with the M.A.T. *Journal of Multivariate Experimental Clinical Psychology,* 1974, *1,* 13–22.

Krug, S. E. *Psychological assessment in medicine.* Champaign, Ill.: Institute for Personality and Ability Testing, 1977.

Lebo, M. A., & Nesselroade, J. R. Individual difference dimensions of mood change during pregnancy identified in five P-technique factor analyses. *Journal of Research in Personality,* 1978, *12,* 205–224.

Pierson, G. R. A specification equation for predicting treatment responses. *Journal of Social Psychology,* 1965, *65,* 59–62.

Pierson, G. R., Barton, V., & Hey, G. SMAT motivation factors as predictors of academic achievement of delinquent boys. *Journal of Psychology,* 1964, *57,* 243–249.

Rickels, K., & Cattell, R. B. Drug and placebo response as a function of doctor and patient type. In P. R. G. May & J. B. Wittenborn (Eds.), *Psychotropic drug responses: Advances in prediction.* Springfield, Ill.: Charles C. Thomas, 1969.

Rickels, K., Cattell, R. B., Weise, C., Gray, B., Yee, R., Mallin, A., & Aaronson, H. G. Controlled psycho-pharmacological research in private psychiatric practice. *Psychopharmacologia,* 1966, *9,* 288–306.

Sweney, A. B. Objective measurement of strength of dynamic structure factors. In R. B. Cattell & F. W. Warburton (Eds.), *Objective personality and motivation tests.* Urbana, Ill.: University of Illinois Press, 1967.

Sweney, A. B. *A preliminary descriptive manual for individual assessment of the Motivation Analysis Test.* Champaign, Ill.: Institute for Personality and Ability Testing, 1969.

Tatro, D. F. The utility of source traits measured by the O–A (objective-analytic) battery in mental hospital diagnosis. *Multivariate Behavioral Research,* 1968, Special Clinical Issue.

Tatsuoka, M. M., & Cattell, R. B. Linear equations for estimating a person's occupational adjustment, based on information on occupational profiles. *British Journal of Educational Psychology,* 1970, *40,* 324–334.

C H A P T E R

7

PERSON VARIABLES IN THERAPEUTIC
CHANGE AND DEVELOPMENT

PAUL KAROLY

Throughout the period of its emergence from the rarefied atmosphere of the laboratory (with its implicitly "rattomorphic" view of the human condition), behavior modification was negatively regarded among the majority of clinical practitioners. To its critics, learning theory represented a school of thought opposed to depth psychotherapy as well as to popular nondirective and humanistic brands of clinical intervention. Behaviorists of the 1950s and 1960s eschewed the speculative, the circular, the nontestable, and the inferential in favor of the manipulable, operational, and quantifiable. To the believers in the tenets of logical positivism and the value of precision over that of richness (cf. Wertheimer, 1972), any attempt to understand the psychology of the normal or abnormal individual by scaling the heights of "personality structure and organization" was roundly repudiated. One simply could not construct a model of the person from the top down—the labyrinth of cognition and emotion being too insidious a trap for even the cleverest of conceptualizers. Experimentally oriented clinicians of the day took solace in what Andrew Salter (1952) called "the healthiest trend of all in the college and university work"—the view that "for practical therapeutic purposes, the human being is largely a habit machine" (p. 154).

As we draw into the 1980s, advocates of the behavioral perspective no longer view for an identity. Their niche seems deep and secure. Their house, constructed from the "ground up" so to speak, is safe from wolves, whether they hail from Vienna or Esalen. But a second mortgage on that sturdy house may be in the offing. Behaviorism now faces the challenges that come from being an essentially self-examining, data-oriented enterprise. There exists no more compelling a challenge than to be able to deal adequately with the demand for durable, meaningful, extendable, and flexible therapeutic learning.

The basic elements of learning-theory-inspired programs of behavior change are by now quite familiar to most students and professionals. Some key material has been outlined in previous chapters of this volume, as well as in a variety of other available sources (e.g., Bandura, 1969; Bergin & Garfield, 1971; Bergin & Suinn, 1975; Goldstein & Stein, 1976; Kanfer & Goldstein, 1975; Kazdin, 1975; Kazdin & Wilson, 1978; Nay, 1976; O'Leary & Wilson, 1975; Yates, 1975). It is generally accepted that measurable short-term alterations in response repertoires can be achieved through behavioral interventions. However, short-term change appears to be a relatively common outcome of many forms of treatment, including psychoanalysis, relaxation, exhortation, and even sugar pills (cf. Kazdin & Wilcoxon, 1976; Orne, 1962; Shapiro & Morris, 1978; Sloane, Staples, Cristol, Yorkson, & Whipple, 1975; Wilkins, 1973). The growing recognition of the desirability of extended therapeutic follow-up notwithstanding, the sobering fact remains that the "demonstration of a successful intervention and an identified therapeutic source plus long-term maintenance of improvement has been about as common as a mute politician" (Mahoney, 1977, p. 9).

The "maintenance problem" is really a combination of problems. Of prime importance is the "outcome problem." Of the literally millions of clinical interventions implemented by various mental health professions, only a fraction ever undergo thorough examination with respect to effectiveness. Of those interventions that do include self-scrutiny, only a small percentage obtain data about extended posttreatment maintenance or transfer of within-therapy learning. Contrary to the beliefs (perhaps, more appropriately, the hopes) of those who would see their therapeutic techniques as being facilitators of long-lasting, adaptive change, patients seldom give evidence of "natural" or "automatic" persistence of treatment gains (Ayllon & Azrin, 1968; Baer, Wolf, & Risley, 1968; Conway

& Bucher, 1976; Franks & Wilson, 1973–78; Kazdin & Bootzin, 1972; Keeley, Shemberg, & Carbonell, 1976; M. A. Lieberman, Yalom, & Miles, 1973; Marholin, Siegel, & Phillips, 1976; O'Leary & Drabman, 1971; Walker & Buckley, 1972; Wildman & Wildman, 1975; Yates, 1975). In addition, evidence for the transfer or generalization of treatment effects across settings or behaviors is scant (Buchwald, 1976). Further, Buchwald (1976) has noted an apparently inexplicable *asymmetry* in generalization. Maladaptive behavior seems to generalize, while behaviors learned in therapy do not:

> Subjects who come for treatment because their behavior constitutes a problem in a setting such as school or home show the same behavior in the treatment setting. However, the behavioral changes produced by operant treatment seldom generalize to the subjects' natural settings. (p. 345)

Perhaps the most critical dimension of the maintenance problem is associated with the manner in which the proposed therapeutic solution is framed. In general, solutions have been of two kinds—technical and theoretical. Many contemporary behaviorists have taken a strongly technological route, on the assumption that the conceptual foundations of their science are essentially correct. Increased resistance to extinction, enhanced generalization, and greater transfer have been sought through such varied means as schedule thinning, booster sessions, programming the extratherapy contingencies, overlearning, and training in the self-management of cues and reinforcers. Because procedural refinements continue to be devised and tested, it is too early to evaluate their success with reasonable reliability. However, there appears to be considerable promise associated with a multielement, active, real-world orientation to the questions of treatment durability and spread of effects.

The purpose of this chapter is to offer another point of view: a conceptual perspective complementary to and compatible with the change-oriented and technique-oriented perspectives of contemporary behavioral psychology. The suggestions to be presented here are based on the premise that the principles of learning, while necessary for understanding many forms of therapeutic behavior modification, are not complete or sufficient in themselves to explain therapeutic change and its long-range effects. Let me hasten to add that the structuralist, insight-oriented, trait, or person-centered approaches are also viewed as being inadequate to account for the myriad forms of change and/or stabilization of human thought and action that characterize the psychotherapeutic encounter.

ON THE INSUFFICIENCY
OF S-R LEARNING MODELS

If we are to assume that the psychotherapy process operates according to the so-called laws of learning, it would behoove us to define just
what is meant by the terms "learning" and "psychotherapy." Unfortunately, precise definitions for these basic terms are presently lacking,
giving our independent and dependent variables a good deal of conceptual space in which to roam. The result of this state of affairs is both
beneficial, to the extent that explanatory systems should appropriately be
open, but disadvantageous, to the degree that communication between
colleagues is often impeded by what appear to be differences in
philosophy and purpose.

Psychotherapy is frequently defined in terms of goals and/or procedures (and often without clear separation between the ideal and the actual; Reisman, 1971). In the beginning, goals of behavioral intervention
tended to center on habit modification, anxiety reduction, and the
development of rudimentary skills. More recently, however, the potential has been recognized for developing learning-based programs the
focus of which has come to be on primary prevention and training in
such skills as coping with everyday stress, decision making, interpersonal
conflict resolution, self-management, relationship building, and the
capacity for adaptive (flexible) lifestyle change. In this context, even the
distinction between "behavioral" and "humanistic" approaches is
beginning to blur (Krasner, 1978; Wandersman, Poppen, & Ricks, 1976).

Clarification of the ambiguities contained within the various definitions of "learning" would, in this writer's opinion, go a long way toward
legitimizing the classical and instrumental conditioning paradigms as applied within the emerging behavior therapy enterprise. Although its
specific objectives may change, the behavior modification movement still
rests on a solid learning foundation. How easily it will rest, however, is
still an open question. It may well turn out that a change in posture will
be demanded.

Perhaps the most salient ambiguity contained in current definitions
of learning is the failure to provide a balance between the emphasis on
the processes of change and on those of stability. Both aspects are clearly
seen as necessary. The latter cannot exist without the former, but the
former is rather pointless without the latter. Learning has traditionally
been defined as a "relatively permanent change in behavior." Tests for
learning commonly include not only the rise of the negatively accelerated
curve of acquisition, but also retention, resistance to extinction, and
generalization. However, the central thrust of learning theory,

methodology and applications have *not* been to examine the course of asymptotic performance (the end point or ultimate objective of acquisition); instead it has stressed the induction of overt performance changes and the fine-grained analysis of the specific experimental manipulations that constitute the "conditions of practice," "reinforcement," or "contiguity." The addition of the qualifier "relatively permanent" to the definition of learning was, in some sense, merely a means of ruling out the effects of such factors as fatigue, illness, or drug influences which are extraneous to the processes of reinforced practice. Similarly, the study of stimulus generalization (a postacquisiton phenomenon) was undertaken by many early investigators only as a means of determining how much control the original training stimulus had over the organism's responding (J. F. Hall, 1976).

On a very concrete level, then, the purpose of much of the learning literature has been to attempt to explain behavioral change and its deteminants. The focus of many learning experiments has been movement, physical and/or psychological. The subject (animal or human) has been required to progress from point *x* to point *y*, whether that progression involves change of locale (e.g., start box to goal box) or change of response probability (e.g., no knowledge of a paired-associate list to 90% correct associations; no preference for response options to discriminative responding on the reinforced alternative; reliable emission of "inappropriate response" to reliable omission of "inappropriate response"). But what happens once the subject achieves *y*? Since the theories pivot around external factors as being responsible for *taking the subject from x to y,* it is quite natural that external factors would still be invoked as being responsible for *keeping the subject at y.* The subject must continue to practice or the contingencies must remain in effect in order to prevent the learner from returning to *x* (or at least to a state of indifference with respect to *y*).

The psychology of transfer may be the only "traditional" topic that addresses long-term outcomes directly. While the term "transfer" is sometimes used to denote "transfer of control," this operant concept is a synonym for classical and instrumental signal learning (stimulus discrimination), and therefore the control involved is considered to reside primarily in the environment (Rachlin, 1976). Transfer, as in transfer of learning (sometimes known as "learning to learn"), places a comparatively strong emphasis on the necessary learning conditions "within the learner" and on the establishment of "capabilities that will be of lasting and general usefulness to the individual" (Gagné, 1970, p. 334). It is interesting to note that the concept of transfer has been used most extensively in laboratory research dealing with motor skills learning, and in educational research (e.g., the concept of "advance organizers"; Ausubel, 1960; Ausubel & Robinson, 1969; Lawton, 1977). Although recommended as relevant to psychotherapy (Goldstein, Heller, & Sechrest, 1966) the phenomena of transfer have not seen widespread application in behavior modification programs (Kazdin, 1978). Indeed, the most notable "learning set" in the clinical behavior-change literature is probably "generalized imitation," a concept not without its critics (cf. Bandura, 1969).

In addition to ambiguities among definitions and omissions of important learning phenomena, data have begun to accumulate which raise doubts about the viability of what Staats (1975) calls the "elemental behavioristic" model of human behavior change and persistence. Among the common arguments against the sufficiency of an S–R account of therapeutic maintenance are the following: (1) classical and operant paradigms may be insufficient to explain response *acquisition* (thereby suggesting inherent limitations to their cogency as models of maintenance); (2) so-called nonspecific elements, often discussed as plausible alternative explanations for the occasional findings of maintenance and generalization, are nonspecific only as they relate to learning theories; (3) the question of change has been judged to be but one side of a two-sided, "systems-oriented" view of human adaptation; it has been suggested that equal attention be devoted to the discovery of principles of stabilization or continuity of responding (in this regard, person variables, the concepts of short- and long-term memory, and culture-specific variables, e.g., transitional roles, sex-role differences, and ethnic differences, have been implicated); and (4) the kinds and conditions of learning studied from within the purview of classical and operant conditioning may not be the most representative of the kinds and conditions of learning actually taking place in psychotherapy.

A brief account of each of these criticisms will precede arguments favoring an "integrated" look at therapeutic learning, and the inclusion of personality factors within an objective psychology of maintenance.

On the Generality of Acquisition Principles

In recent years theoretical accounts of conditioning phenomena have not been dominated by the old, familiar constructs dealing with the motivational properties of external stimuli. Instead, contemporary theories have taken on a decidedly *biosocial* and *cognitive* character. This "new look" in learning is partly the result of the predictive failures of traditional models (Brewer, 1974).

The external programming of animal and human response probability or choice is not accomplished nearly as smoothly as textbooks written in the 1950s and 1960s would have us believe. It does seem to matter what stimuli are employed as CSs and UCSs, what instrumental acts one attempts to strengthen, and how subjects are oriented in an experimental environment. Biological constraints on learning have been noted, species-specific capabilities acknowledged, and the arbitrariness and artificiality of laboratory settings discussed (cf. Revusky & Garcia, 1970; B. Schwartz, 1978; Seligman & Hager, 1972). Of course, biological constraints do not necessarily apply as readily to the human learner, whose actions are far less stereotyped and whose environments are far more complex than those of the laboratory animal (Bandura, 1977a). The associationist model of acquisition may be deceptively simplified in the case of infrahuman species. This condition alone strongly suggests the need for revision of the model in human applications. Far greater emphasis on the learner in the "learning event" appears to be in order (Gagné, 1970).

The data we now possess about the process of acquisition may also be peculiar to the nature of the controlled environments in which they were generated. Because learning is often taken to be synonymous with changes in the frequency of that behavior which is temporally contiguous with the delivery of a reinforcer (Shimp, 1975), it becomes difficult to view the reinforcement contingency as being anything other than the royal road to adaptation. However, in the laboratory, as well as in the "real world," the very ubiquity of reinforcers (both as response-contingent events and as discriminative stimuli) may play a key role in undermining growth and long-term adaptation. With respect to this point, Staddon (1975) has suggested the *Range of Variation Hypothesis:*

The range of behavioral variation is inversely related to the "strength" of a contingency, without regard to its sign. (p. 45)

The widespread emphasis on powerful contingencies (delivered frequently and contingently) is perhaps defensible only if the demonstration of control over the organism is the desired end point. If a restriction of variation under strong contingencies occurs universally (Staddon, 1975), then a total reliance on the law of effect in training should virtually ensure the solidification of a narrow class of behaviors that will not generalize (cf. Chapter 11). Therefore, even if we fully understood the "laws" of acquisition, we might not wish to use them for many practical therapeutic purposes.

Nonspecific Elements

Individual difference psychology remains a discipline quite separate and apart from the experimental approach to "scientific" psychology (Cronbach, 1975). For example, by demanding stable behavioral baselines for purposes of precision, operant investigators have ruled out, or controlled for, many of the learner-mediated effects that field (naturalistic) researchers have deemed critical to the formulation of adequate predictive models (cf. Sidman, 1960; Wachtel, 1973). When individual differences emerge despite the "equalization" of initial states, their influence is termed "nonspecific" or "technique independent."

The well-known brands of nonspecific factor include: motivation to change, expectancy of success (or belief in the efficacy of "treatment"), intellectual capability or aptitude, attention, arousal, knowledge (awareness) of the contingencies, fluctuations in mood, and the differential development of the subject's task-relevant and correlated behavioral repertoire. Such variables, whether found in laboratory or therapy outcome studies, may be considered (depending on one's point of view) as (a) nuisance factors, (b) limiting conditions, or (c) elements to be entered into a complex, interaction equation.

The present criticism of any elemental behaviorism which minimizes nonspecific variables is simple: if knowledge about so-called nonspecific factors is useful in enhancing our ability to predict and control behavior, then they should be included in a theoretical network and promoted from the status of "error term" to full-fledged *variable*! Only an anachronistic radical behaviorist commitment to observability would legislate against recognition of such factors (Karoly, 1972). At the very least the examination of these factors as legitimate phenomena may help us to understand the aforementioned limits on the generality of stimulus and contingency control. All scientific laws, including (perhaps especially) the law of effect, operate within functional domains and are subject to boundary conditions. Therefore, it is appropriate to assume:

that individual differences can be conceptualized as limiting or boundary conditions, and that laws of learning need to consider the assessment of constraints referring to [the] initial state [of the organism] (Glaser, 1967, p. 14)

At another level, individual differences may even be accorded the status of equal partner in the enterprises of behavior theory, assessment, and modification (e.g., Staats, 1975). As Jensen (1967) suggested:

most of what experimental psychologists really want to find out about the nature of learning actually requires an individual differences approach. (p. 118)

This relatively recent, and still controversial, insight on the part of the community of experimental psychologists is antedated by the recognition among many personality theorists of the need for a learning component in their accounts of behavior stabilization (C. S. Hall & Lindzey, 1978; Levy, 1970).

Learning as a Preparatory Step: Acquisition versus Continuity in Social Adaptation.

Another problem with the use of traditional S–R learning models as the scaffolding for a maintenance as well as an acquisition technology follows from the mounting evidence in support of a learning–memory distinction. If learning and retention (coding, storage, and retrieval) are distinguishable (and this does not imply that they are independent), then a monolithic learning-based approach to long-term response stabilization might be likened to a commercial airplane pilot's exclusive reliance on the aerodynamic principles of lift to provide the rationale for the complete management of the plane in flight.

In some sense the differentiation between learning and memory is quite arbitrary. Learning implies the trial-to-trial persistence (retention) of training effects. Likewise, memory (retrieval) implies prior learning (storage) of encountered material. The distinction between experiments concerned with "learning processes" and those concerned with "memory processes" may be seen to lie solely in the experimenter's choice of analytic unit. As J. F. Hall (1976) states:

The utilization of multiple trials almost invariably meant that the investigator was interested in the operation of a particular variable that manifested itself over trials, thus permitting an examination of the influence of that variable on the learning process. When the experimenter permitted a lengthy time period to elapse between the presentation of the material and a subsequent test for recall, the process measured on the recall test was presumed to be memory (or retention). (p. 4)

There are, however, reasons to believe that the distinction between learning and memory involves more than mere procedural variation. First, the postulation of an intimate relationship between learning and memory does not necessarily preclude the existence of separate "mechanisms" underlying these processes. If the principles of "reinforced practice" that might have brought on organism from x to y (be it a discrimination learning or verbal learning experiment) were the same as the principles accounting for retention (stability at y) then all of the following should obtain: (1) equal learning should always produce equal retention; (2) formal training operations should always set the limit on the amount of information the organism held after the retention interval; (3) all experiential variables should affect learning and retention in the same manner; (4) learning and retention should bear the same relationship to each other irrespective of the task; and (5) no new principles (aside from reinforcement or contiguity) should be needed to explain (predict) the course of forgetting. Data exist, however, in dispute of each of these logical corollaries (Flaherty, Hamilton, Gandelman, & Spear, 1977).

Also, in a broad sense learning is often taken to represent a set of operations performed upon the individual (whether through the application of reward/punishment, via instructions, etc.). On the other hand, memory or retention (particularly since the time of Sir Frederick Bartlett's research) has implied an active, dynamic, constructive process wherein the individual performs operations upon information received from the environment. Because constructive processes are believed to be "determined jointly by the immediate context, the cognitive abilities, and the sociohistorical milieu of the individual" (Paris & Lindauer, 1977, p. 37), we are once again encouraged, if not intellectually bound, to examine personality components.

In order to understand or even explore the processes of retention, we must set our sights on where the individual is going, or thinks he is going, and not just on where the individual is now or has been. The human learner has the capacity to restructure and reintegrate past experiences for novel uses, long after the original "stimulus–response pairing." Since interpersonal adjustment involves changing internal as well as external criteria (rather than the achievement of a single "end state"), the constructivist view of retention as a "bridge" or "pathway" rather than as an S–R *bond* more accurately reflects the open-ended nature of human adaptation (Horton & Turnage, 1976; Sechrest & Wallace, 1967). In seeking to address the complex question of behavior maintenance through a parametric extension of S–R theories, whose foci of convenience have been the achievement of short-term behavior change, the contemporary applied behavior analyst may find himself plowing an oddly conservative field.

In addition, we might point to the need for our conceptions to go even beyond constructive memory and response stabilization and to incorporate creativity, innovation, curiosity, independence from environmental contraints, and other "divergent" forms of adaptation. As Dirkes (1978) has suggested:

1. The learning process is based upon intuition, task sequencing and/or an independent production and manipulation of ideas;

2. The divergent production of ideas is characterized by fluency, flexibility, originality, and elaboration. (p. 819)

A model of adjustment that subsumes cultural determinants and the periodic stresses associated with alterations in cultural prescriptions and individual capabilities might well be written in purely S–R terms. But in such a model the individual would probably play a rather minor role—as a mere recipient of ''new programming'' rather than as the initiator and manager of his or her own life transitions. Behavioral flexibility in the pure S–R model would result from the operation of such factors as stimulus and response generalization, but response options would be severely limited. Yet it may ultimately be much more efficient to teach people (after having assessed their prior abilities) how to see the need for new lifestyles, how to divest themselves of the old, and how to use their present skills to acquire and retain additional competencies in the service of adaptation.

On the Representativeness of Therapeutic Learning Tasks

The psychotherapy outcome literature is rife with so-called paradoxes and inexplicable findings. Spontaneous change, spontaneous remission of symptoms, the persistence of maladaptive responding, placebo cures, the occasional superiority of nonprofessional helpers are a few of the puzzles confronting both theorists and clinicians. It is important to remember, however, especially when considering behavior maintenance, that paradoxes are of our own making (Sechrest & Wallace, 1967). Why do the laws of learning operate differently in the laboratory from the ways they do in the consulting room? Perhaps a part of the answer is that we have been looking at an explicable phenomenon, but with conceptual blinders. Not only might it be wise to expand our theoretical models to include factors other than those traditionally incorporated into S–R models, but the very targets of our analytical efforts may need replacement.

In distinguishing among learning (associating and discriminating), constructive retention, and innovation, we have set the stage for our final critical assault on the practice of extrapolating from the animal laboratory to the clinic. Just as there may be distinctive *phases* in the course of successful adaptation involving different *processes*, so too the *tasks* and *boundary conditions* of learning may vary. While it may be true that many instances of therapeutic acquisitions involve the making of skilled motor responses, the control of disorganizing emotional responses, or the establishment of subtle stimulus and/or response differentiations, there is also a wide variety of client problems characterized by functions like verbal and imaginal mediation, abstraction, information processing or problem solving. The conditions governing the acquisition and mobilization of these higher-order forms of performance competency may fall far outside the focus and range of convenience of Skinnerian or Pavlovian theory and technology. The employment of partial schedules, the development of social reinforcers, or the provision of common stimuli in training and in extratherapy settings may be most useful when the tasks of learning involve *being able to behave in the same general fashion under essentially similar setting conditions, or being able to generalize within a definable but narrow range of stimulus and response conditions.*

The view that the therapeutic learning task incorporates divergent productivity as well as the establishment, and/or extinction, of motor and proprioceptive responses is not new (cf. Dollard & Miller, 1950; Rotter, 1954). Yet extrapolations from the realm of language acquisition, concept learning, serial learning, and problem solving to the therapy process have been relatively rare. With the advent of cognitive social learning (e.g., Bandura, 1977a; Kanfer & Phillips, 1970; Lazarus, 1971; Mahoney, 1974; Mischel, 1973; Staats, 1975) has come a softening of the "habit machine" emphasis. Yet it has more often been the mechanisms of learning rather than the problems, goals, or outcomes of learning, that have become diffused and elaborated.

Because of their accent on the shaping and strengthening of instrumental skills or the deconditioning of affective reactions, the contiguity, associationist, and contingency-based models have tended to neglect such important attributes of human adjustment as: the temporal extensivity and multilayered nature of the to-be-learned skills; developmental and normative concerns; the individual's state of readiness for certain kinds of acquisitions; social, economic, and political constraints; and the effects of time-bound decisional and motivational parameters. When the world is represented by a T maze, a Pavlovian harness, or an operant chamber, such concerns tend not to arise.

TOWARD AN INTEGRATED VIEW

Calls for synthesis or integration of differing viewpoints in psychology frequently fall on deaf ears because they appear to imply the repudiation of cherished values, philosophies, and/or methodologies, and because all too often such "calls" amount to little more than empty clamor: sound in the absence of substance, rhetoric in the absence of systemization.

However, the contemporary emphasis on interactionism and general systems theory as metaphilosophical foundations (e.g., Bandura, 1977a; Magnusson & Endler, 1977; Ray & Brown, 1975; Royce & Buss, 1976; Staats, 1975) now provides an atmosphere in which a "unified theory" of behavior, its change and stabilization, may be fruitfully pursued. The goals of humanistic and experimental psychology are no longer seen as being necessarily in conflict. Learning and cognition are no longer at opposite ends of the empirical continuum. Thus personality theorists are now counseled to seek to do more than describe organismic "states" or "traits" in purely subjective terms. Similarly, functionalists are advised to approach the objective psychology of state-to-state transition with a healthy respect for mediational constructs and individual differences. Predictive efficiency is coming to be seen as being best served, then, by explanatory models that begin at a level of complexity commensurate with that of the phenomena under investigation (cf. Kessen, 1962; Sutherland, 1973).

A balanced appreciation of state description, intra- and interindividual personality variation, and transition parameters (going beyond the immediately available cues and reinforcers) as they apply to the multiple and reinterative tasks of clinical treatment should be the goal of a truly empirical approach to psychotherapeutics. Personal development is not a monolithic process. Growth is not a totally predictable, smooth-flowing process. Therefore, only a systematic view that acknowledges the causative and interactive effects of a client's biological, cognitive, affective, and instrumental repertoires in conjunction with the facilitative and nonfacilitative realities of the social milieu can hope to serve as a model for durable therapeutic intervention. The schematic shown in Figure 7-1 represents an attempt to portray, in broad outline, the *interrelated* and-*recurring* goals of treatment, and the relevant mediators of task achievement at each figurative "stage" of therapeutic change and stabilization.

This chapter could just as reasonably have begun with an analysis of the "Insufficiency of Structural (Trait; Psychodynamic) Conceptions" of change and maintenance. However, the psychological literature is well stocked with such critiques. Indeed, there are ample arguments to suggest that the so-called traditional approaches to psychopathology and psychotherapy have yet to establish their *necessity*. On the other hand, starting from a position of acknowledged accomplishment, learning-based models are seen as capable not only of withstanding the preceding critical assaults, but also (when inserted into a central position in our

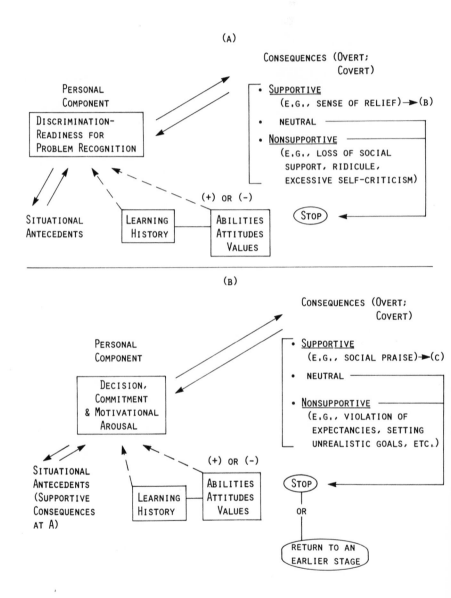

Figure 7-1. Schematic outline of an "open task" cognitive social-learning view of psychotherapy processes.

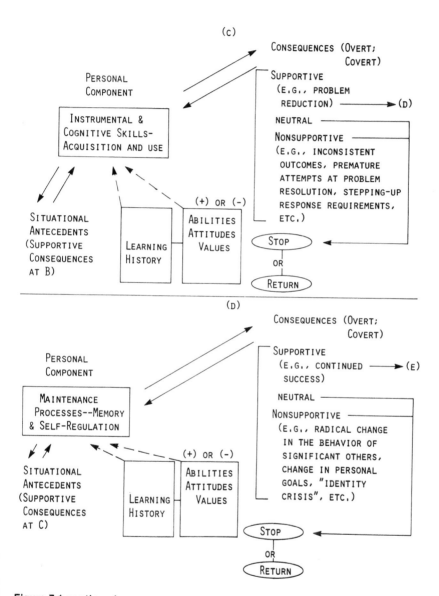

Figure 7-1 *continued.*

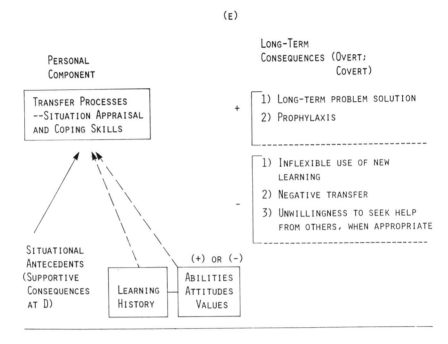

Figure 7-1 *continued*.

conceptual template) of serving as the foundation for a comprehensive clinical paradigm (cf. Staats, 1975).

Some of the salient attributes of this admittedly pretheoretical paradigm are presented below in outline form:

1. It includes ability, attitude, and value factors that are considered capable of either facilitating or impeding the course of learning and maintenance. The impeding components may represent the "non-specific," counterchange elements often overlooked in the analysis of treatment failure.

2. It includes the *content* of therapeutic learning tasks, as well as their putative mechanisms.

3. It includes relatively stable personality dimensions ("personal components") within a system that is explicitly change sensitive and "dynamic" with respect to the sources of psychological input. The locus of both stability and change is *the system*. Each personality component is preceded by situational antecedents and followed by consequences which may or may not support its continued operation.

4. It illustrates the operational, as well as the logical, impossibility of separating the person from the setting for purposes of explanation or intervention.

5. It explicity emphasizes continuity, connectedness, and the probabilistic relationship among elements. Quite clearly no course is inevitable or automatic. Neither "strong egos" nor "behavioral traps" are depicted as shortcuts to successful adjustment.

6. It has the potential for guiding the clinical "troubleshooter" in determining the source(s) of treatment failure. If long-term maintenance of adaptive change does *not* occur, the model suggests not only the possibility of inadequate implementation of learning principles, but the existence of patient-mediated obstacles and/or specific systems dysfunction.

Most important for our present purposes, the outline provides a framework for an organized discussion of the role of person variables within a functional theory of therapeutic learning (change and continuity). To date, the matter of individual differences has received only scattered attention in both the behavior therapy and the learning literatures. I would venture to guess that the general indifference toward personality theory and its constructs is traceable to the historical separation between the traditions of *psychometric-introspectionist-structuralist* psychology and the *manipulative-objectivist-functionalist* version of human science. Applied behaviorists as well as learning researchers have simply not known what to look for. The result has been an "almost-empty-organism" psychology of behavioral intervention, or one in which convenience or popular clinical trends have dictated the occasional incorporation of personality measures for the reduction of error variance.

What graduate student (or seasoned researcher, for that matter) has not contemplated "throwing in" a Rotter I–E Scale or a posttreatment survey of participants' task attributions? But how often have the results of such assessments made the slightest bit of difference in the design of future studies, or in the investigator's interpretation of his or her theoretical commitments?

Having argued against the sufficiency of a *single-process* view of learning and in favor of the need to supplement familiar S–R conceptions with constructs derived from the psychologies of motivation, personality, information processing, memory, and creative problem solving, the next step will be to illustrate *how and where* attention to individual differences with respect to these variables can aid the empirically oriented clinician. In the presentation that follows, I shall not address the various ways in which situational cues and consequences may either bolster or undermine change efforts. The reader will find ample discussion of environmental determinants in several of the other chapters in this volume.

The following presentation may also disappoint readers who insist on finished products rather than blueprints. However, it is a rare finished product of any worth which was not based on a well-delineated set of blueprints. And the potential for research on *learner differences* across the various stages of psychotherapeutic growth is as fresh and exciting as the growing rapprochement between personality and behavior theory. Using the central or individual differences portion of the model (Figure 7-2) as a general topical outline, we will selectively review theory and research dealing with each of the "personal components," illustrating their potential contributions to the clinical psychology of change (learning) and maintenance. This chapter will have fulfilled its purpose if it helps to set in motion a cycle of research relating individual differences to treatment success. As discussed by Rohwer (1976), the four steps in such a research program would include: (1) the establishment of reliable and accurately characterized phenomena; (2) the formulation of hypothesis about learner differences (pinpointing the role of between-person variations in capacity and/or propensity to perform); (3) the verification of hypotheses through the design of compensatory training experiments; and (4) the exploitation of the results of hypothesis verification (the promulgation of improved modes of clinical intervention).

READINESS FOR PROBLEM RECOGNITION

Occasionally in the clinical literature the issue of *client readiness* is addressed. Unfortunately, readiness is often interpreted to mean only the individual's willingness to place himself or herself in the hands of an authoritative therapist or nurturant institution. Willingness to undergo some form of treatment must logically be presumed to depend, however, on a prior discrimination—the discrimination of the existence of stress, conflict, or negative consequences associated with the enactment of a particular behavior or pattern of behavior. In the absence of problem recognition, the yes–no decision to seek therapy is precluded (except in the case of mandatory treatment for criminal offenders and the enforced

Figure 7-2. The processes of therapeutic change and development: a person-centered view.

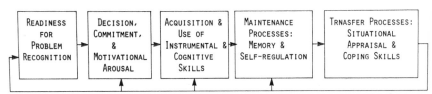

treatment of children—processes about which little is known). Even after the original problem perception and the initiation of therapy, the nature of the voluntary client's problem appraisal is critical to the continued success of treatment.

Since assisting potential clients to make adequate intial problem discriminations might be viewed as being akin to "ambulance chasing", psychologists have generally confined their experimental probes to the nature of client change-related motivation and self-attributions. Such factors are noted in the second stage of our outline, and will be considered shortly. However, our mission at present is to assert the importance of a neglected therapeutic task, i.e., facilitating the client's recognition of the adverse consequences of some segment of his or her actions.[1]

Some of the personality constructs that may play a role in the accomplishment of the task of problem recognition include attentional styles and mode of emotional modulation (e.g.,repression–sensitization). Attitude–value constructs that may be relevant to the task of problem recognition include acceptance/nonacceptance of personal responsibility and the individual's orientation vis-à-vis internal and external "locus of causality" (cf. deCharms, 1968; Rotter, 1966). Finally, an individual's transient and more characteristic levels of arousal may both be influential in determining what aspects of experience are perceived and remembered (Eriksen & Eriksen, 1972; M. W. Eysenck, 1976). Thus, an individual's preparatory set or readiness to discriminate a personal adjustment problem is likely to be a function of physiological state, cognitive-perceptual, attitudinal, and ability factors in addition to the necessary environmental cues and contingencies.

Although this author prefers an integrated concept of *preparatory set*, the literature consists largely of separate and modality-specific appraisals. I will briefly consider some of the better known and to my mind more promising accounts of readiness to perceive, showing how they might apply to the clinical objective of lasting behavior modification.

Certainly among the oldest of learning readiness concepts is the *orienting reflex,* introduced by Pavlov in 1910. As discussed by Sokolov (1960) the orienting reflex (OR) refers to a special kind of unconditioned reflex initiated by a qualitative change, increase, or decrease in the value of a stimulus, and one that is subject to extinction or habituation with repeated presentations. The OR is believed capable of augmenting the discriminatory power (sensitivity) of the perceptual system. While there is little reason to focus on the Pavlovian mechanism per se,[2] it does serve to remind us (1) that learning is predicated on stimulus selectivity and (2) that novelty often acts as an impellent force, helping to convert nominal stimuli into functional stimuli, and setting up the mechanisms for perceptual processing (Medin, 1976). Although theories of discrimination learning have tended to focus on how external stimuli (or stimulus compounds) gain differential control over behavior, the organism is also presumed to orient to self-produced stimuli. Thus, it is reasonable to assume that learning to change (in a therapeutic context) would be preceded by a process of *discriminated self-awareness* (sometimes called *self-monitoring*), and that in addition to situational antecedents there may be acquired cognitive habits that affect *differential* or *selective attention to self*. Of course, this last assertion does not necessarily follow from discrimination learning theories, and may smack of mentalistic thinking—but there are sources for its support.

Space limitations preclude an elaborate defense of the scientific legitimacy of the cognitivist concepts of "attention" and "self." Attention which in the S–R tradition has been objectified as "the selective control of behavior by a subset of the stimuli present during learning" (D.A. Lieberman, 1974, p. 325) has also been interiorized and defined as a process of abstraction, based on limited sensory capacity and involving the selective analysis and filtering of environmental features (cf. Broadbent, 1958; Hebb, 1949; James, 1890; Lashley, 1938; Trabasso & Bower, 1968). There is a variety of psychological and neurophysiological research in support of a complex, central (rather than peripheral) view of attention (Horton & Turnage, 1976; John, 1976; Mackintosh, 1965). Similarly, the concept of "self" has been criticized on the grounds that in philosophical (especially phenomenological) writings it has amounted to little more than the attribution of causality to inner, mental agents whose substance could not be defined a priori (e.g., Skinner, 1953). However, it is useful to differentiate self-as-doer from the individual's attempt to process, store, integrate, and use information relevant to his actions, thoughts, and emotions (just as information about the environment is discriminated, stored, and employed for the tasks of adjustment). Therefore, if it is permissible to examine an individual's abstraction of information from the environment, and if that environment includes his or her own performances (overt and covert), then it should be feasible to conduct a psychological analysis of the factors determining the specific self-relevant features, or dimensions, toward which a person may characteristically orient or "pay attention."

Early work on the selectivity of the personal attentional system focused on the manner by which stimuli of a supposedly threatening nature (i.e., off-color words) were perceived (e.g., Bruner & Postman, 1947; McGuinnies, 1949). However, objections were soon raised dealing with the methodological adequacy of the perceptual defense experiments (Eriksen & Eriksen, 1972). In particular, it was not clear how self-relevant the stimuli were. Further, the experiments involved the selective perception of external, not internal, stimuli (although the target stimuli were hypothesized to stimulate "emotional" reactions). These are the kinds of experiments to which critics still refer when repudiating the selective attention concept. However, in recent research Mischel and his associates (Mischel, Ebbesen, & Zeiss, 1973) have examined the antecedents of individuals' selective attention to information about their own prior performances on a meaningful task (one that ostensibly assessed their intellectual ability). Both situational and dispositional factors were found to be influential in determining the amount of time subjects spent attending to information supposedly bearing on their personality "assets" and/or their personality "liabilities" during a 10-minute period following performance in a concept-learning task. As might be expected, the experiences of success or failure on the concept-learning task had an effect on attentional focus, with successful subjects paying more attention to assets than did the failure subjects. The prior experience manipulation did not influence subjects' attention to their supposed liabilities. Furthermore, the previous effect for success was largely wiped out if subjects were led to expect additional testing, and largely accounted for by subjects scoring as "sensitizers" on the Repression–Sensitization Scale (Byrne, 1964); that is, those subjects who typically use the strategy of intellectualization, and who tend to approach threat, were the ones who responded to the success condition. Correlations between subjects' scores on the Repression–Sensitization Scale and the amount of time they spent looking at assets and liabilities revealed that sensitizers were more likely to look at liabilities and repressors were more apt to attend to assets.

The results of this experiment have several interesting implications in the present context. First, the effects of the success–failure (reward–punishment) experience were mediated by the effects of a subjectively held expectancy about future testing. Thus, while situational antecedents are relevant and powerful (the success condition), their effects can be nullified by a "nonspecific" element such as expectancy. With regard to the repression–sensitization dimension, the following extrapolation to the therapeutic learning situation should be capable of empirical test: that sensitizers (those who are open to, or who focus selectively on, negative input about themselves) will be more likely both to detect (discriminate) a problem in need of treatment and to maintain treatment contact (as compared to repressors) because the sensitizers are more apt to notice therapeutic progress (i.e., "success").

Selective attention to negative information may also lead to emotional disengagement if the input is particularly aversive. Just as individuals may learn to tune in, they may acquire habits of tuning out unpleasant self-relevant feedback. Recall, for example, that the "failure" condition in the Mischel et al. (1973) study did not precipitate a strong desire in subjects to examine their personal liabilities.

Kirschenbaum and Karoly (1977) labeled the recognition and/or recording of positively valued behaviors or attributes as *positive self-monitoring* and the differential attention to negative behaviors or characteristics as *negative self-monitoring*. Further, they postulated that negative self-monitoring can be detrimental to effective self-regulation. In a laboratory-based problem-solving task, college students were instructed to monitor their successes or failures on easy and difficult tasks (after being matched for ability), and were allowed a 10-minute period of self-observation (self-initiated viewing of a videotape of their own prior problem-solving activity). Results indicated that while negative self-monitoring did not differentially diminish attention to self on difficult tasks, it did lower subjects' self-evaluations. Task difficulty was found to be a major source of regulatory dysfunction. According to Kirschenbaum and Karoly (1977):

> high task difficulty negatively aroused participants, which produced a disengagement from effective self-regulation. The course of the disengagement process was unaltered even when subjects were fitted with experimental "rose-colored glasses" (i.e., instructed to positively self-monitor). (p. 1124)

Selective attention to self may be short-circuited and lead to defensive maneuvers if the individual's heightened level of arousal undermines the processing of problem-relevant information (via distraction or by generating defeatist attitudes). Individual differences in "state" and/or "trait" anxiety, social anxiety, introversion–extraversion, frustration tolerance, or in the characteristic manner by which arousal is labeled may play a key role in both the initial and the continued recognition of personal ineffectiveness and in the success of various clinical interventions (cf. Bandura, 1977b; DiLoreto, 1971; Kopel & Arkowitz, 1975; Meichenbaum, 1976; O'Banion & Arkowitz, 1977).

It would be a mistake to focus exclusively on the process of discriminated awareness of internal states (such as anxiety, depression, or confusion) in behavioral self-observation. An equally important process is akin to what Duval and Wicklund (1972) call *subjective self-awareness*. According to these authors, individuals can focus their attentions either on themselves and their conscious states ("objective" self-awareness) or outward on events external to their body, with the resulting perception related to the self as the "source" or originator of action upon the environment (hence the term "subjective self-awareness").[3]

Knowledge of how we affect other people as well as how we affect the inanimate world is considered an essential ingredient in successful adaptation (cf. Mischel, 1976). Clearly, many adjustment problems stem from the absence of such knowledge. Likewise, the initiation of a program of therapy requires that such "insight" be present. In most cases, knowing "what's wrong with me" also involves attributions regarding "what's wrong with me in relation to how I affect outcomes in the social world." It seems reasonable to assume that the awareness of one's tendency to produce negative outcomes is a precursor to behavior change, whether that change be based on acquisition of novel response capabilities, on expectations that new or different responses will lead to positive outcomes (instrumentality), or on attributions that one will be able to execute the desired response (self-efficacy) (Bandura, 1977b; Mitchell & Biglan, 1971).

Over the years, awareness has been implicated in the mechanisms of both classical and operant conditioning (Kanfer, 1968; Postman & Sassenrath, 1961; Ross & Ross, 1976). Typically discussed in terms of the learner's ability to verbalize the operative contingencies, such awareness includes reported knowledge of the relationship between one's behavior and derived outcomes. Despite the controversy over whether organisms (animal and human *do* learn without awareness, it seems safe to conclude that in complex contexts awareness *can facilitate* response acquisition (cf. Bandura, 1977a). It is a short step, then, to the assertion that awareness of one's negative effect on the environment should also facilitate the learner's readiness to expose himself or herself to new learning.

While we have suggested that both of the directional aspects of selective attention to self (i.e., the focus on one's internal state and on one's effects on the environment) are probably critical over the course of therapeutic learning, *differential self-focus* may be involved in the recognition of varied clinical problems and in the subsequent maintenance of adaptive behavior patterns. For example, individuals with self-control problems such as obesity, drug addiction, excessive alcohol consumption, or cigarette smoking, may tend toward the monitoring of internal states of deprivation, and might benefit from a therapy program designed to turn their attention toward the interpersonal consequences of their actions. On the other hand, nonassertive or socially inhibited persons may focus excessively on external standards of conduct and the situational appropriateness of behavior. These persons might be required to learn to adopt a more self-centered attentional orientation. Individual differences in selective attentional focus (in the frequency and accuracy of self-examination as well as its direction) may, therefore, possess diagnostic, prognostic, and prescriptive implications. To test these speculations, researchers may make clinical use of a number of instruments that ostensibly tap various dimensions of attentional tuning (cf., Fenigstein, Scheier, & Buss, 1975; Laird & Berglas, 1975; Mandler, Mandler, & Uviller, 1958; Markus, 1977; Mehrabian, 1977; Rotter, 1966; Sampson, 1978; Snyder, 1974).

DECISION, COMMITMENT, AND MOTIVATIONAL AROUSAL (PROBLEM-ACCEPTANCE AND THE RESOLVE TO CHANGE)

Just as readiness to acknowledge the existence of a problem may fluctuate over the course of therapy (but is almost always necessary for initial clinical contact), so too the level of acceptance or "ownership" of one's recognized clinical dysfunction is subject to all manner of facilitative or interruptive influences. I shall assert that acceptance must achieve a minimum working level to help keep the client exposed to a learning or rehabilitative atmosphere and to help maintain the mobilization of client resources. The majority of contributions from social psychology (cf. S.S. Brehm, 1976; Fishbein & Ajzen, 1975; Janis & Mann, 1977), applied psychology (e.g., Fiedler, 1977), social learning (e.g., Kanfer & Karoly, 1972; Mischel & Ebbesen, 1970; Rotter, 1954), and motivational psychology (e.g., Atkinson & Birch, 1970; Weiner, 1976) have addressed the clinical problem of client persistence or follow-through as a function of a specific cognitive orientation which helps establish the connection between intention and action. In the context of this overview chapter we will briefly consider the contributions of each of the following: self-evaluation theory, achievement motivation research, the expectancy concept, attribution theory, and hypotheses about the binding power of behavioral commitments and intentions. Each will be considered from the perspective of individual differences and the clinical psychology of maintenance.

Self-Evaluative Processes

Once a problematic behavior pattern is identified, efforts to change may be examined as a function of the degree of discrepancy between current outcomes and desired goals. Standards for self-evaluation and goal setting, and the anticipation of their achievement, represent the motivational fuel within a cognitively oriented theory of performance regulation. A mechanism that purportedly fires the fuel in an "active organism'' model of behavior transitions is not external reinforcement, but a putative state of cognitive imbalance (inconsistency, dissonance, or incongruity).[4]

Much has been written about the utility of Festinger's (1957) theory of cognitive dissonance and its modifications (e.g., J. W. Brehm & Cohen, 1962) for the practice of clinical psychology (Goldstein et al., 1966; S. S. Brehm, 1976). Most uses of the dissonance concept have dealt with the process of increasing client attraction to the therapist or therapy program via the induction of belief-discrepant behaviors or attitudes. We shall be touching on the process of altering clients' self-attributions and its effects on the maintenance of behavior change. For now, however, our focus will rest on the mechanisms by which a client's ''natural'' recognition of belief- or goal-discrepant outcomes energizes sustained efforts at behavioral redirection, and the possible impact of individual variations on the operation of the hypothesized mechanism.

Self-evaluation includes an awareness of self as either ''object'' or ''subject'' and a comparison of self-relevant feedback to an ''ideal'' or standard. Self-evaluative standards must not only be available and unambiguous, they must be consistent with the individual's learning history, i.e., they must possess predictive utility (believability) as goals toward which the person *actually* aspires. It is assumed that the content and level of personal goals are taught, directly and indirectly, over the continuing span of socialization. The only truly innate mechanism is the capacity for information processing per se. Perhaps the only controversial aspect of this cognitive view of change motivation is associated with the assumption that the judged discrepancy between how one is currently behaving and how one would like to behave is experienced as an ''aversive'' state which prompts the individual to do something to eliminate or avoid that discrepancy.

There is large body of evidence to suggest that ''*perceptions* of internal states, whether accurate or not, control behavior'' (Weiner, 1976, p. 290). The question remains open as to whether perceptions of incongruence are inherently arousing, and thereby motivating. Sokolov's (1960) neuronal model of the orienting reflex provides an account of how the nervous system stores repetitive inputs, compares new inputs with the stored information, and automatically alerts the cortex (as measured by changes in the EEG, for example) when a qualitative shift in stimulation occurs. Similarly, Hunt (1963) has postulated that information processing per se has motivational properties, but argues that both too little, as well as too much, incongruity is arousing. However, most of the research dealing with the motivational properties of incongruity has focused on sensory and perceptual inputs, rather than on conflicting cognitions (Beck, 1978). With rare exceptions (e.g., Dember & Earl, 1957), individual differences have been ignored.

Recently, Kreitler and Kreitler (1976) presented logical and empirical evidence against a mechanistic interpretation of Sokolov's neuronal model of the orienting reflex:

> the process of matching the input to the neuronal model may pass as purely automatic. But to bring about this matching . . . necessitates a complex act of retrieval of meaning patterns and their translation—possibly even transformation— into neuronal models. Hence, the very determination of whether a stimulus is so new or relevant that an orienting response is required presupposes a complex cognitive act. (p. 51).

We are probably on safer ground if we do not assume that self-evaluative discrepancies are inherently aversive or rewarding hence possessing drive-like properties. It appears, rather, that learned (and modifiable) cognitive reactions to goal-outcome discordance can on occasion precipitate personal efforts to bring behavior in line with desired ends (Kanfer, 1971). Bandura's (1977a) model of the motivational consequencies of performance evaluation specifies a number of factors that influence the judgment process and that are subject to individual variation (see Table 7-1).

Note first that any pattern of behavior is capable of being monitored along a number of different evaluative dimensions. In the measurement of self-referenced natural cognitions it has been found that individuals differ in the content, number, and complexity of concepts used (e.g., Bieri, Atkins, Briar, Leaman, Miller, & Tripodi, 1966; Kelly, 1955), as well as in the personal importance or "centrality" attached to these dimensions (Scott, 1969). It should therefore be possible to assess both the qualitative nature of clients' perceptions and their affective response to their dysfunctional ("problem") attributes or performances. The general omission of such individualized assessment in the behavior therapy literature constitutes a discipline-wide example of the "nomothetic fallacy": the assumption that our clients view the world in the same way we do.

An example of the importance of assessing client-specific affective-evaluative dimensions was provided by Stuart (1977) in a discussion of the success of the Weight Watchers model in comparison to the traditional "professional" modes of intervention in obesity. While psychological and psychiatric appeals to clients' health-related concerns are certainly justified, Stuart noted that the majority of women undergoing weight-loss therapy were primarily motivated by concern over their physical attractiveness. Thus, a treatment program that appealed to these clients' "real-world" preoccupations was judged as standing the best chance for both short- and long-range success (assuming the therapist

Table 7-1
Component Processes in the Self-Regulation of Behavior
by Self-Produced Consequences

Performance	Judgemental process	Self-response
Evaluative dimensions	Personal standards	Self-evaluative reactions
Quality	Modeling sources	Positive
Rate	Reinforcement	Negative
Quantity	Sources	
Originality	Referential	Tangible self-applied
Authenticity	performances	consequences
Consequentialness	Standard norms	Rewarding
Deviancy	Social compari-	Punishing
Ethicalness	ison	
	Personal com-	No self-response
	parison	
	Collective com-	
	parison	
	Valuation of Activity	
	Regarded highly	
	Neutral	
	Devalued	
	Performance	
	attribution	
	Personal locus	
	External locus	

SOURCE: Bandura, 1977, p. 130. © 1977. Reprinted by permission of Prentice-Hall, Inc., Englewood Cliffs, N.J.

had access to data about alterations in central problem perceptions over the course of therapy).

One of the most important individual difference factors involved in the process of self-evaluation is the level (leniency versus stringency) at which standards are set. Persons not only differ in what behaviors, dimensions, or attributes they value, but also in the *degree* of proficiency or integrity they expect from themselves in their personal productions. Clinicians frequently encounter clients who either expect overnight change, or at the other extreme clients who, because of extraordinarily high goal levels, do not really expect to change at all. Goals that are either too high or too low (in the context of a client's current abilities) are seen as capable of disengaging commitment to therapeutic objectives at any time during the course of treatment. Depression proneness and suicidal ideation are among the more extreme consequences of unrealistically high performance standards (Loeb, Beck, Diggory, & Tuthill, 1967; Neuringer, 1974).

Clients' task-specific performance standards and/or their implicit criteria for the self-administration of reward are variables which should be thoroughly investigated by therapists who wish to strengthen their client's self-regulatory skills. Goal levels and self-reward criteria have been shown to vary as a function of such "personal history" dimensions as: previous exposure to models (Marston, 1965); access to information on the task proficiency of peer groups (Karoly & Decker, Note 1); the pattern of previously experienced, task-relevant external rewards (Karoly & Kanfer, 1974); as well as the frequency of prior task successes and failures (Diggory, 1966).

Achievement Motivation

Perhaps the best known hypothesized mediator of task persistence—one strongly linked to personality research—is the construct of achievement motivation. Recent advances in the theory of achievement motivation make it particularly apt for consideration here. First, the revised model emphasizes the interaction between person and environment (as opposed to the traditional appeal to unitary forces within the individual). Second, a constantly active organism is presumed. Finally, the model stresses the study of behavior as a continuous stream rather than as a disconnected series of episodes (Atkinson & Birch, 1978; Raynor, 1969).

It has been noted that both the traditional cognitive (expectancy × value) theory and the S–R (habit × drive) approach to motivation have placed heavy emphasis on the eliciting power of the immediate stimulus situation in determining the strength of the "inclination to act" at any given time. Atkinson and Birch (1978) remind us that

both of these traditional conceptions . . . tend to lull us into the habit of thinking of the subject of study, whether animal or human, as if it were at rest until some critical stimulus in which the observer is interested occurs. (p. 18)

The concept of "resistance to extinction" is the best illustration of the prevalent view that the learner will naturally return to some baseline of inactivity unless "programmed" otherwise.

Leaning heavily on modern neurophysiology, Atkinson and Birch (1978) look to an active organism to make a major contribution to the self-direction via three internal processes: *instigation,* the tendency toward specific ongoing action which is shaped by past experience, physiological state, and genetic makeup; *consummation,* activities that reduce the strength of an action tendency; and *inhibition,* factors that arouse and strengthen the tendency not to act. Of course there are ubiquitous external sources of instigation to action. Similarly, the environment provides the opportunity for most consummatory activity, as well as the signals of impending discomfort or pain that support response inhibition. However, the important message is that in attempting to explain why a person initiates and persists in goal-directed activity, the person's own inclinations (not traits!) must be given proportional attention along with environmental determinants. The objective of a motivation analysis of human performance is not to ascertain what stimuli have goaded movement from x to y, or what environmental arrangements will sustain the individual at y. Rather, since the organism is always moving across a rich variety of behavior settings, the key question becomes: "What generally occurs during an interval of time preceding a change of activity to cause either an increase or decrease in the strength of competing behavioral tendencies?" (Atkinson & Birch, 1978, chap. 1). This "dynamics of action" model has been most notably applied to the reanalysis of the determinants of "success in competition with a standard of excellence"—that is, to the determinants of achievement motivation (McCelland, Atkinson, Clark, & Lowell, 1953).

Since personal success and failure, as well as standards of performance, are salient dimensions for those who voluntarily enter psychotherapeutic treatment, individual differences in the hypothesized components that underlie the tendency toward the instigation, or inhibition, of achievement should variously contribute to the likelihood of an individual's initiating therapy, remaining in therapy (especially when the patient-therapist relationship or the therapeutic "homework" becomes moderately difficult), and persisting in the pursuit of therapeutic goals after the termination of treatment and in the face of occasional failures (cf., Atkinson & Birch, 1978; Feather, 1961; Lewin, Dembo, Festinger, & Sears, 1944). The individual difference factors considered in the revised models of achievement (those of Atkinson & Birch, 1978; and Raynor, 1969) are numerous. The strength of the motive to achieve is seen as a relatively stable, acquired tendency of the person to set high minimal goal levels; one that is present, but not necessarily dominant, in every situation. Also relevant is the strength of the motive or disposition to avoid failure. Other factors include the incentive value (personal importance) associated with success or failure on a particular task (like doing well socially versus academically), subjective estimates of the probability of succeeding or failing on a task, attributions linking success to the person's own effortful actions, and the presence of "future-oriented" expectations (i.e., the belief that success/failure on current tasks is causally linked, by means of what Raynor, 1969, has termed a "contingent path," to psychologically distant outcomes). The conviction that "If I can learn to be successfully assertive in practice sessions with my therapist, I can become the 'stronger person' I want to be with family, friends, and business associates'' is an example of a future-oriented expectation.

Especially important aspects of the revised model of achievement striving include: first, its disavowal of any fixed action tendencies; second, its focus on the continuing stream of an individual's goal-directed activities in contrast to the laboratory-based, segmented, and episodic study of goal choice and persistence; and third, its assumption of a non-resting organism always moving toward some goal (although it may not be the goal with which the observer is concerned). This last point takes on specific significance in that it alerts the clinical investigator to look for active, countertherapeutic goals, attitudes, expectations, or intentions specific to the client that may undercut therapeutic progress during or subsequent to the formal therapy relationship. I have acknowledged in the model the possibility of competing motivational tendencies by the inclusion of "positive" and "negative" ability-attitude-value qualifiers at each stage of the psychotherapy process (see Figure 7-1). The difference between the present call for recognizing the individual's continuing goal striving and the learning-based notion of "behavioral excesses" (such as anxiety) is that with the former, the possibility of permanently extinguishing competing motivational responses is considered neither feasible nor desirable. That is, the fluctuating "motive" to please others may often interfere with the course of assertion training. Yet it is assumed that there are times when approval seeking is adaptive and should be ascendant. The clinician's task is to be aware of the varied personal strivings of his or her clients and to be ready to provide, when necessary, the external impetus that will render the therapeutic motive stronger than the contextually defined "nontherapeutic" one(s).

At this point, the logic of the achievement motivational position might be clear, but its predictive utility may possibly remain in doubt. As the "ultimate" criterion for our adoption of a conceptual perspective is its empirical yield, we will now turn to a brief examination of the achievement literature to see how the interactional (nonstatic) model has fared.

With regard to the process of problem recognition, Tessler and Schwartz (1972) found that low achievers in their sample of college students tended to seek help less than high achievers. The frequent finding that low achievers (typically males) tend to adopt relatively easy goals (Atkinson, 1967) would suggest, however, that only individuals with a comparatively strong achievement need would find the harsh realities of therapeutic work to their liking.[5] Indeed, when research was focused on long-term persistence toward a meaningful goal (in contrast to laboratory-bound, problem-solving activity), the results have supported the view that high achievers are more persistent and hence more successful (cf. Atkinson & Raynor, 1974).

Becker and Maiman (1975) have adapted Atkinson's "value expectancy" model to account for individual differences in compliance with health and medical care recommendations—a domain of direct relevance to psychotherapeutic follow-up, particularly involving pharmacological procedures, and of indirect relevance to the extent that "mental health" recommendations involve components in common with medical advice (i.e., the need for occasional checkups, follow-up appointments, screening tests, booster sessions, and of course the making of preventively-oriented, or early, interventive appointments with health care professionals). Consistent with Atkinson's use of the Yerkes-Dodson law to predict the strength of an individual's tendency to engage in effortful performance, it was discovered that for asymptomatic patients (perhaps the equivalent of therapy patients who fail to recognize the extent of their pathology, or who have achieved some measure of symptomatic relief), both low and high levels of perceived severity of illness were associated with low likelihood of compliance or preventive action. Also consistent with Atkinson's model, generally reliable relationships between compliance and expectancy of future benefits emerged.[6]

Expectancy Effects

Perhaps the most straightforward cognitive mediator of longterm behavior stabilization (persistence) is the individual's expectancy that his or her efforts will result in satisfying outcome. We have previously suggested that clinical investigators should assess their clients' "future-oriented" thinking, and that task difficulty serves as a potent impediment to motivation. A thorough and practical approach to therapeutic expectancy effects would therefore involve: assessing client outcome expectancies during pretreatment, treatment, and posttherapy phases of intervention; examining the relationship between outcome expectancy and task success over the course of treatment and beyond; determining the dimensions of the client's extra therapy environment that contribute to outcome expectancies (good and bad); linking client outcome expectancies to their perceptions relating the amount of meaningful therapeutic benefit to the effect required to achieve it; and asking clients to predict *in advance of follow-up* what factors are likely to undermine successful maintenance. An examination of the maintenance literature reveals that few, if any, of these specific (and rather obvious) expectancy measurements have been taken (cf. also Wilkins, 1973).

Among the less obvious aspects of the outcome expectancy construct is the possibility that under certain circumstances a positive outcome expectancy (that new patterns of behavior or cognition would bring the client closer to therapeutic goals) might undermine, rather than strengthen, persistence motivation.

In an examination of individual differences in social skills training, Marzillier and Winter (1978) discussed a client for whom the learning of new skills and the expectancy that they would be effective may have run afoul of the client's well-established tendency to avoid social encounters and confrontations. When the motivation to avoid failure exceeds the motivation to achieve success, the expectancy of success may indeed be predictive of client disengagement from therapy (e.g., Marzillier and Winter's client dropped out of treatment). This single-case experiment serves to remind us of the folly associated with studying any motivational construct in an idiographic vacuum, and solely within the context of group designs that assess only average forms of responding.

Particular expectancies are not only embedded in a network of beliefs, values, and other expectancies, but they are likewise associated with emotional concomitants. Cognitive (social learning) as well as the more traditional operant learning investigators have avoided the study of "hot cognitive processes" as manifested in therapeutic contexts. According to Janis and Mann (1977), "hot" cognitions refer to constructs designed to "take account of the influence of unpleasant emotions on intellectual judgments when human beings are required to make decisions on highly ego-involving issues" (p. 46). Assuming an individual has entered into a program of psychotherapy (of whatever sort), his or her expectations of success or failure can be framed in terms of the probable conflicting outcomes associated with the enactment of the supposedly "adaptive" patterns of behavior. Traditional psychotherapy theory recognizes the possibility that clients may fear the loss of so-called secondary gains. Janis and Mann (1977) hypothesize four sources of conflict that may "emotionalize" the expectancy construct (usually offered in rather bloodless form). These are (rephrased for the present discussion): (1) "I expect to change as the result of treatment, but there are personal losses as well as gains associated with it"; (2) "I expect to change as the result of treatment, but there are gains and losses for significant others in my life if I do"; (3) "I expect to change, but I will feel a certain loss of self-esteem, along with the obvious gains, if I undergo treatment"; and, (4) "I expect to change, but new behaviors will elicit disapproval, as well as approval, from significant others." Over the course of therapy the individual's focus may shift between utilitarian gains and losses and between the perspective of self versus significant others. The motivation to continue treatment will thereby fluctuate. It is recommended that clinicians be sensitive to the nature of, and the vicissitudes in, their clients' "decisional balance sheets," and the impact of social contingencies (cf. DeVoge, Chapter 10 in this volume; Sulzer-Azaroff & Mayer, 1977).

The call for specificity in the measurement of expectations cannot be made too strongly. This is particularly true since the fascination with "generalized expectancies" in social learning applications seems quite well ingrained (Rotter, Chance, & Phares, 1972) despite warnings as to their limited utility (Rotter, 1975). A recent effort to develop Mental Health Locus of Control and Mental Health Locus of Origin Scales (Hill & Bale, Note 2) represents an advance in the use of the expectancy construct for predicting individual variation in therapeutic outcome and maintenance.

Attribution Theory

A client's motivation to work toward therapeutic change, both in and out of the therapy setting, is assumed to be dependent not only on the client's desire to achieve a valued personal goal and an expectancy that certain responses will lead to goal attainment, but also on the attribution that the *locus of change* is internal (that the "cause" of therapeutic success and failure resides *within* the person's repertoire of skills and labors). As cognitive views of motivation and learning have grown, so too has the use of the attributional perspective, which originated within social psychology (Heider's, 1958, "Naive Psychology," and the work of Festinger, 1954; Schachter & Singer, 1962; Kelley, 1967; and others).

Attribution theory "deals with the rules the average individual uses in attempting to infer the causes of observed behavior" (Jones, Kanouse, Kelley, Nisbett, Valins, & Weiner, 1971, p. x). Particularly important are the processes by which the individual attempts to understand the causes of his or her own behavior, a facet of attributional psychology labeled "self-perception" (Bem, 1967; Kopel & Arkowitz, 1975). It has been suggested that attribution and self-perception figure prominently in the initial therapeutic problem recognition, wherein adjustment failures are commonly perceived as self-generated, as well as in the processes of maintenance of behavior change, wherein success (change) correctly attributed to the client's own efforts has been found to be more sustaining than attributions to external sources such as drugs, an all-knowing therapist, luck, powerful others, and the like (e.g., Bowers, 1975; Davison &

Valins, 1969; Levendusky & Pankratz, 1975; Ross, Rodin, & Zimbardo, 1969; Strong, 1978; Valins & Nisbett, 1971).

Recently, Bandura has proposed an attributional theory of human self-regulation which posits as a central mediator of behavior change and persistence the individual's expectations (attributions) of personal mastery or *self-efficacy* (Bandura, 1977a,b; Bandura & Adams, 1977; Bandura, Adams, & Beyer, 1977). According to self-efficacy theory, an individual's conviction that he or she can successfully execute actions that produce desired (therapeutic) outcomes may influence: what situations or activities are chosen or initiated; how much effort is expended and how long the person persists in the face of obstacles and unpleasant consequences; and how much is eventually learned or unlearned by remaining in the difficult situation.

Bandura (1977a,b) makes no small effort to differentiate self-efficacy expectations from the usual one-shot, broad-based, and unidimensional analyses of outcome expectancy that characterize much of the clinical literature. In addition, Bandura (1977b) notes that expectancies are often confused with unrealistic hopes, wishful thinking, and attributions about the change-engendering power of *external* forces or agents. Efficacy expectations are multidimensional and self-referenced:

> They differ in *magnitude.* Thus, when tasks are ordered in level of difficulty, the efficacy expectations of different individuals may be limited to the simpler tasks, extend to moderately difficult ones, or include even the most taxing performances. Efficacy expectations also differ in *generality.* . . . In addition, expectancies vary in *strength.* Weak expectancies are easily extinguishable by disconfirming experiences, whereas individuals who possess strong expectations of mastery will persevere in their coping efforts despite disconfirming experiences. (Bandura, 1977b, p. 194)

Clearly, self-efficacy is seen as relevant across all phases of the therapeutic enterprise (see Figure 7-1). In several experimental analyses focusing on chronic snake-phobic adults, Bandura and his associates have examined the effects of vaious types of therapeutic intervention on self-efficacy and the degree of congruence between efficacy judgments and performance. Particularly relevant in the context of the present chapter are those findings suggesting that verbally indexed reports of self-efficacy appear to be powerful predictors of performance changes, sometimes even more powerful than behavioral indices (cf. Bandura & Adams, 1977). Although intersubject designs were used, the results of the few self-efficacy experiments reported in the literature indicate that individual differences in performance skill levels and personal history of successes and failures may mediate the effects of self-efficacy. Finally, although the longest thorough follow-up assessment of the effects of training was conducted only 1 month posttreatment, the results (maintenance of gains and some further improvement) are quite encouraging (Bandura, Adams, & Beyer, 1977; also see Mash & Terdal's discussion of follow-up assessment considerations in Chapter 4 of this volume).

An interesting experiment by Carver and Blaney (1977) integrates our stage 1 differential self-focus concept with the self-efficacy (attributional) perspective on therapeutic behavior change. Studying moderately fearful snake-phobic undergraduates, Carver and Blaney (1977) showed that false physiological feedback (sounds of an accelerated heartbeat) led to heightened attention to self and to approach behavior, but differentially so, as a function of initial subject characteristics. Specifically, subjects were divided into those confident of their ability to pick up a snake (similar to Bandura's notion of strong self-efficacy expectations) and those doubtful of their ability eventually to do so. Confident subjects, after being aroused by the false autonomic input, tended to direct their attention to the goal and to their goal-directed behavior, while doubtful subjects become more aware of their fearful attitudes. Confident subjects also approached the aversive stimulus (a 40-inch boa constrictor) significantly more closely than doubtful subjects in the presence of accelerated heartbeat feedback.

From the perspective of the clinical practitioner, however, much work is needed to make cognitive mediators maximally useful in the planning and implementation of treatment. Not only must measurements be taken contextually and regularly, but efforts must be made to ensure that measures are *personally relevant*. In the efficacy research mentioned above, the experimenter provided each subject with the identical list of performance tasks derived from a standardized behavioral avoidance test and took "readings" of self-efficacy reactions in response to these tasks at prearranged intervals over a relatively short span of time. It would be necessary for the clinician who is seeking to tailor a treatment program to the "cognitive orientation" of a particular client to know how the client "unitizes" (i.e., breaks into meaningful segments) the various behavior patterns he or she is attempting to develop, when and where the client self-observes, and for how long, and whether there are any regularities linking client-specific, naturalistic self-judgments (be they expectancies, attributions, decisions, or wishful thinking) and therapeutic learning over the extended course of treatment (cf. Fiske, 1978a). Based on the answers to such questions, treatment programs can be modified and maintenance strategies developed.

Commitment Theory

As a result of the much-discussed failure of attitudes (and motives, intentions, beliefs, etc.) to predict behavior in the real world (e.g., DeFleur & Westie, 1958; Wicker, 1969), those who hold an intervening (personality) variable approach to clinical prediction and intervention have sought to "salvage" and defend the mediational position against the powerful contingency management viewpoint. The essence of the interactionist argument is that the relationship between an individual's desire to engage in a particular pattern of behavior (his or her preference for, evaluation of, belief in, or commitment to an act) and actual behavioral enactment is a complex function wherein ability, opportunity, and environmental stimuli interact with individual choice parameters and the nature of the activity to be performed to determine the probability of action (cf. Bindra, 1974; Fishbein & Ajzen, 1975). Unfortunately, in most experiments on the correspondence between commitment and action the behaviors studied are relatively neutral (compared to clinical problem behaviors) and are already a part of the actor's response repertoire. Despite the complexity and analogue flavor of commitment studies, the conceptual arguments of commitment theorists (e.g., Janis & Mann, 1977; Kiesler, 1971) merit some consideration, especially since our avowed purpose is to suggest new directions for clinical research.

Janis and Mann (1977) have, for example, offered a psychological analysis of "factors that anchor a person to his decision—that impel him to maintain a course of action in the face of adverse feedback and criticism" (p. 279). Such an undertaking has obvious relevance that extends from stage 2 processes until the need for adaptive disengagement from therapeutic plans. Among the hypothesized determinants of commitment (all of which seem capable of assessment in individual clinical cases) are:

1. The individual's tendency to issue public and semiformal statements of intent (cf. also Kanfer & Karoly, 1972; Kanfer, Cox, Greiner, & Karoly, 1974; Marlatt & Kaplan, 1972).

2. The individual's need for social approval which, after public commitment, would serve to constrain deviations from the promised course of action.

3. The individual's characteristic manner of thinking about the planned course of action. According to the work of Tesser and his colleagues (Tesser, 1978; Tesser, Leone, & Clary, 1978) the very act of thinking about a salient object (like a phobic stimulus) while examining the logic (or illogic) underlying one's attitude toward it, should lead to a

reduction in the exaggerated affect directed at that object. On the other hand, the phobic response could become stronger if the individual thinks about the feared stimulus in an unconstrained manner.

THE ACQUISITION OF COGNITIVE
AND INSTRUMENTAL SKILLS

The importance of the distinction between knowning or wanting and capacity cannot be overstated. While many forms of psychotherapy are predicated on the need to achieve stage 1 and 2 "insights" and motivations, they have omitted from consideration the very basic fact that desire and incentives cannot make up for an individual's failure to have acquired the prerequisite skills underlying the enactment of adaptive behavior. Unfortunately, one of the common errors of many learning-oriented practitioners is their assumption that the causal pathway between learning and "personality" is simply a one-way connection, or that personality is learned (is a *dependent* variable).

To be sure, what a person learns and the circumstances of his learning have substantial effects upon his apparent proficiency, but the amount of variation produced by such factors typically falls far short of the amount associated with *differences among learners.* (Rohwer, 1976, p. 71; italics added)

To those who favor conceptions of learning deriving exclusively from the animal laboratory, the contribution of learner differences to long-term task proficiency can only be expected to account for a meager proportion of the outcome variance, especially when compared to the contribution of physiological, physical, and/or temporal and sequential parameters. Person-centered investigators, on the other hand, attribute a sizable piece of the outcome pie to *individual variation in motivation to learn* (propensity), *ability to learn* (capacity), *developmental and contextual readiness to process and perform,* and to learners' *characteristic modes of reaction to success and failure on meaningful learning tasks* (cf. Gagné, 1967, 1970; Karoly, 1977; Mischel, 1973; Nuttin, 1976; Rohwer, 1976).

In the absence of critical experiments comparing the person-centered and technique-centered viewpoints, and in the interests of promulgating the lesser known social behaviorist perspective, the mediational (or person-centered) approach will be briefly presented next.

Motivation to Learn

We have already reviewed quite a few motivational constructs, linked primarily (but not exclusively) to people's willingness to perform "therapeutic" behaviors. However, we might also focus on differences in the way the learner orients to the acquisition of new behavioral information.

As a result of the control which the experimenter has typically executed in traditional learning experiments—over the animal's physiological and physical state and in regard to the task instructions in human learning—there has been little emphasis on subject variations with respect to the motivation to learn. To the extent (1) that the therapeutic learning tasks and laboratory learning tasks share common dimensional characteristics, or (2) that differences in motivation or readiness are controlled for (measured and equated), there may be no need to focus on such subject characteristics. However, since (1) and (2) are rarely true, there is good reason to examine the case in favor of the individual difference model.

An extremely important distinction drawn by Joseph Nuttin (1976; Nuttin & Greenwald, 1968) between open and closed tasks will be useful to our line of discussion. According to Nuttin, rewards and punishments in human response acquisition possess a double function—emotional and informational. These functions relate directly to the manner in which the learning task is conceptualized. Rewards and punishments may serve a momentary emotional function when the subject does not expect to be responding under similar circumstances in the future. Where success and failure are final, we are dealing with what Nuttin calls a "closed task." In Nuttin's framework, the term "task" refers to any large or small behavioral unit that the person intends to perform, and the term "closed" implies that the task objective is reached "by giving a single response to the stimulus, which is expected not to be presented again" (Nuttin, 1976, p. 253). On the other hand, in an open task reward is a signal that the response that preceded it will be useful in the future course of adaptation, while punishment signals the absence of such future utility. The implications of Nuttin's position for the process of behavioral persistence and psychotherapeutic learning are noteworthy:

Formulating the motivation-learning problem in terms of task openness implies a special approach to human behavior itself. Instead of confining behavior within the stimulus-response structure and insisting on the subject's intention (or lack thereof) to learn the association between these two elements, the open-task concept implies that the stimulus-response unit is integrated into a broader cognitive-dynamic structure (a behavioral project or plan). Such motivational structures are future oriented. . . . The important point, then, is to find out to what extent a specific act is part of a broader behavioral structure or, on the contrary, constitutes an independent unit in itself. (Nuttin, 1976, pp. 253-254)

In Nuttin's theory the concept of motivation clearly has specialized meaning. He hypothesizes that humans are satisfied not only by drive-reducing reward objects, but also by the information that rewards convey as to yet unattained, complex, and ever-changing goals or "behavioral units." Few of us are moved to repeat the exact same behaviors in pursuit of the identical outcomes, so the building up of static S-R connections is of limited adaptive utility. Rather, we seek varying ends through varying means. Certainly psychotherapy may be construed as an open, rather than a closed task system.

Thus it may be helpful for practicing clinicians to know: (1) the nature of their clients' perception(s) of the assigned and self-generated tasks of therapy as they vary along the "open-closed" continuum (recall also Raynor's, 1969, '' contingent path" approach to future orientation in achievement motivation); (2) the nature of their clients' idiosyncratic "cognitive-dynamic" structures (i.e., plans, projects, and long-term goals); (3) their client's "latent orientations or interests," referring to the middle-range ends and means that serve to connect present activity to distant outcomes; and (4) the content of clients' changing perceptions regarding the instrumentality of rewards, i.e., the extent to which rewards are seen as informative about the possibility that the behaviors they follow will lead to desired end states.[7] At this time, the most productive means of assessing such perceptions is probably through self-report.

Ability to Learn

Individual variations in ability to learn have been most extensively discussed by Eysenck and his associates in the context of a biologically based approach to personality. According to Eysenck, individuals differ in conditionability as a function of inherited differences in emotionality and introversion-extraversion.

Using retrospective interviews or questionnaires to assess the various outcomes of their subjects' conditioning (learning) histories, British investigators (e.g., H. J. Eysenck, 1967; Gray, 1972) have found a good deal of support for the view that introverts (because of presumably higher levels of cortical arousal) condition faster and extinguish more slowly than extraverts in different settings involving fear, punishment, or frustration. Introversion-extraversion is typically assessed via the Eysenck Personality Inventory (H. J. Eysenck & Eysenck, 1968).

Recently, Kantorowitz (1978) conducted a prospective (rather than retrospective) study in an effort to relate introversion-extraversion to laboratory-based conditioning and deconditioning of sexual arousal. Kantorowitz, following the pattern of findings in the literature, hypothesized that the "typically" nonanxious, hedonistic, and sexually uninhibited extraverts would be highly responsive to tumescence conditioning and would be relatively unresponsive to detumescence conditioning. As expected, the correlation between extraversion (E) and tumescence conditioning was +.88, and the relationship between E and detumescence conditioning was −.76. While introverts may condition better in aversive contexts, extraverts appear "more conditionable than introverts in appetitive contexts" (Kantorowitz, 1978, p. 121).

These results are encouraging, particularly in their shedding light on the role of "personality factors" in sexual treatment. And as the author noted:

The replication and extension of the present findings to clinically relevant populations would represent one of the few instances in clinical psychology in which a basis for factorial allocation of treatment techniques and patient personality characteristics was experimentally clarified. (Kantorowitz, 1978, p. 122)

Further experimental clarification of the relationship between learning and personality awaits the design of appropriate research.

Developmental and Contextual Readiness

The first step in the verification of hypotheses about learner differences in response acquisition is finding an index that will divide a population of learners into those who will, and those who will not, exhibit criterion performance on a given task (Rohwer, 1976). One of the simplest and most predictive indices is age as it interacts with task dimensions.

For example, in attempting to teach children self-instructional responses for use in "temptation" situations, investigators in the domain of self-control have found that younger and older children differ in their "readiness" to follow instructions (e.g., Hartig & Kanfer, 1973; Toner & Smith, 1977). The so-called production deficiency hypothesis (Flavell, Beach, & Chinsky, 1966) has often been invoked to explain the interaction between age and instructional condition—to wit, older children, who spontaneously self-verbalize, are less influenced by training than are preschoolers who do not spontaneously produce self-guiding speech as an aid to learning and performance. On the other hand, a "mediational deficiency" refers to the possibility that a particular capacity or strategy for dealing with a task is unavailable to the child—and cannot be successfully trained.

The message here is clear: the clinical child psychologist who attempts to intervene in the learning processes of children, but without an appreciation for developmental and task-related readiness factors, is likely to experience failure and be unable to localize the cause(s) of program ineffectiveness (i.e., is it the technique, the child, the timing of the intervention, or some complex interaction of these?).

Characteristic Reactions to Success and Failure

To the degree that learning involves exposure to sequences of successes and failures, the manner in which the individual responds (emotionally and cognitively) to behavior-contingent feedback should influence the strength and durability of learning. This broad hypothesis contrasts sharply with the emphasis that S-R theorists have traditionally placed the mechanics of reward and punishment, i.e., on the effects of schedule and sequence of contingent events on response persistence (Amsel, 1958; Capaldi, 1967). However, owing to the work of cognitive theorists, the relevance of subject differences in attention to contingent outcomes, causal ascription of outcomes to internal versus external loci, and emotional adaptability to negative and positive consequences has been established. In so doing the study of success and failure processes has been "humanized."

Age and gender differences in responsivity to consequential feedback are typically neglected in the programmed application of treatment techniques. Some recent studies incorporating these variables demonstrate their potential importance.

Krantz and Stone (1978) reasoned that the elderly (in American society) are likely to feel a loss of personal efficacy and therefore will, when confronted with a difficult problem, more readily give up in the face of failure as compared to a group of college-age subjects. Those elderly individuals who evidence an external locus of control (Rotter, 1966) orientation may be particularly vulnerable. A group of middle-class elderly and college-age females, classified as "internal" or "external" on an abbreviated version of Rotter's I-E Scale, participated in a problem-solving task and were confronted with bursts of loud music which supposedly indicated failure. After experiencing false feedback of success (noise on only 1 out of 12 trials) or failure (noise on 11 out of 12 trials), the participants performed the same task without feedback in what they believed was an unrelated second experiment. Results revealed that internals outperformed externals, and younger subjects outperformed older subjects on the first task. Hence, on this task the hypothesized interaction of age and success/failure experience failed to materialize. However, on the transfer task, a triple interaction was evident: elderly external subjcts who had experienced task failure performed reliably worse than the other groups. The differences might well have been more extreme had the elderly subjects come from an institutional setting rather than being community residents.

The differential effects of success or failure on men and women (and boys and girls) have also been explored. Although much has been written about women's supposed "fear of success," following Horner's (1972) early research, the data bearing on this concept are equivocal. Today, fear of success is not generally considered to be a useful avenue for explaining the differences in achievement between men and women (Frieze, Parsons, Johnson, Ruble, & Zellman, 1978). However, in actual learning situations sex differences in reaction to failure or other forms of evaluative feedback would appear to be a replicable finding. Research by Dweck and her colleagues on the susceptability of young children to the effects of uncontrollable failure experiences revealed that the performance of girls tended to be disrupted to a greater extent than that of boys. Further, the girls who worked the hardest and performed the best prior to the failure experience showed the most deteriorated performance subsequent to it (Dweck & Reppucci, 1973). When boys and girls are required to make explicit statements of their outcome expectancies (a process which heightens evaluative pressure, and which may be a part of many forms of child psychotherapy), the deteriorative effects on girls' task persistence is markedly higher than that noted for boys (Dweck & Gilliard, 1975). Dweck has suggested that young girls in our society may be more concerned about evaluative feedback and are perhaps made more anxious (past the point of optimal arousal) by it. Dweck also found that girls are more apt to attribute task failure to a lack of ability, whereas boys choose to view it as bad luck or the result of their intermittent laziness.

MAINTENANCE PROCESSES: MEMORY AND SELF-REGULATION

At this point, I shall assert that a client's recognition of the existence of a behavior pattern in need of alteration, his or her desire to see it changed, the expectancy that change is possible through personal effort, and actual exposure to new therapeutic learning are all insufficient to ensure long-term adjustment. This is so because the client (1) must yet retain the contents of the new learning and (2) must also be able to motivate himself or herself to employ the new patterns outside of therapy, often in the face of indifferent (nonrewarding) or even hostile (punishing) audiences. Thus, memory and self-regulatory processes are hypothesized as necessary links to a durable therapeutic outcome. The analysis of individual variations in each of these domains will be out next objective. The reader should bear in mind that although these processes are explicitly maintenance oriented, all of the cyclical "stages" or phases of therapeutic change listed in Figures 7-1 and 7-2 are considered to be relevant to the process of long-term stabilization and change. That is, all of the domains of personality already discussed are in fact "maintenance processes."

Memory

Nuttin and his colleagues have investigated individual differences in reactions to success and failure, with emphasis on the learner's perceptions and selective recall of past outcomes as they influence the directions of future behavior (Nuttin & Greenwald, 1968). Memory for past learning events may be crucial in establishing maintenance and transfer functions. Unfortunately, with the exception of the work of Tolman (1959),

systematic behavior theorists have not attributed an important role to the recall of past outcomes in the determination of future behavior. Rather, reward and punishment have typically been credited with automatic effects in the modification of behavior, independently of the learner's recall of them. (Nuttin & Greenwald, 1968, p. 32)

In a series of experiments, Nuttin has shown how "distortions" in impressions of previous task-specific successes and failures could be related to such subject characteristics as "optimism-pessimism" (recall also Carver & Blaney's, 1977, data relating "confidence" to approach performance) and the degree of subject interest ("ego involvement") in the task. Nelson and Craighead (1977) found that depressed college students (high scorers on the Beck Depression Inventory) differed from nondepressed subjects in the amount of reinforcement recalled following a brief experimental procedure. While depressed subjects underestimated rewards received, the nondepressed controls tended to underestimate the amount of punishment received. Further, depressed subjects consistently *self*-reinforced less than controls, suggesting another potential maintenance deficit. If cross-validated with clinical populations such findings would hold obvious implications for a cognitive theory of maintenance. Viewing memory within the framework of an *information-processing* model, contemporary theorists have provided a particularly congenial vehicle for the systematic investigation of individual variation, a vehicle whose potential has hardly been realized in relation to therapeutic outcome. The relative neglect of memory and individual differences in psychotherapy is puzzling in light of the availability of methods for delimiting the stages of processing, of techniques for studying active "control strategies" (i.e., the conscious and deliberate devices that may be used, at the discretion of the memorizer, to aid in coding, storage, organization, or retrieval), as well as the existence of a literature on the relationship between memory and psychopathology (Atkinson & Shiffrin, 1968; Johnson, 1974; Salzman, 1970; S. Schwartz, 1975).

As Johnson (1974) has noted, control processes would be the most logical candidate for an individual differences assault because they are subject determined. Similarly, Campione and Brown (1977) highlight the fact that control processes are trainable and hence are an aspect of competency rather than native endowment.[8] The contributions of memory researchers to improving the formal practices of education (Rohwer & Dempster, 1977) suggest that it is but a short step to the application of the insights from memory laboratory to the *didactic components* of psychotherapy. If differences in the use of control strategies and other "executive" functions can be linked to differential long-term treatment effects (an empirical question), an "instructional approach" (Belmont & Butterfield, 1977) to the tasks of therapy might then be undertaken. Such an instructional approach would involve several steps. First is the assessment of the information-processing and memory strategies employed by the client as new information is presented and novel reponse repertoires are being established. The next step would involve developing means for determining optimal learning strategies for the component "tasks of therapy." Finally, investigators would need to evolve ways of teaching the client to evaluate and revise his or her strategies to conform with situational and task demands. This latter function involves the self-regulation of learning and memory, a topic which will receive separate attention next.

Self-Regulation

Of the numerous behavior-management procedures developed during the past 25 years, few appear more germane to the issue of maintenance than those falling under the banner of "self-regulation" (Kanfer &

Phillips, 1970). Among the most widely employed heuristic models is the "three-stage" conceptualization of self-regulated action popularized by Kanfer and his associates (Kanfer, 1970, 1971; Kanfer & Karoly, 1972; Karoly & Kanfer, 1974) and predicated on the assumption that self-guidance requires discriminated self-observation, followed by a process of comparing one's behavior to a subjective "standard of conduct," leading to self-consequation, or the self-administration of reward or punishment, depending on whether the monitored behavior exceeds or falls below the standard. In this context, both external and mediational factors are presumed to influence the outcome of an individual's efforts at self-regulation (Kanfer, 1977).

In Chapter 8 of the present volume, Sharon Hall has reviewed much of the literature on the application of the self-regulation model to clinical disorders. Therefore, rather than presenting arguments on behalf of the model's clinical relevance and utility, I shall confine my remarks to the role of individual differences in self-regulated behavior.

As in many areas of behavior theory application, individual variations have not occupied a prominent place in clinical research on self-regulation. The topic has not, however, been completely ignored.

For reasons not entirely clear, interest has tended to focus on differences in people's proclivities for self-administered reward. In an early set of studies, Marston (1964) investigated the relationship between positive self-reward (SR +) and subjects' gender, subjects' scores on Rotter's I-E Scale, and their scores on Bass's Orientation Inventory (ORI). The ORI is a self-report measure that presumably permits a classification of persons as either self-oriented (selfish), interaction oriented (sociable), or task oriented (concerned with getting the job done). Marston (1964) found that only task-oriented subjects tended toward increased SR + (over trials, in a learning task), that task-oriented females engaged in more SR + than did task-oriented males, and that Rotter's I-E Scale was not predictive of differences in SR + frequency. The failure of the internal-external dichotomy to predict differences in amount of SR + was also found in a later study by Bellack (1972).

Recently, the emphasis has not been on the antecedents of SR + rate, but rather on the effects of differences in self-reinforcement "style" on treatment outcome. For example, Bellack, Glanz, and Simon (1976) assessed subjects' SR + behavior during a brief laboratory task, prior to providing a behavioral weight-reduction treatment. These investigators found that individuals who were "high" self-reinforcers tended to lose more weight than did "low" self-reinforcers (almost twice as much), and that they also maintained their weight losses during a follow-up period (5 months). Approaching the subject of self-reinforcement from a different slant, Rozensky and Bellack (1974) recruited successful dieters and successful ex-smokers as well as a group of "nonquitters/nonlosers" and again found a positive relationship between SR+ rate (on a laboratory task) and treatment success (albeit retrospectively measured). Obviously, these encouraging findings are in need of replication and extension to behavioral problems other than obesity.

Further, there seems to be no reason to restrict the analysis of individual difference factors to the regulatory component of self-reward. Our previous discussion of factors in self-evaluation and achievement motivation is clearly also relevant to the second "stage" of self-regulation. Individual differences in self-observation have also been addressed. Future research might address the interrelationship of the three regulatory components, their role in children's self-regulation, and ways of assessing their in vivo use in the extratherapy setting (cf. also Hall's extended discussion in Chapter 8 of theoretical and methodological issues in self-regulation).

TRANSFER PROCESSES:
SITUATION APPRAISAL AND PROBLEM SOLVING

In describing the results of a comparative study of the community adjustment of released token economy and nontoken economy patients, Hollingsworth and Foreyt (1975) indicated that "token economy graduates are prepared for life outside the hospital at least as well as, if not better than, releasees from the rest of the hospital" (p. 274). Even had the data consisted of much more than patient responses to an 11-item mailed questionnaire, one would have wondered about the meaning of the phrase "prepared for life outside the hospital." What do psychologists really know of the myriad factors that comprise the adaptive challenges of living within the various social, political, economic, vocational, and interpersonal spheres of American life? Clients of all sorts, whether from middle or lower socioeconomic backgrounds, male or female, young or old, seriously maladjusted or with circumscribed disorders, hospitalized or outpatient, black or white, must one day face the problem of "'reentry" into a complex ever-changing, therapist-free world. What do we know of the various forms of learning what must underlie the therapeutic facilitation of "adjustment" outside the hospital, clinic, or consulting room? An honest answer to the above questions would have to be: "Very little, indeed."

In an effort to shed some light on the maintenance and transfer of therapeutic learning, I am prompted to acknowedge again the impossibility of separating person and context (including both time and place). At any of our arbitrarily bounded "stages" of therapy, the impact of the physical and social environment can either gird or undercut personal change. When we require the client to abstract out of of therapeutic experiences the underlying principles of planned change and to "transfer" or generalize them to new settings, then the interaction of person and environment becomes especially salient. The individual is expected to have acquired some *generalizable skills for dealing with new stressors and with new dilemmas of an interpersonal variety.* To prepare the client for such learning we must know both about the nature of these skills and the stress-producing characteristics of the real-world settings in which the client is preparing to function (e.g., work, school, home, and/or recreational settings).

Therapeutic learning is unlikely to endure or transfer if posttherapy social environments are widely divergent from those simulated or actually mastered during the course of treatment. Included among the hypothesized disruptive changes are alterations in the contingencies of reward and/or punishment which "significant others" emit in response to the client's new patterns of behavior. Transfer is also impeded if general principles of interpersonal problem solving were neither directly taught nor indirectly transmitted to the client during treatment.

Diagnosing the Perceived Environment

It would be a simple matter for a dyed-in-the-wool S-R theorist to ascribe to an interactional credo without changing his metatheoretical commitments in the slightest. This could be done simply by espousing an interest in the interaction of environment and specific behaviors.

While environments mutually interact with behaviors of all kinds, it is the view of social learning theorists that these exchanges are mediated by cognitive processes such as expectancy, attribution, valuation, wishful thinking, and the like. Therefore, essential to a complete conceptualization of therapeutic learning and its cross-situational durability and flexibility is an understanding of how different environments influence cognitive processes. Oddly, "environmentalists" who have poured so much energy into designing or arranging the mechanics of environments have generally neglected to assess their psychological characteristics (Willems, 1977).

The social learning model suggests assessing the nature of the environment *as perceived by the actors within it.* Among the important perceived characteristics of extra-therapy settings that might contribute to successful or unsuccessful transfer are: (1) the degree to which the settings tax or stress the individual's adaptive resources; (2) the availability of social support, especially for the individual's therapeutic commitments; and (3) their stability, predictability, or degree of organization.

Moos (1973), and his associates, have pioneered in the assessment of the perceived "psychological climate" of such diverse real-life contexts as junior high and high school classrooms, the family milieu, work settings, task groups, as well as the within-treatment environments of psychiatric wards, halfway houses, and correctional facilities. To the extent that differential environment perceptions have predictive implications for individual adjustment, perceptual measurements should become standard operating procedure for clinicians concerned with the durability and continuity of their interventions.

An excellent example of the study of the environment's impact on clients' cognitive processes, with particular emphasis on maintenance processes, is Marlatt and Gordon's (1979) analysis of relapse determinants in addictive disorders. Consistent with a theme of the present chapter, Marlatt and Gordon argue that maintenance failure may come about as a result of active, counterchange elements rather than exclusively through weaknesses of the treatment program. Studying groups of smokers, heroin addicts, and alcoholics, Marlatt and Gordon (1979) analyzed 137 "relapse episodes." They found that in fully 76% of the episodes of clients' first use of the taboo substance, the self-reported determinants could be classified into one of three categories of perceived environmental influence: coping with social pressure (24% of the cases), coping with interpersonal conflict (15% of the cases), and coping with negative emotional—intrapersonal—states 37%). The interpersonal conflict situations tended to involve the induction of anger and frustration in the clients.

An obvious implication of these findings is the possibility of identifying "high-risk" situations (those during which the threat of relapse has been empirically ascertained to be a highly likely event), for which a therapeutic program can be expressly geared.

As an example, consider Marlatt and Gordon's (1979) analysis of high-risk situations for heavy drinkers who have pledged themselves to abstinence. These investigators have determined that arguments between the ex-alcoholic client and "significant others" lead to relapse by way of a similar chain of unfortunate events. First, frustration and anger ensue as a direct result of an interpersonal confrontation. Then, instead of adequate assertion, the client turns to drink, as though drinking were "a symbolic act of aggression" toward the other person. According to Marlatt and Gordon, the ex-drinker comes to place his or her faith in the efficacy of alcohol to reduce the unpleasant affect, and concomitantly loses a sense of self-efficacy. The first drink triggers both a sense of guilt and possibly a sense of strength (often via fantasies). Finally, if the client actually acts aggressively there is an easy route to the avoidance of responsibility for it—the "alcohol made me do it."

Prevention of relapse in ex-alcoholics must begin, therefore, with an appreciation of the potential high-risk situations, not just in gross terms but with respect to each of the related elements in the behavior chain leading to social confrontation and its disastrous aftermath. Teaching clients to recognize high-risk situations may require the innovative use of self-monitoring procedures, standard interviews, and/or analogue role-play methods (Marlatt & Gordon, 1979). In each instance, the goal is to ascertain the role of idiosyncratic and predictable social stimuli in fostering substance abuse, so as to permit adequate therapeutic preparations to be made *in advance of the relapse episode.*

It should be mentioned also that in identifying or "diagnosing" environmental impediments to maintenance and transfer, the clinical assessor will encounter client "personality" differences—such as in susceptibility to social pressure, level of ascribed self-efficacy, and de gree of accurate self-awareness—which potentially mediate environmental perceptions. In addition, a most important set of determinants, to which we now turn, has to do with individual differences in clients' ability to cope with the identified stressors of daily living.

Individual Variation in Coping and Problem Solving

In designing intervention programs with high transfer potential, assessing the domain of problem situations is but a first step. An integral part of the total program is the analysis of performance requirements (cf. Goldfried & D'Zurilla, 1969; Gottman & Markman, 1978; Stern, Stein, & Bloom, 1956). By carefully observing individuals who are proficient at handling the kinds of stressors that precipitate relapse in various clinical populations, intervention agents can empirically derive the content of transfer training programs.

As we have noted, it is incorrect to assume that a training program can be applied in a lock-step fashion across individuals. All clients will probably possess some portion of most of the skills necessary for coping with posttreatment stressors. However, they will differ in the degree of organization of their skill repertoires, in their ability to discriminate when and where to use certain forms of responding, in their resiliency under pressure, and so on. It should be helpful, therefore, to construct what Marlatt and Gordon (1979) call a "profile of proficiency" for each client.

If we view adaptation to, and mastery of, changing social conditions, internal states, and physical conditions as *the goal* to be achieved by our clients, we are likely to become bogged down in the search for *global skill factors*—like the ability to manage anxiety, intelligence, rigidity-flexibility, etc. Because the kinds of problems confronting all of us in our daily lives are quite variable, we must expect problem-solving "factors" to be varied and situation specific. Because problem solving is an active and dynamic process, the determinants of proficiency are likely to be related to how well the individual integrates and coordinates varied component skills and not simply to the level of development of molar achievements (Anderson, 1967). Indeed, in a recent investigation, Litman, Eiser, Rawson, and Oppenheim (1979) found that alcoholics who successfully avoided relapse were more likely (than relapsers) to demonstrate flexibility in the use of cognitive coping skills (particularly "positive thinking"), while possessing a broader repertoire of potential coping devices.

In their analysis of interpersonal problem solving and social cognition skills, Spivack, Platt, and Shure (1976) have dealt with constructs of particular relevance to transfer enhancement as we have herein described it. Clinicians would be wise to consider assessing such dimensions as: sensitivity to the variety of potential interpersonal problems; the ability to generate alternative solution possibilities; the capability of articulating step-by-step means for carrying out problem solutions; the tendency to anticipate the varied consequences of an action; and finally, the awareness of or appreciation for the fact that behavior is contextually embedded and motivationally complex. The last component strikes this author as especially important in view of the widespread belief in the maintenance and transfer potential of internalized performance attributions. There will doubtless be many instances in which an internal causal attribution will be inappropriate, engendering a naive, and ultimately futile, attempt to "take charge" of a situation outside the actor's control. Thinking in terms of "reciprocal determinism" may prove far more serviceable across a wider variety of contexts. The reader is referred to Spivack et al.'s *The Problem-Solving Approach to Adjustment* (1976) for examples of how various problem-solving skills might be measured and taught to children, adolescents, and adults.

UNFINISHED BUSINESS

Although a vast amount of territory has been covered in this chapter, much has been left untouched and therefore implicit. By concentrating exclusively on the personal components of the organizational framework, the author has inevitably subordinated stimulus control and contingency factors, whose role is certainly of paramount importance (cf. Karoly, 1975). In addition, while an interactionist perspective was adopted, the author has offered few palpable examples of how "one-variable-at-a-time" thinking can be transcended. In short, the pieces have yet to be tied together in a neat package.

The defense for the above oversights is simple (if not totally acceptable): such is the current state of the art. Perhaps in 5 years a chapter on person or individual difference variables may provide more by way of integration and hard data.

However, there are some attributes of the present chapter that may appear as errors of commission rather than an unavoidable omissions. I would like to attend to three of these before concluding my remarks.

Personality Theory: The View from the "TOPSI"

Readers might wish to know how the author of the present chapter can justify the grafting of a discipline in a state of crisis (personality theory) onto an amorphous enterprise (psychotherapy research) in the expectation that such an operation will contribute meaningfully to the solution of the "maintenance question" (especially as it is rendered within the context of a reasonably healthy framework—learning theory). My answer, in short, is that no such grafting is intended. It is not the body of personality theories, with their attendant ambiguities, but the personality perspective which is being touted here. Psychotherapy is seen as a process involving learning, consolidation, and the creative transfer of skills. The personality perspective merely calls for a recognition of the role of individual differences in relatively stable abilities, in fluctuating propensities or dispositions (which include preferences and expectancies), and in organized modes of information processing, or what Golding (1978) calls "psychological organizing principles"—all of which may enter into complex interactions with the so-called conditions of learning.

It will be necessary to understand that when a clinician discusses an individual difference dimension (like achievement motivation or self-efficacy) he or she is usually assuming that the dimension has generalized predictive utilily. Over the years, however, personality researchers have been guilty of forgetting or overlooking the fact that broad constructs are built upon what Fiske (1978b) has termed "provincial observations" —that is, observations tied into a specific time (T), a particular observer (O) who perceives a phenomenon (P) occurring at a specific point in space (S) and who thereby derives an interpretation (I) of its meaning (hence the acronym, TOPSI). When the observer is the client and the phenomenon an internal response, the data (impressions) that are derived must be closely examined as to their "naturalness," replicability, and generalizability.

This writer is, therefore, in agreement with Bergin and Lambert's (1978) conclusion that traditional personality assessment procedures hold little promise in clarifying the process of psychotherapy outcome. However, the individualized study of therapy-relevant person variables couched within an explicitly interactional framework may well yield important insights into the processes of change and maintenance (cf. also Bergin & Lambert, 1978).

Individual Differences and Interactional Psychometrics

To many, the interaction of personality and learning (behavioral) concepts may seem ideologically feasible, but a practical or genetic impossibility. It is true that structuralism and methodological behaviorism do not mix. Yet a concern for the role of the individual's unique information-processing style as it contacts the cueing, reinforcing, enabling, and informative function of the external environment does not by definition constitute an X-rated perspective. The real perversity lies in the possibility that a marriage calling for a delicate interweaving of viewpoints will end up a shabby affair under the neon sign of "eclecticism."

Personality characteristics are usually thought to be stable aspects of human behavior, providing a *steady organismic state* across a variety of settings or assessment conditions. Based on this consistency assumption, traditional psychometric theory (Nunnally, 1978), and even the more encompassing generalizability theory approach (Cronbach, Gleser, Nanda, & Rajaratnam, 1972) which permits assessment conditions to vary, considers test scores to be "representative" of summarized individuals and essentially repeatable environments (universes). The intrasubject design, the hallmark of behavioral assessment, involves nonindependent observations of a single individual across subject-specific, nonreplicable behavior settings, and is incompatible with the psychometrics of the "true score" (cf. R. R. Jones, 1977). Failure to recognize the basic incongruence between the "pure" learning (change-oriented) and "pure" personality (stability-based) models might foster among enthusiastic and ecumenical investigators the inclusion of I-E Scales, self-esteem inventories, or mood ratings as pre- and posttherapy measures in single-case experiments. The problem, of course, will be to distill out of a change score the portion attributable to the treatment effect and that attributable to measurement error, since a change also represents unreliability. At the other extreme, we are already witnessing the use of such multiple testings as the within-subject factor in ANOVA designs, flying in the face of the "independence-of-observations" assumption. The purpose of the present chapter is not to precipitate the flamboyant use of numbers within either theoretical camp.

We can only assert that for those who acknowledge the utility of the view that people possess organized cognitions and perceptions that transcend, influence, and interact with environmental features, there may be some merit in trying to establish the consistency of personal components, in various client groups, across settings. Similarly, we advocate seeking to develop a taxonomy of situations, and investigating the conditions under which the situation-as-perceived is more useful predictively than absolute indexes of environmental constraint. Finally, we suggest using *integrated measurement or research strategies,* wherein multivariate, intersubject designs are employed in the identification of salient person factors, and then intrasubject experiments are undertaken to test their relevance (external validity) across extended time periods and under varying environmental conditions (see Alker, 1972; Cone, 1977; Golding, 1977; Olweus, 1977; Shine, 1975).

Person Variables over Time

It has been asserted that person variables are relatively stable, as are the tasks of therapeutic learning which the individual confronts. However, as Runyan (1978) has noted:

If behavior is determined by the interaction of persons with situations, then a comprehensive approach to prediction must assess person-behavior-situation configurations, and estimate the probability of alternative configurations developing out of this initial system. (p. 584)

The relative stability of the perceptions, motives, abilities, and modes of information processing relevant to change and maintenance, and our inability graphically to depict sequential, reciprocal interactions, should not obscure the fact that growth within the person and alterations of living conditions are ubiquitous. The temporal (T) facet of Fiske's TOPSI model has nested within it the emergent personal processes of an active organism encountering ever-changing environments. In the context of psychotherapy, our job is to observe and anticipate new configurations within each of the five basic dimensions of change (see Figure 7-2). As noted, some of the newly emerging processes will be supportive of, and others counter to, our treatment objectives. For discussions of how clinicians might go about preparing for the consequences of periodic and growth-enhancing person × environment transactions, the reader is again referred to Marlatt and Gordon (1979) and to Klein's presentation on adult development in Chapter 9.

SUMMARY

This chapter is viewed as an initial attempt to incorporate person variables into a systematic framework for the analysis of individual change and development in psychotherapy. Why individual difference factors should be included, what factors might be most profitably examined, where such factors fit in a stage-like model, and what empirical evidence can be mustered in their behalf were questions that were directly addressed.

The manner in which the process of psychotherapy has been described has tended to reflect the varying theoretical biases of clinical practitioners. Pragmatists have opted for "pretreatment, treatment, posttreatment, and follow-up" models, using *time* as an organizing principle. Another approach has been to make one's descriptive scheme *time- and technique centered,* as in "behavioral baseline, differential reinforcement, reversal, differential reinforcement plus generalization training." Or the focus might rest on hypothesized change mechanisms, such as transference, resistance, and working-through. In this chapter a five-stage, recursive model of open-ended therapeutic tasks was proposed.[9] The framework depends on theory, and is *person centered.* Based on a reasoned rejection of the prevalent behaviorist assumption that change techniques are equally applicable to virtually all populations at all times, a process model based on *person variables* was suggested to complement extant approaches. Consider also the fact that most clinical interventions aspire to be meaningful in the context of the individual's extratherapy life. Taking a larger, systems view, practitioners must look to the individual to provide the necessary continuity in the person × situation × behavior interactions that comprise human adaptation (Pervin, 1978; Runyan, 1978).

Readiness for problem recognition was the first major class of person variables discussed. Differences in the tendency to attend selectively to personal attributes and to person-environment interactions were suggested as having diagnostic, prognostic, and prescriptive implications.

Motivational arousal and the parameters of commitment to engage in a program of lifestyle change were considered next. Individual differences in goal setting, in the mechanisms of self-evaluation, in achievement motivation, in behavior-outcome expectancies (particularly those involving long-term consequences), in attributional systems (including "self-efficacy" beliefs), and in modes of commitment to therapeutic action were addressed. Specificity was urged in the design of assessment procedures.

The acquisition of requisite cognitive and behavioral skills was related to "learner differences" in motivation to learn, in propensity to perform, and in the manner of personal response to success and failure. Nuttin's (1976) distinction between open and closed tasks was suggested as being particularly salient in the conceptualization of psychotherapeutic learning.

Individual differences in maintenance processes (stage 4) were linked to styles of information retention and behavioral self-regulation. The research in this area has been strongly analogue oriented. Extension to clinical disorders is a much-needed and promising direction.

Finally, the process of posttreatment adjustment was considered from the perspective of variations in the nature of perceived extratherapy environments and in individuals' problem-solving strategies.

In general, research on subject variables in the behavioral psychotherapies has been sparce and unsystematic. Perhaps the framework offered in this chapter will contribute, in a modest way, toward the elaboration of therapeutic models, the individualization of clinical intervention, and the cultivation of meaningful long-term outcomes.

NOTES

1. Of course there are clinical problems, such as excessive shyness or nonassertiveness that seem to call for a recognition of the costs associated with *nonaction.* However, here too we might speak of the client's need to acknowledge the consequences of chronic social withdrawal, conformity, acquiescence, or anxiety.

2. But see Maltzman and Raskin (1965) and Maltzman (1967) for a discussion of individual differences in the OR and their effects on learning.

3. Duval and Wicklund's (1972) use of the terms "objective" and "subjective" in the context of their theory, although reasonable, may be somewhat confusing.

4. Recall that we are not advocating an "either-or" perspective on motivation. The importance of environmental support for behavior change efforts is clearly indicated in our structural model (Figure 7-1).

5. Weiner (1976) has suggested that although achievement motivation research shows that high achievers prefer tasks of "intermediate" difficulty, such tasks also possess information value and permit maximum self-evaluative feedback.

Individual differences in preference for information versus reward at various stages of learning might, therefore, prove relevant to the prediction of client dropout from therapy (wherein rewards are often delayed).

6. Apropos of our stage 1 "readiness" notion, perceived vulnerability or susceptibility to illness was also a reliable predictor of compliance.

7. One of the objectives of Nuttin's research program (Nuttin & Greenwald, 1968) has been to show that rewards do not automatically strengthen the behaviors they follow, and that the same reward may fluctuate in its "controlling power" as a function of its perceived instrumentality (cf. also Estes, 1972). For example, might we not expect that a smile coming from a therapist following a client's vain attempt at an "assertive" response to be less predictive of future assertiveness than a response-contingent smile following a successful demonstration of assertiveness? Any attempt to facilitate maintenance by simply "programming" the contingencies in the client's extratherapy world must also take into account the differential informative function of within-therapy and extratherapy "rewarding" events.

8. It is fascinating to note the similarity between the fields of behavior modification and mnemonic training with respect to the growing recognition of the importance of the long-range effects (generalization and transfer) of learning (see Campione & Brown, 1977).

9. The current division into five steps or stages is a matter of personal preference. The reader may wish to consult Marks (1978) in which a similar, but two-stage, framework is provided.

ACKNOWLEDGMENTS

The author thanks R. J. Senter, Will Seeman, and J. T. DeVoge for their careful reading of an earlier version of this manuscript.

REFERENCE NOTES

1. Karoly, P., & Decker, J. *Effects of personally and socially referenced success and failure upon self-reward and self-criticism.* Unpublished manuscript, University of Cincinnati, 1978.

2. Hill, D., & Bale, R. *Development of the mental health locus of control and the mental health locus of origin scales.* Unpublished manuscript, University of Cincinnati, 1978.

REFERENCES

Alker, H. A. Is personality situationally specific or intrapsychically consistent? *Journal of Personality,* 1972, *40,* 1–16.

Anderson, R. C. Individual differences and problem solving. In R. M. Gagné

(Ed.), *Learning and individual differences.* Columbus, Ohio: Charles E. Merrell, 1967.

Amsel, A. The role of frustrative nonreward in noncontinuous reward situations. *Psychological Bulletin,* 1958, *55,* 102–119.

Atkinson, J. W. Introduction and overview. In J. W. Atkinson & J. O. Raynor (Eds.), *Motivation and achievement.* Washington, D. C.: Winston, 1974.

Atkinson, J. W., & Birch, D. *The dynamics of action.* New York: Wiley, 1970.

Atkinson, J. W., & Birch, D. *Introduction to motivation* (2nd ed.). New York: Van Nostrand, 1978.

Atkinson, J. W., & Raynor, J. O. (Eds.), *Motivation and achievement.* Washington, D.C.: Winston, 1974.

Atkinson, R. C., & Shiffrin, R. M. Human memory: A proposed system and its control processes. In K.Spence & J. T. Spence (Eds.), *The psychology of learning and motivation* (vol. 2). New York: Academic Press, 1968.

Ausubel, D. P. The use of advance organizers in the learning and retention of meaningful verbal material. *Journal of Educational Psychology,* 1960, *51,* 267–272.

Ausubel, D. P., & Robinson, F. G. *School learning.* New York: Holt, Rinehart & Winston, 1969.

Ayllon, T., & Azrin, N. H. *The token economy: A motivational system for therapy and rehabilitation.* New York: Appleton-Century-Crofts, 1968.

Baer, D. M., Wolf, M. M., & Risley, T. R. Some current dimensions of applied behavior analysis. *Journal of Applied Behavior Analysis,* 1968, *1,* 91–97.

Bandura, A. *Principles of behavior modification.* New York: Holt, Rinehart & Winston, 1969.

Bandura, A. *Social learning theory.* Englewood Cliffs, N.J.: Prentice-Hall, 1977. (a)

Bandura, A. Self-efficacy: Toward a unifying theory of behavioral change. *Psychological Review,* 1977, *84,* 191–215. (b)

Bandura, A., & Adams, N. E. Analysis of self-efficacy theory of behavioral change. *Cognitive Therapy and Research,* 1977, *1,* 287–310.

Bandura, A., Adams, N. E., & Beyer, J. Cognitive processes mediating behavioral change. *Journal of Personality and Social Psychology,* 1977, *35,* 125–139.

Beck, R. C. *Motivation: Theories and principles.* Englewood Cliffs, N.J.: Prentice-Hall, 1978.

Becker, M. H., & Maiman, L. A. Sociobehavioral determinants of compliance with health and medical care recommendations. *Medical Care,* 1975, *13,* 10–24.

Bellack, A. S. Internal versus external locus of control and the use of self-reinforcement. *Psychological Reports,* 1972, *31,* 723–733.

Bellack, A. S., Glanz, L., & Simon, R. Covert imagery and individual differences in self-reinforcement style in the treatment of obesity. *Journal of Consulting and Clinical Psychology,* 1976, *44,* 490–491.

Belmont, J. M., & Butterfield, E. C. The instructional approach to developmental cognitive research. In R. V. Kail & J. W. Hagen (Eds.), *Perspectives on the development of memory and cognition.* Hillsdale, N.J.: Lawrence Erlbaum, 1977.

Bem, D. J. Self-perception: An alternative interpretation of cognitive dissonance. *Psychological Review,* 1976, *74,* 183–200.

Bergin, A. E., & Garfield, S. L (Eds.), *Handbook of psychotherapy and behavior change: An empirical analysis.* New York: Wiley, 1971.

Bergin, A. E., & Lambert, M. J. The evaluation of therapeutic outcomes. In S. L. Garfield & A. E. Bergin (Eds.), *Handbook of psychotherapy and behavior change* (2nd ed.). New York: Wiley, 1978.

Bergin, A. E., & Suinn, R. M. Individual psychotherapy and behavior therapy. *Annual Review of Psychology,* 1975, *26,* 509–556.

Bieri, J., Atkins, A. L., Briar, S., Leaman, R. L., Miller, H., & Tripodi, T. *Clinical and social judgment.* New York: Wiley, 1966.

Bindra, D. A motivational view of learning, performance, and behavior modification. *Psychological Review,* 1974, *81,* 199–213.

Bowers, K. S. The psychology of subtle control: An attributional analysis of behavioural persistence. *Canadian Journal of Behavioral Science,* 1975, *7,* 78–95.

Brehm, J. W., & Cohen, A. R. *Explorations in cognitive dissonance.* New York: Wiley, 1962.

Brehm, S. S. *The application of social psychology to clinical practice.* Washington, D.C.: Hemisphere (Wiley), 1976.

Brewer, W. F. There is no convincing evidence for operant or classical conditioning in humans. In W. B. Weimer & D. S. Palermo (Eds.), *Cognition and the symbolic processes.* Hillsdale, N.J.: Lawrence Earlbaum, 1974.

Broadbent, D. E. *Perception and communication.* London: Pergamon, 1958.

Bruner, J. S., & Postman, L. Emotional selectivity in perception and reaction. *Journal of Personality,* 1947, *16,* 69–77.

Buchwald, A. M. Learning theory and behavior therapy. In W. K. Estes (Ed.), *Handbook of learning and cognitive processes* (vol. 3). Hillsdale, N.J.: Lawrence Earlbaum, 1976.

Byrne, D. Repression-sensitization as a dimension of personality. In B. A. Maher (Ed.), *Progress in experimental personality research* (vol. 1). New York: Academic Press, 1964.

Campione, J. C., & Brown, A. L. Memory and metamemory development in educable retarded children. In R. V. Kail & J. W. Hagen (Eds.), *Perspectives on the development of memory and cognition.* Hillsdale, N.J.: Lawrence Erlbaum, 1977.

Capaldi, E. J. A sequential hypothesis of instrumental learning. In K. W. Spence & J. T. Spence (Eds.), *The psychology of learning and motivation* (vol. 1). New York: Academic Press, 1967.

Carver, C. S., & Blaney, P. H. Perceived arousal, focus of attention, and avoidance behavior. *Journal of Consulting and Clinical Psychology,* 1977, *86,* 154–162.

Cone, J. D. The relevance of reliability and validity for behavioral assessment. *Behavioral Therapy,* 1977, *8,* 411–426.

Conway, J. B., & Bucher, B. D. Transfer and maintenance of behavior change in children: A review and suggestions. In E. J. Marsh, L. A. Hamerlynck, & L. C. Handy (Eds.), *Behavior modification and families.* New York: Brunner/Mazel, 1976.

Cronbach, L. J. Beyond the two disciplines of scientific psychology. *American Psychologist,* 1975, *30,* 116–127.

Cronbach, L. J. Gleser, G. C., Nanda, H., & Rajaratnam, N. *The dependability of behavioral measurements.* New York: Wiley, 1972.

Davison, G., & Valins, S. Maintenance of self-attributed and drug-attributed behavior change. *Journal of Personality and Social Psychology,* 1969, *11,* 25–33.

deCharms, R. *Personal causation.* New York: Academic Press, 1968.

DeFleur, M. L., & Westie, F. R. Verbal attitudes and overt acts: An experiment on the salience of attitudes. *American Sociological Review,* 1958, *23,* 667–673.

Dember, W. N., & Earl, R. W. Analysis of exploratory, manipulatory, and curiosity behaviors. *Psychological Review,* 1957, *64,* 91–96.

Diggory, J. C. *Self-evaluation: Concepts and studies.* New York: Wiley, 1966.

DiLoreto, A. *Comparative psychotherapy: An experimental analysis.* Chicago: Aldine, 1971.

Dirkes, M. A. The role of divergent production in the learning process. *American Psychologist,* 1978, *33,* 815–820.

Dollard, J., & Miller, N. E. *Personality and psychotherapy.* New York: McGraw-Hill, 1950.

Duval, S., & Wicklund, R. A. *A theory of objective self-awareness.* New York: Academic Press, 1972.

Dweck, C. S., & Gilliard, D. Expectancy statements as determinants of reactions to failure: Sex differences in persistence and expectancy change. *Journal of Personality and Social Psychology,* 1975, *32,* 1077–1084.

Dweck, C. S., & Reppucci, N. D. Learned helplessness and reinforcement responsibility in children. *Journal of Personality and Social Psychology,* 1973, *25,* 109–116.

Eriksen, B., & Eriksen, C. W. *Perception and personality.* Morristown, N.J.: General Learning Press, 1972.

Estes, W. K. Reinforcement in human behavior. *American Scientist,* 1972, *60,* 723–729.

Eysenck, H. J. *The biological basis of personality.* Springfield, Ill.: Charles C. Thomas, 1967.

Eysenck, H. J., & Eysenck, S. B. G. *Manual for the Eysenck personality inventory.* San Diego, Calif.: Educational and Industrial Testing Service, 1968.

Eysenck, M. W. Extraversion, verbal learning, and memory. *Psychological Bulletin,* 1976, *83,* 75–90.

Feather, N. T. The relationship of persistence at a task to expectation of success and achievement related motives. *Journal of Abnormal and Social Psychology,* 1961, *63,* 552–561.

Fenigstein, A., Scheier, M. F., & Buss, A. H. Public and private self-consciousness: Assessment and theory. *Journal of Consulting and Clinical Psychology,* 1975, *43,* 522–527.

Festinger, L. A theory of social comparison processes. *Human Relations,* 1954, *7,* 117–140.

Festinger, L. *A theory of cognitive dissonance.* Stanford, Calif.: Stanford University Press, 1957.

Fiedler, F. E. What triggers the person–situation interaction in leadership? In D. Magnusson & N. S. Endler (Eds.), *Personality at the crossroads.* Hillsdale, N.J.: Lawrence Erlbaum, 1977.

Fishbein, M., & Ajzen, I. *Belief, attitude, intention, and behavior: An introduction to theory and research.* Reading, Mass.: Addison-Wesley, 1975.

Fiske, D. W. *Strategies for personality research.* San Francisco: Jossey-Bass, 1978. (a)

Fiske, D. W. Cosmopolitan constructs and provincial observations: Some prescriptions for a chronically ill specialty. In H. London (Ed.), *Personality: A new look at metatheories.* Washington, D.C.: Hemisphere, 1978. (b)

Flaherty, C. F., Hamilton, L. W., Gandelman, R. J., & Spear, N. E. *Learning and memory.* Chicago: Rand-McNally, 1977.

Flavell, J., Beach, D., & Chinsky, J. Spontaneous verbal rehearsal in a memory task as a function of age. *Child Development,* 1966, *37,* 283-299.

Franks, C. M., & Wilson, G. T. (Eds.). *Annual review of behavior therapy: Theory and practice* (vols. 1-6). New York: Brunner/Mazel, 1973-78.

Frieze, I. H., Parsons, J. E., Johnson, P. B., Ruble, D. N., & Zellman, G. L. *Women and sex roles: A social psychological perspective.* New York: W. W. Norton, 1978.

Gagné, R. M. (Ed.). *Learning and individual differences.* Columbus, Ohio: Charles E. Merrill, 1967.

Gagné, R. M. *The conditions of learning* (2nd ed.). New York: Holt, Rinehart & Winston, 1970.

Glaser, R. Some implications of previous work on learning and individual differences. In R. M. Gagne (Ed.), *Learning and individual differences.* Columbus, Ohio: Charles E. Merrill, 1967.

Goldfried, M. R., & D'Zurilla, T. J. A behavioral-analytic model for assessing competence. In C. D. Spielberger (Ed.), *Current topics in clinical and community psychology* (vol. 1). New York: Academic Press, 1969.

Golding, S. L. The problem of construal styles in the analysis of person–situation interactions. In D. Magnusson & N. S. Endler (Eds.), *Personality at the crossroads.* Hillsdale, N.J.: Lawrence Erlbaum, 1977.

Golding, S. L. Toward a more adequate theory of personality: Psychological organizing principles. In H. London (Ed.), *Personality: A new look at metatheories.* Washington, D. C.: Hemisphere, 1978.

Goldstein, A. P., Heller, K., & Sechrest, L. B. *Psychotherapy and the psychology of behavior change.* New York: Wiley, 1966.

Goldstein, A. P., & Stein, N. *Prescriptive psychotherapies.* New York: Pergamon, 1976.

Gottman, J.,& Markman, H. J. Experimental designs in psychotherapy research. In S. L. Garfield & A. E. Bergin (Eds.), *Handbook of psychotherapy and behavior change: An empirical analysis (2nd ed.).* New York: Wiley, 1978.

Gray, J. A. The psychophysiological nature of introversion–extroversion: A modification of Eysenck's theory. In V. D. Nebylitsyn & J. A. Gray (Eds.), *Biological bases of individual behavior.* New York: Academic Press, 1972.

Hall, C. S., & Lindzey, G. *Theories of personality.* New York: Wiley, 1978.

Hall, J. F. *Classical conditioning and instrumental learning: A contemporary approach.* Philadelphia: J. P. Lippincott, 1976.

Hartig, M., & Kanfer, F. H. The role of verbal self-instructions in children's resistance to temptation. *Journal of Personality and Social Psychology,* 1973, *25,* 259-267.

Hebb, D. O. *The organization of behavior.* New York: Wiley, 1949.

Heider, F. *The psychology of interpersonal relations.* New York: Wiley, 1958.

Hollingsworth, R., & Foreyt, J. P. Community adjustment of released token economy patients. *Journal of Behavior Therapy and Experimental Psychiatry,* 1975, *6,* 271-274.

Horner, M. S. Toward an understanding of achievement-related conflicts in women. *Journal of Social Issues,* 1972, *28,* 157-175.

Horton, D. L., & Turnage, T. W. *Human learning*. Englewood Cliffs, N.J.: Prentice-Hall, 1976.

Hunt, J. McV. Motivation inherent in information processing and action. In O. J. Harvey (Ed.), *Motivation and social interaction: Cognitive determinants*. New York: Ronald Press, 1963.

James, W. *The principles of psychology*. New York: Holt, 1890.

Janis, I. L., & Mann, L. *Decision making: A psychological analysis of conflict, choice, and commitment*. New York: Free Press, 1977.

Jensen, A. R. Varieties of individual differences in learning. In R. M. Gagné (Ed.), *Learning and individual differences*. Columbus, Ohio: Charles E. Merrill, 1967.

John, E. R. A model of consciousness. In G. Schwartz & D. Shapiro (Eds.), *Consciousness and self-regulation: Advances in research* (vol. 1). New York: Plenum, 1976.

Johnson, J. H. Memory and personality: An information processing approach. *Journal of Research in Personality, 1974, 8*, 1-32.

Jones, E. E., Kanouse, D., Kelley, H., Nisbett, R. E., Valins, S., & Weiner, B. *Attribution: Perceiving the causes of behavior*. Morristown, N.J.: General Learning Press, 1971.

Jones, R. R. Conceptual versus analytic uses of generalizability theory in behavioral assessment. In J. D. Cone & R. P. Hawkins (Eds.), *Behavioral assessment: New directions in clinical psychology*. New York: Brunner/Mazel, 1977.

Kanfer, F. H. Verbal conditioning: A review of its current status. In T. R. Dixon & D. L. Horton (Eds.), *Verbal behavior and general behavior theory*. Englewood Cliffs, N.J.: Prentice-Hall, 1968.

Kanfer, F. H. Self-regulation: Research, issues, and speculations. In C. Neuringer & J. L. Michael (Eds.), *Behavior modification in clinical psychology*. New York: Appleton-Century-Crofts, 1970.

Kanfer, F. H. The maintenance of behavior by self-generated stimuli and reinforcement. In A. Jacobs & L. B. Sachs (Eds.), *The psychology of private events*. New York: Academic Press, 1971.

Kanfer, F. H. The many faces of self-control, or behavior modification changes its focus. In R. B. Stuart (Ed.), *Behavioral self-management: Strategies, techniques, and outcome*. New York: Brunner/Mazel, 1977.

Kanfer, F. H., Cox, L. E., Greiner, J. M., & Karoly, P. Contracts, demand characteristics, and self-control. *Journal of Personality and Social Psychology, 1974, 30*, 605-619.

Kanfer, F. H., & Goldstein, A. P. (Eds.). *Helping people change*. New York: Pergamon, 1975.

Kanfer, F. H., & Karoly, P. Self-control: A behavioristic excursion into the lion's den. *Behavior Therapy, 1972, 3*, 398-416.

Kanfer, F. H., & Phillips, J. S. *Learning foundations of behavior therapy*. New York: Wiley, 1970.

Kantorowitz, D. A. Personality and conditioning of tumescence and detumescence. *Behaviour Research and Therapy, 1978, 16*, 117-123.

Karoly, P. On "controls" in psychotherapy research: A plea for innocence. *Psychotherapy: Theory, Research, and Practice, 1972, 9*, 11-12.

Karoly, P. Operant methods. In F. H. Kanfer & A. P. Goldstein (Eds.), *Helping people change*. New York: Pergamon, 1975.

Karoly, P. Behavioral self-management in children: Concepts, methods, issues, and directions. In M. Hersen, R. M. Eisler, & P. M. Miller (Eds.), *Progress in behavior modification* (vol. 5). New York: Academic Press, 1977.

Karoly, P., & Kanfer, F. H. Situational and historical determinants of self-reinforcement. *Behavior Therapy,* 1974, *5,* 381–390.

Kazdin, A. E. *Behavior modification in applied settings.* Homewood, Ill.: Dorsey, 1975.

Kazdin, A. E. *History of behavior and modification: Experimental foundations of contemporary research.* Baltimore: University Park Press, 1978.

Kazdin, A. E., & Bootzin, R. R. The token economy: An evaluative review. *Journal of Applied Behavior Analysis,* 1972, *5,* 343–372.

Kazdin, A. E., & Wilcoxon, L. A. Systematic desensitization and nonspecific treatment effects: A methodological evaluation. *Psychological Bulletin,* 1976, *83,* 729–758.

Kazdin, A. E., & Wilson, G. T. *Evaluation of behavior therapy: Issues, evidence, and research strategies.* Cambridge, Mass.: Ballinger, 1978.

Keeley, S. M., Shemberg, K. M., & Carbonell, J. Operant clinical intervention: Behavior management or beyond? Where are the data? *Behavior Therapy,* 1976, *7,* 292–305.

Kelley, H. H. Attribution theory in social psychology. In D. Levine (Ed.), *Nebraska symposium on motivation* (vol. 15). Lincoln: University of Nebraska Press, 1967.

Kelly, G. A. *The psychology of personal constructs.* New York: W. W. Norton, 1955.

Kessen, W. "Stage" and "structure" in the study of children. In W. Kessen & C. Kuhlman (Eds.), *Thought in the young child: Society for Research in Child Development Monographs,* 1962, *27*(2).

Kiesler, C. A. *The psychology of commitment.* New York: Academic Press, 1971.

Kirschenbaum, D. S., & Karoly, P. When self-regulation fails: Tests of some preliminary hypotheses. *Journal of Consulting and Clinical Psychology,* 1977, *45,* 1116–1125.

Kopel, S., & Arkowitz, H. The role of attribution and self-perception in behavior change: Implications for behavior therapy. *Genetic Psychology Monographs,* 1975, *92,* 175–212.

Krantz, D. S., & Stone, V. Locus of control and the effects of success and failure in young and community-residing aged women. *Journal of Personality,* 1978, *46,* 536–551.

Krasner, L. The future and the past in the Behaviorism–Humanism dialogue. *American Psychologist,* 1978, *33,* 799–804.

Kreitler, H., & Kreitler, S. *Cognitive orientation and behavior.* New York: Springer, 1976.

Laird, J. D., & Berglas, S. Individual differences in the effects of engaging in counter-attitudinal behavior. *Journal of Personality,* 1975, *43,* 286–304.

Lashley, K. S. The mechanism of vision: XV. Preliminary studies of the rat's capacity for detail vision. *Journal of General Psychology,* 1938, *18,* 123–193.

Lawton, J. T. The use of advance organizers in the learning and retention of logical operations and social studies concepts. *American Educational Research Journal,* 1977, *14,* 25–43.

Lazarus, A. A. *Behavior therapy and beyond.* New York: McGraw-Hill, 1971.

Levendusky, P., & Pankratz, L. Self-control techniques as an alternative to pain medication. *Journal of Abnormal Psychology,* 1975, *84,* 165-168.

Levy, L. H. *Conceptions of personality.* New York: Random House, 1970.

Lewin, K., Dembo, T., Festinger, L., & Sears, P. S. Level of aspiration In J. McV. Hunt (Ed.), *Personality and the behavior disorders.* New York: Ronald Press, 1944.

Lieberman, D. A. (Ed.). *Learning and the control of behavior.* New York: Holt, Rinehart & Winston, 1974.

Lieberman, M. A., Yalom, I. D., & Miles, M. B. *Encounter gorups: First facts.* New York: Basic Books, 1973.

Litman, G. K., Eisler, J. R., Rawson, N. S. B., & Oppenheim, A. N. Differences in relapse precipitants and coping behaviour between alcohol relapsers and survivors. *Behaviour Research and Therapy,* 1979, *17,* 89-94.

Loeb, A., Beck, A., Diggory, J., & Tuthill, R. Expectancy, level of aspiration, performance, and self-evaluation in depression. *Proceedings of the 75th Annual Convention of the American Psychological Association,* 1967, *2,* 193-194.

Mackintosh, N. J. Selective attention in animal discrimination learning. *Psychological Bulletin,* 1965, *64,* 124-150.

Magnusson, D., & Endler, N. S. (Eds.). *Personality at the crossroads: Current issues in interactional psychology.* Hillsdale, N.J.: Lawrence Erlbaum, 1977.

Mahoney, M. J. *Cognition and behavior modification.* Cambridge, Mass.: Ballinger, 1974.

Mahoney, M. J. Cognitive therapy and research: A question of questions. *Cognitive Therapy and Research,* 1977, *1,* 5-16.

Maltzman, I. Individual differences in "attention": The orienting reflex. In R. M. Gagné (Ed.), *Learning and individual differences.* Columbus, Ohio: Charles E. Merrill, 1967.

Maltzman, I., & Raskin, D. C. Effects of individual differences in the orienting reflex on conditioning and complex processes. *Journal of Experimental Research in Personality,* 1965, *1,*1-16.

Mandler, G., Mandler, J. M., & Uviller, E. T. Autonomic feedback: The perception of autonomic activity. *Journal of Abnormal and Social Psychology,* 1958, *56,* 367-373.

Marholin, D., Siegel, L. J., & Phillips, D. Treatment and transfer: A search for empirical procedures. In M. Hersen, R. M. Eisler, & P. M. Miller (Eds.), *Progress in behavior modification* (vol. 3). New York: Academic Press, 1976.

Marks, I. M. Behavioral psychotherapy of adult neurosis. In S. L. Garfield & A. E. Bergin (Eds.), *Handbook of psychotherapy and behavior change: An empirical analysis* (2nd ed.). New York: Wiley, 1978.

Markus, H. Self-schemata and processing information about the self. *Journal of Personality and Social Psychology,* 1977, *35,* 63-78.

Marlatt, G. A., & Gordon, J. R. Determinants of relapse: Implications for the maintenance of behavior change. In P. Davidson (Ed.), *Behavioral medicine: Changing health lifestyles.* New York: Brunner/Mazel, 1979.

Marlatt, G. A., & Kaplan, B. Self-initiated attempts to change behavior: A study of New Year's resolutions. *Psychological Reports,* 1972, *30,* 123-131.

Marston, A. R. Personality variables related to self-reinforcement. *Journal of Psychology,* 1964, *58,* 169-175.

Marston, A. R. Imitation, self-reinforcement, and reinforcement of another person. *Journal of Personality and Social Psychology,* 1965, *2,* 255-261.

Marzillier, J. S., & Winter, K. Success and failure in social skills training: Individual differences. *Behaviour Research and Therapy,* 1978, *16,* 67–84.

McClelland, D. C., Atkinson, J. W., Clark, R. A., & Lowell, E. L. *The achievement motive.* New York: Appleton-Century-Crofts, 1953.

McGinnies, E. Emotionality and perceptual defense. *Psychological Review,* 1949, *56,* 244–251.

Medin, D. L. Theories of discrimination learning and perceptual set. In W. K. Estes (Ed.), *Handbook of learning and cognitive processes* (vol. 3). Hillsdale, N.J.: Lawrence Erlbaum, 1976.

Mehrabian, A. A questionnaire measure of individual differences in stimulus screening and associated differences in arousability. *Environmental Psychology and Nonverbal Behavior,* 1977, *1,* 89–103.

Meichenbaum, D. Toward a cognitive theory of self-control. In G. Schwartz & D. Shapiro (Eds.), *Consciousness and self-regulation: Advances in research* (vol. 1). New York: Plenum, 1976.

Mischel, W. Toward a cognitive social learning reconceptualization of personality. *Psychological Review,* 1973, *80,* 252–283.

Mischel, W. *Introduction to personality.* New York: Holt, Rinehart & Winston, 1976.

Mischel, W., & Ebbesen, E. Attention in delay of gratification. *Journal of Personality and Social Psychology,* 1970, *16,* 329–337.

Mischel, W., Ebbesen, E., & Zeiss, A. R. Selective attention to self: Situational and dispositional determinants. *Journal of Personality and Social Psychology,* 1973, *27,* 129–142.

Mitchell, T. R., & Biglan, A. Instrumentality theories: Current uses in psychology. *Psychological Bulletin,* 1971, *76,* 432–454.

Moos, R. H. Conceptualization of human environments. *American Psychologist,* 1973, *28,* 652–665.

Nay, W. R. *Behavioral intervention: Contemporary strategies.* New York: Gardner Press, 1976.

Nelson, R. E., & Craighead, W. E. Selective recall of positive and negative feedback, self-control behaviors, and depression. *Journal of Abnormal Psychology,* 1977, *86,* 379–388.

Neuringer, C. Self- and other-appraisals by suicidal, psychosomatic, and normal hospitalized patients. *Journal of Consulting and Clinical Psychology,* 1974, *42,* 306.

Nunnally, J. C. *Psyuchometric theory* (2nd ed.). New York: McGraw-Hill, 1978.

Nuttin, J. R. Motivation and reward in human learning: A cognitive approach. In W. K. Estes (Ed.), *Handbook of learning and cognitive processes* (vol. 3). Hillsdale, N.J.: Lawrence Erlbaum, 1976.

Nuttin, J., & Greenwald, A. G. *Reward and punishment in human learning: A behavior theory.* New York: Academic Press, 1968.

O'Banion, K., & Arkowitz, H. Social anxiety and selective memory for affective information about the self. *Social Behavior and Personality,* 1977, *5,* 321–328.

O'Leary, K. D., & Drabman, R. Token reinforcement programs in the classroom: A review. *Psychological Bulletin,* 1971, *75,* 379–398.

O'Leary, K. D., & Wilson, G. T. *Behavior therapy: Application and outcome.* Englewood Cliffs, N.J: Prentice-Hall, 1975.

Olweus, D. A critical analysis of the "modern" interactionist position. In D.

Magnusson & N. S. Endler (Eds.), *Personality at the crossroads.* Hillsdale, N.J.: Lawrence Erlbaum, 1977.

Orne, M. T. On the social psychology of the psychological experiment: With particular reference to demand characteristics and their implications. *American Psychologist,* 1962, *17,* 776–783.

Paris, S. G., & Lindauer, B. K. Constructive aspects of children's comprehension and memory. In R. V. Kail & J. W. Hagen (Eds.), *Perspectives on the development of memory and cognition.* Hillsdale, N.J.: Lawrence Erlbaum, 1977.

Pervin, L. C. *Current controversies and isses in personality.* New York: Wiley, 1978.

Postman, L., & Sassenrath, J. The automatic action of verbal rewards and punishments. *Journal of General Psychology,* 1961, *65,* 109–136.

Rachlin, H. *Behavior and learning.* San Francisco: W. H. Freeman, 1976.

Ray, R. D., & Brown, D. A. A systems approach to behavior. *Psychological Record,* 1975, *25,* 459–478.

Raynor, J. O. Future orientation and motivation of immediate activity: An elaboration of the theory of achievement motivation. *Psychological Review,* 1969, *76,* 606–610.

Reisman, J. M. *Toward the integration of psychotherapy.* New York: Wiley, 1971.

Revusky, S. H., & Garcia, J. Learned associations over long delays. In G. H. Bower & J. T. Spence (Eds.), *The psychology of learning and motivation* (vol. 4). New York: Academic Press, 1970.

Rohwer, W. D. An introduction to research on individual and developmental differences in learning. In W. K. Estes (Ed.), *Handbook of learning and cognitive processes* (vol. 3). Hillsdale, N.J.: Lawrence Erlbaum, 1976.

Rohwer, W. D., & Dempster, F. N. Memory development and educational processes. In R. V. Kail & J. W. Hagen (Eds.), *Perspectives on the development of memory and condition.* Hillsdale, N.J.: Lawrence Erlbaum, 1977.

Ross, L., Rodin, J., & Zimbardo, P.G. Toward an attribution therapy: The reduction of fear through induced cognitive-emotional misattribution. *Journal of Personality and Social Psychology,* 1969, *12,* 279–288.

Ross, L. E., & Ross, S. M. Cognitive factors in classical conditioning. In W. K. Estes (Ed.), *Handbook of learning and cognitive processes* (vol. 3). Hillsdale, N.J.: Lawrence Erlbaum, 1976.

Rotter, J. B. *Social learning and clinical psychology.* Englewood Cliffs, N.J.: Prentice-Hall, 1954.

Rotter, J. B. Generalized expectancies for internal versus external control of reinforcement. *Psychological Monographs,* 1966, *80,* (Whole No. 609).

Rotter, J. B. Some problems and misconceptions related to the construct of internal versus external control of reinforcement. *Journal of Consulting and Clinical Psychology,* 1975, *43,* 56–67.

Rotter, J. B., Chance, J., & Phares, E. J. (Eds.), *Applications of a social learning theory of personality.* New York: Holt, Rinehart & Winston, 1972.

Royce, J. R., & Buss, A. R. The role of general systems and information theory in multi-factor individuality theory. *Canadian Psychological Review,* 1976, *17,* 1–21.

Rozensky, R. H., & Bellack, A. S. Behavior change and individual differences in self-control. *Behaviour Research and Therapy,* 1974, *12,* 267–268.

Runyan, W. M. The life course as a theoretical orientation: Sequences of person–situation interaction. *Journal of Personality,* 1978, *46,* 569–593.

Salter, A. *The case against psychoanalysis.* New York: Holt, 1952.

Salzman, L. Memory in psychotherapy. In E. W. Strauss & R. M. Griffith (Eds.), *Phenomenology of memory.* Pittsburgh: Duquesne University Press, 1970.

Sampson, E. E. Personality and the location of identity. *Journal of Personality,* 1978, *56,* 552–568.

Schachter, S., & Singer, J. E. Cognitive, social, and physiological determinants of emotional state. *Psychological Review,* 1962, *69,* 379–399.

Schwartz, B. *Psychology of learning and behavior.* New York: W. W. Norton, 1978.

Schwartz, S. Individual differences in cognition: Some relationships between personality and memory. *Journal of Research in Personality,* 1975, *9,* 217–225.

Scott, W. A. Structure of natural cognitions. *Journal of Personality and Social Psychology,* 1969, *12,* 261–278.

Sechrest, L., & Wallace, J. *Psychology and human problems.* Columbus, Ohio: Charles E. Merrell, 1967.

Seligman, M. E. P., & Hager, J. L. (Eds.), *Biological boundaries of learning.* New York: Appleton-Century-Crofts, 1972.

Shapiro, A. K., & Morris, L. A. The placebo effect in medical and psychological therapies. In S. L. Garfield & A. E. Bergin (Eds.), *Handbook of psychotherapy and behavior change: An empirical analysis* (2nd ed.). New York: Wiley, 1978.

Shimp, C. P. Perspectives on the behavioral unit: Choice behavior in animals. In W. E. Estes (Ed.), *Handbook of learning and cognitive processes* (vol. 2). Hillsdale, N.J.: Lawrence Erlbaum, 1975.

Shine, L. C. Five research steps designed to integrate the single subject and multi-subject approaches to experimental research. *Canadian Psychological Review,* 1975, *16,* 179–184.

Sidman, M. *Tactics of scientific research.* New York: Basic Books, 1960.

Skinner, B. F. *Science and human behavior.* New York: Macmillan, 1953.

Sloane, R. B., Staples, F. R., Cristol, A. H., Yorkston, N. J., & Whipple, K. *Psychotherapy versus behavior therapy.* Cambridge, Mass.: Harvard University Press, 1975.

Snyder, M. The self-monitoring of expressive behavior. *Journal of Personality and Social Psychology,* 1974, *30,* 526–537.

Sokolov, E. N. Neuronal models and the orienting reflex. In M. A. B. Brazier (Ed.), *The central nervous system and behavior.* New York: Josiah Macy Foundation, 1960.

Spivack, G., Platt, J. J., & Shure, M. B. *The problem-solving approach to adjustment.* San Francisco: Jossey-Bass, 1976.

Staats, A. W. *Social behaviorism.* Homewood, Ill.: Dorsey Press, 1975.

Staddon, J. E. R. Learning as adaptation. In W. K. Estes (Ed.), *Handbook of learning and cognitive processes* (vol. 2). Hillsdale, N.J.: Lawrence Erlbaum, 1975.

Stern, G. G., Stein, M. I., & Bloom, B. S. *Methods in personality assessment.* Glencoe, Ill.: The Free Press, 1956.

Strong, S. R. Social psychological approach to psychotherapy research. In S. L. Garfield & A. E. Bergin (Eds.), *Handbook of psychotherapy and behavior change* (2nd ed.). New York: Wiley, 1978.

Stuart, R. B. Self-help group approach to self-management. In R. B. Stuart (Ed.), *Behavioral self-management: Strategies, techniques, and outcome.* New York: Brunner/Mazel, 1977.

Sulzer-Azaroff, B., & Mayer, G. R. *Applying behavior-analysis procedures with children and youth.* New York: Rinehart & Winston, 1977.

Sutherland, J. W. *A general systems philosophy for the social and behavioral sciences.* New York: George Braziller, 1973.

Tesser, A. Self-generated attitude change. In L. Berkowitz (Ed.), *Advances in experimental social psychology.* New York: Academic Press, 1978.

Tesser, A., Leone, C., & Clary, E. G. Affect control: Process constraints versus catharsis. *Cognitive Therapy and Research,* 1978, *2,* 265–274.

Tessler, R., & Schwartz, S. Help-seeking, self-esteem and achievement motivation: An attributional analysis. *Journal of Personality and Social Psychology,* 1972, *21,* 318–326.

Tolman, E. C. Principles of purposive behavior. In S. Koch (Ed.), *Psychology: A study of a science* (vol. 2). New York: McGraw-Hill, 1959.

Toner, I. J., & Smith, R. A. Age and overt verbalization in delay–maintenance behavior in children. *Journal of Experimental Child Psychology,* 1977, *24,* 123–128.

Trabasso, T., & Bower, G. H. *Attention in learning: Theory and research.* New York: Wiley, 1968.

Valins, S., & Nisbett, R. E. *Attributional processes in the development and treatment of emotional disorders.* New York: General Learning Press, 1971.

Wachtel, P. L. Psychodynamics, behavior therapy, and the implacable experimenter: An inquiry into the consistency of personality. *Journal of Abnormal Psychology,* 1973, *82,* 324–334.

Walker, H. M., & Buckley, N. K. Programming generalization and maintenance of treatment effects across time and across settings. *Journal of Applied Behavior Analysis,* 1972, *5,* 209–224.

Wandersman, A., Poppen, P., & Ricks, D. (Eds.), *Humanism and behaviorism: Dialogues and growth.* New York: Pergamon, 1976.

Weiner, B. Motivation from the cognitive perspective. In W. K. Estes (Ed.), *Handbook of learning and cognitive processes* (vol. 3). Hillsdale, N.J.: Lawrence Erlbaum, 1976.

Wertheimer, M. *Fundamental issues in psychology.* New York: Holt, Rinehart & Winston, 1972.

Wicker, A. W. Attitudes versus actions: The relationship of verbal and overt behavioral responses to attitude objects. *Journal of Social Issues,* 1969, *25,* 41–78.

Wildman, R. W., & Wildman, R. W. The generalization of behavior modification procedures: An evaluative review—with special emphasis on classroom applications. *Psychology in the Schools,* 1975, *12,* 432–448.

Wilkins, W. Expectancy of therapeutic gain: An empirical and conceptual critique. *Journal of Consulting and Clinical Psychology,* 1973, *40,* 69–77.

Willems, E. P. Steps toward an ecobehavioral technology. In A. Rogers-Warren & S. F. Warren (Eds.), *Ecological perspectives in behavior analysis.* Baltimore: University Park Press, 1977.

Yates, A. J. *Theory and practice in behavior therapy.* New York: Wiley, 1975.

C H A P T E R

8

SELF-MANAGEMENT AND THERAPEUTIC MAINTENANCE:
Theory and Research

SHARON M. HALL

Imagine a "cure" for obesity in which the therapist spends as little as 10 hours over a 2-month period with the client. At the end of that period the client is able to eliminate overeating, has the skills to reduce to an ideal weight, and of the greatest importance, is able to maintain ideal weight once reached. At the beginning of this decade, many behavioral clinicians and researchers hoped that such treatments and outcomes were on the horizon via "behavioral self-management." Self-management training was being developed not only for obesity, but also for problems as diverse as study habits and cigarette smoking. For all disorders, the goal was to provide the client with skills which could be used during and especially after therapy to produce long-lasting, self-determined change.

The purpose of this chapter is to chart our progress toward the goals of permanent self-management and its companion, stable behavioral change. Addictive behaviors such as obesity and smoking are emphasized because the most work has been done on the treatment of these disorders, but a range of problem behaviors will be considered.

BEHAVIORAL SELF-MANAGEMENT

Behavioral self-management is historically related to the concept of self-control. "Self-management training" was first used with problem behaviors traditionally considered to be caused by deficits in self-control, e.g., excess food intake, poor study habits, inability to give up tobacco. The term was coined as an alternative to "self-control" by behavior therapists who felt the latter was too closely tied to judgmental and circular concepts such as "willpower." ("Why don't you quit smoking?" "I can't. I have no willpower." "How do you know?" "Because I can't quit smoking.")

Generally, "behavioral self-management" refers to a treatment program where: (1) the target behavior is chosen by the client in the relative absence of visible external influence or constraints; (2) the therapist functions mainly as a teacher of skills; and (3) the client is the primary change agent.

This definition needs further explanation. The first statement, that the target behavior is chosen by the client in the absence of visible external influence, illustrates the relative nature of the concept. When external influence is clearly visible to us, subsequent manipulations are not considered instances of self-management. They are more likely to be categorized as such when attempts at influence are more subtle. For example, monitoring cigarette intake would be considered a self-management intervention in an adult who, motivated by an inability to enjoy sports, came to a private therapist with a goal of smoking cessation, but not in a prisoner participating in a study on smoking behavior where participation was rewarded by payment or reduction in sentence.

The second and third parts of the definition emphasize the therapist as teacher and the client as intervention agent. This division of labor differentiates self-management training from those behavioral therapies where the therapist performs certain tasks in the consulting room which are designed to bring about change in the client, and the client's *primary* task is to follow the therapist's directions. Traditional systematic desensitization is an example of such a therapy; the therapist leads the client in the construction of the hierarchy, in relaxation training, and through the scenes of the hierarchy. Although the client contributes material for the hierarchy, the practices relaxation, employment of the technique takes place in the consulting room and is the task of the therapist.

Finally, self-management treatment implies that the client is active in consciously applying the skills in his or her natural environment. This differs from therapies where skills produce a change if practiced in the therapist's office (e.g., desensitization).

MODELS OF SELF-MANAGEMENT

Theories of how individuals learn to control their behavior abound. Even if the analysis is restricted solely to behavioral therories, one must acknowledge the work of Skinner (1953), Blackwood (1972), Logan (1973), Ainslie (1975), and Kanfer and Karoly (1972a, b). In the interest of brevity, we will restrict our discussion to the theories which have had a major impact on the clinical practice of self-management, those of B. F. Skinner (1953) and Kanfer and Karoly (1972a, b).

Skinner's Operant Model

Much of behavioral self-management training evolved from Skinner's (1953) thoughts about self-control as expressed in *Science and Human Behavior*. Skinner noted that we infer self-control to a person when that person (1) delays gratification in some way, whether that gratification is pleasure or relief from pain, and (2) does not appear to be motivated to do so by external constraints. Skinner assumed that such behavior is ultimately controlled by socially engendered guilt and anxiety, threats to health, and social reinforcement and punishment. That is, he assumed self-control behaviors are responses to contingencies and are "ultimately" guided by the same principles that guide any human behavior. He also proposed that, given motivation to control a behavior, there exists a variety of controlling responses which could be implemented. Techniques include use of physical aids and restraints, manipulation of discriminative stimuli, manipulation of deprivation and satiation, manipulation of emotional conditions, use of drugs, and "doing something else" (the only response not also used in controlling the behavior of others).

Skinner raised two issues which have not yet been resolved. The first is whether or not an individual could reinforce or punish himself or herself in the operant sense. (By definition, reinforcement is that which makes a behavior more likely to occur; punishment is an event which makes a behavior less likely to occur.) Although an individual could, for example, allow himself access to friends only after studying, Skinner questioned whether such a manipulation would make studying more likely to occur. Logically, such an occurrence is questionable and Skinner again pointed to the prepotency of external reinforcers and punishers in motivating self-controlling behavior. In spite of this, behavioral clinicians have included self-reinforcement and self-punishment strategies in their treatment programs. Evidence with respect to their efficacy is conflicting. While self-punishment does not appear to be a useful strategy (Mahoney, 1974), evidence on self-reinforcement is mixed (Mahoney, 1974; Jeffrey & Wollersheim, Note 1).

Skinner raised a second issue crucial to maintenance of self-managed behavior: Why should an individual choose to control his or her own behavior? For Skinner, the ultimate answer was the influence of society, in the form of current or historical sanctions or of threats to survival. Most workers in self-management would not argue with this basic tenet. They would, however, indicate that a great deal of work needs to be done to identify precisely how threats to survival and social influence enhance self-management.

The influence of Skinner's formulation can be seen in almost every self-management program which has been developed. Clinicians have taught clients specific skills, most of which were applications of Skinner's ideas on self-control or extrapolations from operant laboratory paradigms. However, emphasis on the importance of social contingencies as ultimate controlling events may have led to a deemphasis on the intricacies of maintaining change. Early workers often assumed that a change would be maintained via social reinforcement if the change was socially valued as adaptive; indeed, they frequently neglected lengthly follow-ups. It was only relatively recently, when several investigators suggested that follow-up data indicated failure of maintenance in self-managed behaviors, that maintenance became an issue (Hall & Hall, 1973; McFall & Hammen, 1971; Stunkard, 1977). Relapse and maintenance are due to a delicate interplay of many factors: some social, some endogenous to the disorder under consideration, and some due to the unique perceptions that the client has of the disorder. While Skinner alluded to all of these, their influence on maintenance is only beginning to be investigated.

Kanfer and Karoly's Negative Feedback Loop

Kanfer and Karoly (1972a, b), also working from an operant base, presented a model of self-control which provides a framework to study the conditions conducive to maintenance of self-managed behaviors. The model, based on a negative feedback loop, suggests that self-controlling behaviors are initiated when a choice point is reached: these points occur either because attention is directed toward a specific behavior (e.g., a physician tells the client that continued smoking will certainly result in emphysema), or because of changes in reinforcement scheduling (e.g., heavy eating formerly reinforced in the family is ridiculed at college), or when expected outcomes are not forthcoming (drug use ceases to bring about euphoria).

At choice points, self-monitoring begins automatically and results in self-evaluation of current behavior, which is compared to a standard. Behavior which meets the performance standard is self-reinforced and strengthened; behavior which does not meet the standard is punished, and the individual seeks out alternative ways of behaving.

This model has led to hypotheses about effective self-management in clinical situations, many of which have implications for maintenance of behavior change. Particularly relevant are formulations of the relationship between behavioral intentions and contracts and the concept of extended self-management. Kanfer and Karoly (1972a, b) suggest that intention statements function as a kind of performance standard, which becomes a self-contract ("Only five cigarettes a day!") or a contract with another individual such as a spouse or therapist. Fulfillment of the contract, or the exercise of the self-controlling responses, is thought to be a function of the explicitness of the contract, mutuality of control, presence of necessary coping skills, feedback about progress (including self-generated feedback), persistence of the aversive consequences of the behavior, past experience of success in similar situations, and continued discrepancies between behavior and goals. Presumably, enhancement of any or all of these factors should lead to continued adherence to the contract, and maintenance of adaptive behaviors. The model has generated a great deal of laboratory analogue research (Kanfer, 1977). Also, several of these variables have been studied in clinical trials. For example, enhancement of coping skills for high-risk drinking situations has been shown to decrease recidivism in alcoholics (Chaney, O'Leary, & Marlatt, 1978) and pretreatment experiences of success in self-control correlate with continued weight loss (Steffen & Myszak, 1978). Further, methods which enhance self-monitoring may encourage maintenance, although evidence to this point is conflicting (Hall, Bass, & Monroe, 1978; Hall, Hall, Borden, & Hansen, 1975); and as mentioned above, evidence as to the efficacy of self-reinforcement and self-punishment is also conflicting.

Also directly relevant to maintenance of change is Karoly's (1977) discussion of extended self-management. Karoly conceptualized the process of self-control in four stages: (1) problem recognition and appraisal; (2) commitment; (3) extended self-management; and (4) habit reorganization. The last is said to take place when the target response is more likely to occur than an alternate response. At this point, self-control is no longer a useful construct. Karoly speculated on several conditions which should facilitate extended self-management, including availability of skills, adequacy of the contract, and of the therapeutic program as a whole, involvement of "significant others," and previous success in treatment.

MODELS OF MAINTENANCE

Since self-management is designed to provide clients with tools to control their own behavior, maintenance is the ultimate test of the usefulness of this form of treatment. As outlined above, both Skinner's original formulation of self-control and Kanfer and Karoly's model directly present, or imply, hypotheses about maintenance of change. Other writers have formulated models specifically directed toward maintenance of behavior, whether the original change be self- or other generated. Among these are the models of Wikler (1965, 1973), Kopel and Arkowitz (1975) and Marlatt (Marlatt, Note 2; Marlatt & Gordon, Note 3).

Wikler's Model: A Classical Conditioning Analysis

Based on work with narcotic addicts, Wikler (1965, 1973) proposed that withdrawal symptoms and other responses, primarily internal responses preceding drug use, become classically conditioned to the environmental stimuli which are associated with them. Later occurrence of these environmental stimuli result in the "conditioned abstinence syndrome." The syndrome includes craving and other cues suggested to be casually related to relapse. The model proposes that the conditioned abstinence syndrome can be extinguished by repeated pairing of the environmental stimuli with no euphoric or withdrawal affect. This theory has been extended to alcohol abuse by Ludwig (1972) and has been proposed as useful in understanding substance misuse in general (Pomerleau, Note 4). Empirical evidence for its usefulness is weak, however. The influence of craving and withdrawal symptoms on relapse is questionable (Marlatt & Gordon, Note 3). On a clinical level, trials with naltrexone, a narcotic antagonist which blocks drug and withdrawal effects, indicate that, contrary to predictions, extinction of opiate use does not occur during antagonist administration, for when administration is terminated, drug use resumes (Meyer, Randall, Barrington, Mirin, & Greenberg, 1976).

Kopel and Arkowitz: An Attribution Analysis

Kopel and Arkowitz (1975) viewed the literature on self-attribution and noted that self-attributed behavior change is maintained to a greater extent than behavior change attributed to an external agent. On the basis of this principle, these writers suggested several strategies for enhancing maintenance, including: (1) using the least powerful reward or punishment so that the saliency of the external agent is reduced; (2) fading therapist involvement over time to shift perceptions from therapist-attributed to client-attributed change; (3) teaching clients self-control skills, especially emphasizing self-generated reward and punishment; (4) allowing the client to play an active role in treatment; and (5) decreasing the use of external aids to which change can be attributed.

Kopel and Arkowitz's contribution has been to suggest application of the findings of attribution research to maintenance in the clinical situation. In the strict sense their model cannot be considered a complete model of maintenance because it does not take into account factors related to maintenance other than those related to attribution. As yet it has not produced a great deal of research. However, its suggestions are clearly testable, and some preliminary investigations have produced resuts consistent with the approach (Coletti, 1977; Kopel, 1974).

Marlatt: Maintenance as Prevention of Relapse

By far the most comprehensive model of maintenance is that proposed by Marlatt and his co-workers (Marlatt, Note 2; Marlatt & Gordon, Note 3). According to this model, certain high-probability situations can be identified as decision points for the "abstainer" (the model was developed in work with alcoholics). If the abstainer has appropriate coping responses available, they will be performed, and the abstainer will continue to perceive self in control and continue abstinence. If no appropriate response is available,, the feelings of self-efficacy decrease and the client engages in the forbidden behavior. This is especially likely to occur if the individual has positive expectations about substance use. Use of the substance results in a phenomenon labeled the abstinence violation effect (AVE), composed of: (1) cognitive dissonance (e.g., drinking behavior is dissonant with the conception of self as abstinent); and (2) personal attribution effect (attribution of the break in abstention to personal weakness). Both of these effects serve to increase the probability that continued abuse will occur.

Marlatt suggests specific skill interventions, including monitoring and assessment of high-risk situations, training in coping skills or desensitization of skills inhibited by anxiety, and interventions designed to develop a more satisfactory lifestyle and strategies to increase control cross-situationally, such as meditation. To combat positive expectations about substance effects, Marlatt suggests education about actual effects, including the emphasis on the "lows" which must inevitably follow the substance-induced "high." To deal with cognitive effects related to initial use of a substance, training in moderation is proposed; to combat the abstinence violation effect, exercises in *programmed relapse* and attempts to change the client's thinking about the meaning of relapse.

Preliminary studies have been completed by Marlatt and his co-workers. A pilot study (Marlatt & Marques, 1977) supported the hypothesis that global coping strategies such as meditation are useful in decreasing alcohol use. (Implications for relapse from this study are unclear since subjects generally stopped meditating during follow-up, and drinking rates tended to increase toward baseline levels.) More pertinent is a study indicating alcoholic inpatients in a "skill training for high-risk situations" condition were less likely to relapse than was a discussion control or a control receiving only the usual inpatient treatment (Chaney, O'Leary, & Marlatt, 1978).

Both Marlatt, and Kopel and Arkowitz, emphasize the role of the individual's skills and perceptions in maintaining adaptive behavior. Both models, but especially Marlatt's, could be considered specialized models of self-management. Conceptually, self-management and maintenance of change are inseparable. Maintenance of change cannot be discussed without inquiry into the client's capability to manage his or her own behavior. Similarly, the ultimate, and perhaps *only,* test of self-management is adaptive changes that continue for extended time periods.

ISSUES IN MAINTENANCE

The discussion so far has dealt with maintenance of therapeutic change and relapse rather loosely, perhaps erroneously implying that precise definitions are available. They are not. Several core issues have yet to be resolved. Central among these are (1) useful definitions of relapse, (2) inquiries into what is maintained, and (3) determination of critical periods for relapse and hence for follow-up periods. These issues are relevant for most, if not all,chapters in this book. In the discussion that follows, it is necessary to focus on them in relation to self-management training and the disorders to which it has been applied.

What is Relapse?

In only three problem behaviors to which self-management has been applied has there been agreement on the nature of relapse. These are alcoholism, illegal drug use, and cigarette smoking. Relapse has been defined as any relatively constant use of the substance after abstinence was achieved. This definition is implicitly based on the "one drink, one drunk" assumption, which suggests that relatively constant use of a problem substance constitutes a treatment failure because such use eventually, inevitably, leads to a complete return to baseline consumption. However, agreement on abstinence as the sole criterion for success in the addictions is disintegrating (Armor, Polich, & Stambul, 1976; Szasz, 1971; Frederickson, Note 5). With the suggestion that moderate drinking and drug use might be acceptable, evaluation of relapse may become as tenuous in these areas as in any other.

Other than failures of abstinence, clear-cut definitions of relapse do not exist. This is due in part to the nondichotomous nature of most behaviors; study skills, excess weight, and anxiety all change by degrees. The research literature reports means, differences between groups, and variability, without attempting to partition successes and failures.

Specific criteria for relapse would provide a standard against which continuing efforts could be judged and would further research into correlates of successful maintenance, as well as promote more definitive criteria for relapse. A useful way to develop criteria is to determine the level of a problem behavior reached at which one's life is impaired on important dimensions, such as social functioning and/or physical health, and consider as relapsers those who exceed this point. In some areas, for example cigarette smoking, relevant data is accumulating (Gori & Lynch, 1978).

At this time, however, lacking specific criteria for relapse, we must base our review of the literature on the form in which it is presented; i.e., the efficacy of self-management strategies will be evaluated relative to other conditions as well as in relation to absolute amount of change.

What is Maintained?

Generally, we have assessed the effects of treatment on some target one step removed from actual self-management behaviors, such as body weight, cigarette consumption, or grade-point average. We have little data to indicate what self-management behaviors are maintained (or for that matter, if they are ever learned). For example, it has been a concern of workers in obesity (e.g., Mann, 1972) that the target indicators used to indicate maintenance of change do not reflect *behavior* change. Assume that a loss of 10 pounds during treatment is observed and that this loss is maintained during follow-up. This prevention of weight gain may represent several alternative outcomes vis-a-vis self-management: clients may use strenuous and unhealthy means to avoid registering increase body weight at follow-up assessments (for example, potent combinations of diuretics, laxatives, and saunas); they may maintain weight loss via "acceptable" means other than the skills taught during self-management treatment (e.g., simple low-calorie diets), or they may, in fact, be employing self-management skills.

This problem is most pressing in the treatment of obesity, where long-term efforts are required and the same goal can be reached temporarily in many different ways. With other disorders, such as smoking or drug use, one could argue that specific skills used are of less importance and that differences in abstinence are crucial. However, even in these instances it is of importance to know what clients actually do to maintain change. While some self-report data on implementation of techniques are available (Brownell & Stunkard, 1978; Hall, Hall, Hanson, & Borden, 1974; Marlatt & Marques, 1977) frequently even self-report data are neglected. Independent assessments of use of skills via informants or experimental observation have been almost totally ignored.

Definition of Optimal Follow-up Periods

Ideally, follow-up should continue until new relapses cease to be found. This requires an examination of the course of a disorder and determination of the danger periods for relapse with each disorder. Little definitive data about such "critical periods" exist. For example, in their often-cited article, Hunt, Barnett, and Branch (1971) found that of those individuals researching abstinence from tobacco, alcohol, and narcotics, 65% in each category had relapsed by 3 months and only 25–30% were still abstinent at 6 months. Relapse rates from 6 months to 1 year were relatively stable, suggesting that follow-ups of at least 6 months are crucial. Unfortunately, these data represent averages over a variety of treatments prior to 1970, and there is some question as to their applicability to more recent treatment programs (e.g., Lichtenstein & Rodriques, 1977). Also, unknown variability in methods of determination of relapse rates across studies raises questions about the usefulness of the relapse rates derived.

Which factors are related to relapse at specific periods is a second level of inquiry. For example, let us say that some x percent of smokers relapse after one week of abstinence, and most of these report that relapse is due to irritability; and that an additional y percent relapse at 5 months, and most of these report that relapse is due to weight gain. If we had such information, we would be better able to indicate the timing and nature of different techniques designed to prevent relapse, and to make precise statements as to which strategies were useful for late and early relapsers. Virtually no data relevant to this point exist.

In summary, issues with respect to relapse, maintenance, and critical periods have not been resolved. In the review which follows, each of these issues will be considered with respect to particular behavior problems.

SELF-MANAGEMENT AND MAINTENANCE: REVIEW OF THE CLINICAL RESEARCH LITERATURE

Addictive Behaviors

As has been noted, addictive behaviors are "relapse prone" (Marlatt & Gordon, Note 3). Because of this, maintaining change has been the focus of considerable interest in obesity, tobacco dependence, and to a lesser extent, alcohol misuse. These disorders are also most appropriate for self-management training, since successful treatment necessarily rests with the client and his or her skill to cope with a variety of pressures, both internal and within the environment, that lead to use. (Despite the conceptual similarity between narcotics addiction and abuse of alcohol and nicotine, we could find no controlled self-management research with addicts.)

Obesity. Self-management programs for obesity are usually multi-faceted and include: training in monitoring food intake and weight change; instructions in ways to limit eating situations; development of self-reinforcement programs; determination of ways to manipulate deprivation and satiation to increase adherence to a lowered calorie regime; methods to modify the act of eating so that the pace become slower and under greater conscious control; and new ways of thinking about food, dieting, and relapse ("cognitive restructuring"). Other skills taught include assertion (the client learns ways of handling food-related social situations) and ways of minimizing stimulus input related to food. The interested reader is referred to Stuart and Davis (1972), Abrahamson

(1977), Jeffrey and Katz (1977), or Fergusen (1975) for detailed descriptions of these techniques.

Self-management treatment programs have repeatedly been evaluated as the most successful treatment for weight loss currently available (Abrahamson, 1977; Hall & Hall, 1974; Leon, 1976; Stunkard, 1972, 1977). This assessment is based on well-controlled studies, most of which indicate that during treatment, self-management is superior to no treatment, to a variety of attention-placebo control conditions, to insight-oriented psychotherapy, and to at least one anorectic drug (Fenfluramine). However, as early as 1973, questions were raised as to the long-term effects of this treatment, especially after therapeutic contact had been terminated (Hall & Hall, 1973).

The problem of obesity brings into focus more general concerns about the conceptual issues surrounding evaluation of self-management treatments. There is little agreement on relapse, maintenance, and/or how long subjects should be followed.

With respect to relapse, it is not unheard of for two writers to consider the same data as indicative of opposite outcomes. For example, Hall (1973), writing from a self-management perspective, assessed 10 subjects and concluded that self-management treatment was not successful because no subject had reached goal weight during the 2-year follow-up. She assumed that continued use of self-management skills would by that time have resulted in weight at or near to goal. The implicit assumption was that "relapse" meant returning to pretreatment eating behaviors. Stunkard (1977), in evaluating the same data, concluded that subjects in this study showed "reasonably good maintenance" because 6 of the 10 subjects reported at least some continued loss. Presumably, Stunkard would consider a return to baseline weight equal to relapse, and was less concerned about the fate of self-management skills.

Closely related is lack of agreement on what we are attempting to maintain. Posttreatment body *weight,* weight loss *rates,* and new eating or activity behaviors are all candidates for consideration. Most investigators, like Stunkard, consider maintenance of posttreatment body weight during follow-up indicative of success. However, there are problems with this criterion. Mean weight loss in the behavioral studies of obesity reviewed by Wing and Jeffery (Note 6) was 11.6 pounds. Such a loss does not indicate completely successful treatment for a person 35–50 pounds overweight (the range of obesity frequently encountered). Ideally, in this respect (and from a self-management perspective) it would seem that weight loss *rate* must be maintained to goal weight if the treatment is to be successful. Second, as discussed above, weight stability is a poor indicator of use of self-management skills.

However, even with weight stability there is disagreement as to (1) whether self-management is responsible for maintenance of weight lost during treatment, and (2) whether the weight is regained. From a series of studies (Hall, 1973; Hall et al., 1974; Hall, Hall, DeBoer, & O'Kulitch, 1977), I have concluded that when clients are given a standard self-management training program, they generally do show gains after treatment termination, such that by 6 months weight losses are not significantly different from pretreatment. The general failure to maintain weight loss has also been noted by Stunkard (1977), who surveyed the literature from a broader perspective. Other writers, however, have concluded that self-management training does produce weight losses that are maintained (Brightwell & Sloan, 1977; Wing & Jeffery, Note 6).

Finally, with respect to what is maintained, researchers have not generally examined the stability of changes in eating or exercise behavior. Anecdotal reports indicate that most individuals cease employing new self-management behaviors after treatment is terminated (Hall et al., 1974). Self-reports obtained via questionnaires present a similar picture (Brightwell, 1976). Indeed, evidence with respect to the role of self-management behaviors during treatment is conflicting (Bellack, 1976; Brownell & Stunkard, 1978; Hall et al., 1977). Collection of data about use of skills is important, for it may provide initial evidence with respect to the processes determining maintenance. If use of behaviors correlates with weight loss, support for self-management as the vehicle of change is increased. If weight remains stable, or if losses occur independent of use of self-management skills, it seems reasonable to assume that maintenance is occuring via some other mechanism.

Lack of agreement on relapse and what is to be maintained makes determination of critical periods for relapse difficult. The data do appear to indicate that weight gains frequently begin immediately after treatment ceases, and may return to near baseline levels within 1 year. However, recently reported data (Stunkard, 1977) indicates that 1-year results may not reflect those at 5 years. At present, the best we can say (rather lamely) with respect to length of follow-up is "the longer, the better" (but see Chapter 4).

Despite this relatively confusing state of affairs, some investigators have implemented programs that produce continuing weight losses after treatment, often of clinically important magnitude. Specific elements of these exceptions may provide clues as to the crucial elements of continuing loss. Program simplicity may increase adherence and maintenence (McReynolds, Lutz, Paulsen, & Kohrs, 1976; Weiss, 1977). Involvement of significant others may also be important. Brownell, Heckerman, Westlake, Hayes, and Monti (Note 7) involved family members in the weight loss process and were able to demonstrate continued loss over an 8½-month period.

Some writers have suggested that failure of self-management behaviors to be maintained is due to the relatively short time periods in which new behaviors are taught and practice is encouraged. Since these behaviors are to supplant those the individual has employed throughout life, it has been argued that a relatively long treatment period, during which new behaviors are encouraged and supported, must be employed. The simplest way of providing such supports is through use of booster sessions. These have been extensively studied.

The booster strategy was initially used by Stuart (1967) in his case study series which provided the impetus for the onslaught of research in self-managed treatment of obesity. Hall et al. (1975), Brightwell (1976), Kingsley and Wilson (1977), and Hall et al. (1978) all found that boosters were valuable in maintaining weight loss, although continued losses were slight or did not occur. In a complex design involving five treatment groups and two cohorts, Ashby and Wilson (1977) failed to find maintenance of weight loss when boosters were used.

However, the weight of the evidence indicates that booster sessions do prevent weight gain. They do not appear to be a means for replacing old eating behaviors with new "self-managed" ones. If they were, marked continuing losses would occur while booster sessions were in effect, and continuing losses or at least maintenance after they were terminated. At best booster sessions may focus clients' attention on weight for a longer time period, but they have a relatively minor impact for the effort expended.

In summary, with respect to obesity it appears that there is now little firm evidence that we are currently teaching people to manage their own eating. What is especially troubling is our ignorance about what behaviors our clients learn, whether they continue to employ them, and how these behaviors relate to maintenance and relapse.

Smoking. The issues in maintaining nonsmoking differ from those in maintaining weight loss. There has been some agreement that abstinence is the ultimate criterion. Relapse is generally the subject's report that he or she smoked *any* cigarettes at a constant rate. The rationale for this rather strenuous criterion is that one cigarette will eventually lead to a return to baseline rates. There is also some agreement over the minimum length of time over which follow-ups should be completed (i.e., 6 months). However, data obtained by Lichtenstein and Rodriques (1977) call into question such relatively short-term follow-ups; these investigators followed subjects who had participated in rapid smoking studies, and who had obtained 6-month abstinence rates of 60%. At 2–5 years these rates had dropped to 25–35%, rates that are similar to those reported by other investigators at a comparable time period (Schwartz, 1977). Again, the dictum "the longer, the better" may be appropriate.

In attempting to look more closely at what is maintained, several unanswered questions emerge. First, subjects' reports of abstinence indicate nothing about behaviors employed to maintain this state. "Not smoking" in itself is not a behavior. We do not know what alternative behaviors are employed to maintain nonsmoking or how these behaviors are developed, nor do we know which self-management behaviors are used, if any.

Use of techniques at different points after treatment termination may have different implications. Early in abstinence, when nicotine withdrawal effects may be present, employment of self-management behaviors may be needed to combat smoking resumption. Over time, if withdrawal symptoms dissipate, use of self-management devises may become unnecessary. Thus, if a nicotine chemical dependency model is a useful one, failure to find that self-management behaviors are employed a considerable time after treatment may not weaken support for their efficacy, but report of failure to use them immediately after treatment termination would do so.

Lichtenstein and Danaher (1976) in their comprehensive review, list a total of seven different techniques that fit the definition of self-management and that have been evaluated either in single-case studies, in case series, or in controlled studies: use of stimulus control techniques; methods to increase the interval between cigarettes by establishing a gradually faded smoking cue; hierarchical reduction; establishment of self-reward and self-punishment programs; contingency contracting; and development of cognitive control. Recent years have seen little research on single-focus techniques, since for the most part these have not been effective (Lichtenstein & Danaher, 1976).

Broad-spectrum self-management programs have not fared a great deal better. Ober (1968), in an early study, found no difference between a multifocal self-management program, aversion, and transactional analysis a termination and a 1-month follow-up. Pomerleau, Adkins, and Pertschak (1978) reported at 61% abstinence rate at the end of an 8-week treatment period, but only 32% and 29% abstinence at 1 and 2 years, respectively. Their program consisted of baseline data collection, gradual reduction to abstinence, and follow-up meetings.

McGrath and Hall (1976) compared a self-management program similar to that used in obesity studies to a nonspecific (social pressure plus self-monitoring control) and a no-treatment control, and found no difference between self-management and nonspecific control at treatment termination, but at the relatively short follow-up (80 days posttreatment) self-management subjects reported significantly less consumption than the other two groups.

The problem with such short-term follow-up was highlighted in a study by Brockway, Kleinman, Edelson, and Grunewald (1977), who compared a multifaceted self-management program with a no-treatment control condition. Their treatment program, which included alternative response training, gradual reduction via hierarchies, behavioral rehearsal of nonsmoking, and in vivo practice of nonsmoking, produced significant differences in number of cigarettes smoked at posttreatment and at 3 and 6 months, but these differences had dissipated by 1 year. Similar negative results of self-management programs, when used alone, have been reported by Katz, Heiman, and Gordon (1977), and Levinberg and Wagner (1976).

In retrospect, it is not surprising that self-management training does not produce abstinence. The focus of such techniques is on modification of patterns related to tobacco use, rather than elimination of its use.

The addition of self-management as an adjunct to abstinence-targeted strategies, however, may be worthy of further exploration, especialy if techniques specifically selected for their applicability to prevention of relapse to smoking are employed.

The few studies of follow-up treatments to enhance maintenance of nonsmoking have reported favorable results. Chapman, Smith, and Layton (1971) enhanced abstinence after aversive conditioning via training in self-management and posttreatment monitoring. (The self-management training consisted of several techniques, again similar to those used in obesity studies.) Delahunt and Curran (1976) found "negative practice" (smoking twice the usual number of cigarettes) plus self-management superior to either treatment alone or to controls, both in percentage reduction of cigarette smoking and abstinence rates at 6-month follow-up. Sutherland, Amit, Golden, and Roseberger (1975) also reported positive results when they compared rapid smoking plus deep muscle relaxation with either treatment alone or with two control conditions. Lando (1978) compared negative practice and negative practice plus self-management. At 6 months, negative practice alone produced abstinence rates of 35%; the combined condition produced 76% abstinence, which is among the highest reported in the literature.

Unsuccessful combinations of self-management programs with aversion treatments have been reported by Danaher (1977) and Lando (1978). In a factorial design, Danaher provided subjects with either rapid-smoking treatment or normal-rate smoking and with either self-management training prior to rapid smoking or with "filler" discussion. Not only did the self-management training interfere with cessation, but it also resulted in higher relapse rates during 6-month follow-up. The self-management program in this study was quite complex, consisting of instructions in the use of stimulus control, deep muscle relaxation, substitute behavior, cognitive controls for strengthening averision and countering rationalizations and self-reward.

Lando (1978) attempted to determine the effective components of his earlier, successful multifocal program (Lando, 1977). His attempt, characterized by a complex experimental design and a multifaceted treatment program, produced high attrition rates and poor results at follow-up.

As is the case in obesity, there is little information available on implementation of self-management techniques during follow-up; one study found that use of techniques was correlated with self-reported decreases in smoking during follow-up (McGrath & Hall, 1976). These results must be viewed with more than the usual scientific caution, however, as both variables were determined solely from self-report.

In summary, self-management in smoking treatments is less frequent than use of such techniques in the treatment of obesity. Early use of single-focus self-management techniques was not effective, and the attention of the field shifted to aversion treatment such as rapid smoking. Recognition of the limits of such techniques has led to renewed interest in combining these with training in self-management. Such combined treatments seem particularly useful when they are simple and targeted at maintaining abstinence rather than effecting it. Again, there is ignorance about what is maintained, and at what situations or withdrawal symptoms techniques should be targeted. We do not know what sort of withdrawal symptoms need to be alleviated, if any; nor do we have much information on the sort of situations which result in relapse. Finally, few data has been collected on the implementation of self-management techniques.

Alcohol Abuse. Outcome research in alcohol treatment has lagged far behind that in obesity and smoking cessation. Both difficulties in implementation (Henderson, Hall, & Lipton, 1979) and ethical consideraions (Miller, 1977) are responsible for this dearth of research.

Most outcome studies have focused on aversive conditioning treatments, and generally have only very limited self-control components, if any at all (Lovibond & Caddy, 1970; Sobell & Sobell, 1973).

Recently, however, a major study has been reported by Miller (1977), who compared three treatments designed to produce controlled drinking in heavy drinkers recruited via newspaper advertisements. These were (1) aversive (electric shock) counterconditioning, (2) self-control (record-keeping, identifying antecedents of drinking, methods to control drinking rates, and finding alternative ways to achieve the effects of alcohol), and (3) a composite treatment, the self-control training program plus discriminative aversion training (Lovibond & Caddy, 1970) and directed practice in controlled drinking including avoidance of high-rate drinking (Sobell & Sobell, 1973, 1976). Dependent variables included clients' and significant others' report of drinking rate, daily record cards, complex improvement ratings, and measures of general psychological functioning. With a few minor exceptions these measures showed marked similarity both among groups and over time. In general, behavioral self-control and the controlled drinking composite both showed marked posttreatment reduction, which was maintained at 3- and 12-month follow-ups. The aversive conditioning group showed less reduction and appeared to relapse at 3 months, but at 1 year showed a level of drinking no different from the other two groups who decreased consumption from treatment termination. Given the complexity and expense of the controlled drinking composite, the author's preference for the self-management condition is understandable.

At termination subjects were randomly assigned to either receive or not receive a self-management manual (Miller & Munoz, 1976). The effects of the manual are not clear, since at 3-month follow-up subjects who received the manual and read it differed from those who did not receive it, but so did those subjects who received the manual but did not read it. Miller (Note 8) has completed several replications attesting to the usefulness of self-management training for individuals with problem drinking.

Miller's work to teach controlled drinking represents an excellent start in this field for self-management training. However, abstinence is the usual criterion for success in alcoholism treatment, and will probably continue to be the goal for most alcoholics (Nathan, 1976). Extrapolating from the smoking literature, we would not expect self-management to be of great value in effecting abstention, but might be useful in preventing relapse from abstention. One might well consider Chaney et al.'s (1978) demonstration of the usefulness of coping skills in preventing relapse to be a step in that direction. Major issues, such as the fit between self-management behaviors and problems occurring upon termination or reduction of alcohol use, use of self-management techniques, descriptions of situations and symptoms related to relapse, remain untouched, with few exceptions (e.g., Marlatt & Gordon, Note 3).

General Conclusions. Several conclusions are possible from our survey of the addictive behaviors. First, in spite of the relatively large number of studies available, the overall impression is one of superficiality and ignorance about the processes involved in maintaining change. Universal needs appear to be (1) to investigate what skills subjects employ after treatment is terminated; (2) to study how to enhance use of skills, since the little evidence available indicates adherence is low; (3) to investigate more thoroughly the course of changes in relapse rates and withdrawal symptomatology, for longer time periods; and (4) to determine what factors are related to these changes. Alcohol abuse research is the exception in that even more basic outcome studies are also needed; for example, those which explore the usefulness of self-management in preventing relapse from abstinence. Within the context of such studies we would hope to see attention devoted to the more fine-grained issues which also trouble obesity and smoking.

Adherence to behavioral prescriptions may well be a central issue. In obesity, and to a lesser extent in smoking, researchers have tended to employ programs which included many different techniques, some of which require considerable creativity and determination to implement. The implicit expectation seems to be that ineffective techniques will eventually drop out while effective ones will continue to be used. However, most of us have also urged clients to implement all the techniques in a treatment program, at least during the intensive treatment period, so that the technique will be given a chance for success, as well as to foster uniformity of treatments in outcome studies. From the client's perspective, however, we may be urging him or her to spend a good deal of time learning new behaviors only a few of which seem to have an effect on the target behavior. The result may be that we lose credibility in our client's view, and also that this very low partial reinforcement schedule is not sufficient to maintain the new behaviors (cf. also Brehm and McAllister's analysis of therapeutic reactions in Chapter 11). In terms of other demands on the subject's life, the cost is too much for the benefit received, and new behaviors are abandoned or clients leave treatment. An examination of data on adherence to treatment regimes in other areas (Kasl, 1975) indicates that behavioral psychologists are doing precisely what the medical literature suggests would result in a low rate of adherence; complex treatments are prescribed when simple ones are more likely to produce adherence (Clark & Troop, 1972).

In large part this is due to lack of knowledge about what the subject experiences upon modification of eating or drug use patterns. Data on withdrawal symptoms (e.g., Ludwig, 1972; Schacter, 1977; Shiffman & Jarvik, 1976), exists, but much of them are not sufficiently specific to be of use in designing treatment programs, and only Marlatt and Gordon (Note 3) have related them to relapse. A second problem is ignorance about situational factors related to relapse.

Other Health Behaviors

No field has attracted the attention of researchers and clinicians interested in self-management to the extent of the addictive behaviors. However, promising early applications of self-managed therapies are found with respect to other disorders, especially those related to other health-related behaviors. In most instances, the techniques are used to provide self-control treatments for disorders assumed to be related to anxiety and traditionally modified by medication.

Insomnia. Almost all the work reported has dealt with *predormital insomnia* i.e., difficulty in falling asleep. The core of the treatment program has been self-generated relaxation practiced at or before bedtime. Case reports and studies employing single-subject designs have presented follow-up data for periods as long as 6 months; generally, changes appear to be maintained across such periods (Haynes, Price, & Simons, 1975; Kahn, Baker, & Weiss, 1968; Weil & Goldfried, 1973). Several controlled studies have also supported the efficacy of self-induced relaxation to amerliorate insomnia, at least when subjects' progress is examined during the treatment period, but most studies lack long-term follow-ups (Borkovec & Favelo, 1973; Lick & Heffler, 1977; Steinmark & Borkovec, 1974). An important exception is the work of Nicassio and Bootzin (1974), who compared autogenic training and progressive relaxation with two controls. At posttreatment, the two structured relaxation groups fell asleep significantly faster than did controls, and the change was maintained at 6 months with little relapse noted. Self-control procedures relying primarily on stimulus control have also been reported, but few controlled evaluations of them have been published (Bootzin, 1977). Haynes et al. (1975), using A-B-A-B design, were able to demonstrate improvement in sleep behavior in four chronic insomniacs via stimulus control principles, and maintenance of improvement at a 9-month follow-up.

Headache. Work on control of tension headaches has primarily used self-induced relaxation applied in tense situations or at headache onset to decrease headache episodes. Promising results have been reported by Mitchell and White (1977) with a chronic headache sufferer (5–6 headaches a week). Headaches were entirely eliminated, and this change was maintained at a 6-month follow-up. Other favorable reports are available (Holroyd, Andrasik, & Westbrook, 1977), indicating that self-management produces a reduction in headache episodes and pain that is maintained or even slightly improved at follow-ups from 4 to 6 months in duration (Cox, Freundlich, & Meyer, 1975). However, a recent report (Holroyd & Andrasik, 1978) questions the specific impact of self-management; further work is clearly needed. Some very preliminary work on migraine headaches indicates the usefulness of a treatment program focused around relaxation and desensitization, and promising short-term maintenance (Mitchell & White, 1977).

Miscellaneous Health Disorders. An intriguing early self-management study was that reported by Efron (1957) who used a chain of conditioned responses to inhibit epileptic seizures. The patient paired the odor of jasmine (which had automatically arrested the seizures on previous occasions) with the sight of a bracelet. After repeated pairing, when the patient experienced preseizure symptoms, the thought of the bracelet was used to abort the fit. At 14 months posttreatment the patient was symptom free.

Other case reports of applications of self-management techniques include the use of relaxation, covert imagery, and cognitive relabeling to reduce chronic abdominal pain (Levendusky & Pankratz, 1975), use of self-relaxation to avoid or reduce bronchiospasm in asthma (Sirota & Mahoney, 1974), self-relaxation combined with desensitization to eliminate motion sickness (Saunders, 1976), and development of incompatible responses to eliminate inflammatory scratching. All of these case studies reported moderately long follow-ups; the range is from 6 to 19 months. All reported maintenance of change with no indications of relapse.

As this review indicates, research in health disorders other than the addictions is at the case study stage. However, the cumulative effect of this relatively weak data base is such that we may have cause to be optimistic about maintenance of effects in these areas. On the other hand, it might be argued that when the research in the addictions was at a stage comparable to that in these areas, the results were comparably optimistic. Only after early enthusiasm had faded to manageable proportions and techniques became used by many practitioners and clinical researchers did the issue of maintenance become clear-cut, and the need to focus on it became obvious.

However, these health disorder data do appear to follow a different curve than that found in addictive behaviors. Successful studies frequently show lower rates of the problem at follow-up, or a complete amelioration of the problem that does not return at all. This is more promising than the slow, gradual upward turn of data points during followup hailed as a success of addictive behaviors treatment.

There are several conceptual differences between the addictive behaviors and other health problems which may make the latter more amenable to permanent change. In the studies discussed in this section, the techniques used are not "costly" to those using them, either in terms of time or social visibility. Most of these interventions have employed relaxation training, which also has the benefit of being enjoyable in and of itself, and of being a plausible treatment of any disorder which the popular mind believes is caused by stress. As discussed above, simplicity of treatment prescription appears to promote adherence. A second factor related to promotion of adherence is rapid alleviation of aversive states (e.g., medication for urinary tract infection is more likely to be taken than for hypertension; Berkowitz, Malone, Klein, & Eaton, 1963). A striking feature of the disorders discussed in this section is that when the self-management techniques are employed, they result in fairly rapid elimination of the aversive state which brought the client into treatment. The most stable instance of this is the use of the bracelet image to avoid the preseizure aura, but it is also reflected in other therapies which use relaxation; self-generated behavior terminates sleeplessness and reduces headache pain or its precursors. In one sense, discussions of criteria for relapse, and questions about what is maintained and critical periods, seem premature in this area. It seems safest to say that not enough outcome data have accumulated to indicate that techniques employed are truly promising, and that more outcome studies are needed. However, researchers in other health areas might do well to heed the (negative) example of workers in the addictions and incorporate at an early point repeated, long-term follow-up assessments, evaluations of implementation of skills taught, and if needed, careful thought about relapse.

Anxiety Reduction

Conceptually, self-management work with phobias and pervasive general anxiety is closely related to the treatment of health problems assumed to be caused by excess tension. In both instances, a negative state (pain, insomnia, or the experience of excess anxiety) is alleviated by the client's instituting another state or performing an alternative behavior. Research literature in this area is not as voluminous as that in addictive behaviors, but what does exist is quite sophisticated methodologically.

Goldfried (1977) has divided self-management approaches into two categories: self-induced relaxation and "cognitive restructuring." Goldfried (1971) originally proposed that systematic desensitization, as described by Wolpe (1958), works because it indirectly teaches clients general anxiety-reduction skills. He suggested several modifications to emphasize the self-managed aspects of desensitization. These include: (1) complete explanations to promote understanding and ability to use the procedure in real life; (2) allowing the client to experience anxiety during the visualized scene and to use relaxation to "relax away" tension; (3) teaching the client to use internal tension cues to relax; and (4) to use the same techniques to "relax away" tension in real-life situations. Goldfried (1977) reported successful removal of long-standing pervasive anxiety via this technique, and 5-month self-report data indicated virtually no relapse. Evidence from controlled studies indicates that the procedure is useful for reducing anxiety. It appears to work as well as or better than systematic desensitization. The reader is referred to Goldfried and Trier (1974), Zenmore (1975), Goldfried and Goldfried (1977), and Goldfried, Linehan, and Smith (1978). Of greatest importance is that if change is achieved during treatment, reduction is not only maintained but continues (Goldfried & Goldfried, 1977; Goldfried & Trier, 1974; Jachs, 1972, as cited in Goldfried, 1977). In a related line of investigation, Sherman (1975) found that most subjects reported continual use of self-relaxation taught 2 years earlier in a study on speech anxiety.

Another approach to anxiety reduction has been to examine the kinds of verbalizations clients make to themselves in anxiety-producing situations, to note the irrational and self-defeating aspects of such statements, and to encourage the client to modify self-instructions so that they become more rational, and facilitate rather than distract from the task at hand (Holroyd, 1976; Meichenbaum, Gilmore, & Fedoravicius, 1971; Trexler & Karst, 1972). Results produced by such cognitive modification strategies parallel those produced by self-induced relaxation.

Such treatments are generally found to reduce or entirely alleviate fear, both on self-report and behavioral measures. Follow-ups are usually short-term (generally 1–3 months), but during this time measures of anxiety tend either to remain stable, or more generally, to decrease.

With respect to fear reduction, then, the picture is quite different from what we observe in the addictions, and more closely resembles that obtained in treatment of other anxiety-related problems. While some similar issues remain unresolved, they may probably remain so because they are less problematic. For example, there seems to be less need to define relapse because it is not the norm. Follow-up periods are extremely short, but it must be admitted that continued improvement, rather than evidence of relapse, renders this less crucial than in the addictions. Since there is no evidence, and little reason to believe, that some critical period occurs after 3 months, the time periods used to date may be adequate. Longer periods would be desirable to be certain that this is so. The question of what is maintained is not answered by available data, however. Surprisingly, even when techniques are relatively discrete and countable, such as instances of self-relaxation, investigators have not reported data about their use. To be sure, anxiety inventory scores do decrease during treatment, and it seems plausible to assume that this reflects use of relaxation skills. With respect to maintenance, there is little evidence as to the time periods over which most subjects consciously use techniques, or if and when a neutral or relaxed state as opposed to an anxious state becomes the prepotent one. The comments about self-management and anxiety reduction parallel those with respect to health behavior. The disorder and the treatment are such that one would expect maintenance once an initial change has been made. Not surprisingly, the evidence to date, derived primarily from short follow-ups, appears to indicate that the change is in fact maintained. Once again, however, there is no indication that these early follow-ups will correlate with later ones.

Other Behavior Problems

Other behavior problems to which self-management techniques have been applied are numerous. Most are case studies; controlled studies are not sufficiently available to allow conclusions about the efficacy of techniques during treatment, much less estimates of maintenance potential. Case reports include successful treatment of several obsessive-compulsive states via techniques as diverse as relaxation training, thought stopping, and self-monitoring (Alban & Nay, 1976; Campbell, 1973; Horton and Johnson, 1977; Melamed & Siegal, 1975); trichotillomania, via self-monitoring (Bayer 1972); aggression and anger via relaxation, self-instruction, and preparation for anger-evoking incidents (McCollough, Huntsinger, & Nay, 1977; Novaco, 1977); and a variety of "nervous habits" (e.g., nail biting) via habit reversal (i.e., awareness training and competing response practice; Azrin & Nunn, 1973; Nunn & Azrin, 1976). Inconclusive data on changes in study behavior as a function of self-management training have been reported (Beneke & Harris, 1972; McReynolds & Church, 1973). Recently, Richards and Perri (1978) have produced data which indicate that training in a self-control program which includes use of self-monitoring, stimulus control, and reinforcement does not produce long-lasting change, but addition of training in problem solving (D'Zurilla & Goldfried, 1971) may enhance maintenance of study skills over the long term.

OVERVIEW

A picture of the state of the art in self-management and the variables influencing it emerges from the data we have reviewed. First, when the target problem is related to anxiety, whether the problem be manifested in a health disorder or in a specific phobia, symptom amelioration and related anxiety reduction occur, and are generally maintained. The clinical picture may even improve after treatment is terminated. Improvement seems to be maintained whether the treatment is self-induced relaxation or changes in internal dialogue.

In the addictive behaviors, the picture differs. Outcomes using self-management treatments, either alone or in combination with other techniques, are often superior to controls. However, although the course of relapse is slower, relapse rates remain high. We may find that they are equivalent to those noted in traditional treatments in the long term, except that they take longer to reach baseline levels. To date, we have not generated dramatic changes in the shape of the relapse curve for these disorders.

Differences in maintenance for anxiety-related versus addictive disorders may be related to several factors. First, anxiety-related disorders have a single identifiable core problem. As a result, treatment programs involve use of few techniques. This is not the case with addictions. The behaviors, emotions, cognitions, and physiological factors behind the problem are unknown. For example, in obesity we are not even certain whether the obese eat more or differently from normals (Wooley, Wooley, & Dyrenforth, 1979). Or the same behavior may reflect different mechanisms in different individuals, and to further complicate matters, these mechanisms may differ over time. Such may be the case with cigarette smoking, where there is some evidence that individual smokers differ in what aspects of smoking are reinforcing to them (Horn and Waingrow, 1966). Further, an individual may smoke for different reasons at different times; a smoker who initially smoked to reduce anxiety may over time become addicted physiologically.

A second difference is the immediacy of noticeable beneficial change. Relaxation training produces an immediate reduction in an unpleasant state; this reduction may never before have been experienced by the client. Employment of self-management techniques may not produce a perceptible change and resulting reinforcing feedback. A related factor is the relapse-prone nature of the addictions. Temporary changes may well have been experienced previously by the client, only to be followed by relapse. The reinforcing value of initial changes may be weakened when such changes have been followed previously by repeated failures.

Finally, related to ignorance about the "cause" of addictive behaviors is ignorance about withdrawal symptoms and situations related to relapse. Given the dearth of our knowledge about these two factors, it may be that many are not even addressed in the most complex of treatment programs.

A WORKING MODEL

Several factors can be identified as influencing and interacting with adherence to self-management strategies. These variables and their relationship are shown in Figure 8–1, and are discussed below.

Costs and Benefits

From a psychological perspective, "cost" and "benefit" indicate the subjective expectancy of reinforcement and punishment, respectively, resulting from applications of relapse-prevention strategies of abstinence. Costs of giving up a problem behavior include withdrawal symptoms, loss of social reinforcement ("secondary gain"), and loss of pleasant drug effects. Benefits of abstaining from the problem behavior include better health, endurance, and social approval. Costs resulting from use of coping skills include loss of time and money, and possible

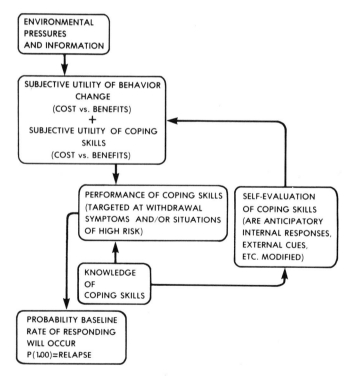

Figure 8–1. A working model of self-management processes and adherence.

embarrassment; benefits of performance of skills themselves may be minimal, but could include social reinforcement from concerned others (cf. also Karoly's discussion of motivational variables in behavior change in Chapter 7).

To increase adherence, therapies must increase the benefits of relapse prevention and minimize costs of applications of coping skills. Theoretically, maximizing the costs of relapse and the benefits of coping skills should also increase adherence. However, practical difficulties render both of these less useful. Coercive attempts to increase actual costs, e.g., applications of a punishing stimulus, are usually met with countercontrol responses. Increasing the benefits of skill use is difficult since most may have few "intrinsic" rewards.

The cost–benefit ratio can be shifted via environmental pressure and information, feedback about the benefits of coping skills in maintaining change, selection of skills, and knowledge about their use.

Environmentally Provided Information and Pressure

To some extent, any attempt to change on the part of the individual is motivated by advertising, information provided and values promoted by the mass media, legislation, fads, and other social variables. We may well find that variables such as these explain a large proportion of the variance involved in behavior change and maintenance.

A second level of environmental pressure comes from the social unit of which the individual is a part—the family, the ethnic group, the peer group, and other cultural units. The role of the family in weight reduction is well illustrated by the work of Brownell (Note 9; Brownell et al., Note 7); of the subculture, in Stunkard's (1975) discussion of obesity with respect to social class, ethnic group, and generational membership. Environmental pressures and information, far from being the most obvious and easily manipulable sources of influence, probably represent the most complex classes of variables and influence outcome in several ways. The mass media and other information sources provide information about the ultimate reinforcement to be expected as a function of extended self-management. This may interact with treatment modalities in unrecognized ways. For example, while the surgeon general's report in and of itself may have been only minimally effective in producing smoking cessation, one wonders how many of those who have abstained from smoking via "effective" treatment, such as rapid smoking, would have done so had the surgeon general not indicated that smoking causes lung cancer.

The media and experience with social models in significant subgroups may directly or indirectly modify attempts to maintain therapeutic change by providing information about the potential success of extended self-management attempts. Continued adherence to abstinence-oriented strategies in an ex-heroin addict might be disrupted by reading a popular book on the subject, which informs the ex-addict that addiction is a disease and that the metabolic cause of the disease is such that relapse is inevitable. Models of failure may provide similar information—a perpetually dieting, and perpetually obese, parent suggests that the probability of successful weight reduction is low.

Perhaps even more subtle and complicated are subgroup norms that support a destructive behavior. Moving from a small rural high school where smoking is considered deviant by most students to a large urban school where it is reinforced by a large number of influential peers may rapidly destroy adherence to maintenance-oriented strategies for an adolescent smoker.

Finally, within some subgroups, particularly the family and marital units, any behavior can become part of an ongoing system in ways that act for or against maintenance. An example is the client in our smoking clinic who fell from abstinence when, after an argument, his mate left an almost-full, open pack of cigarettes on the kitchen counter near where the client was doing the dishes.

The multiplicity of such factors should make us wary, but need not make us pessimistic. Many of these factors can be dealt with via therapeutic techniques already in our armamentarium. Information on the long-term benefits of change and on the positive outcome can be emphasized via presentations in treatment programs of suitable information, assertiveness skills to deal with subtle attempts to engender relapse can be taught, and models provided by the change program can counter those of deviant subgroups.

Knowledge of Coping Skills

Knowledge of coping skills necessarily directly influences long-term performance of these skills. Self-management treatments to date have focused almost exclusively on developing and teaching clients coping skills. Interestingly, studies in the area generally neglect to determine if skills were in fact correctly learned, much less performed. This is important, because incomplete or incorrect understanding of skills can lead to poor outcome. For example, an obese individual who believed that monitoring would be equally effective if done at the end of each day than if done prior to each meal might see little change in intake and pounds as a function of monitoring, and might abandon the strategy. Thus not only does knowledge of skills act directly on outcome, it indirectly influences adherence over time via feedback about outcome related to its performance.

Self-Evaluation

A crucial aspect of adherence to use of a self-management strategy is whether or not a particular strategy is self-evaluated as effective in changing problem behavior. Primary among sources of information used to make a judgment is the client's perception of whether coping skills change the problem behavior in the desired direction. Purely social influences, such as advice or endorsements by experts, novelty, or group pressure, will effect adherence for the short term, but have little impact on long-term adherence. First among those factors which do influence long-term adherence is actual change in the target problem, for example, weight losses in obese individuals, or the ability of an ex-speech phobic to deliver an "A" speech. A second important source is changes anticipatory to changes in the target problem. For example, a client who believes that reduced caloric intake is related to weight loss will continue to adhere to strategies that cause decreases in caloric intake, at least initially, even if weight changes are not immediately forthcoming. Eventually, if experience proves that the client's initial assumptions are faulty (e.g., if reduced intake does not eventually result in weight loss), adherence will decrease. This analysis suggests that self-monitoring is important, at least in part because it focuses the client's attention on the desired change (e.g., charting weight loss ensures the client's awareness of long-term, as well as day-to-day, changes in weight) as well as on improvements in "signal changes," such as caloric intake.

Performance of Coping Skills

Skill performance is a function of the subjective cost–benefit ratio. While all of the above factors feed into this ratio, so too do the nature of the skills and the program into which they are combined. "Expensive" techniques are those which are potentially embarrassing (e.g., easily visible bite counters, or buzzing cigarette cases) or which are difficult or time-consuming for the client to implement (e.g., self-reinforcement programs for clients with limited access to reinforcers) or which deprive the individual of important satisfactions of a normal life (e.g., access to other people during meals). Simple, nonvisible, non-time-consuming techniques are most likely to be implemented over the long term (e.g., making eating a "pure experience").

As this review indicates, the range of possible coping strategies available is enormous; thus, one approach has been to include a large number in "shotgun" or "multimodal" treatment programs. The hope is that each client will select and use those which prevent relapse. However, an alternate approach, and one which is in keeping with this model, is to select specific therapeutic techniques which are likely to be effective for a particular problem and then further modify these to fit the individual. This means identifying specific difficulties inherent in changing specific problems, such as fears about detoxifying in addicts, the role of indirect social pressure in smoking cessation (Marlatt & Gordon, Note 3), and the impact of social variables of family support in obese individuals (Stunkard, 1975; Brownell et al., Note 7). The need for such strategies is particularly clear in the addictive behaviors, where careful analyses of withdrawal symptoms, situations related to relapse, and the course of these over time, are possible and would indicate what skills are useful and at what point. Such an analysis would greatly reduce the complexity and "costs" of treatment by eliminating theoretically *appealing* techniques that are *in fact irrelevant*.

The Link between Performance of Coping Skills and Relapse

A crucial question is "Which coping skills or self-management behavior will be effective for a particular disorder?" As has been stressed repeatedly in this chapter, we need data on the withdrawal symptoms, high-risk relapse situations, and other manifestations of relapse, particularly in the addictions, to choose technique skills which seem most fitting. However, treatments can be better matched to characteristics of disorders, even with the limited data we have available. We know, for example, that anxiety is characteristic of smoking withdrawal (e.g., Schacter, 1977), and we have in our armamentarium effective techniques to reduce anxiety; we know that social pressure enters into relapse in tobacco dependence and heroin addiction, and assertiveness skills are available to deal with such pressure.

At this point I can envision that the most favorable growth of our field would be selection from a large armamentarium of therapeutic techniques those logically matching the characteristics of disorders, beginning with the current data on these characteristics with continued interplay between descriptive and clinical studies. At our laboratory we are beginning pilot work on a maintenance strategy for ex-smokers based on this general concept. In addition to rapid and magnified feedback about change to enhance commitment during "critical periods," the program includes simplified training in relaxation and in dealing with social situations that provide cues to smoking. These techniques were selected because the data extant indicate that ex-smokers experience relapse in situations producing high levels of negative emotions, as well as in situations where the ex-smoker experiences direct or indirect social pressure to smoke (Shiffman & Jarvik, 1976; Marlatt & Gordon, Note 3). We have specifically refrained from developing a comprehensive, time-consuming program, hoping that the benefits in increased adherence to a few techniques will prove more fruitful than the complicated, multifocal programs of the past.

ACKNOWLEDGMENT

Preparation of this paper was supported in part by National Institute of Drug Abuse Demonstration Grant No. 1R01-DA-01978. The author wishes to thank Robert Hall for reading and critiquing the manuscript, and Peter Loeb for assistance in library work.

REFERENCE NOTES

1. Jeffrey, D. B., & Wollersheim, J. P. *Cognitive theories: Application and limitations in weight control.* Paper presented at the meeting of the American Psychological Association, Toronto, September 1978.

2. Marlatt, G. A. *Craving for alcohol, loss of control, and relapse: A cognitive behavioral analysis.* University of Washington Alcoholism and Drug Abuse Institute Technical Report No. 77–05, 1977.

3. Marlatt, G. A., & Gordon, J. R. *Determinants of relapse: Implications for the maintenance of behavior change.* Paper presented at the Tenth International Conference on Behavior Modification, Banff, Alberta, Canada, March 1978.

4. Pomerleau, O. *Similarities in the understanding and treatment of self-management problems: Smoking, problem drinking, obesity and heroin use.* Paper presented at the meeting of the National Institute on Drug Abuse on behavioral approaches to analysis and treatment of substance abuse, Reston, Va. February 1978.

5. Frederickson, L. *Controlled smoking.* Paper presented at the meeting of the National Institute on Drug Abuse on behavioral approaches to analysis and treatment of substance abuse, Reston, Va., February 1978.

6. Wing, R. R., & Jeffery, R. W. *Outpatient treatments of obesity: A comparison of methodology and clinical results.* Unpublished manuscript, Stanford University, 1976.

7. Brownell, K., Heckerman, C. L., Westlake, R. J., Hayes, S. C., & Monti, P. M. *The effects of couples training and partner cooperation: New in the behavioral treatment of obesity.* Paper presented at the meeting of the Association for the Advancement of Behavior Therapy, Atlanta, December 1977.
8. Miller, W. R. *Alcoholism and substance abuse: Behavioral perspective.* Paper presented at the meeting of the National Institute on Drug Abuse on behavioral approaches to analysis and treatment of substance abuse, Reston, Va., February 1978.
9. Brownell, K. *Obesity, activity, and adherence to behavior programs.* Paper presented at the meeting of the National Institute on Drug Abuse on behavioral approaches to analysis and treatment of substance abuse, Reston, Va., February 1978.

REFERENCES

Alban, L. S., & Nay, W. R. Reduction of ritual checking by a relaxation delay treatment. *Journal of Behavior Therapy and Experimental Psychiatry,* 1976, *7,* 151-154.

Abrahamson, E. E. *Behavioral approaches to weight control.* New York: Springer, 1977.

Ainslie, G. Specious reward: A behavioral theory of impulsiveness and impulse control. *Psychological Bulletin,* 1975, *82,* 463-496.

Armor, D. J., Polich, M. J., & Stambul, H. B. *Alcoholism and treatment.* Santa Barbara, Calif.: The Rand Corporation, 1976.

Ashby, W. A., & Wilson, G. T. Behavior therapy for obesity: Booster sessions and long-term maintenance of weight loss. *Behaviour Research and Therapy,* 1977, *15,* 451-464.

Azrin, N. H., & Nunn, R. G. Habit reversal: A method of eliminating nervous habits. *Behaviour Research and Therapy,* 1973, *11,* 619-625.

Bayer, C. A. Self-monitoring and mild aversion treatment of trichotillomania. *Journal of Behavior Therapy and Experimental Psychiatry,* 1972, *3,* 139-141.

Bellack, A. S. A comparison of self-reinforcement and self-monitoring in a weight reduction program. *Behavior Therapy,* 1976, *7.* 68-75.

Beneke, W., & Harris, M. B. Teaching self-control of study behavior. *Behaviour Research and Therapy,* 1972, *10,* 35-41.

Berkowitz, N. H., Malone, M. F., Klein, M. W., & Eaton, A. patient follow through in the outpatient department. *Nursing Research,* 1963, *12,* 16-22.

Blackwood, R. O. *Mediated self-control: An operant model of rational behavior.* Akron, Ohio: Exordium Press, 1972.

Bootzin, R. R. Effects of self-control procedures for insomnia. In R. B. Stuart (Ed.), *Behavioral self-management.* New York: Brunner/Mazel, 1977.

Borkovec, T. D., & Favelo, D. C. Controlled investigation of the effect of progressive and hypnotic relaxation on insomnia. *Journal of Abnormal Psychology,* 1973, *82,* 153-158.

Brightwell, D. R. One year follow-up of obese subjects treated with behavior therapy. *Diseases of the Nervous System,* 1976, *37,* 593-594.

Brightwell, D. R., & Sloan, C. L. Long-term results of behavior therapy for obesity. *Behavior Therapy,* 1977, *8,* 895–905.

Brockway, B. S., Kleinman, G., Edelson, H., & Grunewald, K. Non-aversive procedures and their effect on cigarette smoking. *Addictive Behaviors,* 1977, *2,* 121–128.

Brownell, K., & Stunkard, A. J. Behavior therapy and behavior change. *Behaviour Research and Therapy,* 1978, *6,* 301.

Campbell, L. M. A variation of thought stopping in a twelve year old boy: A case report. *Journal of Behavior Therapy and Experimental Psychiatry,* 1973, *4,* 69–70.

Chaney, E., O'Leary, M., & Marlatt, G. A. Skill training with alcoholics. *Journal of Consulting and Clinical Psychology,* 1978, *46,* 1092–1104.

Chapman, R. F., Smith, J. W., & Layton, T. A. Elimination of cigarette smoking by punishment and self-management training. *Behaviour Research and Therapy,* 1971 *9,* 255–264.

Clark, G. M., & Troop, R. C. One tablet combination drug therapy in the treatment of hypertension. *Journal of Chronic Disease,* 1972, *25,* 57–64.

Colleti, G. *The relative efficacy of participant modeling, participant observer and self-monitoring procedures as maintenance strategies following positive behaviorally based treatment in smoking reduction.* Unpublished doctoral dissertation, Rutgers University, 1977.

Cox, D. J., Freundlich, A., & Meyer, R. G. Differential effectiveness of electromyograph feedback, verbal relaxation instructions and mediation placebo with tension headache. *Journal of Consulting and Clinical Psychology,* 1975, *43,* 892–898.

Danaher, B. G. Rapid smoking and self-control in modification of smoking behavior. *Journal of Consulting and Clinical Psychology,* 1977, *43,* 1068–1075.

Delahunt, J., & Curran, J. P. Effectiveness of negative practice and self-control techniques in the reduction of smoking behavior. *Journal of Consulting and Clinical Psychology,* 1976, *44,* 1002–1007.

D'Zurilla, T., & Goldfried, M. R. Problem solving and behavior modification. *Journal of Abnormal Psychology,* 1971, *78,* 107–126.

Efron, R. The conditioned inhibition of uncinate fits. *Brain,* 1957, *80,* 251–262.

Fergusen, J. M. *Learning to eat.* Palo Alto, Calif.: Bull, 1975.

Goldfried, M. R. Systematic desensitization as training in self-control. *Journal of Consulting and Clinical Psychology,* 1971, *37,* 228–234.

Goldfried, M. R. The use of relaxation and cognitive relabelling as coping skills. In R. B. Stuart (Ed.), *Behavioral self-management.* New York: Brunner/Mazel, 1977.

Goldfried, M. R., & Goldfried, A. P. Importance of heirarchy content in self-control of anxiety. *Journal of Consulting and Clinical Psychology,* 1977, *45,* 124–134.

Goldfried, M. R., Linehan, M. M., & Smith, J. L. The reduction of test anxiety through rational restructuring. *Journal of Consulting and Clinical Psychology,* 1978, *46,* 32–39.

Goldfried, M. R., & Trier, C. S. Effectiveness of relaxation as an active coping skill. *Journal of Abnormal Psychology,* 1974, *83,* 348–355.

Gori, G. B., & Lynch, C. J. Toward less hazardous cigarettes. *Journal of the American Medical Association,* 1978, *240,* 1255–1259.

296 Self-Management and Therapeutic Maintenance

Hall, S. M. Behavioral treatment of obesity: A two year follow-up. *Behavior Research and Therapy,* 1973, *11,* 453-454.

Hall, S. M., Bass, A., & Monroe, J. Follow-up strategies in obesity treatment. *Addictive Behaviors,* 1978, *3,* 139-147.

Hall, S. M., & Hall, R. G. Behavioral control of obesity: A review. *American Psychological Association Journal Supplement and Abstract Service,* 1973, *3,* 57.

Hall, S. M., & Hall, R. G. Outcome and methodological considerations in the behavioral treatment of obesity. *Behavior Therapy,* 1974, *5,* 353-364.

Hall, S. M., Hall, R. G. Borden, B. L., & Hanson, R. W. Improvement of posttreatment performance via monitoring and limited contact in obese subjects. *Behaviour Research and Therapy,* 1975, *13,* 167-172.

Hall, S. M., Hall, R. G., DeBoer, G., & O'Kulitch, P. External reinforcement and self-management in the treatment of obesity. *Behaviour Research and Therapy,* 1977, *15,* 89-95.

Hall, S. M., Hall, R. G., Hanson, R. W., & Borden, B. L. Permanence of two self-managed treatments of overweight in university and community populations. *Journal of Consulting and Clinical Psychology,* 1974, *42,* 781-786.

Haynes, S. N., Price, M. G., & Simons, J. B. Stimulus control treatment of insomnia. *Journal of Behavior Thearpy and Experimental Psychiatry,* 1975, *6,* 279-282.

Henderson, J. B., Hall, S. M., & Lipton, H. Self-destructive behaviors. In G. Stone, N. Adler, & F. Cohen (Eds.), *Trends in health psychology,* San Francisco: Jossey-Bass, 1979.

Holroyd, K. A. Cognition and desensitization in group treatment of test anxiety. *Journal of Consulting and Clinical Psychology,* 1976, *44,* 991-1001.

Holroyd, K. A., & Andrasik, F. Coping and self-control of chronic tension headache. *Journal of Consulting and Clinical Psychology,* 1978, *46,* 1036-1045.

Holroyd, K. A., Andrasik, F., & Westbrook, T. Cognitive control of tension headache. *Cognitive Therapy and Research,* 1977, *1,* 121-133.

Horn, D., & Waingrow, S. Some dimensions of a model for smoking behavior change. *American Journal of Public Health and the Nation's Health,* 1966, *56,* 21-26.

Horton, A. M., and Johnson, C. H. Treatment of homicidal obsessional ruminations by thought stopping and covert assertion. *Journal of Behavior Therapy and Experimental Psychiatry,* 1977, *8,* 339-340.

Hunt, W. A., Barnett, L. W., & Branch, L. G. Relapse rates in addiction programs. *Journal of Clinical Psychology,* 1971, *27,* 455-456.

Jeffrey, D. B., & Katz, R. C. *Take it off and keep it off.* Englewood Cliffs, N.J.: Prentice-Hall, 1977.

Kahn, M., Baker, B. L., & Weiss, J. M. Treatment of insomnia by relaxation training. *Journal of Abnormal Psychology,* 1968, *73,* 556-558.

Kanfer, F. H. The many faces of self-control, or behavior modification changes its focus. In R. B. Stuart (Ed.), *Behavioral self-management.* New York: Brunner/Mazel, 1977.

Kanfer, F. H., & Karoly, P. Self-control: A behavioristic excursion into the lion's den. *Behavior Therapy,* 1972, *3,* 398-416. (a)

Kanfer, F. H., & Karoly, P. Self-regulation and its clinical application: Some additional considerations. In R. C. Johnson, P. R. Dokecki, & O. H. Mowrer (Eds.), *Conscience, contract and social reality.* New York: Holt, 1972. (b)

Karoly, P. Behavioral self-management in children. In M. Hersen, R. M.

Eisler, & P. M. Miller (Eds.), *Progress in behavior modification.* New York: Academic Press, 1977.

Kasl, S. V. Social psychological characteristics associated with behaviors which reduce cardiovascular risk. In A. J. Enelow & J. B. Henderson (Eds.), *Applying behavioral science to cardiovascular risk.* Seattle: American Heart Association, 1975.

Katz, R. C., Heiman, M., & Gordon, S. Effects of two self-management approaches to cigarette smoking. *Addictive Behaviors,* 1977, *2,* 113–119.

Kingsley, R. G., & Wilson, G. T. Behavior therapy for obesity: A comparative investigation of long-term efficacy. *Journal of Consulting and Clinical Psychology,* 1977, *45,* 288–298.

Kopel, S. *Effects of self-control, booster sessions and cognitive factors on the maintenance of smoking reduction.* Unpublished doctoral dissertation, University of Oregon, 1974.

Kopel, S., & Arkowitz, H. The role of attribution and self-perception in behavior change: Implications for behavior therapy. *Genetic Psychology Monographs,* 1975, *92,* 175–212.

Lando, H. A. Stimulus control rapid smoking and contractual management in maintenance of non-smoking. *Behavior Therapy,* 1978, *5,* 962–963.

Leon, G. R. Current directions in the treatment of obesity. *Psychological Bulletin,* 1976, *83,* 557–578.

Levendusky, P., & Pankratz, L. Self-control techniques as an alternative to pain medication. *Journal of Abnormal Psychology,* 1975, *2,* 165–168.

Levinberg, S. B., & Wagner, M. K. Smoking cessation: Long-term irrelevance of mode of treatment. *Journal of Behavior Therapy and Experimental Psychiatry,* 1976, *7,* 93–95.

Lichtenstein, E., & Danaher, B. G. Modifying of smoking behavior: A critical analysis of theory, research, and practice. In M. Hersen, R. M. Eisler, & P. M. Miller (Eds.), *Progress in behavior modification.* New York: Academic Press, 1976.

Lichtenstein, E., & Rodriques, M. P. Long-term effects of rapid smoking treatment for dependent cigarette smokers. *Addictive Behaviors,* 1977, *2,* 109–112.

Lick, J. R., & Heffler, D. Relaxation training and attention placebo in the treatment of severe insomnia. *Journal of Consulting and Clinical Psychology,* 1977, *45,* 153–161.

Logan, F. A. Self-control as habit, drive, incentive. *Journal of Abnormal Psychology,* 1973, *81,* 127–136.

Lovibond, S. H., & Caddy, G. Discriminated aversive control in the moderation of alcoholics' drinking behavior. *Behavior Therapy,* 1970, *1,* 437–444.

Ludwig, A. M. On and off the wagon: Reasons for drinking and abstaining by alcoholics. *Quarterly Journal of Studies in Alcohol,* 1972, *23,* 91–96.

Mahoney, M. J. Self-reward and self-monitoring techniques for weight control. *Behavior Therapy,* 1974, *5,* 48–57.

Maiman, L. A., & Becker, M. H. The health belief model: origins and correlates in psychological theory. In M. H. Becker (Ed.), *The health belief model and personal health behavior.* Thorofare, N.J.: Charles B. Slack, 1974.

Mann, R. A. The behavior-therapeutic uses of contingency contracting to control an adult behavior problem: Weight control. *Journal of Applied Behavior Analysis,* 1972, *5,* 99–109.

Marlatt, G. A., & Marques, J. K. Meditation, self-control and alcohol use. In R. B. Stuart (Ed.), *Behavioral self-management*. New York: Brunner/Mazel, 1977.

McCollough, J. P., Huntsinger, G. M., & Nay, W. R. Self-control treatment of aggression in a 16 year old male. *Journal of Consulting and Clinical Psychology*, 1977, *49*, 322–331.

McFall, R. M., & Hammen, C. L. Motivation, structure and self-monitoring: The role of non-specific factors in smoking reduction. *Journal of Consulting and Clinical Psychology*, 1971, *37*, 80–86.

McGrath, M., & Hall, S. M. Self-management of smoking behavior. *Addictive Behaviors*, 1976, *1*, 287–292.

McReynolds, W. T., & Church, A. Self-control, study skill development and counseling approaches to improvement of study behavior. *Behaviour Research and Therapy*, 1973, *11*, 233–235.

McReynolds, W. T., Lutz, R. N., Paulsen, B. K., & Kohrs, M. B. Weight loss resulting from two behavior modification procedures with nutritionists as therapists. *Behavior Therapy*, 1976, *7*, 283–291.

Meichenbaum, D. H., Gilmore, J. B., & Fedoravicius, A. Group insight versus group desensitization in treating speech anxiety. *Journal of Consulting and Clinical Psychology*, 1971, *36*, 401–421.

Meichenbaum, D. H. Cognitive modification of test anxious college students. *Journal of Consulting and Clinical Psychology*, 1972, *39*, 370–380.

Melamed, B. G., & Siegal, L. J. Self-directed *in vivo* treatment of an obsessive-compulsive checking ritual. *Journal of Behavior Therapy and Experimental Psychiatry*, 1975, *6*, 31–38.

Meyer, R., Randall, M., Barrington, C., Mirin, S., & Greenberg, I. Limitations of an extinction approach to narcotic antagonist treatment. In D. Julius & P. Renault (Eds.), *Narcotic antagonists: Naltroxone*. Rockville, Md.: National Institute on Drug Abuse, 1976.

Miller, W. R. Behavioral self-control training in the treatment of problem drinkers. In R. B. Stuart (Ed.), *Behavioral self-management*. New York: Brunner/Mazel, 1977.

Miller, W. R., & Munoz, R. F. *How to control your drinking*. Englewood Cliffs, N.J.: Prentice-Hall, 1976.

Mitchell, K. R., & White, R. G. Behavioral self-management: An application to the problem of migraine headaches. *Behavior Therapy*, 1977, *8*, 213–221.

Nathan, P. E. Alcoholism. In H. Leitenberg (Ed.), *Handbook of behavior modification*, Englewood Cliffs, N.J.: Prentice-Hall, 1976.

Nicassio, P., & Bootzin, R. A comparison of progressive relaxation and autogenic training as treatments for insomnia. *Journal of Abnormal Psychology*, 1974, *83*, 253–260.

Novaco, R. W. Stress inoculation: A cognitive therapy for anger and its application to a case of depression. *Journal of Consulting and Clinical Psychology*, 1977, *43*, 600–608.

Nunn, R. G., & Azrin, N. A. Eliminating nail-biting via the habit reversal procedure *Behaviour Research and Therapy*, 1976, *14*, 5–67.

Ober, D. C. Modification of smoking behavior. *Journal of Consulting and Clinical Psychology*, 1968, *32*, 543–549.

Pomerleau, O., Adkins, D., & Pertschuk, M. Prediction of outcome and recidivism in smoking cessation treatment. *Addictive Behaviors*, 1978, *3*, 65-70.

Richards, C. S., & Perri, M. G. Do self-control treatments last? An evaluation of behavioral problem solving and faded counselor contact on treatment maintenance strategies. *Journal of Counseling Psychology,* 1978, *25,* 376–383.

Saunders, D. G. A case of motion sickness treated by systematic desensitization and *in vivo* relaxation. *Journal of Behavior Therapy and Experimental Psychiatry,* 1976, *7,* 381–382.

Schacter, S. Nicotine regulation in light and heavy smokers. *Journal of Experimental Psychology,* 1977, *6,* 5–12.

Schwartz, J. L. Smoking cures: Ways to kick an unhealthy habit. In M. E. Jarvik, J. W. Cullen, E. R. Gritz, T. M. Vogt, L. J. West (Eds.), *Research on smoking behavior.* Rockville, Md.: National Institute on Drug Abuse, 1977.

Sherman, R. A. Two year follow-up of training in relaxation as a behavioral self-management skill. *Behavior Therapy,* 1975, *6,* 419–420.

Shiffman, S. M., & Jarvik, M. E. Smoking withdrawal symptoms in two weeks of abstinence. *Psychopharmacology,* 1976, *50,* 35–37.

Sirota, A. D., & Mahoney, M. J. Relaxing on cue: Self-regulation of asthma. *Journal of Behavioral Therapy and Experimental Psychiatry,* 1974, *5,* 65–66.

Skinner, B. F. *Science and human behavior.* New York: Macmillan, 1953.

Sobell, M. B., & Sobell, L. C. Individualized behavior therapy for alcoholics. *Behavior Therapy,* 1973, *4,* 49–72.

Sobell, M. B., & Sobell, L. C. Second year treatment outcome of alcoholics treated by individualized behavior therapy: Results. *Behaviour Research and Therapy,* 1976, *14,* 195–215.

Steffen, J. J., & Myszak, K. A. Influence of pretherapy induction upon the outcome of a self-control weight reduction program. *Behavior Therapy,* 1978, *9,* 404–409.

Steinmark, S. W., & Borkovec, T. D. Active and placebo treatment effects on moderate insomnia under counter demand and positive demand instructions. *Journal of Abnormal Psychology,* 1974, *83,* 157–163.

Stuart, R. B. Behavioral control of overeating. *Behaviour Research and Therapy,* 1967, *5,* 357–365.

Stuart, R. B., & Davis, B. *Slim chance in a fat world.* Champaign, Ill.: Research Press, 1972.

Stunkard, A. J. New therapies for the eating disorders: Behavior modification of obesity and anorexia nervosa. *Archives of General Psychiatry,* 1972, *26,* 391–398.

Stunkard, A. J. Presidential address—1974. From explanation to action in psychosomatic medicine: The case of obesity. *Psychosomatic Medicine,* 1975, *37,* 195–236.

Stunkard, A. J. Behavioral treatment of obesity: Failure to maintain weight loss. In R. B. Stuart (Ed.), *Behavioral self-management.* New York: Brunner/Mazel, 1977.

Sutherland, A., Amit, Z., Golden, M., & Roseberger, Z. Comparison of three behavioral techniques in the modification of smoking behavior. *Journal of Consulting and Clinical Psychology,* 1975, *43,* 443–447.

Szasz, T. S. The ethics of addiction. *American Journal of Psychiatry,* 1971, *128,* 33–38.

Trexler, L. D., & Karst, T. O. Rational emotive therapy, placebo, and no-treatment effects on public speaking anxiety. *Journal of Abnormal Psychology,* 1972, *79,* 60–67.

Weil, A., & Goldfried, M. R. Treatment of insomnia in an eleven year old child through self-relaxation. *Behavior Therapy,* 1973, *4,* 282–284.

Weiss, A. R. A behavioral approach to the treatment of obesity. *Behavior Therapy,* 1977, *8,* 720–726.

Wikler, A. Conditioning factors in opiate addiction and relapse. In D. I. Wilner & G. G. Kassebaum (Eds.), *Narcotics.* New York: McGraw-Hill, 1965.

Wikler, A. Conditioning of successive adaptive responses to the initial effects of drugs. *Conditional Reflex,* 1973, *8,* 193–209.

Wolpe, J. *Psychotherapy by reciprocal inhibition.* Stanford, Calif.: Stanford University Press, 1958.

Wooley, S., Wooley, O. W., & Dyrenforth, S. R. Theoretical, practical, and social issues in the treatment of obesity. *Journal of Applied Behavior Analysis,* 1979, *12,* 3–25.

Zenmore, R. Systematic desensitization as a method of teaching general anxiety reducing skills. *Journal of Consulting and Clinical Psychology,* 1975, *43,* 157–161.

C H A P T E R

9

CHANGE IS NORMAL:
Adult Development Theory, Research, and Clinical Applications

EDWARD B. KLEIN

This chapter presents an overview of theoretical developments and research findings in the area of adult development. A summary of major trends in this emerging field includes an evolving set of age- and task-specific stages for adults. Next, since biographic investigatory methods are not as well known as other approaches, a description of the research procedures involved in one of the most recent studies in adult development is presented. The last section of the chapter will indicate how adult development theory may be applied to clinical work. In particular, normal changes that occur at different stages over the life span will be highlighted so that a balance is provided against the tendency to overinterpret change (lack of consistency) as being pathological in nature.

A major bias in treatment is that clinicians seek to maintain therapeutically induced change. An adult development perspective would suggest that we all go through periods of change as well as stability.

Focusing on the maintenance of change per se negates the individual's developmental tasks which include normal periods of lifestyle alternation between stable and transitional stages. Research in the psychology of adulthood indicates that one does adapt, develop, and cope over time in response to both internal and external pressures for change.

Although clinicians may find the view presented in this chapter to be different from their own, the intent is *not* to assert that a developmental perspective is better than a clinical one. Rather, a developmental viewpoint provides historical continuity for understanding how one's client developed into the person who is now seeking aid, and for conceptualizing the kinds of tasks that are central for this particular time in the client's life. Therefore, adult development and clinical approaches are compatible in therapeutic work.

BACKGROUND, THEORY, AND RESEARCH

Historically, in the area of human development there has been considerable literature on childhood and adolescence, and a small but growing body of knowledge on the aged. The period of early and middle adulthood (roughly from ages 20 to 60) has been marked by neglect. Until recently, the best sources for what happens in adulthood have been dramatic portrayals in plays, novels, biographies, and autobiographies. Social scientists, with a few exceptions, have only recently begun to look at adult development and to propose tentative theories about the life span.

Within psychiatry, Jung (1933) has made a significant contribution to our understanding of adulthood. He viewed adult development as the process of individuation. Jung suggested that age 40 is central, in that a person at the midpoint in life turns inward and takes stock as opposed to looking without and following the dictates of others. Jung saw this internal movement as part of a growth process which allows one to be more in touch with formerly denied aspects of the self, leading to a greater sense of being a whole or balanced individual. This growth often comes about by addressing various polarities within the person such as young versus old and masculine versus feminine.

Other writers have taken a more sociopsychological view. The person who has perhaps made the greatest contribution to the field of adult development is Erik Erikson. Erikson (1950) enumerated eight stages of development across the life span. In his epigenetic chart he posits that each stage has a psychosocial crisis which has to be addressed before one can move on to the next stage. Erikson went beyond Freud by providing a sociocultural perspective, showing an appreciation of the historical moment and expanding his stage theory throughout adulthood. His in-depth studies of Martin Luther (Erikson, 1958) and Gandhi (Erikson, 1969) provide a developmental view of the lives of two great religious-political leaders. Bühler (1955) has also proposed a stage theory of development from a humanistic perspective, listing five stages over the life span.

A number of researchers in psychology have described changes in adult personality which occur after midlife. For instance, Neugarten (1965) studied two groups of adult men and women at 40 and 60 years of age. She found that the older, in comparison to the younger, men were more likely to express the "softer," more caring, collaborative aspects of themselves. Similarly, older women manifested their more assertive, aggressive, self-centered, competitive side. Both sexes, then, became more expressive of stereotypic, other-gender role behavior which had been minimized or denied earlier in life.

Jaques (1965) noted that the late 30s and early 40s was a time of painful reappraisal of one's life involving a confrontation with the inevitability of death. Using a sample of over 300 creative artists, Jaques described their work as being precipitous, or quick and not as thought-out, before age 35, and more sculptured or formed during what he describes as the "midlife crisis." Early in their careers the artists dealt with the lighter aspects of life, often in the form of comedy, and with the broader, more profound and tragic later in their careers.

Although there has been an interest in adult development from a social psychological perspective, particularly around the midlife transition or crisis (about age 40), little work has been done to integrate theory and research in this area. Analysts have very general ways of referring to this time in life: Jung (1971) speaks of the "noon of life"; Singer (1977), the development of "androgyny"; and Jaques (1965), the "encounter with death." Researchers such as Neugarten (1965) have noted the difficulties of measuring personality components over time. She cites the dilemmas of assessing any single personality variable over various time spans, and suggests combinations of measures in order to increase, predictability.

The extensive study of adulthood over the past decade from a developmental perspective has culminated in the publication of three major books in 1 year. Vaillant, in *Adaptation to Life* (1977), reported the longitudinal study of the adult lives of a highly selected sample of 94 male Harvard students through extensive yearly or biennial questionnaires and personal interviews up to 30 years after graduation. This work is an advance over traditional psychoanalytic theory in that it takes account of social, familial, and economic realities. The book deals primarily with the quality of a man's overall adjustment in adulthood, showing that it is mainly influenced by personality mechanisms of defense and coping. Although the focus is on personality and adjustment, not development, Vaillant provides evidence of significant changes from ages 20 to 50. He particularly stresses the use of more "mature" defenses (humor, anticipation, suppression, and sublimation) over 30 years of life in a group that had notable difficulties even with the privileges of an excellent educational background.

Gould, in *Transformations* (1978), initially investigated a mixed sample of male and female patients in couples and group therapy, later expanding his study to nonpatients. He notes a number of age-linked stages in adult development, each with its own emotional and philosophical challenges stemming from the contradictions between child and adult views of the current situation. This work primarily stresses the process of growth and personal unfolding, and with excellent clinical examples, notes the changing nature of society, particularly the effects of the women's movement on both genders.

The third investigation is *The Seasons of a Man's Life* by Levinson, Darrow, Klein, Levinson, and McKee (1978; hereafter referred to as *Seasons)*. This book was based on 10 years of research and used a biographic methodology to study 40 men between the ages of 35 and 45 (10 each of academic biologists, published novelists, industrial workers, and business executives). Results revealed an age-linked sequence of developmental eras and periods from which the authors generated a psychosocial theory of male adulthood. The writers proposed that the basic unit of the life cycle is the *era*, which lasts roughly 20 years. They note a uniform sequence of stable, structure-building periods, lasting 6–8 years; these periods alternate with transitional restructuring periods lasting 4–5 years, embedded within four 20-year ears of life. The eras are: preadulthood (birth to age 20); early adulthood (20–40); middle adulthood (40–60); and late adulthood (60 to death). Each era has its own distinctive character. Moving from one era to another is considered a major step, requiring a transitional period of from 4 to 5 years. The origins of the eras and developmental periods are found in the interpenetration of the individual's biology, the psychological polarities of the self, and the multigenerational nature of society.

The major concept in *Seasons* is that of the individual life structure. The life structure is the underlying design of a person's life at a given time. it is a patterning of self-in-world and requires a joint consideration of both the person and the world he inhabits. The life structure is neither static nor constantly changing. Rather, it evolves in a systematic pattern through an alteration of stable and transitional stages. In stable periods, a person works at building a life structure to enrich his existence. The shorter, transitional stages involve altering the life structure built during stable periods and changing it in some way in anticipation of the next stage. Adult development is, therefore, the evolution of the life structure over time. The periods (age ranges with ±2 years on either side) and developmental tasks to be addressed in each, are as follows:

The Early Adult Transition (17–22): The task is to terminate preadulthood by leaving the dependency of adolescence, centered in family and school, and initiate early adulthood by becoming more autonomous and self-reliant in college, military service, or work.

Getting into the Adult World (22–28): The tasks involve entering the adult world by forming an occupation and social and love relations, often in the form of marriage and family.

The Age 30 Transition (28–33): The primary task is to question and modify the initial adult life structure formed in the 20s. Developmental crises commonly occur near the 30th birthday when the first life structure is experienced as flawed in some way.

Settling Down (33–40): There are two tasks: "settling down," which involves a greater sense of commitment to work, family, and community; and in the late 30s, "making it" or becoming one's own man, particularly in the world of work.

The Midlife Transition (40–45): The developmental tasks are to question the current life structure, terminate early adulthood, and create a new basis for entering middle adulthood. Many men try to become more individuated by addressing various polarities such as young–old, masculine-feminine, destructiveness-creativity, and attachment-separateness.

These three new works on adult development all have in common a view of change as a normative pattern in the lives of adults. The kind of stability some authors have spoken about or the completely individualistic development favored by others is not supported in these studies. Although Vaillant (1977) and Levinson et al. (1978) have small, highly selected male samples and Gould (1978) reports primarily about patients (including men and women), there may be some basis for generalizing to other groups. All studies address the influence of social class, family background, early life experiences, and opportunities. Gould (1978) and Levinson et al. (1978) independently arrive at a similar age-linked pattern of stages. What needs to be done is further to test out these observations and findings with larger samples, including women and minorities.

Seasons provides the most comprehensive and integrated sociopsychological developmental theory of the three above-mentioned works. Although it is based on the lives of men, there are a number of central developmental concepts which may possess cross-sex relevance. These include the Dream, the Mentor, the Special Woman (or Man), and the Ladder. The Dream is an important element in the life structure which usually emerges during the 20s and early 30s and has impact during subsequent developmental stages. The Dream is a vision of self in the adult world, starting early in life as a vague and rather unformed sense of future possibilities. Over time, it becomes more articulated. For men it is work centered, rarely involving other people. One of the tasks of early adulthood is to place the Dream into the adult life structure.

The course of the Dream's development is facilitated by relationships with two important persons, the Mentor and the Special Woman. A Mentor fosters the young person's growth as an adult. All of the Mentors in the *Seasons* were men and tended to be a half generation (8–12 years) older than the subject. The Mentor endorses the protégé and his Dream through an intense personal relationship. The import of the relationship can be measured by the feelings produced when the bond is broken. It is not unusual for the protégé to feel that the formerly close, facilitating older man has now betrayed him. The Special Woman is a young woman who is connected to the man's developing Dream. She encourages the growth of the Dream and aids the young man in putting it into the world. In general, a man who accomplished much of his Dream was fortunate enough to have a Mentor and a Special Woman (often his wife) both of whom aided him in this process.

Another important concept was the Ladder. Many men, both in conscious descriptions of their lives and their responses to projective tests (TAT), saw themselves as climbing up a ladder, although it was not always clear whether they would reach the top or fall before reaching the last rung. The image of the Ladder may be seen externally in messages communicated by bosses to the young man about his achievements, and internally in feelings about success and how the man views himself in the world. In his 20s a man is an apprentice, in his early 30s he becomes a junior member, and during his late 30s he strives to become a senior member of his enterprise. In each of the above periods, the man is on some low rung starting out to climb a ladder and, although possibly reaching the top by the end of the period, starts the next stage on another low rung. This pattern may apply in many arenas: work, social position, money, union, church, and community.

Although *Seasons* demonstrates that men go through a series of stages that are marked alternately by stability and transition, there are identifiable patterns that they seem to follow. These patterns are based on personality, life circumstances, social class, race, health, and other external factors. All men are not alike, but what is remarkable is that the stages show great uniformity and that the men's developmental course is age linked.

As in many of the social sciences, our knowledge is based on restricted samples. For instance, most psychological research involves such captive groups as children in schools, college students in the freshman subject pool, patients in mental institutions, members of the armed forces, prisoners, and elderly citizens in homes for the aged. In addition, such research is typically biased toward the study of white, middle-class, male subjects. Similarly, in the area of adult development, most of the research is also based on investigations into the lives of men (Erikson, 1958, 1969; Levinson et al., 1978; Vaillant, 1977).

Recently, Stewart (1976) extended the work of Levinson et al. (1978) to women. She studied a small group of women and found that they went through similar developmental periods in their 20s and early 30s. Stewart noted that there was great variability in how developmental tasks were accomplished by women. Her conclusion was that this variability is related to the woman's Dream, and to whether the initial life structure was formed around marriage or occupation.

The more traditional women had a difficult time during their age 30 transition. Most of their own identity stemmed from the mother, there were few Mentors, and it was hard for them to form a more individual adult self. The career-oriented women experienced a high degree of internal conflict in their early 30s with regard to becoming a parent. Stewart saw this as being related to an ambivalent mother–daughter relationship earlier in life. Parallels to the findings of Gould (1978) and Friday (1978) are worth noting. Given the similarities between *Seasons* and Stewart's (1976) exploratory research, it seems that the age 30 transition may be more problematic for women than for men. Part of this may be due to the fact that women's Dreams are more relational than men's. In addition, age 30 demarkates a physiological timeliness related to reproduction, a fact often highlighted by obstetricians. Women have two major decisions to make: marriage and children, or furthering their career. For Stewart's women, the struggle was to come to terms with their relationship to their own mothers and perceptions of their mother's lives. This often proved to be a very difficult and painful reevaluation.

Another recent study on women has been influential in understanding adulthood. Hennig and Jardin (1977) investigated the development of 25 upper management women who had line, not staff, authority in medium-to large-size firms. This is a highly selected, elite sample drawn from the 100 most successful women in the nation, and is somewhat similar to Vaillant's (1977) group of men. In general, these women tend to be only or first-born children, and their lives are marked by a special type of close relationships to their fathers. The father facilitated their development by encouraging them to pursue more masculine as well as feminine interests and activities, thus bestowing a sense of potency, which was nurtured in the family and maintained in the face of traditional feminine attitudes at school and within the peer group. The 25 most successful career women were college graduates with Mentors, usually their first bosses. They and their Mentors moved up the organizational hierarchy together. These women consciously centered their first postcollege decade completely around work. What distinguished them from women who never made the jump from middle to top management was that at about age 35 they took a brief psychological break from their preoccupation with work and attended to more personal and feminine concerns. All who married did so during this period to men who were about 10 years older and occupied higher status jobs. To some extent marriage was now possible because the father was older, often ill, and the women had moved away from their initial Mentor. This study raises a question about whether the midlife transition may start at age 35 (at least for these special women) as opposed to age 40 in men.

In order to investigate further the generalizability of the above to women, our research group (Klein, Allinsmith, Burlew, Correa, Dember, Duff, Gleser, Hiller, & Newman, Note 1) has been meeting for 1½ years and has conducted some pilot interviews with women in the Cincinnati area. This preliminary work suggests that a Special Man may play a role in the lives of some women similar to the role of a Special Woman has been shown to have for a young man. In addition, we think that the Ladder is not the most appropriate symbol for women's development. Rather, a concept such as the Lattice, with movement back and forth between work and family, may help us better to understand adult development in women. We plan to test empirically, in a large randomly selected sample, whether there are similar age- and task-specific stages for women as *Seasons* and other work indicates is the case for men.

What all of the above theory and research suggests is that change is normal. In general, it appears that there is an orderly sequence of stages or periods, alternately transitional and stable in nature, that adults traverse. In addition, there are individual differences in development which may occur due to social class, race, gender, the historical moment, and personality. Even with these differences, it is clear that there is more uniformity of development for adults than previously thought.

RESEARCH DESIGN, SAMPLING,
AND INTERVIEWING METHODS FOR *SEASONS*

Having reviewed some history, theory, and research in adult development, I will now describe in detail how one of the major investigations in
this new field was actually conducted. This detail is included since the
area involves biographic methods which are not well known to researchers who use other approaches. The procedures used also highlight the
role that change plays in the lives of normal men. This method of investigation has implications for clinicians in treatment settings which will be
specifically addressed later. The interdisciplinary research group that
produced *Seasons* started to meet in 1967. The book was published in
1978. The following will provide some background about the difficulties
involved in carrying out this type of study.

Based on the professional literature and the contributions of creative
artists, we decided to study one decade in male adult life, the period from
ages 35 to 45. We viewed this decade as a transition from early to middle
adulthood. Since there was no organized body of theory or data about
the problems of men in the midlife decade, we had to make a number of
difficult research decisions. This part of the chapter reviews how we
organized the investigation. The following pages describe the purpose,
focus, research strategy and contract, sample, interview techniques, and
data analyses.

Purposes

The primary purposes of this investigation were to describe the most
common characteristics of the age 35–45 period in a sample of normally
functioning American men, and to study the frequency with which this
period was marked by stability or crisis. If such crisis existed, we wanted
to note any regularities in its nature and outcome. We wished to determine individual processes of change in the lives of men and investigate
major influences which determine the course of the period. This would
include a consideration of sociocultural as well as personality factors involved in each man's development.

One goal was a description of "lives-in-progress" over the course of
the midlife decade; this would provide other investigators with rich data.
Second, we wanted to propose a theory that would be tested in later
phases of research. We used a variety of sociological theories and findings on occupation, career, marriage, and family as factors influencing
the course of individual lives. The work of Erikson, Jung, and Jaques
supplied important concepts for our emerging ideas of personality de-

velopment. When we started the investigation in 1967, none of these theories had been consistently applied to the study of the evolving lives of normal people. There was no other current or historical study in this area, no "field" which would govern the methodology to be used.

In attempting to understand normal functioning men, we became increasingly aware of the "normality" of change, development, and even crisis, in men's lives. As we explored the literature and talked to colleagues, it became apparent that many common occurrences in people's lives are viewed by professionals through "psychopathologically colored glasses." Much of this viewpoint has to do with our clinical training. But part of the bias is determined by the lack of a normal, socially accepted framework from which to view changes and developments in the lives of adults. We also hoped that a more human, less rigid research methodology would be developed in the study which could be used by future investigators.

The Focus

It was clear that we had two choices. We could conduct a large-scale survey with a highly structured interviewing procedure and a limited number of predefined variables and hypotheses. This field approach would be like public opinion studies carried out by survey research institutes. The other choice was to perform an intensive analysis of fewer cases, to provide a more in-depth view of developments in a man's life. After months of exploration we decided not to proceed with a large-scale, structured study, adopting instead a systematic case analysis method for men selected to represent the most varied kinds of occupations and lifestyles. After this step we decided that the samples should reflect many factors currently influencing society (i.e., race, class, ethnicity, and marital status). We were interested in how mobile men were within occupation, how many were single, married, or in a second marriage. We wanted to investigate both innovative and traditional occupational settings, since we thought that more traditional settings would attract different kinds of persons, possibly more stable, than innovative settings. Having opted to look at the nature of the difficulties involved in turning 40, we determined that half of our sample should be 35–40 years old and the other half, 40–45.

The final sample contained 40 men, 10 in each of four occupational categories; business executives, blue-collar workers, professionals, and artists. On theoretical grounds, occupation was made the primary basis for sampling. From a sociological perspective, work is the major vehicle by which a man engages the world; from a psychological perspective, the man's work career is of crucial importance in his adult development.

As the study proceeded, a variety of questions arose. For the managers and the production workers, we decided that half of each group should come from a more traditional stable company and half from a newer, technological, sophisticated work setting. We hoped in this manner to sample more broadly and study a major influence in our society, namely, the effects of innovative work settings (a new plant producing new products) on the development of individual men.

In the case of the professionals and artists, we had a choice of selecting 10 men from a variety of occupations within each broad category, or narrowing the scope to one specific profession and artistic medium. We picked the latter course. Within the professions we chose university professors (to the exclusion of lawyers and physicians, people like the research group, surely a reason why this research has not been done before). We selected biologists employed in a university setting. Within the arts, we picked writers (to the exclusion of painters, musicians, etc.), and more specifically, novelists. The selection of a particular occupation in each category increases the opportunity for taking careful account of the man's *work world,* including occupation and workplace, and the part it plays in his development.

We picked biologists from academe for ease of selection and availability. University-based biologists are also in a somewhat less rigidly defined career than biologists in industry or government. At the most flexible end of the continuum are artists, who often function in a more individually defined work world. Our idea about creative artists was that many men have chosen these endeavors in part as a reaction against the business world. In addition, a small, less formally organized work setting may have particular psychological importance for creative men. Artists have greater freedom to define their work and activities in contrast to managers, production workers, and scientists. It may be that they are doing, or think that they are doing, "their own thing" more than an industrial manager, for example, who seems more engaged in doing someone else's thing. By sampling in this manner we highlighted social-class differences (i.e., years of formal education, family of origin, and background). We hoped this would make the final sample more representative of the worlds of work.

The final sample allowed us to investigate various occupations (managers, production workers, academic biologists, and novelists) within different institutional settings (stable versus innovative) to see if issues such as activism, dependence, conformity, and creativity differ in these groups. We wished to learn why men choose particular careers and what these choices meant in terms of a man's sense of responsibility and authority. We wished to know in what ways work influences other parts of the man's life; family, leisuretime activities, sexuality, self-image, a sense of mortality, and social values. We were interested in each man's view of his success and what costs were involved in it.

We were not sure whether development proceeded at the same rate in all areas of man's life (work, family, social and community life). If a man were less successful or invested in the world of work, would he try harder or compensate by developing social or community life to a greater extent? We were also interested in the meaning of friendship in the various occupational groups, particularly as one gets older. Finally, we realized that this intensive interview procedure would present problems for both the men and the interviewers.

The Research Strategy

We developed a rather novel research approach. The research was carried out by a small group comprised of the five authors of *Seasons* plus Douglas Derrer, a psychologist with interests in Erikson, and Ray Walker, a Jungian-trained medical student. The seven of us conducted all 40 interviews. We formed a larger adult development seminar which included faculty members from a variety of disciplines. In the faculty seminar we had biweekly meetings in which the overall theory, research strategy, and actual cases were discussed. This enhanced the overall perspective and prevented any one theory from dominating our evolving viewpoint. Sociologists Theodore Mills and Kai Erikson emphasized the contribution of social class in development. Psychiatrists Gerald Klerman and Daniel Schwartz explored the role of personality in adult development. Peter Newton, a younger psychologist, helped us to investigate more thoroughly the time period leading up to the midlife decade.

The work in the seminar led to the idea of each interviewer's being paired with another faculty member, outside of the study group proper, analogous to a therapy supervisor in clinical work. We spaced interviews once a week for a period of 2–3 months. Interviewers met with a faculty supervisor to review each case with regard to background, personality dynamics, and the interviewing process. This was particularly important since in the pilot work we discovered that each man had a "secret." The men were more than eager to talk, but needed interviewer support and a developing rapport to tell about their secrets (extramarital affairs, unethical behavior, illness, impotency, etc.). The collaborative supervisor relationship aided the interviewer in getting the men to tell about their lives more fully.

We learned that the best way to proceed was to have each man start the interview by discussing where he was now in his life. It became apparent that beginning with what was most comfortable for each man allowed more collaborative exploration of a life in depth. Telling each man what we were up to produced a greater sense of comfort, and did not make him feel like a "subject" who was being manipulated. Many psychological investigations are marked by duplicitous instructions; we did not wish to have that occur in this study. By stating our interests, we facilitated the interviewee's talking about his life from his own perspective. This explicit research contract helped in another way. Each man was able to help us conceptualize some of the major issues, problems, and achievements of the midlife decade. Both parties were engaged in understanding the man's life and in the exploration of the broader meanings of the decade that the researchers might have overlooked. This may sound like clinical work, but supervision helped us to maintain a research focus.

We had to decide what number of interviews would be large enough to provide depth and would also be realistic, given our resources. Initially, we estimated that 5 hours would be enough, but we soon realized that a larger number of interviews conducted over a 3-month period would be a better strategy. A reason for increasing the number and spacing of interviews is that it allows both the men and the interviewer to obtain distance from the material. Each man could then see not only the pattern of his life, but exceptions as well. The time between interviews would allow both parties to prepare for the next session. We thought that we could ask each man to keep diaries of his daily activities, but for practical reasons we scrapped the idea. Instead, it became apparent that adults are more than interested in the development of their lives and would raise questions between interviews that would then be reflected in the next session. When the men taught us that each could collaborate in the exploration of his life, the responsibility was then shared. Together we worked on issues that change over time, as well as unique aspects of each man's life. The supervisory relationship aided the interviewer in exploring the material, developing hypotheses to be investigated later, and understanding the man's life from a threefold perspective: the views of the man, interviewer, and supervisor. As this multiple perspective developed, it was discussed both in the study group and in the faculty seminar. In this way we simultaneously addressed the individuality of the man's life and regularities which occur over lives that only can be discerned in a shared fashion. The interviewer and the supervisor emphasized the uniqueness of each man, whereas the faculty seminar stressed patterns across men. This strategy combined both the individual aspects of the person with a more structured view of age-linked stages of development.

It became apparent that we needed more than interviews, and so we decided that half an hour should be spent in a more formal testing procedure. Since we were studying men of different social classes, they might differ in their degree of psychological mindedness. We felt that working-class men would be less in touch with the "deeper" aspects of their own personalities and would be more uncomfortable talking about their fantasies, wishes, and fears than would be the case for the better educated, middle-class professionals. We used the Thematic Apperception Test (TAT) as a fantasy-eliciting technique in order to investigate the more psychological aspects of a man's life. The TAT is a standard projective technique, but we modified it for the purposes of this study. To be consistent, we used five cards in a regular sequence with each man; the interviewer then had the option of using one or more additional cards based on the situation at the time of testing.

In addition, we wanted to get some external view of the man either by interviewing family members, co-workers, or friends, or by observing him at home or work. Suggestions were made about attending a family dinner, meeting with the wife and children, or interviewing a mistress or lover. For every man we attempted to interview an important woman, spend time with the family, or visit his place of employment. A follow-up interview a year later was the last part of the research contract. This procedure allowed us to have additional contact with the man, ask about other areas of his life, test out more formal hypotheses, and most important, see if further changes had occurred.

The Sample

Business Executives. Two companies, T (traditional) and I (innovative), provided workplaces from which to draw both the managers and production workers. Company T is a division of a large corporation. It has manufactured a small number of products for many decades; a strength of the company. It is highly involved in the military-industrial complex and produces products for both government and private sectors. Historically, its technology and organizational structure have remained fairly constant. Company I is a new and rapidly growing firm in the modern communication–information–processing field. It has one manufacturing facility and only four products to which its fortunes are tied. The founders of Company I left national corporations and had a dream that their small company would shortly become a giant corporation rivaling its forebearers. The chief operating officers either directly or by delegation provided us with the names of all top- and middle-management executives who fit our qualifications. For each company we made five selections, choosing men so as to have a good distribution on age, organizational rank, ethnicity, and other background factors.

Among the managers, we had no dropouts; all completed the basic series of interviews as well as the 1-year follow-up; and most would readily have continued for a longer period had this been possible. This work with executives has important positive implications for research with "noncaptive" adults (e.g., nonstudents, nonpatients) who are asked to give a great deal of time, effort, and intimacy to a research enterprise.

Production Workers. The workers also were drawn equally from Companies T and I. In company T, where 60% of the hourly labor forces are black, we selected three black and two white workers. The men varied in age, occupational level, union status (two shop stewards), and years with the company. In company I, all of the production workers were white and, therefore, five white men were invited to participate. Company I workers meet the same criteria as used in the other company except for union status. Of the 10 men selected from the two different companies, all participated.

Academic Biologists. Biology is experiencing rapid change, and is seen as increasingly socially relevant (i.e., medicine, genetic control, warfare). The 10 biologists came from an excellent private university on the eastern seaboard. We had to talk to 13 biologists in order to obtain 10 participants. There were some dropouts, which makes this group somewhat different from the previous samples.

Novelists. Our approach, as with other samples, was ethnographic. We explored the world of the novelists, the institutions, work conditions, and the career problems faced by such men. We discovered that few novelists spend all of their time at writing; most of them have "hyphenated" careers: they also work as critics, teachers, journalists, and businessmen. We used two major indicators in selecting the sample: first, that a man had published at least two novels, and second, that in his mind, being a writer is of central importance. As opposed to other samples, all novelists were interviewed in their own homes or offices. We had the most difficulty in obtaining this sample; four refused participation and one dropped out. It took at least 15 contacts to provide the final group of 10 novelists.

The Research Contract. Each man was seen for approximately 15 hours in a weekly series of 1½-hour interviews. This strategy took into account the available research hours and the estimated time required to establish a relationship and gather the necessary material. Interviews were held in our offices, in the workplace, or in the home of the participant, whichever was the most mutually convenient location. Each man was seen by an interviewer who conducted the whole series of weekly interviews. Since the interviewers varied in age, sex, and interview experience, and settings differed, these affected the men in a nonsystematic fashion. Supervision helped to control some of this bias. The most marked differences were in the way the men discussed sex with male and female interviewers. There was marked boasting with male interviewers and more serious discussions with the woman interviewer. The total interview time varied from a low of 10 to a high of 22 hours. Not unexpectedly, it was found that the more articulate participants, usually the biologists and novelists, required more time.

As part of the research contract, participants were told what the study was about, namely, a focus on how men get through the midlife decade and the problems, satisfactions, and changes that occur in a man's life. It was noted that the study included men in four different occupations for comparative purposes. The research was being carried out within the Yale University Department of Psychiatry and was supported by a grant from the United States Public Health Service. We said that the investigation was not psychiatric in the sense of focusing primarily on problems. Rather, we wished to understand each man and how he lived. We emphasized the multidisciplinary aspect of the research. It was clearly stated that our interest was in human development in adulthood and how this is affected by circumstances at work, in the family, personal commitments, and changes in the larger society.

Each man was interested in how he was chosen. We explained the selection of the four occupations, and then how lists were provided by either the companies, university departments, or our own research on the novelists. We said that 10 men within the midlfie decade were picked in order to get distribution by age and other attributes. We tried to convey that the man's performance or potential was not critical, so that he did not have a sense of being evaluated. While this was not as difficult as we at first thought, it did present a problem for a few men.

We discussed our agreement with the sponsoring authorities, if there were any. For the managers and production workers, their companies gave their approval and moral support but were not otherwise involved. We assured anonymity and stated that we would write up the findings both for professional journals and a more general audience. We tried to use our creditability as academic investigators to elicit cooperation.

Each man was told that we would meet in weekly sessions over a few months. The conversations would be with one interviewer and would be tape-recorded. The tapes were used so that the researcher would be more involved in the interview process. Tapes would be transcribed later for analysis, and only members of the research team would hear or see them. Once transcribed, interviews would be coded so that anonymity could be insured. We said that there would be one formal psychological test and that we would discuss its rationale and answer any questions *after* it was conducted. We stated an interest in having a later interview with the wife or another significant woman. We suggested the possibility of having dinner with the family and seeing the man in his work setting. We noted the need for a single follow-up interview a year after the initial series ended. It was suggested that this would be useful to both the men and ourselves to understand additional developments in their lives. All of these procedures were overdrawn since the men were more than cooperative once the interviews started.

We strongly stressed the collaborative nature of the work, "that you and I together will try to get a picture of your life: the world you live in, what you do, how you experience it, and how things are changing. It is not our purpose to put you under a microscope but rather for both of us to be working at a common task, learning together about your life."

In terms of what was offered to the man, three things were noted: first, learning about one's development, "how you got there, and where you want to go"; second, after the formal talks have been completed, "if you wish, we will be glad to have a final meeting in which you ask most of the questions and I can offer any thoughts about what I've learned about you"; third, that we would show each man what we have written, "that it would not be so much about you as a separate individual but how your life and that of others reflects common patterns; that would be interested in your suggestions for improving anything we write." Finally, "if we do write in more detail about your life, we will give you the opportunity to edit any comments which you find too revealing, inaccurate, or misleading."

In general, this procedure was most straightforward with the executives and production workers. There was greater negotiation with the academic biologists who questioned us more thoroughly. The novelists demanded the greatest assurance of anonymity. For many of them, we had to send letters spelling out in detail our research ideas and procedures. Again, as with other field studies, artists presented the greatest problem in obtaining cooperation.

The Interview. There was no standard interview format, but there were 10 predefined areas to be covered. In general, we started with work, occupation, and career. The family included marriage, lifestyle, and children. Family of origin focused on parents and memories of early relationships. Discussion of social class included income, residential area, and style of living. Under ethnicity and religion we talked about the man's ideology, affiliation, identity, membership, and reference groups. In the political area, we asked about local, state, and national political affiliation, his general political ideology, and specific attitudes toward civil rights, poverty, and war (the Vietnamese War was at its height during the interviews). With regard to leisuretime activities, we questioned each man about recreation, cultural interests, how he spent weekends and vacations, his social networks (both personal and familial), friendships and acquaintances, and the intimacy of these relationships. We were particularly interested in the experience of declining bodily powers and capacities, including such specific change as baldness, graying hair, lessened physical attractiveness, diminishing capacity for athletics, reduced sexual capacity or desire, and illness.

We were curious about the man's thoughts regarding his own death or immortality. We ascertained the occurrences of illness and death of important people in his life. The man's view of his legacy (i.e., relationships, material benefits) was obtained. Finally, we asked how he sees the past, the present, and the future, and their connection. We tried to get the man to focus on his interior sense of self (often a difficult task since it was easier to talk about work, wife, family, or childhood than self), his origins, what paths he has taken, and where he sees life leading. We sought to determine how he evaluated himself, his life, and his legacy. Of what significance was it to him that he was "*x*" years old?

Data Analysis. One reason this project took so long had to do with developing a theory and refining a methodology at the same time, particularly in an uncharted area of exploration. As one illustration, the magnitude of the organzing task was often experienced as overwhelming. Interviews averaged 60 typed pages; usually there were eight interviews for a total of 480 pages per participant. With 40 men in the sample, there was a grand total of 19,200 pages of material to organize in a coherent fashion. As the first step, after an interview series ended the man was discussed in the study group and then in the faculty seminar. Over a period of years we developed coding procedures and worksheets which led to a set of guidelines to describe and organize the man's life in a number of areas: social background and family of origin; schooling; sexual history; family of procreation; fatherhood; occupation and social class; military service; work history; relations with man; leisure interest; death, illness, disturbance, and bodily decline; psychological difficulties, crisis, and contact with mental health professionals; religion and philosophy of life; current life issues; and stages of the interview.

As work continued on these guidelines and case analysis, we developed additional concepts. We formulated more adult development stages based on staff discussions. After 5 years we realized that we were now engaging in the work of biography. Over time, we had become social psychological biographers who were developing a method to describe the unique richness of each man's life. The evolving concepts allowed us to see a man's life in terms of stages of normal adult development. We became aware that a number of concepts such as the role of the Mentor, the Special Woman, and the Dream played a particularly prominent role in the lives of the men in their 20s. As we struggled with the issues of the 30s and the settling-down process it became apparent that there was a transitional period which occurred around the 30th birthday. These recognitions made us reorder the material we had collected on each man and structure his life in a way which made it more understandable. As the biographic form evolved, we were able to test it with many of the men in subsequent case analysis, and this helped further to refine our theory. As we developed new ideas, we were able to move beyond coding, worksheets, and guidelines to more age-linked adult development stages. This culminated in the adoption of a biographic approach with regard to the treatment of the interviews, projective techniques and other material collected from, and with, each man. Often, the interview with the wife aided greatly in further understanding the man's life. The biographic method made for a fuller description of each man's life. This method allowed for direct comparison of a man to others within his own occupation, as well as comparison of the four occupational groups. We considered these painstaking and time-consuming theoretical and methodological advances to be major contributions to the study of normal adult development.

CLINICAL IMPLICATIONS OF AN ADULT DEVELOPMENT VIEW

The first part of this chapter reviewed theory and research in the area of normal adult development and described how a major biographic investigation in the field was actually conducted. We now turn to the application of an adult development view in clinical work.

Before doing this, it should be noted that the author had to review the work of a number of theorists in the areas of behavioral and humanistic therapy. This is the case since his own training and practice involves a combination of psychodynamic and social systems theories. It is apparent that all three therapy orientations (dynamic, humanistic, and behavioral) have often been viewed in a somewhat pejorative fashion by the other approaches. More recent work (Wachtel, 1973; Wandersman, Poppen, & Ricks, 1976) has begun to address similarities as well as differences between these theories and actual treatment. It is clear that dynamic writers, although strong on transferential aspects of the therapeutic relationship, overemphasize early childhood development and often overinterpret psychopathology. In part this has to do with a dynamist's overly deterministic view which places a disproportionate stress on the child's earliest experiences in the family. These formative relationships are seen as powerful forces which influence almost all subsequent behavior, including therapy. But the nature of the actual authority structure in therapy as opposed to transference has only recently been reviewed from a social systems viewpoint with important consequences for treatment (Newton, 1973). Implicit sets of assumptions underlie dynamic therapies about what is the normative way to develop and grow in infancy, childhood, and adolescence. Deviation from such developmental progression is then viewed as neurotic or pathological in nature. Only recently have dynamically oriented writers, influenced by the work of Erikson (1950), seriously focused on the importance of broader social, cultural, and economic factors, such as class, race, ethnicity, and gender, in treatment.

Behavioral therapists stress the specific details of treatment and have conducted impressive research, but they display a tendency to adopt an ahistoric, adevelopmental view of clients. This tendency is confounded by a limited environmental viewpoint. Behaviorists focus on the generalization of behavioral procedures and are concerned about the transfer of training (change) from the treatment situation to other aspects of life. This is done so that training and treatment can be linked to contingencies of reinforcement across situations. The problem is that no two social environments are exactly alike. For instance, if a client learns to be more assertive or aggressive with his therapist, it may get him into difficulty in the family or work setting, or the larger community. This possible outcome is not due to behaviorists' theoretical naïveté but rather because the larger sociocultural context is often underestimated. Only recently have behaviorists given serious consideration to reprogramming the extra-therapy contingencies (see Chapter 2).

Behaviorists (Kanfer & Saslow, 1969) adovocate that therapists only take into account the client's past in order to determine the individual's learning history, and to discard other material since it is not helpful in deciding on the type of treatment which would be most beneficial. But how can therapist ascertain quickly the major life difficulties of the client? A developmental perspective is necessary in order to place the client in his life, not the therapist's view of his current situation. Of course, one must focus on treatment eventually, but a nondevelopmental view does damage to the complexity of the client, often reducing him or her to a disembodied set of presenting symptoms.

The time dimension is a critical aspect in development and treatment, and its importance is often minimized. For instance, Kanfer and Grimm

(1977) list numerous marker events that are important in all of our lives; unemployment, divorce, growing up of children, retirement, extended vacations, or other changes in lifestyle. These events are certainly important, but what is lacking is a developmental context in order to understand the meaning of such events for the client. Specifically, a divorce which occurs during a transitional time has quite different effects than one that happens during a more stable period of adult development. Since questioning of one's life structure is a normal part of a transitional period, divorces, job changes, or even career shifts are more likely to occur during such times than in more stable periods. For the behavior therapist, this framework provides a normal way of viewing adult behavior. All ages and stages are *not* the same.

Most behaviorists' concerns about the temporal arrangements between a behavior and its consequences are limited. The time dimension tends to be in terms of hours, days, weeks, or months. For adults, this is too small a sampling of changes that occur over a much broader time span. This is an example of how an ahistoric approach interferes with untold consequences for maintenance of changes in the treatment situation and afterward.

In behavior theory there tends to be a lack of emphasis on the behavior of the therapist. There is a norm of presenting the therapist as a neutral scientist exploring behavior. But as we all know, the therapeutic relationship is important for effective treatment. Therefore, therapists have to understand their own behavior. In terms of this chapter, what is critical is the stage of life that the therapist is in and how this influences treatment. For instance, if the client is in a developmental crisis during the midlife transition and so is the therapist, he may have great difficulty treating the client unless he is aware of the meaning of such transitional times for both the client and himself. This illustration raises the question of the appropriateness of such treatment and the need for consultation. At a minimum, it is important for both client and therapist to know the developmental stage they are collaboratively working in. This knowledge aids them in setting obtainable goals and expectations about treatment and the client's life during the immedite posttherapy future.

The process is further confounded by an ahistorical approach to clinical work itself. That is, behaviorists tend to view treatment as time limited; ending with the last session. One of the concepts that therapists might borrow from an adult development framework is the notion of the Mentor as explicated in the *Seasons*. A few people in a person's life may play a Mentor-like role, including a "good enough" therapist. For any close relationship to occur, time is necessary for its development. In terms of psychotherapy, one important implication is that whatever occurred in the treatment may be useful to the client in the time *after* the formal therapy has ended. Clients are influenced in treatment; therefore, they will test out, after therapy, ideas, concepts, and behavioral strategies suggested by the therapist during the actual treatment. Again, if one adopts a developmental perspective, this posttreatment phase is a time in which the "internalized therapist" will, hopefully, influence the former client in his ongoing daily life. Therefore therapists ought to consider psychotherapy as a phase in their client's life, with potential additional learning and change, rather than an end point in itself. Also, behaviorists might adopt a view of themselves as Mentor to lessen the charges of exploitation of positive transference and of increasing clients' dependency.

A criticism one might make of humanistic therapies is the primary focus on the "here and now." This is not the case for all humanists, but certainly some have distorted the sensitive clinical approach and work of Fritz Perls (1969), leading to treatment marked by a rejection of both the past and the future. Writers associated with this view, including many in the human encounter movement, stress the current, immediate awareness of feelings and emotions. It is a psychology that disproportionately looks within people without an adequate view of their environment and the social roles they are asked to play. This therapeutic bias leads many humanists to an ahistoric, theoretical position. What is lost is a temporal dimension which allows one to become aware of, and let go of, the past in order to attempt an integration of past, present, and future goals. A nondevelopmental perspective disproprtionately focused on the "here and now" ignores most of one's life and reduces the complexity of the lived life to the moment. Patients in humanistic treatment tend to be young and seen at university-based clinical facilities. Such people are often in a transitional stage and the therapist can serve as a role model, and hopefully a Mentor. Humanistic treatment is very demanding, but without some theory of "transference" clients may experience themselves as extremely dependent on therapists. Many humanistic psychologists (Rogers, 1967) are aware of the dilemmas of dealing with a dependent client, but others rarely take into account problems of transference and countertransference in the actual treatment. There is research (Bergin, 1971) suggesting that humanists help their clients. Nevertheless, they might be more effective if they took a developmental perspective which encourages changes over longer periods of time.

We have briefly outlined some shortcomings, particularly with regard to the time dimension, of the major theoretical approaches to treatment. Now, we will apply an adult development perspective to clinical work. For the sake of clarity, this section will be divided into four areas: training, assessment, treatment, and follow-up or maintenance.

Clinical training usually includes two major biases: an ahistorical, nondevelopmental view and a psychopathology perspective with regard to the understanding of adult problems. The first is seen in an overemphasis on the influence of early childhood on later development. This is most clearly stressed by dynamically oriented authors who concentrate on the importance of the first 1 (Klein), 3 (Mahler), 5 (Freud), or 13 (neo-Freudians) years of life. How the child goes through certain developmental tasks in interaction with mother, father, siblings, and peer group is viewed as the major determinant of later development. There are age- and stage-specific tasks for these earlier periods, and clinicians are trained to appreciate their significance. Later events such as leaving home, first job, marriage, parenthood, geographic moves, loss, economic depression, war, and death are seen as marker events, but without a developmental framework in which their occurrence can be understood. It is as if development does have a timetable up until a certain period in life, and then it becomes idiosyncratic.

An adult development perspective offers the opportunity to see a life as an evolving process from birth until death. It is made up of changing and stable weaves, but is of whole cloth, if we can only see the total pattern. The clinician's ahistorical bias may be a defense against the constancy of change and the challenge that that represents to each of us. After all, stages with specific tasks that one needs to address throughout life is a threatening idea to many people, including therapists, particularly when viewed within the context of growing older.

The other major bias in clinical training is an overemphasis on pathology. Nonphysicians blame this on the "medical model," but in all the mental health disciplines it has more to do with the absence of a life span perspective. Without an understanding of normal development, it is no accident that people and their situations are overinterpreted as pathological in nature. For instance, if questioning of the structure of one's life is developmentally appropriate at age 30, is a client who does this neurotic, in conflict, or normal? The latter is often the case, but clinicians are not taught to take into account such appropriate developmental tasks. This is not to deny that pathology exists, but even mentally ill people have developmental issues which have to be recognized along with their intrapsychic problems.

Generally, in assessment work, dynamically oriented clinicians place a disproportionate emphasis on early childhood; behaviorists do not adequately weigh maturational and developmental aspects; and humanists tend to be ahistoric, stressing the current situation. For instance, it is inadequate for a dynamically oriented therapist to interpret the dilemmas of the 21-year-old about to get his first full-time job solely in terms of competition with father at age 5. To address only such early life influences for a 40-year-old's midlife transition is insensitive. To do the same with a 62-year-old preretirement patient is a serious distortion. Similarly, a behaviorist needs to know the client's history in detail with regard to what reinforcers and punishers were effective in what stage of their life and how the contingency arrangements have changed over time. Without this detailed behavioral history, plus some understanding of adult tasks, one can administer inappropriate incentives to a 45-year-old. Humanists without a full appreciation of development can inadvertently attack a client's long-standing defenses and produce destructive outcomes if they focus disproportionately on the current situation. Placing a client in a developmental framework allows the clinician to judge what is normal and what is pathological. That is, how is the client doing in comparison to age cohorts in performing common life tasks? Of course, additional work in this area is needed to make ever-finer distinctions. But the assessment process must take into account the whole person, including his or her history. Without a knowledge of our client's childhood and adult past, the present is unclear and the future unknowable. Again, a biographic perspective places the client into his *own* developmental history so that assessment is formed by a fuller understanding of the individual's total life to date.

In treatment, this model aids the clinician to appreciate the developmental significance of psychological crises. A client can be helped to see the crisis as stemming from devastating failures to carry out age-linked life tasks. Once the clinician sees how the client is doing on his age-specific tasks compared to other people his age, and within the context of his own personality, the therapist can then plan treatment including a reasonable prognosis. For instance, a large percentage of clients at the University of Cincinnati Walk-In Clinic (a crisis center), both from the university and the larger community, are between 17 and 22 years old, the transition into early adulthood. How they address the task of leaving the dependency of adolescence and entering the adult world, with its stress on automy and self-reliance, is critical. Many "first-break" schizophrenics also show up at this time in life. This is not surprising since this can be a stressful transitional period. But without an appreciation of the task of this stage, we are all too likely to institutionalize and increase the numbers of occupants of the sick role. The stresses such young people face may be seen as a developmental crisis where the individual experiencces his life structure as unsatisfactory or intolerable. The combination of stress, poor life structure, and a feeling of lack of options (helplessness) leads them into mental health facilities. Clinicians working with such clients also feel that they have no, or limited, options. Instead of denying pathology by focusing only on the situation or placing all of the problems in the client, the clinician can help the client to understand his life, to move out of the house into a more appropriate environment (halfway house, commune, etc.), so as to have a choice between the psychologically disturbing family of origin and the total institution.

As an illustration of how an adult development framework can be clinically useful, I will now describe the treatment of a client. Before presenting this case, I would like to note a number of "rules of thumb" a clinician might keep in mind using this developmental approach. First, it is helpful to know the base rate for various activities (i.e., exploration of relationships, education, work history) for clients at particular ages. Second, the tasks of different stages of life (i.e., exploration of choices and options in the 20s, questioning of life structure during the age 30 transition, the settling-down tendencies of the early 30s) need to be remembered. Third, do not use psychopathological labels when describing clients' behavior, since this tends to create more distance in the therapeutic relationship than what already exists given the social role and authority differences of the two participants. Also, labeling overemphasizes deviation or pathology and does not acknowledge appropriate changes that occur in normal development. Fourth, maintain a present orientation without being overly concerned with early childhood experiences, since an exclusively past focus can result in a pessimistic view of the possibilities for change and growth. Fifth, stress life goals so that treatment has a future thrust. Sixth, keep in mind the importance of "working through" issues, including enough time spent on termination so that the client internalizes the therapeutic work and relationship, thus enhancing the possibility for using afterward what was gained in treatment. This last point is important if one is thoroughly to address the issue of maintenance of change, or follow-up.

Joan was a 30-year-old white woman working as an art teacher in a private school in New York. When I saw her, she was single and living alone in an apartment. Most of her friends were from work and her family lived hundreds of miles away. Joan grew up in a large family. Her father served in the Second World War and was away until she was 4 years old. Her mother was a Mormon and her father was Catholic: "Mother felt it was a sin to marry a man who drank coffee and liquor." The family secret was that the father was not a Mormon. During Joan's early development her father was away often, since he had to travel for his company. He was the disciplinarian in the family and insisted on her keeping a neat room. She found it very difficult to please him. Initially, her father supported Joan's artistic interests and she had many sensuous fantasies about him, but he became progressively less reasonable as he got older. Although her mother worked all of her life, and is viewed as a success, she is said to have spent most of her time at home crying. Joan was very successful in college but complained that she did not have a good enough education. Her father also restricted her social life. After college graduation she spent an exciting year in Europe studying art. She returned to New York and obtained an excellent job. A year later, when Joan was 27, her father died of a heart attack. Joan blamed both her mother and herself for her father's death; "We overfed him." Joan's relations with men had been very limited, unhappy, and primarily involved older or married men who were unavailable for building longer term relationships.

Therapy, like adult development, goes through stages. Joan was seen over a period of 6 months in twice-a-week therapy. Initially, we focused on her weight problem. Being overweight made it difficult for her to attract men. She was also a workaholic, often working over 60 hours a week: "When I started to teach, I felt like God in front of the children." Her dream was to have an excellent art program which would change the school and society. Given this unrealistic approach, Joan reported that she worked so hard during the week that "If I don't work on weekends, I get depressed." She described herself as "aggressive at work and passive in social life." This passive, withdrawing stance interfered with any attempt at building a social life. During this first phase of therapy I was struck by how much she spoke about work and the passion and fire it generated in her. School meetings were described in sexual and aggressive terms. Her talk about work was marked by pleasurable, stimulating, and often exciting affect.

After 2 months of treatment, Joan's perspective broadened. Instead of just saying "I'm waiting for my life; it's out there somewhere" and speaking as if she couldn't do anything about it, she began to see her own contribution to her dilemma. For instance, her overwhelming sense of responsibility and lack of authority at work interacted with the school system which perpetuated this unpleasant situation. I pointed out how she participated in bringing this about. If she could do this and was now aware of her collusion in a hurtful system, she could also change how she behaved, which could indeed effect some aspects of her life. Joan then began to think about ways to change. She subsequently spent the first nonwork weekend with friends. This was an important event which led her to question her constricted, work-focused lifestyle. She then went on a week's vacation, met some interesting people, and continued to broaden her views. Joan was able to see how her need for love, attention, and respect from children, parents, and teachers was a way to use work as a defense against developing a social life. She also became aware, through interpretation, how sexual issues were expressed at work, leaving little energy for social/sexual contacts.

In the last, or termination, stage of therapy, she became less work oriented, started career planning, and worked on redefining her job. As Joan faced these issues she became less depressed and passive. It became apparent to Joan that she could leave her job, which she had grown to hate, without some overwhelming sense of guilt. She developed better relations with women, but still had unrealistic expectations about men. Joan knew I was leaving town, and managed to take an art workshop in Washington: she left me before I could leave her. This represented the difficulty of having another man leave, an all-too-painful experience in her life. At our last session Joan presented me with a present, a dream full of food, mansions, and beautiful people.

Dynamically, one could view Joan as playing out a strong father attachment by becoming involved with older or unavailable men. She strongly identified with mother's professional role but hated her social/personal role. Her greatest fear was to become like her mother (lose control, cry, and be hysterical). Certainly, work was used as a defense against personal involvement. Eating, therefore, can be seen as leading to her becoming unavailable as an attractive, sexual woman. By the end of this course of therapy she had had a number of successes and presented herself less as a starved child in her dreams of food, houses, and lovely people. A dynamic view would hold that regression is necessary, but this is more likely to occur in stable periods. During transitional stages, both life structure and personality are in flux. The therapeutic relationship supported development and Joan in her belief that nature, not mental illness, was encouraging such change.

In adult development terms, Joan can be seen as in her age 30 transition, questioning the meaning of her life. During her 20s she appropriately explored education and work. Because of her family background and religious beliefs, social/sexual relations were ignored. She has now decided that the trip has not been worth the price. Joan knows that she can be an effective teacher but now wants more authority in an administrative position in the work world. She also would like to have a more rounded life. What Joan will do about these issues is problematic, since development is a lifetime enterprise not subject to cure or final solutions.

As an adult, Joan still had problems with dependency on others, particularly men. Work and living alone made her feel independent. Intimacy and mature dependency threatened her with loss of control, leading to feelings of depression. Nevertheless, Joan was addressing normative issues for her stage of life. My sharing a developmental viewpoint was helpful in explicating Joan's dilemmas and allowing her to make a

number of choices. She no longer had to feel so guilty about even thinking about leaving her work situation. This freedom, then, allowed Joan
to plan for appropriate next steps. She was in the process of change,
questioning her whole life structure. This is part of a normal age 30 transition. To have overinterpreted Joan's behavior as complete or un-
qualified pathology would be to deny her own normal development and
discount the dilemmas women have when they are seriously committed to
work and wish to take on more authority as a responsible adult. Our
work together facilitated Joan's not blaming herself, or feeling guilty or
angry at people in her past, for things beyond her own control. This current orientation realistically allowed Joan to work on the tasks of her
own stage of development. I also used adult development concepts so we
collaboratively could look at the relationship between two adults trying
to understand Joan's life. Early childhood history helps in working on
transference, but with adult patients the real authority relationshp
(Newton, 1973) has to be explored if developmental issues are to be
understood. I might mention that, being in a transitional period myself
at the time, this was not the easiest client to treat. Consultation with
others was helpful in sorting out what were her and what were my issues.

With regard to follow-up of treatment and the maintenance of
change, an adult development perspective focuses on two issues. First, it
addresses a time dimension with regard to treatment and its effects, with
enough space for termination work. Second, it addressses age-specific
tasks with regard to the client's stage of life. As noted previously, clinicians need to consider treatment as an ongoing process in the client's life.
The end of formal therapy is not the end of change produced by a particular treatment. Rather, clients need time to integrate the new learnings, perspectives, and changes begun during therapy. In addition, clinicians ought to allow their clients the adult right to evaluate treatment and
take in the more mentoring, helpful, and supportive aspects of the
therapy. In advancing this view, I have in mind both client's and clinician's being somewhat more sanguine about the time needed for change
instead of rushing to produce immediate effects both within the treatment and shortly after termination. This stance frees both parties in
terms of evaluating the maintenance of change over a longer time dimension. Since therapy involves a relationship, it does not end after the last
session. Rather, the therapist often influences the client in many ways
posttreatment. If the therapy was "good enough," then there will be
positive movement by the client after termination. A focus on immediate
effects may get in the way of a more formed perspective on the part of
both clinician and client. Appropriately allowing for long-term effects
reduces immediate pressure which often leads to conformity responses.

That is, pushing clients gets them to "please" the therapist by the display of particular behaviors. To avoid some of these problems, the clinician can plan for an appropriate end to treatment with enough time in the termination phase to work on critical issues including both the transferential and real authority aspects of therapy. Joan's treatment was conducted with the explicit knowledge that it was time limited. Her workshop then is understandable as a resistance against the already known time boundary around the therapy. Its meaning in terms of avoiding another loss of a man in her life could be explored. Unfortunately, it wasn't done well enough since she terminated without adequate notice, but even that type of "acting-out" was understandable to both parties. Indeed, some of Joan's changes may have been done to please me, but her earlier than planned termination expressed the other side of her ambivalence: fear of intimacy and loss of control.

One implication of an adult developmental stance would be extending the time dimension for evaluative studies of treatment. If sensitive clinical research is to be conducted, follow-up should include enough time after treatment to assess the client's integration of what was learned and experienced in the therapy. This would be facilitated if clinicians made enough room in therapy for a termination phase which could serve as a bridge between therapy and posttreatment situations.

An adult development view underscores the nature of stable and transitional periods in life. Since we all go through stable periods followed by transitional ones, it is critical to keep this in mind in the treatment situation. Transitional periods, by their very definition, involve more questioning by the person and changes in the life structure. It is therefore no accident that most patients like Joan seen in public facilities are indeed in transitional stages. Change also occurs during stable periods as well, but the magnitude of such changes is smaller than what occurs in transitional or crisis times. In transitional periods, individuals are changing their life structure in anticipation of the next stage. In stable periods, individuals may modify their life structure to make it fit in better with the tasks of the current period. Both the client and the clinician should know what stage and tasks they are working on together, this is necessary in order to have realistic goals and expectations for treatment. It is also important to keep this in mind in order to evaluate the maintenance of therapeutic effects. For instance, changes are greater in transitional times, independent of treatment. The therapist can side with the positive push toward changing in untenable life structure in such times. There can clearly be dramatic changes which, if understood, can be maintained over time. During more stable periods the maintenance of major change is harder to obtain. This is the case because the nature of stable periods has to do with "putting one's house in order." The task of such stages facilitates a more stable, ordered, and consistent life structure. If a clinician or researcher wishes to measure the maintenance of change, two things need to be kept in mind: first, that the time dimension is long enough; and second, what stage of life the client is currently dealing with. Without both aspects as central, the evaluation of change will either be too short (and thus superficial), or insensitive to the constancy and changes involved in different stages of adult development. Finally, it is clear that a developmental view can be used with a clinical perspective in treatment since the two are *not* incompatible. In fact, the two in a combination enrich assessment, treatment, and maintenance since there is a balance between normative and pathological approaches to understanding the person's current dilemmas in light of the total life experiences.

REFERENCE NOTE

1. Klein, E. B., Allinsmith, B., Burlew, A. K., Correa, M. E., Dember, C., Duff, N., Gleser, G., Hiller, D., & Newman, J. *Adult development in women.* Unpublished manuscript, University of Cincinnati, 1978.

REFERENCES

Bergin, A. E. The evaluation of therapeutic outcomes. In A. E. Bergin and S. Garfield (Eds.), *Handbook of psychotherapy and behavior change: An empirical analysis.* New York: Wiley, 1971.
Bühler, C. The curve of life as studied in biographies. *Journal of Applied Psychology,* 1955, *19,* 405–409.
Erikson, E. H. *Childhood and society.* New York: W. W. Norton, 1950.
Erikson, E. H. *Young man Luther.* New York: W. W. Norton, 1958.
Erikson, E. H. *Gandhi's truth.* New York: W. W. Norton, 1969.
Friday, N. *My mother myself.* New York: Delacorte, 1977.
Gould, R. *Transformations.* New York: Simon & Schuster, 1978.
Hennig, M. & Jardin, A. *The mangerial woman.* New York: Doubleday, 1977.
Jaques, E. Death and the mid-life crisis. *International Journal of Psychoanalysis,* 1965, *46,* 502–514.
Jung, C. G. *Modern man in search of a soul.* New York: Harcourt, 1933.
Jung, C. G. The stages of life. In Joseph Campbell (Ed.), *The portable Jung.* New York: Viking, 1971.
Kanfer, F. H., & Grimm, L. G. Behavioral analysis: Selecting target behaviors in the interview. *Behavior Modification,* 1977, *1,* 7–28.
Kanfer, F. H., & Saslow, G. Behavioral diagnosis. In C. Franks (Ed.), *Behavior therapy: Appraisal and status.* New York: McGraw-Hill, 1969.

Levinson, D. J., Darrow, C. H., Klein, E. B., Levinson, M. H., & McKee, B. *The seasons of a man's life.* New York: Knopf, 1978.

Neugarten, B. A developmental view of adult personality. In J. E. Birren (Ed.), *Relations of development and aging.* Springfield, Ill.: Charles C Thomas, 1965.

Newton, P. M. Social structure and process in psychotherapy: A sociopsychological analysis of transference, resistance, and change. *International Journal of Psychiatry,* 1973, *11,* 480–512.

Perls, F. *Gestalt therapy verbatim.* Lafayette, Calif.: Real People Press, 1969.

Rogers, C. R. Carl Rogers. In E. G. Boring and G. Lindzey (Eds.), *A history of psychology in autobiography.* New York: Appleton-Century-Crofts, 1967.

Singer, J. *Androgyny.* Garden City, N.Y.: Anchor Press, 1977.

Stewart, W. *A psychosocial study of the formation of the early adult life structure in women.* Unpublished doctoral dissertation, Teacher's College of Columbia University, 1976.

Vaillant, G. *Adaptation to life.* Boston: Little, Brown, 1977.

Wachtel, P. Psychodynamics, behavior therapy, and the implacable experimenter: An inquiry into the consistency of personality. *Journal of Abnormal Psychology,* 1973, *82,* 324–334.

Wandersman, A., Poppen, P., & Ricks, D. *Humanism & behaviorism: Dialogue and growth.* New York: Pergamon, 1978.

PART IV

Dyadic, Social, Ecological, and Political Systems

CHAPTER

10

RECIPROCAL ROLE TRAINING:
Therapeutic Transfer as Viewed from
a Social Psychology of Dyads

J. T. DeVOGE

It has been argued that interpersonal theory is an important context from which to view behavior therapy since the working arrangement for much of this therapy is a dyad (therapist–client) and the goals of treatment frequently involve alterations in a client's interpersonal relationships (DeVoge & Beck, 1978). This chapter is not intended as a broad critique of behavior therapy. The focus, instead, will be on one of the more serious problems for behavior therapy suggested by interpersonal theory—the transfer of therapeutic training. After all, it is into a social context, a network of interpersonal relationships, that a client carries his newly acquired behaviors. Judging from reports of a lack of favorable results regarding transfer of training (e.g., Burtle, Whitlock, & Franks, 1974; Davidson & Seidman, 1974; Gomes-Schwartz, Hadley, & Strupp, 1978; Hersen & Bellack, 1976; Jeffrey, Christensen, & Katz, 1975; Kazdin & Bootzin, 1972; Keith & Lange, 1974; Levine & Fasnacht, 1974; Liberman, McCann, & Wallace, 1976; Miran, Lehrer, Koehler, & Miran,

1974; Sobell & Sobell, 1976), there are grounds to suspect that something is amiss.

Helping a client toward a more satisfying adjustment in his social world appears to be a frequent theme in behavior therapy, and recent social learning theories focus on the interrelationships among personal, behavioral, and contextual factors in the determination of human social behavior (e.g., Bandura, 1969, 1974, 1978; Mischel, 1973, 1977). Yet in the consulting room clients continue to receive exposure to forms of behavioral intervention which largely ignore social context effects (Willems, 1974; Wahler, Note 1). Thus while behaviorists in increasing numbers wander into the community in hopes of affecting societal change (Franks & Wilson, 1975), modern-day behavior therapy remains largely a science focused on the modification of specific acts through the application of techniques fundamentally similar to those developed in animal laboratories.

This trend is apparent even in behavioral techniques geared to effect cognitive alterations. While social learning theorists speak of complex cognitive phenomena such as strategies, plans, and subjective stimulus values (e.g., Mischel, 1973, 1977), these concepts seem as yet to have made little impact on the cognitive therapies of behaviorists. As a result, cognitive behavioral approaches tend to be difficult to distinguish from noncognitive behavioral interventions, the distinction often being little more than a shift in focus from a motor act to a specific thought (Ledwidge, 1978).

Not that all this attention to specific act alteration has been without merit. Even while critics have described technical problems (Davison, 1973; DeVoge & Beck, 1978) and theoretical contradictions (Yates, 1975), or have assigned treatment results to nonbehavioral factors (e.g., Bergman, 1976; Wolowitz, 1975), the results from a variety of investigations generally support the view that behavioral techniques are effective ways to change behavior in therapeutic settings (Gomes-Schwartz et al., 1978). Possibly because of the influence of behaviorists, more has been empirically established regarding the science of modifying specific acts than has been established about any other "change" concept in psychotherapy. Nonetheless, their narrow conceptualization of human social behavior has left behaviorists with the dilemma of knowing better how to change behaviors in therapeutic confines than how to maintain changed behaviors in a social context.

According to interpersonal theory, part of the problem is that persons may operate socially in ways which most behaviorists do not yet fully appreciate (Bowers, 1977; Carson, 1969; DeVoge & Beck, 1978; Wachtel, 1973, 1977a,b). Especially troublesome from an interpersonal perspective is a currently popular behavioral notion concerning the issue of social reinforcement. While behaviorists contend that this phenomenon generally operates in a simple and unilateral way (for instance, praise and approval are "generalized" social reinforcers), interpersonal theorists posit that social reinforcement is a complex, subtle process whose outcome may seem paradoxical in some cases. In fact, it is precisely these paradoxes which may suggest some direct explanations for poor transfer or maintenance of training from behavioral programs (see also Chapter 11).

It is not the point to belabor theoretical issues in this introduction. However, the next two sections will be devoted to a clarification of theoretical differences between behaviorists and interpersonal theorists. Unless these differences are clearly sorted out, there exists the possibility that more practical issues about transfer of training may be misunderstood. Therefore the sequence of this chapter will include theoretical discussions of social behavior, an outline of deficiencies in some current behavioral models pertinent to transfer of training, and a theoretical alternative—reciprocal role training. Clinical suggestions will be offered in an appendix.

BEHAVIORAL VIEW OF THE SOCIAL WORLD

At a theoretical level, recent years have witnessed a growing appreciation among behaviorists of the complex interplay between the human organism and the environment (Bandura, 1969, 1974, 1978, Mahoney, 1974; Mischel, 1973, 1977). The concept of a social context which operates in a continuous, reciprocal relationship with an organism's behavior represents not only a significant departure from more classic, "bedrock" behaviorism (e.g., Skinner, 1975), but a point of view quite similar to present-day interactionism (e.g., Magnusson & Endler, 1977).

Nonetheless, social learning theory in its present form remains too vague to be readily usable to a clinician in the practice of behavior therapy. For example, while the theory emphasizes the reciprocal, interactive nature of person and situational factors, social behaviorists have not speculated reading the specific form of this interaction, or the general principles that might be involved in the regulation of the interaction. Golding (1975) has stated that unless person–situation interactions can be broken down into meaningful patterns, they remain theoretically ambiguous. One result of this ambiguity is that in spite of its conceptual advance, social learning theory has stimulated little new in the way of direct clinical application. In fact, Kunkel (1975) has left the impression that the social learning model does not require interventions substantially different from those currently in use.

Two examples from recent behavioral literature underscore this point. The first example is a study conducted by Mariotto and Paul (1975) in which person versus situation effects were examined on two inpatient wards. Balanced rotation of staff members between the two wards allowed the same staff to conduct treatment on both wards, thus equalizing effects due to "relationship" factors. In addition, continuous and reliable observations were obtained through time-sampling techniques on such dimensions as cognitive dysfunction, social interaction, and staff responses to patient behavior. In all, 8 consecutive weeks of data from 34 patients were examined for this study. What is striking about this investigation is that in the midst of this sophisticated research methodology, the behavior *therapy* employed consisted of the usual prompts, tokens, and "social reinforcement" (undefined).

The second example is a case study reported by McCullough, Huntsinger, and Nay (1977). The report describes a self-control treatment conducted on an adolescent boy with a history of temper outbursts. The authors stated that the case represented an illustration of the relevance of an interactional model as a rationale for self-control treatment. Yet the treatment consisted of rehearsal plus praise to increase self-control, and attempts to alter the natural environment by programming teachers to praise the boy when he held his temper. While programming natural environments is a strategy that predates reformulated social learning theory (Baer, Wolf, & Risley, 1968), rehearsal is a technique which hardly requires a social learning rationale. In addition, the use of contingent praise is traditional operant practice.

There appears to be little evidence in either example of any special contribution to the therapeutic strategy provided by a social learning model, although both studies show an operant influence. This influence may mirror a trend. In the absence of influence on clinical procedures from a social learning model, operant models have maintained a predominant position (e.g., Cautela & Upper, 1975; Goldfried & Davison, 1976; Kazdin, 1975; O'Leary & Wilson, 1975; Wilson, Hannon, & Evans, 1968).

In an operant model, two primary assumptions apply to social behavior. The first pertains to the organization of social behavior. From an operant perspective, there are *no* laws describing abstract organizational principles or patterns of social behavior. Particularly disregarded have been notions about person factors, especially concepts resembling personality traits (see Chapter 7, and Bowers, 1973; Wachtel, 1973,

1977a). While recognition has been given to the fact that two or more responses may covary and form a response *class,* it has been contended that there are no a priori bases for predicting which responses will covary (Wahler, Note 1). Presumably this is a matter for empirical discovery with each individual case. Thus the clinical focus in behavior therapy has remained on a specific response, its cueing stimuli, and its immediate, observable consequences.

While the organization of social behavior has been viewed as unique for each individual, hence given no central concern by operantly oriented behaviorists, a contrasting emphasis has been placed on the more generalized property of praise and approval as social reinforcers. Frequently, praise and approval emerge as such universally desirable outcomes that they are casually referrd to as "social reinforcement," the terms seemingly interchangeable (DeVoge & Beck, 1978). The assumption has been that socially desirable stimulation such as praise and approval is an effective reinforcer for nearly every individual.

A corollary to this assumption has been the belief that behaviors will be maintained which are effective in leading to praise and approval, while those behaviors which do not result in praise and approval will extinguish. Accordingly, behavioral clinicians from Wolpe and Lazarus (1966) to Goldfried and Davison (1976) have advocated a warm, friendly, and dominant role for the therapist to enhance the "reinforcing" value of his praise and approval. Further, to facilitate transfer of training, one popular strategy has been the programming of a client's natural environment to "reward" new behaviors through contingent praise and approval (e.g., Kazdin & Bootzin, 1972).

There is an accumulation of evidence which indicates that there are problems with the operant view of the social world. First of all, in a number of investigations results have been obtained which suggest a specific structural organization for social behavior. Although this material will be presented in the next section, it seems appropriate to point out here that this organization does suggest a priori grounds for formulating assumptions about the kinds of behaviors which may covary.

In addition, the results of a number of studies on verbal conditioning lead to the conclusion that there are subject populations who do not respond well when praise and approval are employed as reinforcers. One group shown repeatedly to be unresponsive to praise and approval is hospitalized schizophrenics (Buss & Lang, 1965; Caulfield & Martin, 1976; Frankel & Buchwald, 1969). In fact, it has been demonstrated that schizophrenics have actually outperformed (i.e., offered assistance more frequently to a patient who had fallen from his crutches) college students when there was no apparent opportunity to earn a reward (Tolor, Kelly, & Stebbins, 1976). In order to make social stimuli such as the word "good" reinforcing, this stimulus has had to be paired with nonsocial reinforcers (e.g., Drennen, Gallman, & Sausser, 1969; Hurwitz, 1969; Miller & Drennen, 1970; Stahl, Thompson, Leitenberg, & Hasazi, 1974), a pheonomenon analogously reported with juvenile delinguents (Schwitz-gebel, 1967, 1969; Slack, 1960).

While reasons for this nonresponsiveness have not been empirically established, there is the likelihood that a contributing factor involves preferences that certain people have regarding how they behave toward others and how others act in return (DeVoge & Beck, 1978). Thus there may be individuals who not only do not prefer praise and approval from others, but who may experience such stimulation as aversive. Needless to say, when these people encounter praise and approval in a social exchange, responses which led to this outcome are likely to be discarded. When this happens because of responses acquired in therapy, the result could be lowered transfer of training.

To summarize, social learning theory appears to be similar to modern interactional accounts of human social behavior, but has made few novel contributions to clinical practice because it is vague about the particulars of person–environment interaction. Operant views, by contrast, have had noteworthy impact on clinical behavioral treatment, but may be misleading because of a deemphasis on person factors and their neglect of the nuances of social reinforcement.

PARAMETERS OF INTERPERSONAL BEHAVIOR

Universals in Dyadic Behavior

Recently, Triandis (1978) has commented on some "universals" of interpersonal behavior. By his definition, a variable could be considered universal if there were some evidence of its transcultural similarity concomitant with an absence of contradictory findings. Using these criteria, Triandis identified four bipolar universals for the measurement of interpersonal behavior: association–dissociation, superordination–subordination, intimacy–formality, and overt–covert behavior.

The first two dimensions refer to stylistic features of interpersonal behavior (DeVoge & Beck, 1978). Whether one considers the over manifestations of a specific interpersonal act (such as voice tone, message content, manner, body gestures) or by contrast seeks to organize social behavior around broad, underlying factors, these two emerge repeatedly as the dimensions which define the universe of interpersonal behavior. Briefly, association–dissociation refers to the distinction between behaviors which are friendly, cooperative, or affiliative in nature and behaviors which are unfriendly, hostile, competitive, or disaffiliative. Similarly, superordinate–subordinate distinguishes behaviors which are assertive, active, or dominant from those which are submissive, passive, or dependent.

The intimacy–formality dimension refers to a contrast about the extent to which occasions (or situations) for social behavior exert an influence on the behaviors performed in them. Accordingly, situations might be classified by the relative amount of behavioral *constraint* they exert (Endler & Magnusson, 1976; Magnusson & Endler, 1977; Price & Bouffard, 1974; Schneider, 1973). In formal situations constraint is significant, and behaviors tend to be similar across individuals. Conversely, the distinguishing feature of intimate situations is their absence of constraint. Under these circumstances, situational factors are relatively unimportant, behavior being determined primarily by the participants.

For example, the groom at a wedding is expected to express, among other intentions, his affection for the bride. Yet during the ceremony his behaviors for doing this are limited (constrained) to a few rehearsed statements and a brief embrace. Alone with his bride after the ceremony, his affectionate behavior, no longer constrained by formality, is apt to assume different forms. Privately, the primary constraining factor on the groom's behavior, if any, would be the behavior of the bride.

The intimate–formal polarity shares similar characteristics with the distinction drawn between "manded" and "tacted" behaviors (Bem, 1967; Skinner, 1958; Tedeschi, Schlenker, & Bonoma, 1971). The basis for this distinction is an individual's subjective impression of the amount of personal freedom he has regarding his behavior in a given circumstance. To the extent that there is perceived external pressure to perform a specific set of responses, behavior would be manded. In the absence of this pressure, performed behaviors would be tacted.

The final dimension discussed by Triandis referred to the distinction between covert and overt interpersonal behaviors. While the distinction is not conceptually difficult, and both kinds of behavior have been studied by psychologists, they have rarely been investigated in the same studies (Triandis, 1978). As a result, not much is known about the relationships between overt and covert social behavior, even though this relationship has been the focus of interesting speculation (e.g., Powers, 1973). For our present purposes, it is sufficient to keep in mind that the dimension of overt–covert is a universal social phenomenon.

Together, these four "universal" dimensions offer a conceptual framework for interapersonal behavior. While this framework would be primarily only a descriptive system for classifying interpersonal responses, these dimensions have been used as the building blocks for interpersonal theories which attempt to explain more of the "dynamics" of social behavior as well. In one particular interpersonal theory, the Leary system (Carson, 1969; Hine, 1972; Leary, 1957), seven of the eight polar positions are given systematic representation (those positions being association, dissociation, superordination, subordination, intimacy, overt, and covert). In other words, the domain of the Leary system is the social behavior of human beings in relatively intimate encounters. The theory has recently been extended to include speculations about possible links between covert operations and overt actions (Carson, 1969, in press; DeVoge & Beck, 1978). This theoretical account not only rests on a surprising amount of empirical support, but more important to our present purposes, casts the matter of unfavorable transfer of training in an interpersonal perspective.

The Leary System

The Leary system is a schema for the classification of interpersonal responses and the relationships among those responses. Descriptively, the classification is structured within a circular space defined by the intersection of two bipolar, independent dimensions essentially similar to association–dissociation (labeled love–hate in the Leary system) and superordinate–subordinate (called dominance–submission). There has been considerable empirical evidence substantiating this two-factor description of interpersonal behavior (Benjamin, 1974; Berzins, Welling, & Wetter, 1978; Briar & Bieri, 1963; Mehrabian, 1972; Rinn, 1965; Triandis, 1978; Wiggins & Holzmuller, 1978; Wish, Deutsch, & Kaplan, 1976; Berzins, Welling, & Wetter, Note 2). Even analyses of social behavior among animals have indicated that these dimensions best account for the behavioral variance (Mason, 1964; Zajonc, 1972). So, at least descriptively, the Leary system seems to rest on factors of consensual validity.

In the Leary classification these two dimensions are typically grouped into four quadrants around the circular space, each quadrant consisting of one pole of the love–hate dimension and one of the dominance–submission dimension (Carson, 1969; DeVoge & Beck, 1978). Thus the quadrants have been referred to as friendly dominance, friendly submission, hostile submission, and hostile dominance, respectively.

Briefly, friendly dominance refers to a response class consisting of behaviors that communicate (to others) the sender's sense of self-confidence, strength, or competence along with warm feelings toward the receiver. Offers of help, guidance, leadership, or sympathy would be included in this category. Similarly, friendly submissive behaviors convey a feeling of warmth, but in the context of weakness rather than strength. Examples of this category are deferent cooperation, dependency, and agreeability.

The weakness message continues in the hostile submissive quadrant, but mixed with an unfriendly set toward self and others. Self-doubt, cynicism, and wariness of others are included here, the overall social impact constituting a message of "I'm not OK, and you're not OK either" (Harris, 1967). The unfriendly set toward others continues in hostile dominance, but paired with a self-reference of strength or pride. The sarcasm, narcissism, or sadistic features of this category communicate to others a message of "I'm OK, but you're not."

As was mentioned previously, in studies investigating the variability of social behavior dominance–submission and love–hate emerge as the two independent dimensions which best account for observed variance. While research of this kind establishes validity for these dimensions at an abstract level, the results of other studies indicate that these dimensions can be distinguished at lower levels of abstraction as well. For example, warm–cold is a distinction frequently mentioned by behaviorists in theoretical discussions involving a therapist's behavioral style. This dimension has been the focus of study in behavioral laboratories for years in studies ranging from verbal operant conditioning to systematic desensitization (e.g., McGlynn, 1976; Morris & Suckerman, 1974, 1976; Namanek & Schuldt, 1971; Reece & Whitman, 1962; Vitalo, 1970). While dominance–submission has not received the amount of scientific attention in the behavioral literature that has been given warm–cold comparisons, nonetheless promising operational differentiations exist in the literature for concepts related to this dimension, such as "expert" versus "inexpert" (Schmidt & Strong, 1970; Strong & Schmidt, 1970). Furthermore, in studies more directly concerned with Leary phenomena, it has been shown repeatedly that these dimensions can be reliably observed by raters (Dittman, 1958; Heller, Myers, & Kline, 1963; Raush, Dittman, & Taylor, 1959; Raush, Farbman, & Llewellyn, 1960; Shannon & Guerney, 1973). In view of this evidence, it seems reasonable to speculate that these dimensions constitute useful response classes whose characteristics can be meaninfully separated from each other. As such, they offer the a priori grounds for predicting covariation between discrete responses, a possibility disclaimed by Wahler (Note 1).

Characteristics of Response Classes. In addition to their descriptive distinctiveness, Leary response classes have been presumed to bear interesting relationships among one another. The organizing concept for these interrelationsips is the principle of *reciprocality* (Carson, 1969; DeVoge & Beck, 1978; Leary, 1957). According to this principle, one characteristic of a response class is its tendency to pull from a social context a predictable consequential response. In other words, a person behaving in a manner consistent with one of the Leary quadrants is likely to elicit from others a particular quadrant-type behavior in their counter-response. While there are several reasons to predict that this elicited response will not be uniform (including such phenomena as intense situational constraint, inability of the receiving person to perform the reciprocal response, etc.), nonetheless the theory suggests that each Leary category will elicit, by and large, a most likely response from others. While Leary (1957) speculated that these relationships might be uniform to the extent of resembling reflexive, automatic behavior, it would appear more empirically accurate, given situational and personal limitations, to consider reciprocal responses as "modal" elicited responses.

In terms of the Leary dimensions, like poles are believed to be reciprocal for love–hate phenomena while unlike poles are thought to be reciprocal for dominance-submission. More specifically, love is reciprocal to love and hate is reciprocal to hate, while submission is reciprocal to dominance and vice versa. In an interaction, then, a person behaving in a friendly, loving manner will most likely elicit friendly behavior from others, while a person behaving in an unfriendly manner will tend to elicit hostility in exchange. By contrast, a person behaving in a dominant fashion will most likely elicit submissive behaviors from others, while a person engaging others in a submissive style will likely elicit dominant behaviors in return.

If we examine reciprocality in terms of Leary *quadrants,* the following relationships emerge. For friendly dominance, the reciprocal response would be friendly submission (like pole for friendliness, opposite pole for dominance). Likewise, for friendly submission the reciprocal response is friendly dominance. The same relationships hold for hostile dominance and hostile submission (that is, they should be mutually reciprocal).

In several studies general support for these response–response bonds has been obtained. For example, both Shannon and Guerney (1973) and Heller et al. (1963) found results mainly in line with these theoretical hypotheses, although there seemed to be some difficulty in eliciting hostile dominance from college students (except as a response to hostile dominane; Shannon & Guerney, 1973). In addition, both Kelley and Stahelski (1970) and Raush et al. (1960) discovered that these reciprocal relationships held particularly well for friendliness and unfriendliness. In some ways the study by Heller et al. (1963) has special pertinence to the area of psychotherapy, because the reciprocal effects occurred in interviewers as the result of "programmed" behaviors from clients.

Characteristics of Social Exchanges. Another way of conceptualizing the implications of the Leary system is to consider the available possibilities by Leary criteria for an ongoing social exchange. To reiterate, friendly dominance and friendly submission were formulated to be mutually reciprocal, as were hostile dominance and hostile submission. What this means at the level of social exchanges is that either category of a mutually reciprocal pair could elicit its reciprocal, which as a further consequence should elicit more of the original, and so on. Thus we might think of a mutually reciprocal pair of response classes as being mutually *eliciting* and *sustaining*.

Using Leary criteria, there are two kinds of social exchanges which could therefore achieve the status of an *ongoing* social exchange—friendly-dominant/friendly submissive, and hostile-dominant/hostile-submissive (DeVoge & Beck, 1978). Thus if a person wishes to enter into an ongoing exchange in which he would send, say, hostile dominance, he would "need" to encounter someone willing to engage him from a position of hostile submission. If any other class of response (other than hostile submission) were to follow hostile dominance, the hostile dominant behavior would not be eliciting a reciprocal response, hence would not be sustained itself. In such cases it is doubtful that the encounter would endure long enough to achieve any "ongoing" status (Carson, in press). The same process can be used to speculate about any response class behaviors sent in a social exchange. Either the response class is reciprocated by the receiver's subsequent behavior (which opens up the possibility of an ongoing exchange) or it is not reciprocated by the receiver's actions (which either closes out the exchange or offers exchange possibilities of a different kind).

These two kinds of social exchanges offer four options for the individual wishing to get involved in an ongoing exchange. On the friendly side, a person can be dominant (send help, advice, leadership, support) with a submissive partner (who in return sends admiration, dependency, cooperative following), or he can be submissive with a dominant partner. Likewise, in a hostile exchange one could be dominant (send narcissism, criticism, rebuke, rejection, or attack) with a submissive partner (who in return sends self-rebuke, resentment, disappointment, or defeat), or submissive with a dominant partner. Any forms of exchange involving nonreciprocal response classes will either be short-lived or eventually resolve along reciprocal lines.

Characteristics of Persons. In the Leary system, a person could be conceptualized on the basis of a response repertoire regarding the four response classes. Whereas some people are equipped with a variety of responses under each response class (even though some classes may be better supplied than others), other people may be grossly undersupplied in some classes. When a person demonstrates a range of different response classes in his overt behavior, especially when a variety of behaviors appears without undue environmental pressure to perform certain classes of responses, the term "flexible" is applied to that person's behavior (DeVoge & Beck, 1978). In the absence of behavioral variety, a person's behavior is defined as "rigid."

The major aspect of behavioral rigidity is that it should result in a fairly narrow experience (with others) for the person so behaving (Carson, in press). In other words, through exchange processes dependent on reciprocality, a person behaving in a rigid fashion should generate a fairly uniform response from others, particularly from those of long-standing relationships. In a sense, rigid people, through the uniformity of their own behavior, come to constrain the exchange options of others, and thereby also restrict their own future options.

This constraining phenomenon may constitute a particular problem for persons whose behavior is rigidly hostile or submissive (or both). Available evidence suggests that rigidly hostile or submissive behaving may result in a greater amount of subsequent restriction than friendly or dominant behaving (Carson, in press). For example, dominant behaviors may be countered by reciprocal submission or a dominant challenge (e.g., Shannon & Guerney, 1973). For instance, a person issuing a command may receive refusal or compliance from another person. However, it is difficult to imagine an exchange in which submissive responses are countered by other submissive responses. In such an encounter, one would wonder just who would intiate, since both may be attempting to follow the other's lead. Probably such exchangs occur, but do not endure long enough to get much of an exchange underway. Likewise, friendly responses may be reciprocated with friendliness or demonstrated that hostility will be primarily countered through reciprocal hostility (Kelley & Stahelski, 1970; Raush et al., 1960). Even when paired with a person who is likely to respond in a cooperative manner it takes but a brief encounter before the rigidly hostile person begins to elicit reciprocal hostility from his partner (Kelley & Stahelski, 1970).

Thus the consequences of behaving in a rigid manner are dependent on the form of that rigid behavior. The most uniform experience that a person has with others will result from personal behavior which is rigidly hostile or submissive. As a result of the restriction in other's behavior concomitant with rigid hostility or submission, the rigidly hostile or submissive actor will over time accumulate experiences with others which (by comparison with a flexible actor) are statistically skewed or biased. In particular, his experience will be deficient in the reception of friendliness and/or submission from others (Carson, in press).

Unfortunately, in all probability this bias is not limited to a person's overt experience with others. If we consider that a person's cognitive activity regarding others is at least influenced by his firsthand experience with them, then it follows that experiential biases will result in cognitive biases as well (DeVoge & Beck, 1978), a hypothesis that has received empirical support (Golding, 1977; Kelley & Stahelski, 1970; Golding, Note 3). In general, these cognitive biases tend to parallel the kinds of biases present in an individual's experience with others (Carson, in press; DeVoge & Beck, 1978). In other words, persons whose behavior is rigidly hostile, for example, tend to "recognize," and perhaps even anticipate, more hostility (in others' behavior) than friendliness. Likewise, rigidly submissive people tend toward perceptual biases emphasizing dominance in others. Thus one cognitive result of behaving rigidly is a tendency to overperceive familiar behavior in others (i.e., reciprocal behavior) and underperceive unfamiliar (nonreciprocal) behavior.

It is also likely that these kinds of cognitive biases have a tendency to result in "self-fulfilling prophecies" (Merton, 1948). Whether it is speculated that because of a well-defined perceptual bias an individual is made uncomfortable by nonconfirming evidence (e.g., Powers, 1973), or simply selectively attends to confirming evidence (Sullivan, 1953), it has been demonstrated that these biases tend to create the social reality they predict (Snyder & Swann, 1978; Snyder, Tanke, & Berscheid, 1977). In other words, even when an attribution regarding another person is incorrect, a perceiver may act in such a way as to elicit from the other a confirming set of behaviors.

The net result of this dual behavioral-cognitive bias is that a rigid individual operates on his social environment in ways which serve to maintain his rigidity. If we consider the rigidly hostile person in this contxt, the circularity of his predicament becomes obvious. In the first place, he behaves in a way which tends to elicit only hostile resposes from others. In turn, these hostile behaviors from others increase the likelihood of his future hostility, and so on. All the while, his ability to perceive others' behavior accurately is restricted to a hostile range of behaviors, a bias which also tends to delimit his behavior as well as his evaluation of others' actions. In essence, his entire behavioral-cognitive apparatus is geared to function most elaborately in the context of hostile–hostile exchanges.

If it is also assumed that a person is an organism who can plan, reflect, etc. (e.g., Mischel, 1973, 1976), it is quite likely that these activities, at least as they are applied to interpersonal matters, reflect the same biases apparent in one's overt behavior and interpersonal percepts.

Carson (1969) has used the term "tactics" to apply to sequences of exchange behavior in which overt responses are deployed by an individual in order to elicit perception-confirming behaviors from others. For the rigid individual, tactics may involve long, complex sequences, utilizing more than one response class, but they *eventuate* in a familiar exchange. At any rate, the purpose of these maneuvers is to reduce uncertainty associated with exchanges unfamiliar to the individual by causing others' behavior to meet preexisting percepts (Carson, 1969; Leary, 1957; Powers, 1973).[1] For example, a person who prefers hostile exchanges and outcomes with others may engage *temporarily* in friendly-friendly transactions with those others. However, as friendliness continues over time, the person will likely become uncomfortable with the lack of hostility in the encounter and begin maneuvers to alter the exchange into a hostile outcome. Berne's (1964) games of RAPO and NIGYSOB are examples of just such maneuvering.

Thus rigidity may not be defined solely in terms of a limited overt response repertoire. At a tactical level, while a person may demonstrate some discrete response flexibility, rigidity may manifest itself as a recurrent outcome with others which terminates a series or sequence of transactions.

Implications for Transfer of Training

In the main, behavior modification attempts to change observable behavior. From the perspective of dyadic phenomena, a salient issue concerns the *consequences* of an altered overt repertoire due to the effects of behavior therapy. In this regard, complications may be expected because changes in overt behaviors produce reciprocal changes in others' behavior. These reciprocal changes may be anxiety producing because they are misunderstood or because, while generally regarded as socially desirable, they are often *not* individually preferable.

For the flexible client, the consequences of change seem fairly straightforward. Possessing a relatively unconstricted view of others (stemming from his already more varied experience with others), this individual is able to perceive accurately the change in others resulting from his own changed response. In all likelihood, the perceived change in others simply signals to the flexible perceiver the opportunity for a different exchange, one that could be expected to be more socially, as well as individually, desirable. In this case the goals of therapy would be compatible with the goals of the client, and therapeutically acquired change could be expected to endure (i.e., transfer) beyond treatment.

For the rigid client things seem a bit more complicated. If therapy results in an altered overt repertoire without concomitant changes in covert operations, then reciprocal changes in others' responses are *not* likely to be perceived accurately. Even if newly reciprocal behaviors are given vague recognition as "novel" (or outside the boundaries of preexisting perceptual categories), they are likely to be experienced as confusing and discomforting since they run counter to the client's tactics. Paradoxically, therapeutic change has led the rigid individual into a dilemma. Either he must reorganize his covert repertoire to render it more synchronized with his new overt patterns, or cease to perform new behaviors in order to preserve old, familiar patterns. The simple choice in this bind is to avoid newly acquired responses.

This bind may be especially intense for clients who were rigidly hostile and/or submissive prior to therapy. Preferring exchange outcomes such as hostility, resentment, failure, or rejection, these clinets are ill-equipped to cope with responses from others which are generally reegarded as socially desirable (DeVoge & Beck, 1978). As was previously mentioned, notable in this respect are schizophrenic populations who are typified by their avoidance of socially desirable exchanges (Carson, 1971) and by their lack of responsibility to socially desirable stimulation. With these clients, it becomes likely that the goals of therapy may be incompatible with their own tactical "goals," making it doubtful that newly acquired responses transfer beyond treatment.

These speculations hinge, of course, on the possibility that overt responses can be altered in treatment without accompanying covert changes. From an interactional view, this possibility may depend on the degree of similarity between the treatment setting and the posttreatment social setting, a relationship previously noted as important for transfer (Goldstein, Sprafkin, & Gershaw, 1976). In short, a critical parameter of treatment may be the extent to which the performance of a response in treatment resembles the performance of that response in a social context. The more treatment settings differ from the social context, the less likely they are to expose the client to enough contextual features to enable joint behavioral-cognitive changes to take place. From interpersonal theory, the hypothesis would be that when this occurs, newly acquired responses extinguish soon after treatment.

AN INTERPERSONAL APPRAISAL
OF SOME BEHAVIORAL TREATMENTS

Admittedly, it is impossible to ascertain precisely all that is "learned" in any therapeutic program. However, it is possible to make inferences about how much is learned from an account of the number of contextual elements present in a particular instructional paradigm. At least, as the number of critical elements increases, the opportunities for learning enlarge. By contrast, the absence of specific elements should preclude learning about any phenomena involving those elements.

Since several important elements of social behavior have been identified (Triandis, 1978), these "universals" will serve as a basis for evaluating some behavioral treatments in the following analyses. From an interpersonal view, the critical aspect of treatment is the extent to which it can be assumed that tactical (cognitive) changes have occurred in treatment which will allow overt behavioral changes to be maintained posttreatment. An exception to this premise would be the instance in which an overt behavioral change was consistent with existing tactical cognitions. The likelihood of this instance's arising with a rigid client is fairly little. Especially with these clients, transfer of training may rest on the availability of tactical learning concomitant with overt behavioral training in the treatment program.

The Token Economy

Basically, this approach is the systematic application of operant technology suitable for controlled settings. An appealing feature of the token economy is that the procedures can be adapted to a wide range of behaviors and treatment settings without wholesale alteration. Another advantage of token economics is their applicability to groups of clients as well as to individuals (cf. Chapter 2).

In this treatment model the formula for behavioral change consists of arranging the environmental contingencies so that desirable behavior results in reward while undesirable behavior leads to no reward or punishment. Reward typically consists of portable "tokens" (or tickets, points, chips, etc.) which can be exchanged for nonsocial reinforcers such as food, cigarettes, or opportunities to participate in preferred activities. Although punishments are usually held to a minimum, elimination of extremely undesirable behaviors may be facilitated through response cost or time-out procedures.

Especially with severely disturbed clients, the most common strategy in token economies is to begin clients on a reward system which emphasizes exclusively the tokens and their backup reinforcers. Over time, praise is introduced as a stimulus paired with tokens, and in many cases no doubt derives some of its reinforcing "value" through this pairing (classical conditioning). While not done routinely, it is nonetheless possible with this arrangement to fade token reinforcement once praise has become an established reward, leaving praise as the sole reinforcer.

Using token reinforcement contingencies, behaviors representative of any Leary quadrant could conceivably be targeted and modified, since these procedures seem well suited to deal with the overt responses of clients. However, despite their adaptability to a variety of social responses, token economies offer clients very little in the way of social exchange.

First of all, the most salient social outcome in these systems is praise, a response with distinctly friendly dominant characteristics (Davis, 1971; DeVoge & Beck, 1978; Jones, 1964). While friendly dominance may be reciprocal for a range of behaviors associated with acting in a friendly manner (quite possibly a therapeutic goal for many clients in token programs), it is not reciprocal for responses which require a client to behave more assertively (show initiative, refuse unreasonable requests, etc.). In fact, it is difficult to imagine just how a token economy prepares a client for being more dominant in a social context. In the present reveiw of the literature there was no clear evidence of a token program in which dominant responses from clients resulted in contingent submissive responses from program staff. More typical were attempts to fade the trappings of the token program near the end of treatment to help the client become more independent of external contingencies and begin to evaluate his own performance. While such tactics may help a client gain experience with his own independence, they do not guarantee that the client obtains experience with others' compliance or submissiveness, a critical occurrence if dominance responses are to transfer. Moreover, there is the danger during this phase of treatment that if the staff's response (to the client's independence) becomes less praising in style, the client will experience the alteration as punishing (because of the conditioned reward value of praise). On the other hand, if the staff continues to praise independence, the client remains in an artificial environment strikingly different from social context realities.

Second, even though friendly dominance is reciprocal for many kinds of cooperative client responses, the type of friendly dominance offered in token economies is an unlikely imitation of responses which will be encountered socially. For one, these friendly dominance responses are delivered in the context of an extremely formal exchange system. Not only is the response specifically delimited to a few verbalizations (okay, fine, good) plus a smile and friendly tone, but the rules for its occurrence are clearly spelled out (i.e., the operational contingencies of the program) and prominently displayed in the program setting. In fact, formality in the delivery of response consequences is a hallmark of token systems. As a result, a client is in the position of knowing exactly what to expect in these exchanges, a phenomenon not likely (particularly for a client who may have formerly operated in a rigidly hostile manner) in the less formal exchange patterns of a social context.

Furthermore, in the token program these friendly dominant staff responses tend to signal the termination of the exchange sequence. In other words, once the praise has been delivered, the contingency has been completed. While such a pattern of exchange fulfills the requirements of an operant conditioning model, it falls short of an adequate learning experience for positive social intimacy. For example, it could be expected that if a client became skilled at behaving in a friendlier manner, someone in his social context will, in the process of reciprocating friendliness, invite the client into an ongoing positive exchange. To a client inexperienced with friendly intimacy, any failure of the friendly exchange to terminate immediately may constitute a significant contrast with token economy experiences, and could provide a source of aversive stimulation.

In summary, the resemblance between a token economy and a social context is less than striking. While any response class may conceivably be modified in such a program, these systems offer no reciprocal exchange opportunities for dominance responses. Further, those friendly behaviors which occur contingent on friendly client responses tend to be overly formal and brief. In short, token systems do not typically offer a client the chance to learn about others' submissive or friendly intimacy.

Assertion Training

Assertion training is a clinical application of operant conditioning and modeling principles aimed primarily at overt behavior change. While the direction of change is often toward friendlier responses in clients who are too hostile (Fensterheim & Baer, 1975; Hersen & Bellack, 1976; Hersen, Eisler, & Miller, 1973; Lazarus, 1971), the most frequent goal of assertion training is to help passive individuals behave more actively, dominantly, independently, or assertively. With a heavy emphasis on the client's performance skill, the bulk of this behavioral change program involves role-playing and behavioral rehearsal as "practice" vehicles. Within practice sessions, repeated use is made of behavioral shaping and contingent praise.

For example, in a typical assertion training episode, a "scene" may be created which resembles a real-life situation with which the client has admitted having had prior coping difficulties. After appraising the client's current performance in the scene, the therapist would outline an appropriate assertive response for the client, to replace less adaptive responses. During subsequent rehearsals, the client would be encouraged to perform the new response. Adequate performance of the assertive response would be followed by praise, while inadequate performance would usually result in more practice and rehearsal. For responses that are quite difficult for the client to perform, shaping procedures could be introduced to help him acquire the response gradually. This procedure would also increase the likelihood that the partial response would be performed adequately, thereby increasing the probability that the client would receive praise for his efforts.

If necessary (for example, to enlist the cooperation of a difficult client), assertion training techniques can be blended with tokens or non-social rewards. However, assertion training is frequently much less formal than a token system, especially in the delivery of response consequences. For example, in contrast to the rigorously formalized delivery of praise in token economies, in assertion training there are few rules governing the administration of praise other than making it contingent on adequate performance by the client. Rather, in assertion training formal emphasis is placed on the client's skill in the performance of the assertive response, not on the behavior of the therapist. Accordingly, the therapist may assume a variety of roles vis-à-vis the client, including instructor, coach, model, co-actor, and eventually, reinforcing agent. It is interesting to note that most of these roles for the therapist are dominant ones, in that he advises, instructs, demonstrates, and evaluates.

Interpersonally, the noteworthy aspect of assertion training is the paradox created by requiring a passive client to perform dominance responses in order to obtain friendly dominance (praise) as an outcome. Overtly, such a procedure is in keeping with the principles of operant conditioning, and should produce a significant change in the client's repertoire, the goal of assertion training. Ostensibly, once new responses are acquired which can be skillfully performed, and which lead to successful experiences with others (such as their compliance or respect), such responses should be retained posttreatment. In fact, to facilitate performance of new behavior, one clinical behavioral source recommends that a therapist take particular care to discuss new outcomes with a client, to help him recognize the positive benefits of his new behaviors (Goldfried & Davison, 1976).

Nonetheless, at a tactical level this procedure results in complexities which may interfere with posttreatment performance. To follow another's (therapist's) directions, or to perform responses another has requested, places one in a compliant (submissive) position vis-à-vis that other, *regardless* of the stylistic features of the particular responses (e.g., Haley, 1963). When one receives praise as a result of his compliance, and increases his performance of responses which lead to further praise, the exchange epitomizes a friendly-dominant/friendly-submissive interaction. Thus, in an assertion training paradigm the client can become enmeshed in the situational paradox of performing stylistically dominant responses while remaining in a submissive position to the therapist. When this paradox predominates the treatment relationship, assertion training does not reflect social realities and does not provide the formerly passive client with an opportunity to grow comfortable with others' submission to him. Pointing out the "positive" benefits of assertive behavior to such a client is not likely to correct this treatment deficiency.

Dyadic Contracting

Among the techniques of behavioral therapy there is no operant conditioning treatment which is more closely attuned to dyadic processes than marital contracting (e.g., Azrin, Naster, & Jones, 1973; Jacobsen & Weiss, 1978; Lederer & Jackson, 1968; Patterson, Hops, & Weiss, 1975; Stuart, 1969; Weiss, Birchler, & Vincent, 1974). Combining the social exchange theory of Thibaut and Kelley (1959) with the operant parameters of stimulus and reinforcement control, the theory supporting dyadic contracting is an interpersonal one employing a conceptual language similar to the one being used in this chapter. While these authors attach some different meanings to similar terms, and vice versa, their theoretical ideas are nonetheless interpersonal by design. And while they theoretically underplay person factors in a traditionally operant fashion, in treatment there is a clear focus on the interpersonal cognitive plans (i.e., the "strategies" of reinforcement) between marital partners (Stuart, 1969; Weiss et al., 1974). In several ways marital contracting procedures deal with social "universals."

Regarding dyadic phenomena in marriage, marital contract therapists have identified two interactional patterns of social reinforcement: reciprocity and coercion (Patterson & Hops, 1972; Patterson & Reid, 1970; Stuart, 1969). Reciprocity as used here denotes a marital relationship in which partners attempt to maximize mutual benefits and rewards while minimizing penalties. This pattern has been found to be more typical of successful marriages than of unsuccessful ones (Wills, Weiss, & Patterson, 1974; Birchler, Weiss, & Wampler, Note 4). Operationally, in a "reciprocal" relationship the partners exchange pleasurable outcomes in a far greater ratio than they exchange unpleasantries, a pattern equivalent to a love-love relationship. By contrast, in a coercive pattern partners exchange a low rate of rewards and basically attempt to minimize punishment. Sequentially, coercive tactics involve one partner's aversive request for a positive outcome (e.g., "I will stop nagging you if you carry out the garbage") followed by the other partner's resentful compliance, escalation, or withdrawal. Typical of unsuccessful marriages, this pattern meets definitional requirements for a hate-hate transaction.

Beginning with the assumption that married persons are more attracted to (prefer) pleasant exchanges (Stuart, 1969), marital contract therapists attempt to move marital interactions away from coercive patterns toward predominantly reciprocal ones. This is done primarily through a series of negotiated two-party agreements called "contracts." In addition, a fair amount of preparatory work is done with the couple before formalized contracts are drawn up. Notable in this regard are didactic lessons about the observational bases of "personality" impressions held by each partner regarding the other, and the interactional logic of altering one's own behavior in order to witness a change in a spouse's behavior. From these lessons, clients are supposed to learn an expanded view of the outcomes possible with their spouses and the interpersonal contingencies involved with each outcome. According to the thesis being developed in this chapter, these are the critical covert changes which must accompany lasting overt changes. In addition, attention is focused on negotiating skills, especially the specific, descriptive communication between partners of particular spouse behaviors and their subjective stimulus values. This style of interpersonal communication seems identical to the style of feedback promoted by sensitivity (t-group) trainers (e.g., National Training Laboratories, Note 5). To the extent that precontract training renders partners more equal in negotiating skills and/or encourages more passive partners to become more vocal, it may serve to lessen the extent of dominance-submission polarities in these relationships (Eisler, Miller, Hersen & Alford, 1974).

Two different kinds of contracts have been used in this treatment model. The first, called a quid pro quo model, is nothing more than an explicit "this for that" agreement between partners (Lederer & Jackson, 1968; Stuart, 1969). Each spouse agrees to accelerate the delivery of one (or more) positive payoffs to the other spouse contingent on some accelerations by the other spouse. While conceptually simpler, quid pro quo contracts have the disadvantage of being vulnerable to sabotage by the failure of either partner to carry out the negotiated behaviors (Weiss et al., 1974). Because of this mutual stimulus control explicit in the quid pro quo, there is no way for partners to work on their accelerations independently, a factor which could undermine therapy, especially in the initial stages.

This drawback can be circumvented in the second kind of contract, the "good faith" model (Weiss et al., 1974). Under this agreement, each partner agrees to specific accelerations not made contingent on the other partner's negotiated accelerations. While contingencies can be added to the contract as incentives, targeted accelerations are not contingency linked between spouses.

Although contracting methods seem quite formal, along a formal–informal dimension, methods have been devised for shaping some degree of informality. For example, Stuart (1969) has made the suggestion of using token reinforcement within a quid pro quo contract. This would permit immediate reward for spouse accelerations, a maneuver which may be helpful early in contractng with couples largely void of reciprocity. Over time, tokens can be faded and quid pro quo arrangments made increasingly noncontiguous. Likewise, Weiss et al. (1974) have recommended good faith contracts supplemented initially with contingencies for nonsocial rewards from the therapist. This strategy avoids one spouse's becoming a punishment agent for the other, yet permits maintenance of contingency controls with any spouse reluctant to change. Therapist contingencies can be faded in favor of simpler good faith bargains involving only the marriage partners.

In summary, dyadic contracting appears to be a significant improvement over individualized operant methods toward sound interpersonal treatment. The procedures deal directly with overt–covert, formal–informal, and love–hate issues, and at least indirectly with dominance–submission. In addition, these methods engage the matter of transfer of training in a unique manner. By working with the marital dyad and fading the therapist from the negotiating process, a treatment situation is created which maximally resembles optimal posttreatment conditions. Thus performing new responses in treatment becomes highly similar to performing them after treatment. While additional research is needed to determine if this approach does facilitate transfer (Greer & D'Zurilla, 1975), preliminary data suggest favorable results (e.g., Hickok & Komechak, 1974; Rappaport & Harrell, 1972).

Nonetheless, from an interpersonal perspective there remains one stumbling block with this model. In all their attention to dyadic phenomena, these authors have failed to account for dyadic processes which operate between client and therapist (Gurman & Knudson, 1978). While this oversight may be of no consequence with fairly flexible clients who simply have established coercive relationships with their spouses, it could pose problems for rigidly hostile clients, who are not likely to cooperate in treatment with a therapist. Indeed, these may well be the spouses who refuse to enter marital therapy. Although marriages involving such people probably involve a high degree of coercion, it is doubtful that rigidly hostile clients would accept didactic explanations of interpersonal change, especially if delivered by a warm, friendly therapist. Nor would they be expected to deal openly about their real preferences for spouse behavior. In fact, the whole idea of negotiating a more "pleasant" relationship may be aversive to them.

These possibilities lead to the speculation that marital contracting may have its maximum benefits with less rigid couples. Some limited findings lend credence to this hypothesis. Vincent (1972) for example, found that in a sample of couples fairly representative of the kinds of subjects employed in marital contracting research, spouses from distressed marriages displayed normal problem-solving skills when paired with cross-sexed strangers. Actually, few results attest to the efficacy of this approach with severely disturbed couples (Gurman & Kniskern, 1978), the bulk of the evidence being limited to couples with "mild to moderate" distress (Jacobsen & Weiss, 1978). Furthermore, Wiemann, Shoulders, and Faar (1974), in comparing effects of contracting on behaviors with which a couple had either prior skill or prior skill deficits, found diminished results with the latter behaviors. This result was manifest in spite of extensive didactic counseling to "ready" the couple for contracting with these behaviors. This finding casts particular doubt on the effectiveness of didactic methods for correcting severe disturbance (Greer & D'Zurilla, 1975).

Procedures to Reduce Avoidance Behavior

One symptom which has attracted an abundance of behavioral attention is the avoidance of normally nontreating stimuli by individuals who claim to be excessively fearful of such stimuli. Several types of avoidance reduction treatments are currently available including extinction, flooding, implosion, and the modern prototype for these methods, systematic desensitization (Marks, 1972; McNamara, 1972; Morganstern, 1973; Stampfl & Levis, 1967, 1968; Wolpe, 1958, 1973; Wolpe & Lazarus, 1966). While all these procedures represent strategies for reducing anxiety through repeated presentation of the phobic stimuli to the client, debate about the theoretical underpinnings of these techniques has consumed volumes (Nay, 1976; Yates, 1975). The main differences among these treatments involve the presence or absence of relaxation training, the use or nonuse of hypothetical material, the order of presentation of phobic stimuli, and the presentation of stimuli through imagery or in vivo.

Arguments abound regarding the actual curative elements in these procedures, no doubt reflecting both the number of treatment elements involved and the fairly arbitrary manner in which procedural rules have been laid down by originators. In addition, research in the area is clouded by the likelihood of differential responsiveness of high- and low-fearful persons (Borkovec, 1972, 1973) coupled with the fact that a preponderance of results has come from analogue studies employing low-fearful subjects (Nay, 1976). Furthermore, especially with systematic desensitization, it appears that major alterations in procedure can occur without significant decrements in outcome (Yates, 1975).

Needless to say, given these amorphous conditions procedural differences have captured most of the attention of researchers mainly interested in comparative effects. Interpersonally, however, similarities involved in these treatments seem more interesting. For one, all of these treatments deal with phobic symptoms. From an interpersonal vantage, a phobic symptom is an expression of submission (Andrews, 1966; Leary, 1957), so much so in fact that even early behavioral formulators suggested assertive responses as counteractive of excessive fearfulness (Salter, 1949; Wolpe, 1958). Nay (1976) has referred to approach behavior as indicative to peers of bravery or mastery. In essence, a phobic symptom signals to others that the phobic individual is *unable* to behave like others because of the debilitating effects of the phobia. Through claims of poignant helplessness, phobic individuals can become quite manipulative of others' behavior (Haley, 1963), restricting them to reciprocal dominance behavior. Features of this kind of exchange can be observed frequently in psychiatric clinics, for example when physicians decide that a phobic "must" be given additional medication or treatment in order to prevent further psychological deterioration, or when family members try unsuccessfully to escape from forced patterns of excessive caregiving (e.g., Hand & Lamontagne, 1976).

Given this quality of clinically phobic behavior, it is not surprising that the typical posture outlined for the therapist using these techniques is one of considerable dominance. In all of these treatments the client is guided and instructed actively by the therapist, being told precisely what to do and how to do it at virtually every step in the treatment procedure. The therapist provides relaxation training, determines most of the order, magnitude, and duration of stimuli presentation, and presents the imagined scenes. In addition, therapist praise and approval probably accompany most client progress (Nay, 1976). Even in procedural variations in which the therapist is partially or completely removed (e.g., Lang,

Melamed, & Hart, 1971), directional input is merely transferred to tape-recorded instructions.

Thus, as in assertion training, the client is in the paradox of performing assertive responses in order to remain compliant with a dominant other. Fortunately, this paradox may not be altogether different from social realities that occur posttreatment. In some cases, phobic stimuli are nonsocial (open spaces, closed places, heights, animals, etc.) objects that are not associated with the performance of behaviors which are also feared by the client. Certainly most snake phobias among college students fit this category. Moreover, as approach behavior is witnessed by intimate associates aware of the client's phobia, they are likely to give praise to the client contingent on the approach behavior. In these instances, performance in therapy leads to consequences similar to those of performance in the social context, conditions which should facilitate transfer even among quite rigid clients.

However, in some clinical phobias the feared objects are intimately intertwined with the performance of feared behaviors (Lazarus, 1971). Witness, for example, the corporate executive who is afraid to fly on airplanes because company flights often lead to business encounters in which he must make independent decisions, an activity he dreads. In general, transfer should be deleteriously influenced in any situation in which a rigidly submissive client is being desensitized to stimuli which elicit dominance responses. None of these treatments includes dominance training, other than approach behavior, and none includes helping the submissive client prepare for others' submission, should he or she perform dominance responses. Similar predicaments might face rigidly hostile submissive clients with fears of stimuli which elicit friendly behaviors, or rigidly friendly submissive clients with fears of stimuli which elicit hostility. In any such dilemma, it must be tempting for a rigid client to try to prolong or preserve treatment in order to stay in a preferred position and avoid a nonpreferred one, maneuvers which would also diminish transfer results. It is not surprising in this context to note reports of emergent fears or exacerbations of interpersonal conflicts in fairly disturbed clients when avoidance reduction has taken place rapidly (Foa & Steketee, 1977; Hand & Lamontagne, 1976).

RECIPROCAL ROLE TRAINING

To summarize, the thesis of this chapter has been that sustained behavioral change may be undermined by the combined stress of changing overt responses and subsequently being confronted with the altered behavior of others. Old responses, even while leading to personal disenchantment, are nonetheless familiar, comfortable to perform, and by and large evaluate in predictable outcomes. While it is presumed that existing behavioral methods are sufficient to produce overt behavioral change, the goal of reciprocal role training is to enable a client to adjust to the social consequences of a newly acquired behavioral repertoire. These consequences consist of the reciprocal behaviors (i.e., reciprocal role) others will predictably assume upon exposure to the new behaviors of the client. In practice reciprocal role training will require different strategies depending on a client's position on a flexible–rigid dimension, but these strategies contain common theoretical elements despite differences in actual procedure.

Elements of Reciprocal Role Training

The various elements which constitute reciprocal role training can be divided into two groupings—procedures designed to prepare a client, interpersonally, for overt behavioral change, and procedures for supporting and maintaining overt change as it develops. Preparation for overt change consists of orienting clients in interpersonal logic, and providing them with an awareness of the alterations in their social dealings implied by the impending overt change. Maintenance procedures are a combination of exposures to newly reciprocal behavior and practice in auxiliary responses which assist the client to delve into relatively novel exchanges in a systematic rather than haphazard fashion.

The elements which prepare clients for overt change form a constellation of therapeutic activity which should serve to identify the client's role as a causal agent in troubles with others, and should result in an increase in anxiety surrounding old habitual, preferred ways of engaging others. The basic procedure in this process is negotiation between therapist and client, focused on the behavior of the client, aimed at producing a *mutual* agreement regarding the specific stylistic features of the "problem" behavior(s). In this negotiating process it is imperative that the *client* comprehend that certain responses lead to personally undesirable outcomes, and that to attain different outcomes, new behaviors are required. To ensure that this learning has occurred, the therapist can attempt to elicit clear statements from the client about these points.

When these developments have transpired in the therapeutic process, the stage is set to negotiate a specific, goal-oriented change contract, and to begin overt change maneuvers. The preparatory process should clearly establish the interpersonal rationale for overt change, and the increased anxiety with current behavior should both facilitate change and discourage reversion to old habits as change develops.

Concomitant with overt change, the therapist may initiate dialogue with the client about temptations to avoid change caused by the initial awkwardness of new behavior and the paradoxical discomfort of socially desirable but personally novel social exchanges. This kind of dialogue seems to be especially effective when the therapist *predicts* some reversion, and the reasons for it, before any reversions occur. It is also very important that the client receive reciprocal behaviors in treatment, as a preparation for posttreatment realities. This exposure helps highlight paradoxical anxiety while simultaneously working toward its extinction.

As part of the exposure to reciprocal behaviors, it may also be helpful to train the client in the use of auxiliary responses that might be called "graceful exit" responses. The function of these responses is to enable a client to avoid new exchanges which are simply too intense and intimate for him to handle, but to do so in a manner which preserves the opportunity for the exchange at a later date. These responses amount to a kind of social "rain check," and further reduce the temptation to revert to old habits in the face of desired, but anxiety-provoking outcome possibilities.

Alternate Strategies

The need for alternative strategies for reciprocal role training arises because the flexible client, compared to the rigid client, may be easier to train about social phenomena. There are several reasons why this is so. First of all, flexible clients have the advantage of a less constricted view of others' behavior. Not only should this facilitate their comprehension of the interpersonal rationale for overt change, but perhaps more important, it should help them perceive the behavior of the therapist more accurately. Specifically, to the extent that a client can comfortably engage the therapist from a position of friendly submission, the more likely it becomes that he will be influenced by the therapist in a therapeutically desired direction (DeVoge & Beck, 1978). This should also facilitate a client's acceptance of the rationale offered by the therapist and should make agreement about identification of problem behaviors easier. There is little doubt, furthermore, that a warm, directive approach by the therapist would enhance client cooperation in these instances. Finally, since they have experienced a broader range of interpersonal exchanges, reciprocal role behavior will be relatively less anxiety provoking for them, simplifying the training concomitant with overt change.

Consequently, with many flexible clients reciprocal role training can be done in a very direct manner through didactic therapist interventions akin to those described by the dyadic contract therapists (see above). This is especially true of reciprocal role training preparatory to overt change. Explanations followed by requests for the client to agree or disagree should provide adequate training for these clients. Then as these clients begin overtly changing, minimum counseling about paradoxical anxiety, plus some repeated exposure to reciprocal role behavior (through role-plays), should be sufficient to maintain the new behaviors after treatment.

However, with many rigid clients the friendly submissive position is either so aversive that cooperation and agreement are an extremely low probability, or the position is so preferable that they will emit high rates of cooperative agreement behavior regardless of the therapist's actions. In the former situation a struggle ensues because the client will not reciprocate cooperation, while in the latter case the struggle develops because the client, while agreeable, avoids any concrete approach to change (i.e., maintaining that he is too sick, weak, stupid, or crazy even to try to be different). With either type of rigid client it is doubtful that didactic maneuvers will provide adequate new learning to prepare for or maintain overt change. This is likely to be especially true regarding the early phases of treatment, wherein rigid clients will be busily attempting to structure this new relationship along old, familiar lines, maneuvers which may be expected to increase in intensity if the therapist does not fall into place along reciprocal lines.

The delicacy of the circumstances of early phases is underscored by the possibility of premature termination if reciprocal behavior is not forthcoming or by the establishment of a nontherapeutic alliance if the therapist does begin to reciprocate. Obviously, the situation calls for therapeutic maneuvering somewhere between these two extremes (clearly nonreciprocal or clearly reciprocal behaviors), these maneuvers including an avoidance of "nice guy" responses by the therapist.

The overall strategy for dealing with this situation has been thoroughly described by Cashdan (1973). The goal of this strategy is to use the current, here-and-now relationship between client and therapist as the vehicle for interpersonal learning. While the tactics to be described include some novelties, the sequencing of maneuvers is directly borrowed from Cashdan's approach. In essence, the therapist allows the relationship to develop somewhat along the lines desired by the client, but he withholds reciprocation of the client's behavior. Rather, he attempts to clarify with the client the client's tactics. Once this is done, he begins the painful process of teaching the client the limitations involved in the client's approach and the opportunities for exchange being overlooked.

The first step in this process is for the therapist to give the client the impression that a relationship of the kind preferred by the client is possible, but to do this in a nonreciprocal way. One way of doing this is for the therapist to communicate to the client his *personal interest* in the relationship, but to communicate this message in a style that to the therapist is dimensionally "neutral" (i.e., as near the midpoints of the status and affect dimensions as possible). If the maneuver is successful, the client will begin to perceive the relationship as an opportunity for a familiar exchange at an intimate level, and will begin to send out behaviors toward this end.

Usually these tactics are not communicated in clear syntax (e.g., "I want you to take care of me and protect me forever"), but the behaviors pull for a reciprocal class of responses through intense stylistic features (e.g., patient cries, bemoans his fate, makes poignant claims of helplessness). When this process is clearly underway, the next step is for the therapist to focus on these behaviors and attempt to clarify them with the client. The goal of this phase is to elicit from the client clear, undistorted statements about what he is doign vis-à-vis the therapist and what the client expects as an outcome. Mutual agreement on these points is essential.

The next step involved is for the therapist to begin leveling with the client about how the client's behavior really affects him. The critical element in this maneuver is to be able to *inform* the client of these effects without *behaving* in a manner reciprocal to the client's behavior. Such responses have been called "asocial" responses (Beier, 1966; Carson, 1969) because of their lack of reciprocal social value to the client. Tactically, Cashdan (1973) has described the maneuver as refutation–affirmation; the behavior of the client is refuted, but the therapist's continuing interest in a relationship with the client is affirmed.

These maneuvers, needless to say, can prove to be quite disruptive to the tactics of the client, and may produce threats of termination (Cashdan, 1973). However, the prior and continuing interest of the therapist will hopefully counterbalance this disruption and motivate the client to continue therapy. At this point the therapist continues his feedback to the client and begins to lay out in a general fashion just how things might be different between them. Again, mutual agreement about these points (undesirability of old patterns, relative desirability of new ones) is critically important *before* change contracting is begun.

After this preparatory (to overt change) work is completed, the latter stages of therapy resemble therapy with flexible clients. The primary difference is that the relatively greater anxiety that will in all likelihood accompany the reception of reciprocal behaviors may necessitate a more gradual, more painstaking approach. In fact, more formal desensitizing methods (other than repeated exposure) may be required to lessen this anxiety, and "graceful exit" responses may have to be inserted very soon after initial overt change has developed.

SUMMARY

The central theme of this chapter has been the promotion of interpersonal learning (i.e., reciprocal role training) as an adjunct procedure to behavior modification for the specific purpose of facilitating the transfer of therapeutic training. Such an addition to standard behavioral techniques was seen as necessary for two reasons.

First, the consensus of results from the investigation of behavior therapy outcomes with a variety of client "types" is that many clients do not maintain therapeutic gains once therapy has terminated. In far too many instances it has been demonstrated that behavioral techniques can lead to changes in the therapeutic environment per se, changes which do not hold up satisfactorily in the posttreatment social context. The continual replication of this outcome suggests the need for some kind of alteration in the conduct of behavior therapy.

Second, available evidence concerning the behavior of people in relation to others (i.e., in dyads) suggests that praise and approval (commonly regarded by behaviorists as generalized or "universal" social reinforcers) do not function as social rewards for some people. In fact, exposure to praise and approval may be aversive to many clients, especially those whose behavior is generally restricted to submissive and/or hostile exchanges with others. For such clients, treatment through standard behavioral procedures may represent a paradox. Since the frequent goal of behavior therapy is to equip clients with "new" behavioral responses which will result in the reception of praise and approval (or related socially desirable outcomes, such as success), behavior modification may be moving many clients toward goals which are aversive to them. It was speculated here that when this paradox develops, a likely resolution for the client is to discontinue the performance of "new" behaviors once therapy has terminated.

Reciprocal role training was suggested as a procedure for working therapeutically with this dilemma. While part of these techniques are focused on expanding clients' cognitive processes regarding their behavior in relation to others, another facet of reciprocal role training is aimed at reducing clients' anxiety at socially desirable outcomes. It was posited that the combination of interpersonal learning and behavior modification would better prepare a client to transfer his newly acquired repertoire to extratherapy contexts.

APPENDIX: RECIPROCAL ROLE TRAINING
WITH RIGID CLIENTS

The special problems presented by the rigid client are the focus of this section because, quite possibly, they call for procedures which rule out purely didactic methods. Keep in mind, further, that while much of what will be discussed here concentrates on the interpersonal, cognitive aspects of relearning in therapy, much of what transpires in my own therapeutic work includes an approximately equal share of "traditional" behavioral therapy. The difference is that, especially with quite rigid clients, the more traditional behavioral methods are embedded in interpersonal methods and are the focus of therapeutic activity at a particular point in the sequence. Also, although I shall be describing the therapist's contributions to dyadic encounters, I do not view these methods as limited to individual therapy. Meeting with small, open-ended groups, I have used these methods for years with severely disturbed, psychiatric inpatients. Finally, while I shall describe the process of reciprocal role training as a strict sequence of stages, "real" therapeutic encounters often evolve in a bit less orderly fashion. It is not unusual, for example, to discover the appearance of a "new" interpersonal dilemma rather late in a therapy process, say, well after specific change procedures have been under way (stage 4). Nonetheless, when this happens I usually work on such an issue beginning with clarifying (stage 2) maneuvers, then anxiety-arousing tactics (stage 3), then back to the issue of specific change (stage 4 again). Thus, while the "new" dilemma gets dealt with out of sequence, the sequence of therapists' behaviors in dealing with the dilemma still follows the original outline.

Stage 1: Hooking

These maneuvers are designed to do two things: (1) to remove the therapist from his role as a cold, objective professional and make him seem more of an interested, personal helper; and (2) to keep the therapist's profile low enough that his behavior does not override the client's perceptual bias. In other words, the therapist (T) wants the client (C) to see him as a therapist he wants to see (because of something personal developing between them) while letting C come to his own conclusions about the personal attributes of T. Here are some hooking tactics:

1. Active Listening. In these tactics T is busy as a listener and attempts to show C that he really cares about getting C's story right. Particularly, I try to play a bit "dumb" and let C elaborate his own items, even while they may be fairly clear at the outset. Also, I try to have him explain feelings and emotional states in clear terms. Here are some specific remarks from T:

"That's not all of it, I guess. How did you feel about it?"

"So you figure he is a 'mean' person?"

" 'Upset,' you say. How do you mean, 'upset'?"

"Could you use another word than 'freaked' to describe it for me?"

2. Showing Interest. Another way of getting a message to C that T is interested is to tell him so, rather directly. For example:

"That *does* sound interesting. Could you tell me more?"

"I would like to understand it exactly the way you do."

"If it's important to you, I sure would like to hear about it."

3. Emotional Coupling. Here, T wants C to know that T can appreciate C's troubles beyond a mere intellectual comprehension. While T may not have C's involvement in the issue, he can see that C's feelings are painful, and can come close to having some of the same "gut reactions" as C describes. Examples:

"I could hear the disappointment in your voice. It must still hurt to talk about."

"Gee, that must've been very rough."

"I can see that it's painful. I appreciate your being candid with me about it."

4. Sequencing. Although this maneuver is just a particular kind of active listening, I give it special attention because it so often opens up interesting areas for further discussion, and because it is a way to get an interpersonal focus to things early and without concentrating on T and C's relationship. Basically, C is often quite arbitrary in telling a particular story or describing a specific event. Either he recalls it only as it supports his complaint or he just did not tune in to critical elements in the sequence. This maneuver is designed to fill in such gaps:

"So you had a nice dinner prepared, but your husband angrily refused to eat. . . . What happened then?"

"Well, back to this particular instance. You made a request, then he turned and yelled at you? . . . What did you do then?"

"Well, no. I'm not sure I have it straight yet. What did you say after she made that remark?"

"So, you gave it a try, but it didn't work out. . . . Is that all there was to it?"

Stage 2: Clarification

Whereas in stage 1, the tactic was for T to appear interested and reduce himself as a situational constraint, in this stage T abandons that position to some extent. While he continues to remain somewhat "client
centered," T also begins to focus directly on the here-and-now relationship desired by C. In other words, if hooking was successful, C will begin
his attempt to engage T along familiar lines. T, with the help of this firsthand evidence, then tries to convert C's nonarticulated behaviors into
clearly labeled messages. Tactics for doing this include:

Focusing. T uses focusing statements to get C talking about the
here-and-now relationship. Coupled with active listening, T continues to
teach C to be careful and precise with his language in therapy. Examples
include:

"How do you think I react when you tell me that?"

"How would you prefer that I react?"

"You mean you want me to notice, in particular, that you are [fero-
cious, nice, capable, unworthy, sick, crazy, etc.]?"

"When you say I'll be 'only' your doctor, what kinds of things do
you *not* want me to do?"

"You say it's like that with everyone. Does that include me, too?"

"Just how would you like me to behave toward you?"

Especially since C's articulated preferences for a relationship with T
will be the focus of painful learning, it is imperative that stage 2 not be
abandoned prematurely. Remarks from C which mark the end of clarification need to meet these criteria:

1. The statements carry an operational definition of T's and C's role
in the here-and-now relationship (as preferred and described by C).

2. Supporting phrases or statements describe clearly C's perception of
the qualities of T (and C) which necessitate such a relationship.

3. T and C mutually agree on C's reasons and preferences (that is,
they agree that this is how C sees it and wants it).

The following examples demonstrate "end points" with which I can
comfortably proceed to stage 3:

"So, it's help for pay. I'll be the cold, advising expert and minister to
you because you're so incapable." *Support:* "I couldn't possibly like
you." "We will not get involved because you have nothing to offer."

"So, I'll be the fall guy. We will argue and you will win because of
your superior wits." *Support:* "You don't need help, especially from
me." "It's other people who are messed up." "I'm like them, but you
are together."

"In other words, we will like each other a lot. I will tell you how to
act and you will dutifully obey." *Support:* "I am the respected doctor

and know what is best." "You are capable of a lot, but only with proper guidance." "Arguments solve nothing . . . and are best avoided."

"So . . . what you're proposing is that we meet here once a week and make love . . . forget about 'therapy'." *Support:* "I am irresistibly charming to you." "You are hopelessly in love with me." "You are unable to control your real feelings. . . . You have such a crush on me that you must have me."

"That's it, huh? I will eventually just reject you because you are hardly worth my concern." *Support:* "I must certainly have better things to do with my time." "You are totally unworthy in every respect; no re-deeming qualities of any kind do you possess."

". . . We will fight it out, but you will lose because I have the 'system' on my side." *Support:* "I'm just another powerful son-of-a-bitch who is unworthy of your affection." "I'm like all the rest . . . another pushy adult interested only in telling you how to run your life." "You have a lot of love to give . . . but you're not going to waste it on some arrogant ass." "You would rather fight me than do anything else you can think of."

". . . You will tell me about your life and I will listen and admire your competence. Is that what you're proposing?" *Support:* I could be more helpful with others who need it more than you." "You are strong, really don't need help." "In fact, you frequently help others, so obviously you don't need it for yourself."

Stage 3: Anxiety Arousal

This phase of interpersonal learning is very actively launched by T. This is at once a very direct assault by T on C's preferences regarding a relationship with T and a delicate reassurance by T of his continuing in-terest in a relationship with C. Here it becomes evident why a mutual agreement over C's preferences is so important. Once T begins his assault on C's position, C will begin to experience pain. If the focus of T's attack is on a topic that has not been clearly established as C's "position," it be-comes possible for C to attempt anxiety reduction by claiming that he has been misunderstood, that T is making much ado over trivialities, etc.

The stylistic features of stage 3 maneuvers are also crucial to their success. Since the goal of these tactics is to provide C with information which is anxiety arousing, it is important here that the content of T's message be communicated. Thus T's remarks should carry impact from content, but be delivered in a careful manner void of intense status or af-fect characteristics. Otherwise T will run the risk of either reciprocating C's behavior or giving C the idea that T simply wants to terminate the relationship.

Here are some tactics that I have found useful for doing this:

1. Incredulity. This is a more intense claim to disbelief than the "playing dumb" tactic utilized in hooking. For example:

"I'm puzzled. I've told you before that when you come on like this I get nervous . . . yet you keep on doing it. I don't like it."

"I don't know . . . if you're helpless how the hell can I help you?"

"I don't get it. How do you get what you want by behaving like this?"

"Is this the best we can do?"

"You want this? You want me to believe you are helpless [sick, crazy, etc.]? How does that help you?"

"Is there something that you're getting out of this that I don't understand?"

2. Sarcasm. The object here is to provide C with a response that neither confirms his own suspicions nor implies that he must continue to be a certain way forever. Needless to say, here it becomes extremely important for T to tone down stylistic features. Examples:

"I have to hand it to you . . . when you decide to put yourself down you certainly do a professional job."

"Those are your only grounds for thinking of yourself as incurably homosexual? I thought you had 'proof.' I was expecting something much more serious."

"[calmly] If you are trying to get me angry with you, you're doing a superb job."

"Let's say you convince me that you are worthless . . . then what?"

"Okay, you win. I'm wrong and you're right. Now, what shall we do next?"

"For someone who claims to be helpless, you certainly win your share of arguments with me."

"Gee, I'm amazed! I could never think up so many ways to make myself miserable."

"I see. You've got things so figured out in your life that you don't need help. Well, tell me, then . . . how'd you end up here [in treatment, in a hospital, etc.]?"

"Ordinarily I have no qualms about kicking someone in the pants . . . but with you I just don't see the point."

"Why do you want my punishment, too? Isn't your own plenty?"

"Boy, you do seem down today . . . must've been working overtime on that 'put down' skill, huh?"

"So you want to quit, huh? Well, I'm not that easy to get rid of. I'll be here next week."

"Oh, yes . . . the list of faults again. I was afraid you might omit [lazy, crazy, stupid, sick, etc.]."

3. Interpersonal Feedback. In this gesture, T tells C what C is doing and how it makes T react (in feelings and/or thoughts). Examples:

"When you do _____ [here T describes C's actions], I get annoyed."

"I do find you attractive, but I could never enjoy having sex with a client. . . . It makes me nervous when you bring it up."

"When you _____, I become frightened of you."

"When you describe yourself that way, I find myself thinking, 'If she continues that, I may come to believe her.' "

"When you refuse to get angry, I find it very frustrating. . . . I don't respect your sweetness."

4. Refutation/Affirmation. This is a special form of feedback that in addition to feedback includes a clear statement from T that he intends to continue the relationship. Examples:

"I came prepared to be cooperative with you . . . enjoy your progress with you. . . . But you make it difficult by continuing to put yourself down."

"Frankly, I don't enjoy arguing with you . . . it becomes disgusting to me. . . . I would think there is a better way for us to spend our time."

"I am certainly interested in continuing to see you . . . but not on these terms."

"I think you have a lot of potential . . . it's that [particular behavior] I find obnoxious."

5. Interpretation. While I make some interpretations, I keep these at a low level of abstraction and use them only after a lot of previous stage 3 dialogue. Examples:

"I get the idea that if I rejected you, you would know exactly what to do. What you seem afraid of is my liking you."

"You practically shove your sexuality down my throat, so to speak. . . . I get the idea that you feel you have nothing else to offer."

"Everytime I offer you a little praise, you blow up. I think you're afraid of success . . . why wouldn't you be? It would be novel for you!"

"Just because you're angry isn't much of a reason. There are dozens of things you can do when you're angry that don't amount to that. I think you want me to get mad and fight you . . . maybe things have gotten a little too friendly in here."

"You know how to fight . . . God knows you've been in enough of them. . . . I think it's affection that scares you off."

6. Dealing with Paradoxes. In this maneuver T feeds back to C his own observations about mutually exclusive desires mentioned by C. Along with interpretations, these tactics not only loosen C's faith in old beliefs and habits, but may provide a general glimpse of how things might be if they were indeed better. Examples:

"You want to do everything your parents don't want you to do . . . yet you want them to like you. Isn't that unlikely?"

"You say you want respect, yet you go out of your way to belittle yourself. It doesn't add up . . . [maybe you want to avoid respect?]."

"You say you hate being rejected, yet you systematically set it up . . . [maybe you're afraid not to be rejected?]."

"So everyone gets turned off to you. I guess, seeing as how people are somewhat different, the intriguing question to me is how you manage to get everyone to do that."

Stage 4: Specific Change

While things may get intense and disruptive during stage 3 (it is not unusual for a client to threaten to leave at this point), the end of stage 3 is marked by a willingness by C to engage T in a less pathological manner and to tolerate discussion about the interpersonal positions being avoided by C. As this kind of talk develops, therapy can rapidly proceed to a negotiation of specific ways for change, T's methods for helping C attain specific goals, etc. In other words, therapy can become much more "traditionally" behavioral at this point, because the peak intensity of interpersonal learning will have passed. In this stage, most of the therapeutic work I do is probably quite familiar to most behavior therapists.

However, there are two interpersonal tasks that still need to be monitored. The first is the temptation to revert to old habits, often just as C appears to be making solid progress. Stage 3 tactics should help here. For example: "Well, back to the fault list, huh? Maybe you couldn't stand a little prosperity?" "Well, things that you want are scary because they're new. You've just quit doing them, that's all . . . got back into old stuff."

Sometimes it is helpful to predict that there will be periodic returns to old ways: "Well, things seem to be progressing very nicely. I should think you'll get nervous about these [old ways] sometimes." "Well, I wouldn't be surprised if . . ." "Sure, two steps forward, one back. . . ."

The other problem that may arise here has to do with intensely new reciprocal behavior from others. Clients need to learn how to be different toward others, yet maintain control over how much of it they get involved with at a time. In addition to role-playing experience with newly reciprocal behavior, I try to expose clients to the intense forms of it, in order to teach them graceful exits. It requires that C learn to bargain straightforwardly with others in terms of the occasion and the amount of behaviors to be exchanged, without scaring off or turning off the other. Consider this response from a previously hostile-submissive C trying to be friendlier and more outgoing with a boyfriend:

Friend: Well, let's go steady. I love you—you love me, so let's go!

C: I'm flattered by your enthusiasm, but this is all very new to me. I want to date around a little before I decide to go steady.

Friend: But . . . uh . . . [sadly] I thought you liked me . . .

C: I do. I just don't want to go steady yet.

Learning these responses (which expressed feelings she believes she would "never" get out) helped this C become more socially outgoing. Previously, even after successful progress in therapy, she remained somewhat shy with me because of a specific fear of this exchange. I have noted similar specific fears in clients attempting to become less rigidly dominant, passive, or even friendly. This response helped a passive and overly friendly man become more dominant:

C: Excuse me, but you stepped in front of me in line.

2nd man: So what? You wanna make something of it?

C: No, I don't want to fight, I just wanted to be sure that you understood that I didn't like it. You're being pushy and I don't care for it.

2nd man: You don't like it, huh? Wanna do something about it?

C: Not at all, I've satisfied myself.

Otherwise, stage 4 is primarily involved with behavioral change. While there may also be a stage 5, perhaps "termination," it usually is not a major therapeutic involvement. By the time stage 4 begins to wind down, most of my clients are eager to "try it on their own," even though they get a little tense thinking about it. Usually the biggest part of termination is the mutual recognition by T and C that there is not much left to do or talk about, that C is ready to exit.

NOTE

1. A contrast may be drawn between *descriptive* integrity (response class) and *functional* integrity (tactics). At a tatical level, descriptive different behaviors may have the same effect on others. For example, whiney self-criticism may elicit disgust, just as friendly chatter toward someone busily trying to finish a task might do the same; although descriptively different, in sequential context the two function similarly. Likewise, descriptively similar responses may lead to different outcomes (flirting with your own date versus someone else's date). Thus tactics are sequential, contextual maneuvers which could be classified according to their outcome effects on others (DeVoge & Beck, 1978). Here, then, is a second alternative to Wahler's (Note 1) disclaimer regarding an a priori basis for grouping behaviors together.

REFERENCE NOTES

1. Wahler, R. G. *The indirect maintenance and modification of deviant child behavior.* Paper presented to a symposium "The Child in His Environment" of the Houston Behavior Therapy Association, May 1972.
2. Berzins, J. I., Welling, M. A., & Wetter, R. E. *Androgynous vs. traditional sex roles and the interpersonal behavioral circle.* Paper presented at the annual meeting of the American Psychological Association, Washington, D.C., September 1976.
3. Golding, S. L. *Individual differences in the construal of interpersonal interactions.* Paper presented at the Symposium on Interactional Psychology, Stockholm, Sweden, June 1975.
4. Birchler, G. R., Weiss, R. L., & Wampler, L. D. *Differential patterns of social reinforcement as a function of degree of marital distress and level of intimacy.* Paper presented at the Western Psychological Association, Portland, Orego, April 1972.
5. National Training Laboratories Institute for Applied Behavioral Science. *Feedback and the helping relationship.* NTL Institute Reading Book. Washington, D.C.: NTL Institute, 1967. (mimeographed)

REFERENCES

Andrews, J. B. W. Psychotherapy and phobias. *Psychological Bulletin,* 1966, *66,* 456–480.

Azrin, N. H., Naster, B. J., & Jones, R. Reciprocity counseling: A rapid learning-based procedure for marital counseling. *Behaviour Research and Therapy,* 1973, *11,* 365–382.

Baer, D. M., Wolf, M. M., & Risley, T. R. Some current dimensions of applied behavior analysis. *Journal of Applied Behavior Analysis,* 1968, *1,* 91–97.

Bandura, A. *Principles of behavior modification.* New York: Holt, Rinehart & Winston, 1969.

Bandura, A. Behavior theory and the models of man. *American Psychologist,* 1974, *29,* 859–869.

Bandura, A. The self system in reciprocal determinism. *American Psychologist,* 1978, *33,* 334–358.

Beier, E. G. *The silent language of psychotherapy: Social reinforcement of unconscious processes.* Chicago: Aldine, 1966.

Bem, D. J. Self-perception: An alternative interpretation of cognitive dissonance phenomena. *Psychological Review,* 1967, *74,* 183–200.

Benjamin, L. S. Structural analysis of social behavior. *Psychological Review,* 1974, *81,* 392–425.

Bergman, R. L. Extinction and interpersonal closeness treatment techniques in chronic schizophrenia: A serendipitous case study comparison. *Psychotherapy: Theory, Research and Practice,* 1976, *13,* 395–396.

Berne, E. *Games people play: The psychology of human relationships.* New York: Grove Press, 1964.

Berzins, J. I., Welling, M. A., & Wetter, R. E. A new measure of psychological androgyny based on the personality research form. *Journal of Consulting and Clinical Psychology,* 1978, *46,* 126-138.

Borkovec, T. Effects of expectancy on the outcome of systematic desensitization and implosive treatments for analogue anxiety. *Behavior Therapy,* 1972, *3,* 29-40.

Borkovec, T. D. The role of expectancy and physiological feedback in fear research: A review with special reference to subject characteristics. *Behavior Therapy,* 1973, *4,* 491-505

Bowers, K. S. Situationism in psychology: An analysis and critique. *Psychological Review,* 1973, *80,* 307-336.

Bowers, K. S. There's more to Iago than meets the eye: A clinical account of personal consistency. In D. Magnusson and N. S. Endler (Eds.), *Personality at the crossroads.* Hillsdale, N.J.: Lawrence Erlbaum, 1977.

Briar, S., & Bieri, J. A factor analytic and trait inference study of the Leary Interpersonal Checklist. *Journal of Clinical Psychology,* 1963, *19,* 193-198.

Burtle, V., Whitlock, D., & Franks, V. Modification of low self-esteem in women alcoholics: A behavioral treatment approach. *Psychotherapy: Theory, Research and Practice,* 1974, *11,* 36-40.

Buss, A. H., & Lang, P. J. Psychological deficit in schozphrenia: I. Affect, reinforcement, and concept attainment. *Journal of Abnormal Psychology,* 1965, *70,* 2-24.

Carson, R. C. *Interaction concepts of personality.* Chicago: Aldine, 1969.

Carson, R. C. Disordered interpersonal behavior. In W. A. Hunt (Ed.), *Human behavior and its control.* Cambridge, Mass.: Schenkman, 1971.

Carson, R. C. Phenomenological implications of interactionism in the study of interpersonal relations. In R. L. Burgess and T. L. Huston (Eds.), *Social exchange in developing relationships.* New York: Academic Press, in press.

Cashdan, S. *Interactional psychotherapy: Stages and strategies in behavioral change.* New York: Grune & Stratton, 1973.

Caulfield, J. B., & Martin, R. B. Establishment of praise as a reinforcer in chronic schizophrenics. *Journal of Consulting and Clinical Psychology,* 1976, *44,* 61-67.

Cautela, J. R., & Upper, D. The process of individual behavior therapy. In M. Hersen, P. M. Miller, & R. M. Eisler (Eds.), *Progress in behavior modification* (vol. 1). New York: Academic Press, 1975.

Davidson, W. S., & Seidman, E. Studies of behavior modification and juvenile delinquency: A review, methodological critique, and social perspective. *Psychological Bulletin,* 1974, *81,* 998-1011.

Davis, J. D. *The interview as arena: Strategies in standardized interviews and psychotherapy.* Stanford, Calif.: Stanford University Press, 1971.

Davison, G. C. Counter control in behavior modification. In L. A. Hammerlynck, L. C. Handy, & E. J. Mash (Eds.), *Behavior change: Methodology, concepts, and practice.* Champaign, Ill.: Research Press, 1973.

DeVoge, J. T., & Beck, S. The therapist–client relationship in behavior therapy. In M. Hersen, R. M. Eisler, & P. M. Miller (Eds.), *Progress in behavior modification* (vol. 6). New York: Academic Press, 1978.

Dittman, A. T. Problems of reliability in observing and coding social interactions. *Journal of Consulting Psychology,* 1958, *22,* 430.

Drennen, W., Gallman, W., & Sausser, G. Verbal operant conditioning of hospitalized psychiatric patients. *Journal of Abnormal Psychology,* 1969, *74,* 454-458.

Eisler, R. M., Miller, P. M., Hersen, M., & Alford, H. Effects of assertive training on marital interaction. *Archives of General Psychiatry,* 1974, *30,* 643-649.

Endler, N. S., & Magnusson, D. Toward an interactional psychology of personality. *Psychological Bulletin,* 1976, *83,* 956-974.

Fensterheim, H., & Baer, J. *Don't say yes when you want to say no.* New York: Dell, 1975.

Foa, E. B., & Steketee, G. Emergent fears during treatment of three obsessive compulsives: Symptom substitution or deconditioning? *Journal of Behavior Therapy and Experimental Psychiatry,* 1977, *8,* 353-358.

Frankel, A. S., & Buchwald, A. M. Verbal conditioning of common associations in long-term schizophrenics: A failure. *Journal of Abnormal Psychology,* 1969, *74,* 372-374.

Franks, C. M., & Wilson, G. T. Commentary (behavior therapy and the natural environment: Community-societal issues). In C. M. Franks and G. T. Wilson (Eds.), *Annual review of behavior therapy, theory and practice: 1975.* New York: Brunner/Mazel, 1975.

Goldfried, M. R., & Davison, G. C. *Clinical behavior therapy.* New York: Holt, Rinehart & Winston, 1976.

Golding, S. L. Flies in the ointment: Methodological problems in the analysis of the percentage of variance due to persons and situations. *Psychological Bulletin,* 1975, *82,* 278-288.

Golding, S. L. The problem of construal styes in the analysis of person-situation interactions. In D. Magnusson and N. S. Endler (Eds.), *Personality at the crossroads.* Hillsdale, N.J.: Lawrence Erlbaum, 1977.

Goldstein, A. P., Sprafkin, R. P., & Gershaw, N. J. Structured learning therapy: Training for community living. *Psychotherapy: Theory, Research and Practice,* 1976, *13,* 374-377.

Gomes-Schwartz, B., Hadley, S. W., & Strupp, H. H. Individual psychotherapy and behavior therapy. *Annual Review of Psychology,* 1978, *29,* 435-471.

Greer, S. E., & D'Zurilla, T. J. Behavioral approaches to marital discord and conflict. *Journal of Marriage and Family Counseling,* 1975, *1,* 299-315.

Gurman, A. S., & Kniskern, D. P. Behavioral marriage therapy: II. Empirical perspective. *Family Process,* 1978, *17,* 139-148.

Gurman, A. S., & Knudson, R. M. Behavioral marriage therapy: I. A Psychodynamic systems analysis and critique. *Family Process,* 1978, *17,* 121-138.

Haley, J. *Strategies of psychotherapy.* New York: Grune & Stratton, 1963.

Hand, I., & Lamontagne, Y. The exacerbation of interpersonal problems after rapid phobia-removal. *Psychotherapy: Theory, Research and Practice,* 1976, *13,* 405-411.

Harris, T. A. *I'm OK—you're OK.* New York: Avon, 1967.

Heller, K., Myers, R. R., & Kline, L. V. Interviewer behavior as a function of standardized client roles. *Journal of Consulting Psychology,* 1963, *27,* 117-122.

Hersen, M., & Bellack, A. S. Social skills training for chronic psychiatric patients: Rationale, research findings, and future directions. *Comprehensive Psychiatry,* 1976, *17,* 559-580.

Hersen, M., Eisler, R. M., & Miller, P. M. Development of assertive responses: Clinical, measurement, and research considerations. *Behaviour Research and Therapy,* 1973, *11,* 505-521.

Hickok, J. E., & Komechak, M. G. Behavior modification in marital conflict: A case report. *Family Process,* 1974, *13,* 111-119.

Hine, F. R. Psychodynmics of the individual. In F. R. Hine, E. Pfeiffer, G. L. Maddox, P. L. Hein, & R. O. Friedel (Eds.), *Behavioral science—a selective review*. Boston: Little Brown, 1972.

Hurwitz, B. A. A conditioned reward for chronic schizophrenics. *Dissertation Abstracts International,* 1969, *30,* 1360.

Jacobsen, N., & Weiss, R. L. Behavioral marriage therapy: III. The contents of Gurman et al. may be hazardous to our health. *Family Process,* 1978, *17,* 149–163.

Jeffrey, D. B., Christensen, E. R., & Katz, R. C. Behavior therapy weight reduction programs: Some preliminary findings on the need for follow-ups. *Psychotherapy: Theory, Research and Practice,* 1975, *12,* 311–313.

Jones, E. E. *Ingratiation: A social psychological analysis.* New York: Appleton-Century-Crofts, 1964.

Kazdin, A. E. *Behavior modification in applied settings.* Homewood, Ill.: Dorsey Press, 1975.

Kazdin, A. E., & Bootzin, R. R. The token economy: An evaluative review. *Journal of Applied Behavior Analysis,* 1972, *5,* 343–372.

Keith, K. D., & Lange, B. M. Maintenance of behavior change in an institution-wide training program. *Mental Retardation,* 1974, *12,* 34–37.

Kelley, H. H., & Stahelski, A. J. Social interaction basis of cooperators' and competitors' beliefs about others. *Journal of Personality and Social Psychology,* 1970, *16,* 66–91.

Kunkel, J. D. *Behavior, social problems and change: A social learning approach.* Englewood Cliffs, N.J.: Prentice-Hall, 1975.

Lang, P. J., Melamed, B. G., & Hart, J. A. Psychophysiological analysis of fear modification using an automated desensitization procedure. *Journal of Abnormal Psychology,* 1970, *76,* 220–234.

Lazarus, A. A. *Behavior therapy and beyond.* New York: McGraw-Hill, 1971.

Leary, T. *Interpersonal diagnosis of personality.* New York: Ronald Press, 1957.

Lederer, W. J., & Jackson, D. D. *Mirages of marriage.* New York: W. W. Norton, 1968.

Ledwidge, B. Cognitive behavior modification: A step in the wrong direction? *Psychological Bulletin,* 1978, *85,* 353–375.

Levine, F. M., & Fasnacht, G. Token rewards may lead to token learning. *American Psychologist,* 1974, *29,* 816–820.

Liberman, R. P., McCann, M. J., & Wallace, C. J. Generalization of behavior therapy with psychotics. *British Journal of Psychiatry,* 1976, *129,* 490–496.

Magnusson, D., & Endler, N. S. Interational psychology: Present status and future prospects. In D. Magnusson and N. S. Endler (Eds.), *Personality at the crossroads.* Hillsdale, N.J.: Lawrence Erlbaum, 1977.

Mahoney, M. *Cognition and behavior modification.* Cambridge, Mass.: Ballinger, 1974.

Mariotto, M. J., & Paul, G. L. Persons versus situations in the real-life functioning of chronically institutionalized mental patients. *Journal of Abnormal Psychology,* 1975, *84,* 483–493.

Marks, I. M. Flooding (implosion) and allied treatments. In W. S. Agras (Ed.), *Behavior modification: Principles and clinical applications.* Boston: Little, Brown, 1972.

Mason, W. A. Sociability and social organization in monkeys and apes. In L.

Berkowitz (Ed.), *Advances in experimental social psychology.* New York: Academic Press, 1964.

McCullough, J. P., Huntsinger, G. M., & Nay, W. R. Self-control treatment of aggression in a 16-year-old-male. *Journal of Consulting and Clinical Psychology,* 1977, *45,* 322–331.

McGlynn, F. D. Comments on the Morris and Suckerman study of therapist warmth as a factor in automated systematic desensitization. *Journal of Consulting and Clinical Psychology,* 1976, *44,* 483–489.

McNamara, J. Systematic desensitization versus implosive therapy: Issues in outcomes. *Psychotherapy: Theory, Research and Practice,* 1972, *9,* 13–16.

Mehrabian, A. *Nonverbal communication.* New York: Aldine-Atherton, 1972.

Merton, R. K. The self-fulfilling prophecy. *Antioch Review,* 1948, *8,* 193–210.

Miller, P. M., & Drennen, W. T. Establishment of social reinforcement as an effective modifier of verbal behavior in chronic psychiatric patients. *Journal of Abnormal Psychology,* 1970, *76,* 392–395.

Miran, M., Lehrer, P. M., Koehler, R., & Miran, E. What happens when deviant behavior begins to change? The relevance of a social systems approach for behavior programs with adolescents. *Journal of Community Psychology,* 1974, *2,* 370–375.

Mischel, W. Toward a cognitive social learning reconceptualization of personality. *Psychological Review,* 1973, *80,* 252–283.

Mischel, W. *Introduction to personality* (2nd ed.). New York: Holt, Rinehart & Winston, 1976.

Mischel, W. The interaction of person and situation. In D. Magnusson and N. S. Endler (Eds.), *Personality at the crossroads.* Hillside, N.J.: Lawrence Erlbaum, 1977.

Morganstern, K. Implosive therapy and flooding procedures: A critical review. *Psychological Bulletin,* 1973, *79,* 318–334.

Morris, R. J., & Suckerman, K. R. Therapist warmth as a factor in automated systematic desensitization. *Journal of Consulting and Clinical Psychology,* 1974, *42,* 244–250.

Morris, R. J., & Suckerman, K. R. Studying therapist warmth in analogue systematic desensitization research—a reply to McGlynn. *Journal of Consulting and Clinical Psychology,* 1976, *44,* 485–489.

Namanek, A. A., & Schuldt, W. J. Differential effects of experimenters' personality and instructional sets on verbal conditioning. *Journal of Counseling Psychology,* 1971, *18,* 170–172.

Nay, W. R. *Behavioral intervention: Contemporary strategies.* New York: Gardner, 1976.

O'Leary, K. D., & Wilson, G. T. *Behavior therapy: Application and outcomes.* Englewood Cliffs, N.J.: Prentice-Hall, 1975.

Patterson, G. R., & Hops, H. Coercion: A game for two: Intervention techniques for marital conflict. In R. Alrick & P. Mountjoy (Eds.), *The experimental analysis of social behavior.* New York: Appleton-Century-Crofts, 1972.

Patterson, G. R., Hops, H., & Weiss, R. L. Interpersonal skills training for couples in early stages of conflict. *Journal of Marriage and the Family,* 1975, *37,* 295–303.

Patterson, G. R., & Reid, J. B. Reciprocity and coercion: Two facets of social systems. In C. Neuringer and L. Michael (Eds.), *Behavior modification in clinical psychology.* New York: Appleton-Century-Crofts, 1970.

Powers, W. T. *Behavior: The control of perception.* Chicago: Aldine, 1973.

Price, R. H., & Bouffard, D. L. Behavioral appropriateness and situational constraint as dimensions of social behavior. *Journal of Personality and Social Psychology,* 1974, *30,* 579–586.

Rappaport, A. F., & Harrell, J. A behavioral exchange model for marital counseling. *Family Coordinator,* 1972, *21,* 203–212.

Raush, H. L., Dittman, A. T., & Taylor, T. J. The interpersonal behavior of children in residential treatment. *Journal of Abnormal and Social Psychology,* 1959, *58,* 9–27.

Raush, H. L., Farbman, I., & Llewellyn, L. G. Person, sitting and change in social interaction: II. A normal-control study. *Human Relations,* 1960, *13,* 305–333.

Reece, M. M., & Witman, R. N. Expressive movements, warmth and verbal reinforcement. *Journal of Abnormal and Social Psychology,* 1962, *64,* 234–236.

Rinn, J. L. Structure of phenomenal domains. *Psychological Review,* 1965, *72,* 445–466.

Salter, A. *Conditioned reflex therapy.* New York: Creative Age Press, 1949.

Schmidt, L. D., & Strong, S. R. "Expert" and "inexpert" counselors. *Journal of Counseling Psychology,* 1970, *17,* 115–118.

Schneider, D. J. Implicit personality theory: A review. *Psychological Bulletin,* 1973, *79,* 294–309.

Schwitzgebel, R. L. Short-term operant conditioning of adolescent offenders on socially relevant variables. *Journal of Abnormal Psychology,* 1967, *72,* 134–142.

Schwitzgebel, R. L. Preliminary socialization for psychotherapy of behavior-disordered adolescents. *Journal of Consulting and Clinical Psychology,* 1969, *33,* 71–77.

Shannon, J., & Guerney, B., Jr. Interpersonal effects of interpersonal behavior. *Journal of Personaity and Social Psychology,* 1973, *26,* 142–150.

Skinner, B. F. *Verbal behavior.* New York: Appleton-Century-Crofts, 1958.

Skinner, B. F. The steep and thorny way to a science of behavior. *American Psychologist,* 1975, *30,* 42–49.

Slack, C. W. Experimenter–subject psychotherapy. *Mental Hygiene,* 1960, *44,* 230–256.

Snyder, M., & Swann, W. B., Jr. Behavioral confirmation in social interaction: From social perception to social reality. *Journal of Experimental Social Psychology,* 1978, *14,* 148–162.

Snyder, M., Tanke, E. D., & Berscheid, E. Social perception and interpersonal behavior: On the self-fulfilling nature of social stereotypes. *Journal of Personality and Social Psychology,* 1977, *35,* 656–666.

Sobell, M. B., & Sobell, L. C. Second year treatment outcome of alcoholics treated by individualized behavior therapy: Results. *Behavior Research and Therapy,* 1976, *14,* 195–215.

Stahl, J. R., Thompson, L. E., Leitenberg, H., & Hasazi, J. E. Establishment of praise as a conditioned reinforcer in socially unresponsive psychiatric patients. *Journal of Abnormal Psychology,* 1974, *83,* 488–496.

Stampfl, T., & Levis, D. Essentials of implosive therapy: A learning theory-based psychodynamic behavioral therapy. *Journal of Abnormal Psychology,* 1967, *72,* 496–503.

Stampfl, T., & Levis, D. Implosive therapy: A behavioral therapy? *Behaviour Research and Therapy,* 1968, *6,* 31–36.

Strong, S. R., & Schmidt, L. D. Expertness and influence in counseling. *Journal of Counseling Psychology,* 1970, *17,* 81–87.

Stuart, R. B. Operant-interpersonal treatment for marital discord. *Journal of Consulting and Clinical Psychology,* 1969, *33,* 675–682.

Sullivan, H. S. *The interpersonal theory of psychiatry.* New York: W.W. Norton, 1953.

Tedeschi, J. T., Schlenker, B. R., & Bonoma, T. V. Cognitive dissonance: Private ratiocination or public spectacle? *American Psychologist,* 1971, *26,* 685–695.

Thibaut, J. W., & Kelley, H. H. *The social psychology of groups.* New York: Wiley, 1959.

Tolor, A., Kelly, B. R., & Stebbins, C. A. Altruism in psychiatric patients: How socially concerned are the emotionally disturbed? *Journal of Consulting and Clinical Psychology,* 1976, *44,* 503–507.

Triandis, H. C. Some universals of social behavior. *Personality and Social Psychology Bulletin,* 1978, *4,* 1–16.

Vincent, J. P. *The relationship of sex, degree of intimacy, and degree of marital distress to problem solving behavior and exchange of social reinforcement.* Unpublished doctoral dissertation, University of Oregon, 1972.

Vitalo, R. L. Effects of facilitative interpersonal functioning in a conditioning paradigm. *Journal of Counseling Psychology,* 1970, *17,* 141–144.

Wachtel, P. L. Psychodynamics, behavior therapy, and the implacable experimenter: An inquiry into the consistency of personality. *Journal of Abnormal Psychology,* 1973, *82,* 324–334.

Wachtel, P. L. Interaction cycles, unconscious processes, and the person-situation issue. In D. Magnusson and N. S. Endler (Eds.), *Personality at the crossroads.* Hillsdale, N.J.: Lawrence Erlbaum, 1977. (a)

Wachtel, P. L. *Psychoanalysis and behavior therapy: Toward an integration.* New York: Basic Books, 1977. (b)

Weiss, R. L., Birchler, G. R., & Vincent, J. P. Contractual models for negotiation training in marital dyads. *Journal of Marriage and the Family,* 1974, *36,* 321–330.

Wiemann, R. J., Shoulders, D. I., & Farr, J. H. Reciprocal reinforcement in marital therapy. *Journal of Behavior Therapy and Experimental Psychiatry,* 1974, *5,* 291–295.

Wiggins, J. S., & Holzmuller, A. Psychological androgyny and interpersonal behavior. *Journal of Consulting and Clinical Psychology,* 1978, *46,* 40–52.

Willems, E. P. Behavioral technology and behavioral ecology. *Journal of Applied Behavior Analysis,* 1974, *7,* 151–165.

Wills, T. A., Weiss, R. L., & Patterson, G. R. A behavioral analysis of the determinants of marital satisfaction. *Journal of Consulting and Clinical Psychology,* 1974, *42,* 802–811.

Wilson, G. T., Hannon, A. E., & Evans, W. I. M. Behavior therapy and the therapist–client relationship. *Journal of Consulting and Clinical Psychology,* 1968, *32,* 103–109.

Wish, M., Deutsch, M., & Kaplan, S. J. Perceived dimensions of interpersonal relations. *Journal of Personality and Social Psychology,* 1976, *33,* 409–420.

Wolowitz, H. M. Therapist warmth: Necessary or sufficient condition in behavioral desensitization? *Journal of Consulting and Clinical Psychology,* 1975, *43,* 584–585.

Wolpe, J. *Psychotherapy by reciprocal inhibition.* Stanford, Calif.: Stanford University Press, 1958.

Wolpe, J. *The practice of behavior therapy.* New York: Pergamon, 1973.

Wolpe, J., & Lazarus, A. A. *Behavior therapy techniques.* New York: Pergamon, 1966.

Yates, A. J. *Theory and practice in behavior therapy.* New York: Wiley and Sons, 1975.

Zajonc R. B. *Animal social behavior.* Morristown, N.J.: General Learning Press, 1972.

C H A P T E R

11

A SOCIAL PSYCHOLOGICAL
PERSPECTIVE ON THE MAINTENANCE
OF THERAPEUTIC CHANGE

SHARON S. BREHM AND DAVID A. McALLISTER

One of the most difficult aspects of writing a chapter involving "a social psychological perspective" is to define social psychology. Many people think of social psychology as the field that examines psychological processes that are distinctly social in nature. Thus, studying the processes that occur in group settings would be an easily recognized focus within social psychology. Actually, much of what goes on under the label of "social psychology" has little to do with social interaction per se. Theories such as dissonance, self-perception, and reactance focus on intrapsychic processes that may be influenced by social interaction, but are not restricted to social settings. The present chapter reflects a combination of these two types of social psychology. While the more intrapsychic theories will form the basis of our discussion, we will always focus on a distinctly social setting: the interaction between therapist and client (cf. also, Chapter 10).

In any discussion of the application of social psychological theory to clinical endeavors that is addressed primarily to an audience of clinicians, it is probably worthwhile to consider attitudes toward social psychology that may already be held by at least some members of this audience. Many clinicians are acquainted with social psychological research, and for some, this acquaintance may have led them to be doubtful about the possible relevance of social psychology for clinical issues. After all, they may think, isn't social psychology based on esoteric little two by two experimental designs with college sophomores? Therapeutic change, on the other hand, deals with real people in the real and very complex world. How could an approach based on social psychology have any useful benefits for clinical practice?

These are legitimate questions to pose, and ones that are frequently encountered. In attempting an answer to them, it will be useful to provide some historical background. Forty years ago, for example, these questions probably would not have arisen. It is doubtful that people like Kurt Lewin and Gordon Allport perceived any difficulty about being social psychologists who also addressed clinical issues. Furthermore, it is doubtful that their colleagues viewed their behavior as anything out of the ordinary. It may be noted as evidence of these shared "roots" that as late as 1964, social and clinical psychologists contributed to a common journal: the *Journal of Abnormal and Social Psychology*. The subsequent division of this journal into two separate journals (*Journal of Abnormal Psychology* and *Journal of Personality and Social Psychology*) marked the beginning of an increasing separation of the two professional groups.

The reason for this separation (and indeed for the division of the journal itself) is easy to see. Starting in the late 1950s, psychology entered into almost two decades of explosive growth. As more and more professional literature produced by more and more professionals literally flooded the field, it became difficult to keep a foot in both camps. Specialization became the preferred, and in many instances a necessary way of life. While there have been some attempts to bridge the gap (for example, Frank's *Persuasion and Healing,* 1961/1973; Goldstein, Heller, & Sechrest's *Psychotherapy and the Psychology of Behavior Change,* 1966; Carson's *Interaction Concepts of Personality,* 1969; Valins & Nisbett's *Attribution Processes in the Development and Treatment of Emotional Disorders,* 1971; and S. S. Brehm's *The Application of Social Psychology to Clinical Practice,* 1976), in general, most clinical psychologists today do not speak the social psychological language, and vice versa.

Rather paradoxically, however, during the same period that social and clinical psychology were becoming increasingly separated, clinicians were becoming more interested in and influenced by another area of "academic" psychology—the psychology of learning. A variety of approaches to human learning, ranging from the relatively mechanistic models of operant and classical conditioning to more cognitive perspectives such as Rotter's (1954, 1966) and Bandura's (1969; see also Bandura's recent theory of self-efficacy, 1977) social learning theories, created the still-burgeoning coalition between basic learning principles and clinical practice known as behavior modification and/or behavior therapy. In this case—perhaps because of the impact of leading figures such as Skinner, Ullman, Krasner, Bandura, and Lazarus, who persuasively demonstrated the benefits of the clinical application of learning principles—the enormous growth of psychology worked for integration into clinical practice rather than for separation from it.

This contrast between the current major influence of learning theories and the minor influence of social psychological theories on clinical activities strikes some of us as a bit surprising. If the complexity and richness of real-world behavior in general and of clinical problems in particular are to be grounds for theoretical preferences, one might have expected the opposite outcome. After all, while research conducted primarily with college sophomores may be objectionable, research conducted originally with white rats and pigeons would seem even more so.

Comparative advocacy of one rather than the other general theoretical perspective has, however, probably become unnecessary. In recent years the need for ideological purity has decreased (London, 1972) and the parity between specific clinical approaches has become increasingly evident (Sloane, Staples, Cristol, Yorkston, & Whipple, 1975). What is now of paramount concern is the need to increase the effectiveness, efficiency, and long-term impact of therapeutic endeavors. Clinical practice has become more than ever before a free marketplace for the competition of specific ideas and techniques, with individual clinicians more interested in the effectiveness of a given approach than in its ideological pedigree.

While it is hard to view this kind of practicality and eclecticism with anything but unconditional positive regard, at least one potential drawback should be noted. The absence of ideological fervor and the emphasis on practical effectiveness should not be construed as indicating the death of theory and conceptual models. While theoretical proclivities have been used on occasion as an opportunity to throw brickbats at the opposing theoretical camp, this is not the sum and substance of theoretical concerns. In fact, all clinicians depend on theory. One simply cannot erase one's mind and begin again with each individual client. One must generalize to the individual from a more global set of concepts. The issue, then, is not theory or no theory: the issue is *which* theory under *which* circumstances. If the new eclecticism becomes an amorphous illusion of theory-free endeavor, it will offer us and our clients little advantage. If on the other hand, the new eclecticism takes a more sophisticated approach to theory that continues to recognize the need for and debt to theoretical conceptualizations, then some crucial advances may become possible.

This more sophisticated approach to theory is composed of several components. First, it must rest on a clear recognition of the necessity of securing empirical support for the theoretical model. Armchair speculation that does not lead to a creative interplay with ongoing research is simply an indulgence that an applied science cannot practically or ethically afford. Second, such an insistence on empirical support will probably entail the realization that global theories of human functioning, such as many psychodynamic theories, are too general and too imprecise. Finally, the need for empirical support will probably mean that we will have to lower our aspirations and use conceptual models that apply to limited areas of human functioning. Once a limited-domain perspective is adopted, it should become apparent that theories will have differential utility for different behaviors and that some behaviors may be best approached through a combination of various theories. Thus, the task of an eclectic approach becomes much more difficult than that of the ideological purist. It is not a matter of knowing one theory well and applying it to all clients under all circumstances. It becomes a matter of knowing a variety of theories well, appreciating their respective domains of relevance, and being capable of creating techniques based on the innovative integration of jointly applicable theories.

All of which brings us back to our original goal of discussing the relevance of social psychology to clinical practice. The perspective that will be taken in this chapter will be a composite of a number of existing social psychological theories. Our efforts at eclectic integration will occur on two levels. First, we shall try to show that, regardless of theoretical orientation, clinicians use some basically similar techniques and, consequently, encounter similar problems in maintaining therapeutic gains. Second, we will propose that the various social psychological theories that are discussed converge to produce rather similar recommendations for how best to ensure desired maintenance.

In contrast to these rather inclusive goals, two limitations of the present chapter should be noted. Since our purpose is to provide a review of a selected set of theoretical issues relevant to the maintenance of therapeutic gains, we have limited accordingly those social psychological theories that we review. Consideration of a broader range of clinical issues and social psychological theories may be found in S. S. Brehm's 1976 book. In addition, for those theoretical issues that we do discuss, we will present a general overview, rather than a detailed description of specific empirical findings and points of theoretical dispute. For a more detailed examination of such issues, we refer the reader to the reviews of the literature cited in this chapter.

Throughout our discussion of a social psychological perspective on the maintenance of therapeutic change, we hope to display the potential advantages of enlarging the cross-fertilization between basic theoretical research and applied clinical practice. In our concluding remarks, we shall describe various kinds of research activities that can serve to promote this process.

THERAPEUTIC CHANGE
INDUCED BY POSITIVE REINFORCEMENT

The use of positive reinforcement as a method of obtaining a desired change is a common practice. Although theoretical systems vary in the degree of emphasis that they place on this mechanism and in the language in which they discuss it, positive reinforcement may be thought to be an element in all therapy.

The clearest example of the use of positive reinforcement is found, of course, in behavior modification. Here, the primary method if increasing the frequency of a desired behavior is the enforcement of a contingency such that a positive reinforcer is obtained only when the behavior is emitted. Whether the reinforcer is an M&M, a token, or social praise is of little consequence; the same methods of contingency management are used.

The use of positive reinforcement is by no means restricted to behavior therapists. In the more traditional schools of therapy, the reinforcers tend to be mainly social in nature and the contingencies may be less explicit, but are still present. In psychoanalysis, for example, the low frequency with which the therapist interacts with the client can be viewed as establishing a "deprivation" situation. In such a situation, the infrequent "uh huh's" and "yes, go on's" that therapists do emit probably carry unusual reinforcement value.

Group therapy also relies on social reinforcement. It has been said that a primary "curative factor" of group therapy is its provision of a new socializing experience (Yalom, 1970). This process of socialization is probably based, at least in part, on the provision of large doses of "positive feedback" when a desired and effective behavior appears.

Consideration of group therapy leads to another point about the use of positive reinforcement in therapeutic settings. Although any group member may provide feedback to another member, it is usually true that the therapist's comments have the most impact. In group therapy, as in all therapy, the therapist's role is that of expert. It has also been proposed by Goldstein et al. (1966) that the attractiveness of successful therapists will be high. Both expertise and attractiveness can make the therapist a potential reinforcing agent.

All of this suggests, then, that positive reinforcement is a ubiquitous and powerful element in virtually all therapeutic endeavors. This is a conclusion that has been reached repeatedly by authors from a variety of theoretical perspectives (e.g., Krasner, 1962; Truax & Carkhuff, 1966), so this conclusion is hardly to be considered a provocative point if it is viewed in isolation. If viewed in the context of certain social psychological theories, however, this conclusion has crucially important implications for the process of therapy. There are two social psychological theories particularly useful in analyzing the influence of positive reinforcement on the generalization and maintenance of therapeutic change which we will now discuss.

The Forced-Compliance Perspective on Positive Reinforcement

One body of social psychological literature that provides a useful view of positive reinforcement and its effects on maintenance is a large group of studies collectively entitled "forced-compliance" research. This research was conducted to test various predictions derived from the theory of cognitive dissonance. In order to understand the relevance of the "forced-compliance" situation to the maintenance of therapeutic change, it is necessary to have some familiarity with the underlying theoretical perspective, and the following summary of the theory is presented for this purpose (see Wicklund & Brehm, 1976, for an extensive consideration of the theory and its empirical support, especially chapters 3 through 5, which summarize a number of forced-compliance studies).

Dissonance is an aversive psychological state that is said to arise when "cognitions" (i.e., a person's knowledge about himself or the environment) do not "fit together" or are inconsistent with each other. According to the theory, the individual confronted with an inconsistency among cognitions will be motivated to reduce the dissonance this inconsistency produces. The strength of this motive will depend on the amount of inconsistency that is present and the importance of the cognitions that are involved. In order to reduce dissonance, dissonant cognitions can be eliminated, consonant cognitions can be added, the importance of dissonant cognitions can be reduced, and/or the importance of consonant cognitions can be increased.

While the possible ways in which dissonance can be reduced are thus numerous, the theory does provide specification about which is more likely to occur in a given situation. It is recognized that some cognitions are difficult to change, while some are easy to change. Dissonance reduction processes should, then, center around those cognitions that are *least* resistant to change. Frequently, this will mean that cognitions about recent, overt behaviors are not likely to change, while cognitions about less recent, more ambiguous, or covert behaviors are more likely to change. Finally, it should be noted that "recent research has made it abundantly clear that dissonance reduction as we know it takes place only when the dissonant elements have been brought together through the personal responsibility of the individual who experiences dissonance" (Wicklund & Brehm, 1976, p. 7). While personal responsibility can arise in various ways, the element of choice is seen as crucial.

Now let us try to flesh out the bare bones of the theory as presented above. Consider a person who regards himself as unassertive but who finds himself behaving in an assertive manner. This inconsistency between the person's self-concept and his knowledge of his overt behavior (both important cognitions to the person) should create dissonance, and the person should be motivated to attempt to reduce this dissonance. How can he do this? Two alternatives would seem most obvious: he can change his self-concept, or he can deny his behavior. While we can all think of people who would deny their behavior (i.e., actually deny they engaged in it) rather than change their self-concept, such people are relatively rare. For most people the knowledge of recent, overt behaviors will be difficult to deny. Attitudes (toward the self or the environment) are, however, frequently more ambiguous, less well articulated, and simply less salient than behavior. In such cases, dissonance reduction should take place in regard to the attitude, and the attitude should come to be more in line with the behavior. In our example, the person should begin to think of himself as more assertive than before.

All of this will take place, however, only if the person views himself as responsible for the dissonant elements. Since the attitude existed prior to the behavior and dissonance was created only when the behavior was performed, the issue of responsibility is particularly crucial in regard to the behavior. If the person was forced to engage in the behavior, he should not feel personally responsible and no dissonance (and thus no attitude change) should result. In terms of our example, if the person who views himself as unassertive behaves assertively because he is forced to, a change in self-concept would not be expected. Only when he believes he is personally responsible—most frequently through voluntarily engaging in the behavior—would dissonance theory predict an ensuing change in self-concept.

The forced-compliance literature has provided substantial documentation of this kind of process. In a forced-compliance study, subjects are induced to behave (or at least to commit themselves to behaving) in a way that is inconsistent with an existing attitude. Some subjects are induced to engage in this "counterattitudinal" behavior by the presentation of large rewards (such as money), or are not given any choice about the matter (i.e., they are ordered to engage in the behavior by the experimenter). Other subjects are given only a small reward or are told that they have a choice about engaging in the behavior and that their participation is strictly voluntary. It has been found in numerous studies of this sort that subjects change their attitudes, bringing them more into line with their behavior, only when rewards are small or the counterattitudinal behavior is perceived as freely chosen.

There are several important implications for the therapeutic process that can be derived from forced-compliance research. First, it indicates that changes in people's attitudes can be brought about by inducing behaviors that are inconsistent with these attitudes. Although the relationship between attitudes and behavior is certainly not perfect, one may expect that the new attitude that is consistent with the new behavior will be a factor contributing to the maintenance of the new behavior in the future and to its generalization to nontherapeutic settings. Second, forced-compliance research has indicated that large rewards can serve to undermine the person's perceived freedom of choice. Large rewards constitute an offer the person cannot refuse. Indeed, in forced-compliance research the provision of a large reward is used interchangeably with forcing a person to do something by a direct command, and both have similar effects. In sum, the provision of a large reward has been shown to short-circuit the dissonance and attitude-change processes (as noted previously, Wicklund & Brehm, 1976, provide a detailed review of this research).

At this point it may be helpful to return to our example of the unassertive person. Let us suppose that this person enters into therapy and that one goal of the therapy is to increase his assertiveness. Regardless of the specific orientation of the therapist, it is quite likely that some sort of positive reinforcement contingency will be used to increase the frequency of the client's assertive behavior. While positive reinforcement would be likely to be effective in increasing the desired behavior, it may also be perceived by the client as decreasing his choice about whether or not to act in assertive ways, thus decreasing his personal responsibility for his new behavior. If personal responsibility is decreased, dissonance theory would predict that changes in self-concept are unlikely to occur and thus that the intrapsychic foundations for continued engagement in the behavior—outside of the reinforcement contingency framework—should not be created. Assertive behavior may occur in the therapeutic setting while therapy is continuing, but may not be generalized to other settings or be maintained when therapy is terminated.

It would appear, then, that the therapist is in a bind. One of the methods that may be used to induce new behaviors may have the consequence of reducing the likelihood of maintaining those behaviors. This concern about the effects of positive reinforcement is not restricted to dissonance theorists. Another research literature has developed from a different theory that leads to a similar conclusion.

The Overjustification Perspective on Positive Reinforcement

The overjustification literature is based on a prediction derived from any one of several attribution theories. Bem (1972), deCharms (1968), Deci (1975), and Kelley (1967, 1973) all provide theoretical frameworks that have been applied to overjustification. In order to avoid redundancy, only Bem's theory will be presented here. The choice is based simply on personal preference and in no way implies denigration of the other theoretical approaches.

Bem's self-perception theory states that people come to hold beliefs regarding their intrinsic motives and desires "partially by inferring them from observation of their own overt behavior and/or the circumstances in which this behavior occurs" (Bem, 1972, p. 2). Specifically, the theory proposes that overt behavior will be used by a person as evidence of an intrinsic motive to the degree that the reinforcement contingencies for that behavior are subtle or undiscernible. If the reinforcements for a behavior are not obvious, a person will be led to the conclusion that he/she perform the behavior for intrinsic reasons. On the other hand, when the reinforcements for a behavior are readily apparent, the person will conclude that he/she performed for extrinsic reasons (i.e., in order to get the desired reinforcement).

The overjustification hypothesis is a simple derivation from these basic postulates that applies to situations in which people are aleady intrinsically motivated to perform a particular behavior. In such a situation, a person who expects and is given a significant reward for engaging in the behavior will come to perceive himself or herself as less intrinsically motivated than a person who has engaged in the behavior without such a reward. The reinforcement contingency provides the person with an extrinsic rationale for the behavior, and this information undermines the person's perception of intrinsic motivation. It is readily apparent that the overjustification hypothesis has implications relevant to the issue of maintaining a behavior outside of the therapeutic setting. In particular, a person who perceives himself or herself as less intrinsically motivated should be less likely to engage in the behavior in any setting where the reinforcement contingency does not apply.[1]

An example will be useful in clarifying the essence of the overjustification situation, and to provide one, we may return to the example of the unassertive client. Suppose we have a client who actively seeks assertiveness training. This behavior demonstrates at least some intrinsic interest in being assertive, and further evidence of motivation is shown if the baseline rate of assertive behaviors is above zero. The well-meaning clinician may decide that such a client will benefit from a contingency that positively reinforces assertive behaviors, and these good intentions will seem to be realized by the increased rate of assertiveness that soon appears. During the contingency period, however, the client could undergo a self-observation process that undermines the intrinsic motives necessary to maintain the new behavior: "Sure I'm acting assertive," the client may say, "who wouldn't under these circumstances?" The client may come to the conclusion that the increase in assertive behavior does not reflect an intrinsic motive at all, so that once the contingency is terminated, the behavior itself will not be especially attractive and the likelihood of continued engagement in the behavior will be low. Once again we have arrived at the conclusion that the use of positive reinforcement may have negative implications for the achievement of therapeutic maintenance.

The overjustification hypothesis has generated a good deal of research in the past several years, much of which has been reviewed by Condry (1977) and Notz (1975). In general, this research has supported the hypothesis, and certainly should create concern about any indiscriminate use of positive reinforcement. One limitation of the overjustification literature should, however, be noted. Thus far most of the research has been addressed relatively cognitive and relatively novel activities. It is likely that more well-learned activities may be affected to a lesser extent by reinforcement. It is also unknown whether the use of reinforcement would serve to undermine intrinsic interest in more fundamental behaviors such as eating and sexual behavior, or indeed more highly driven behaviors in general such as additions or aggression.

A Comparison of Forced Compliance and Overjustification

Two perspectives have been offered that may be of use in understanding the effects of positive reinforcement on the maintenance of therapeutic change. Both of these empirically supported theories suggest that maintenance is most likely when a perception of being personally responsible for a behavior is present, and both suggest that use of positive reinforcement may undermine such personal responsibility. There are, however, some fundamental differences between forced compliance and overjustification. Most important among these differences may be the domains to which the theories apply (see also Fazio, Zanna, & Cooper, 1977). The forced compliance analysis is best applied to attitude-change phenomena that accompany engagement in attitudinally discrepant behavior. The overjustification hypothesis is best applied to behaviors that are congruent with a person's existing attitudes, or are at least irrelevant to those attitudes.

In terms of the clinical setting, forced compliance may be most appropriately applied to behaviors that the client is reluctant to perform. This includes those situations in which the use of reinforcement is intended to induce the client to engage in behaviors that are discrepant with an existing belief or self-concept. The overjustification paradigm may be most applicable when the goal of therapy is to increase the frequency of behaviors that the client already regards as desirable or that he/she has no strong feelings about. These two perspectives, then, have a certain complementarity that collectively covers most, if not all, possible uses of positive reinforcement, and both raise serious concerns about the use of this method of inducing therapeutic change.

Concern about the negative effects of positive reinforcement is not confined to the social psychology literature. For example, in a review of token economy programs, Kazdin (1975) states:

There is considerable evidence that responses developed with token reinforcement are not maintained once the contingencies are withdrawn and are not likely to transfer automatically to nontreatment settings. (p. 252)

Something that is unique about the social psychology perspective on positive reinforcement, however, is that it not only makes sense out of problems that have been empirically observed, it also offers a theoretical framework for generating strategies to overcome such problems. Moreover, the emphasis on the central role of self-determination and self-mastery derived from both dissonance and self-perception theories is consistent with recent therapies advocating self-control techniques (e.g., Thoresen & Mahoney, 1974). Thus the social psychology perspective may be useful in understanding the effectiveness and growing popularity of such therapies (cf. also Chapter 8).

Specific methods that are well known among behavior therapists to be helpful in "preventing extinction" fit quite well with maintenance strategies that may be generated from the social psychology perspective. It has long been a fiat of behavioral approaches to avoid excessively large rewards in favor of more frequent, small rewards (e.g., Homme, Csanyi, Gonzales, & Rechs, 1970; Smith & Moore, 1966). Small rewards are, of course, less likely to create overjustification or short-circuit dissonance, so the greater maintenance achieved through this technique is consistent with the theories presented here. The use of intermittent reinforcement schedules is also frequently recommended by behavior therapists (Kazdin, 1975). From the social psychological perspective, such schedules allow clients to observe themselves performing their new behaviors without obtaining rewards, thus reducing the negative psychological impact of such rewards. Other techniques for increasing maintenance suggested by the social psychological perspective would include the use of verbal cues to influence the client's attributions about his or her own behavior (Grusec, Kuczynski, Rushton, & Simutis, 1978; Kiesler, Nisbett, & Zanna, 1969). In such a cognitive "reframing" approach, the therapist would discredit the importance of the reinforcement contingency and stress the client's personal responsibility for any change that has taken place. Another strategy is derived specifically from dissonance theory. This view suggests that the therapist may facilitate positive changes in the client's self-concept by pointing out inconsistencies between the new behavior patterns and the client's former self-concept. Such "confrontation" would be likely to heighten the dissonance aroused and would thus serve to increase changes in self-concept.

Our interest in presenting this discussion of positive reinforcement is not to propose that the technique be abandoned. Rewards are an effective way of achieving relatively quick changes in behavior, and they have appropriate uses. However, we have highlighted here the potential drawbacks of rewards for the goals of generalizing and maintaining behavior change. The therapist must keep in mind that techniques that offer immediate efficiency may also have costs in terms of long-term effectiveness. It would be very easy to be impressed with the immediate therapeutic gains produced by large and conspicuous rewards and to be less sensitive to the issue of maintaining these gains outside of the therapeutic context. The social psychological perspective, however, has the value of focusing one's attention on the delicate relationship between situationally induced behavior (i.e., immediate gains) and self-determined behavior (i.e., generalized maintenance of changes).

THERAPEUTIC CHANGE
INDUCED BY AVERSIVE EVENTS

It was pointed out above that the use of positive reinforcement in therapy is nearly ubiquitous. A similar argument may be made regarding the use of aversive experiences. For this analysis it is important to distinguish between specific aversive contingencies and more diffuse aversive events that may occur on a noncontingent basis. This distinction allows for the analysis of the role of aversive events in therapy in terms of two different social psychological perspectives. One theory stresses the potential negative effects of contingent aversive consequences, while the other indicates the potential value of nonspecific aversive experiences. Consideration of both points of view should contribute to a more comprehensive understanding of how aversive aspects of therapy may be most effectively applied.

Aversive Contingencies and
Psychological Reactance

One important perspective on the effects of aversive contingencies is provided by J. W. Brehm's theory of the psychological reactance (see J. W. Brehm, 1966, and Wicklund, 1974, for extensive reviews of this literature). This theory is based on the premise that every individual has certain behavioral freedoms—behaviors that the person has engaged in in the past, is engaging in during the present, and/or plans to engage in in the future. Whenever a behavioral freedom is threatened with elimination, the person should be motivated to reduce reactance by acting to restore the behavioral freedom. The most direct way to restore freedom is to engage in the threatened behavior.

Reactance theory, then, has a general application to those circumstances under which the client feels forced to engage or *not* to engage in a specific free behavior. In the former case, for example, a large reward that "forces" the client to engage in a therapeutically desirable behavior should arouse reactance and the client should be motivated to reestablish his/her freedom by engaging in the behavior. Thus reactance theory raises concerns about the use of positive reinforcement that are consistent with the dissonance and self-perception analyses in the previous section.

While large rewards can be seen to have the psychological effect of "forcing" behavior, the issue of force is perhaps more salient in regard to aversive contingencies. Whenever a client expects to be punished for a response, this punishment should be perceived as "forcing" him/her to relinquish the behavior and thereby threatening his/her freedom to engage in the behavior. According to reactance theory, increased motivation to engage in the "forbidden" behavior should then result.

The applicability of reactance theory to clinical practice is considerably enlarged when the definition of "punishment" is closely considered. There are, of course, direct, physical punishments used, for example, in aversion therapy. There are also more subtle forms of punishment that may be quite frequent in many types of therapy. The therapist is an important figure in the client's life, and actual or feared disapproval from such an important person can constitute a distinct punishment. Moreover, there is punishment by omission as well. When a client expects approval from the therapist and such approval does not occur, this may be perceived as highly aversive and punishing by the client. From this more general standpoint, then, contingent aversive consequences are likely to be experienced by many clients in many types of therapy, and the reactance theory analysis can be applied to a broad range of specific therapeutic interventions.

The potential seriousness of reactance arousal during therapy can be illustrated by returning to our example of the client who seeks assertion training.[2] While this client may wish to become more assertive (and indeed has entered therapy to accomplish this), being unassertive is a well-established and important (in the sense of affecting a large part of the person's life and helping the person to predict other people's responses to him) freedom. Suppose, then, that the therapist has strongly urged this client to become more assertive and has accompanied this urging with a mixture of promised reward for compliance ("I will approve of your behavior if it is assertive") and punishment for noncompliance ("I will disapprove of your behavior if it is not assertive"). Such a strong persuasive communication might well be perceived by the client as contituting a threat to the freedom to behave unassertively and might arouse reactance. The client can reduce reactance by direct engagement in the threatened freedom—that is, by engaging in *un*assertive behaviors. Thus reactance arousal and subsequent restorative efforts can produce behavior reversals—the client's engaging in the opposite of what has been urged by the therapist—that in a clinical context would be seen as "deterioration effects" (cf. also DeVoge's analysis in Chapter 10 of complementary roles for an alternative explanation of this phenomenon).

Faced with such a possibility, the therapist may believe that stronger persuasive efforts and/or contingency management are needed to overcome the client's "resistance" to therapeutic change. It should be noted, however, that the theory of psychological reactance states that stronger threats to freedom will increase the magnitude of reactance arousal. Thus the stronger communication and/or contingency is likely to produce more engagement in the undesirable behavior rather than less.

This issue has been discussed by Worchel and Brehm (1971) in terms of the two forces elicited by persuasive communications. Worchel and Brehm note that any persuasive communication elicits both a tendency to comply and a tendency to oppose; whichever tendency is stronger will determine whether the person complies with the communication or opposes it. The analysis by Worchel and Brehm seems to suggest that increases in compliance and reactance tendencies are not identically related to increases in the strength of the communication. It appears that when one goes from a moderately strong persuasive communication to a very strong one, there may well be a greater increase in reactance than in the tendency to comply. Thus the very elements (such as a command rather than a request, high attractiveness of the communicator, offers of rewards and/or punishments that cannot be refused) that can contribute to compliance can, if present in too much force, create powerful oppositional tendencies.

In terms of the therapeutic situation, it is particularly important to consider when and where such oppositional tendencies are likely to be expressed. Most reactance research has dealt with immediate opposition. The research paradigm has typically been to present a strong threat to a behavioral freedom and then to allow subjects to restore freedom directly by engaging in the threatened behavior. While such immediate opposition has implications for a variety of undesirable behaviors that may be seen during therapy (such as derogation of the therapist, resistance and opposition to therapeutic recommendation, and premature termination of therapy; see Stivers & Brehm, Note 1), direct opposition does have the virtue of coming immediately to the therapist's attention. Moreover, a study by J. W. Brehm and Mann (1975) suggests that when immediate opposition has been expressed, removal of the pressure to comply can lead to compliance. This paradigm may serve as an explanatory model for the so-called vacation cures commonly noted in clinical folklore. Separation from the therapist may reduce the pressure to comply, thus reducing reactance arousal and allowing increased compliance with therapeutic injunctions to take place.

The above model, however, should only operate in those instances where opposition has been expressed in overt behavior during therapy. There are some situations where such direct expression will not occur. There are situations, for instance, where the cost of expressing opposition may be too high, and thus even though the motivation to oppose is high, overt behavior will continue to be compliant. Not infrequently, therapeutic settings may constitute just such a situation. Many clients may perceive the cost of directly opposing their therapists as being prohibitive. They may be emotionally invested in gaining their therapists' approval and they may believe that direct opposition may harm their therapeutic progress. However, once therapy is terminated, the client's emotional investment in the therapist should decline considerably and the issue of therapeutic progress should become less salient. If reactance arousal has been high, direct expression of this motive may now occur and these clients may restore their freedom by engaging in the forbidden behavior(s).

These considerations lead to a set of recommendations aimed at avoiding the deterioration effects that may be caused by arousal of reactance. First, it should be clear that to minimize client opposition during therapy, strong attempts at persuasion (which involve strong threats to behavioral freedoms) should be avoided—regardless of whether they are based on the anticipation of a reward or a fear of punishment, and whether these rewards and punishments are primary, secondary, or social in nature.

Less obvious ways of avoiding reactance arousal during therapy can be derived from a consideration of two other factors that affect the magnitude of reactance: the importance of freedoms, and implications for other freedoms. In terms of the importance of freedoms, the relationship is a direct one; the more important the freedom that is threatened, the more reactance will be aroused. At first blush this proposition would seem rather unhelpful in the therapeutic situation. Therapy, after all, tends to deal with important behaviors, not unimportant ones. Therapists who concentrate on unimportant freedoms may in fact not arouse reactance, but would they be doing anything therapeutic? As is usual in psychology, the answer to this question depends on how we define our terms. If we define "important" to mean "psychologically significant" to the client, then it is true that therapy must deal with important freedoms and probably must threaten them to some extent. If, however, we look at other constructions of the meaning of importance, we may find some therapeutically relevant information. For example, a study by Wicklund and Brehm (1968) defined importance in terms of perceived competence. These investigators reasoned that if a person feels incompetent regarding some behavior—that is, unable to have a knowledgable opinion or make an informed decision about the behavior—then the behavioral freedom cannot be regarded as an important one. Their results were consistent with this reasoning and indicated that the more competent a person felt on an issue, the more likely that person was to experience reactance in response to a threat to freedom. Thus it would seem that as long as the therapist is perceived as relatively more competent than the client vis-à-vis a specific behavior urged by the therapist, reactance arousal is unlikely to be high. In practice this may mean that therapists need to make their field of expertise clear to their clients. Also of value in this regard would be statements making clear to clients areas where the therapists claim no more expertise (and sometimes less) than they. The delineation of areas of both superior and inferior expertise should help to define clearly the therapist's expertise and make it more credible.

The other determinant of reactance arousal, implications for other freedoms, may be particularly useful in reducing reactance arousal in therapy. Reactance arousal is a function of the proportion of freedoms threatened; the greater the proportion that is threatened, the greater will be the arousal of reactance (Wicklund, Slattum, & Solomon, 1970). Thus, assuming the number of freedoms to be constant, threats to freedom that by implication threaten other freedoms will arouse more reactance than threats that are isolated to one freedom. Therapeutically, this proposition suggests that the broader the class of behaviors urged by the therapist, the more likely reactance arousal will become. For instance, the therapist who recommends that a client reduce consumption of one undesirable substance is less likely to arouse reactance than the therapist who recommends reduction in a variety of substances. Also, reactance is less likely if a client is advised to increase a given behavior in one situation rather than in a number of situations. In general, then, the more precisely defined and limited the therapeutic recommendation, the fewer freedoms will be threatened and the less reactance should result.

The above recommendations are concerned with preventing reactance arousal during therapy. It is presumed that if reactance arousal is sufficiently low during therapy, the possibility of deterioration effects after therapy will also be low. But, one should ask, how is a therapist to tell that reactance arousal is *sufficiently* low? After all, a non-reactance-producing therapy would look the same as a highly reactance-producing therapy in which the client was constrained from overt opposition. In both, compliance and not opposition would occur during therapy.

Fortunately, there is one sure way to determine whether or not the therapeutic situation is overly constraining the client and thus obscuring from the therapist any reactance motivation that may be present. This is to elicit noncompliance during therapy. In fact, the eliciting of noncompliance may not take much active endeavor from a therapist who utilizes the types of theoretical analyses already discussed in this chapter. Any therapist who is keeping both rewards and punishments low will likely find that on occasion these inducements to compliance are so low that the client does not comply. This outcome indicates two factors to the therapist: (1) in order to induce compliance, rewards and/or punishments will have to be increased; and (2) the therapeutic situation is certainly not too powerful and thus any reactance motivation that is aroused can be revealed during therapy. If, on the other hand, the therapist finds that any inducement, no matter how apparently small, leads to behavioral compliance, then the therapist may be concerned that the pressures on the client to comply are in fact undesirably high. This situation would raise the possibility that reversals of therapeutic gains could occur after termination.

In such an instance, it might well be helpful for the therapist to induce the client to oppose a therapeutic recommendation. For example, by threatening an important behavior on which the client feels competent and/or expanding the implications for other freedoms of a given threat to freedom, it should be possible for the therapist to obtain overt opposition. This opposition can then be made salient to the client as evidence of the client's freedom in therapy to comply *or* to oppose, and the likelihood of maintaining therapeutic change should be increased. It should be noted that this method of induced reactance should be relatively safe to use within therapy as long as the therapist threatens a behavior in which direct engagement is available to the client and will not be harmful By allowing the client to restore feedom directly by engaging in the threatened behavior, reactance from the specific threat to freedom will be reduced and should not have any undesirable effects after therapy is completed.

Finally, one must consider the possibility that even after active attempts to arouse reactance, no overt opposition will be displayed by the client. This state of affairs is quite ambiguous: perhaps the client's behavior is overwhelmingly constrained and thus one needs to be concerned about maintenance, or perhaps the client is simply "ready" to make dramatic and extensive behavior change and no concerns about maintenance are warranted. To sort out these possibilities, it is probably reasonable to move very quickly in therapy, but then to institute a lengthy maintenance period in which therapeutic contacts are spread out over a considerable period of time. If therapeutic changes are maintained during the maintenance period, then therapy will have been notably effective and efficient. If, however, therapeutic gains diminish or even reverse during the maintenance period, renewed efforts by the therapist to establish the client's perceptions of behavioral freedom will probably be necessary.

Noncontingent Aversive Experiences and Cognitive Dissonance

The above discussion has focused on aversive contingencies and the resultant restrictions on behavioral freedoms that can occur. In contrast to these situations, there are aversive aspects to therapy that are not part of the specific persuasion process and/or contingency management administered by the therapist, but instead occur in a general and diffuse way throughout the therapeutic process. Sometimes these aversive aspects are relatively dramatic, as when clients in desensitization or implosion therapy concentrate on those things that make them afraid. In other instances these aversive aspects are less clear-cut and simply involve those vague feelings of discomfort, awkwardness, and embarrassment that virtually all clients feel at some point during therapy.

Many therapists have of course sought to reduce such unpleasant aspects of therapy. They have endeavored to create an acccepting, benevolent atmosphere in therapy in which the client feels comfortable and secure. Even in such situations, however, it has not usually been possible to eliminate the effort that therapy involves. Clients have to expend time and effort to arrive for the therapeutic sessions, they usually have to pay for therapy in some way, they have to concentrate on their problems, and they are usually expected to make and effort between sessions to overcome these problems.

Thus it can be stated that therapy is a high-effort situation frequently involving at least some aversive consequences for the client, and that these features of effort and aversive consequences characterize a broad range of different forms of therapy. If this description is accepted as valid, then it is only a small step to the conclusion that *when clients engage in therapy voluntarily,* a state of cognitive dissonance should be aroused.[3] The belief that something is aversive and choosing to engage in it simply do not "fit"; such a choice does not follow from the belief that is held, so cognitive dissonance should result.

There are many studies in the dissonance literature indicating that dissonance is aroused and attitude change is induced when people voluntarily undergo unpleasant experiences and/or effortful endeavors (see Wicklund & Brehm, 1976, especially chap. 10 and 11, for a review). The issue that is less well resolved involves what specific attitude will be changed. The most direct reduction of dissonance would probably involve becoming more favorable toward the unpleasant and/or effortful task, viewing it as more pleasant and/or less effortful, and therefore being willing to endure more of it. This type of dissonance reduction has certain benefits for the client—by reducing the likelihood of premature termination of therapy—and obvious benefits for the therapist's bank account, but is not directly relevant to the issue of therapeutic change. On the other hand, a less direct but perhaps equally likely mode of dissonance reduction in therapy would involve the client's perception of the effectiveness of therapy. Dissonance should be considerably reduced if clients believe that therapy (the unpleasant/effortful endeavor they are voluntarily participating in) is working through production of those problems that brought them into therapy. This belief that therapy is working may be a critical factor in inducing both immediate and long-lasting behavior change. For the belief that therapy is effective (and worth the effort) to be created and maintained, changes in behavior and self-concept that are implied by that belief must actually come about.

This type of analysis of therapeutic interventions has at least two important implications. First, it would suggest that efforts to reduce the unpleasant/effortful characteristics of therapy may be well intended but misleading. Certainly, therapy has to be pleasant enough that clients will come to it and stay in it for a period of time. Past this critical minimum of pleasantness, however, the unpleasant and effortful characteristics may be crucial to therapeutic success. Indeed, the dissonance analysis is quite clear on this point: as long as the individual continues to engage in the behavior voluntarily, the greater the effort and/or unpleasantness of the behavior, the more dissonance should be created. The more dissonance that is created, the more attitude change should take place, and if our analysis is correct, the greater should be the desired behavior change and maintenance.

Second, mention should be made of the timeliness of considering relatively nonspecific explanatory models of therapeutic success. Recent concern over the importance of nonspecific effects in social-learning-based anxiety reduction techniques such as systematic desensitization (see reviews by Kazdin & Wilcoxon, 1976; Lick & Bootzin, 1975), and Sloane et al.'s (1975) finding of essentially equivalent effectiveness for experienced behavior and psychotherapists, suggest that our analysis of the therapeutic process may need to be enlarged. This is not to say that a return to global, nonempirical conceptual schemes is recommended, but it does now appear that an effort to discover theoretically precise and empirically supported models that can cut across various specific therapeutic modalities would be highly appropriate. While all of the theoretical perspectives discussed in this chapter would seem to have a considerable contribution to make to this endeavor, it is quite possible that the conceptualization of therapy as an effort justification process is the most far-reaching, and thus potentially the most powerful.

CONCLUSIONS AND DIRECTIONS FOR FUTURE RESEARCH

At this point it should be quite evident that the various social psychological theories discussed here converge on a general recommendation concerning maintenance of therapeutic change. Whether one wishes to speak of the need for dissonance-induced attitude change or for attribution to intrinsic motivation or for avoiding reactance, the conclusion is the same: it is crucial that clients perceive their behaviors in therapy as voluntary and not coerced by external rewards or punishments. Moreover, while the present chapter has focused on rewards and punishments, the same concerns apply to the use of any external agent (such as medication—Davison, Tsujimoto, & Glaros, 1973; Davison & Valins, 1969) that could serve as a causal explanation of or justification for therapeutic change. The essence of the social psychological perspective on maintenance is quite simply that clients need to feel that they "own" their own gains in therapy and are responsible for them. If these conditions are met, therapeutic change stands a good chance of being maintained; if these conditions are not met, therapeutic changes may disappear or even be reversed once the special circumstances of therapy are removed.

This need of clients to feel responsible for their behavior is, of course, not a particularly new idea in clinical circles. A variety of significant figures in clinical work, including such diverse individuals as Sigmund Freud and Carl Rogers, have constructed therapeutic approaches that minimize the overt control of the client by the therapist. Furthermore, humanistic approaches to therapy have been quite emphatic in their respect for the client's freedom and self-initiative.

It is important to be aware, however, that the social psychological perspective discussed in this chapter is somewhat—perhaps even radically—different from many of these previous concerns with the client's freedom. The social psychological approach advocates maximizing the client's *perception* of freedom within a context that is in fact controlled by the therapist. The perception of freedom is seen as desirable not because of any general philosophical position, but because it is a critical ingredient in effecting the long-lasting behavior change desired by the client. The social psychological approach is then quite similar to that of behavior therapy. The therapist is seen as responsible for manipulating the environment to create specific effects on the client. The difference between the social psychological approach and approaches based on various learning theories lies in the variables they consider most important, not in their general approach to the therapeutic endeavor.

Furthermore, the social psychological approach recognizes that the way in which the client's perception of freedom is created may vary considerably depending on the specific therapeutic circumstances. For some clients, perceived freedom may be enhanced by decreasing the client's emotional attachment and attraction to the therapist. For others, the therapist will need to increase such an attachment to counter the more coercive effects (as perceived by the client) of significant others in the client's social milieu. There is no one format of therapy that can be derived from a consideration of social psychological theories. There are, however, a number of important psychological factors indicated by such theories, and these factors may typically be operationalized in numerus ways. Thus the clinician is faced with a multitude of decisions each time a client enters the office. It is the need to choose which of the many factors and which of the many ways of manipulating it are most appropriate for each client that constitutes the "art" of the clinician.

Acknowledgment that the use of psychological theory in applied settings remains something of an art does not deny the need for or the value of scientific research. The social psychological approach to therapeutic maintenance presented here has been based on existing research findings. The research findings have, however, been "basic" in nature rather than applied; they have been obtained from research with normal populations rather than clinical ones. In our concluding remarks, we would like to address the relationship between basic and applied research and the way in which they can both contribute to our understanding of the therapeutic enterprise.

First, it is our opinion that any approach to therapy needs to be grounded in a strong foundation of basic research: (1) because of the greater control available in the laboratory than in the real world, basic research can specify precise relationships that might be virtually impossible to "pull out of" the booming, buzzing confusion of real life; and (2) because basic research is typically easier and cheaper to perform than full-blown therapy outcome research, it provides a necessary proving ground for ideas. Moreover, it seems only ethically responsible to make sure that the basic theoretical and conceptual frameworks that we wish to use in therapy rest on relationships that have received clear (that is, replicated by numerous, independent investigators) support in the laboratory.

Second, once a conceptual framework or theory has received ample support at the basic laboratory level, then analogue studies offer a valuable method of adjusting the basic research paradigms closer to actual clinical concerns. Analogue studies—including such approaches as role-playing by subjects from normal populations and the use of subjects with minor psychological difficulties such as circumscribed phobias and mild anxiety states—appear to have come into disrepute recently. This may be based on a misunderstanding of the contribution of such studies to clinical knowledge. Analogue studies cannot, by their very nature, serve to prove the clinical effectiveness of any approach. They can serve, however, as a screening device (would one really want to test any approach on a clinical population that failed to be effective in an analogue study) and as a forum to indicate the clinical implications of various approaches. Thus it would seem that analogue studies not be dismissed as having no value, but that the nature of their contribution must be understood and not overstated.

At the third level, full-scale therpay outcome studies with experienced clinicians and clinical populations are necessary to document the effectiveness of any specific approach. Note here the emphasis on *effectiveness*. Due to both ethical and practical constraints, it is extremely difficult to use therapy outcome studies to make an initial determination of the relative importance of specific factors within any given general approach. Clinicians tend to "overbuild" their bridges; they tend to use a variety of factors to work in combination toward therapeutic goals. And well they should. However, this does produce an important limitation on this sort of research. Since many factors are being used with different frequencies by the therapists in these studies, information about which of the factors is the "most effective ingredient" is difficult to obtain. Therapy outcome studies will thus be more helpful in establishing whether an approach is more effective than no treatment and/or an alternate treatment than in determining how to improve the effectiveness and/or efficiency of therapy.

Improvement of our clinical services, however, calls for maximizing both effectiveness (total change) and efficiency (change per unit of time). It is at this point that analogue studies again become useful. Once a general approach has obtained good empirical support for its effectiveness (and even today this state of affairs is only beginning to exist), then follow-up analogue studies can begin to address what aspects of the general treatment approach are *most* effective. Presumably, such follow-up analogues could in time create a new general approach based on those factors that appear most effective and deleting those factors that have little or no impact. This new general approach could then be subjected to the rigors of a full-scale therapy outcome study.

This view of research is, obviously, a highly inclusive one. It maintains that a variety of research approaches have important and different contributions to make to clinical concerns. It is also an approach that is highly consistent with a social psychological perspective. In social psychology, there are many theories with good empirical documentation obtained in the laboratory. Increasingly, there are some analogue studies that begin to address clinical concerns more directly. We view this as a good beginning, but no more than a beginning. It is our hope that this chapter will serve to stimulate more consideration of the relevance of social psychological theory and findings to clinical practice, and that from this consideration will come further steps down the long road of research on the maintenance of therapeutic change.

NOTES

1. While the need for a client to make a "self-attribution" concerning his or her engagement in therapeutically desirable behaviors is quite evident from a consideration of the overjustification literature, this does not imply that self-attributions are always beneficial. Both Valins and Nisbett (1971) and S. S. Brehm (1976) have argued that, in general, *extrinsic* attributions for *un*desirable behaviors may be preferable.

2. It will presumably be obvious that applications of social psychological theory are not restricted to problems encountered in attempting to increase assertive behavior. This one example has been used throughout the chapter to facilitate comparison of the different theories being discussed.

3. Note, then, that the following discussion would not be applicable to clients who are clearly coerced (e.g., by court order, by staff order for persons living in a "total institution" such as a prison or committed to an inpatient facility or by one's parents if one is a minor) into participating in therapy.

REFERENCE NOTE

1. Stivers, M., & Brehm, S. S. *The influence of perceived personal control on responses to communications concerning sources of control.* Unpublished manuscript, University of Kansas, 1978.

REFERENCES

Bandura, A. *Principles of behavior modification.* New York: Holt, Rinehart & Winston, 1969.

Bandura, A. Self-efficacy: Toward a unifying theory of behavioral change. *Psychological Review,* 1977, *84,* 191–215.

Bem, D. Self-perception theory. *Advances in experimental social psychology,* 1972, *6,* 1–62.

Brehm, J. W. *A theory of psychological reactance.* New York: Academic Press, 1966.

Brehm, J. W., & Mann, M. The effect of importance of freedom and attraction to group members on influence produced by group pressure. *Journal of Personality and Social Psychology,* 1975, *31,* 816–824.

Brehm, S. S. *The application of social psychology to clinical practice.* Washington, D.C.: Hemisphere, 1976.

Carson, R. C. *Interaction concepts of personality.* Chicago: Aldine, 1969.

Condry, J. Enemies of exploration: Self-initiated versus other-initiated learning. *Journal of Personality and Social Psychology,* 1977, *35,* 459–477.

Davison, G., Tsujimoto, R., & Glaros, A. Attribution and the maintenance of a behavior change in falling asleep. *Journal of Abnormal Psychology,* 1973, *82,* 124–133.

Davison, G., & Valins, S. Maintenance of self-attributed and drug-attributed behavior change. *Journal of Personality and Social Psychology,* 1969, *11,* 25–38.

deCharms, R. *Personal causation.* New York: Academic Press, 1968.

Deci, E. L. *Intrinsic motivation.* New York: Plenum Press, 1975.

Fazio, R. H., Zanna, M. P., & Cooper, J. Dissonance and self-perception: An integrative view of each theory's domain of application. *Journal of Experimental Social Psychology,* 1977, *13,* 464–479.

Frank, J. D. *Persuasion and healing* (rev. ed.). Baltimore: The John Hopkins University Press, 1973. (Originally published 1961.)

Goldstein, A. P., Heller, K., & Sechrest, L. B. *Psychotherapy and the psychology of behavior change.* New York: Wiley, 1966.

Grusec, J., Kuczynski, L., Rushton, J. P., & Simutis, Z. M. Modeling, direct instruction, and attributions: Effects on altruism. *Developmental Psychology,* 1978, *14,* 51–57.

Homme, L., Csanyi, A. P., Gonzales, M. A., & Rechs, J. R. *How to use contingency contracting in the classroom.* Champaign, Ill.: Research Press, 1970.

Kazdin, A. E. Recent advances in token economy research. In M. Hersen, R. M. Eisler, & P. M. Miller (Eds.), *Progress in behavior modification* (vol. 1). New York: Academic Press, 1975.

Kazdin, A. E., & Wilcoxon, L. A. Systematic desensitization and nonspecific treatment effects: A methodological evaluation. *Psychological Bulletin,* 1976, *83,* 729–758.

Kelley, H. H. Attribution theory in social psychology. In D. Levine (Ed.), *Nebraska Symposium on Motivation* (vol. 15). Lincoln: University of Nebraska Press, 1967.

Kelley, H. H. The process of causal attribution. *American Psychologist,* 1973, *28,* 107–128.

Kiesler, C. A., Nisbett, R., & Zanna, M. On inferring one's belief's from one's behavior. *Journal of Personality and Social Psychology,* 1969, *11,* 321–327.

Krasner, L. The therapist as a social reinforcement machine. In H. H. Strupp & L. Luborsky (Eds.), *Research in psychotherapy* (vol. 2). Washington, D.C.: American Psychological Association, 1962.

Lick, J. R. & Bootzin, R. R. Expectancy factors in the treatment of fear: Methodological and theoretical issues. *Psychological Bulletin,* 1975, *82,* 917–931.

London, P. The end of ideology in behavior modification. *American Psychologist,* 1972, *27,* 913–920.

Notz, W. W. Work motivation and the negative effects of extrinsic rewards: A review with implications for theory and practice. *American Psychologist,* 1975, *30,* 884–891.

Rotter, J. B. *Social learning and clinical psychology.* Englewood Cliffs, N.J.: Prentice-Hall, 1954.

Rotter, J. B. Generalized expectancies for internal versus internal control of reinforcement. *Psychological Monographs,* 1966, *80* (1, Whole No. 609).

Sloane, R. B., Staples, F. R., Cristol, A. H., Yorkston, N.J., & Whipple, K. *Psychotherapy versus behavior therapy.* Cambridge, Mass.: Harvard University Press, 1975.

Smith, W. I., & Moore, J. W. *Conditioning and instrumental learning.* New York: McGraw-Hill, 1966.

Thoresen, C. E., & Mahoney, M. J. *Behavioral self control.* New York: Holt, Rinehart & Winston, 1974.

Truax, C. B., & Carkhuff, R. R. Reinforcement and non-reinforcement in Rogerian psychotherapy. *Journal of Abnormal and Social Psychology,* 1966, *71,* 1–9.

Valins, S., & Nisbett, R. E. *Attribution processes in the development and treatment of emotional disorders.* Morristown, N.J.: General Learning Press, 1971.

Wicklund, R. A. *Freedom and reactance.* Hillsdale, N.J.: Lawrence Erlbaum, 1974.

Wicklund, R. A., & Brehm, J. W. Attitude change as a function of felt competence and threat to attitudinal freedom. *Journal of Experimental Social Psychology,* 1968, *4,* 64–75.

Wicklund, R. A., & Brehm, J. W. *Perspectives on cognitive dissonance.* Hillsdale, N.J.: Lawrence Erlbaum, 1976.

Wicklund, R. A., Slattum, V., & Solomon, E. Effects of implied pressure toward commitment on ratings of choice alternatives. *Journal of Experimental Social Psychology,* 1970, *6,* 449–457.

Worchel, S., & Brehm, J. W. Direct and implied social restoration of freedom. *Journal of Personality and Social Psychology,* 1971, *18,* 294–304.

Yalom, I. D. *The theory and practice of group psychotherapy.* New York: Basic Books, 1970.

12

MODIFYING SETTINGS AS A STRATEGY FOR PERMANENT, PREVENTIVE BEHAVIOR CHANGE:
Flexible Work Schedules and the Quality of Family Life

RICHARD A. WINETT AND MICHAEL S. NEALE

In a recent book on behavioral approaches to community psychology, a basic tenet of the "behavioral community" position was stated: "The development and patterning of human behavior is the result of a transactional process between the person and the environment . . . and, as a consequence, efforts to alleviate social problems necessarily entail modification of *both* environmental events and human behavioral repertoires" (Nietzel, Winett, MacDonald & Davidson, 1977, p. 1). There is also a growing belief in clinical and community psychology that the usual rehabilitative approach has been costly, of limited effectiveness, and that more of our efforts need to be directed toward *prevention* (Cowen, 1973).

The two major concepts that formed the basis for the research program that will be described below were modification of settings (Sarason,

1972) or environmental design (Winett, 1976), and prevention. These concepts were overlaid, as we shall see, with an *ecological* view of behavior (Bronfenbrenner, 1977). Simply stated, this overall framework highlights the need to: (1) examine various systems that directly and indirectly affect behavior; (2) consider modifying such systems or settings as an intervention strategy; and (3) focus on preventive interventions and strategies.

If we examine the issue of maintenance, this framework suggests why permanent behavior change through therapeutic endeavors has often been elusive. Virtually all maintenance strategies have been *person-centered*. In one way or another, the person-centered approach attempts to train clients to *adapt* to environments that essentially caused, or are related to, the presenting problems. Person-centered maintenance strategies include various self-control and cognitive approaches, skill development involving training in the "natural environment" and in multiple settings, teaching skills that are reinforceable by significant others, and procedures that entail fading of reinforcement contingencies (Kazdin, 1975).

Obviously, person-centered approaches are important. It is not always possible to "reprogram the environment." Person-centered maintenance strategies are becoming increasingly sophisticated, multimodal, and at least for some problems, more effective (Best & Block, in press; Lando, 1977).

However, person-centered approaches to behavior change and maintenance seem a poor choice when: (1) problems are experienced by a significant proportion of the population; (2) such problems, in part, are readily attributable to deficiencies in specific systems and settings; and (3) the targeted environments are potentially modifiable, or new structures can be embedded into existing systems (e.g., Fairweather, Sanders, & Tornatzky, 1974). In this chapter we will examine how this ecological perspective was applied to problems experienced by families with young children.

THE CHANGING FAMILY

The "ideal American family," composed of the male "breadwinner," the female "caretaker," and children, is the basis for the rules and regulations that govern many of our social systems. For example, the typical school system's hours of operation assume that someone (mother) is always available to watch children after 3 P.M., and of course assume that a full-time caretaker is available during the summer, numerous holidays, and "conference" days. Yet the ideal American family is now a *statistical minority*. For example, the single-breadwinner family comprises only 13% of existing American households (Ramey, 1978), and in only 34% of husband–wife families is the husband the sole breadwinner (Hayghe, 1976). By 1976, 54% of married women with school-age children worked outside their home (U.S. Department of Labor, 1977). For families with preschool children, 37% of married mothers worked outside their home in 1976 compared to 13% in 1948 (National Academy of Sciences, 1976; U.S. Department of Labor, 1977).

Keniston (1977) puts both the trend and current status of families in focus for us:

> To be sure, changes in American family structure have been fairly continuous since the first European settlements, but today these changes seem to be occurring so rapidly that the shift is no longer a simple extension of long-term trends. We have passed a genuine watershed: this is the first time in our history that the *typical* school age child has a mother who works outside the home. (p. 5)

We also know that the major variable influencing the pattern of our lives today (even more striking than socioeconomic status) is whether or not we work outside the home (J.P. Robinson, 1977). For example, if we know that a person is employed full-time outside the home, it is a relatively straightforward process to predict his or her daily schedule of activities and behavior settings.

What, then, are some of the problems that are encountered by dual worker families?

PROBLEMS ENCOUNTERED BY DUAL-WORKER FAMILIES

Given traditional role structures and prevailing systems, the increasing entrance of women with school-age children into the labor market has created numerous pressures and problems for many American dual-worker families. The sheer amount of work (job, child care, and home chores) performed by a dual-worker family is greater than that performed by a single-worker family. Where does the time and (human) energy to perform work and home functions come from, and at what social-psychological costs (e.g., time from spouse, friends, and children)? Who will care for the children before and after school (or other child-care situations)? How good is child care outside the home for young children (Winett, Fuchs, Moffatt, & Nerviano, 1977)? How are men and women developing new role relationships? These are some of the problems and issues being raised as family life is affected by the world of work.

It certainly is not surprising that a sample of dual-worker families reported to us a host of "clinical" symptoms (fatigue, stress, anxiety, guilt) and difficulties (not enough time with children; no time for friends, spouse, relaxation, or recreation; and difficulty in completing all morning activities; Winett & Neale, Note 1). If these are common problems for many dual-worker families, how are such problems to be approached?

The typical American approach to social problems has been to focus on the individuals involved even when it is apparent that such problems are a product of significant changes that have taken place in our society. We tend to view individuals and families as self-sufficient and blame them for their failures to cope with external (structural) pressures (Keniston, 1977; Ryan, 1971):

> Blaming parents and giving them advice both spring from the assumption that the problems of individuals can be solved by changing the individuals who have the problems. This implies a second assumption as well: that families are free-standing, independent, and autonomous units, relatively free from social pressures. If a family proves less than independent, if it is visibly needy, if its members ask for help, then it is by definition not an "adequate" family. Adequate families, the assumption runs, are self-sufficient and insulated from outside pressures. (Keniston, 1977, p. 9)

Thus the usual approach to helping dual-worker families consists of advice giving, parent training, marital counseling, etc. Obviously, some of these types of interventions are needed and are quite useful. However, if numerous dual-worker families experience similar problems, such person-centered efforts will have limited "reach" and will not change a major environmental determinant of dual-worker family problems—the nature of work in our society.

WORK AND FAMILY LIFE

When we first started to review the literature on work and family life, one crucial aspect of the literature quickly became apparent. There is, of course, an abundant literature on children, families, marriage, and so on. An equally rich literature exists on work settings, organizational structure, personnel selection, etc. However, there is very little literature concerned with the *interface of work and family*. Consistent with themes developed above and the perspective of others (e.g., Bronfenbrenner, 1977), each system or setting has unfortunately been studied in *isolation* from each other. It is, for example, as if systems external to the family exert no influence on parental and child behaviors, and family concerns have no place at work. Rapoport and Rapoport (1965) have summarized this situation:

Specialists in family sociology and occupational psychology have tended to treat each of these areas as a relatively closed subsystem. It is as though family structure, organization, and functioning depended entirely on factors associated with the family and the individual personalities within it, while the organization and functioning of work groups could be explained exclusively in terms of the work situation. (p. 382)

Recent studies investigating the relationships between work and family life have at least in part been stimulated by changing patterns and attitudes toward women's, particularly mothers', employment (Hoffman & Nye, 1974; Mason, Czajka, & Arber, 1976). More specifically, the entrance of increasing numbers of women of childrearing years into the labor force and their gradual ascendancy into some formerly "male" jobs has heightened the interest in exploring the relationships (and often conflicts) between the home and family. Investigations have focused on the meshing of home and work responsibilities, aspects of childrearing, the division of labor at home, and changes in sex-role orientation and tasks by the wife and husband as a consequence of employment. Most often, the literature's primary focus is on women (i.e., not on changes in men).

A literature is also starting to develop concerning the dual-career family. Although much of that literature apparently still consists of case studies (e.g., Holmstrom, 1972; Rapoport & Rapoport, 1971), some incisive points germane to this chapter have been made. A consistent theme that emerges is the stress and strain that such families experience when two persons try to combine career and family responsibility (Hunt & Hunt, 1977). To alleviate these problems, arrangements are usually made so that various child-care and household chores are shared, as opposed to more "traditional" families where these tasks are usually the almost exclusive domain of the wife (Winett et al., 1977). In addition, some household services and, of course, child care during working hours are provided by other persons.

However, given the fact that the whole fabric of contemporary society is woven with the conventional patterns implicit, it is not possible for more than a small proportion of those who ideally might like a dual-career family to actually make such a structure work. (Rapoport & Rapoport, 1971, p. 8)

One of the greatest impediments to the dual-career family is how work is structured (e.g., number of hours required, scheduling of work), although other facets of work and career (e.g., the single-minded devotion to career that is often needed) assuredly also present conflicts. The pervasive influence of employment in the organization and synchronization of all other facets of daily activity has been carefully documented by J. P. Robinson (1977) and noted above. While earlier reports (Holmstrom, 1972; Rapoport & Rapoport, 1971) tended to stress the adaption of the dual-career family to such impediments, more recent literature has emphasized the *need for change in the work setting if such families are to be viable* (Hunt & Hunt, 1977; Pleck, 1977). Interestingly, Holmstrom (1972) indicated that in the dual-career families she studied, the most important aspect of work which allowed for the merging of work and family reponsibilities was flexible work schedule (see Holmstrom, 1972, p. 90). The number of hours of work per se seemed less significant.

Part-time employment may not appeal to many families for two reasons: (1) there are very few career-oriented part-time positions; and (2) in a time of rapid inflation, families often need two full-time salaries to surrive (Winett, Moffatt, & Fuchs, 1975). For example, the mean purchase price of a home in the Washington, D.C., metropolitan area is over $85,000. The issue of part-time employment and other family-oriented policy changes will be returned to briefly at the end of this chapter.

The major thesis of the research project to be described in this chapter is that flexible work schedules—a change in the structure of work—*may* enhance the life of dual-worker families with young children. Before reviewing the scope of the project and some preliminary findings, several points will be made:

1. Modifying the work to help dual-worker families with young children is consistent with the framework set forth in the beginning of this chapter. That is, such an intervention has an ecological and preventive focus. Further, if possible effects are demonstrated, it is a type of intervention that can be used in numerous work settings to help families now and in the future.

2. If at least some aspects of problems are attributable to the environment, e.g., settings and systems, then modifying that environment should result in relatively *permanent* problem solution or changes (*but,* see below).

3. With any social or behavior change, there are likely to be both positive and negative outcomes, or at least we can say that change in one sphere is likely to produce or influence change in other spheres (some anticipated and some not, e.g., Willems, 1974).

4. Social innovations require careful documentation in terms of outcome before they should be widely disseminated (Fairweather et al., 1974).

In the case of flexible work schedules, for example, the popular press and even the professional literature were describing the many benefits to working mothers (hardly ever saying *working parents*) that could accrue from "flexitime" *before* any formal evaluations had been done. In reviewing 42 flexitime studies and reports (see Table 12-2, below), we found only 8 that inquired into family practices affected by flexitime. These inquiries generally involved one to several items on "post" questionnaires, hardly an adequate evaluation of this important issue.

It seemed more likely that multiple outcomes would result from flexitime, some possibly quite positive, and some negative. It could be that flexitime, while providing benefits for the enactment of one role or set of tasks (e.g., child care), could also create difficulties in other areas. For example, flexitime (to be described below) involves minimal changes in work hours compared to shiftwork, yet Brown's (1975) analysis of role and time coordination in shiftwork seemed relevant for consideration with flexitime:

A common time schedule thus helps ensure that individuals in the differentiated sets of roles they occupy in advanced societies are available to perform particular roles when the people demanding these role performances expect them to be. Shiftwork threatens this time synchronization and makes social integration problematic by reducing the possibilities for certain forms of social interaction. (p. 232)

The person arriving at work early, under flexitime, in order to be with his/her child in the afternoon quite possibly will not eat lunch with peers and not stay up late enough in the evenings to enjoy adult company. In addition, there may be effects on other systems. For example, if a building operating under flexitime is open for more hours, energy costs may rise. In choosing to come to work at different times, workers may decrease their use of car pools and public transportation.

These types of "trade-offs" are also the focus of our research project. The important point germane to the framework of this chapter is that *it was predicted that a change in one system would result in multiple changes in other systems.*

FLEXITIME: A REVIEW

The reader should be aware that *flexitime is not being offered as a panacea* to the problems experienced by dual-worker families. It is one minimal type of intervention in the world of work that may prove beneficial. The problems discussed previously are also attributable to other environmental, economic, and social pressures. The high cost of living today, a suburban sprawl, outmoded transportation systems—all these factors certainly affect family life.

Flexitime systems were apparently first developed in European countries, particularly West Germany, in the late 1960s (Elbing, Gadon, & Gordon, 1974). It is now estimated that approximately 2.5 million West German workers, 40% of the workers in Switzerland, and 35% of those in France use flexitime (Federal Energy Administration, Note 2; Haldi Associates, Note 3; Sharko & Price, Note 4). A similar proliferation has been predicted for this country (Elbing et al., 1974; Martin, 1975; D. Robinson, 1976; Sharko & Price, Note 4), and, indeed, recently passed legislation mandating experiments in the federal government with flexitime should have the effect of initiating more flexitime programs throughout the country (Public Law 95-390, passed by the 95th Congress on September 29, 1978).

Under flexitime systems, workers are generally allowed to decide when they wish to arrive in the morning and depart in the afternoon or evening. Workers are usually, however, obligated to work during certain *core* hours and maintain a full 5-day, 35- to 40-hour week. Table 12-1 presents a typical flexitime schedule. Employees could start work any time between 6:30 A.M. and 9:30 A.M. and depart from work after completing their designated hours (e.g., 8 hours). However, as noted before, they must be present during the core period. The place of employment would be operational from 6:30 A.M. to 6 P.M., the bandwidth. Variations of this basic system are prevalent and include: (a) shorter and longer bandwidths, flexitime, and core time periods; (b) flexible time periods in the middle of the day; (c) governing rules requiring an employee to adhere to one schedule for a given period, or systems in which daily schedule changes are permissible; and (d) systems allowing working different amounts of time each day, but with hour totals designated for a week or month.

The amount of time worked per day by an employee has generally been monitored manually, although automatic cumulative recording devices are available and have been used (Commercial Union Assurance Group, Note 5; Williams, Note 6).

Table 12-1
A Typical Flexitime Schedule

6:30 – 9:30	9:30 – 3:00	3:00 – 6:00
A.M.　　　A.M.	A.M.　　　P.M.	P.M.　　　P.M.
Flexible Time	Core Time[a]	Flexible Time
◄───────────────────────	Bandwidth	───────────────────────►

[a]One-half hour allowed for lunch.

The rationale of flexible work schedules can be placed in three categories: organizational, environmental systems, and personal-social.

Organizational

Flexitime has been conceptualized as a "humanistic" organizational development strategy focusing on *structural change* (Friedlander & Brown, 1974; Golembiewski, Itilles, & Kango, 1974; Schein, Maurer, & Novak, Note 7). Flexitime has been viewed as a method to give workers control of their work schedules and hence develop a "climate" of trustworthiness. Worker morale would presumably be higher in such a setting, contributing to increased productivity (Golembiewski et al., 1974; Schein et al., Note 7). The flexibility in the work schedule has also been seen as a way to decrease, if not eliminate, tardiness; decrease unnecessary absences and leave time; and reduce overtime (Golembiewski et al., 1974; Schein et al., Note 7). Improvements in tardiness, absences, and decreased overtime pay could result in substantial savings to an organization (Golembiewski et al., 1974). Varying schedules may facilitate cross-training for different jobs or tasks. The larger bandwidth also presents the possibility of giving the public increased time for service.

Environmental Systems

Flexible work schedules (and staggered work schedules; Remak & Rosenbloom, Note 8 & 9) are seen as one mechanism to decrease commuting time by reducing the rush hour or peak use of public and private transportation. With commuting spread more during morning arrival and afternoon departure times, transportation facilities should be less crowded and more efficient (Remak & Rosenbloom, Notes 8 & 9). Air quality should also be improved (Haldi Associates, Note 3); accident rates might be reduced as commuters drive under less stressful conditions. Often overlooked in discussions of environmental impacts of flexitime is the possibility of reducing peak-load residential use of electricity and natural gas (Kohlenberg, Phillips, & Proctor, 1976). Besides the contemporary relevance for including environmental criteria as evaluative outcomes for social programs, the peak-load question is of particular importance to flexitime since increased hours of operation may mean greater overall energy use (Hill, Note 10).

Personal-Social

Flexitime has been advocated as a means of allowing persons greater freedom and more opportunities in scheduling educational, recreational, social, and family pursuits (Haldi Associates, Note 3). As noted above, flexitime has also been discussed as an important change needed in work conditions to accommodate an increasingly common and stressful situation in our society: families with preschool or school-age children where both parents work (and of course one-parent families with such children; Bronfenbrenner, 1974, 1977; Levine, 1976). Flexible work schedules may facilitate the sharing of child-care responsibilities by allowing parents to plan their work schedules with maximum time devoted to their children and decrease (although not eliminate) the reliance on external child-care arrangements (Haldi Associates, Note 3). Flexible work schedules may also eliminate the "latch-key child syndrome," e.g., a child returning home from school to an empty house, apparently a situation related to childhood and adolescent problems (Bronfenbrenner, 1977). While potential impacts on family life have usually been discussed as "women's issues," it is apparent that men are increasingly becoming involved in child care and household management, particularly when both parents work and children, of necessity, are placed in child-care settings (Winett et al., 1977). Such issues are thus *"parenting issues."*

In order to assess the extent to which these multifaceted objectives have been fulfilled as a result of implementation of flexitime programs, a review was made of evaluative data available on flexitime. Thus the focus of the literature search was *not* on *articles explaining* flexitime and its potential impact, but rather *actual reports* on programs that were enacted. The results of this search are found in Table 12–2.

Several conclusions are readily apparent:

The primary focus of evaluations has been on the work organizational setting. Morale, and to some (minimal) extent productivity, have been improved under flexitime. Unexcused absences have decreased and tardiness has been virtually eliminated. Not included in the table, but of obvious significance, are indications that supervisory and time-accounting problems under flexitime are minimal. Most agencies or businesses also noted plans in their reports to implement flexitime on a wider basis as a result of initial programs. Such decisions were highly endorsed by employees.

Commuting time has been decreased with no apparent reduction in car pooling or use of public transportation. Not represented on the table, but also highly significant in terms of environmental systems, are data indicating that in most flexitime programs about 60% of employees opt for revised work schedules, with many persons apparently preferring earlier arrival and departure times. While the effects of this spread in arrival and departure time has been documented in the transportation area (Fiss, Note 11; Port Authority, Note 12), the potential favorable impact of such a spread in peak-load residential use of electricity and natural gas, as noted previously, has been unexplored.

Table 12-2
Review of Flexitime Studies: Evaluative Criteria[a]

Site	Number of employees	Time of study	Measures improved	Type evaluation
U.S. Dept. of Agriculture Economic Research Service	Not available	Start late 1976	Not available	Focus on organizational productivity; no data available
Headquarters, Air University, Alabama (case report)	100 and expanded to 1100	1975	Morale, personal-social (see Table 12-3)	Post-questionnaires
Headquarters, U.S. Army Computer Systems Command, Virginia (case report)	82	1975	Morale, productivity, leave time, initiate educational experiences	Post-questionnaires
U.S. Army Material Development, Readiness Command, Washington, D.C.	Not available	1976	Not available	Focus on organizational productivity
U.S. Army Military Personnel Center, Virginia	70 400	1975 1976	Not available	Focus on organizational productivity
U.S. Army Natick Laboratories, Massachusetts (case report)	1200	1975	Morale, tardiness	Subjective
U.S. Army Research Institute for the Behavioral & Social Sciences, Virginia	200	Start 1976	Not available	Not available
U.S. Army Tank Automotive Command, Michigan (case report)	5400	1974– 1975	Morale, leave time, traffic	Post-questionnaire

Table 12-2 (continued)

Site	Number of employees	Time of study	Measures improved	Type evaluation
Army Depot, Sacramento, California (case report)	355	1974–1975	Morale, leave time	Post-questionnaire and interview
Regional Planning Council for Metropolitan Baltimore, Maryland (case report)	Not available	Start late 1976/ early 1977	Not available	Focus on community problems
City of Berkeley, California (experiment)	230	1974	Morale, leave time, overtime (reduced), personal-social (see Table 12–3)	Post-questionnaires and performance data
Berol Corporation, Canada	Not available	1974	Not available	Focus on organizational productivity
Berol Corporation (diverse U.S. sites) (case report)	Not available	Diverse	Morale, leave time, tardiness, absences, traffic	Post-questionnaire, pre-post performance data
Bureau of Alcohol, Tobacco & Firearms, Dept. of the Treasury, Washington, D.C. (case report)	25	1975	Morale, productivity, leave time, tardiness supervision	Post-questionnaire and and performance data
Bureau of Drugs, Food & Drug Administration, HEW, Maryland	More than 100	1976	Not available	Not available
Bureau of Health Insurance, U.S. Civil Service Commission, Georgia (case report)	92	1976	Morale, absences, leave time, overtime (reduced), personal-social (see Table 12–3)	Post-questionnaires

Table 12-2 (*continued*)

Site	Number of employees	Time of study	Measures improved	Type evaluation
Bureau of Indian Affairs, U.S. Dept. of the Interior, New Mexico (case report)	290	1972–1976	Morale, productivity, tardiness, absences	Subjective
Bureau of Policies & Standards, Civil Service Commission, Washinton, D.C. (case report)	250	1975–1976	Commuting, other data to be analyzed	Pre-post questionnaire
Bureau of Training Civil Service Commission, Washington, D.C. (case report)	199	1975	Satisfied with Flex system	Post-questionnaire
U.S. Civil Service Commission, San Francisco, California (case report)	686	1976	Morale, adherance to rules, tardiness, personal-social (see Table 12-3)	Post-questionnaire report)
U.S. Civil Service Commission, Seattle, Washington (case report)	129	1975	Morale, commuting	Post-questionnaire
Control Data Corp., Minnesota, Canada (case report)	1544	1972–1976 (series of studies)	Morale, turnover, absences, tardiness, leisure time, traffic (combined results)	Pre-post questionnaire and performance data
Bureau of Community Health Services HEW, Washington, D.C. (case report)	232	1976	Not available	Pre-post questionnaire

Table 12-2 (*continued*)

Site	Number of employees	Time of study	Measures improved	Type evaluation
Fiscal Service, Bureau of Government Financial Operations, Washington, D.C. (case report)	About 800	1976	Supervision, tardiness, transportation, personal-social (see Table 12-3)	Post-questionnaires
Environmental Protection Agency, Washington, D.C.	3500	1976	Not available	Not available
Geological Survey, U.S. Dept. of the Interior, Reston, Virginia (case report)	11,500	1975 and 1976	Morale, absences, tardiness, overtime (reduced), work conditions, commuting, personal-social (see Table 12-3)	Post-questionnaires
Hewlett-Parker Co., Palo Alto, California (case report)	Not available	1974	Morale, productivity, tardiness, commuting	Post-questionnaires
Industrial Indemnity, Los Angeles, California	Not available	1974	Not available	Not available
U.S. Information Agency, Washington, D.C. (case report)	35	1975	Morale, tardiness, turnover	Subjective
Library of Congress, Washington, D.C.	Not available	1977	Not available	Focus on organizational productivity
Division of Management, National Institutes of Health, Bethesda Maryland (case report)	32	1975–1976	Leave time, transportation, personal-social (see Table 12-3)	Post-questionnaire

Table 12-2 (*continued*)

Site	Number of employees	Time of study	Measures improved	Type evaluation
Metropolitan Life Insurance Co., New York, New York (case report)	404	1974	Morale, pro-productivity, tardiness	Post-questionnaire
National Oceanic & Atmospheric Admin., U.S. Dept. of Commerce, Colorado	Not available	1976	Not available	Not available
National Oceanic & Atmospheric Admin., U.S. Dept. of commerce, Maryland	150	1976	Not available	Not available
National Security Agency, Center Security Service, Maryland (case report)	Not available	1976–1977	Morale, absences, tardiness, productivity	Post-questionnaire
Navy Finance Center, Department of the Navy, Ohio (case report)	68	1975	Morale, tardiness, "work life"	Pre-post questionnaire
Port Authority of New York & New Jersey (experiment: transportation aspect; case report: other aspects)	850	1974–1975	"work satisfaction," personal-social (see Table 12-3)	Pre-post questionnaire, interviews, analysis of transportation
Pacific Gas & Electric, San Francisco, California (case report)	Not available	1974–1975	Morale, leave time, productivity, commuter time	Post-questionnaire

Table 12-2 (continued)

Site	Number of employees	Time of study	Measures improved	Type evaluation
Pan American Health Organization, World Health Organzation, Washington, D.C.	Not available	1976	Not available	Not available
Naval Ship Missile Systems Engineering Station, California (case report)	1700	1975	Morale, quality and quantity of work	Post-questionnaire
SmithKline Corp., Pennsylvania (case report)	3000	1972	Morale, productivity, work life, traffic	Two post-questionnaires
SmithKline Corp., Pennsylvania (experiment)	48	1973	Morale, productivity, work life, traffic	Pre-post questionnaires and performance data
Social Security Administration, HEW, Baltimore (case report)	353 2000	1974 1975	Morale, tardi-tardiness, commuting, work quality, personality-social (see Table 12-3)	Post-questionnaire

[a]Given that virtually all these data were not found in published reports, other reports on flexitime experiments may be available, and certainly more will be forthcoming.

The impact of flexitime on educational, recreational, social, and family pursuits remains unclear, since virtually all of the listed studies have not focused on these areas. For example, Table 12–3 presents questions asked of employees about their family life with flexitime.

Although responses are suggestive of more available family time and greater ease in child-care arrangements, the questions' superficiality should be apparent. We simply have no clear understanding of the impacts of flexitime in the personal-social area.

While evaluations of innovations by governmental agencies and private industry are admirable, only three of the studies can be considered true experiments. Evaluative methodology has primarily consisted of postquestionnaires (and at times pre- and postquestionnaires) completed by employees, supplemented where possible by pre- and postmeasures of tardiness, absences, and in some instances, productivity.

Table 12-3
Review of Flexitime Studies with
Personal-Social Evaluative Criteria

Site	Focus	Comment
Headquarters Air University	Family time	One question: some employees indicated spent more time with families
City of Berkeley	Family time	One question: about 25% responded to questions, and of these, 57% indicated spent more time with family.
Civil Service Commission, Georgia	Family, child welfare	One question for each area: 14% of respondents reported more convenience for child care; 35% reported more time given to family.
Civil Service Commission, California	Nonwork life	Two general questions: of respondents, 63% indicated more time for outside activities and 42% indicated more time for educational courses.
Fiscal Service, Bureau of Government Financial Operations	Nonwork life	General questions: reported helped to participate in family, community, and social activities. 183 of respondents were working parents. Of the 183, 182 reported beneficial in arranging for child care (1 question).
Geological Survey	Nonwork life	General questions: 69% of survey respondents reported spent more time with family; 58% reported more time in recreational activities, and 43% reported more time in educational activities.
National Institute of Health	Nonwork life	One question for each area: 6 of 8 for whom question relevant reported made caring for children easier. 15 of 32 respondents said spent more time with family; 11 of 32 respondents said spent more time on outside activities; 5 of 32 said more time spent on educational courses; 21 of 32 reported easier to fit work and nonwork together.
Social Security Administration, Baltimore	Family, child care	One question each area: large number of female and one-parent families. Of 118 employees indicating having major responsibility for care of one or more children, school age or younger, 82% reported flexitime made child care easier. 78% of employees reported flexitime allowed more time for family.

The potential methodological problems in such evaluations have been well documented (Campbell, 1969; Fairweather, 1967; Parsons, 1974; Weiss, 1972).

Overall, several conclusions are apparent. Flexitime will probably be rapidly implemented in government and private industry. While there are a number of benefits accruing from flexitime to the operation of an organization or agency, and positive impacts on transportation systems and air quality, little is known about another primary impact area: family life and educational, social, and recreational pursuits. The possible alleviation of peak-load residential energy use has also not been investigated.

PRELIMINARY RESULTS OF FLEXITIME/FAMILY LIFE STUDIES

In order to evaluate empirically the family impact of flexitime, two studies were conducted with two large federal agencies in Washington, D.C. The first study, a pilot effort, was conducted during Fall 1977 and Spring 1978; while the second, larger study was implemented in Spring 1978, and is at the two-thirds point at the time of this writing. The procedures, measures, and some preliminary findings from these projects will now be discussed.

Settings and Participants

Both settings performed primarily administrative functions and were their agency's central headquarters. In both federal agencies, prior to flexitime employees were working an 8-hour day (8:45 a.m. to 5:15 p.m. in Agency 1; 8:15 a.m. to 4:45 p.m. in Agency 2) with 30 minutes for lunch. Both flexitime programs were relatively simple. In the first agency, workers could arrive as early as 7:30 a.m. or as late as 9:30 a.m. and leave from 4:00 p.m. to 6:00 p.m. In the second agency, the bandwidth is also presently 7:30 a.m. to 6:00 p.m. In both agencies, extra time could be taken for lunch, and time was accounted for by sign-in systems (no time-accumulator equipment). Employees in consultation with their supervisors were free to change their schedules frequently, but *time could not be saved* (i.e., an 8-hour day was still in effect). Obviously, in both agencies, the flexitime programs were *limited*. However, the bandwidth did allow employees to avoid at least some of the traditional rush-hour havoc in Washington, D.C.

All participants in both projects had one characteristic in common. They were all parents from families having at least one young child (less than 12 years old). Some participants were single parents, others were from dual-worker families, and some participants were from dual-parent families where they were the only one working outside the home. About two-thirds of the participants were women. We thought that comparisons between types of families would be particularly interesting, but we cannot yet report those results.

All participants had volunteered to participate in the projects and received payment of about $75 each for completing forms and interviews.

Design and Measures

Because of practical constraints, participants in each study could not be randomly assigned to treatment condition. Rather, after a baseline period in which regular work hours were in effect, all departments in an agency, on a staggered-weeks basis (Study 1), or across the board (Study 2), implemented their flexitime program. Invariably, when flexitime programs had been initiated in other agencies, some employees changed their hours of work while other employees retained their original schedules. This situation occurred in both of our studies, creating one group of employees who changed their hours of work and a comparison group who remained on their regular schedules.

In Study 1, the baseline period averaged about 1 month, and data were collected during the flexitime period for about 3½ months. In Study 2, the baseline period was about 2 months, and data will be collected for about 9 months during flexitime.

The following measures were used:

1. Time–Activity Logs. Two or three times per week participants completed an hour-by-hour log on which they indicated the activity engaged in, place of activity, and persons involved in the activity with them. Participants also rated their enjoyment of each activity. The logs provided highly interpretable, microlevel data on activities and time spent by the participant with family members. The quality of the log data was improved in Study 2 by training which involved modeling and feedback procedures described in detail elsewhere (Winett, Neale, & Williams, Note 13). Several methods were also used in Study 2 to ascertain the reliability of the logs. Reliability appears to be at an acceptable level (Kazdin, 1975). In addition, procedures were used so that over 90% of all forms distributed were returned to us completed (see Winett et al., Note 13).

2. Work and Nonwork Survey. Once a week (Study 1), or seminmonthly (Study 2), participants completed a 15-item survey on which they rated (on a 7-point scale) the ease or difficulty in coordinating aspects of work and family life, particularly in relationship to hours of work. For example, "the hours I work make spending time in the evening with my child (children) _____." Five open-ended questions also focused on aspects of coordinating work and family life. In this way, it was possible to evaluate the effects of flexitime on particular aspects of family life as perceived by the participants.

3. Weekend Checklist. For every weekend, participants in Study 2 indicated activities engaged in by themselves and other family members. In this way, we will assess if flexitime helps to enhance weekend activities by, for example, allowing more chores to be completed during the week.

4. Parent Interview Schedule. Following an instrument used previously (Winett et al., 1977), home interviews were conducted with the participant and his/her spouse. The interview focused on the distribution of effort by the husband and wife in completing specific child-care and household chores. Additional material was obtained concerning parent–child interactions and leisuretime activities. The interview was given once in Study 1 to ascertain if family patterns were related to changes in family life attributable to flexitime. In Study 2, interviews will be given three times, not only to investigate family patterns, but also to determine if flexitime modifies parental roles, e.g., distribution of effort. In each study, single parents were also interviewed to find out how they managed family tasks and functions usually completed by two parents.

5. Work-Related Measures. In Study 2, more detail will be available from participants' activity logs to examine the effects that flexitime may have on work activities. Data on leave time, tardiness, and absenteeism will be collected, and additional information will also be available on the overall effects of the flexitime program at the agency.

6. Other Measures. Additional data were collected on commuting and residential use of heating and cooling to ascertain the effects of flexitime on transportation and home energy use during peak-load periods (available in Study 2).

GENERAL RESULTS AND SOME PRELIMINARY FINDINGS FROM STUDY 1

While flexitime is a major focus of our studies, our research more generally is concerned with family life and the world of work. Our data from Study 1 verify a number of points made by other researchers (Bronfenbrenner, 1977) and, we may add, by working parents. The logs and surveys indicated that, at least during the week, the time involved in working and commuting left little time for family life and other pursuits, a situation many participants found very difficult and stressful. However, even in our dual-worker families, more of the burden of coordinating home and work life *still* rested with the woman. For example, women performed about 75% of the child-care tasks and household chores. The inequity in the distribution of labor at home will be a point further investigated in Study 2.

Flexitime, however, seemed to help some families. From the 33 participants in Study 1, we found 10 people who changed their schedules by at least 30 minutes and 11 people who retained their original hours.[1] Workers who changed their schedule were a bit younger and had younger children than those retaining their schedules; however, both groups were at the same mean government level. Table 12–4 shows the mean start of work time for each group before and during flexitime. The "change" group moved their start time up by almost 1 hour [$t(18) = 8.85, p < .001$], while the no-change group remained the same.

All participants who changed their schedules opted for earlier hours. They got up earlier each day during flexitime [$t(18) = 3.48, p < .01$], but went to bed about the same time as before (Table 12–5). Again, the no-change group retained their original schedule.

We found some provocative results across measures that we will be following up in Study 2.

Time-Activity Logs

For each activity log from each participant, activities were categorized as engaged in with spouse, with children, with spouse and children, or alone, during a.m. or p.m. In this way, for each recording day a specific amount of time could be computed for each category. For the group that changed work hours, it was found that they increased their P.M. time with their children alone, or spouse and children, by almost an hour per day during flexitime [$t(18) = 2.41, p < .05$]. The group that did not change work schedule maintained about the same amount of p.m. time with their children, or spouse and children, as before flexitime. These findings are shown in Table 12–6.

Table 12–4
Mean Start of Work Time

Group	Before	Flexitime
Change	8:41 A.M.	7:45 A.M.
No change	8:35 A.M.	8:34 A.M.

Table 12-5
Mean Time Waking Up and Going to Bed

	Before		Flexitime	
Group	Wake	Bed	Wake	Bed
Change	6:28 A.M.	10:52 P.M.	5:50 A.M.	10:39 P.M.
No change	6:31 A.M.	11:01 P.M.	6:34 A.M.	11:00 P.M.

Six of 10 change participants increased their time with their children and spouses by at least 35%, while only 1 of 11 no-change participants increased their time with their children and spouses by this magnitude. Figure 12–1 shows individual time-series data for the 10 participants and group time-series data for the no-change group (N = 11).

Participants 2, 4, and 9 did not change the amount of time spent with their spouses and children. The other seven participants showed a pattern of increased, although quite variable, time with their spouses and children following their change to an earlier work schedule. The comparison group data (bottom) tend to obscure the day-to-day variability of the individual data, but clearly show *no* increasing trend during the recording months. The initials on the left-bottom of each individual graph indicate the sex of each participant and the work status of each family.

P.M. time alone or with spouse was evidently not affected by a change in work schedule. The time data indicate that as a group, participants who did not change their work hours tended to spend more time with their spouse (alone) than participants who changed their schedules. No changes were found in A.M. time allotted to different categories, and A.M. time with family members was extremely limited.

Work and Nonwork Survey

The survey data indicate that as a group, participants who changed their schedules initially reported *more* difficulty in coordinating family life and work, but it appears that flexitime may have reduced difficulties experienced by participants to a level about equal to that of the comparison group. Table 12–7 shows mean ratings for survey items for

Table 12-6
Mean Time in Hours with Children
Alone and Spouse and Children

Group	Before	Flexitime
Change	2.42	3.52
No Change	2.13	2.20

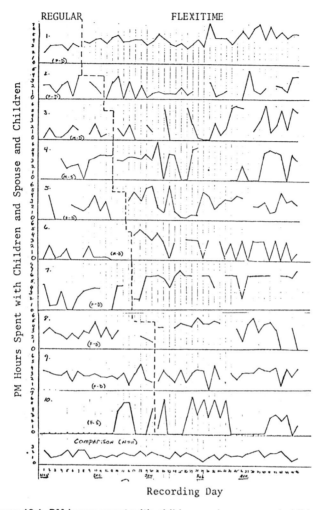

Figure 12-1. PM hours spent with children and spouse and children.

periods before and during flexitime for both the group that changed work schedule and the group that retained the original hours. Note that activities which logically would seem unaffected by a change to an earlier schedule, that still only permitted returning home by late afternoon, were rated as no less difficult than before flexitime (items 1, 2, 4). The three change participants who did not increase their amount of time with their children and spouses showed an overall change score acorss the 15 items of about 0. Note also that there were no significant changes in ratings by participants who retained their original schedules.

Table 12–7
Survey Ratings Baseline and Flexitime
by Change and No-Change Groups[a]

Item	Change group Baseline	Flexitime	No-change group Baseline	Flexitime
1. The time I start to work makes getting my child (children) to school or a child-care setting _____ .	4.12	4.06 NS	3.33	2.84 NS
2. If my child (children) should become ill during the day, my work situation makes it _____ to be sure the child is receiving care.	4.52	3.99 NS	3.05	3.57 NS
3. The time I *leave* work makes it _____ to spend afternoon time with my child.	5.97	4.08 $p < .025$	5.78	5.52 NS
4. Because of my work hours, breakfast time with my child (children) is _____ .	4.79	5.29 NS	4.55	4.12 NS
5. My work hours make picking up my child (children) after school or from a child-care setting_____.	5.10	3.73 $p < .05$	4.61	4.29 NS
6. Because of my work hours, it is _____ to spend time with my spouse/partner during the work week.	5.22	3.64 $p < .025$	4.91	4.03 NS
7. My work hours are such that it is _____ to see friends during the work week.	5.45	3.65 $p < 0.25$	4.51	4.18 NS
8. My work hours are such that it is _____ to share lunchtime or a coffee break with friends at work.	2.25	2.97 NS	2.57	3.50 NS
9. Because of my work hours, commuting to and from work is _____ .	4.38	3.55 NS	3.25	3.03 NS
10. The hours I work make having dinner with my spouse/partner and/or child (children) _____ during the work week.	3.76	2.69 $p < .10$	3.27	3.05 NS
11. The hours I work make spending time in the evening with my child (children) _____.	4.55	2.69 $p < .01$	3.27	3.62 NS
12. The hours I work make pursuing additional educational (formal and informal) opportunities _____.	5.27	3.41 $p < .01$	3.88	3.94 NS

Table 12-7 (continued)

Item	Change group Baseline	Flexitime	No-change group Baseline	Flexitime
13. The hours I work make engaging in recreational pursuits and hobbies _____ .	4.70	3.29 $p < .025$	4.05	3.87 NS
14. The hours I work make completion of shopping and household chores _____ .	5.28	4.03 $p < .025$	4.48	4.08 NS
15. The hours I work make it _____ to have relaxed evenings during the week.	5.20	3.82 $p < .01$	4.01	3.65 NS

[a] 1 = easy; 7 = difficult. NS = not significant.

Parent Interview Data

Although, as noted above, men were apparently only responsible for about 25% of household chores and child-care tasks, one interesting difference was found between families where a participant changed hours and families where a participant retained his/her original hours. In "change" families, fathers were more involved in child-care tasks $[t(15) = 1.43, p < .20]$, and reported engaging in more activities with their children than "nonchange" families $[t(15) = 1.92, p < .10]$. These patterns only emerged when two categories on the interview schedule were combined: tasks or activities men reported doing *alone* and *together with their spouses.*

The children in "change" families were younger ($\bar{X} = 4.5$ years) than children in "nonchange" families ($\bar{X} = 6.5$ years). These findings suggest, as has been found in other family research (Winett et al., 1977), that different types of families may simply prefer or benefit from different kinds of services or structural changes.

Commuting Data

There were minimal changes in commuting patterns in either group. However, one participant in the change group switched from part-time use of mass transit to full-time use of a private car with the onset of flexitime. One participant in the no-change group switched from full-time use of a private car to mass transit.

With regard to the third group of participants, who tended to be variable in their work schedules, no changes were found for any of the measures.

Summary

The preliminary results from our first study indicate that a flexitime program may help some working parents change their hours of work so that they can start work earlier, leave work earlier, and spend more time in the afternoon and evening with their families. These changes were apparently accomplished by simply getting up earlier in the morning. Parents who changed their hours of work reported decreased difficulty in coordinating many important aspects of home and work. Not surprisingly, there was some evidence that characteristics and patterns may differ in families where a working parent decides to alter his or her work schedule. Finally, the commuting data suggested that flexitime may promote some minimal changes in mode of transportation.

These findings will be followed up in the larger and longer longitudinal study that will also be able to assess the impacts of flexitime in a number of other areas of work and family life, transportation, and energy use. For example, the more detailed data from our second study should indicate if increased time with one's family is perceived as more enjoyable or satisfying (for example, compared to loss of sleep), indicate specific behaviors affected, clarify transportation issues, and also examine peak-load use of air conditioning and heating.

Overall, the impression we have gained from the first study is encouraging, particularly in light of the scope of this flexitime program, which was quite modest.

CONCLUSIONS AND DIRECTIONS

While further conclusions regarding flexitime's effects on family life await reports from the larger study and from other research projects focused in this area (Bohen, Note 14), hopefully several points have already been demonstrated: (1) modifications of one setting can affect behaviors in other settings; (2) such interventions can be preventive in nature; (3) social innovations can be evaluated before large-scale diffusion; and (4) the world of work has great influence on family life.

Clearly, what is needed in this area are many more investigations of the "family impacts" of other social policies and structures. Such a movement is well on its way (Keniston, 1977). In addition, policy makers, social scientists, concerned citizens, and parents need to look to several other Western countries that have specifically developed programs to help families.

Sweden provides a good model. Here is a partial list of family-related programs in Sweden (Ministry of Health and Social Affairs, 1977):

1. National health insurance.

2. General allowance (payment) for all children under 16.

3. Economic support for childbirth and when one parent must stay away from work to care for a sick child. This childbirth system allows for the benefits (7 months' insurance coverage) to be shared by *both* parents, or used by *either* parent.

4. Home furnishing loans and housing allowances (subsidies).

5. Domestic assistance when a child is sick.

6. Liberal abortion laws.

7. An extensive child-care system.

8. Availability of part-time work (although mostly in traditional women's occupations) and flexible work hours.

Some of these social and economic policies will probably not be adopted in this country; others may well be implemented in the next decade. Clearly, however, these policies, other proposed innovations, and many additional structures exert a profound influence on family life. The analysis, implementation, and evaluation of change in social, economic, and physical systems and settings is a prime task for the social scientist concerned with facilitating larger scale, sustained improvement in the quality of life.

More generally, the flexitime research is supportive of the perspective that one effective approach to changing family patterns on a large-scale, preventive, and more permanent basis may rest with the analysis and modification of important systems that impinge on parents and children.

NOTE

1. For "change" and "no-change" participants, *baseline* data include all data from before flexitime. *Flexitime* data include data from the point the department implemented flexitime (all no-change participants) or from the point workers changed their work schedule by at least 30 minutes (some change participants).

ACKNOWLEDGMENTS

This research was supported by Grant No. MH-30585 to the Institute for Behavioral Research from the Center for the Study of Metropolitan Problems of the National Institute of Mental Health, and Grant No.

5S07-RR05636 from the Division of Research Resources of the National Institutes of Health.

The authors are grateful to Barbara Fiss and Tom Cowley for allowing them access to the files on flexitime at the Civil Service Commission, Washington, D.C., and for the time they graciously gave to them for discussions; and to Ken Williams, who helped conduct the day-to-day work in the flexitime/family life studies.

REFERENCE NOTES

1. Winett, R. A., & Neale, M. S. *Family life and the world of work: A preliminary report on the effects of flexitime.* Paper presented at the meeting of the American Psychological Association, Toronto, September 1978.

2. Federal Energy Administration. *Energy efficient report: Flexible work hours.* Washington, D.C.: Author, 1976.

3. Haldi Associates, Inc. *Alternative work schedules: A technology assessment.* Report prepared for the National Science Foundation, Washington, D.C., 1975.

4. Sharko, J. R., & Price, J. P. *Impacts of energy conservation measures applied to commuter travel.* Report prepared by Regional and Environmental Studies Group, Mathematica, Inc., Philadelphia, for Office of Planning and Evaluation, U.S. Environmental Protection Agency, Washington, D.C., 1976.

5. Commercial Union Assurance Group, *Flexible working hours.* Undated.

6. Williams, L. *Summary report on flexitime test program.* City of Berkeley, California, November 1974.

7. Schein, V. E., Maurer, E. H., & Novak, J. F. *Flexible working hours as an organizational development intervention.* Paper presented at the meeting of the American Psychological Association, Washington, D. C., September 1975.

8. Remak, R., & Rosenbloom, R. *Peak-period traffic congestion: State of the art and recommended research.* Report prepared for the National Cooperative Research Program, Transportation Research Board, National Research Council, Washington, D.C., 1976.

9. Remak, R., & Rosenbloom, R. *Solutions to peak-period travel congestion: Options for current programs.* Report prepared for the National Cooperative Highway Research Program, Transportation Research Board, National Research Council, Washington, D.C., 1976.

10. Hill, J. A. Letter to the assistant secretary of defense, The Pentagon. Files of the Federal Energy Administration, Washington, D.C., 1976.

11. Fiss, B. L. *Report of the Bureau of Policies and Standards Flexitime Committee.* Civil Service Commission, Washington, D.C., 1975.

12. Port Authority of New York and New Jersey, Planning and Development Department. *Flexible work hours experiment,* 1975.

13. Winett, R. A. Neale, M. S., & Williams, K. R. *Effective field research procedures: Recruitment and quality data acquisition.* Manuscript submitted for publication, 1978. (Available from Institute for Behavioral Research, 2429 Linden Lane, Silver Spring, MD 20910)

14. Bohen, H. Study in progress on flexitime. Family Impact Seminar, George Washington University, Washington, D.C., 1978.

REFERENCES

Best, J. A., & Bloch, M. Compliance and the control of cigarette smoking. In R. B. Haynes, D. W. Taylor, & D. L. Sacket (Eds.), *Compliance with therapeutic and preventive regimens.* Baltimore: John Hopkins University Press, in press.

Bronfenbrenner, U. Development research, public policy, and the ecology of childhood. *Childhood Development,* 1974, *45,* 1-5.

Bronfenbrenner, U. Toward an experimental ecology of human development. *American Psychologist,* 1977, *32,* 513-531.

Brown, D. Shiftwork: A survey of the sociological implications of studies of male shiftworkers. *Journal of Occupational Psychology,* 1975, *48,* 231-240.

Campbell, D. T. Reforms as experiments. *American Psychologist,* 1969, *24,* 409-429.

Cowen, E. L. Social and community interventions. *Annual Review of Psychology,* 1973, *24,* 423-472.

Elbing, A. O., Gadon, H., & Gordon, J. R. M. Flexible working hours: It's about time. *Harvard Business Review,* 1974, *52,* 1-6.

Fairweather, G. W. *Methods for experimental social innovation.* New York: Wiley, 1967.

Fairweather, G. W., Sanders, D. H., & Tornatzky, L. G. *Creating change in mental health organizations.* New York: Pergamon, 1974.

Friedlander, F., & Brown, L. D. Organization development. *Annual Review of Psychology,* 1974, *25,* 313-341.

Golembiewski, R. T., Itilles, R., & Kango, M. S. A longitudinal study of flexitime effects: Some consequences of an OD structural intervention. *Journal of Applied Behavioral Science,* 1974, *4,* 503-532.

Hayghe, H. Families and the rise of working wives—an overview. *Monthly Labor Review,* May 1976, 10-19.

Hoffman, L. W., & Nye, F. I. *Working mothers.* San Francisco: Jossey-Bass, 1974.

Holmstrom, L. L. *The two-career family.* Cambridge: Schenkman, 1972.

Hunt, J. G., & Hunt, L. L. Dilemmas and contradictions of studies: The case of the dual-career family. *Social Problems,* 1977, *24,* 407-416.

Kazdin, A. E. *Behavior modification in applied settings.* Homewood, Ill.: Dorsey Press, 1975.

Keniston, K. *All our children.* New York: Harcourt Brace Jovanovich, 1977.

Kohlenberg, R., Phillips, T., & Proctor, W. A. Behavioral analysis of peaking in residential electrical-energy consumers. *Journal of Applied Behavior Analysis,* 1976, *9,* 13-18.

Lando, H. A. Successful treatment of smokers with a broad-spectrum behavioral approach. *Journal of Consulting and Clinical Psychology,* 1977, *45,* 361-366.

Levine, J. A. *Who will raise the children? New options for fathers (and mothers).* Philadelphia: Lippincott, 1976.

Martin, V. H. *Hours of work when workers can choose.* Washington, D.C.: Business and Professional Women's Foundation, 1975.

Mason, K. O., Czajka, J. L., & Arber, S. Change in U.S. women's sex-role attitudes, 1964-1974. *American Sociological Review,* 1976, *41,* 573-596.

Ministry of Health and Social Affairs. *Catalogue of social services.* Stockholm, Sweden: Author, 1977.

National Academy of Sciences. *Toward a national policy for children and families. Report of the Advisory Committee on Child Development.* Washington, D.C.: Author, 1976.

Nietzel, M. T., Winett, R. A., MacDonald, M., & Davidson, W. *Behavioral approaches to community psychology,* Elmsford, N.Y.: Pergamon, 1977.

Parsons, H. M. What happened at Hawthorne? *Science,* 1974, *183,* 922–932.

Pleck, J. H. The work-family role system. *Social Problems,* 1977, *24,* 417–427.

Ramey, J. Experimental family forms—the family of the future. *Marriage and Family Review,* 1978, *1*(1), 19–26.

Rapoport, R., & Rapoport, R. Work and family in contemporary society. *American Sociological Review,* 1965, *30,* 381–394.

Rapoport, R., & Rapoport, R. *Dual career families.* London: Penguin, 1971.

Robinson, D. *Alternate work patterns: Changing approaches to work scheduling.* Scarsdale, N.Y.: Work in America Institute, 1976.

Robinson, J. P. *How Americans use time: A social-psychological analysis of everyday behavior.* New York: Praeger, 1977.

Ryan, W. *Blaming the victim.* New York: Vintage, 1971.

Sarason, S. B. *The creation of settings and the future societies.* San Francisco: Jossey-Bass, 1972.

U.S. Department of Labor. Married persons' share of the labor force declining, BLS study shows. *Department of Labor News,* March 8, 1977, No. 77191.

Weiss, C. *Evaluation research.* Englewood Cliffs, N.J.: Prentice-Hall, 1972.

Willems, E. P. Behavioral technology and behavioral ecology. *Journal of Applied Behavior Analysis,* 1974, *7,* 151–166.

Winett, R. A. Environmental design: An expanded behavioral research framework for school consultation and educational innovation. *Professional Psychology,* 1976, *7,* 631–636.

Winett, R. A., Fuchs, W. L., Moffatt, S. A., & Nerviano, V. J. A cross-sectional study of children and their families using different child care environments: Some data and conclusions. *Journal of Community Psychology,* 1977, *25,* 149–159.

Winett, R. A., Moffatt, S. A., & Fuchs, W. L., Social issues and research strategies in day care. *Professional Psychology,* 1975, *6,* 145–154.

C H A P T E R

13

PSYCHOLOGY, HEALTH PLANNING, AND COMMUNITY MAINTENANCE PROGRAMS

WILLIAM R. MEYERS AND MARK KEMPNER

It is the authors'view that the psychologist who provides clinical services finds himself enmeshed in an increasingly regulated health care system. In particular, *aftercare programs* are typically delivered by corporate entities such as community mental health centers, hospitals, halfway houses, or other social agencies. This delivery system places the client and provider squarely within the regulatory framework of the health care system. To deliver care of adequate quality, or to develop needed new services, requires that the psychologist know how the system is organized and financed. It also requires that he or she understand the decision criteria and decision-making structures in the health care system. Therefore we argue in this chapter that systematic training in health planning and related areas would benefit psychologists and the people they serve. While making that argument, we present an extremely brief overview of some of the structures of the health care system. This is included not to obviate a course of specific training in health planning, but rather to give a general flavor of how the system is organized.

One of the authors of this chapter is a psychologist and the other is a health planner. Our aim is to help psychologists cope with the flood of regulations and administrative complexities that have engulfed us; for it is astonishing how little of this complex structure has reached public awareness. As an example, consider the federal Health Planning and Resources Development Act (Public Law 93-641), which we shall discuss in detail later in this chapter. This law, passed by Congress in 1974, is the nation's most important piece of health legislation; yet comparatively few people, even behavioral scientists, have ever heard of it (see *Behavior Today,* Feb. 27, 1978, pp. 1-3, and March 27, 1978, pp. 4-6). The act creates an immense regulatory structure, much of which affects mental health programs and facilities. Mental health professionals were so much asleep at the switch that the act as passed in 1974 does not once mention mental health, and so contains no provisions taking mental health programming needs into account. Yet these programs are often controlled by the act. Worse, owing to the ignorance and apathy of mental health professionals in respect to this legislation, there are indications of a lack of sensitivity to mental health issues in the implementation of the act. The regulatory bureaucracy set up by this law has tended to give mental health programs a low priority when they compete, as they often do, for funds against other health programs. As a result, mental health does not get its fair share of health program monies controlled by this legislation. This situation is in part owing to the fact that the top administrators of the Health Systems Agencies (HSAs) set up by this act are most often trained in business management, not in the social or behavioral sciences (*Behavior Today,* Feb. 27, 1978, pp. 1-3, and March 27, 1978, pp. 4-6). To be fair to mental health professionals, the rest of the public is also so unaware of this regulatory structure that the Aetna Life Insurance Company took a two-page advertisement in *Time* magazine explaining what Health Systems Agencies are, explaining the Health Planning and Resources Development Act, and urging citizens to participate in HSA decision-making processes in order to gain control of costs in our health care system (*Time,* April 23, 1979).

As an introduction to the maze of health planning legislation and regulation, and as a prelude to considering what kinds of training would benefit psychologists in these areas, let us begin with a brief examination of the history of the health care system in this country.

THE HEALTH CARE SYSTEM:
THE BEGINNINGS OF REGULATION

With the beginning of the Medicaid and Medicare programs in 1965, the federal government started paying for the medical care received by nongovernment personnel, leading to a "system" over which the government had no real control. The economic consequences of this arrangement were not understood and still give economists ample opportunity to parade a host of theories and analyses about demand curves and a free-market economy before a weary public. The rapidly increasing cost of health care since 1965 (see Figure 13–1) has necessitated the imposition of government regulation in an effort to control rising costs.

Regulation of the health care system certainly has precedent in other sectors of the economy. A more direct precedent is that the public's health has been regulated by a variety of laws spanning hundreds of years. The power to examine, quarantine, and treat people suspected of carrying contagious disease has long been one of the legal powers of the state. Compulsory vaccination, serologic tests of people getting married, fluoridation, sanitation, automobile safety standards, and fire laws are further examples of the state's power to act when it is judged that the action is related to the public's health. An even more ambitious effort on the part of government is the process of controlling the levels of some 70,000 chemical substances in our environment produced by industry, as well as new substances before they enter the marketplace. This complex, impossible task became law in January 1977 with the passage of the Toxic Substance Control Act of 1976.

Given the history of the government's legal and regulatory role in the maintenance of the public's health, it is not surprising that government has begun to exercise control over the medicl care delivery system as the share of government money supporting that system increases. But even with the increased cost to government for medical care, control and regulation of the health care system is a recent phenomenon. Controlling the quality of medical education in the United States took place only after World War I. As late as the 1940s, many states did not even require hospitals to be licensed.

Many authors have discussed the emerging role of government regulation of the health care system in some detail (e.g., Silver, 1976; Wing, 1976). The purpose of this chapter is not to summarize these works, but to discuss the impact of this increasing regulation on the practice of clinical psychology, particularly the development of aftercare services, and to suggest methods that would increase the effectiveness of clinical psychologists in program development and administration.

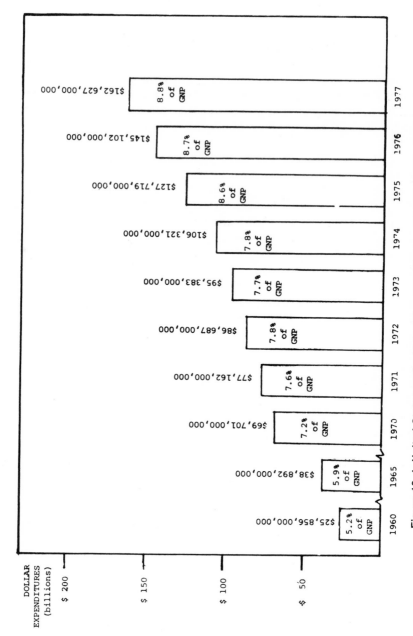

Figure 13-1. United States national health expenditures and national health expenditures expressed as a percentage of GNP. *Source:* U.S. Depart. of Health, Education and Welfare. *Social Security Bulletin,* 1978, *41*(7). Prepared by Health

GOVERNMENT REGULATION OF THE HEALTH CARE SYSTEM: ITS POLITICAL, SOCIOLOGICAL, AND LEGAL BASES

Before turning to an examination of the legal constraints placed on program development by health planning legislation, it is necessary to understand the sociological, political, and legal bases for the increasing regulation of the health care system.

The Role of Science and Technology

The organization and practice of medicine in this country is primarily the result of the interaction of economic and sociological factors, not scientific discoveries (Silver, 1976). The validity of this statement rests in part on the role of basic scientific *discoveries* versus the development of sophisticated *technology* in the practice of medicine. *Basic scientific discoveries* such as immunization are often made outside the practice of clinical medicine. These discoveries enter the medical care system through the private physician. Preventive practices such as immunization for polio, diphtheria, and typhoid, enter the system very slowly, due to the treatment rather than preventive orientation of medical education. In such instances, the government is often forced to mandate preventive measures in order to fulfill its responsibility to maintain the health of the public.

Advances in technology, on the other hand, have proved sophisticated diagnostic equipment such as computed axial tomography (CAT scanners), ultrasound, and "dedicated" laboratory computers. The impact of such equipment on medical education (and the cost of medical care) is profound, yet such equipment does little to affect the health status of the population. New medical specialities, even subspecialities such as radiotherapy and oncology, have resulted from advances in technology rather than advances in our basic understanding of disease-producing mechanisms. Such technology is the handmaiden of modern medicine and is much desired by physicians. Given that this technology has been focused on the individual patient, there has been little effort to regulate its development and use until recently. And medical education continues to focus its teaching on the skillful use of sophisticated *diagnostic* equipment and *treatment* by surgical and chemical means, rather than the *prevention* of the onset of disease. The result of this high technology is an increasingly costly medical care system, medical education designed to understand and use this technology, and case-by-case care rather than systemic change and disease prevention. We seem to be willing to spend an infinite number of dollars and engage in heroic efforts to save a single life, yet this same resolve is not present when confronted with the death caused by drunken driving, tobacco, carcinogenic substances, or lack of exercise. This viewpoint has created a two-tiered system in which the health of the public has become a major responsibility of the state, and the health of the individual rests with individuals and depends on their ability to enter the health care system as needed.

The Role of the Hospital

The interaction of factors such as technology, the individual clinical versus social systemic nature of medical practice, and our free enterprise system has resulted in a system in which medical care is centered about a relationship between an individual patient and an individual doctor. In fact, the hospital was originally merely a facility where physicians treated the seriously ill patient, a facility that offered "hospitality" and was not considered to be a participant in the treatment of the patient. The role of the hospital has undergone a profound change during the past 35 years. In a significant number of medical encounters the relationship is between a patient and an institution, and often the institution is a hospital. Clearly the physician is still intimately involved in the treatment of a hospitalized patient, deciding when to admit, what treatment is to be received, and when to release the patient. But hospitals now play a significant role in these processes. The hospital provides equipment, services, and personnel that are directly responsible for the care of the patient. Hospitalized patients no longer see themselves as only "in the care of the physician" but also "in the hospital." This change in the hospital's role raises the question of the hospital's liability, and argues against the fiction that they do not practice medicine. This liability of a hospital founded on the reasonable principles of general supervision of care, consultation in certain categories of cases, and requiring that nurses report cases they believe are being mismanaged was stated in *Darling v. Charlestown Community Memorial Hospital* (33 Ill. 2d 326, 211 N.E. 2d 253 [1965]). This decision marked a profound change in the legal liability of hospitals, making their malpractice liability consistent with their role in the care of the hospital patient.

The *Darling* decision reflects the fact that modern medicine is increasingly dependent on the role of institutions providing sophisticated treatment and diagnostic equipment. Whether or not this trend is necessary or desirable, it is likely that the future medical care delivery system will be organized around large medical centers and networks or hospitals using telemetry, designated phone lines, and other sophisticated communications to link expensive technology together in an institutionally based system of care. It is likely that one response to this trend will be an increase in the amount and scope of government regulation.

The Gradual Growth of
Government Regulation

The regulation problem is peculiar to the United States. In almost all other developed nations, the government *owns* or *directly controls* health facilities. Consistent with our economic system, health facilities are privately owned, with some important exceptions. Of the some 7000 hospitals in the United States, only 2000 are state, county, or district hospitals. Another 500 hospitals are operated by the federal government through the Public Health Service and the Veterans Administration. The remaining 4500 are privately owned.

Even though our system of health facilities is predominately privately owned, many of these facilities were built with government funds and currently receive a substantial portion of their operating revenue from government-supported medical insurance programs. Federal and state government indirectly subsidizes privately owned hospitals that are incorporated as nonprofit institutions by exempting their income from state and federal taxes. Even with government subsidy for construction and maintenance of health facilities, and the payment for medical services to nongovernmental facilities, it is only recently that government has been willing to improve the regulation of hospitals and other health facilities and providers. Government regulation has been in the areas of licensure and physical plant requirements such as fireproofing, ventilation, and sanitation. Attempts at regulating the cost, distribution, and quality of medical services is a recent phenomenon. As this hesitancy to regulate hospitals has decreased, government involvement in regulation of the entire health care system has also begun. The new role of government has raised such issues as: To what extent should the government control health care facilities? Can the government effectively regulate the quality of care? Should the government regulate the distribution of medical personnel and medical facilities? Should the government set rate schedules for services not paid directly by the government? A clear trend is emerging, although the pace is still an explosive political issue. This trend is to the health care system as a public utility. The licensing, certification, accreditation, and federal health planning legislation establishes regulatory mechanisms consistent with viewing the health care system as a public utility.

Licensing, Accreditation, and Certification as Steps toward Regulation

Virtually all states require that hospitals and nursing homes be licensed. The licensing procedure attempts to control the quality of care by setting minimum standards. Often licensing requirements focus only on the physical adequacy of facilities and on minimum staffing patterns. But to the extent that these requirements deal with the physical safety of patients, they address issues of quality. To what extent the government can involve itself in quality assurance is still hotly debated. A complication of those licensing procedures that attempt directly to ensure quality of care is that each state sets its own standards, and state licensing statutes usually include a statement that facilities must be in "substantial compliance" with the state licensing standards. The state-by-state approach allows for considerable variation in standards, and the "substantial compliance" language permits political pressures to interfere with the licensing process. At best, state licensing procedures have eliminated only the very worst facilities.

Unlike licensing, accreditation is voluntary and is awarded by private associations of health and health-related facilities. By far the most important of these associations is the Joint Commission on Accreditation of Hospitals (JCAH), organized during the 1950s and sponsored jointly by the American Hospital Association, American Medical Association, American College of Physicians, and the American College of Surgeons. The JCAH developed its own standards and its function is similar to state licensing procedures. But there are differences between licensing and accreditation, since accreditation is a voluntary process conducted by a private nongovernmental agency. JCAH representatives function as a consultant firm hired by the hospital to inspect and evaluate its physical plant and offered services. JCAH standards deal more extensively and directly with patient care than do state licensure standards.

Since accreditation is voluntary, it meant little more than added prestige—until 1965. In that year accreditation was linked directly to the Medicare certification process. Eligibility for participation as a provider in the Medicare program was based on certification by the Department of Health, Education and Welfare (HEW). Certification by HEW is also voluntary, but few facilities could afford the financial loss they would incur by forfeiting Medicare reimbursement. Certification to participate in the Medicare program as a provider is contingent on meeting a number of requirements including: (1) that a health facility be licensed under its own state licensing law; and (2) that the facility meet HEW "Conditions of Participation," which are standards of quality outlined in the Medicare statute. The 1965 legislation authorized HEW to set requirements necessary to the health and safety of patients, but such standards may not be higher than those established for accreditation by the JCAH. This is the link between accreditation and certification. The constitutionality of this statute was questioned by some, but not tested in the courts. In 1972, Social Security amendments changed the statutory basis for Medicare certification. HEW may, if it chooses, impose higher standards than those of the JCAH or have the option of relying on the JCAH standards. This change is more consistent with the constitutional principle of government regulation of a government function.

Certificate of Need Laws

All of the above regulations are attempts to ensure that the quality of health facilities and their services meet minimum standards. During the past 10 years, states and particularly the federal government have become involved in imposing even more direct and far-reaching controls over health facilities. These controls have taken the form of federal health planning legislation and state certificate of need laws. Certificate of need statutes were passed by state legislatures during the late 1960s and early 1970s. Each state law differs in scope and in the administrative structures set up to carry out the law. However, all certificate of need laws empower an administrative agency or agencies to determine the public's "need" and approve or disapprove requests for expansion or new construction of specific categories of health facilities. Most state certificate of need statutes also grant approval and disapproval powers for proposed expansions of services as well as for changes of services. Although certificate of need laws are too new to permit us to assess their impact and effectiveness, they are a clear attempt at state government regulation of both the growth and the distribution of health facilities and services offered to the public.

The federal government adopted the certificate of need concept in 1972. Social Security amendments passed in that year required that a certificate of need review process be undertaken for all agencies receiving Medicaid, Medicare, and Maternal and Child Health funds. This review was to be done by Comprehensive Health Planning Agencies or other designated planning agencies within a state. If a provider engaged in capital expansion found to be "unnecessary" or not in conformity with state and local planning activities, HEW could reduce the reimbursement for the above services in proportion to the extent to which a provider had exceeded certificate of need guidelines. This process, known as "1122 Review," took place only in those states where the state governor and

HEW came to an agreement specified in the federal statute and regulations.

Federal Health Planning Legislation

In 1974 the Congress passed Public Law 93-641, the National Health Planning and Resources Development Act. This act consolidates the activities of a variety of agencies and gives regional health planning agencies some "teeth" to implement their plans. Public Law 93-641 established three basic kinds of organizations: the Health Systems Agency (HSA), the Statewide Health Coordinating Council (SHCC), and a designated State Health Planning and Development Agency (SHPDA).

1. Functions of the HSA. To understand the functions of the various agencies, it is important to distinguish between *local-* and *state*-level health planning. Local health planning is the responsibility of the HSAs. Specifically, the responsibilities of the HSA as defined by statute are:

1. improving the health of residents of a health service area,
2. increasing the accessibility (including overcoming geographic, architectural, and transportation barriers), acceptability, and quality of health services provided them,
3. restraining increases in the cost of providing them health services, and
4. preventing unnecessary duplication of health resources; each health systems agency shall have as its primary responsibility the provision of effective health planning for its health service area and the promotion of the development within the area of health services, manpower, and facilities which meet identified needs, reduce documented inefficiencies and implement the health plans of the agency. (Section 1513 [a], Public Law 93-641)

These rather grand goals are to be accomplished through a number of activities. HSAs are mandated to compile data on the available health services in their area. This effort is to include surveys, or analysis of existing data, on the health status of area residents and on the utilization of existing services. It also includes evaluation of the effectiveness of the area's health services, and assessment of environmental and occupational health exposure factors. These activities will lead to the development of two planning documents, a Health System Plan (HSP) and Annual Implementation Plan (AIP). The HSP will state long-range goals for issues determined by the HSA as priorities for the area. The AIP will state short-term objectives for the area, and identify projects to be implemented to meet the long-range goals of the HSP. The act also provides for an Area Health Services Fund to be administered by the HSA. Grants can be made by the HSA from this fund to encourage the development of services consistent with the HSP and AIP. Although this "carrot" approach was authorized in Public Law 93-641, it has not yet been funded, owing to lobbying by hospitals and physicians. This section, if it were funded, could begin to create a HSA control the slope of the cost curve of the health care system, but do not change the fundamental economic organization of the system.

2. *HSAs and Applications for Federal Funds.* HSAs also have the authority to review and comment on applications for federal funds under a number of federal health and health-related programs. These programs include community mental health centers, community health centers, National Health Service Corps personnel, and substance (drugs and alcohol) abuse programs. This review-and-comment process ("HEW funds review") is not binding on a federal funding source (although it is often de facto determinative), but new federal regulations on the Proposed Use of Federal Funds (PUFF) give HSAs increased authority in this area effective November 1979. Psychologists should note that this new review process will affect aftercare services in a direct way. All such services that are funded by HEW money will be subject to a review-and-approve process by HSAs prior to HEW funding decisions. Each HSA will prepare guidelines and criteria for review of such funding requests, and an analysis of each request will be prepared by HSA staff for a decision by their governing body. Such decisions by an HSA will be de jure binding on HEW.

3. *HSAs and Certificate of Need Review.* HSAs also review and comment to the state-level certificate of need office on applications requesting grants or loans for health facility development and certificate of need requests. Community mental health centers, for example, are sometimes subject to certificate of need review. Final authority for approval of certificate of need requests rests with the state. Although the HSA's role in this process is advisory, it is infrequent that an HSA decision is overturned by a state certificate of need office.

The certificate of need process is often a tedious task requiring enormous specificity on the part of the applicant. Review questions for an applicant will routinely cover such areas as the physical design of a facility, linkages with other parts of the health care system, community involvement in the planning process, incidence and prevalence of a disease or condition that necessitates the application, special efforts to accommodate racial and linguistic minorities, and whether the proposal represents the most cost-effective approach.

All of the above questions have been asked of applicants seeking to expand or develop mental health services. What is of particular interest is that with the exception of the question of incidence and prevalence, *the knowledge base to answer the above would not be found in a traditional graduate program in psychology.* This places the applicant agency from the mental health field in a potentially costly bind. The use of consultants is common if the necessary expertise is not present within the staff of applicant agency. However, the review process byh an HSA includes oral probing of the applicant's written responses. This aspect of the process requires a thorough knowledge of the areas under discussion and implies that mental health professionals need training in these areas.

4. HSA "Appropriateness Review." Finally, HSAs are mandated to review the "appropriateness" of existing institutional health services and make recommendations regarding continuation and growth of such services. "Appropriateness review" is the tool that an HSA and the state health planning agency will use to close facilities found to offer inappropriate services. This form of review has not yet begun, but HEW regulations for such review are expected in 1979. This type of review must take into account the community view of the appropriateness of institutional services. This will require an HSA to engage in a rather complex process, including both an assessment of current community attitudes and an effort at public education. Many health planners question the ability of an HSA to implement "appropriateness review" both on methodological grounds and because of limitations of staff resources. It is our own view that this type of review process will be implemented slowly and with a considerable degree of uneven expertise from HSA to HSA. It is clear that this type of review is amenable to political pressure. The effectiveness of both HSAs and institutions in dealing with this process will rest on the community organization skills of the parties involved, including psychologists on the staff of the HSAs. As noted later, Health Systems Agencies are a growing source of employment for clinical psychologists.

5. The Organizational Structure of HSAs. HSAs plan and review on a *local and regional* basis. Regions rarely cross state lines. The size of an HSA planning area is determined by population. This has resulted in a few HSA regions' being coterminous with states, such as in West Virginia, Vermont, Utah, and Wyoming. An HSA may be a governmental unit or a nonprofit agency that engages solely in health planning and development. The governing body or board of an HSA must be composed of at least 10 members, the majority of whom must be consumers "broadly representative" of the constitutents of the area. The rest can be "providers." Moreover, Public Law 93-641 is very specific in its definition of a provider. Section 1531 of the act defines a provider as someone:

(A)   who is a direct provider of health care (including a physcian, dentist, nurse, podiatrist or physician assistant) in that the individual's primary current activity is the provision of health care to individuals or the administration of facilities or institutions (including hospitals, long-term care facilities,

outpatient facilities, and health maintenance organizations) in which such care is provided, and when required by state law, the individual has received professional training in the provision of such care or such administration and is licensed or certified for such provision or administration; or
(B) who is an indirect provider of health care in that the individual
   (i) holds a fiduciary position with, or has a fiduciary interest in, any entity described in subclause (II) or (IV) of clause (ii);
   (ii) receives (either directly or through his spouse) more than one-tenth of his gross annual income from any one or a combination of the following:
      (I) Fees or other compensation for research into or instruction in the provisions of health care.
      (II) Entities engaged in the provision of health care or in such research or instruction.
      (III) Producing or supplying drugs or other articles for individuals or entities for use in the provision of health care.
      (IV) Entities engaged in producing drugs or such other articles.

   (iii) is a member of the immediate family of an individual described in subparagraph (A) or in clause (i), (ii), or (iv) of subparagraph (B); or
   (iv) is engaged in issuing any policy or contract of individual or group health insurance or hospital or medical service benefits.

All individuals not defined as providers are considered consumers. This governing board of the HSA has the responsibility for the development of the HSP, AIP, and all other mandated functions of Public Law 93–641 described above. Professional staff of the HSA engage in the work necessary to meet the legal mandates, but final authority rests with the governing board. All governing board meetings must be public with adequate notice given of such meetings. All records and data compiled by the governing board are available to the public upon request.

Given the public nature of the HSAs, it is not an uncommon experience for institutions to attempt to influence the decisions of an HSA governing board. The ability to marshall data to support a position or request before an HSA governing board is becoming an increasingly important skill in the day-to-day business of the health care system. Data available for analysis are often also amenable to interpretation, producing situations of judgment about the "need" versus "no-need" decision. Thus, both analytical and political skills are needed by professionals on the staff of HSAs and the institutions they regulate.

State-Level Health Planning in Public Law 93–641

Before discussing the skills needed for effective intervention in the health planning process, we must complete the explanation of *state*-level health planning specified in Public Law 93–641. The act provides for two *state*-level health planning bodies, the State Health Coordinating Council (SHCC) and a State Health Planning and Developing Agency (SHPDA) designated by the governor of a state to (1) administer a state certificate of need program, (2) act as the state agency for the federal "certificate of need" program ("1122 Review" described above), (3) review HSA recommendations regarding appropriateness of existing facilities and make such reviews public, and (4) develop a state medical facilities plan for the purpose of allocating resource development funds.

1. The State Health Coordinating Council. The SHCC serves as an advisory group to to the state health planning agency and must review the state health facilities plan and other activities of the stage agency. A majority of the members of the SHCC must be consumers, and at least one-third of the providers on the SHCC must be direct providers as defined in the legislation.

2. The State Health Planning and Development Agency. The SHPDA may or may not have all of the responsibilities outlined above. It is fairly common for states to establish a separate office to administer certificate of need programs. In addition, the SHPDA may serve as professional staff for the State Health Coordinating Council (SHCC). It is not within the scope of this chapter to delineate all of possible organizational arrangements that exist, but it must be noted that every state does have a SHCC and a SHPDA, and they are powerful.

The Health Maintenance Organizations

In addition to establishing the system of planning and regulating agencies we have been describing, Public Law 93-641 also mandated one of the few *structural* changes in the health care delivery system undertaken at a national level, in that Health Maintenance Organizations (HMOs) were made a part of the governing board of every HSA in which a fully certified HMO existed. To understand the impact of this part of the act, it is necessary to understand how HMOs, a new type of *delivery* system, differ from the traditional organization of our health care system. An HMO is simply a prepaid medical practice with all personnel being on salary plus bonus. The fact that makes HMOs markedly different is that for them to be financially viable they must keep hospitalization rates for their members to a minimum. By contrast, for a private fee-for-service physician, the most secure income is from third-party payors. Given that outpatient services are either not insured or are minimally insured, the economic incentive encourages the maximum use of hospitals. With an HMO the incentive is just the opposite. An HMO member, for a fixed annual premium, is entitled to the unlimited medical services offered by their HMO. The most expensive of services is hospitalization. In order for an HMO to survive financially it must keep hospitalization rates to a minimum; thus prevention becomes an integral part of the HMO concept. Two drawbacks of HOMs have been alleged: (1) the HMO member must see a physician employed by the HMO; and (2) HMOs cannot afford to serve the elderly and the poor because they are the least healthy groups in our population. The first point is valid. The second drawback is dependent on the number of enrollees; that is, the larger HMO, the larger the potential dollar surplus that can be applied to unhealthy populations. The issue is still being debated and resolution awaits the continued existence of HMOs so their economic realities can be studied more carefully. Drawbacks aside, HMOs represent a fundamentally different way of delivering health care and it is noteworthy that they are identified in Public Law 93-641 not only for representation on HSA governing boards, but also on a form of medical care organization to be encouraged by HSAs.

THE REVIEW PROCESS IN THE HSAs, AND THE ROLE OF HEALTH PLANNING

Of all the *planning and regulatory* agencies discussed above, the Health Systems Agencies, which are very powerful, are the closest to the communities they serve both in terms of their limited geographical area and their legal mandates. The requirement that the members of their governing body live within the geographic community served by the HSA assures that this body will be sensitive to the planning area, and makes them accessible to those most directly affected by their decisions. Accessibility is a double-edged sword, since to the extent that it means that a public agency can be manipulated by political pressure it may produce a loss of confidence in an agency's ability to be rational and consistent. Moreover, the absence of a coherent medical care system and a coherent national policy regarding the development of a system makes it easier to influence HSAs by political pressure.

Ideally, decisions on certifcate of need and the use of HEW money are made on the basis of the components identified in the Health Systems Plan (HSP) of an HSA. This plan is an effort to construct, on a local and regional basis, the ideal health care system. "Ideal" is defined as that system which assures the accessibility and availability of quality health care at reasonable costs. Emphasis, for obvious political reasons, is often placed on the reasonable cost or cost-containment aspects of the HSP in the project review process within an HSA. Often the other variables of the HSP, if implemented, would increase costs. Many argue that the increased costs related to accessibility, availability, and quality of care are short-term increases, and that the process of eliminating duplication and underutilized services will limit cost increases over the long run. Underlying this argument is the assumption that a more equitable delivery of health care services will improve the health status of a population, a debatable assumption. A full discussion of this premise is beyond the scope of this chapter. Suffice it to say here that many authorities believe that immunization, better nutrition, exercise, cessation of smoking, full employment, and adequate housing would likely do more to improve the health of the population than the guarantee of medical care for the entire population (Belloc, 1973).

The issue of cost control and the argument about the role of medical care is improving the health status of the population make HSAs particularly vulnerable to political pressures. The vulnerability is compounded by the fact, as noted, that we do not have a national policy that specifies what type of health care system would best serve the needs of the American people.

1. Health Planning and National Health Insurance

In this atmosphere, planning becomes the process of forecasting both the availability of resources and the political forces that will dictate such availability. A short history of recent attempts to legislate national health insurance (NHI) will serve to demonstrate the problems of predicting the future when action is dependent on the political process. Following the adoption of Medicare and Medicaid in 1965, the consequent and seemingly out-of-control rise in health care costs, proposals for NHI were introduced in Congress. These proposals had the dual purposes of removing economic barriers to health care and the containment of costs. During subsequent congressional sessions there was a great deal of political debate as to whether or not we should enact NHI. In the early 1970s the basic battle seemed to be won, and attention focused on what form NHI should take. NHI became part of the platforms of presidential candidates, and President Carter indicated strong support for the concept of NHI. But the "taxpayers revolt" spawned in California with the passage of Proposition 13 is resulting in a further delay of legislative initiative for NHI. The arguments about the costs of NHI have taken on even more of a liberal-versus-conservative political overtone, further impairing the ability of planners to predict the outcome of this fundamental proposal. The detailed effects of NHI, if it is passed, on the health care system are calculable only if one knows what benefits will be included, to whom, and how NHI will be financed. In general, it is safe to say that if the impact of Medicare and Medicaid was dramatic, the impact of NHI will be awesome. The Health Systems Plans of HSAs consistently ignore the impact of some form of NHI, which is understandable only when you know that the HSP is oriented toward current decisions.

2. The Future of Health Planning

The frustrations health planners feel are underscored by the political battle over NHI and the lack of a coherent national health care policy. But as federal involvement in the health care system expands in terms of dollars, federal regulation of that system will also increase. Health Systems Agencies or State Health Planning Development Agencies will probably be given this increased regulatory responsibility. Health planners and Health Systems Agencies are already significant actors in the process of determining the allocation of resources within the health care system, and are currently influenced both by the presentation of reasoned, well-researched projects and by political pressure. This analysis suggests that there is a basic set of skills that are needed to interact successfully with an HSA in both the development of its Health Systems Plan and its project review functions.

HEALTH PLANNING SKILLS

Understanding the current role of HSAs and possessing the skills to interact with its planning and regulating functions are requisite for anyone involved with the delivery and growth of health services. The first step is to acquaint oneself with the HSA's plan. Federal regulations require that the Health Systems Plan of each HSA be available to the public. A copy of this plan must be available in every major library in the service area of an HSA. The priorities of the local HSA are spelled out in the HSP, and are subject to annual review and update by the HSA. This update activity is a public process, since HSAs are mandated to be responsive to public comments, and have their public hearing as a vehicle for receiving such comment. Large turnouts by community groups and other special-interest groups at public hearings held by HSAs on their Health Systems Plan are a frequently used strategy for affecting the priorities of the Health Systems Plan. Changing the priorities of a Health Systems Plan can take up to a year's time, but given the HSP's importance as a template for project review, it is time well spent. Community organizaiton skills are a critical component of these lobbying efforts.

Of more immediate concern to health care institutions is getting what they want from an HSA review. This review is based on taking an applicant's stated basis of need and his proposal for meeting that need, and assessing the validity of the proposal in relation to other similar or competing services. Some of the criteria used to determine validity are: (1) demonstrated need and a sufficient population to sustain the program; (2) the appropriateness of the particular response to this need (i.e., is this the best way to meet this need?); (3) the cost implications of such a program for the health care system; and (4) integration of this service with other appropriate services and institutions in the health care system. This list suggests some of the skills needed to develop such an application. Determination of a population in need of a given service requires basic skills in demography and epidemiology. The use of the concepts of incidence and prevalence are critical to any defensible statement of need. Given that health planning uses population data as the basis for decision making, the manipulation and interpretation of such data are essential in the review process.

The ability to present a program budget, in the context of costs in the health care system, increases the likelihood that your position will be reviewed favorably. Besides a knowledge of program budgeting and cost–benefit analyses, this type of presentation requires a basic understanding of health care organization and the economic variables in the health care system. Simply balancing an inertial budget is not sufficient because it ignores the economic variables that dictate costs in the health care system.

A common concept in the planning arena is "linkages and capacity building." This means identifying agencies and services that augment and support your services and integrating them, when possible, in the development of new services. This is a cost-savings device and begins to address the development of a regional, coordinated health care system. The development of linkages, and therefore capacity building, requires a thorough knowledge of health care organization and an understanding of how to exchange benefits with other agencies in order to build bonds of cooperation.

Finally, a general rule of thumb in program development, based on current economic and political trends, is that any program that significantly raises costs in the health care system is not likely to be approved unless it can be documented in a compelling way that such a program is the only possible response to a demonstrated need. Rapidly rising health care costs have necessitated this response. Moreover, government's share of these rising costs has increased both as a percentage and as an amount of dollars spent. For example, in 1950 the government share of the $10.4 billion spent on personal health care was 20%. In 1976 the government share of the $120.4 billion spent was 40%. Even more dramatic is that the government paid 55% of the $55.4 billion expended on hospital care in 1976.

It is conceivable that Health Systems Agencies as we know them may not exist 10 years from now, but the regulation that is being imposed on the health care system is here to stay. Even under a national health insurance plan, for example, mechanisms will exist to control the growth and cost of the health care system. It is our view that many psychologists are not adequately prepared to compete effectively in this system when they find themselves in an administrative or program development role. Hence, their ability to influence the long-range adjustment of their patients is significantly reduced.

SUGGESTED READINGS IN HEALTH PLANNING

As will be discussed below, health planning draws on a number of fields, including sociology, economics, and epidemiology. It will become clear that these are complex subjects as they apply to health planning and administration, and systematic coursework would be helpful. Some readings can be recommended as a prelude to coursework, or where necessary, a partial substitute for it. These include works by Blum (1974), Feldstein (1971), Fuchs (1972, 1975), Hyman (1975) and MacMahon and Pugh (1970) to provide an introduction to the organization of the health care system, health economics, health planning, and epidemiology. A practical orientation to health planning can also be found in various U.S. government publications, especially the *Health Planning Information Series.* The most important volume in this series is the first, *Trends Affecting the U.S. Health Care System* prepared by the Cambridge Research Institute (1976). This is an analysis of the economic, technological, governmental, and social factors affecting our health care system. Another valuable resource is the *Vital and Health Statistics Series* (known as the "Rainbow Series") of the Health Resources Administration, National Center for Health Statistics, which includes all data from the national health interview survey and selected studies of special interest to health administrators.

PSYCHOLOGISTS IN THE MENTAL HEALTH SYSTEM

We believe that topics can usefully be suggested for a curriculum for psychologists working or planning to work in the health field. Since psychologists are the intended audience for the curriculum, attending will be given to mental health programs and issues, and their relation to aftercare, a crucial program category. However, in many caes aftercare issues and mental health or community mental health issues cannot be fully separated from broader health care issues. The curriculum proposed will in some cases address them jointly.

The History of Psychology: A Brief Note

The preceding discussion of the health care system, and the drastic changes occurring or imminent in it, suggests that many psychologists know little of the relevant material in the health care fields. Psychology graduate training programs rarely cover such matters as the nature of HSAs, HMOs, the function of Public Law 93-641, or epidemiology. These omissions are natural and understandable, considering the history of the discipline of psychology. The field developed first as a kind of applied biology, the study of organisms in respect to mental states and perceptions, based on a model of 19th-century physics. A typical issue was the creating of a mathematical equation for relating the perceived intensity of a stimulus, such as a noise, to the actual intensity of the stimulus. Later, more general concerns about the nature of mind became important. Issues of human interaction and of the behavior of crowds became important as social psychology began to develop. Attitudes and values became an issue of study from a social point of view, and motives were studied, usually from a biological point of view. Cognitive and behavioral interpretations of human nature also emerged. Psychologial theories were applied to the raising of children, and social psychology was applied to survey research investigations. But *clinical* psychology did not fully develop until World War II, when there was a critical shortage of psychiatrists and other clinically trained personnel in the armed services. Psychologists trained in psychometrics or experimental psychology were pressed into service as clinical psychologists. Training programs in clinical psychology did not emerge until after World War II. Clinical psychologists struggled to define their role as more than psychological testing, that is, to include psychotherapy and administration, and to become a competing profession with psychiatry. At the same time, social work and nursing were developing branches called psychiatric social work and psychiatric nursing, also in uneasy competition with psychiatry.

Psychologists and Community Mental Health

Through this period, clinical psychology remained primarily individual oriented. But with the passaage of the Community Mental Health Centers Act, federal mental health funding began to stress community-oriented programs in addition to the old hospital-oriented ones. In terms of the crucially important competition with psychiatry, psychology's position as in part a social science (as well as in part a biological science) meant that clinical psychology could claim special competence in the community area not possessed by psychiatrists; and community mental health began to be defined as a field. Community mental health training programs in graduate departments of psychology sprang up. Naturally, psychiatrists in competition began to speak of community psychiatry, note here that the Washington area is one of the most lucrative in the nation for the private practice of psychotherapy, owing to the concentration there of federal workers who have available the 80% deductible clause of their government-provided health insurance. In this environment, it is unlikely that the failure to volunteer is only because psychiatrists are too hard-pressed financially.

The greater willingness of psychologists to work with the financially needy appears to have several roots. Attitude surveys indicate that psychologists are more politically liberal than psychiatrists and than phy- and even of social psychiatry. But clinically trained psychologists began to dominate the field, by dint of numbers (psychiatry was restricting the number of people it was willing to train, as were all branches of medicine) and by dint of social science orientation (a smattering of sociology, and perhaps more of social psychology). Perhaps most important, psychiatrists with their private practices were sometimes unenthusiastic about community mental health with its overtones of volunteerism, helping the impoverished, and government regulation of fees. Clinical psychologists, on the other hand, saw the field of community mental health as a way of extending their arena of operations and a way of laying claim to special competences. This is not to deny that some of the key and most original founders of community mental health, such as Gerald Caplan, are psychiatrists.

Not all psychologists receive community mental health training, and some of those who do are not trained very intensively. Clinical psychology graduate students have training placements in hospitals, and to a lesser extent in community mental health agencies (the latter do not have training funds for psychologists), but little in their training is devoted to explaining how those agencies work, how they are funded, and how they relate to other health agencies.

Moreover, few clinical psychologists receive broad systematic training about the organization of the health care system. This omission is unfortunate since a substantial proportion of psychologists (mostly clinical psychologists, but also some social psychologists) work in the health care system after receiving their degrees. For example, they are staff members of mental hospitals, community mental health centers, or university counseling centers. This means that they work in a system whose organization and functioning they frequently do not understand systematically.

Job Trends and the Health Care System

Once source of jobs for psychologists, academia, has contracted greatly in recent years. The job scarcity for psychologists generally may become more severe, since there are at present more students in graduate school in psychology than the total of all psychologists now working. Moreover, the chances to start off immediately as a private practitioner of psychotherapy are very limited owing to difficulties in obtaining referrals for private practice if one is not affiliated with a health care agency. As a result of these job trends in psychology, we can expect more psychologists to seek work in the expanding health care area. With the growth of HSAs, the advent of HMOs, and the ultimate arrival of some kind of national health insurance, these opportunities should become more marked. It makes sense for psychologists moving in this direction to get appropriate health planning training so that they can become more useful earlier in their careers, with fewer expensive mistakes.

Special Qualifications of Psychologists

Psychologists do have some things to offer to start with that make them especially able to learn and use the necessary health care systems training. For one thing, psychologists may have more of a public than a private orientation as compared with psychiatrists. Dr. Brenda Gurel (1978), who served as the American Psychological Association's administrative officer for ethics for the years 1973–1978, cites an article in the *Washington Monthly* to the effect that of the 1100 psychiatrists who practice in Washington, D. C., not one volunteers as much as 1 hour a week to work in the community health centers, and only three have offices in the needier northeast and southeast quarters of town. We would note that attitude surveys indicate that psychologists are more politically liberal than physicians generally. These attitudinal differences may be due to the distinctly lower social class origins of psychologists than psychiatrists and other physicians. It is not surprising, for example, to discover that an entire class of candidates at a medical psychoanalytic institute had voted for Richard Nixon in 1972. When queried, they replied that they were "comfortable in pursuing their self-interest." The competing professions—psychology, social work, and psychiatric nursing—because their social class origins are lower than those of psychiatrists, appear to be more at home with working with financially needy populations. (By "social class origins" here is meant what the sociologist would call "father's occupation, education, and income.") These professions therefore have something special to offer in the health care and aftercare areas, where the populations involved are typically not drawn from the higher social strata.

Psychologists in particular have other "traits" of interest for their work in the health care administration and aftercare fields. Many psychologists have an intellectualizing, rational, systematic, precise way of approaching things. These are marked advantages for persons in administrative positions, because such roles require one to be careful, systematic, planful, orderly, rational, precise, and concerned about the future. In particular, psychologists seem to like to be rational and precise about human concerns, as contrasted with engineers and physical scientists who like to be rational and precise about impersonal matters.

The research orientation of psychologists also increases their ability to contribute in the health care systems field, since a research orientation leads to influenceability by data, a most desirable trait in administrators. It also involves comfort in handling quantitative data (a help in epidemiology) and some degree of comfort with statistics. The interest in approaching problems systematically, shared by good managers in all fields, is thus reinforced by the research orientation of most psychologists. Some psychologists are even blessed with an inquiring turn of mind, which can be very important in planning and administrating in a rapidly changing field like health care systems. This trait is too rare in administrators generally, with the result that bureaucracies often do the wrong thing, efficiently.

Some psychologists also have knowledge of biological factors although many do not have as much to offer in understanding the biological aspects of health care systems problems as do nurses and physicians. But most psychologists do have some training in understanding the social factors in illness. While frequently innocent of knowledge of sociology and of social structural considerations, they often have a social psychological orientation that permits them to become sensitive to cultural and ethnic differences in the populations served. These differences are unfortunately often slighted in their training, as compared with the training of social workers. This training deficiency is extremely unfortunate for those who will work with aftercare patients, many of whom come from the most disadvantaged economic and ethnic groups.

Additional Qualifications Needed by Psychologists

What then needs to be added to this complex of traits, styles, interests, training, and proficiencies that psychologists bring to the health care systems field? The answer depends to some extent on the specific role the psychologists will play. The roles of clinician and administrator are very different in terms of the kinds of things one must know well. The clinician needs an understanding of the organization of the health care system, but the administrator needs a great deal more. But is is useful to give some caveats about the contrast between the roles of clinician and administrator.

For one thing, there is mobility between the two roles since psychologist clinicians are often promoted to administrative-managerial roles, because of the tendency to recruit from within the organization, and because psychologists with their rationalistic tendencies are often good at administration. Moreover, even without promotion, many administrative tasks, such as grant writing, program evaluation, and community consultation, get assigned to the psychologist. It is a rare psychologist who is allowed to be a clinician full time in a health care agency. A final qualification is that managerial insights are useful to most applied psychologists in the more limited sense of helping them to organize their time, set priorities, measure progress, and so forth.

For psychologists working in the health care system, with its demands for administrative activities and skills, what has happened to the classic clinician–scientist model of clinical psychology? Is a revised model, *a clinician-scientist-administrator model,* feasible? We do not think so. All three functions are so demanding that we think any two of them are in practical terms exclusive of the third. Some health administrators can do clinical work at the same time, and some can do research at the same time, but very few health system administrators can do significant amounts of both clinical work and research while at the same time filling a major administrative role.

Broad Training about the Health Care System

What training concerning the health care system will be most useful to a psychologist working in it? The most basic need for the psychologist working either as clinician or administrator is to understand the organization of the health care system. For the psychologist in the clinical role this is perhaps the only urgent need. Such an understanding indicates where a patient can go for further help; that is, it helps the clinician provide continuity of care and make referrals to other agencies intelligently.

It helps the clinician understand the health insurance system, and so be able to advise patients about reimbursement for their treatment. An understanding of the organization and functioning of the health care system also helps the clinician understand the nature of the institutional or community background from which the patient may have emerged (see Lamb, 1976; Pasamanik, Scarpetti, & Dinitz, 1967). With aftercare patients, psychologist–clinicians are aware of the harsh realities of life that the patient has experienced inside the large state mental hospitals that constitute the alternative to remaining in the community. They are aware that it is the advent of the psychoactive drugs, not primarily the community mental health movement, that has led to the emptying of the state mental hospitals. Psychologist–clinicians are also aware of the extent to which the desire of state legislatures to save money (sometimes, as in Massachusetts, the State Department of Mental Health is both the most expensive state agency and the largest state government employer) that has also led to this emptying out, in the rush to close some state mental hospitals. They know the realities of the life of many discharged aftercare patients, including wretched conditions at the SRO (single room only) hotels in large cities all over this country. They know that despite the emphasis on returning them to the community, the majority of aftercare patients live alone. This knowledge of the realities of the health care system helps the clinician understand his patients by understanding their environment, and therefore helps the clinician plan for them better.

For the psychologist in the role of administrator, a knowledge of the health care system has additional uses. It enables psychologist-administrators to do better health care planning for their facilities, and to do better health care administration. Health care planning means, in the current health system, raising money; and health care administration means spending money wisely. An understanding of the health care system involves at least the following topics that should be part of the training of psychologist–health administrators. The first is *health legislation,* that is, the rules and regulations that govern the raising and spending of money, the standards which must be met, the purposes for which the money may be used under various programs, and the procedures of certification or peer review, and so forth.

A second aspect of the organization of the health care system is the *politics of health.* This includes an understanding of the political forces, lobbies, and pressure groups behind the shifting policies in health care. A proper understanding will help the psychologist-administrator predict and prepare for some of the changes that will occur in the health care system. Of critical importance are the political acumen and sophistication necessary to raise funds through federal, state, and local grant, subsidy, and reimbursement application. This sophistication includes knowing the political reasons a program is being established by the government so that the application can say the politically appropriate things. Proposals writing is an important skill. However, the technical parts of proposal writing, such as organization and format, are easier to learn than the policy analysis and political analysis necessary to formulate a proposed program in a way that is fundable from a legal and political point of view.

A third aspect of learning to cope with the health care system involves *preparing for the advent of national health insurance.* As noted earlier, national health insurance of some sort appears to be likely sometime in the near future, say within 5–10 years, despite the taxpayer revolt. In fact, it may become less expensive to have national health insurance than not to have it, given rapidly rising hospital and other health care costs. It is important, therefore, to keep up with the legislation and the debates in Congress so that programs can be planned and facilities designed so as to be maximally effective and fundable under the coming insurance system.

A fourth aspect of the organization of the health care system is particularly important for the psychologist–administrator. This is an understanding of the *special problems of aftercare.* A number of these have been mentioned already, but there are other aspects, such as the relation of aftercare programs to funding under Title XX of the welfare legislation. A major problem is the social isolation of the aftercare patient. Another is the "dumping" of large numbers of "former mental patients" in communities that do not want them, such as the Upper West Side of Manhattan. This is a problem in many modern nations. A third problem is the squalid life of many aftercare patients in SRO hotels. The heavy use of drugs in aftercare treatment (raising questions of logistics and of armed robbery of drug caches) is another issue. Also problematic is the location of aftercare day-treatment centers in the community, which usually does not want former hospitalized mental patients coming into residential areas for treatment. Halfway houses raise the ire of the local residents, who object to aftercare patients' living near them.

A separate difficulty is the placement of aftercare programs in community mental health centers. The centers were not set up to handle patients with severe disabilities, but rather to give inexpensive psychotherapy or social casework to income groups that could not otherwise afford it; as a result, community mental health centers' staffs are often unfamiliar with the needs and treatment of aftercare patients. Thus it is not unusual to have inappropriate treatment plans. For example, a classic measure of success with very hard-to-reach patient groups, such as skid-row alcoholics, was the number of times the patient came to treatment (see, for example, Blane & Meyers, 1963, 1964; Chafetz, Blane, & Hill, 1970; Meyers & Blane, 1970). But nowadays it is not unusual for the measure of success in evaluations of the aftercare programs to be the "ability" of the client not to have to come in for treatment (see Kiresuk, 1975). This reflects not so much the needs of the aftercare patients (some may need to be seen therapeutically much of the rest of their lives) as of the facility. The overload on the facility causes therapists to try to clear their calendars "by any means possible" in order to be able to accept new patients from the incoming flood. Coping well with the flood of aftercare patients requires both fundraising and program design, and perhaps innovation, by the psychologist–administrator.

Besides a general understanding of the organization of the health care system, there are specialized skills needed by the psychologist–health administrator, and we shall briefly describe some of these. But it is the broader understandings and skills that are the more important. For example, health economics is even more important than budgeting skills. Policy analysis and political analysis are even more important than quantitative skills. Planning theory is even more important than planning techniques such as demography and working with vital statistics data. And the ability to write clearly is more important than is skill in statistical analysis.

Specialized Skills Needed

Having said all this, we can describe briefly some specialized skills likely to be helpful to the psychologist–health administrator. Perhaps most important, as painful experience has shown, is *community organization*. Community organization skills are necessary to create a "demand" for health care services. The administrator needs citizen support in making his or her case with politicians, legislators, hospitals, and health agency officials, and the agencies that approve or reject the administrator's proposals for health care programs and facilities. Support by local citizens is necessary to force needed programs through. It is also a legal retirement since many federal programs require "citizen participation." Community organization subsumes many subskills, such as forming community groups, leading them, negotiating with them, and working with citizen advisory or governing boards for hospitals, community mental health centers, HMOs, and other health care facilities such as halfway houses and day-treatment centers. It includes being able to run a meeting, chair, form, or appoint a committee, draft a constitution for an organization, plan and follow through on lobbying with citizens, contact legislators, raise money from individuals, agencies, and local governments, and so forth. In the mental health and aftercare areas, citizen mental health and retardation catchment area boards (often establish ed by legislation) are important factors, as are the governing boards of community mental health centers, private mental health associations, and private mental retardation associations. In the aftercare context, Alcoholics Anonymous is one key group. For reasons of deprivation and discrimination, aftercare patients are disproportionately of low social class background and minority ethnic status. Consequently, skill in working with groups representing welfare clients, the poor, and minorities is important. Another dispossessed group is the elderly. The psychologist–administrator would do well to learn to obtain their political support (given their increasing proportion in the population), and understand their needs. They are highly represented among aftercare clientele. According to our experience and observation, the need for community organization skills in health care administration far exceeds the supply.

A need more specific to the aftercare field is *an understanding of community mental health ideology.* Many of the key propositions can be found in the Mental Health Ideology Scale (Baker & Schulberg, 1967, 1969). A somewhat deeper look is given by a measure of antiauthoritarian attitudes about how psychotherapy ought to be done and supervised, called the Democratic Values Scale (Lerner, 1973). Judging from these scales, and our own experience, we believe that community mental health ideology stresses the following points: reaching the financially needy, being anticustodial, dispersing services into the community and away from the hospitals, being responsive to community needs and demands, and taking power away from the doctors. This is not a growth model; it is a model of redistribution of power from the hospital to the community. Therefore strong community affiliations by the psychologist–health administrator will be crucial, especially in the politically hot climate of aftercare. The antiphysician, antihospital flavor means that the psychologist–administrator can expect some resistance from doctors, since community-based programs make them less important as administrators, and from hospitals, since community programs shift resources away from hospitals. The mental health field has not been short of examples of hostility between state mental hospitals and neighboring community mental health centers. As for physicians, the legislative debate over national health insurance has been marked by struggles between psychologists and physicians over whether outpatient mental health services, mainly psychotherapy, by psychologists should be reimbursable even though not performed under the supervision of a physician. This conflict suggests that skill in negotiating with or circumventing the medical bureaucracy will come in handy to the psychologist–administrator in aftercare.

A more general issue is that mental health programs are competing for governmental dollars with other kinds of health care programs, namely, physical health. It is up to professionals working in mental health, and citizens, to make sure that mental health gets its fair share of health care dollars. Has mental health competed effectively? We think not, and we believe that the psychologist–health administrator in the aftercare area must take steps to rectify this maldistribution. The problem is particularly acute in aftercare programs. Just as children are too young to be their own advocates, aftercare patients are usually too impaired to form adequate lobbying groups. It therefore behooves professionals in the field to make special efforts in their behalf and to be especially vigilant with respect to their interests. This requires political, administrative, negotiating, and bargaining skills.

A very general skill needed by the psychologist–administrator is of course *administration*. What subskills constitute administration? In our sense, they include accounting, traditional budgeting, and program budgeting. (The latter comprises the planning–programming–budgeting system [PPBS], cost–benefit and cost-effectiveness analysis, zero-base budgeting, and similar techniques.) Moreover, we specifically have found management by objectives to be a useful perspective in administration. On the other hand, we are not among the throngs following PPBS like lemmings to the sea. Rather, we are skeptics. But the floodtide of interest in PPBS and related skills runs so high that we believe it is necessary to be knowledgable about them, despite Wildavsky's (1975) convincing argument that PPBS has never worked anywhere, anytime. (See also the skeptical treatment by one of us of this technique in the context of program evaluation; Meyers, forthcoming). Budgeting skills of *some* sort, even traditional line-item budgeting, are necessary. Few psychologists receive any budgetary training as part of their graduate work, despite the fact that so many psychologists work as administrators.

Program evaluation is another skill needed by the psychologist-health administrator. Program evaluation is one of the few booming fields in the social sciences. There is currently a deluge of literature appearing; graduate courses in the area (not to mention graduate degree programs in evaluation) are growing in number and size. Many of the crucial areas in program evaluation can be subsumed under the following categories: experimental and quasiexperimental designs; measurement applications; survey methods; fieldwork and ethnographic methods; and, much oversold, program budgeting and cost-effectiveness methods. Courses that cover these areas will be valuable to psychologists and other working in health administration, according to the experience of our students. Three things must be recognized in considering the topics we have suggested. One is that the proper evaluation of programs involves not only attention to the program outcome, but also to the understanding of how the program operates in actuality, that is, what is called "process evaluation." Process evaluation usually requries methods of a field of work, ethnographic case study variety. Second, political considerations are crucial in program evaluation. Third, planning is the obverse of evaluation, so that the plan for a program should include a plan for evaluating the program. The evaluation results in turn should become part of the next cycle of the planning process. Consequently, program evaluation in the health field can with some profit be conceptualized as part of the health planning process.

Another area of skills important for the psychologist–health administrator is *epidemiology.* This field includes some attention to demography the analysis of vital statistics data, and the modes by which disease processes spread or are controlled. A course in epidemiology will provide these. But to some extent the disease process is only a metaphor when applied to mental health. There are even some, such as Szasz (1961), who argue that the "health" in "mental health" is a misnomer. They believe that mental illness is not an illness: it is a different personal orientation or a different set of values held by the individual. Thus there is a conflict about the extent to which insights from the health area really apply to mental health. Consequently, each psychologist studying epidemiology must come to his or her own conclusions about the extent to which epidemiological phenomena characterize aftercare phenomena, or for that matter mental health phenomena more generally. We believe that at least the concepts of incidence and prevalence are useful in these contexts.

A further area of knowledge useful for the psychologist–administrator is the *sociology of the community.* This is essential for health aftercare programs, since these programs are intended to be "community based" (located in the community and supported by the community) and are intended to serve the community. There is a great deal of loose thinking and self-serving formulation in the community mental health field, including the aftercare field. Much of it can be clarified with a proper understanding of the elements of community sociology, as was originally pointed out in a brilliant and insufficiently appreciated article by Jerome Manis (1968). For example, it is often not clear what community a "community-oriented" program is serving. Drawing catchment area boundaries on a map does not make the enclosed area a community. Therefore, an issue to be explored in a community sociology course for psychologist–health administrators in the health field is defining properties of a community, as contrasted with mere lines drawn on a map.

Another central problem is the tendency of psychologists and other mental health researchers, such as psychiatrists, to analyze communities by means of concepts suited not to collectives but to members (see Manis, 1968; Meyers, 1966; Meyers, Dorwart & Kline, 1977). Therefore, such a course should examine the difference between properties of members (such as individuals) and properties of collectives (such as communities) as outlined by Lazarsfeld and Menzel (1964) and Etzioni and Lehmann (1967). These are not dealt with in the usual "community psychology" course with its inappropriately individualistic bias. It is hard to plan and administer community-oriented health maintenance and aftercare programs if the community one is considering the no social reality, or is composed of conflicting communities or parts of communities whose characteristics have not been analyzed. Moreover, the salience for community mental health programs, including aftercare, of communities that are nongeographic is often igored. A large industrial firm may constitute a community for its employees, and in terms of its importance for their careers, incomes, lifestyles, and mental health, may be a more salient community than the local geographic one where their residence is located. Once this is understood, community-based programs addressed to the firm become possible, and indeed there exist many industrial alcoholism programs of this sort. With aftercare the issue becomes important if the patients are to any extent employable; also, institutions within the catchment area, such as a local church group, can sometimes constitute health-sustaining communities of greater significance to the patient than is the alleged community represented by the catchment area. Training in community sociology can also examine issues discussed earlier under the rubic of community organization. In addition, close attention to community power structure, formal and informal, will repay the psychologist–administrator amply when it comes time (all the time) to raise money or secure political support for a program. For example, knowing the local chief of police personally will tend to diminish problems caused by halfway houses for delinquent teenagers, since the police will be less tempted toward vindictive and counterproductive "drug busts." Another topic is the needs of special groups within the community, such as ethnic groups, residents of public housing, residents of SROs, unemployed teenagers, and so forth.

Programs That Could Include These Topics

This list of topics we believe to be of most use to the psychologist–health administrator working in the health care system, and particularly in aftercare, is not all-inclusive. For example, the sociology of bureaucracy would be helpful but not as crucial; so would training in philanthropic fundraising from private sources, and so also would public relations. But there is not time for everything. The question arises as to how to fit those things we have recommended most urgently into the training of psychologists. As we have suggested above, for psychologists working only as clinicians in the health care system, a semester course in the organization of the health care system would perhaps be sufficient to make a difference in the way they plan for the care of their patients. The course could be included as an option in the standard clinical psychology training program. For the psychologist–administrator, however, there are courses needed in the organization of the health care system (including health care legislation and the politics of health care); epidemiology; administration, management, and budgeting; finding and developing funding sources (perhaps best covered under the organization of the health care system); program evaluation; and community sociology. This would constitute the equivalent of a semester or a year of coursework. How should this be fit into the training of psychologists interested in health administration generally, or programs like aftercare in particular? Several methods appear feasible. One would be a separate master's program in health planning. A few such programs already exist. Some of the training we suggest above is also available in master's programs in public health. There are also programs in "health administration," but most of these were formerly titled "hospital administration" and are not the most relevant for our purposes. A fourth alternative is to offer a year of such training as a speciality within an existing doctoral program in clinical psychology. A fifth alternative is postdoctoral training covering these topics. To be most attractive to psychologists already practicing, such a program could be nonresidential for some students, and could also be available on a part-time basis. It would probably be most appealing if a master's degree in health administration or health planning could be awarded at the conclusion, given the fact that psychologists with both the PhD in clinical psychology and a master's in health planning are in great demand even in these days of recession, perhaps because they are appropriately trained to face the problems they will encounter and to work effectively in the health care administration field. With politically loaded highly conflictful programs like aftercare, the argument for such training is even stronger.

SUMMARY

There exists a complex health care system comprising a great deal of federal regulation that is not well understood by most psychologists, even those working in community and aftercare programs. We have mentioned briefly some of the salient features of this regulatory system, and have discussed various kinds of training that might be most helpful to psychologists who have to cope with it in order to give good patient care and develop needed community and aftercare services. Some of the kinds of formal training programs already available, or that might be made available, have been noted. A few introductory readings about the health care system itself have also been suggested.

REFERENCES

Baker, F., & Schulberg, C. The development of a community mental health ideology scale. *Community Mental Health Journal*, 1967, *3*, 216–225.

Baker, F., & Schulberg, C. Community mental health ideology, dogmatism and political-economic conservatism. *Community Mental Health Journal*, 1969, *5*, 433–436.

Belloc, N. B. Relationship of health practice and mortality. *Preventive Medicine*, 1973, *2*, 67–81.

Blane, H. T., & Meyers, W. R. Behavioral dependence and length of stay in psychotherapy among alcoholics. *Quarterly Journal of Studies in Alcohol*, 1963, *24*, 503–520.

Blane, H. T., & Meyers, W. R. Social class and the establishment of treatment relations by alcoholics. *Journal of Clinical Psychology*, 1964, *20*, 287–290.

Blum, H. L. *Planning for health: Development and application of social change theory.* New York: Human Sciences Press, 1974.

Cambridge Research Institute. *Trends affecting the United States health care system (Health Planning Information Series,* vol. I). Washington, D.C.: U.S. Government Printing Office, 1976.

Chafetz, M. E., Blane, H. T., & Hill, M. S. *Frontiers of alcoholism.* New York: Science House, 1970.

Etzioni, A., & Lehmann, E. W. Some dangers in "valid" social indicators. *Annals of the American Academy of Political and Social Science*, 1967, *373*, 1–13.

Feldstein, M. S. *The rising cost of hospital care.* Washington, D. C.: Information Resources, 1971.

Fuchs, V. R. (Ed.). *Essays in the economics of health and medical care.* New York: Columbia University Press, 1972.

Fuchs, V. R. *Who shall live? Health, economics, and social choice.* New York: Basic Books, 1975.

Gurel, B. D. Arrogance and altruism—a bit of preaching. *American Psychological Association Monitor*, 1978, *9*(2), 2.

Hyman, H. H. *Health planning: A systematic approach.* Germantown, Md..: Aspen Systems Corporation, 1975.

Kiresuk, T. Goal attainment scoring and quantification of values. In Guttentag, M., Kiresuk, T. Oglesby, & Cahn, J. (Eds.), *The evaluation of training in mental health.* New York: Behavioral Publications, 1975.

Lamb, H. R. & Associates. *Community survival for long-term patients.* San Francisco: Jossey-Bass, 1976.

Lazarsfeld, P. F., & Menzel, H. On the relation between individual and collective properties. In A. Etzioni (Ed.), *Complex organizations: A sociological reader.* New York: Holt, Rinehart & Winston, 1964.

Lerner, B. Democratic values and therapeutic efficacy. *Journal of Abnormal Psychology,* 1973, *82,* 491-498.

MacMahon, B., & Pugh, T. F. *Epidemiology: Principles and methods.* Boston: Little, Brown, 1970.

Manis, J. G. The sociology of knowledge and community mental health research. *Social Problems,* 1968, *15,* 488-501.

Meyers, W. R. Social attitudes and community renewal. In Arthur D. Little, Inc. (Ed.), *Community renewal programing.* New York: Praeger, 1966.

Meyers, W. R. *Program evaluation.* San Francisco: Jossey-Bass, forthcoming.

Meyers, W. R., & Blane, H. T. Social isolation, social dependence and the formation of treatment relations by alcoholics. In H. E. Chafetz, H. T. Blane, & M. J. Hill (Eds.), *Frontiers of alcoholism.* New York: Science House, 1970.

Meyers, W. R., Dorwart, R., & Kline, D. Social ecology and citizen boards: A problem for planners. *Journal of the American Institute of Planners,* 1977, *43,* 169-177.

Pasamanik, B., Scarpetti, F. R., & Dinitz, S. *Schizophrenics in the community.* New York: Appleton-Century-Crofts, 1967.

Silver, G. A. *A spy in the house of medicine.* Germantown, Md.: Aspen Systems Corporation, 1976.

Szasz, T. J. *The myth of mental illness.* New York: Hoeber, 1961.

Wildavsky, A. *Budgeting: A comparative theory of the budgeting process.* Boston: Little, Brown, 1975.

Wing, K. R. *The law and the public's health.* St. Louis, Mo.: C. V. Mosby, 1976.

AUTHOR INDEX

SUBJECT INDEX

A

Abstinence violation effect, 81, 242-243, 269-270
Achievement motivation, 222-225
Adaptation to Life (Vaillant), 303
Addictions
  alcohol abuse
    lifestyle, 18
    self-management of, 279-281
  drug abuse
    lifestyle, 18
    research, 273
  erosion of treatment success over time, 13
  ignorance of causes, 287
  obesity
    self-management of, 273-276
  smoking
    reasons for, 287
    self-management of, 276-279
Adherence
  to behavioral prescriptions, 281
  to medical recommendations, 225, 250
Adjustment process analysis, 179-181, 185-186
Adult development
  age thirty transition, 305, 319, 327

in artists, 303, 310-312, 315
and behavior therapy, 320-322
in blue collar workers, 310-312, 315
in business executives, 310-312, 314-315
clinical implications, 319-330
and clinical training, 323
in early adulthood, 302, 304
early adult transition, 305
the era, 304
getting into the adult world, 305
in Harvard students, 303
and humanistic therapy, 322
individuation, 302
late adulthood, 304
life structure, 304
in middle adulthood, 302, 304
midlife transition, 302, 304
in professionals, 310-312, 315
and psychodynamics, 319-320
psychopathological perspective, 310, 319-320, 323
psychosocial crisis, 302-303
research methods in, 301, 304, 307, 318-319
and schizophrenia, 324-325
settling down, 305
stages and tasks, 301, 306-307, 318-319, 320, 321, 323